THE HOOVER
ADMINISTRATION

From the drawing by Clarence R. Mattei

THE
HOOVER
ADMINISTRATION

A DOCUMENTED NARRATIVE

BY

WILLIAM STARR MYERS
Professor of Politics, Princeton University

AND

WALTER H. NEWTON
Member of Congress, 1919-1929
Secretary to the President, 1929-1933

CHARLES SCRIBNER'S SONS · NEW YORK
CHARLES SCRIBNER'S SONS · LTD · LONDON
1936

COPYRIGHT, 1936, BY
CHARLES SCRIBNER'S SONS

Printed in the United States of America

*All rights reserved. No part of this book
may be reproduced in any form without
the permission of Charles Scribner's Sons*

A

PREFACE

IN preparing the State Papers of President Hoover for publication, Mr. Myers became impressed with the enormous value in these troubled times of a knowledge of the actual policies, methods and measures of the Hoover Administration. Although history usually is written years afterwards, when its lessons have but little direct application to the problems of the day, yet we still are dealing with the problems of the depression, and the experience gained for the nation during the four years when Herbert Hoover was President of the United States is of real public importance.

In compliance with our desire to present these experiences, Mr. Hoover has placed at the disposal of the authors and Mr. Arch W. Shaw the whole of his files, diaries and information. This has been supplemented by Mr. Newton's records and from the current press. Mr. Newton, as Secretary to President Hoover, participated in many of the conferences described, especially those pertaining to legislative policy. Mr. Shaw furnished valued counsel and advice for which the authors are much indebted. He thus added, to Mr. Myers' study of these official documents and Mr. Newton's actual participation in many of the events described, a perspective that grew out of years of close association with Mr. Hoover. This association began at the outbreak of the World War, when Mr. Shaw became chairman of the Commercial Economy Board of the Council of National Defense, and later chairman of the Conservation Division of the War Industries Board. It continued through the period of Mr. Hoover's services as Secretary of Commerce and as President.

Mr. Hoover has placed certain limitations upon the use of the material: that foreign affairs should not be touched upon except in purely economic relations (a subject that may be dealt with at some future time); and that material which might be unfairly interpreted so as to give pain to honest individuals, should not be used. This is American history, as seen from the vantage point of the White House.

The constant aim of the authors is to present actual facts in a plain, direct manner. The opinions and policies cited as Mr. Hoover's are from his own public or private declarations. Any other comment is that of the authors, and is reduced to a minimum. It is based upon the public records of the day and is merely in explanation of those forces which formed the background for the actions taken. On account of the type of sources used, it has been thought best to present the material in the form of a daily log. When documents have been abridged or given in outline form, the full text may be found in the *State Papers and Other Public*

Writings of Herbert Hoover, edited by William Starr Myers (2 vols., 1934).

The story of the interim between the November election and the inauguration of President Roosevelt, which culminated in the bank panic of March 1933 (Chapters XV-XIX inclusive) is substantially as presented in *The Saturday Evening Post* (June 8, 15, 22, 29, 1935). It is here included by the gracious permission of the editors of that publication.

On June 15, 1928, in response to a telegram of the Honorable George H. Moses from Kansas City, Missouri, which informed him of his nomination for the Presidency, Mr. Hoover used the following words:

You convey too great a compliment when you say that I have earned the right to the Presidential nomination. No man can establish such an obligation upon any part of the American people. My country owes me no debt. It gave me, as it gives every boy and girl, a chance. It gave me schooling, independence of action, opportunity for service and honor. In no other land could a boy from a country village, without inheritance or influential friends, look forward with unbounded hope.

My whole life has taught me what America means. I am indebted to my country beyond any human power to repay. It conferred upon me the mission to administer America's response to the appeal of afflicted nations during the war. It has called me into the Cabinets of two Presidents. By these experiences I have observed the burdens and responsibilities of the greatest office in the world. That office touches the happiness of every home. It deals with the peace of nations. No man could think of it except in terms of solemn consecration. . . .

The government is more than administrations; it is power for leadership and co-operation with the forces of business and cultural life in city, town and countryside. The Presidency is more than executive responsibility. It is the inspiring symbol of all that is highest in America's purpose and ideals. . . .

The authors are confident that a reading of the following pages will demonstrate how sincerely and fully Herbert Hoover lived up to these principles of purpose and policy. And always he was animated by that spirit so well stated years ago by Auguste Comte: "It is for the heart to suggest our problems; it is for the intellect to solve them."

WILLIAM STARR MYERS,
WALTER H. NEWTON.

August 15, 1935.

CONTENTS

PART I
THE BATTLE ON A HUNDRED FRONTS

	PAGE
PREFACE	v
INTRODUCTION	3

CHAPTER

I. THE COMING OF THE STORM ... 14

II. THE FIRST CRISIS OF THE DEPRESSION. OCTOBER–NOVEMBER, 1929 ... 21

III. LIQUIDATING THE STOCK BOOM. DECEMBER, 1929–NOVEMBER, 1930 ... 32

IV. MEASURES TO ALLEVIATE THE DEPRESSION. DECEMBER, 1930–MARCH, 1931 ... 57

V. THE SECOND STAGE OF THE DEPRESSION—A SURVEY. APRIL, 1931–JULY, 1932 ... 73

VI. THE GERMAN MORATORIUM AND THE STANDSTILL AGREEMENT. APRIL–JULY, 1931 ... 81

VII. THE AMERICAN DEPRESSION RELIEVED. JULY–SEPTEMBER, 1931 ... 109

VIII. BRITISH DIFFICULTIES AND THE AMERICAN REPERCUSSION. SEPTEMBER–NOVEMBER, 1931 ... 118

IX. THE OPENING OF CONGRESS AND THE CLOSE OF THE YEAR. NOVEMBER–DECEMBER, 1931 ... 142

X. REMEDIES FOR THE DRAIN UPON GOLD AND THE CONTRACTION OF CREDIT. JANUARY–FEBRUARY, 1932 ... 159

XI. PRESIDENT HOOVER AND CONGRESS—THE STRUGGLE OVER TAXATION AND ECONOMY. FEBRUARY–APRIL, 1932 ... 174

XII. PRESIDENT HOOVER AND CONGRESS—THE STRUGGLE TO BALANCE THE BUDGET. MAY–JULY, 1932 ... 201

XIII. THE THIRD STAGE OF THE DEPRESSION—A PERIOD OF ECONOMIC RECOVERY. JULY–NOVEMBER, 1932 ... 238

CONTENTS

CHAPTER		PAGE
XIV.	Extracts from the Speeches of Mr. Hoover in the Presidential Campaign, 1932	248
XV.	World Economic Stabilization and War Debts	275
XVI.	Preventing a Balanced Budget	303
XVII.	Breaking Down Confidence by Delay in Banking and Bankruptcy Reform and Publication of R. F. C. Loans	315
XVIII.	Fear of Currency Tinkering Stops Recovery	329
XIX.	The Gold Panic	347
XX.	Conclusion	368

PART II

THE NORMAL TASKS OF ADMINISTRATION

Introduction		373
I.	Launching the Administration. The Special Session of the Seventy-first Congress. Farm Legislation, and the Struggle Over the Tariff. April–November, 1929	374
II.	The First Regular Session of the Seventy-first Congress. The Development of Administrative Policy. The Children's Charter. December, 1929–December, 1930	414
III.	The Short Session of the Seventy-first Congress and the First Session of the Seventy-second. The Check Upon Constructive Legislation. December, 1930–September, 1932	462
IV.	Extracts from the Speeches of Mr. Hoover in the Presidential Campaign of 1932. A Summary of the Constructive Policies of the Administration	503
V.	Carrying On. November, 1932–March, 1933	522
VI.	The Cabinet and the Executive Departments of the Government	530
Index		543

THE HOOVER
ADMINISTRATION

PART I

THE BATTLE ON A HUNDRED FRONTS

INTRODUCTION

WHEN Herbert Hoover came to the Presidency the world was on the eve of one of the greatest economic crises since the aftermath of the Napoleonic Wars. That crisis and the evils which flowed from it dominated his entire period in the White House. For any comprehensive view of the period and the reasons for action during that time, we must examine the causes and the events which led up to it.

President Hoover was the first President in our history to offer Federal leadership in mobilizing the economic resources of the people, and in calling upon individual initiative to accept definite responsibility for meeting the problem of the depression. This leadership, pioneering as it was, he confined to an arena of action clearly within the Constitutional powers of the Federal Government. In some cases, when the threat to our economic or financial systems came from abroad, he extended this leadership to world-wide action. The depressions that arose in the Van Buren, Buchanan, Grant, Cleveland, Theodore Roosevelt, or Wilson Administrations were practically ignored by the government in any official action. An examination of Presidential messages will show that but little of importance was done officially by previous Presidents to relieve either depression, distress or unemployment, or to cushion the financial and business situations that resulted from such conditions. The history of this depression, and indeed the history of our times, cannot be understood or written without a full knowledge of the leadership of President Hoover in piloting the country through the most dangerous stages of this terrible human experience.

In the larger perspective the depression in the United States fell into two major stages—first, the collapse of a gigantic bubble of stock speculation, and second, and far more severe, the impact from a financial collapse in Europe due to lingering war causes.

The course of the depression, which began with the stock collapse in 1929, was a slow movement downward. It was marked by a series of major and minor crises and major and minor recoveries. This slow downward movement can be considered in three distinct periods. First, there was the period of the domestic collapse, which was caused partly by post-war and partly by boom conditions, and which turned toward recovery early in 1931. Second, there followed the period that was under the influence of the European collapse of 1931, and which caused us to sink to greater depths, but from which the final turn of recovery came in the summer of 1932. Third, there came the period that was under the influence of our party politics, when the prospect of an abrupt change in policy following the election of November brought upon us the economic collapse in the fall and winter of 1932 that culminated in the bank panic of March, 1933.

Fundamentally, the causes of the great depression lay in the Great War. It necessarily developed to world-wide dimensions. No one can maintain that such a calamity would have come to humanity had there been no war. Its acute characteristics, as they gradually unfolded, were chiefly monetary, credit and fiscal—that is to say, a financial crisis dominated the disturbed industrial conditions. We can here only attempt a summary of the forces which produced this gigantic catastrophe.

1. The direct and indirect death rate of the war probably exceeded 20,000,000 men, women and children. The maimed and debilitated people probably amounted to an equal number. And war destroys the best; it devitalizes nations for years to come.

2. The physical destruction of property was enormous, running into many billions.

3. During the war the combatant nations had increased internal governmental debts from $20,000,000,000 to $200,000,000,000. They had created over $50,000,000,000 of intergovernmental debts, including borrowings and reparations. Everywhere the financing of the war had been accompanied either by credit or by currency inflation, or by both. Values, both of land and property, had mounted stupendously and a vast structure of private debt had been built up on these inflated values. The agricultural debts had increased from $3,320,000,000 in 1910 to $7,857,000,000 in 1920 in the United States, mostly during the war, and despite the high prices the farmers had received during the war.

4. There had been a vast world-wide expansion of productive capacity in those commodities that were required by the war or induced by inflated prices. For example, the acreage of wheat increased in the United States during the war years by nearly seventeen per cent. Likewise the production of copper, coal, lead, zinc, rubber, and steel was greatly expanded.

5. The peace treaties had resulted in great political instability; the normal channels of trade were disrupted. Old hates were perpetuated and the germs of militant nationalism were planted. Russia had become Communist and was a constant threat to a weakened world.

During the years that immediately followed the war the nations staggered under many burdens, and frantically endeavored to find a stable footing. The burdens and the desperate struggles for relief likewise can be summarized.

1. Readjustments in the over-expanded production of agriculture, of minerals, rubber and things used in the manufacture of munitions, played a leading part in the post-war difficulties. Also the rapidity of technical advance in industry created elements of instability, among which technological unemployment was but one expression. But the dominant continuing disturbance over the whole world was the ill-balance of agricultural and industrial prices. That has been universal for a long period following every great war.

2. The uneconomic boundaries resulting from the peace treaties stifled industry and commerce. The high fever of nationalism added more artificial restrictions of one kind or another to trade movements. In many countries the pre-war standards of living and consumption of goods have not yet been regained.

3. The combatant nations were confronted by the expensive necessity of finding employment for their demobilized armies. They faced stupendous taxes to provide the pensions demanded for millions of widows, orphans, and disabled men.

4. Suspicion and political instability found expression in the creation and maintenance of armies and navies upon a vastly extended scale, except in those nations of Central Europe that had been disarmed by treaty requirements. This was at an annual cost to the world equal to four times that before the war. And in no year since 1919 has the world been free from demoralizing threats of renewed conflict.

5. Some of the nations rid themselves of private and governmental debts by complete currency inflation. This was true of Germany and Austria and in a sense of Russia. Others reduced the effect of their financial burdens by devaluing their currency, as did France, Italy, and ultimately Great Britain. These were attempts at recovery, but they merely resulted in further demoralization.

6. Every nation obligated for payments outside its borders constantly was agitating for reduction by its creditors. German reparations were readjusted three times and finally repudiated. Russia repudiated its debts to all its old allies. France temporarily settled its war-debts to the United States for about fifty cents on the dollar only to repudiate them in the end. Great Britain settled with the United States at seventy-five cents, and Italy at twenty-five cents on the dollar, Belgium at twenty cents. All of them, except Finland have practically refused to pay their external war obligations.

7. Many governments were unable or unwilling to balance their budgets of after-war burdens in the face of internal opposition. Other nations tried to rebuild or to expand their industries in order to compete

for foreign trade with money borrowed from abroad and on any terms that expediency or profit dictated. A vast hidden debt in short term obligations was created.

8. Upon this general instability was piled worse instability by the erratic flight of private capital from one country to another, as the result of every suspicion that a domestic currency could not retain its value or that international controversies would flame into war.

9. In spite of all this, somehow the world made progress and finally, five to seven years after the war, most nations had re-established the gold standard in an heroic struggle to promote internal stability and a world interchange of goods. Unfortunately, while so doing, they introduced other forms of instability, for some of these governments in Central Europe were not in a position to protect their gold bases against unbalanced budgets and unbalanced trade except by steady foreign borrowing. Others established the gold content of the currency on too high a level. Great Britain did so, and with her enormous debt payments could not hold it against the pressure of foreign trade and of debts.

In the meantime, the United States almost alone of the important combatant countries was solidly convalescing from war injuries. Following the short post-war depression, the whole economy of the United States was growing in strength during the years from 1922 until 1927. Sound currency, a balanced budget, annual and substantial reduction of the national debt, opportunity, initiative, and increased efficiency among the people, were steadily maintained, and were advancing toward the increased prosperity of all the people. The over-expansion and inflation of war-time agriculture still remained out of balance with industry, although the situation was steadily improving. Also the war inflation in the prices of farm lands was causing bad results which were felt in the foreclosure of farm mortgages and in the closing of country banks. There was the same situation in the overproduction of soft coal and in a few other industries. But despite these difficulties we slowly were finding adjustment and an advancement in the general standard of living.

We now may examine the more immediate causes of the crisis in the United States. Above all, of course, was the accumulation of destructive forces in Europe which we have already noted. But we had our own store of domestic and economic problems from war effects, of ill-balance between agriculture and industry and in other quarters, and from the rapid advance of labor-saving appliances. Also there were other forces which were to contribute greatly to the development and creation of the crisis. One of them was the weakness in our banking organization which lent itself to the boom and gave inadequate protection during the collapse.

Another was the development of gigantic speculation in the United States which in itself had certain origins in the after-war situation in Europe.

We had in 1929 a total of nearly 24,000 independent banks, a large part of them with inadequate capital. Many were incapably managed. The State banks, representing the large majority, were independently regulated by forty-eight different systems of State laws. Many of these State regulatory laws were inadequate or unsound. Only the National banks were under Federal inspection. While the Reserve System extended over a portion of the State banks, that organization had no adequate regulatory control of its members as against the deficiencies of State laws. Even in the prosperous years there were continuous failures, more than in any other leading commercial country. During the years 1927, 1928 and 1929, the net failures of National banks, after deducting re-openings, were 199 with deposits of about $177,000,000 as against 1,387 State banks with some $362,000,000 deposits. Even after allowing for the larger number of State banks, the failures in that class were in proportion about three times the number of those of the National banks. In this three-year period of prosperous times the deposits in failed banks were about one percent of the average total of deposits.

During the crisis years of 1930, 1931 and 1932, the total net failures of National banks were 773 with deposits of $721,000,000, while there were 3,604 net State bank failures with deposits of $2,031,000,000. The ratio in proportion to numbers was again about three to one against the State banks. The total deposits of net bank failures during these three years were about five percent of the average total deposits. While the major weakness was plainly in the State systems, even the National bank failures were unparalleled among commercial nations.

The origins of the stock boom are of great importance. The more remote causes lay in the optimism due to the natural growth of real wages and the enlarging consumption of goods which was due to a steady growth in industrial efficiency. A further instance of the more remote causes was the heavy taxes imposed by our government on capital gains, for this made owners of stocks and real estate hesitate to sell, since a large part of the accrued gain would go to the government. Thus an abnormal "scarcity" of stocks and real estate was created which contributed to rising prices.

Another of these more remote causes of the boom and the depression was the effect of the international movement of gold. The subject has not yet been adequately examined, but it may here be pointed out as at least a contributory factor. The practice had grown up in the post-war years of foreign governments and foreign central banks shipping a considerable part of their gold reserves for currency and banking purposes to the United States and depositing them at interest in American institutions. They then carried these as gold reserves upon their books and gained interest upon their reserves. It subsequently developed that there were approximately $1,500,000,000 of such deposits in the United States. The effect in a measure was to build up in the United States an expansion of credit upon this gold base which really did not belong to us and which stimulated domestic speculation. When the collapse abroad came in the year 1931, the withdrawal of these reserves acted as a powerful deflationary force and was a contributory cause of our domestic difficulties.

Yet another of these remote contributions to our difficulties was the flight of capital to the United States resulting from unstable European conditions. There were considerable amounts of such capital in the United States before the boom. At different periods afterwards it was heavily withdrawn and, in fact, our own citizens engaged in this. Such movements inward had an inflationary effect while movements outward were deflationary. Naturally both movements came at the wrong time if we were to hope to achieve stability.

Another economic factor should be mentioned here which, although it had very little to do with creating the speculative booms of 1927-29, did have some effect upon the economic situation later on. In 1921 the country was in the immediate slump from the war inflation and was confronted with considerable unemployment. The world was short of the goods which America could supply, but possessed only partially the means to pay for these goods. The obvious way to remedy unemployment and to rescue agriculture was to extend credit to foreigners so as to enable the purchase of goods from the United States. All agencies—labor, agriculture, manufacture, governmental and private, including Congress, favored such a policy. In consequence, net private long-term loans (after deducting refunding and repayments) were made to the extent of between seven and a half and eight and a half billion dollars during the period from 1921 to 1929, inclusive. Of these loans, about two to three billions have been partially or wholly defaulted during the depression, but no doubt much of this will be made good with recovery.

During this period America sold about $42,000,000,000 worth of goods abroad. The loss on loans, even if no recovery were made, if spread over the whole would amount to about six percent. Whatever the results were, they maintained full employment in the United States from 1922 to 1929—a condition that no other great commercial country enjoyed during this period. It was the cheapest unemployment and agricultural relief ever known. The losses on these loans would have been much

INTRODUCTION

less had our people heeded the advice of Mr. Hoover from time to time, who was then the Secretary of Commerce, and of which some mention later on will be made.

As already stated, the private foreign loans had little to do with creating the "boom." Of course the defaults during the world depression added to our difficulties.

It is not possible here to review at length general economic history prior to President Hoover's Administration. But one current illusion should be pointed out. That is the assertion that the United States "sucked the gold out of the world" betwen the end of the war and the beginning of the Hoover Administration. If we deduct from the total the gold deposited in the United States by foreign government banks and by private individuals for interest and safety purposes, our country actually lost gold during this period.

A far more important and immediate cause of the boom was the deliberate credit inflation policy undertaken by the Federal Reserve System and the important central banking systems of Europe in the year 1927. These institutions aimed to bolster a weakening Europe, believing that they could prevent the inevitable liquidation of the war. This inflation of credit, coming at a time of natural optimism from the steady growth of the country, transformed that optimism from a valuable force into an actual madness. The result of this policy on America was to produce a mass speculation unparalleled in American history. We were engulfed in an unrestrained orgy of greed.

The whole event is of the greatest historic importance when viewed in the light of the economic dislocation and human misery which it caused. It reached a climax in a terrific shock to the entire economic and social order in the United States, and in the world.

This inflation of credit, of course, deserves a more extensive treatment than can be given here, but at least a short review is necessary for an understanding of the ills which followed. The whole period in retrospect becomes more clear than at the time.

In late 1925 the Federal Reserve Bank of New York, through its governor, Benjamin Strong, entered into the discussion of a program of joint action with Montagu Norman, governor of the Bank of England. This was joined in by the officials of various central banks of continental Europe. The objects were the expansion of credit, "easy money policies" by "open market" operations, and the manipulation of the discount rates. The purpose of the arrangements was to strengthen the situation in Europe.

At the time these arrangements were under discussion, Mr. Hoover, then Secretary of Commerce, protested vigorously to Governor Daniel R. Crissinger of the Federal Reserve Board. Certain senators also became alarmed and sought Mr. Hoover's views upon it. In order to clarify the situation he prepared at their suggestion the drafts of a series of letters which were transmitted by Senator Irvine L. Lenroot of Wisconsin to Governor Crissinger. In this correspondence Mr. Hoover made a true and ominous prophecy. His letter of November 25, 1925, after referring to the proposed American-British financial understanding and noting the already speculative atmosphere in the United States, said:

> As to the effects of these Reserve policies upon the United States, it means inflation with inevitable collapse which will bring the greatest calamities upon our farmers, our workers and legitimate business. . . .

The opposition apparently was effective at the time. The records of the Federal Reserve System show that "open market" operations, mildly undertaken in November, 1925, were abandoned by February, 1926, and the policy was checked for the time being.

During the first days of July, 1927, Montagu Norman, governor of the Bank of England, Dr. Hjalmar Schacht, president of the Reichsbank, and Professor Charles Rist, deputy-governor of the Bank of France, visited the United States. At this time the economic situation in Europe was more perilous and the overdue débâcle was impending. These gentlemen, along with Governor Strong of the Federal Reserve Bank of New York, now won over the majority of the Reserve Board to their proposals. A determined policy aimed to inflate credit was entered upon for the stated purpose of assisting the business situation in Europe by open market operations and by discount action. The United States was not in need of credit expansion. Our industry and commerce were amply supplied.

Mr. Hoover was not aware of the policies in progress, for during this period from April until September, 1927, he was in the Southern States, engrossed in moving 1,500,000 people out of the way of the Mississippi Flood and in solving the relief problem growing out of it, and he was not informed of these matters.

The Board gave assurance that if anything in the nature of unhealthy speculation resulted they would at once reverse the process. The trouble with every inflation is that there is a long interval between the injection of the stimulant and its result in speculation and, likewise, there is a long interval between the injection of the sedative and the lowering of the speculative fever. Once it gets under way it feeds on and generates its own stimulants. The injection took place during the latter half of 1927.

INTRODUCTION

The fever began strongly to arise in the latter half of 1928 and when sedatives were applied they did not work until nearly a year had elapsed.

Under the program, open market operations to inflate credit were begun by the Federal Reserve Banks in July, 1927. The discount rate was lowered in August. The importance of this is shown by the fact that at the end of June, 1927, the total Federal Reserve credits outstanding were $1,034,000,000; but by the end of December, 1927, approximately $500,000,000 had been injected into the System. This raised the outstanding Reserve credit to $1,592,000,000.

This expansion of the basis of credit by such action on the part of the Federal Reserve System, when the country was already in an optimistic mood, was greedily taken advantage of by the gambling public and credit quickly expanded. The theoretical ratio of expansion of ten to one was fully employed, and more. The volume of inflation during the next two years due to this and other causes is shown by the increase in bank debits to individual depositors in 141 cities, from $53,600,000,000 at the end of June, 1927, to $82,400,000,000 eighteen months later. There was an increase in all bank loans from $37,400,000,000 in June, 1927, to $41,500,000,000 two years later. There was an increase in New York loans to stockbrokers on securities from $3,560,000,000 in June, 1927, to $7,070,000,000 two years later. The amount rose to over $8,000,000,000 before the crash. The effect upon common stocks is shown in the Reserve Board Bulletins by the ascent of the index of prices.

	Common Stocks
June, 1927	115
Dec., 1927	133
June, 1928	145
Dec., 1928	171
June, 1929	190
Sept., 1929	225

That commerce, industry and agriculture gained little from the inflation is easily shown by the same indices of business. In fact, they also demonstrate how largely the movement was one of stock speculation and promotion, and not one of expansion in commodity prices or business volume.

	Wholesale Commodity Prices	Factory Employment	Freight Car Loading	Department Store Sales (adjusted index)
June, 1927	94.1	99.5	104	106
Dec., 1927	96.4	96.5	98	106
June, 1928	96.7	96.7	100	107
Dec., 1928	95.8	99.8	106	111
June, 1929	95.2	102.7	108	113

The inflation of credit was participated in by the European central banks, and the speculation was spread over the whole world. While there are economists who do not agree that this manipulation of credit by a half-dozen men in different parts of the world was the sole cause of the speculative orgy of 1927-1929, yet all agree that it was a large influence. The world will never be able to measure the calamity that was produced. One of its most regrettable effects has been to furnish unlimited material for attacks upon our social and economic system through the representation that the waste, fraud and greed that flowed from it and the slump that came from it were typical of our civilization, and not the exception to it.

The inflation served to postpone the inevitable European after-war collapse for a time—possibly for two years. Such an European collapse would have brought depression to the United States, but had we not been so weakened by our domestic excess we never would have reached the depths of misery we have experienced.

It is not to be judged that these international banking actions were inaugurated for the selfish purposes of the gentlemen concerned or for that of their friends. Undoubtedly, they were acting in the hope of preventing a European collapse with consequent great damage to world-wide employment and to agriculture. That action of such gigantic moment may be undertaken in a democracy without adequate public consideration or check gives it an importance parallel with the effects of other undue powers in the hands of mere individuals, governmental or private.

Early in 1928, the Federal Reserve System ceased further injections of inflation and later started withdrawals of credit. But it had done enough. The fever was beyond control. By the end of 1928 its members themselves were alarmed. Mr. Strong had died on October 8th of the same year.

On February 7, 1929, the Board under Governor Roy A. Young, issued public notice of "direct action" to the banks, restraining indirect use of Federal Reserve Credits for speculative loans. It had but little effect.

Mr. Hoover had retired from President Coolidge's Cabinet in June, 1928, and after his election in November had journeyed to South America, returning to Washington for the inauguration on March 4, 1929. The retiring President had called the Senate into special session for the transaction of executive business. It met on March 4th and adjourned to March 5th. In the meantime, the President had announced his Cabinet as follows:

INTRODUCTION

Henry L. Stimson, Secretary of State;
Andrew W. Mellon, Secretary of the Treasury;
James W. Good, Secretary of War;
William D. Mitchell, Attorney-General;
Walter F. Brown, Postmaster-General;
Charles Francis Adams, Secretary of the Navy;
Ray Lyman Wilbur, Secretary of the Interior;
Arthur M. Hyde, Secretary of Agriculture;
Robert P. Lamont, Secretary of Commerce;
James J. Davis, Secretary of Labor.

The Senate promptly confirmed all nominations. One of the President's former colleagues, Frank B. Kellogg, was asked to remain as Secretary of State until Mr. Stimson could return from the Philippine Islands and assume his new duties. Secretary Mellon and Secretary Davis were continued in the offices they had held in the Cabinet of President Coolidge.

CHAPTER I

THE COMING OF THE STORM

WHEN Mr. Hoover took office as President the country was enveloped in an unparalleled orgy of stock speculation and gambling. The collapse some months later introduced the Great Depression and contributed to undermine the strength of the country against the impact of the ultimate European financial débâcle which arose from causes born of the war.

Indeed, the boom had reached the stage of a craze of madness throughout the world. Like other similar crazes in world history, moral restraints were thrown overboard. Speculation was not confined to Wall Street. A "Wall Street" grew up like a mushroom in every village. Every type and level of citizen was authorizing its local town and village Wall Street to speculate in his or her behalf in some form or other.

Aside from its directly vicious features, the mania was drawing credit from legitimate industry and thus threatened to cause a whole sequence of disasters. President Hoover at once undertook the difficult task of putting on the brakes. The only government implement was the Federal Reserve System.

Stated chronologically, the events in this connection were as follows:

March 6, 1929: The President conferred with the Federal Reserve officials upon additional action that should be undertaken by the Reserve Board to reduce credit for speculative purposes. The Board determined to insist that banks should not be allowed credit from the Federal Reserve while directly or indirectly they were financing speculation, and to urge banks further to reduce loans on speculative securities.

March 15, 1929: At the President's suggestion, Andrew W. Mellon, the Secretary of the Treasury, issued a statement to the press which was intended as a warning, but for obvious reasons was phrased as a suggestion. He said:

> The present situation in the financial markets offers an opportunity for the prudent investor to buy bonds. Bonds are low in price compared to stocks.

Secretary Mellon added that he was in full agreement with the Federal Reserve Board in the restriction of credits for speculative purposes.

March 16th: Governor Young of the Federal Reserve Board, in a public address appealed to the banks of the country for co-operation with the Board in the restriction of credit used for speculation.

March 25th-27th: These policies began to have an effect which resulted in a rise of interest on market loans for speculative securities to a rate as high as twenty percent per annum. Just at the moment when it appeared that speculators would be brought under control, under instructions of its chairman, Charles E. Mitchell, the National City Bank of New York suddenly defied the Reserve Board's program and offered large credits to the stock market. Senator Carter Glass of Virginia and others bitterly attacked Mr. Mitchell for "slapping the Reserve Board in the face and treating their policies with contempt and contumely."

The President was assured by Governor Young that, despite the Mitchell defiance, the advance of stock prices and the increase in the market absorption of credit had been stopped, also that pressure back to orderly markets would be continued with the co-operation of most of the banks. These actions were greatly resented in "Wall Street" and on *March 30th,* to allay the pressure upon the Reserve Board, the White House informed the press that the President supported the Board's policies. A continued forcing of stock exchange loan rates to fifteen and twenty percent had some effect. The check was sufficient to hold speculative stock prices within a price rise of not over three percent until the middle of June. However, a speculatively crazed people cares little for interest rates, and the policy of restraining speculation had not only little public support but also met with active opposition. This is shown by the fact that on *April 20th* many of those attending a meeting of the American Newspaper Publishers Association expressed "grave doubts" as to the wisdom of the efforts of the Federal Reserve Board.

During this time, Chairman Louis T. McFadden of the Committee on Banking and Currency of the House, and other members of Congress, vigorously attacked these restrictive policies of the Board.

April 3, 1929: The Federal Reserve Board issued a statement that unless there were voluntary restriction of credit for speculation they would "adopt other methods of influencing the situation."

In April and May, the President communicated with the publishers of several leading newspapers and urged that they should inaugurate campaigns in their columns that should warn the public against speculation. A few journals co-operated.[1]

May 15, 1929: President Hoover announced that he would not approve the joining by the United States in the World Bank (the Bank for Inter-

---
[1] *The Kansas City Star* responded with a series of editorials which warned the public of speculation and the consequent restriction of credit needed for production purposes. See also *The New York American,* April 16, 1929, and May 16, 1929.

national Settlements) then being created in Europe as an agency for revision of reparations. His major reason was that he suspected that the bank might become another vehicle for inflation or deflation of credit.

May 17, 1929: Certain of the New York banks and the New York Federal Reserve Bank recommended a raise in the discount rate on commercial loans to six percent on the ground that this would check speculation. This probably would have been the case, but meanwhile it would penalize legitimate business in a shaky world. Governor Young announced that the Board would not approve such an action. He again called upon the banks to co-operate by ceasing to supply speculative credits, and thus not to penalize the whole country.

In June the President instructed the Department of Justice to make a drive to prevent the bucketshops and market tipsters from using the mails to stimulate speculation. This was the only means by which the Federal Government could obtain jurisdiction and take action. These bucketshops were violating the laws of the State of New York, but the officials of that State had failed entirely to prevent these violations of State laws. He hoped that this exposure would open the eyes of the public. Some fifty such establishments were closed. The press noted that telephone calls in New York decreased by 150,000 per day since the drive was started and accounted for it as the drying-up of bucketshops and tipsters. Subsequently, the reports of the Better Business Bureau stated that this was the most significant clean-up in the history of the Exchange.

About the end of June the situation took another turn to speculation. It perhaps was contributed to by the rush of money from private and foreign sources into the call market, attracted by the high rates. The Federal Reserve Board, still reluctant to impose penalties upon general business, finally raised the discount rates in August as the only remaining method of bringing things to check.

The foreign propaganda that the depression began in the United States, and that the collapse of other countries was due to our domestic financial madness, is untrue. Stock speculation was world-wide and already had collapsed in eight or nine countries in Europe, also in South America and Australia. In the London stock market a leading speculator failed in September and brought that market to a stop (the Hatry affair). The impending stock crash was hastened by a sharp rise in European discount rates in September. Even the European central banks, which so largely had contributed to bring about this speculation, could support it no longer.

The inevitable stock market crash came in the United States in the middle of October, 1929. A few days of "weakness" developed into a panic fall of the stock market on October 23rd and again on October 26th and 29th. Thenceforward, until November 13th, there were alternate crashes and partial recoveries. From October 14th to November 13th, industrial stocks fell forty-three percent. At the middle of November a temporary recovery set in so that they closed the year at about thirty percent below the mid-October levels. During this period of two and one-half months, brokers' loans were reduced from over $8,000,000,000 (mid-September) to $3,328,000,000. During the crash, securities were thrown on the market in panic with the same crazy recklessness that had marked the speculative rise.

The crash in the stock market did not fail to affect the prices of agricultural commodities and also employment. From October 15th to November 13th the price of cash wheat fell from $1.29 to $1.12 per bushel. Cotton, which had stood at 17.48 cents per pound on October 15th, reached 16.18 cents on November 13th. The employment index of the Department of Labor showed a decrease from 98.3 per cent in mid-October to 86 per cent at the end of December. But all these were merely first symptoms.

One of the economic lessons that may be gained from this experience is that while lowering interest rates can stimulate speculation and open market operations can inflate credit, yet, when the madness is on, an increase of rates counts for little with the speculator. He is going to make one hundred per cent in a week and an interest rate of fifteen per cent per annum does not stop him.

Before discussing the crash, we well may pause for a résumé of the events from 1927 to 1929, for in retrospect certain facts can be stressed. We somewhat anticipate the course of the depression in order that the picture may be more complete.

1. Europe was destined for a depression in 1927 or 1928 on account of an unliquidated war and its fictitious financial bolstering.

2. The deliberate inflation of credit delayed this European collapse perhaps for a year or eighteen months.

3. This planned inflation created a mad speculation in the United States, the economic and moral effects of which will last for many years.

4. The United States no doubt would have suffered from the depression in Europe if that had been allowed to come earlier, but we should have been far stronger to meet it without the inflation and resultant moral degeneration brought by the speculative period.

5. The depth of the depression would have been far less, at least in the United States, without our inflation.

6. The weakness of our banking organization not only deprived us of a rightful shock absorber, but in its own failures added immensely to the difficulties.

President Hoover was confronted not only by a difficult but also by a most dangerous situation. Inevitable liquidation must follow all booms. Especial danger lay in the world-wide character of the calamity, and in the unknown capacity of foreign countries, by reason of their own war weaknesses, each to meet its peculiar situation. The dimensions of the impending movement could not be foreseen. At least, our own boom inflation and speculation had to be met and the results liquidated. Time was required for readjustment, particularly in the inflated values of stocks, real estate, and the fictitious debts founded upon them. Also the waste, bad management and extravagance in industry incident to the speculation must be eliminated. Above all, it was necessary to adjust the minds of individual citizens and of the nation as a whole to a different order of moral and physical values, to a less extravagant form of life and business, and also to bring about necessary economic and social reforms.

In order to gain a more clear understanding of the situation, it is desirable here again to anticipate somewhat and to outline the movement of the depression which divided itself into four definite periods. President Hoover was under the necessity, during each of these periods, of adapting his policies to meet the new forces of destruction.

The first period extended from the market crash in the United States in October, 1929, to the beginning of the collapse of Central Europe in May, 1931.

The second period included the main force of the European débâcle, and extended from May, 1931, until July, 1932, when the world-wide tide of economic deterioration was definitely turned.

The third period was one of definite world-wide recovery which began in July, 1932, and continued in the United States until the time of the Presidential election in November of the same year.

The fourth period was one of deterioration in this country, during which time we parted from the upward course of the general world movement toward economic recovery. This period began at the election in November, 1932. It was caused by a prospective change in policies and especially by a prospective devaluation of the dollar. The destructive effects still remain with us.

During the administration of Mr. Hoover the country was five times turned back from a like number of crises, any one of which threatened to produce the destruction which can come from an acute public and banking panic.

The first crisis was the result of the stock market crash of October-November, 1929.

The second crisis was the result of the Central European financial collapse of June, 1931.

The third crisis was due to the abandonment of the gold standard by England in September, 1931, which caused the departure of twenty to thirty countries from the gold standard.

The fourth crisis was caused by the near approach of conditions which threatened to force the United States from the gold standard in February, 1932.

The fifth crisis was caused by the breakdown of public confidence due to obstruction in Congress in June, 1932.

A sixth crisis was the actual panic in February, 1933, brought about by the collapse of banks which certainly was caused in large part by the approach of the New Deal and by the acute fear of the currency and budgetary policies of Mr. Roosevelt.

On each of these occasions, except the last, the tide was turned almost wholly through the battles fought by President Hoover and his associates. The country gradually gained strength after each crisis was passed—only again to be swept by a new hurricane of economic trouble.

In order to give any comprehensive understanding of the course of these events it is necessary to indicate the fundamental policies of the President. These policies, as distinguished from actual means and methods, were continuous throughout the depression. The means and methods that were used increased in amount and in intensity to meet each new crisis, but their foundation of principle was the same.

Stated in brief form, the aims of President Hoover were:

1. To co-operate with other nations in meeting the problems of the world-wide depression.

2. To prevent industrial conflict and social disorder.

3. To cushion the inevitable downward readjustments of wages and prices, and the effects of the unbearable debts so as to prevent widespread bankruptcy and consequent dispossession of property, and to avoid the destruction that would result from senseless panic.

4. To preserve the financial strength of the United States Government as the bulwark of all stability by a balanced budget and a sound currency, and to preserve America as the one credit and currency Gibraltar in the world; in other words, to demonstrate that America paid

every debt, and to insure "that the dollar should ring true on every counter in the world."

5. To provide against any suffering from hunger and cold among our dislocated and unemployed people.

6. To sustain the courage and the morale of the people.

7. To secure business and fundamental economic reforms that were imperative; but, where there was danger that reform would delay the process of recovery, to suspend reform by placing recovery in employment and agriculture first, lest drastic treatment of a sick nation might bring greater illness.

8. While working out this program, to maintain the Constitution, and the liberties of the people. We shall see the methods by which these principles were expanded as the depression shifted.

President Hoover gave his own explanation of the spirit behind these aims in an address at Indianapolis on June 15, 1931.[2]

> For the first time in history the Federal Government has taken an extensive and positive part in mitigating the effects of depression and expediting recovery. I have conceived that if we would preserve our democracy this leadership must take the part not of attempted dictatorship, but of organizing co-operation in the constructive forces of the community and of stimulating every element of initiative and self-reliance in the country. There is no sudden stroke of either governmental or private action which can dissolve these world difficulties; patient constructive action in a multitude of directions is the strategy of success. This battle is upon a thousand fronts. . . . Some . . . people . . . demand abrupt change . . . in our American system. . . . Others have indomitable confidence that by some legerdemain we can legislate ourselves out of a world-wide depression. Such views are as accurate as the belief we can exorcise a Carribean hurricane by statutory law.

[2] State Papers, Vol. I, p. 572.

CHAPTER II

THE FIRST CRISIS OF THE DEPRESSION
OCTOBER–NOVEMBER, 1929

THE mental unpreparedness among business and economic leaders at the time of the stock crash and their disbelief in the realities of the situation are of interest in establishing the state of public mind generally. The following public statements were partly the result of a genuine attempt to prevent panic and partly the result of a total lack of knowledge and appreciation of the real situation. They are proof that people seldom recognize inflation or its dangers while it is in progress, or even during the first stages of the collapse.

October 22, 1929: Professor Irving Fisher of Yale said: "Even in the present high market the prices of stocks have not caught up with their real values. Yesterday's break was a shaking out of the lunatic fringe that attempts to speculate on margin." During the next few weeks he predicted a "ragged market returning eventually to further steady increases." *October 24th:* Charles E. Mitchell, of the National City Bank of New York: "This reaction had badly outrun itself." *The New York Times* of the same date stated: "Confidence in the soundness of the stock market structure notwithstanding the upheaval of the last few days was voiced last night by bankers and other financial leaders." Thomas W. Lamont, of J. P. Morgan & Co., said: "Prices of many important issues had been carried down below the levels at which they might be fairly expected to sell." Senator Carter Glass, of Virginia, said: "The present trouble is due largely to Charles E. Mitchell's activities. That man more than forty others is responsible for the present situation." *October 29th:* The press generally made optimistic statements. John D. Rockefeller issued a statement asserting conditions were sound and announced that he was buying stocks. *October 30th:* It was too much to expect partisan politics to remain out of the picture. Senator Joseph T. Robinson of Arkansas, the Democratic leader, made the statement that President Hoover was responsible for the crash but said stocks would recover their prices. The Democratic National Committee, over the name of Senator Millard E. Tydings, of Maryland, blamed the President for the stock crash. John J. Raskob, in a statement in *The New York Times,* declared: "Prudent investors are now buying stocks in huge quantities and will profit handsomely when this hysteria is over and our people have opportunity in calmer moments to appreciate the great stability of business by reason of the sound fundamental economic conditions in this great country of ours." Mr. Raskob was asked by an interviewer if he believed that the decline in the stock market would have great effect on business. He answered that he did not believe the effects would be other than temporary, lasting probably two or three months, and that he did not believe that they would be drastic in other than luxury industries. Albert Conway, New York State Commissioner of Insurance under Governor Franklin D. Roosevelt, recommended that life insurance companies buy common stocks. *The Buffalo* (N. Y.) *Courier* stated: "The attitude of the Federal Reserve Board . . . for a year undoubtedly carried a warning."

November 1, 1929: Stuart Chase, popular writer and radical economist, said that "the stock markets will not affect general prosperity." *November 2nd:* Alfred P. Sloan, Jr., president of the General Motors Corporation, stated: "Business is sound." *November 18th:* William Butterworth, president of the United States Chamber of Commerce, was quoted as saying that "industry and commerce will maintain the levels they have reached subject only to seasonal fluctuation." *November 22nd:* William Green, president of the American Federation of Labor, announced: "All the factors which make for a quick and speedy industrial and economic recovery are present and evident. The Federal Reserve System is operating, serving as a barrier against financial demoralization. Within a few months industrial conditions will become normal, confidence and stabilization in industry and finance will be restored." *December 7th:* Again William Green reassured the public: "We are going to move forward until I think in a few months we will be back to a normal state in the industrial and economic life of our nation." *December 8th: The New York Times* stated: "That there has been a distinct change of sentiment on the outlook for business in 1930 during the last month is apparent. The credit for this impression is given by business leaders to plans under way for industrial expansion during the next year, as revealed at the conference called by President Hoover with key men in all lines. Lack of widespread commercial failures, the absence of serious unemployment, and robust recovery in the stock market have been factors calculated to dispel the gloominess which threatened . . . in the country as a result of the market collapse in October and November." *December 23rd: The New York Journal of Commerce* said: "As a matter of fact there is nothing fundamentally unsound as far as can be learned in our present situation."

January 1, 1930: The public expressions of the administration for the new year were reserved but hopeful. Secretary of the Treasury Mellon said: "Forecasting the future course of business can never be done with any certainty. . . . It is hazardous to attempt to do so. . . . I see nothing in the situation which warrants pessimism. . . . There is plenty of credit available." Likewise, Secretary of Commerce Robert P. Lamont said: "It is impossible to forecast what temporary ups and downs may occur . . . but one may predict for the long run a continuance of prosperity and progress."

President Hoover was still apprehensive of the boom and its consequences. He naturally felt it wise not to discourage the country in so serious a situation by publishing any misgivings. At the same time he steadily refused to be drawn into discussion of the value of stocks. On *October 25th,* in response to the press clamor, the President declined to issue any statement as to the stock market, but said: "The fundamental business of the country, that is, production and distribution, is on a sound and prosperous basis." Treasury officials stated that "the break was the result of undue speculation." On *November 15th* one influential newspaper made a demand that the President urge the people to invest in stocks, with the assurance that they were cheap. The President ignored this editorial demand, for he had no intention to lead the public in the stock market at that or any other time.

The crash soon realized the President's worst and underlying fears in the extent of its damage to business, employment, and agriculture. The first and most urgent problem of the moment was to prevent the development of the stock panic into a general banking panic. Within thirty days securities had shrunk $30,000,000,000 in value. Brokers' loans of almost $8,000,000,000, made mostly to speculators, in two and a half months made a precipitous descent to $3,500,000,000. The persons owing this money of necessity were forced to reduce their bank deposits or to borrow elsewhere. A graphic indication of the shrinkage of business was the fact that bank debits to individual accounts in 141 cities decreased from $95,000,000,000 to $60,000,000,000 in three months, although loans did not decrease.

The immediate necessity was to maintain public morale and to assure banking stability and a supply of credit to meet the shock. Fortunately, Roy A. Young, the governor of the Federal Reserve System, was a sound, experienced, and courageous banker from the mid-West. He resolutely co-operated with the President, as his frequent communications with and calls at the White House showed.

The primary purpose of the Federal Reserve System now was fulfilled in a real service to the country. It enabled the tremendous shrinkage and deflation of credits to be cushioned without bringing down the banks to ruin. Reserve credit, through purchase of eligible paper and government bonds, was expanded by about five hundred million dollars in the last quarter of the year 1929. Discount rates were lowered on November 1st to five per cent and on the 15th to four and one-half per cent. These policies and facilities now were being applied to offset deflation and for American needs, and not for inflation for foreign benefit as was the case two years before.

The crash in the stock markets quickly created panic conditions in the markets for farm products. These markets were in great peril because the farmer, who had produced the nation's supply for the year on credit and had not sold all of it, was greatly indebted for loans against his products. A sudden drop in prices and the calling of loans threatened to force vast quantities of commodities into the markets through liquidation to pay the loans. During the October stage of the stock crash, wheat fell seventeen cents per bushel and cotton $7.50 per bale.

The Federal Farm Board, upon the President's recommendation, had been created earlier in the year with a revolving fund of $500,000,000 for the purpose of advancing co-operative marketing of farm products, by encouraging such united action among farmers themselves, and thus giving greater stability to their markets. This experiment had been recommended originally by President Coolidge and was promised in the Republican Platform of 1928. Under the provisions of the Agricultural Marketing Act, cotton and wheat co-operatives had organized themselves into national marketing corporations. On October 24th, the day after the stock crash, in view of the emergency, and in order to prevent panic spreading to all these markets the Farm Board under the chairmanship of Mr. Alexander Legge advanced funds to the existing co-operatives to cushion the fall of prices in the agricultural markets. On October 26th, the Board authorized the Farmers' National Grain Corporation to loan upon wheat and the Cotton Co-operatives to loan upon cotton at agreed prices. The cushioning of wheat and cotton helped the other agricultural markets. Wheat prices recovered their entire losses by the end of December. Cotton at the end of the year showed a fall of only about six percent.

November 15, 1929: An indication of the seriousness of the situation is shown in a confidential report to the President from the Federal Reserve officials a few days before, which had stated: "The situation is far from liquidated . . . it is honeycombed with weak spots . . . it will take perhaps months before readjustment is accomplished." Other information of even wider dangers came to hand. The President, considering the situation as extremely critical, began the issue of a series of calls for the business, industrial and labor leaders of the country to meet with him at the White House to secure co-operation by industry, labor and business in solving the problems of stability, unemployment, and industrial peace. His whole concept was to stimulate and lead the initiative of the country itself in meeting the situation; that it was the sum of individual effort in the country which would eventually overcome the depression. Through leadership the co-operative action of the country to these ends could be secured. In his announcement of the conferences he said: "Words are not of any great importance in times of economic disturbance. It is action that counts." Owing to the short time available not all those asked were able to attend, but the groups were later expanded to be more widely representative.

November 18, 1929: As Secretary of Commerce, Mr. Hoover had been the chairman of the Unemployment Conference of 1922. He was on that occasion probably the first person to propose that useful public works and construction work generally should be expanded in times of depression as an aid to unemployment and business stability. He now took the first step to apply the idea practically and arranged with Secretary Mellon that he propose to Congress, as soon as it should meet, an immediate increase in the Federal Public Buildings program of $423,000,000.

November 19, 1929: President Hoover's first conference was with the nearby railroad presidents in the Cabinet Room of the White House. His purpose was to secure co-operation by the railways through a conference of executives which already had been scheduled to meet in Chicago within a few days. The subject discussed at this preliminary meeting was in large part the maintenance of normal construction work. Among those present at this conference were: The President, the Secretary of the Treasury, the Secretary of Commerce, Richard H. Aishton, W. W. Atterbury, J. J. Bernet, P. E. Crowley, Agnew T. Dice, Fairfax Harrison, L. F. Loree, Jeremiah Milbank, J. J. Pelley, Fred W. Sargent, Hale Holden, Arch W. Shaw, and William Butterworth, president of the United States Chamber of Commerce. The press statement, issued after the meeting, said:[1]

The railway presidents were unanimous in their determination to co-operate in the maintenance of employment and business progress. It was stated that the railways which they represented would proceed with full programs of construction and betterments without any reference to recent

[1] State Papers, Vol. I, p. 134.

stock exchange fluctuations; that they would canvass the situation as to further possibilities of expansion, and that amongst these particular railways it appeared that the total volume of such construction work already indicated an increase during the next six months over the similar period of last year.

It was agreed that the whole question should be taken up at the meeting of the railway executives convening in Chicago next Friday, with view to securing co-operation of all railways in the United States. . . .

This Chicago meeting not only pledged its co-operation but also at once established an organization to carry it into effect.

November 21, 1929: Leaders connected with the major industries met with the President, at his request, in the Cabinet Room. Among those present were: The Secretary of the Treasury, the Secretary of Commerce, Henry Ford, Julius Rosenwald, Clarence M. Woolley, Walter Teagle, Owen D. Young, Matthew S. Sloan, E. G. Grace, Myron C. Taylor, Alfred P. Sloan, Jr., Pierre duPont, Walter Gifford, Samuel W. Reyburn, Jesse I. Straus, William Butterworth, E. J. Kulas, George Laughlin, A. W. Robertson, Redfield Proctor, Philip H. Gadsden, Ernest T. Trigg, Julius Barnes, and Arch W. Shaw.

The discussions were confidential in order that those present could express themselves freely without danger of sensational or partial reports disturbing the public mind. The President requested each person to give his views of the situation. They varied in the degree of seriousness with which they regarded it. Some believed the trouble might be but temporary. He asked their views upon the action the government should take. They all expressed the feeling that the President should take the lead in stimulating the co-operation of the government with industry. The President's statement can be summarized from his prepared note at the time. He outlined the situation. He said that he would not have called them were it not that he viewed the crisis more seriously than a mere stock market crash; that no one could measure the problem before us or the depth of the disaster; that the depression must last for some time; and that there were two or three millions unemployed by the sudden suspension of many activities. He warned them that we could expect a long and difficult period at best; that there must be much liquidation of inflated values, debts and prices with heavy penalties on the nation; that no one could at this time measure the destructive forces we must meet, since the stock boom and collapse were world-wide; that Europe was still under the influence of the destructive aftermath of the war.

The President further proceeded to point out that our immediate duty was to consider the human problem of unemployment and distress; that our second problem was to maintain social order and industrial peace;

THE FIRST CRISIS OF THE DEPRESSION

the third was orderly liquidation and the prevention of panic, and the final readjustment of new concepts of living. He explained that immediate "liquidation" of labor had been the industrial policy of previous depressions; that his every instinct was opposed to both the term and the policy, for labor was not a commodity. It represented human homes. Moreover, from an economic viewpoint such action would deepen the depression by suddenly reducing purchasing power and, as a still worse consequence, it would bring about industrial strife, bitterness, disorder, and fear. He put forward his own view that, in our modern economy and on account of the intensified competition from shrinkage in demand and the inevitable loss of profits due to a depression, the cost of living would fall even if wages were temporarily maintained. Hence if wages were reduced subsequently, and then no more and no faster than the cost of living had previously fallen, the burden would not fall primarily on labor, and values could be "stepped down." Thereby great hardships and economic and social difficulties would be avoided. In any event the first shock must fall on profits and not on wages.

President Hoover held the fundamental view that wages should be maintained for the present; that planned construction work should be maintained by industry, and governmental agencies even should increase construction to give as much employment as possible; that the available work should be spread among all employees by temporarily shortening the work-week of individuals; and that each industry should look after distress among its own employees. By these means industry would help to "cushion down" the situation.

A discussion followed in which the industrial representatives expressed major agreement. The program was accepted subject to its approval by labor leaders and the agreement by them that they would initiate no strikes or demands for increased pay during the present situation. It was also agreed that those present would sponsor a larger meeting of industrial leaders in Washington on December 5th to further organize the program of co-operation by industry as a whole.

The same afternoon (November 21st) the President held conferences with the outstanding labor leaders and secured their adherence to the program. This co-operation required the patriotic withdrawal of some wage demands which already had been made. The labor leaders loyally carried out their part in these withdrawals. Among the leaders who met with President Hoover and Secretary of Labor James J. Davis were William Green, Frank Morrison, T. A. Rickert, Matthew Woll, John L. Lewis, William L. Hutcheson, William J. McSorley, John P. Frey, B. M. Jewell, A. Johnston, Timothy Shea, A. F. Whitney, and E. P. Curtis.

A brief announcement given to the press as to measures taken at both conferences was as follows:[2]

The President was authorized by the employers who were present at this morning's conference to state on their individual behalf that they will not initiate any movement for wage reduction, and it was their strong recommendation that this attitude should be pursued by the country as a whole.

They considered that aside from the human considerations involved, the consuming power of the country will thereby be maintained.

The President was also authorized by the representatives of labor to state that in their individual views and as their strong recommendation to the country as a whole, no movement beyond those already in negotiation should be initiated for increase of wages, and that every co-operation should be given by labor to industry in the handling of its problems.

The purpose of these declarations is to give assurance that conflicts should not occur during the present situation which will affect the continuity of work, and thus to maintain stability of employment.

November 22, 1929: The President called a conference of leaders in the building and construction industries and secured from them an undertaking to aid in maintaining and stimulating those industries. Those present were: The President, the Secretary of Commerce, T. T. Flagler, Sam Hotchkiss, Frank H. Smith, Harry H. Culver, Wilford Kurth, Frederick J. Reimer, Samuel Eckels, E. L. Carpenter, F. W. Reimers, Arthur W. Berresford, W. M. Wood, A. Trieschmann, D. T. Riffle, A. M. Lewin, and Darwin P. Kingsley.

November 23, 1929: The President by telegraph requested the governors and mayors throughout the country not to decrease public works, but to co-operate with him in expanding them in every practical direction, to take up the slack in employment.[3]

With view to giving strength to the present economic situation and providing for the absorption of any unemployment which might result from present disturbed conditions, I have asked for collective action of industry in expansion of construction activities and stabilization of wages. . . . I should like to feel that I have the co-operation of yourself and the municipal, county, and other local officials in the same direction. . . .

November 24, 1929: The President directed the Secretary of Commerce to set up a definite organization for co-operation with governors and mayors during the forthcoming year in the expansion of public works. A temporary bureau was set up in the Department of Commerce for this purpose.

November 25, 1929: Telegrams in reply were received as follows

[2] State Papers, Vol. I, p. 136.   [3] State Papers, Vol. I, p. 137.

from many governors. *John C. Phillips, Arizona:* ". . . our wholehearted approval . . . our State expansion [of construction] program already begun. . . ." *Franklin D. Roosevelt, New York:* ". . . expect to recommend to legislature . . . much needed construction work program . . . limited only by estimated receipts from revenues without increasing taxes. . . ." *Albert C. Ritchie, Maryland:* ". . . assure you of my cooperation . . . will proceed with its construction work . . . energetically." *John S. Fisher, Pennsylvania:* ". . . do all in my power to carry into effect . . . full harmony . . . in furthering your great purpose." *Doyle E. Carleton, Florida:* ". . . Complete co-operation in your program . . . will call State, county, and municipal departments to carry on. . . ." *Flem D. Sampson, Kentucky:* ". . . hearty co-operation . . . have road program which will continue two years . . . commencing immediately highway and bridge program. . . ." *William T. Gardiner, Maine:* ". . . gladly co-operate. . . ." *Charles W. Tobey, New Hampshire:* ". . . promise full and hearty co-operation . . . causing a survey to be made. . . ." *Myers Y. Cooper, Ohio:* ". . . full sympathy with program . . . my active co-operation . . . have most extensive program for the immediate future in the history of the state. . . ." *Henry H. Horton, Tennessee:* " . . . complete sympathy . . . with plans. . . . Tennessee co-operates fully. . . ." *Walter J. Kohler, Wisconsin:* ". . . will co-operate to fullest extent. . . ." *Bibb Graves, Alabama:* ". . . concerted movement timely and wise . . . Alabama will go with you all the way. . . ." *Harvey Parnell, Arkansas:* ". . . heartiest cooperation . . . immediate survey . . . State, county, municipal, and private interests with view to expediting. . . ." *C. C. Young, California:* ". . . heartily endorsed . . . will convey to cities and counties. . . ." *William H. Adams, Colorado:* ". . . anxious to co-operate . . . as fast as state finances permit. . . ." *L. G. Hardman, Georgia:* ". . . glad to co-operate. . . ." *H. C. Baldridge, Idaho:* ". . . co-operate wholeheartedly . . . wiring county officials also. . . ." *Harry G. Leslie, Indiana:* ". . . co-operate in every way possible . . . efforts wise and timely. . . ." *Louis G. Emmerson, Illinois:* "You may depend on State of Illinois to do its part. . . ." *John Hammel, Iowa:* ". . . will co-operate with you . . . will also urge municipal, county and local officials." *Frank G. Allen, Massachusetts:* ". . . fully co-operate . . . program for public works in Massachusetts the most ambitious one yet undertaken. . . ." Similar messages were received from Governors C. D. Buck, of Delaware; John H. Trumbull, of Connecticut; Fred Green, of Michigan; A. J. Weaver, of Nebraska; F. B. Balzar, of Nevada; Morgan Larsen, of New Jersey; R. C. Dillon, of New Mexico; O. Max Gardner, of North Carolina; George F. Shafer, of North Dakota; Wm. T. Halloway, of Oklahoma; I. L. Patterson, of Oregon; John C. Richards, of South Carolina; John E. Weeks, of Vermont; Harry F. Byrd, of Virginia; William Conley, of West Virginia; Frank C. Emerson, of Wyoming; T. E. Erickson, of Montana; and the mayors of several cities.

November 25, 1929: The leaders of the national agricultural organizations met with the President, the Secretary of Agriculture, the directors of the Farm Board and the chairman of the Federal Land Banks. The representatives of the agricultural organizations expressed their approval of the steps already taken by the government agricultural agencies and assured their co-operation with other groups.

Those meeting with the President, Secretary Hyde, and Mr. Alexander Legge of the Federal Farm Board were: C. E. Huff, C. S. Barrett, C. S. Talbot, Louis Chambers, C. H. Rogers of the Farmers' National Union; Fred Brenckman and S. S. McClosky of the National Grange; H. S. Thompson and Earl Smith of the American Farm Bureau Federation; Lerot Melton and P. C. Betts of the Farmers' Equity Union.

November 27, 1929: President Hoover conferred with representatives of the public utility industry. There were present: Owen D. Young, New York; Samuel Insull, Chicago; S. Z. Mitchell, New York; Charles Edgar, Boston; Frederick Dame, New York; W. A. Jones, New York; B. C. Cobb, New York; Thomas McCarter, New Jersey; C. E. Grosbeck, New York; Haljord Erickson, Chicago; George M. Kidd, New York; John P. Zimmermann, Philadelphia; P. G. Gessler, New York; W. W. Freeman, New York; George B. Cortelyou, New York; John B. Miller, Los Angeles; Floyd L. Carlisle, New York; Herbert A. Wagener, Baltimore; Matthew S. Sloan, New York; J. N. Shanahan, Omaha; J. B. Barnes, Louisville; Guy A. Richardson, Chicago; J. H. Hanna, Washington; P. E. Paige, Brooklyn; S. P. Hulswit, New York; G. H. Clifford, Boston; Paul Clapp, New York; L. E. Storrs, Baltimore; N. A. Draper, Cincinnati; P. A. Gadson, Philadelphia; B. L. Mulvaney, Chicago.

The situation was fully canvassed, and all those present were in agreement with the President's program except Samuel Insull, who deprecated all such activities and asserted that there was nothing in the industry he represented which indicated any seriousness in the situation. But industry in general promised full co-operation in continuing and expanding construction work, and in the other items of the program, such as the spreading of employment, the maintenance of wages, etc.

These utility organizations reported the results of their efforts to stimulate construction. *B. T. Mullaney,* president of the American Gas Association, reported: "Expenditures for construction by the gas industry in 1930 will aggregate approximately $425,000,000, an increase of about six per cent over 1929." *Matthew S. Sloan,* president of the National Electric Light Association, reported the result of their canvass: "Electric light, power, gas, and electric railway utilities assure expenditure $1,400,-000,000 during 1930 for new construction . . . an increase over 1929 of $110,000,000. In addition they will spend in maintenance $410,000,-000." Also the railway organizations reported the results of their undertaking to co-operate. *J. N. Shanahan,* representing the electric railways of the country, reported: "Canvass . . . ninety-seven per cent of executives responded . . . indicates that this industry which during 1929 is spending approximately $1,000,000 a day for maintenance, betterments . . . to maintain or exceed this . . . during 1930." *R. H. Aishton,* president of the American Railway Association, reported: "The railway executives who were called into conference by you in Washington have as you requested communicated with their associate executives at their meeting in Chicago . . . representing ninety-one per cent of total railway mileage . . . capital expenditures program (coming year) $1,247,792,000 compares with $902,307,000 same date last year."

November 28, 1929: The President directed the Postmaster General to expedite the letting of contracts for ocean mail carriage, to be conditional upon the undertaking of immediate new ship construction. This was a further aid to employment.

CHAPTER III

LIQUIDATING THE STOCK BOOM

DECEMBER, 1929–NOVEMBER, 1930

December 2, 1929: Congress convened in regular session. The House of Representatives was under the control of a Republican majority. The relations between the administration and these members were to prove most co-operative, as had been the case in the previous (special) session. The President found the leaders most friendly and cordial. Among them were Speaker Nicholas Longworth and Representatives Tilson, Snell, Purnell, Wood, Williams (Ill.), Hawley, Parker, Hoch, Haugen, Lehlbach, Mapes, Treadway, Williamson, Porter, Johnson (S. D.), Ramseyer, Leavitt, Graham (Pa.), Underhill, White (Me.), Vestal, Elliot, Dempsey, Free, Cramton, Chindblom, Strong (Kans.), Wm. E. Hull (Ill.), Johnson (Wash.), Luce, Fort, Michener, and Simmons. Personal conferences were frequent and an infinite amount of legislative detail and exchange of ideas was expedited by telephone. The first telephone ever on the Executive desk was on that of President Hoover.

The situation in the Senate had developed in the special session to be one of extreme difficulty and it was so to continue. The regular Republicans in the upper House were in a minority. There were but forty-two of them against thirty-nine Democrats, fourteen "Progressive Republicans," and one Farmer-Labor, a total of fifty-four, who were to act as a coalition of obstruction to the President. Nor were some of the regular Republicans of the so-called Old Guard always to be depended upon to co-operate. The origin of these attitudes is somewhat obscure. Mr. Hoover was essentially a real Republican liberal, in the older meaning of that term, in his approach to public questions. He had been a "Bull Mooser" in 1912. He had been opposed by the stand-pat groups in the pre-convention campaign for the nomination in 1928, especially by certain banking and big-business elements in New York City and other centers. Several of the Old Guard senators also had been candidates for the Presidential nomination at that time. Several of the "Progressive Republicans" had supported Senator Norris, of Nebraska, in the pre-convention campaign.

It was obvious at the very start, and before the policies of the administration had begun to develop, that the "Progressive Republicans" were united in opposition. That opposition best can be explained on the particular ground that these men in general had been in opposition to any administration; and on the further ground that such a course invites larger public attention to themselves. In any event they united with the Democrats, whose principal desire was to destroy the possibility of the retention in power of the Republican Party. The extremes to which the "Progressives" would subordinate their own professed ideas were indicated by their later opposition to the flexible tariff which had appeared as a plank in all "Progressive" declarations.

The fact cannot be ignored that the political, economic, and social views of President Hoover represented a middle-of-the-road liberalism which was displeasing both to the reactionaries and to the radicals of the Senate. In consequence, he was forced to attempt to find methods of bringing these groups into co-operation during his whole four years in order to get through the Senate what proved to be a very extensive program of legislation and to secure its passage generally with a majority of the Senate antagonistic to him. In the Seventy-first Congress (April, 1929–March, 1931) this was much more easily accomplished by the loyalty and co-operation of the Republican majority in the House, who joined in forcing the Senate to give up many policies of obstruction.

December 3, 1929: The first annual message of President Hoover to Congress reviewed for that body the economic situation in a very restrained manner, in order not to alarm the country:[1]

. . . a wave of uncontrolled speculation in securities, resulting in . . . the inevitable crash . . . a reduction in consumption . . . number of persons thrown temporarily out of employment . . . agricultural products . . . affected in sympathy with the stock crash.

Fortunately, the Federal Reserve System had taken measures to strengthen the position against the day when speculation would break. . . . There has been no inflation in the prices of commodities and no undue accumulation of goods . . . past storms of similar character had resulted in retrenchment of construction, reduction of wages, and laying off of workers. . . . I have . . . instituted systematic . . . co-operation with business . . . State and municipal authorities, . . . that wages and therefore consuming power shall not be reduced and that a special effort shall be made to expand construction work . . . a very large degree of industrial unemployment and suffering . . . has been prevented. . . .

The President's message urgently recommended increased public works, banking reform, the expansion of the merchant marine, the regulation of inter-State distribution of electric power, the consolidation of railroads, the development of public health services, and departmental reorganization for greater economy.

[1] State Papers, Vol. I, p. 145.

December 4, 1929: The President presented to Congress the budget for the fiscal year beginning July 1, 1930. This showed that reductions made in many directions would permit the proposed additional appropriations for the revolving fund of the Farm Board and for an increase in public works during the next fiscal year, and all this without an appreciable increase in total expenditures.

December 5, 1929: At the White House conference on November 21st between the President and industrial leaders, it had been determined to call general meetings of leaders from industrial and labor groups to meet two weeks later. The President addressed a conference of several hundred representatives. In concluding, he stressed the responsibility of business and asked for its co-operation. He said:[2]

> The cure for such storms is action. The cure for unemployment is to find jobs.
> All of these efforts have one end—to assure employment. . . .
> The very fact that you gentlemen come together for these broad purposes represents an advance in the whole conception of the relationship of business to public welfare. You represent the business of the United States, undertaking through your own voluntary action to contribute something very definite to the advancement of stability and progress in our economic life. This is a far cry from the arbitrary and dog-eat-dog attitude of the business world of some thirty or forty years ago. And this is not dictation or interference by the government with business. It is a request from the government that you co-operate in prudent measures to solve a national problem. A great responsibility and a great opportunity rest upon the business and economic organization of the country. The task is one fitted to its fine initiative and courage.

The conference adopted the program of November 21st and created a temporary organization to make it effective.

The *Journal* of the American Federation of Labor stated January 1, 1930: "The President's conference has given industrial leaders a new sense of their responsibilities. . . . Never before have they been called upon to act together . . . in earlier recessions they have acted individually to protect their own interests and . . . have intensified depression."

December 13, 1929: Secretary Lamont appointed Dr. John M. Gries to head the temporary bureau for co-ordination and stimulation of construction work.

January 2-10, 1930: The President discussed the increased public works program with various Congressional leaders. The principal items for which he sought authorization were an increase in the Public Building program up to $500,000,000, Rivers and Harbors authorizations up

---
[2] State Papers, Vol. I, p. 181, *et seq.*

to $150,000,000, Public Roads to $75,000,000, and the dam in the Colorado River to $60,000,000.

February 3, 1930: After consultation with the President, the Federal Farm Board adopted further measures to cushion the cotton market, which in the past few days had fallen fractionally below the sixteen cents a pound basis on which the Board had based its loans.

February 12, 1930: The New York Times stated editorially: "Indication is that the patient at the end of January has begun to recover."

February 18, 1930: In the Cabinet discussion it was agreed that the danger of a banking panic from the stock collapse definitely had passed. The stockbrokers' loans of eight and a half billion had been liquidated to three billion with the help of the Federal Reserve System. Collapse in the farm commodity markets had been prevented by the Federal Farm Board. It was obvious that although the banks had sustained great losses from customers' withdrawals and the depreciation of securities, uneasiness among depositors generally had been prevented.

The President now was able to announce to the press that the preliminary shock of the collapse had abated; also that the Department of Labor index of all employment, which had dropped from 93.3 in October to 86.0 at the end of December, had by this date increased to 92.8, which indicated the return of several hundred thousand men to work. The governors' reports and independent surveys showed that in thirty-six States no important distress had developed from unemployment, and that in the other twelve States measures put in operation by private and local authorities were meeting the situation. The danger of a general panic in finance and industry had been averted.

February 20, 1930: The President made a public exposure of proposals by certain Congressmen for unnecessary additions to the budget of over $1,700,000,000. He stated to the press: "We have enough resources to take care of the budget and special marginal cases of disabilities among veterans, and for the speeding up of public works in aid to unemployment, but this is not the time for expansion of general public expenditure."

March 17, 1930: The New York Board of Trade reported to Governor Franklin D. Roosevelt that the peak of unemployment was passed in February and that since then conditions had shown a "decided improvement."

April 18, 1930: President Hoover, in a letter to the chairman of the House Appropriations Committee, Representative W. R. Wood, of Indiana, again protested against the passage of certain legislation authorizing additional appropriations, pointing out that falling revenues already forecast a budget deficit for the next year.

The President announced to the public the details of the Public Buildings Program for the forthcoming year which was to be expanded as an aid to employment.

April 30, 1930: President Hoover had directed that a complete house-to-house census of employed and unemployed should be made, coincident with the general decennial census. This never had been undertaken before, and gave for the first time in our history an accurate knowledge of the current employment situation. The census showed:

Persons gainfully employed	45,644,662
Persons out of work able to work and looking for employment	2,429,062
Persons temporarily laid off	758,885
Total unemployed	3,187,947
Total persons eligible for gainful occupation	48,832,609

There are generally considered to be in the best of times about 2,000,000 of unemployed persons who fall in two categories. One is of the unemployables and the other is of those workers who are temporarily between jobs. The latter workers, as measured over the year, have an income but at the precise instant of the census are out of work. This census helped to verify this assumption by the fact that about 1,200,000 of those enumerated as unemployed had been out of work for less than one month. Thus the true number of unemployed due to the depression at this time was apparently about 1,900,000.

This census has furnished the basis for all calculations and estimates of unemployment since that time. Most of these calculations, such as those of the American Federation of Labor, are based upon the application, with some modification, of the index numbers of the Department of Labor to this base.

May 1, 1930: The President in an address to the United States Chamber of Commerce expressed an optimistic view and said: "I am convinced with unity of effort we shall rapidly recover." He condemned destructive speculation and insisted that it could and must be controlled. As shown later, this view as to recovery was shared by economic leaders.

May 9, 1930: Senator Robinson (Arkansas) criticized the President for being optimistic concerning the future, but now acknowledged, "The President of course did not bring about the panic." Secretary of Labor Davis replied: "Conditions would be far worse if not for the President."

May 9, 1930: Charles M. Schwab, of the Bethlehem Steel Corporation, in a public statement said that trade was on the upward swing.

May 30, 1930: The commercial trade reviews, the Federal Reserve

Board, the National Industrial Conference Board, all presented a more optimistic view in their surveys of the situation during the month. On May 21st, in the press reports of a trade convention, various economists asserted that the "recession in prosperity" had run its course and that definite improvement was certain.

June 1, 1930: The Farm Board withdrew further loans for the cushioning of agricultural prices. Through the co-operatives, and the stabilization corporations which they had created, prices had been supported during the panic months from October and November to the end of May. In this time the farm co-operatives accumulated a net amount of about eight per cent of the wheat crop and ten per cent of the cotton crop. The dairy, wool, and other products had been supported without accumulation. Prices of wheat had declined slowly from $1.29 per bushel at the time of the crash to $1.05 per bushel at the end of May. Cotton receded from 17.48 cents to about 15 cents per pound. Since the farmer by this time had marketed his crop which had been produced at the high costs of 1929, the Board considered the cushioning should end for the present to allow for readjustment. Panic had been prevented and the farmer had realized hundreds of millions more for his 1929 crop than otherwise would have been the case, and was thus enabled better to adjust himself. A more economical production of his new crop now was possible due to the fall in prices which he must pay for living and farming materials.

In explanation of the operations of the Federal Farm Board, Mr. Alexander Legge, the chairman, had made the following statement on February 25, 1930:

> Some objection has developed in the grain trade against the action of the Farm Board in financing farm co-operatives in the purchase of wheat and cotton in the present situation. . . .
> In connection with these objections I should like to make this statement as a conservative business man, addressed to the conservative business men of the country.
> The country as a whole was thrown into depression through the collapse of speculation on the New York Stock Exchange. The action of the President in securing co-operation of the business world absolutely prevented this collapse from developing into a panic and has enormously mitigated its effects upon employment and business, including agriculture.
> The co-operation of the great employers of the country in upholding wages, and therefore the buying power of the public, the action of the railways, the public utilities, the industries, the Federal Government, the States, the municipalities in undertaking great programs of construction, are greatly mitigating unemployment and giving protection to the workman and stability to business.

The farmer also was the victim of this collapse. His products and his labor were jeopardized the same as the other workers through the currents started in considerable part from the same causes. His only direct support in this emergency is the Farm Board, through powers conferred upon it. The Board is endeavoring through finance of the farmer's own organization, to help restore stability and expedite recovery from a crisis which the farmer did not create and for which he is not responsible.

The measures taken are purely emergency measures on the par with those taken by other business agencies of the country, and I am confident that the Board deserves and will receive the support of all thinking business men in its endeavor to contribute its part toward the swift recovery of the country as a whole from this situation. . . .

The President had expressed his own ideas in connection with the emergency activities of the Farm Board in a letter to Chairman Legge, on March 15, 1930:

. . . I note the reasons which induced the Board's decision to undertake a large operation in wheat under Section 9 of the Agricultural Marketing Act. A stabilization under this section is practically subject to the determination of the Board as to the circumstances under which it should be made use of.

I recognize that in the form which Congress established the Farm Board, its responsibilities are independent of the President, thus constituting an entirely independent agency, and therefore my views are more those of a friendly interest than authority. In this spirit I should like to take this occasion to express my views upon this section of the Act.

The major purpose of the Board, as you say, is to build up farmer-owned, farmer-controlled marketing organizations under the other sections of the act. This will require years of steady building toward a reorganized marketing system, but without this foundation I see no permanent realization of our hopes of a new day for agriculture. In any event it has been my view that "Stabilization" in any form was absolutely dependent upon building up competent farmer-owned and farmer-controlled marketing organizations in the different commodities to a point where they are in position to provide first, stability through orderly marketing and elimination of waste; second, to accumulate sufficient capital to constitute a real equity under loans made by the Board; and third, to assure storage and other marketing facilities—and above all, to be equipped with competent and experienced staff so as to conduct their business without interference and detailed direction from the Board. At least until this is done the "stabilization" section in the act as finally formulated, is to my mind of very doubtful value, and susceptible of injury to agriculture and the whole country. That this should be first accomplished is the whole difference between private initiative and the Government in business, and it seems to me a prerequisite of any success in permanent relief to agriculture.

The Board has unanimously determined that the collapse in the wheat market which arose from the boom and slump of the stock exchange presents a national emergency to agriculture of the first importance, which in its many ramifications through this and foreign countries has definitely interfered with the free flow of supply and demand in respect to wheat, and that the Board should in this emergency exert every power at its disposal not to fix prices, but to maintain and restore to the farmer a free market based upon the realities of supply and demand even though the prerequisites I have mentioned are not all of them present. I have accepted the views of the Board and have given it my support by recommending the appropriation asked for.

I am glad to know from you that the operation has so far been successful in stemming a panic and slowing the fall in prices so that the grain farmer has realized prices much above the point he would otherwise have secured, and has thus saved many hundreds of millions directly and indirectly to them and contributed to reestablish stability in business in general. It is of course too early to see the final results of this action. The difficulties and dangers to the farmer which have already developed in it are indeed an indication that nothing but a most unusual emergency warrants its use. Whatever the results are it will have compensations in experience.

But I am concerned with the necessity of drawing for the future a complete defined separation of the government from stabilization activities and the building of a sound system of independent farmer-marketing institutions through other powers of the Board.

Yours faithfully,

HERBERT HOOVER.

June 19, 1930: William Green, the president of the American Federation of Labor, informed President Hoover that according to his belief the employment situation had reached the "point of improvement," and was "decidedly encouraging." He so announced to the press.

June 30, 1930: The President, in a radio address to the annual convention of governors at Salt Lake City, urged further action by the States and municipalities in public works to aid unemployment. He called attention to the fact that this was the first time that the Federal government had concerned itself in such problems, and expressed his appreciation of their co-operation in relief activities.

July 1, 1930: The expenditures and receipts of the government for the past fiscal year ending June 30th were made available to the President.

As the readers of this book may have become accustomed to a new form of arranging the Federal budget, the tables here given have been recast in accordance with the practice inaugurated by the present administration.

The Roosevelt Administration has adopted a separation of "emergency" expenditures from "general" expenditures, while under the Hoover

Administration all receipts of the Treasury were credited on one side of the ledger and every kind of outlay on the other. Under the present procedure practically all public works and construction of all kinds are charged to "emergency." Certain "trust accounts" and the tax receipts for the local government of the District of Columbia have been eliminated from the totals of expenditures and receipts by the Roosevelt Administration. In the accounting of both administrations postal expenditures paid from postal receipts are excluded. The statutory debt retirement is omitted from the expenditures as the results show in the fall of debt.

In order to make comparisons possible, we present the expenditures analyzed in this way:

	1929	1930
General Expenditures	$ 2,942,750,423	$ 2,740,011,582
Emergency Expenditures:		
Agriculture		10,958,911
Public Works, other construction and other items	356,529,781	410,420,141
Loans to Farm Cooperatives through Farm Board		148,591,009
[Total Emergency]	356,529,781	569,970,061
Grand Total	$ 3,299,280,204	$ 3,309,981,643
Total National Debt at End of Period:	$16,931,197,000	$16,185,308,000

It will be noted that the loans, so far as recoverable, would ultimately reduce the burden upon taxpayers by that much.

July 3, 1930: Congress adjourned, having passed the President's recommendations for new authorization of Rivers and Harbors improvements, $145,000,000; Public Buildings, $530,000,000; Public Roads subsidies to the States, $75,000,000; and appropriations for starting the Colorado River Dam which, with its subsidiary works, was to cost $165,000,000. The cost of this dam—$65,000,000—is to be repaid, with interest, to the government from contracts for sale of power. The subsidiary works—$100,000,000—are to be constructed by municipal and private participation and irrigation districts. Mr. Hoover had been for years its most persistent and effective advocate. Following an established custom of naming these large reservoir dams for a President of the United States, Secretary Wilbur, on September 18, 1930, named this the Hoover Dam. There had previously been named the Roosevelt Dam in Arizona, the Wilson Dam in Alabama, and the Coolidge Dam in Arizona. It may be of interest to note that, notwithstanding this action, based upon well-established custom and supported by Mr. Hoover's long and continued efforts in behalf of the dam, within a few days after he ceased to be President, the administration which had succeeded his issued an order changing the name of the dam to Boulder Dam. The President in signing these measures stated (July 4th): [3]

> It was with particular satisfaction that I signed the Rivers and Harbors Bill as it represents the final authorization of the engineering work by which we construct and co-ordinate our great systems of waterways and harbors, which I have advocated for over five years; it was promised in the last campaign and in my recommendations to Congress.
>
> We can now build the many remaining segments of a definite canalization of our river systems through which modern barge trains of 10,000 to 15,000 tons of burden can operate systematically through the Mid West and to the Gulf of Mexico, and through the Lakes to the Atlantic. The system, when completed, will have 12,000 miles of waterways and will give waterway connections between such great cities as New Orleans, Memphis, Knoxville, Chattanooga, St. Louis, Kansas City, Omaha, and Sioux City, Keokuk, Minneapolis, St. Paul, Chicago, Evansville, Cincinnati, Wheeling and Pittsburgh. Through the Great Lakes and the Erie Canal many of those points will have access to central New York and the Atlantic. By its authorization for deepening of lake channels we shall support the present commerce of the Great Lakes and make preparation for ocean shipping by the ultimate deepening of the St. Lawrence. It authorizes numerous improvements in our harbors.
>
> It is a long view plan for the future. It will require many years to complete its construction. I do not propose that we should proceed in a haphazard manner, but that we should approach the problem on sound engineering lines, completing the main trunk systems and gradually extending the work outward along the lateral rivers. . . .
>
> In aggregate this inland waterway undertaking represents a larger project than even the Panama Canal. It will provide employment for thousands of men. It should be fruitful of decreased transportation charges on bulk goods, should bring great benefits to our farms and to our industries. It should result in a better distribution of population away from the congested centers.

July 5, 1930: The legislation now being completed, the President requested Secretary of the Interior Ray Lyman Wilbur to start work at once at the dam on the Colorado River, in order to aid employment. The work at Boulder City began on July 8th.

The President announced a complete reorganization of the administration of the Federal public works under the War Department into decentralized districts, under command of specially qualified army engineers in order to secure still more effective action. Major General Lytle Brown, Chief of Engineers, was placed in charge.

[3] State Papers, Vol. I, p. 349.

July 15, 1930: It was clear that government revenues were falling, under the stress of the depression. President Hoover therefore devoted a special session of the Cabinet to the consideration of measures for reducing expenditures below the Congressional appropriations for the forthcoming fiscal year. Afterwards, the President announced to the press that Cabinet members and heads of independent agencies had begun "a searching inquiry" into every governmental branch to see where savings could be made without interfering with the program designed to aid employment and agriculture.

July 29, 1930: The President directed the departments of Justice and Commerce to undertake an exhaustive investigation of bankruptcy law and practice with a view to the elimination of malpractice, and to develop a more constructive method of readjustment of debts, so as to avoid many bankruptcies and foreclosures. This was to lead to one of the most important of the recovery measures that later were enacted.

July 31, 1930: The President again publicly emphasized the need for economy on the part of all governmental departments and bureaus. He reminded them of the request made two weeks before for cuts in expenditures not absolutely necessary at this time so as to equalize by this means the increases due to emergency expenditure for relief.

August 4, 1930: William Green of the American Federation of Labor stated that the stabilizing effects of the President's policies were "becoming more and more apparent." He praised the maintenance of wage standards by employers.

August 5, 1930: A great drought began to threaten the farming States. The President directed the Department of Agriculture to make a detailed investigation at once. Its report, received a few days later, showed that the area mainly affected lay in the valleys of the Potomac, Ohio, and lower Mississippi and in certain northwestern States. About one million farm families were affected and twenty million animals, which forecast the most widespread drought in recent history. This called for extensive relief measures for which he felt personally responsible. For this reason he gave up the trip to California he already had planned which had included stopping en route in the Grand Teton National Forest in Wyoming.

The President secured agreements with railroads to haul feed to drought sufferers at fifty per cent reduction in rates. He instructed the Department of Agriculture to set up a joint organization with the railways to administer the arrangement.

August 8, 1930: The President requested the governors of the States affected by the drought to come to Washington in order to devise measures of co-operation in relief plans.

August 13, 1930: The President directed the Department of Justice to report publicly any attempts to profiteer in food as a result of the drought.

August 15, 1930: The President presided at the conference at the White House of governors and Federal officials for drought relief. The governors who attended were Leslie of Indiana, Cooper of Ohio, Caulfield of Missouri, Hammil of Iowa, Emmerson of Illinois, Conley of West Virginia, Pollard of Virginia, Erickson of Montana, Weaver of Nebraska, Reed of Kansas, Commissioner Fitts for the Governor of Tennessee, Harvey T. Harrison for the Governor of Arkansas, and Senator Robsion for the Governor of Kentucky, also Mr. Stone and Mr. Wilson of the Federal Farm Board, Chairman Bestor of the Farm Loan Board and Chairman Payne of the Red Cross. A program of relief measures was adopted. The Secretary of Agriculture and the Chairman of the Red Cross were appointed to put the plan in action in co-operation with the State authorities.

President Hoover directed that the Federal share of road funds be applied in drought States to give employment to drought-stricken farmers. Secretary Hyde apportioned the necessary funds and started this road-building program on August 17th.

August 19, 1930: Upon conclusion of the conference of governors of the drought States, the President stated to the press:

In accordance with the conclusions of my conference with the governors, I have appointed a committee to undertake co-ordination between Federal and State activities under Secretary Hyde as chairman of the National Drought Committee. The members of this Committee are:

    Chairman Legge, of the Federal Farm Board.
    Chairman Bestor, of the Federal Farm Loan Board.
    Governor Young, of the Federal Reserve Board.
    Chairman Payne, of the Red Cross.
    Chairman Aishton, of the American Railway Association.
    Henry M. Robinson, Chairman of the Security and First National Bank of Los Angeles.

Mr. Robinson has consented to serve on the committee for purposes of co-ordinating Federal with State and private credit activities. The headquarters of the National Drought Relief Committee are being set up in the Department of Agriculture.

The governors of the various States are moving rapidly in the creation of their organizations. The governors of Illinois and Virginia have reported their committees, comprising men of high leadership in their States. These committees are already actively creating their county organizations.

Continuing reports confirm the severity of the situation and the inevitability of distress over the winter in the acutely affected counties, which now apparently number something over 300. The rains of the last few days have stemmed the spread of the drought and greatly improved the situation outside of the acutely affected area. In those areas the destruction of crops has proceeded to a point that is beyond any great degree of recovery, although pasturage should improve. It must be borne in mind that from a relief point of view the burden of the problem in the acute area will show very much more vividly over the winter than at the present minute.

I have received from all sections of the drought area high appreciation of the railways for their prompt and constructive action. . . .

In order that there may be no failure to cover any case of distress pending the time when the States have completed their detailed organization, the Red Cross has given instructions to all their county agencies to take care of the situation.

August 24, 1930: The President directed the speeding up of governmental waterways and flood-control projects in certain areas to relieve unemployment caused by the drought. The War Department apportioned special funds for this construction.

August 29, 1930: The President called for a report from the Secretary of Commerce upon the progress of the expedited merchant ship construction under the Federal subsidies. The report showed that 487,000 tons of merchant ships were in construction on July 1, 1930, as compared with 170,000 tons on July 1, 1929. The increase, at the cost of about $180,000,000 to the shipping companies, gave employment to a large number of men, with further increases impending.

August 31, 1931: The President urged the treasury and postoffice officials to reduce the red tape in the Federal building program. He likewise asked them for a budget estimate for new construction which would end the necessity for expensive postoffice rents.

September 6, 1930: A revolution in the Argentine created financial disturbance in the world markets.

Eugene Meyer was appointed governor of the Federal Reserve Board, Roy Young having resigned to accept the governorship of the Federal Reserve Bank of Boston. Mr. Meyer had served as chairman of the War Finance Corporation and chairman of the Farm Loan Board.

September 9, 1930: The President announced his determination to stop all immigration into the United States as a measure of aid to unemployment and issued instructions to that effect. He stated that the quota entrants amounted to about 150,000 per annum and the immigration from non-quota countries to about 100,000 per annum. The law provided that persons likely to be public charges should be excluded, and as most immigrants were seeking work which was not available, they or the persons they displaced would be actual or potential public charges. As estimated later, this action prevented the addition of several hundred thousand persons to the unemployed within the next three years.

September 14, 1930: Fascists and Communists made great gains in German elections. This caused much apprehension in Europe and affected American prices of agricultural products.

September 15, 1930: The New York Times reported the European situation was threatening as the result of the German elections, and also noted heavy bear raids on the stock markets and a heavy fall in security, wheat, copper and other prices over the world.

September 20, 1930: The President was informed that the Soviet Government was selling wheat short on the Chicago Board of Trade. He at once directed the Secretary of Agriculture to investigate. The following day, Secretary Hyde confirmed the report that the Soviet authorities had sold large quantities of wheat short in that market. On September 23rd, the press dispatches from Europe stated that the Soviet authorities had started dumping large quantities of wheat in European markets at below world prices. The price of wheat fell precipitately in Chicago. Secretary Hyde reported that the Soviet authorities stood to make large profits in their short operations. Certain banks demanded larger margins on wheat loans and thus further precipitated the situation. On September 24th, the Federal Reserve officials, after conference with the President, announced special extensions of credits to hold wheat from the market in order to protect holders of wheat from loan pressure. On September 25th, the Farm Board directed the Farmer's National Grain Corporation to support the market against the Soviet raid. On September 25th, Delgass, a vice president of *Amtorg* (the Soviet commercial agency in the United States) resigned. He stated publicly that the purpose of the Soviet Government was to create disorganization and disturbance to farmers in other countries by such operations as this of *Amtorg*. In the meantime, President Hoover called upon the directors of the Chicago Board of Trade and other centers to take action to protect American markets from such raids. Otherwise, he announced, the Federal Government would be forced to do it. On the same date the directors of the various produce markets installed rules preventing direct or indirect dealings by any foreign government in American markets.

September 30, 1930: Frank R. Kent, special writer for the Baltimore *Sun,* in an article in *Scribner's Magazine,*[4] stated:

---

[4] September, 1930, Vol. LXXXVIII, No. 3, p. 290. Mr. Shouse had been appointed April 30, 1929 and Mr. Michelson on June 9, 1929.

46   THE HOOVER ADMINISTRATION

". . . the political agency in Washington that more than any other has helped to mould the public mind in regard to Mr. Hoover, magnifying his misfortunes, minimizing his achievements . . . [is] an illuminating illustration of the amazing power of unopposed propaganda in skilful hands . . . the new Democratic publicity bureau . . . 'Charley' Michelson . . . director . . . not in the least understood by the country as a whole . . . [is] the most elaborate, expensive, efficient and effective political propaganda machine ever operated in the country by any party, organization, association or league. . . . Mr. Raskob, Chairman of the Democratic National Committee, agreed . . . to underwrite the activities of the Democratic Committee for a period of three years to the tune of $250,000. He selected the astute, politically seasoned and personally popular Mr. Jouett Shouse of Kansas City to act as Executive Chairman . . . [and a] suite of offices, nearly a whole floor in the National Press Building. . . . [He] picked Mr. Michelson . . . many years chief of the Washington bureau of the New York *World* . . . a Democrat with a real capacity for mischief . . . [and] gave him a free hand. . . . The goal set for him was to 'smear' Mr. Hoover and his administration. That is what he is there for and all he is there for. That is his job and it would be hard to imagine a man with his heart more completely in it . . . paid $25,000 a year. . . . It has been his pleasant task to minimize every Hoover asset and magnify all his liabilities . . . to obscure every Hoover virtue and achievement. . . . His employment is to get into the daily and weekly press of the country as much stuff putting Hoover and the Hoover Administration in an unfavorable light as he can . . . a solid year and a half of this sort of thing . . . could not fail to have an effect. . . . [He has] kept himself in the background. . . . His game is to 'plant' interviews, statements, and speeches with Democratic members of the Senate and House of sufficient standing and prominence to make what they say news. . . . He does not have to draft them now, they volunteer. . . . [It is] priceless personal publicity for such men. . . . Speeches, interviews, articles, statements, he has written for them . . . have appeared as their own. . . . Every move Hoover has made is followed by the firing of a Michelson publicity barrage. . . . Editorials and news items have streamed through the mails to small papers hitting Hoover, the Administration and the Republican party in a hundred different ways."

October 2, 1930: The President addressed the American Bankers Association at Cleveland. He said:[5]

. . . The problem today . . . is not a problem in academic economics. It is a great human problem. . . .

. . . no one can occupy the high office of President and conceivably be other than completely confident of the future of the United States. Perhaps as to no other place does the cheerful courage and power of a confident people reflect as to his office. There are a few folks in business

[5] State Papers, Vol. I, p. 375.

and several folks in the political world who resent the notion that things will ever get better and who wish to enjoy our temporary misery. To recount to these persons the progress of co-operation between the people and the government in amelioration of this situation . . . only inspires the unkind retort that we should fix our gaze solely upon the unhappy features of the decline. And, above all, to chide the pessimism of persons who have assumed the end of those mighty forces which for 150 years have driven this land further and further toward that great human goal —the abolition of intellectual and economic poverty—is perhaps not a sympathetic approach. . . . This is no time . . . to talk of any surrender . . . the spirit of this people will never brook defeat. . . .

I wish to revert to the influence of the bankers . . . in expedition of our recovery . . . at this juncture the responsibility of those in control of money and credit is very great. Without faith on your part . . . the early return to full prosperity cannot be accomplished. . . .

. . . there comes a time in every depression when the changed attitude of the financial agencies can help the upward movement in our economic forces. . . .

It appears from the press that someone suggested in your discussion that our American standards of living should be lowered. To that I emphatically disagree. I do not believe it represents the views of this association. Not only do I not accept such a theory, but on the contrary, the whole purpose and ideal of this economic system which is distinctive of our country, is to increase the standard of living by the adoption and the constantly widening diffusion of invention and discovery amongst the whole of our people. Any retreat from our American philosophy of constantly increasing standards of living becomes a retreat into perpetual unemployment and the acceptance of a cesspool of poverty for some large part of our people.

Our economic system is but an instrument of the social advancement of the American people. It is an instrument by which we add to the security and richness of life of every individual. It by no means comprises the whole purpose of life, but it is the foundation upon which can be built the finer things of the spirit. . . .

October 3, 1930: The Congressional elections were to come in November, 1930. *The New York World,* a Democratic newspaper, started a series of articles, nationally advertised and syndicated, which charged great scandals to Secretary of the Interior Wilbur in leasing oil shale lands in the West. It developed that the *World* had paid twelve thousand dollars to a discharged government employee for the preparation of these articles. The President at once directed an investigation into the facts by the Department of Justice. The Attorney-General today reported:

Kelley [the discharged employee] has made an effort to give the public the impression that oil shale lands presently worth untold billions have been or are about to be lost to the Government. In his charges he uses such expressions as "oil shale worth forty billions" and "surrender of billions of dollars of oil lands." The facts are that oil shale has no substantial present commercial value; that the cost of mining the shale and extracting the oil greatly exceeds the value of the product. . . . While oil shale may have a potential value . . . the wild and reckless statements made in Kelley's charges respecting values reflect on the accuracy of all his statements.

The Geological Survey estimates a total of 8,257,791 acres of oil shale land in Wyoming, Utah, and Colorado, where the big shale deposits are found. Of that amount, only 175,724 acres have been patented during this and all previous administrations. During the present administration only 42,840 acres have been patented, and of that amount the patent of 23,057 acres was approved by Kelley himself. Patents on 15,778 acres were required to be issued as a result of the Krushnic decision by the Supreme Court, leaving only 7,278 acres patented, the patent of which Kelley disapproved in whole or in part or said nothing about. The United States still owns 97% of all its original oil shale lands. . . .

There is Kelley's charge that Assistant Secretary Finney wanted to destroy some papers relating to applications by claimants . . . the papers in question never were destroyed and are in their proper places in the files. . . .

There stands out the fact that Kelley, when placed in charge of this oil shale matter in your Washington office, immediately got in touch with a newspaper, refrained from presenting any of his complaints to you, and sold his story to the press, and refused then to give to authorized public officials any statement of the matter. It is a just inference that his refusal to assist the Assistant Attorney General in his inquiry was merely to protect the news value of his proposed newspaper articles. . . .

Despite this, the *World* persisted in the publication of these articles until the Congressional election in November, after which, upon threats of legal proceedings for libel by Secretary Wilbur, the newspaper apologized and admitted there was no basis for the assertions. On October 28th, after presenting the facts and reviewing the Department of Justice's report, the President stated:[6]

I may say at once that proper inquiry or proper criticism by the press is the safeguard of good government. But this investigation was more than that. . . .

The charges . . . were instantly denied by Secretary Wilbur and proof offered . . . of their falsity . . . yet despite all these opportunities to test the truth these agencies have persisted in broadcasting them for the last six weeks by every device of publicity. . . . As a piece of journalism . . . it certainly does not represent the practice of better American journalism. As a piece of politics it is . . . below the ideals of political partisanship. . . . But there is another and more important phase. I am interested and have a duty of the preserving and upbuilding of honest

[6] State Papers, Vol. I, p. 409.

public service . . . when reckless, baseless and infamous charges in the face of responsible denial are broadcast with no attempt at verification . . . the ultimate result can only be damage to public service as a whole . . . damage to the whole faith of our people in men. There is hardly an administrative officer of importance in the Federal Government who is not serving the government to the sacrifice of the satisfactions and remuneration he or she could command from private life. Aside from service of their countrymen, the only thing they can hope for is the enhancement of their reputations. . . . Men of a lifetime of distinction and probity . . . should not be subjected to infamous transactions of this character.

October 6, 1930: President Hoover addressed at Boston the annual meeting of the American Federation of Labor. He said:[7]

In his invitation that I should address you on this occasion President Green spoke in terms of high praise of the benefits to labor from the nation-wide co-operation initiated at the White House last November for mitigation of the effects of the present depression.

At those White House conferences the leaders of business and industry undertook to do their utmost to maintain the rate of wages. They also undertook in case of shortened employment to distribute work as evenly as possible over their regular body of employees. The leaders of labor undertook to urge effort in production and to prevent conflict and dispute. . . .

We have now had nearly a year in which to observe the working of these arrangements. These, the first undertakings of this character in our history, have been carried out in astonishing degree. There are, of course, exceptions, but in the large sense our great manufacturing companies, the railways, utilities, and business houses have been able to maintain the established wages. Employers have spread their employment systematically. For the first time in more than a century of these recurring depressions we have been practically free of bitter industrial conflict. . . .

. . . Our freedom from strike and lockout is well evidenced by the statement of the Department of Labor that in the last depression there were more than 2,000 labor disputes, many of them of major character and accompanied by great public disorder, as compared with less than 300 disputes in this period, and these mostly of minor character. . . .

The undertakings made at that time represent a growing sense of mutual responsibility and a willingness to bend private interests to the general good.

Your chairman has spoken of my interest in the development of an American basis of wage. Both the directors of industry and your leaders have made great progress toward a new and common ground in economic conceptions, which, I am confident, has had a profound effect upon our economic progress during the last few years. That is the conception that industry must be constantly renovated by scientific research and invention; that labor welcomes these labor-saving devices; that labor gives

[7] State Papers, Vol. I, p. 390.

its full and unrestricted effort to reduce costs by the use of these machines and methods; that the savings from these reduced costs shall be shared between labor, employer, and the consumer. It is a philosophy of mutual interest. It is a practice of co-operation for an advantage that is not only mutual but universal. Labor gains either through increase of wage or reduction of cost of living or shortened hours. Employers gain through enlarged consumption, and a wider spread distribution of their products, and more stable business. Consumers gain through lower cost of what they buy. Indeed, mass production must be accompanied by mass consumption through increased standards of living.

A conception of this sort does not at once find universal application. We ought not to forget that it is something new in the world's economic life. And there are, of course, those who do not yet believe. It is as far apart as the two poles from the teachings of the economists of 100 years ago, who took it for granted that the well-being of the worker could be purchased only at the expense of the well-being of the employer or some other group in the community, and further that wages could never rise above subsistence or the number of workers would so increase as to pull the weaker back into the cesspool of poverty. . . .

It is this process of readjustment that partly causes our present difficulties in the bituminous-coal industry. In that industry the encroachments of electrical power, of natural gas, of improvements in consumption, have operated to slow down the annual demand from its high peak, leaving a most excessive production capacity. At the same time, the introduction of labor-saving devices has decreased the demand for mine labor. In addition to its other difficulties must be counted the effect of the multitude of 6,000 independent mine owners among 7,000 mines, which has resulted in destructive competition and final breakdown of wages.

All these conditions have culminated in a demoralization of the industry and a depth of human misery in some sections which is wholly out of place in our American system. . . . One key to solution seems to me to lie in reduction of this destructive competition. It certainly is not the purpose of our competitive system that it should produce a competition which destroys stability in an industry and reduces to poverty all those within it. Its purpose is rather to maintain that degree of competition which induces progress and protects the consumer. If our regulatory laws be at fault they should be revised.

But most of these problems are problems of stability. With the job secure, other questions can be solved with much more assurance. You, as workers, know best of all how much a man gains from security in his job. It is the insurance of his manliness, it upholds the personal valuation of himself and of his family. To establish a system that assures this security is the supreme challenge to our responsibility as representatives of millions of our fellow workers and fellow citizens. The discharge of that responsibility does not allow present difficulties to rob us of our clear vision or the wholesome faith and courageous aggressive character for which our country has been long the leader of the world. . . .

The President was presented to the convention by William Green, its president. In doing so Mr. Green referred to the conference of representatives of labor and industry which the President had called at the White House in November, 1929, shortly after the crash came. He said:

At that conference he suggested that peace be preserved in industry and that wages be maintained during the period of unemployment through which we are passing. The great influence which he exercised upon that occasion served to maintain wage standards and to prevent a general reduction of wages. As we emerge from this distressing period of unemployment we are permitted to understand and appreciate the value of the service which the President rendered the wage earners of the country and industry when he convened the White House conference to which I have just referred.

In the convention of the same organization held at Vancouver in 1931, the executive council in its report expressed appreciation of the President's efforts and the substantial success attending them.

Realization of the pernicious effects of wage reductions has prevented a widespread liquidation of wages such as we had in the depression of 1921. Growing adherence to the high-wage principle, strengthened by the President's stand against wage cuts, has brought effective support from the leading industrialists of the country.

In the full year of 1921 there were ninety-two wage cuts per hundred firms reporting to the Bureau of Labor Statistics, while in the full year of 1930 there were only seven firms per hundred firms reporting.

Although wage-cuts have increased in 1931, there still has been no widespread tendency toward a liquidation of wages such as we experienced in 1921.

In the first seven months of 1931 the number of cuts reported per hundred firms was twelve compared to fifty-four in 1921.

October 7, 1930: Revolution broke out in Brazil. After much fighting the Brazilian Government was overthrown on October 24th. A severe fall in Brazilian securities was precipitated in the world markets.

October 10, 1930: The President announced that a partial list of reductions in Federal expenditures for the current fiscal year amounted to $67,000,000. Many departments as yet had not been heard from.

October 13, 1930: President Hoover sent for the officials of the New York Stock Exchange. He informed them that, despite the fact that primarily the Exchange for purpose of regulation was under the jurisdiction of the government of the State of New York and not under the Federal Government, unless the Exchange reformed its rules and conduct so as to eliminate the manipulation then generally going on, and enforced those rules, attempts to force Federal regulation were inevitable. He informed them further that he would make no public statement at that time, in order that they might first have the opportunity to correct the situation themselves.

October 17, 1930: The President announced to the press that for some weeks he had been in consultation with Federal officials and governors of States preparatory to the organization of a nation-wide program of measures for relief of distress during the winter of 1930-31. He stated in a single sentence a new and enlarged concept of national duty: "As a nation we *must* prevent hunger and cold to those of our people who are in honest difficulties." The President was able to call upon a large experience in relief. He had organized and administered relief on a wider scale than any man in history. It had included the Belgian Relief of 10,000,000 people during four years of war; the relief of 150,000,000 people in Central Europe during the Armistice; the relief of 10,000,000 children in Europe in the winter following; the relief of 20,000,000 people in Russia in 1922-23, and the Mississippi Flood Relief of 1927. This experience had demonstrated that such measures could be organized efficiently only upon certain principles:—that the whole must be decentralized; that no central administration could competently direct such widespread activities; that no paid bureaucracy could be trained and organized during an emergency; that voluntary service of the leading citizens of every community on a non-political basis must be secured for administration; that these decentralized agencies must be given full authority with sufficient checks to see that the work was effectively done. In no other way could efficient relief be adapted to community and individual needs, and politics, waste and corruption be avoided.

October 21, 1930: The President appointed Colonel Arthur Woods, of New York, who had organized unemployment relief under Secretary Hoover in 1921, to direct Federal relief activities and to organize and co-ordinate national, State and private agencies.

At the press conference the President gave warning against exaggeration of the unemployment situation. Agitators and partisan-minded persons were talking about "five million destitute families." "The situation was bad enough and one for great anxiety . . . but based upon the application of the Department of Labor index to the April census of unemployment, the real number was about four million, five hundred thousand persons unemployed. Of these about one and a half millions were persons normally between jobs who had a living but at a given moment were in the process of a shift from one job to another. About 500,000 were estimated as the unemployables. Of the two and one half million which might be called depression unemployment, there were 1.7 breadwinners per family which would indicate about 1,500,000 families without breadwinners. The load would increase with winter and the country might need to give aid to 2,000,000 families."

October 22, 1930: A conference of industrial and educational leaders at Chicago predicted an immediate revival of business.

October 30, 1930: The President, in co-operation with Colonel Arthur Woods, established "The President's Committee for Unemployment Relief," the membership of which under the chairmanship of Colonel Woods, was composed of Sewell Avery, Frank Bane, Edward Bernays, John Blandford, Douglas Brown, Lewis Brown, W. Clifford Clark, Fred C. Croxton, Alice Dickson, Harold Fabian, Leonard Fox, Lillian Gilbreth, Erving P. Hays, Thad Holt, Willard Hotchkiss, James Lawrence, Porter Lee, John F. Lucey, Lewis Meriam, Franklin Miller, William Phillips, Beardsley Ruml, Bryce Stewart, Walter Stewart, James Taylor, Joseph Willits and Leo Wolman.

Colonel Woods reported to the President that, in co-operation with the governors and State authorities on unemployment relief, there had now been erected, in practically every State, a State-wide non-partisan relief committee of leading citizens; and that municipal and county committees were proving able and effective. Steps were being taken by the organization to co-ordinate during the winter the private activities in each locality with the local and Federal Government services. Colonel Woods expressed himself satisfied that with nationally stimulated private funds and county and municipal funds, and with the Federal public works program and the national stimulation of private construction work, the situation could be met during the winter. Practically no State governments had found it necessary as yet to make direct relief appropriations, and thus the second line of defense after the local community had not yet been called upon. The President, in conference with the nation-wide committee members, again stressed the necessity for decentralized organization and administration of relief through committees of leading citizens, and that all available local and State resources should be first exhausted. He insisted that if the Federal Government were forced to pay for and administer direct relief as was advocated by members of Congress it would result in politics, graft and waste such as we had never witnessed. He stated that if the Federal Government as its contribution were forced to go outside of genuine public works to prevent privation, then it should do so by supplementing resources of the State committees and not by a direct Federal bureaucracy as was being proposed. He felt strongly that any breach of the responsibilities of the State and local governments or any centralization or bureaucracy of relief would be disastrous. It has so proved.

November 1, 1930: A new crisis arose in the world agricultural markets in which grain prices collapsed in Europe to an equivalent abroad of less than fifty cents per bushel in the American market. European trade restrictions, Soviet dumping and excessive world supplies had combined to produce such an outcome. The Farm Board authorized the farmers' grain co-operatives again to undertake systematically the cushioning of our grain and cotton markets for the next few months. This operation was continued until the following June, 1931. The new crop had been produced at less cost than the previous year. Wheat prices were held at from seventy-five to eighty cents per bushel, and cotton at nine and one-half to ten and one-half cents per pound for the period necessary to market the crop of 1930. The prices for wheat thus ranged from twenty-five to thirty-five cents per bushel above parity in Liverpool. Through these activities all agricultural prices were held more steady, and the farmers received a great deal more for the 1930 crop than they otherwise would. Of the government advances to the co-operatives to aid in marketing the 1929 and 1930 crops, probably less than $150,000,000 were lost. The benefits to the farmer were many times the amount of loss by the government and represented the margin necessary to hold the agricultural industry from bankruptcy with all the consequent suffering and contagious disorganization. And this bankruptcy would have extended widely into the mercantile and banking world. The solution was not perfect, but there is no complete solution in a world collapse which so severely reduces demand, following a tremendous world increase in supply.

November 4, 1930: In the Congressional elections, the Democratic Party, conducting a campaign largely blaming the President for the depression, obtained a sweeping victory in the House of Representatives. The President, in answer to a press request for his comment on the election, said: "The job for the country now is to concentrate on further measures of co-operation for economic recovery." The Democratic gains would not affect the short session, from December until March 4, 1931, of the Seventy-first Congress. But the situation a year hence, beginning with the Seventy-second Congress in December, 1931, would be changed. While the Senate, in the Seventy-first Congress, had contained a majority against the President, the House of Representatives now would be Democratic in the new Congress. Some seats inevitably must remain in doubt until the meeting of the new Seventy-second Congress. The indications were that the alignment would be: in the Senate, 48 Republicans, 47 Democrats, 1 Farmer-Labor. But twelve of the so-called

Republicans were "Progressives," and would co-operate with the Democrats, as did the Farmer-Labor member. This meant that the potential alignment would be 36 Republican supporters of the administration, and 60 in the opposition coalition. In the House of Representatives, the returns showed, on the surface, 218 Republicans, 216 Democrats, and 1 Farmer-Labor. But a like defection of "Progressive Republicans" must be expected, which meant that the administration must face opposition in both Houses of Congress. In fact, Mr. Hoover, during the entire four years of his administration, lacked real majority support in the Senate, and in the next Congress must face majority opposition in both bodies.

November 7, 1930: In the month prior to the election, and in anticipation of the result, industrial stocks had declined by from ten to fifteen percent. They declined further in the days immediately following. Today certain Democratic political leaders both in and out of Congress, apprehensive of the effect of this slump upon their party, issued a statement pledging that they would provide a full program of legislation for recovery in the next Congress and that they would give full co-operation to the Administration. ". . . The Seventy-second Congress will not be an obstructive body. It will not seek to embarrass the President of the United States, but will be glad to co-operate with him and with the members of the opposition party in the House and Senate in every measure that conduces to the welfare of the country. There will be no interruption to the steady progress of the business of government. There will be no holding up of necessary appropriations. . . ." The program never was offered and the character and extent of the "co-operation" will become clear in subsequent chapters.

November 9, 1930: The President announced that he would ask Congress for still further appropriations to enlarge Federal public works already authorized and to care for farm sufferers from the drought.

November 10, 1930: President Hoover publicly welcomed the promised co-operation from the Democratic leaders. He promptly opened negotiation with them to determine whether or not this meant co-operation during the forthcoming short session to pass needed legislation for relief to employment and agriculture, likewise banking reform and other constructive measures.

November 13, 1930: Congressman Garner was reported in the press as saying:

For my part, if we organize the House, politics will be a secondary consideration.

As a result of these discussions the President announced that the Senate leaders of the Republican and Democratic sides agreed to co-operate upon such a program for relief. Practically nothing was accomplished during the session.

November 15, 1930: At preliminary sessions, the general chairmen of the five train-service unions, in response to a request from the President, conferred on plans for alleviating unemployment among railway men by a greater sharing of work.

November 17, 1930: Wheat in Winnipeg and Liverpool fell eighteen cents per bushel, but was held steady in the United States by the Farm Board. The situation was so critical that the directors of the Chicago Board of Trade, according to a *New York Times* dispatch (November 19th), expressed the opinion that the action of the Board had averted a panic in agricultural products. On previous occasions, the Chicago Board had been in disagreement with the policies of the Farm Board.

CHAPTER IV

MEASURES TO ALLEVIATE THE DEPRESSION

DECEMBER, 1930–MARCH, 1931

December 2, 1930: The President's second annual message to Congress reviewed the economic situation:[1]

During the past twelve months we have suffered with other nations from economic depression. . . . The origins of this depression lie to some extent within our own borders through a speculative period . . . had [this] been the only force operating we would have seen recovery many months ago. World-wide causes . . . over-production of certain commodities abroad . . . financial crises in many countries . . . political agitation in Asia; revolutions in South America, and political unrest in some European States . . . methods of sale by Russia of her . . . agricultural exports . . . our own drought,—have all contributed to prolong and deepen the depression.

In the larger view, the major forces of depression now lie outside of the United States . . . fear and apprehension [are] created by these outside forces. . . .

Economic depression cannot be cured by legislative action or executive pronouncement. . . . Recovery can be expedited and its effects mitigated . . . [by] agreement of leading employers to maintain the standards of wages . . . [We have] freedom from the public disorder which has characterized previous depressions, . . . co-operation . . . to distribute . . . work to the maximum number of employees . . . [and] the largest public construction in years . . . in addition . . . [the co-operation of] public utilities, railways . . . [and the] organization . . . of committees for local employment . . . [and] relief of distress. . . . We have as a nation a definite duty to see that no deserving person in our country suffers from hunger or cold. . . . I have set up a more extensive organization . . . to relieve individual distress. . . . The Federal Government is engaged upon the greatest program . . . of improvement in all our history . . . [which] will exceed $520,000,000 for this fiscal year . . . compares with $253,000,000 last year. . . . I favor still further temporary expansion of these activities in aid to unemployment, . . . an expenditure upon construction . . . of over $650,000,000 during the next twelve months. . . .

[As a] . . . combined result of the tariff and the operations of the Farm Board . . . wheat prices at Minneapolis . . . [are] thirty per cent higher than at Winnipeg . . . corn prices at Chicago are over twice as high as at Buenos Aires. Wool prices . . . [are] eighty per cent higher . . . than abroad and butter is thirty per cent higher . . . than Copen-

[1] State Papers, Vol. I, p. 428.

hagen. . . . We have had the most severe drought . . . [To meet this emergency] I appointed a national committee, . . . railway rates . . . [have been] reduced . . . 50,000 cars of [feed and livestock] transported. . . . [The] Red Cross [has] established a preliminary fund of $5,000,000 . . . [the] Federal Farm Loan Board has extended credit . . . [and the] Farm Board has given financial assistance. . . . In order that the government may meet its full obligation toward our countrymen in distress . . . I recommend an appropriation . . . for purpose of seed and feed. . . . The Red Cross can relieve the cases of individual distress. . . .

[The] . . . budget estimates of receipts and expenditures for the current year . . . [were] formulated . . . [a year ago] when it was impossible to forecast the severity of the business depression. . . . A surplus of about $123,000,000 was estimated for this fiscal year . . . revised estimates . . . of receipts . . . indicate a decrease of about $430,000,000. . . . Legislation . . . by Congress . . . enlarging construction work, . . . [and] for increase in veterans' services . . . has increased expenditures by about $225,000,000. . . . [This will] adversely change . . . [the] budget . . . by $655,000,000, . . . offset by [various items] . . . and economies . . . to an estimated deficit of about $180,000,000. . . . While . . . necessary . . . to further increase expenditures . . . in aid to unemployment and aid to the farmer . . . I cannot emphasize too strongly the absolute necessity to defer any other plans. . . . The budget for next year indicates . . . a surplus of only about $30,000,000. Most rigid economy is . . . necessary. . . .

I have . . . recommended effective regulation of . . . electrical power [which] should preserve the independence and responsibility of the States, . . . an inquiry into the working of the anti-trust laws, . . . [the] wasteful and destructive use of national resources . . . [the] destructive competition which may impoverish the producer and wage earner . . . [an] inquiry to determine if these evils can be remedied without sacrifice of fundamental purpose . . . [I] recommend a study of capital gains tax . . . [and] revision of immigration laws. . . .

December 3, 1930: The President, in presenting the budget to Congress, stated: "This is not a time when we can afford to embark upon any new or enlarged ventures of government. It will tax our every resource to . . . provide for employment and relief."

December 5, 1930: Representatives of all the railway labor organizations were called to meet in Washington at the President's request to consider again how to aid about 50,000 unemployed railroad workers by shortening the work-week.

December 9, 1930: Certain senators criticized President Hoover as heartless and unfeeling toward the unemployed, the drought sufferers and the farmers, and demanded larger appropriations and direct organization of relief by the Federal Government instead of through the States and local communities. One can imagine how this must have hurt a man who had devoted so much of his life to alleviating human suffering. The President countered by charging these men with "playing politics at the expense of human misery." His statement at a press conference was: [2]

I observe that measures have been already introduced into Congress and are having advocacy, which, if passed, would impose an increased expenditure beyond the sums which I have recommended for the present and next fiscal year by a total of nearly four and one-half billions, and mostly under the guise of giving relief of some kind or another. . . .
Prosperity cannot be restored by raids upon the public treasury. . . . Some of these schemes are ill-considered; some represent enthusiasts and some represent the desire of individuals to show that they are more generous . . . than even the leaders of their own parties. They are playing politics at the expense of human misery.
Many of these measures are being promoted by organizations and agencies outside of Congress and being pushed upon members of Congress. . . . Some of these outside agencies are also engaged in promoting political purposes. The American people will not be misled by such tactics.

December 12, 1930: The Bank of the United States, of New York City, with 400,000 depositors and $180,000,000 deposits, closed its doors. While its name might indicate otherwise, it was a State bank solely under State inspection and regulation. Subsequent investigation showed its failure was due to fraud and that the inspection by the authorities of New York State had been grossly negligent. The failure of an old and nationally known bank of that size had an alarming effect upon the public mind.

December 16, 1930: The House Committee on Appropriations reported on a measure appropriating $30,000,000 for drought relief. The President urged the leaders to secure its passage before Christmas. Senator Robinson, Democratic leader, demanded $60,000,000. This fund was finally compromised between the two Houses at $45,000,000.

December 23, 1930: The President ruled that wages paid in government work generally should be at the rate prevailing in the locality. From his own experience, President Hoover was fully convinced that "made" work in the sense of requiring some effort on useless projects in return for relief, as distinguished from a serious man's job at full pay and full effort, was even more deteriorating and damaging to men's self-respect than direct relief. He therefore insisted that whatever the Federal Government did by way of employment upon needed public improvements should be at full pay, regular work, and no shirking.

[2] State Papers, Vol. I, p. 459.

December 31, 1930: The President some time since had initiated negotiations between all the railways in the territory east of the Mississippi to consolidate the lines into four systems for the purpose of securing lower operating costs and greater financial stability. Agreement upon this consolidation was announced today and approved by the President as being a move in consummation of the spirit of the transportation law. This agreement was subject to the approval of the Interstate Commerce Commission.

December 31, 1930: The American Economic Association, meeting in Cleveland, stated that recovery by the spring of 1931 seemed assured.

An estimate of the unemployed by the governmental departments as of December showed a total of about 4,900,000. Deducting the normal "between jobs" and unemployables of 2,000,000, the total was about 2,900,000, which number represented about 2,000,000 families without breadwinners. At the direction of the President, a re-survey of progress was made by the Unemployment Relief Organization under the direction of Colonel Woods. This showed that distress would be well cared for over the winter.

A report to the President by the Department of Commerce (as of December 31st, but formulated some weeks later), showed that the President's organized drive for increased construction work by the Federal, State, and local governments and by public utilities in relief of unemployment had resulted in the following accomplishment:

	1929	1930
Federal Construction	$ 384,000,000	$ 493,000,000
State and Municipal Construction	2,838,000,000	3,054,000,000
Public Utility and Railways	2,038,000,000	2,845,000,000
	$5,260,000,000	$6,392,000,000
Other private construction	$3,391,000,000	$1,974,000,000

There thus was an increase of $1,130,000,000 in activity of the public and utility groups over the boom year, as compared with a decrease of $1,420,000,000 in private construction. The normal course of depression without the President's effort would have been a pro-rata decrease in public and utility construction. Thus the success of the drive was represented probably by over $3,000,000,000 of stimulated work. In human returns, it meant continued employment for at least a million families more than otherwise would have been the case.

The Red Cross had been taking care of the drought sufferers since August. It had been intended to make a public appeal for $10,000,000 further to finance their program as soon as the Community Chests had

MEASURES TO ALLEVIATE THE DEPRESSION 61

completed their annual drive. This would bring the total of the Red Cross resources for the purpose up to $20,000,00. President Hoover in conference with Judge Payne today decided that the appeal should be issued.

January 1, 1931: Senator Couzens, Chairman of the Senate Committee on Interstate Commerce, criticized the railway consolidation as "a proposal to help the railroads out of their financial difficulties."

January 2, 1931: The President in a press conference stated:

> . . . the railways . . . are one of the greatest economic problems confronting the country. . . . The competition of electrical transmission of power, the busses, trucks, automobiles, waterways, gas and oil pipe lines . . . contributed to steadily undermine railway traffic. . . . We must look forward either to reorganization or continued distress . . . to our largest single industry . . . must reorganize . . . the weak roads [are] a menace . . . railways need expend annually $1,500,000,000 on improvements . . . consolidation leads to economy and stronger finance. . . . Congress itself laid down this line of action years ago. . . . If Senator Couzens blocks it, that will add sensibly to our depression difficulties. . . .

The legislation necessary for this consolidation was opposed in the Senate, which prevented its passage. The government subsequently had to lend hundreds of millions of dollars to prevent bankruptcy in those railroads.

January 4-6, 1931: Senators Robinson, of Arkansas, Borah, and others made a proposal in the Senate to appropriate Federal money for the Red Cross for drought relief, or to increase the $45,000,000 drought fund by $25,000,000 to be used for "human relief" by direct distribution by the Federal Government. Their action greatly embarrassed the Red Cross drive for voluntary contributions which had been advertised to begin January 10th. On January 6th, Chairman Payne informed Congress that the Red Cross could meet any further demands for human relief from drought if the Federal Government would keep its hands off and only provide a loan fund for seed and feed. The Red Cross drive proceeded under the leadership of the President and Chairman Payne and ultimately attained its goal despite the difficulties placed in its way.

January 7, 1931: A Senate committee summoned Colonel Woods, who testified that the President's relief organization and measures were meeting the situation.

January 10, 1931: The President issued the public call for an additional $10,000,000 for Red Cross drought relief; $5,000,000 already had been appropriated by the Red Cross from its reserve fund.

January 18, 1931: The President appointed a nation-wide committee under the chairmanship of ex-President Coolidge to sponsor the voluntary relief call. The money was subscribed in full.

January 20, 1931: Despite the Red Cross assurances of adequate funds, the Senate, under the leadership of Senator Robinson, of Arkansas, passed a resolution appropriating $20,000,000 additional for the Federal distribution of relief. The Central Committee of the Red Cross protested again that it could meet the situation. On January 28th, Chairman Payne, summoned before the House Appropriations Committee, protested that the sum was not necessary. On January 29th, the House Appropriations Committee rejected Senator Robinson's proposal. The charge was made in Congress that there was a desire to enlarge the authority of the Department of Agriculture so that relief would be delivered to cotton planters and by them doled out to their tenants. Thereby the negro tenant would be kept in control and peonage. This resulted in a revision of the legislation.

January 26, 1931: Surveys of relief in thirty-five States showed that breadlines in 120 cities had now been found unnecessary and had been abandoned.

February 3, 1931: The attacks upon the relief measures of President Hoover continued in Congress. The President insisted to his advisers, both from Congress and the Administration, that relief should be conducted (a) as work-relief through *genuine* public works programs; (b) direct relief by local and State authorities through the committee system of leading citizens which he had erected; (c) that the Federal Government should not appropriate for direct relief until local and State resources were exhausted; (d) if that should occur, the resources of the State committees should be supplemented only to the amount of their need, and they in turn should supplement with the addition of State money to local committees, who also should be compelled to contribute some part; (e) that the Federal Government must not set up any organization of direct relief, for it would destroy local responsibility, and introduce graft, politics, waste and mismanagement.

Nevertheless, the President issued through the press a conciliatory reply to the attacks in the Senate.[3]

Certain senators have issued a public statement to the effect that unless the President and the House of Representatives agree to appropriations from the Federal Treasury for charitable purposes they will force an extra session of Congress.

I do not wish to add acrimony to a discussion, but would rather state this case as I see its fundamentals.

[3] State Papers, Vol. I, p. 496.

This is not an issue as to whether people shall go hungry or cold in the United States. It is solely a question of the best method by which hunger and cold shall be prevented. It is a question as to whether the American people, on one hand, will maintain the spirit of charity and mutual self-help through voluntary giving and the responsibility of local government as distinguished, on the other hand, from appropriations out of the Federal Treasury for such purposes. My own conviction is strongly that if we break down this sense of responsibility of individual generosity to individual and mutual self-help in the country in times of national difficulty and if we start appropriations of this character we have not only impaired something infinitely valuable in the life of the American people but have struck at the roots of self-government. . . .

And there is a practical problem in all this. The help being daily extended by neighbors, by local and national agencies, by municipalities, by industry and a great multitude of organizations throughout the country today is many times any appropriation yet proposed. The opening of the doors of the Federal Treasury is likely to stifle this giving and thus destroy far more resources than the proposed charity from the Federal Government.

The basis of successful relief in national distress is to mobilize and organize the infinite number of agencies of self-help in the community. That has been the American way of relieving distress among our own people, and the country is successfully meeting its problem in the American way today.

We have two entirely separate and distinct situations in the country; the first is the drought area; the second is the unemployment in our large industrial centers—for both of which these appropriations attempt to make charitable contributions.

Immediately upon the appearance of the drought last August, I convoked a meeting of the governors, the Red Cross and the railways, the bankers and other agencies in the country and laid the foundations of organization and the resources . . . to meet the situation. . . .

The organization has stretched throughout the area of suffering, the people are being cared for . . . no one is going hungry and no one need go hungry or cold.

To reinforce this work at the opening of Congress I recommend large appropriations for loans to rehabilitate agriculture from the drought and provision of further large sums for public works and construction in the drought territory, which would give employment in further relief to the whole situation. . . .

In the matter of unemployment outside of the drought areas, important economic measures of mutual self-help have been developed such as those to maintain wages, to distribute employment equitably, to increase construction work by industry, to increase Federal construction work from a rate of about $275,000,000 a year prior to the depression to a rate now of over $750,000,000 a year; to expand State and municipal construction—all upon a scale never before provided or even attempted in any depression. But beyond this to assure that there shall be no suffering, in every town and county voluntary agencies in relief of distress have been strengthened and created and generous funds have been placed at their disposal. They are carrying on their work efficiently and sympathetically.

But after and coincidently with voluntary relief our American system requires that municipal, county, and State governments shall use their own resources and credit before seeking such assistance from the Federal Treasury.

I have indeed spent much of my life in fighting hardship and starvation both abroad and in the Southern States. I do not feel that I should be charged with lack of human sympathy for those who suffer, but I recall that in all the organizations with which I have been connected over these many years, the foundation has been to summon the maximum of self-help. I am proud to have sought the help of Congress in the past for nations who were so disorganized by war and anarchy that self-help was impossible. But even these appropriations were but a tithe of that which was coincidently mobilized from the public charity of the United States and foreign countries. There is no such paralysis in the United States and I am confident that our people have the resources, the initiative, the courage, the stamina and kindliness of spirit to meet this situation in the way they have met their problems over generations.

. . . *I am willing to pledge myself* that if the time should ever come that the voluntary agencies of the country together with the local and State governments are unable to find resources with which to prevent hunger and suffering in my country, *I will ask the aid of every resource of the Federal Government because I would no more see starvation amongst our countrymen than would any senator or congressman.* I have faith in the American people that such a day will not come.

The American people are doing their job today. . . .

The whole business situation would be greatly strengthened by the prompt completion of the necessary legislation of this session of Congress and thereby the unemployment problem would be lessened. . . .

February 4, 1931: Today began a number of disquieting disclosures arising from the failure of the Bank of the United States in New York City which, as already stated, was outside the jurisdiction of Federal regulation and inspection. These disclosures showed the most questionable banking practices and made plain the complete failure of New York State bank supervision and inspection in its most primary duties. The effect was greatly to disturb public confidence in all banks due to the age, size, and wide reputation of this bank.

At this time there was a strong movement over the country to authorize the payment of fifty per cent of the face value of the soldiers' adjusted compensation certificates. The House Committee on Ways and Means was conducting hearings. Owen D. Young, conservative and nationally known industrialist and financier, appeared before that committee and urged the passage of such a law. The result was a breaking down of the committee's resistance and a new impetus toward the passage of a bonus bill.

The Arkansas senators charged that the Red Cross was starving their constituents, who were "rioting." The President at once dispatched Colonel Campbell B. Hodges of the army to investigate and report. He went to Arkansas, made a thorough investigation, and reported that the charges were baseless.

February 7, 1931: The President sent word to the Republican members of the Senate and House committees in charge of the legislation that he would veto the proposed bonus bill.

February 12, 1931: President Hoover, in a radio address on Lincoln's Birthday, delivered from the Lincoln study in the White House, issued an appeal to the country to avoid further centralization of power in the Federal Government; to resist temptation to put pressure upon the Federal Government to that end; and to assume the full burdens of local and individual responsibility. He warned against the disastrous effects of centralization upon the nation, and said:[4]

> ... The moment [that] responsibilities of any community, particularly in economic and social questions, are shifted from any part of the nation to Washington, then that community has subjected itself to a remote bureaucracy. . . . It has lost a large part of its voice in the control of its own destiny. . . . Where people divest themselves of local government responsibilities they at once lay the foundation for destruction of their liberties. . . . At once when the government is centralized there arises a limitation upon the liberty of the individual and a restriction of individual opportunity . . . can lead but to the superstate where every man becomes the servant of the State and real liberty is lost.

February 13, 1931: The House Committee on Ways and Means reported a bill to pay fifty per cent of the bonus in cash, stating that it would "only" cost $700,000,000. The President sent word that it would cost $1,300,000,000, which later proved to be correct.

February 15, 1931: A compromise between the House and Senate was

---

[4] State Papers, Vol. I, p. 500. When Mr. Hoover entered the White House, the old Lincoln study was in use as a bedroom. It had been for many years. The President wanted his study to be the same room that Lincoln used. The room was restored. Books again lined the walls. A large steel engraving of Lincoln and his cabinet was hung over the mantel of the white marble fireplace. This picture Mr. Hoover had carried with him in his travels over the world for many years. Four of the Lincoln cabinet chairs were found in the attic. They were much the worse for wear. They were restored and placed in the room. Upon the fireplace is an inscription reminding the reader that in this room Lincoln signed the Emancipation Proclamation. Looking out from the windows which face south the visitor can see the Washington Monument and the hills of Arlington. It was in this room, so filled with the spirit of Lincoln, that Herbert Hoover chose to do his work. It was here that he loved to hold his conferences and in this atmosphere to thresh out the problems of government.

reached on the drought relief bills, and $20,000,000 was appropriated for loans for specific purposes to be administered by the Department of Agriculture. As appeared later, only $35,000,000 out of the first fund of $45,000,000 ever was used and only $3,600,000 of the additional fund of $20,000,000. The Red Cross expended less than $12,000,000 of its privately raised $15,000,000 fund. The whole debate for over two months was largely of a partisan character and designed to make the President appear heartless toward the distressed.

President Hoover signed the act creating a small statistical body called the Federal Stabilization Board. He stated to the press that it was an admirable measure in which the constructive suggestions of the various government departments, for co-ordination of public works, had been adopted, and the credit was due to Senator Wagner, of New York, its Senatorial sponsor, and to Edward Eyre Hunt and Otto Mallery, by whom the principles in the legislation first were proposed.

Despite the protests of the President to the House leaders, the House of Representatives passed the Bonus Bill, which authorized a cash loan to the veterans of fifty per cent of the deferred World War bonus. Some of the President's critics desired to pass the bill through the Senate during the closing days of the session, affording the President an opportunity to kill the legislation by means of a pocket veto. By exercising a pocket veto he would not be required to state his reasons and would not have the same opportunity to justify his action. But the President did not propose to evade responsibility. An editorial in *The New York Times* commented as follows: "President Hoover has let it be known that he is not behind the manœuver to enable him to kill the veterans bonus by pocket veto. Let the Senate pass the bill as soon as it please following the precipitous action of the House yesterday and then he will veto it promptly and so throw back the responsibility where it belongs. This is the frank and bold way of going about the business."

The President sent for several senators in an endeavor to stop the passage of the bonus through the Senate.

February 18, 1931: President Hoover sought to end the postal deficit caused by constant Congressional legislation for increases of pay, extension of the franking privilege, and by the lowering of postage. He asked the Congressional leaders to secure the authorization of an inquiry into methods of placing the postoffice on a full paying basis in preparation for legislation at the next session. Congress refused.

Senator Reed Smoot, of Utah, chairman of the Committee on Finance of the Senate, requested the views of President Hoover on the pending bonus legislation. The President replied, and pointed out that if all who were entitled to it should claim the bonus, this would entail a payment of about $1,300,000,000 from the Federal Government: [5]

. . . I have supported and the nation should maintain the important principle that when men have been called into jeopardy of their very lives in protection of the nation, then the nation as a whole incurs a special obligation beyond that to any other group of its citizens. . . . Over 700,-000 World War veterans or their dependents are today receiving . . . allowances. . . . The country should not be called upon, however, to support or make loans to those men who can by their own efforts support themselves . . . the largest part of this huge sum . . . is to be available to those who are not in distress. . . . Such action may . . . result in prolongation of this period of unemployment and suffering. . . . These burdens . . . cannot but have a damaging effect. . . . The one appealing argument for this legislation is for veterans in distress. . . . Placing a strain upon savings needed [for reconstruction] . . . by a measure . . . for a vast sum beyond the call of distress . . . will not only nullify the benefits to the veterans but inflict injury to the country as a whole.

February 19, 1931: The President directed the Secretary of Labor to draft and submit to Congress a bill providing for the revision of the employment service of the Federal Department of Labor into an adequate system of United States employment offices to work in co-operation with the States, and in substitution for Senator Wagner's bill for subsidies to the States. The reason for this action was to avoid a long delay and to prevent the enactment of legislation giving political control of industrial employment offices, which would place an enormous amount of industrial patronage at the disposal of State and local political organizations. In the meantime, the President had secured an increased appropriation of $750,-000 for expansion of the existing Federal Employment Service and had appointed Mr. John R. Alpine of New York, long experienced in labor and employment questions, as special assistant to the Secretary of Labor to direct it. This service was based upon co-operation with, but independence from, other agencies.

February 24, 1931: Senator Vandenberg of Michigan assured the Senate that the Treasury reserves of about $785,000,000 to meet the bonus should cover any possible demand. This was $515,000,000 under the President's estimate of $1,300,000,000.

February 26, 1931: The President received a report from General Frank T. Hines, the administrator of Veterans' Affairs, upon distress among veterans. This investigation had been undertaken at the President's request. The report stated:

[5] State Papers, Vol. I, p. 507.

I am inclosing herewith as complete information as it has been possible to secure as to the number of veterans and veterans' families who are receiving relief through organized charity.

These returns represent the reports from eighteen cities whose veteran population is estimated as approximately 898,469. While, in my opinion, the figures on relief extended are indexes only including, as they doubtless do, some duplication, and on the other hand in some instances probably not including all cases to whom relief is being extended, it is interesting to note that from these figures the per cent of veteran population represented who is actually in receipt of relief approximates 8, as some 72,310 cases are represented by the attached reports. If we apply this per cent to the 3,400,000 holders of bonus certificates there would result a figure of approximately 272,000, which is at least indicative of the number of veterans at this time so in need as to seek relief from organized society.

I might add it is my personal opinion, however, that these figures on the average are higher than probably the actual facts warrant when we take into account possible duplications and also minor forms of relief which may be comprehended. I would say that a better average figure might be 6%. Further, I have checked back on certain reports originally received, and modified figures have been used.

The President vetoed the Bonus Bill (February 26th) with a vigorous message amplifying his former statement: [e]

There is not a penny in the Treasury to meet such a demand. The government must borrow this sum through the sale of reserve fund securities . . . or impose further taxation. . . . This proposal . . . is a requirement . . . to provide an enormous sum . . . to a vast majority who are able to care for themselves. . . . Among them are 387,000 veterans and 400,000 dependents . . . already receiving . . . support from the Federal Government. . . . These services now total an annual expenditure of . . . $800,000,000. . . . It is argued that . . . it would stimulate business. . . . We cannot further the restoration of prosperity by borrowing from some of our people, pledging the credit of all the people, to loan to some of our people who are not in need of the money. . . . It can be of no assistance to the return of real prosperity . . . if this argument is correct, we should make government loans to the whole people. . . . I have no desire to present monetary aspects . . . except so far as they affect the human aspects. Surely it is a human aspect to transfer to the backs of those who toil, including veterans, a burden of those who by position and property can care for themselves. It is a human aspect to incur the danger of . . . continued unemployment. . . . Of much graver importance is the whole tendency to open the Federal Treasury to a thousand purposes, many admirable in their intentions . . . many . . . insidiously consume more and more of the savings . . . of our people . . . each of them breaks the barriers of self-reliance and self-support in our people.

[e] State Papers, Vol. I, p. 512.

February 27, 1931: The Senate over-rode the veto of the bonus by the vote of 76-17. At one time the President had thirty-two senators pledged to support the veto, lacking only two of the necessary number; of these, some fifteen promises were conditional upon his securing the full thirty-four. Senators Vandenberg and Glass led the fight to sustain the veto.

The President stated to the press:[7]

Although I have been greatly opposed to the passage of the bonus legislation in its provisions for loans from the Treasury to people not in need, now that it is a law we propose to facilitate the working of it in every way possible.

Inasmuch as the physical task of making loans to 3,500,000 veterans, or even half that number, who might apply, will require many months, even with the most intensive organization, I have requested General Hines to give complete priority to applications from veterans who are in need, and have asked him to set up some machinery for the certification of these cases, especially giving regard to the certification of the veterans service organizations and the various relief organizations dealing with unemployment. The recent survey of the larger cities shows, in the opinion of the administrator of Veterans' Affairs, that about six and one-half per cent of the total number of veterans in industrial centers are now receiving support from the local unemployment and other relief committees. . . .

At this time the *Federal Reserve Bulletin* stated: "The output of most important industries increased more than seasonally in February."

March 4, 1931: The first session of the Seventy-first Congress expired in a filibuster.

During the session the President vetoed eleven measures, including the Muscle Shoals Bill, which were designed unnecessarily to increase government obligations. Two of these vetoes, those of the Spanish War Veterans' pensions and the Bonus Bill, were over-ridden by Congress. The following letter is a judgment of value:

Embassy of the United States
of America
London, March 10, 1931

MY DEAR MR. PRESIDENT:

Distance gives perspective, just like time—and away from distracting local occurrences as I am over here, I think my view of what you have achieved during the last session of Congress may be of interest to you and Mrs. Hoover. I have not often written personally to you, as apparently some past Ambassadors over here have written to their Chief (possibly for publication after his death) for which you are no doubt grateful.

[7] State Papers, Vol. I, p. 517.

But if you were neither my friend, nor I your appointee, I would write to you at this juncture as an American citizen to a great President of the United States. You have successfully endured the severest test of statesmanship during the past few months. No other President since the war has experienced during his whole term the difficulties and crises you have met during the past six months. Where some of these situations were in general similar, yours were always the more acute. To veto a bonus bill in a time of National prosperity is both commendable and courageous. To veto one during the worst of an unprecedented business depression, at a time when the bill prompted by demagogism could be represented as one to relieve suffering, is an heroic thing—as well as being commendable. Your steadfastness—when so many from whom it was not expected have weakened—in defense of our American system of relief as distinguished from the dole principle and of private, as distinguished from Governmental ownership of utilities, were all the more difficult for the same reason. Your opponents were able to use a public calamity as an excuse for the violation of a fundamental principle of good government. When public opinion was distracted by conditions temporarily very adverse, you stood for a principle when you knew you would go down with it for the time. From now on you will come up with it. From such things only does greatness come. Whatever the future holds from now on—whether or not you are re-elected—whether times get better or worse—you have stood the test and have "won out." Your name will always be respected and revered as one of our greatest Presidents.

It is upgrade every way from now on. As is always the case the reaction in your favor in time will be proportionate in its strength to the injustice, bitterness and misrepresentation of the recent criticisms you have braved.

Mrs. Dawes joins me in best remembrances and greetings to you and Mrs. Hoover. Am planning my next trip to Chicago some time this summer or next fall.

Yours

CHARLES G. DAWES.

March 21, 1931: Germany and Austria announced their consummation of a customs union. An immediate protest was made by France and England that it would not be permitted. A sharp slump took place in the German and Austrian markets.

Though not recognized at the time, this was the spark which, like the assassination of the Grand Duke at Sarajevo in June, 1914, set fire again in the tinder box of Europe. This time it was not the collapse of European peace, but the collapse of European finance.

March 25, 1931: Great Britain demanded a review of the German-Austrian Customs Agreement by the League of Nations.

March 27, 1931: The Government of Peru defaulted on payment of its public debt.

March 28, 1931: Civil rights were suspended by the German Government.

The general spirit in the United States at the end of March, 1931, was more confident. The passage of the Bonus Bill had been a considerable blow, but current press and economic opinions everywhere were voicing evidences of recovery. On March 22nd, the Federal Reserve Board reported an improvement in the banking situation and a decrease in commercial failures in the United States. March 23rd, economic writers in *The New York Times* and elsewhere concluded that the depression had reached bottom and that recovery signs were showing. March 24th, the Federal Reserve Board reported increasing industrial output for February. March 30, 1931, the *Federal Reserve Bulletin* stated: "Further increase in the industrial activity was reported for the month of March which usually shows little change from February." As the result of a detailed economic survey of the whole country, carried out by the American Telephone and Telegraph Company, it was announced that the economic tide had turned. The commercial page headlines in the press were: "Further gains in business"; "Definite upturn at close of first quarter"; "All commodities stronger."

These opinions were confirmed by many statistical indices. The enormous speculative account in stocks had been liquidated, without serious impairment to the financial structure. Bank failures had abated. According to the Federal Reserve Board report for January, 1931 (page 126), since the crash these had been a little over two per cent of the deposits. While the cost of living had decreased by twelve per cent, the rate of wages generally had been upheld. Unemployment, which reached its deep point in January, 1931, began to recover. A realignment of the public mind against extravagance had taken place, and serious reforms had been achieved in business management. The average prices of industrial securities in the stock exchange reflected business sentiment by showing a gradual increase of about ten per cent in prices from mid-January.

Some of the important economic indices of the Federal Reserve Board show the steadying up of the situation.

	January, 1931	*February, 1931*	*March, 1931*
Factory payrolls	68	73	75
Factory employment	78	78	78
Prices of common stocks	112	119	121
Freight car loadings	82	80	80
Construction contracts awarded	71	79	77
Industrial production	83	86	87
Department store sales	99	99	97
Wholesale commodities	78	77	76

Thus the economic picture of the United States at the end of March, 1931, and in fact for the first third of April, showed not only an ending of the decline but a tendency to upturn in the depression. The United States was steadying up and it was clear that, if no external influences intervened, the country was making for general recovery. But the collapse of Europe was yet to come—and to come from weakness created basically by the destruction of the war and by the subsequent artificialities of finance, trade, and political settlements.

The measures taken by the President had been effective in cushioning the shocks. The destitute had been cared for. There had been no industrial friction. The depression up to this time was not serious as depressions go. It is true that the stock crash was dramatic, and had brought great hardship upon individuals, but the productivity of the country still was running strongly. Unemployment had not exceeded that of the short post-war depression of 1921 or, in proportion, that of the depression of 1907-1908, from both of which recuperation had been easy and rapid.

CHAPTER V

THE SECOND STAGE OF THE DEPRESSION—A SURVEY
APRIL, 1931–JULY, 1932

THE lowest depth of the world depression was reached during the period from April, 1931 to July, 1932. At this time was fought and won the great battle to save the country from economic chaos.

The whole world was weakened by the collapse of speculation and the slow recovery from the effects of the war. The canker of war and subsequent disintegration, the story of which was outlined in the Introduction, had eaten deeply into the whole political, financial and industrial structure of Europe. Its inflations and its artificial economic structures had been due for a liquidation since 1927. The postponement through the forced inflation of credit in that year could no longer be continued. And the United States, while on the road to recovery, was weakened by the collapse of speculation which arose from this period of credit inflation.

Early in April there appeared in various world centers the signs of new fears over the economic situation. Whence they came, or how justified they were no one knew. At that time no one could have known the utterly hollow structure of finance which had been built up in Europe, though the impact of its fall, upon an already weakened world, was to shake the foundation of civilization. It was not until a full view could be gained that the world saw its dreadful proportions. The men who saw it fought bravely everywhere to salvage as much as possible, to save the public welfare from destruction.

A cold and formal statement of the progress of this new tide of world disintegration is to be found in the report of the Bank for International Settlements, published a year later. This institution, the creation of the central banks of twenty-six countries, was in a position to know. On May 10, 1932, it reviewed the whole world situation:

When at the end of March, 1931, the Bank for International Settlements closed its books for the first financial year, the depression, although characterized by an unusually sharp fall in prices, still showed in most respects the main tendencies of an ordinary depression. On the capital markets there was a large supply of short-term funds at declining rates . . . government credit had not yet been seriously weakened. . . . It is now possible to estimate that the total amount of short-term international indebtedness which existed at the beginning of 1931 aggregated more than $10,000,000,000 At that time the magnitude of this indebtedness was not known . . . central banks began to realize . . . a danger and they endeavored . . . to strengthen their reserves of foreign exchange . . . the menace . . . did not appear as self-evident as it does today . . . when . . . short-term funds are recalled . . . as the result of the breakdown of confidence . . . almost certain to break the situation at some point. . . . The liquidation in a single year [was] of more than six billion of short-term indebtedness . . . of the balance . . . still outstanding, a substantial part has in fact become blocked. . . . It is unnecessary to emphasize the havoc wrought . . . or to dwell upon the stagnation that resulted. . . . Each contributed their part to the persistent fall in prices . . . [and] accentuated the deflationary forces which are oppressing world economy. . . . In an effort to cope with the situation . . . new forces, themselves dislocating, were introduced into the international economic system of the world . . . a whole series of steps designed to arbitrarily arrest the continuation of transfers and to protect home currencies, such as exchange control, stand-still agreements, restrictions on imports . . . temporary suspension of the gold standard . . . [and] consequent depreciation of currencies . . . [with] exchange restrictions . . . to control capital movements and especially to prevent the flight of capital . . . [also] to control imports . . . [with] allotted foreign exchange for import of "necessary" raw material . . . governments have established import quotas or clearing arrangements. Exchange control . . . forces trade into a kind of strait-jacket. . . . This interference offers no solution . . . [but] aggravates.

Little of this picture of Europe referred to the United States except in one direct particular. Our relation to it was that a large number of our banks had loaned an aggregate of some $1,200,000,000 to $1,500,000,000 on this short-term paper from Central Europe and elsewhere, a considerable part of which funds could not be paid on demand. Neither our government nor our citizens had borrowed from foreign countries. We had established no restrictive trade or capital control, and we had made no default in payment. Our currency and fiscal system were sound. Our trade, however, was restricted and demoralized by the action of foreign nations. We did not build this financial and economic structure of Europe and we could not control it. We did not even know its full weakness, nor did others. But we suffered grievously from it.

The immediate cause of explosion arose from the fact that Germany, Austria, Hungary, Poland, Czechoslovakia, certain countries of South America, and other states, both governments and citizens, who found the long-term money markets exhausted as early as 1927, had been borrowing increasingly vast sums on thirty- to ninety-day bank acceptances, notes, trade-bills, etc. These short-term loans had been placed abroad on the assumption that they were simply normal advances upon goods in export trade. The fact was that a great deal of this short-term money had been invested in capital improvements. It lay in brick and mortar through improvements of factories; or in ships; or was frittered away in purposes which should have been met by taxation, such as the support of armies, avoiding imposition of new taxes for balancing budgets, paying reparations, pensions to disabled veterans, old-age pensions, and doles to the unemployed. Each of these governments and its banks borrowed independently from a multitude of foreign banks, each contributing its part to create an unparalleled structure of short-term paper.

A further force contributing to the disintegration of Europe—and like all such forces, its relative might is not measurable—was the German reparations to the European Allies. The structure of short-term and other debts of that country had been, to some extent, built up in an endeavor to meet these payments, which had in fact become impossible. The comparatively small amounts of payments from the Allies to the United States were a burden during a depression even if insignificant when compared to other forces in action.

We previously have mentioned another factor which was to have great effect upon the United States. That was the practice by foreign governments and foreign national banks of sending their gold or currency reserves abroad on deposit, particularly to the United States and Great Britain, and then of carrying such deposits on their own books as if they were gold. By this method they could earn interest on their reserves. Something like $1,500,000,000 of such deposits from foreign countries were in the United States. France alone placed over $900,000,000 here. In turn, our institutions loaned this money to our own citizens, or on these doubtful foreign bills, or used this gold to build up credit. When the crash came, and foreigners demanded their money, the American banks could not collect upon these bills of other foreigners which they held, and they had to call domestic loans. Thus there was established upon a gigantic scale a drain away from our whole financial system.

Great Britain, with a reputation built by two centuries of financial integrity as a depository, likewise held vast sums of this character. She had loaned a larger proportion of it to foreign countries, on short-term bills, and had less domestic reserves to rely upon. She held probably $600,000,000 of French deposits alone. When the collapse came and those who deposited with her wanted their money, she could not collect her loans. She defaulted upon gold payments.

Still a third factor which greatly affected world stability was the uneasy "flight" of capital. As the result of losses to individuals by former currency depreciations in France, Germany and elsewhere, every time there was the suspicion of financial weakness in any country, the citizens of that country at once sought to move their capital into some other country they regarded as more safe. Such flights of capital always implied gold and exchange movements, weakening currency reserves, a period of frantic borrowing by the weak country, restrictions on exchange and trade, all of which cumulated in an ultimate collapse. Not alone did this flight of capital further weaken the situation in the country under pressure, but its frightened citizens threw their marketable assets upon the markets with a consequent depression of values in the weak country. Mr. Hoover subsequently described these movements of gold and exchange as "like a cannon loose on the deck of the world in a storm." The final repercussions in the United States were manifold, all of them disastrous.

Thus a situation, entirely new to the world, confronted the President. Its dimensions could not be known. It only unfolded itself fully during the six months from April to October, 1931.

It was in fact a most critical peace-time situation which confronted the American people, for the financial stability of the whole world was shaken. Hitherto, in the course of the depression, our problems had been those of economic readjustment from domestic inflation and mad speculation which were intensified by the fact that they were world-wide. Now we were subjected to a crisis from abroad that broke through our very doors. Had the President not held America firm, we should have fallen upon years of much greater difficulty.

The President's policies now widened to meet the situation of April-June, 1931. They were as follows:

1. Co-operation with foreign governments to localize the world difficulties.
2. Maintenance of the impregnability of the credit of the United States Government against these shocks through balancing the budget, in spite of falling revenues and increasing expenditures in relief.
3. Holding the American dollar and American credit sound and free as a Gibraltar of strength in a world crumbling in every quarter.
4. Maintenance of the stability of banks, insurance companies, and other financial institutions of the United States by expansion of credit and government loans.
5. The expansion of relief measures to meet the growing distress.
6. The creation of a vast machinery of reconstruction by the government, and its co-operation with industry.

Although somewhat out of place in sequence of time, we introduce here President Hoover's graphic description of this situation in a speech at Des Moines, Iowa, on October 4, 1932.[1]

[1] State Papers, Vol. II, p. 298.

I wish to describe one of the battles we have fought to save this nation from a defeat that would have dragged farmers and city dwellers alike down to a common ruin. This battle was fought parallel with other battles on other fronts. Much of what I will tell you has been hitherto undisclosed. It had to be fought in silence, for it will be evident to you that had the whole of the forces in motion been made public at the time there would have been no hope of victory because of the panic through fear and destruction of confidence that very disclosure would have brought. . . .

Our own speculative boom had weakened our own economic structure, but the critical assaults and dangers swept upon us from foreign countries. We were therefore plunged into a battle against invading forces of destruction from abroad to preserve the financial integrity of our government; to counteract the terrific forces of deflation aligned against us; to protect the debtor class who were being strangled by . . . the demands for payment of debt; to prevent our being pushed off the gold standard . . . to preserve the savings of the American people.

We were fighting to hold the Gibraltar of world stability because only by holding this last fortress could we be saved from a crashing world, with a decade of misery and the very destruction of our form of government and our ideals of national life.

When eighteen months ago the financial systems of Europe were no longer able to stand the strain of their war inheritances and of their after-war economic and political policies, an earthquake ran through forty nations. Financial panics; governments unable to meet their obligations; banks unable to pay their depositors; citizens, fearing inflation of currency, seeking to export their savings to foreign countries for safety; citizens of other nations demanding payment of their loans; financial and monetary systems either in collapse or remaining only in appearance. The shocks of this earthquake ran from Vienna to Berlin, from Berlin to London, from London to Asia and South America. From all those countries they came to this country, to every city and farm in the United States.

First one and then another of these forty nations either abandoned payment in gold of their obligations to other countries, or restricted payments by their citizens to foreign countries, so as practically to amount to at least temporary or partial repudiation of public and private debts. Every one of them in a frantic endeavor to reduce the expenditures of their citizens, imposed drastic restrictions upon their imports of goods. These events were not as children playing with blocks. They brought revolutions, mutinies, riots, downfalls of governments, and a seething of despair which threatened civilization.

The first effect of these shocks on us was from foreign dumping of American securities on our markets which demoralized prices upon our exchanges, foreign buying power stagnated because of their internal paralysis and this in turn stifled the markets for our farm and factory products, increased our unemployment and by piling up our surpluses demoralized our commodity prices.

The frantic restrictive measures on exchanges and the abandonment of gold standards made it impossible for American citizens to collect billions of the moneys due to us for goods which our citizens had sold abroad, or short-term loans they had made to facilitate commerce. At the same time citizens of those countries demanded payment from our citizens of the moneys due for goods they had sold to our merchants and for securities they had sold in our country.

Before the end foreign countries drained us of nearly a billion dollars of gold and a vast amount of other exchange.

Then we had also to meet an attack upon our own flank by some of our own people, who, becoming infected with world fear and panic, withdrew vast sums from our own banks and hoarded it from the use of our own people, to the amount of $1,500,000,000. This brought its own train of failures and bankruptcies. Even worse, many of our less patriotic citizens started to export their money to foreign countries for fear we should be forced onto a paper money basis. . . .

Three of the great perils were invisible except to those who had the responsibility of dealing with the situation.

The first of these perils was the steady strangulation of credit through the removal of three billions of gold and currency by foreign drains and by hoarding from the channels of our commerce and business. And let me remind you that credit is the lifeblood of business, of prices, and of jobs.

Had the full consequences of this action been allowed to run their full extent, it would have resulted, under our system of currency and banking, in the deflation of credit anywhere from twenty to twenty-five billions, or the destruction of nearly half the immediate working capital of the country. There would have been almost a universal call for payment of debt which would have brought about universal bankruptcy, because property could not be converted to cash, no matter what its value.

And there were other forces equally dangerous. The tax income of the Federal Government is largely based upon profits and income. As these profits and income disappeared, the Federal revenues fell by nearly one half, and thus the very stability of the Federal Treasury was imperiled. The government was compelled to borrow enormous sums to pay current expenses.

The third peril, which we escaped only by the most drastic action, was that of being forced off the gold standard. . . .

I believe I can make clear why we were in danger of being forced off even with our theoretically large stocks of gold. I have told you of the enormous sums of gold and exchange drained from us by foreigners. You will realize also that our citizens who hoard Federal Reserve and some other forms of currency are in effect hoarding gold, because under the law we must maintain forty per cent gold reserve behind such currency. Owing to the lack in the Federal Reserve System of the kind of securities required by the law for the additional sixty per cent of coverage of the currency, the Reserve System was forced to increase their gold reserve up to seventy-five per cent. Thus with $1,500,000,000 of hoarded

THE SECOND STAGE OF THE DEPRESSION

currency there was in effect over $1,000,000,000 of gold hoarded by our own citizens.

These drains had at one moment reduced the amount of gold we could spare for current payments to a point where the Secretary of the Treasury informed me that unless we could put into effect a remedy, we could not hold to the gold standard but two weeks longer because of inability to meet the demands of foreigners and our own citizens for gold.

Being forced off the gold standard in the United States meant utter chaos. Never was our nation in greater peril, not alone in banks and financial systems, money and currency, but that forebode dangers, moral and social chaos, with years of conflict and derangement.

In the midst of this hurricane the Republican administration kept a cool head and rejected every counsel of weakness and cowardice. Some of the reactionary economists urged that we should allow the liquidation to take its course until we had found bottom. Some people talked of vast issues of paper money. Some talked of suspending payments of government issues. Some talked of setting up a council of national defense. Some talked foolishly of dictatorship—any of which would have produced panic itself. Some assured me that no man could propose increased taxes in the United States to balance the budget in the midst of a depression and survive an election.

We determined that we should not enter the morass of using the printing press for currency or bonds. All human experience has demonstrated that the path once taken cannot be stopped, and that the moral integrity of the government would be sacrificed, because ultimately both currency and bonds would become valueless.

We determined that we would not follow the advice of the bitter-end liquidationists and see the whole body of debtors of the United States brought to bankruptcy and the savings of our people brought to destruction.

We determined we would stand up like men and render the credit of the United States Government impregnable through the drastic reduction of government expenditures and increased revenues until we balanced our budget. We determined that if necessary we should lend the full credit of the government thus made impregnable, to aid private institutions to protect the debtor and the savings of our people.

We decided upon changes in the Federal Reserve System which would make our gold active in commercial use and that we would keep the American dollar ringing true in every city in America and in the world; that we would expand credit to offset the contraction brought about by hoarding and foreign withdrawals; that we would strengthen the Federal Land Banks and all other mortgage institutions; that we would lend to the farmers for production; that we would protect the insurance companies, the building and loan associations, the savings banks, the country banks and every other point of weakness.

We determined to place the shield of the Federal Government in front of the local communities in protection of those in distress and that we would increase employment through profitable construction work with the aid of government credit.

In fighting the forces of depression there were times when the situation was so critical that it would have been fatal to disclose the whole story. As a result, President Hoover was repeatedly handicapped in presenting the matter to the public. This was the case even in his Des Moines address, on October 4, 1932. Important as was that address from the standpoint of his own political fortunes, he refrained from telling the entire story, for fear of aggravating the situation. He did not tell the story of that discouraging day in July, 1931, when he discovered that more than a hundred American banks, from the Atlantic to the Pacific, with total deposits of billions of American citizens' money, held huge amounts of uncollectable European short-term bills.

When that speech was made, the situation had been greatly repaired; yet the breath of suspicion might again have set panic afloat. The President knew what bank panics would mean to the American home. The people were not to know until after his authority and leadership, which so long had saved them, had been removed by the election. Several months later they were to experience the consequences.

CHAPTER VI

THE GERMAN MORATORIUM AND THE STANDSTILL AGREEMENT

APRIL–JULY, 1931

THE course of the depression and the actions of President Hoover to meet it unfold themselves in day-to-day events during the sixteen months from April, 1931, to July, 1932. During this time a world battle against chaos was fought.

This difficult period was ushered in by the announcement of the German-Austrian customs agreement on March 21st. The consequences of this—another minor incident in the general political instability—were enlarged by the demand of Great Britain on the twenty-fifth of the month for its review by the League of Nations and by the subsequent announcement of the French Government that it would not permit the customs agreement. To outward appearances this was all that happened. It seemed to be only the usual European squabble, and no doubt it soon would be patched up. But the major consequence, unknown at that time, was that France, which was a large holder of German and Austrian short-term securities, at once demanded payment, and this started a strain upon the finances of those countries. The full amount of French holdings is not known, but probably it exceeded $300,000,000. The demand presumably was an act of political pressure. But immediately these debtor countries began frantically trying to borrow elsewhere, and apprehension was at once created, although the world did not know its cause.

A reaction—of apprehension—immediately was felt in the United States. In the ten days after March 25, 1931, industrial stocks in New York City fell ten index points. They continued to fall throughout April until, at the end of the month, they had fallen twenty per cent.

Immediately following the adjournment of Congress on March 4th, President Hoover had gone on a short inspection trip to Puerto Rico. On his return about two weeks later he was confronted by a world transformed from hope to anxiety. The story of the events may be followed from day to day.

April 12, 1931: A revolution broke out in Spain and the monarchy was overthrown on the fourteenth. This added to the general uncertainty.

April 15, 1931: The President directed an inquiry by the Treasury and Commerce departments as to what was changing the situation from the recent favorable outlook. Both departments reported that there was no domestic reason for alarm, but that there was considerable European selling of American investments and apparently some flight of capital toward the United States. The press noted a decrease in European buying of American commodities.

April 20, 1931: The prices of securities and commodities were falling in European markets and this was reflected in American markets. The President directed that the cabled reports from our commercial and other agents abroad should be brought to him. They indicated that the economic situation in Central Europe was steadily becoming worse but no one was able to assign a special reason for it.

April 27, 1931: The anxiety in the President's mind was indicated by his guarded statement in a speech before the Gridiron Club at Washington: [1]

If, by the grace of God, we have passed the worst of this storm, the future months will be easy. If we shall be called upon to endure more of this period, we must gird ourselves for even greater effort, for today we are writing the introduction to the future history of civilization in America. The question is whether that history shall be written in forms of individual responsibility, and the capacity of the nation for voluntary co-operative action, or whether it shall be written in terms of futile attempt to cure poverty by the enactment of law, instead of the maintained and protected initiative of our people. This is a period when the ideals and hopes which have made America the envy of the world are being tested. So far our people have responded with courage and steadfastness. If we can maintain this courage and resolution we shall have written this new chapter in national life in terms to which our whole idealism has aspired. May God grant to us the spirit and strength to carry through to this end.

April 30, 1931: During the month of April the prices of commodities had fallen all over the world, the decline of wholesale prices in the United States being 1.6 per cent. Cotton fell 10 per cent to 9.11 cents per pound. The prices of securities fell sharply in all markets of the world, the fall in industrial stocks in the United States being about twenty per cent. Unemployment had sensibly increased. With the economic barometer steadily falling, a storm was impending.

May 4, 1931: The President spoke before the meeting in Washington of the International Chamber of Commerce, saying: [2]

... I wish to give emphasis to one of these war inheritances in which international co-operation can... reduce tax burdens of the world, remov-

[1] State Papers, Vol. I, p. 558.   [2] State Papers, Vol. II, p. 559.

ing a primary cause of unrest. ... That is the ... reduction of armament. ... The world armament expenditure ... is now nearly five billions of dollars yearly, an increase of about seventy per cent over that previous to the great war. ... International confidence cannot be builded upon fear.

May 6, 1931: Ambassador Sackett arrived in Washington from Berlin. Lawyer, business executive, and experienced in public affairs, he was in a position to observe and keep his government informed. He advised the President that the situation in Germany and Central Europe was gradually developing toward a crisis. Mr. Sackett did not feel there was any immediate danger, but he was convinced that, unless the tide should turn by autumn, Germany would collapse. He stated that capital was in flight, foreign loans were being withdrawn, and credit was greatly restricted; the pressure of reparations so heavy that he did not believe that the democratic government would continue. Unemployment was increasing, the misery of the people was so great, and the internal political disturbances were so extreme, that there was real danger of a Communist revolution. This would greatly affect the situation in Europe and, in turn, in the United States. Europe was infected with fear of such a result and the entire world was apprehensive.

May 7, 1931: The President was now convinced of the location of the center of the storm which was affecting the United States. He directed that the State and Commerce departments should make a full survey of the financial condition in Central Europe. He caused a canvass to be made of the views of delegates to the International Chamber of Commerce, then in conference in Washington, as above noted. The reports showed that the German and Central European delegates were gloomy. The French were certain that there was nothing wrong except what they called the usual German perverseness in trying to avoid reparations. The British were equally certain that all human happiness depended upon cancellation of their war debts by the United States. Not one delegate mentioned the impending financial panic in Central Europe.

May 11, 1931: Other reports made to the President showed that the total annual interest payments on reparations and inter-governmental debts were about $1,000,000,000 and that they were proving a heavy burden on international exchange and currency stability. About $250,000,000 of this sum was due to the United States. President Hoover therefore requested the Secretary of State to consider as a means of relieving international strain the possibility of readjusting during the depression all inter-governmental debts to a basis nearer the capacity to pay. A study was to be made of the amount of such reductions at might be necessary.

May 13, 1931: A dispatch from the American legation at Vienna brought the startling news that the largest private bank in Austria, the Creditanstalt, was in difficulties and had appealed to the government for assistance. The government and other private banks made temporary advances to it.

May 14, 1931: There was heavy foreign realization upon the New York stock market. Commodity prices weakened on the slackening demand from Europe.

A European conference to consider the economic situation was assembled at Geneva. President Hoover requested the Secretary of State to seek through his agents to learn the views of the representatives to this conference as to what might be impending.

The President today gave out a report upon the effect of the State Department's instruction to consuls, issued in accordance with his instructions September 8, 1930, relative to restriction of immigration. The report showed that before the instruction was issued immigrants were entering the United States at a rate of 22,000 per month. Eight months' experience showed a reduction to 3,000 per month, while deportations and departures were running at a rate of 7,000 per month. Instead of our unemployment burden being increased by immigration at a rate of 200,000 per annum, it was being decreased at a rate of 50,000 per annum. A more rigorous enforcement of deportation laws was reflected in the record of increasing departures.

The total deportations for the fiscal year ending June 30, 1931, was 18,142, for 1932 it was 19,426, for 1933 the figure was 19,865. Of late there has been a great falling off in the number of deportations. In 1934 this had dropped to 8,879. There had been a substantial shrinkage also during the year 1934 of undesirables who had voluntarily migrated back to avoid being deported.

May 15, 1931: The American legation at Budapest reported great excitement in Hungary created by the rumors of an impending financial collapse in Austria.

May 16, 1931: The French and German governments again clashed over the German-Austrian Customs Union.

May 18, 1931: An obscure financial dispatch carried the information that the Bank for International Settlements had offered a loan to the National Bank of Austria to meet the "financial crisis." This was the first intimation of any European financial difficulties to appear in the American press and it appears to have passed unnoticed by the economic writers. It was reported from New York City to the President that a single European financial institution had sold $100,000,000 of American investments.

Wheat and cotton prices dropped in foreign markets and this was reflected in the United States.

May 20, 1931: The President held several conferences with members of the Federal Reserve Board on this and succeeding days. He stated the results of the European surveys made at his request. It was evident that there were large sums from France and other parts of Europe on deposit in the United States and Americans held large amounts of European short-term paper. The French were calling in Austrian and German bills and a flight of capital was starting from those countries. Difficulties were impending for us.

The Federal Reserve officials gave assurance that the Reserve System could absorb any withdrawals without shock. They also informed him that there were many foreign trade-bills in American banks, but they believed them merely to represent goods shipped and to be self-liquidating. There would be no danger from this quarter of failure to meet payments. This opinion, so far as it related to the immediate ability to pay these bills, proved in large part erroneous.

May 21, 1931: The Soviet Government representatives at the International Wheat Conference in London announced that they would continue to dump wheat. There were further recessions in the world price of this commodity.

The European Economic Conference at Geneva adjourned without reaching any conclusions. The members divided on political rather than economic grounds.

May 22, 1931: The President in reply to certain radical senatorial demands for an immediate session of Congress said that distress was being taken care of and that "we cannot legislate ourselves out of this depression." He especially had in mind the storm coming from Europe.

May 25, 1931: Partisan politics again came to the fore. The Democratic National Committee and some of its leaders blamed President Hoover for the falling prices of securities and commodities. In the meantime veterans' bonus payments, imposed over the President's veto, already exceeded the sum of $750,000,000.

May 26, 1931: Official American dispatches from Austria indicated that no hopeful solution of the difficulties yet had been found. The situation of the Creditanstalt was jeopardizing the stability of the Austrian National Bank, and therefore the stability of the government. Prices of grain and cotton continued to fall in the European markets.

May 27, 1931: Press reports from Germany for the first time made public mention of "economic difficulties" in that country. Dispatches from Vienna warned that the gravity of the Austrian financial crisis was growing from hour to hour, and that it was difficult to see the end. The American press today began to take note of the European situation, although mostly in the financial columns.

May 28, 1931: The American legation at Vienna advised that the Austrian Government had guaranteed all bank deposits, but expressed little confidence that this would solve the situation. Advices arrived from Paris that the French officials considered Germany "shamming" in order to escape reparations, and that the French were insisting that Germany and Austria should dissolve the Customs Union as the price of financial assistance.

During the past few days, the British, German, and American banks had agreed upon a loan to the Austrian National Bank. The French refused to participate. The American banks consulted the President upon the question of their participating. His view was that if they distributed the burden and took proper security, it was urgent that they assist in stopping the financial crash which was imminent. The loans subsequently were repaid.

May 30, 1931: Business declined during the month instead of showing the seasonal increase. Prices continued to fall throughout the world and unemployment continued to increase. Wholesale prices in the United States declined 2.7 per cent, industrial stocks fell sixteen per cent, making a total fall in the latter of thirty-six per cent since the end of March.

May 30, 1931: President Hoover, with mind on the impending storm, in a Memorial Day speech at Valley Forge appealed to the nation for steadfastness: [3]

The peculiar significance of Valley Forge in our American annals should strike with especial force in this particular moment of our national life—another Valley Forge . . . an hour of unusual stress and trial . . . is beset with difficulties. . . . These temporary reverses in the march of progress . . . the penalty of excesses of greed, failure of crops, the malign inheritances of the Great War and a storm of other world forces beyond our control . . . all know the misgivings of doubt and grave concern for the future . . . temptations under the distress of the day to turn aside from our true national purposes, from wise national policies and fundamental ideals of the men who builded our Republic. Never was the lure of the rosy path to every panacea and of easy ways to imagined security more tempting.

For the energies of private initiative, of independence, and a high degree of individual freedom of our American system we are offered an alluring substitute in the specious claim that everybody collectively owes each of us individually a living rather than an opportunity to earn a living, and the equally specious claim that hired representatives of a hundred

[3] State Papers, Vol. I, p. 566.

million people can do better than the people themselves, in thinking and planning their daily life. . . .

We are still fighting this war of independence. We must not be misled that the source of all wisdom is in the government. We know that the source of wisdom is in the people; that the people can win anew the victory. But that wisdom is not innate. Rather it is born out of experience, and most of all out of such experience, as is brought to us by the darkest moments—the Valley Forges—of our individual and national careers. It is in the meeting of such moments that are born new insights, new sympathies, new powers, new skills. . . .

Sirens still sing the song of the easy way for the moment of difficulty . . . but the truth which echoes upward from this soil of blood and tears, the way to the nation's greatness is the path of self-reliance, independence, and steadfastness in times of trial and stress.

Valley Forge met such a challenge to steadfastness in times and terms of war. Our test is to meet this challenge in times and terms of peace. . . . If we weaken, as Washington did not, we shall be writing the introduction to the decline of American character and the fall of American institutions. If we are firm . . . we shall be writing the introduction to a yet more glorious epoch in our nation's progress. . . .

. . . Freedom was won here by fortitude, not by the flash of the sword. Valley Forge is our American synonym for the trial of human character through privation and suffering, and it is the symbol of the triumph of the American soul. If those few thousand men endured that long winter of privation and suffering, humiliated by the despair of their countrymen, and deprived of support save their own indomitable will, yet held their countrymen to the faith, and by that holding held fast the freedom of America, what right have we to be of little faith?

May 31, 1931: The German Chancellor, Herr Bruening, announced that he would visit England in an endeavor to secure financial assistance for Germany. The announcement created further uneasiness in the commodity and security markets of the world.

June 1, 1931: The American Minister at Vienna, Gilchrist B. Stockton, reported that the situation was more hopeful and that he had reason to believe the crisis had passed.

June 2, 1931: Advices from our Berlin embassy indicated that the German Government was contemplating drastic taxation in an attempt to balance the budget and to meet the Young Plan reparations payments. These payments amounted to $475,000,000 per annum, of which $175,000,000 were unconditional and $300,000,000 could be temporarily postponed with the consent of the Allied governments.

June 2, 1931: Ambassador Sackett was asked by the President to shorten his vacation in Kentucky and return to Germany, as the situation was daily becoming more acute.

June 5, 1931: The German Ministry issued their emergency decrees calling for about twenty-five per cent increase in taxes and ten per cent decrease in expenses, cutting veterans' allowances, unemployment doles, and government officials' pay. A strong appeal, the serious tone of which indicated great necessity, was issued to the people to accept the drastic steps proposed. A dispatch from *The New York Times* correspondent in Berlin a few days later (June 7th) described this step as "the one last desperate attempt to save the Reich from collapse by the imposition of staggering new burdens on an already sorely laden land."

June 5, 1931: A bank crisis developed in Chicago. Treasury and Federal Reserve officials and leading bankers co-operated in giving immediate attention to it. As a result of their efforts the large Foreman banks were taken over by one of the other banks, with private guarantees. A number of small State banks collapsed before they could be rescued. It developed later that many of the banks had been mishandled and their funds used in promotion and speculation.

The same day, President Hoover summoned to the White House the Cabinet officers concerned, Secretaries Stimson, Mellon and Mills, and stated to them his view that the European situation was deteriorating rapidly, and that there was great danger of financial collapse. We already were being affected by the sale of American securities by foreign institutions, by the fall in our commodity markets and the general apprehension. He feared that if we were not to be involved in a general European financial crash we must take some action. The disintegration of leadership in Europe was evident and offered little hope, but leadership from America might save the situation and restore a measure of confidence throughout the world. While the President did not think the situation had yet reached the acute stage, the United States must be prepared to take the leadership.

The President proposed suspension of all payments on all inter-governmental debts for one year. He expressed the opinion that certainly the French were not yet alarmed sufficiently to accept such a proposal, but that a week or two of increased difficulty would serve to convince them. He asked Secretary Mellon, who was sailing to Europe the next day for a vacation, to survey the situation and report his views at once by cable.

June 6, 1931: The German Chancellor, then in London, issued a public statement that Germany must have financial assistance.

June 7, 1931: After a joint conference in London, German and British ministers issued a public statement:

. . . special stress was laid by the German Ministers on the difficulties of the existing situation in Germany and the need for alteration. The

British Ministers . . . called attention to the world-wide character of the depression. . . . Both parties were agreed . . . the revival of confidence and prosperity depended upon international co-operation.

It was reported by American officials that what really happened in London was that the German ministers told the British that the crash in Austria was having disastrous effects in Germany; that their own situation was critical but not likely to be acute for two months or so, unless there were further withdrawals of short-term credits and a flight of capital. The British considered that any negotiations by them with the French were hopeless. The Germans were sent away with reassuring words of a desire to co-operate.

June 12, 1931: Important German firms suspended payments, and Department of Commerce representatives in Germany advised the Washington Government that others would follow.

June 13, 1931: The withdrawals from the German Reichsbank for the past thirteen days amounted to forty per cent of its reserves in gold and foreign exchange. The bank raised the discount rate to seven per cent.

June 15, 1931: The Acting Secretary of State, William R. Castle, Jr., advised the President that, as the result of the failure of the visit to London of the German ministers to secure assurances of help, the situation in Germany had apparently been precipitated. Runs had developed upon most of the banks.

Ambassador Sackett, who now had returned to Germany, advised that widespread outbreaks of public disorder were likely to develop any moment and that there was doubt that the German Government could survive.

This same day there was a revolution in Costa Rica.

June 15, 1931: The President delivered an address in Indianapolis, at a dinner of the Republican Editorial Association of Indiana. He had intended to use this forum to outline the foreign situation and the policies he proposed, but during the week the situation had taken such a dangerous turn that any discussion without action might only make things worse. The field was not yet prepared for action. His only reference to the foreign situation was: [4]

> As we look beyond the horizons of our own troubles . . . we know that the main causes of this extreme violence and the long continuance of this depression came not from within but from without the United States. Had our wild speculation; our stock promotion with its infinite losses and hardship to innocent people; our loose and extravagant business methods; our unprecedented drought been our only disaster, we should have recovered months ago.

[4] State Papers, Vol. I, p. 574.

A large part of the forces which have swept our shores from abroad are the malign inheritances in Europe of the Great War. . . . Without the war we would have no such depression. . . .

June 16, 1931: The President had called Republican Congressional leaders to meet him at Indianapolis and at various places en route to that place, in order to discuss the action he now was planning, and which resulted in the "Moratorium."

June 17, 1931: The Bank of England, to avert a collapse of the National Bank of Austria, advanced that institution twenty-five millions of dollars and asked that French banks should participate. The French refused to do so unless Austria agreed to "abjure" the German-Austrian Customs Union. France gave Austria three hours to accept or refuse, and that country refused. The British advances were made and the American legation in Vienna advised that the aid given had enabled a new ministry to be formed. The acting government had gone to pieces with little prospect of reorganization. The American banks participated in the British advances.

The same day the German Ambassador von Hoesch in Paris laid before the French Government the critical situation in his country.

June 18, 1931: Secretary Mellon reported by cable that the situation suddenly had become very critical. President Hoover returned to Washington from Indianapolis and at once began conferences with Democratic congressional leaders upon the situation and upon his proposal for a moratorium of inter-governmental debts. The President was advised by the State Department that an appeal for his intervention was being formulated by President von Hindenburg on behalf of the German people. The message arrived a day later and read as follows:

HERBERT HOOVER, PRESIDENT OF THE UNITED STATES,
MR. PRESIDENT:

The need of the German people which has reached a climax compels me to adopt the unusual step of addressing you personally.

The German people has lived through years of great hardship, culminating in the past winter, and the economic recovery hoped for in the Spring of this year has not taken place. I have, therefore, now taken steps, in virtue of the extraordinary powers conferred upon me by the German Constitution, to insure the carrying out of the most urgent tasks confronting the Government and to secure the necessary means of subsistence for the unemployed. These measures radically affect all economic and social conditions and entail the greatest sacrifices on the part of all classes of the population. All possibilities of improving the situation by domestic measures without relief from abroad are exhausted. The economic crisis from which the whole world is suffering hits particularly hard the German nation which has been deprived of its reserves by the consequences of the war. As the developments of the last few days show, the whole world lacks confidence in the ability of the German economic system to work under the existing burdens. Large credits received by us from foreign countries have been withdrawn. Even in the course of the last few days the Reichs Bank has had to hand over to foreign countries one third of its reserves of gold and foreign currency. The inevitable consequence of these developments must be a further serious restriction of economic life and an increase in the numbers of unemployed who already amount to more than one third of the total number of industrial workers. The efficiency, will to work, and discipline of the German people justify confidence in the strict observance of the great fixed private obligations and loans with which Germany is burdened. But, in order to maintain its course and the confidence of the world in its capacity, Germany has urgent need of relief. The relief must come at once if we are to avoid serious misfortune for ourselves and others. The German people must continue to have the possibility of working under tolerable living conditions. Such relief would be to the benefit of all countries in its material and moral effect on the whole crisis. It would improve the situation in other countries and materially reduce the danger to Germany due to internal and external tension caused by distress and despair.

You, Mr. President, as the representative of the great American people, are in a position to take the steps by which an immediate change in the situation threatening Germany and the rest of the world could be brought about.

PRESIDENT VON HINDENBURG.

Today (June 18th) the British Ministry, though not favoring the Customs Union, expressed to our representatives great surprise at the French attitude of forcing a financial débâcle in Austria in order to prevent the Customs Union. Meanwhile, our representatives in Paris advised that it was probable that the French would resist any relief to Germany and that they would not co-operate. But the French, rather than see the British go it alone, finally joined in the credit to Austria.

June 19, 1931: Further heavy withdrawals from the Reichsbank in Berlin amounted to a panic.

During these two days (June 18th-19th) President Hoover telephoned to thirty out-of-town congressional leaders with reference to his proposed moratorium. Congress was not in session, and it was necessary to be absolutely sure of congressional approval if the move were to be made. Other nations, knowing that the Senate frequently has refused approval of international agreements, might be doubtful of our good faith or hang back pending approval many months hence. Senator Robinson, Democratic leader of the Senate, refused to give an assurance and John N. Garner, who was slated to be Speaker of the House, refused to approve, so that the President had to make sure of enough Democratic rank and file to carry both Houses.

June 19, 1931: President Hoover instructed the Secretary of State to call in the interested foreign ambassadors and ministers in Washington and give to them the general lines of his proposed action so that they could communicate it to their governments in advance. He proposed to make public his action on Monday morning, June 22nd. He had determined not to make it a matter of advance confirmation by the foreign governments, as that might result in refusals or attempts at modification among the seventeen nations involved and might lose its force in a fog of international propaganda, leaks and intrigues. It was open diplomacy openly arrived at, and the President trusted that the few disturbers would not oppose the opinion of the world.

Although the President's conversations with congressmen had been confidential, some of them had begun to talk and, in order to prevent inaccurate accounts being given, he made a short statement to the press.[5]

Since my return from the Central West I have conferred with those leaders of both political parties who are present in Washington with respect to certain steps which we might take to assist economic recovery both here and abroad. These conversations have been particularly directed to strengthening the situation in Germany ... the responses ... are most gratifying. Any statement of any plan or method is wholly speculative and is not warranted by the facts.

June 20, 1931: This was Saturday. The President learned that certain senators, with whom he had conferred, had disclosed portions of his proposals to the press and those newspapers that had the information planned to publish it the following (Sunday) morning. The President first requested the press, as a matter of courtesy and patriotic duty, to "hold" the story until the foreign governments concerned could be officially informed. Some refused to do so. To risk the story appearing in garbled form was out of the question. As a result, the President was forced to make his proposals public at once. The statement was prepared late that Saturday afternoon, and then given to the press for Sunday morning release (June 21st). This was before it had been possible to consult with some of the foreign governments that were concerned in the situation. All this resulted in criticism for his apparent lack of diplomatic courtesy in not giving notice to some foreign countries in advance of the newspapers. The American and foreign press both made this comment.

The moratorium statement of President Hoover was:[6]

---
[5] State Papers, Vol. I, p. 591.   [6] State Papers, Vol. I, p. 591.

THE GERMAN MORATORIUM

The American Government proposes the postponement during one year of all payments on inter-governmental debts, reparations and relief debts, both principal and interest, of course not including obligations of governments held by private parties. Subject to confirmation by Congress, the American Government will postpone all payments upon the debts of foreign governments to the American Government payable during the fiscal year beginning July 1st next, conditional on a like postponement for one year of all payments on inter-governmental debts owing the important creditor powers.

This course of action has been approved by the following senators: Henry F. Ashurst, Hiram Bingham, Wm. E. Borah, James F. Byrnes, Arthur Capper, Simeon D. Fess, Duncan U. Fletcher, Carter Glass, William J. Harris, Pat Harrison, Cordell Hull, Wm. H. King, Dwight W. Morrow, George H. Moses, David A. Reed, Claude A. Swanson, Arthur Vandenberg, Robert F. Wagner, David I. Walsh, Thomas J. Walsh, James E. Watson, and by the following representatives: Isaac Bacharach, Joseph W. Byrns, Carl R. Chindbloom, Frank Crowther, James W. Collier, Charles R. Crisp, Thomas H. Cullen, George P. Darrow, Harry A. Estep, Willis C. Hawley, Carl E. Mapes, J. C. McLaughlin, Earl C. Michener, C. William Ramseyer, Bertrand H. Snell, John Q. Tilson, Allen T. Treadway and Will R. Wood. It has been approved by Ambassador Charles G. Dawes and by Owen D. Young.

The purpose of this action is to give the forthcoming year to the economic recovery of the world and to help free the recuperative forces already in motion in the United States from retarding influences from abroad.

The world-wide depression has affected the countries of Europe more severely than our own. Some of these countries are feeling to a serious extent the drain of this depression on national economy. The fabric of inter-governmental debts, supportable in normal times, weighs heavily in the midst of this depression.

From a variety of causes arising out of the depression such as the fall in the price of foreign commodities and the lack of confidence in economic and political stability abroad there is an abnormal movement of gold into the United States which is lowering the credit stability of many foreign countries. These and the other difficulties abroad diminish buying power for our exports and in a measure are the cause of our continued unemployment and continued lower prices to our farmers.

Wise and timely action should contribute to relieve the pressure of these adverse forces in foreign countries and should assist in the re-establishment of confidence, thus forwarding political peace and economic stability in the world.

Authority of the President to deal with this problem is limited as this action must be supported by the Congress. It has been assured the cordial support of leading members of both parties in the Senate and the House. The essence of this proposition is to give time to permit debtor governments to recover their national prosperity. I am suggesting to the American people that they be wise creditors in their own interest and be good neighbors.

I wish to take this occasion also to frankly state my views upon our relations to German reparations and the debts owed to us by the Allied governments of Europe. Our government has not been a party to, or exerted any voice in determination of reparation obligations. We purposely did not participate in either general reparations or the division of colonies or property. The repayment of debts due to us from the Allies for the advance for war and reconstruction were settled upon a basis not contingent upon German reparations or related thereto. Therefore, reparations is necessarily wholly a European problem with which we have no relation.

I do not approve in any remote sense of the cancellation of the debts to us. World confidence would not be enhanced by such action. None of our debtor nations has ever suggested it. But as the basis of the settlement of these debts was the capacity under normal conditions of the debtor to pay, we should be consistent with our own policies and principles if we take into account the abnormal situation now existing in the world. I am sure the American people have no desire to attempt to extract any sum beyond the capacity of any debtor to pay and it is our view that broad vision requires that our government should recognize the situation as it exists.

This course of action is entirely consistent with the policy which we have hitherto pursued. We are not involved in the discussion of strictly European problems, of which the payment of German reparations is one. It represents our willingness to make a contribution to the early restoration of world prosperity in which our own people have so deep an interest.

I wish further to add that while this action has no bearing on the conference for limitation of land armaments to be held next February, inasmuch as the burden of competitive armaments has contributed to bring about this depression, we trust that by this evidence of our desire to assist we shall have contributed to the good will which is so necessary in the solution of this major question.

The effect of this proposal in Europe can be illustrated by the following incident. That evening, within an hour after the release had been given out, the editor of one of the large London papers called the White House from London by trans-Atlantic radio telephone, and asked to talk with the President. He was informed that the President was en route to the Rapidan Camp in Virginia. The editor then talked with Secretary Newton. In the course of the conversation which ensued the editor said, "We [the public] look upon it as the greatest thing since the signing of the Armistice."

A few days later in commenting upon the action of the President, the Rt. Hon. Ramsay MacDonald, the British Premier, in speaking before the annual Independence Day dinner of the American Society, said it was "an action of great wisdom, courage and deep insight."

On July 7th *The Washington Post* commented as follows: "The

Moratorium carries with it such a powerful stimulus that it may well mark a definite turning point toward prosperity."

Each government immediately was notified of the forcing of the President's hand by certain of the press.

June 21-23, 1931: The President was continually in touch by telephone with our ambassadors and ministers in each important capital.

June 22, 1931: The action of President Hoover seemed to have transformed the whole international situation. During early June the economic condition of the world had continued to sink to a still lower level under the continuous influence of the growing panic in Europe. Immediately after the news of the moratorium became public, prices and business activity responded in every part of the world. In the United States wheat rose four to five cents per bushel, cotton almost twenty per cent, industrial stocks nearly thirty per cent. The retail trade at once improved. Men were taken back into employment. The whole world breathed easier. Panic no doubt had been prevented. *The New York Times* editorial a few days later (June 29th) said: ". . . great results [are] already achieved . . . that a severe financial crisis was hanging over Germany is fully established . . . that danger . . . not only to Germany but of all Europe and the United States was removed. . . . We cannot but wonder with the rest of the world at the happy revulsion of feeling which everywhere followed. . . ."

The public reception of the moratorium was good in all parts of America and Europe except in Paris where the French Ministry unofficially informed the American ambassador that they approved (with the usual) "in principle" but that they would not accept the inclusion of the "unconditional reparations" and "reparations in kind" from Germany. The "unconditional reparations" were an annual priority payment amounting to $175,000,000 of which about $110,000,000 were to go to France, and, together with "reparations in kind," comprised the bulk of the reparations payments collected by France. In other words, the French would hold to about $130,000,000 per annum from Germany, but would be glad to be relieved of the $120,000,000 a year that they were paying the United States and Great Britain upon their war debts. This attitude was not unexpected by President Hoover and was precisely the reason for public action instead of private negotiation. The President now requested Secretary Mellon to join Ambassador Walter E. Edge in Paris.

June 23, 1931: The President telegraphed to all the members of the Senate and the House whom he had not consulted previously and asked if they approved the moratorium. A majority of the members of both Houses responded favorably. Also, the President instructed Ambassador

Edge informally to say to the French authorities that anything short of a clean sweep would not accomplish his purpose. "This is the restoration of public confidence throughout the world. . . . Nothing short of such a major purpose would justify him in asking the American people to make such a sacrifice." He pointed out that if the moratorium were withdrawn, the Germans in any event could default under the terms of the "conditional" reparations and "payments in kind," of the Young Plan, and leave France only $110,000,000 per annum. Furthermore, he stressed the opinion that the United States and Great Britain no doubt would claim their war-debt payments from France and therefore that country would gain nothing in the end. The world would return to panic through the breakdown of the plan. The government-inspired press in France was antagonistic and bitter, with personal abuse of the American President.

The Italian Government and the British Government accepted unconditionally, with thanks to the President for his intervention.

President Hoover instructed the Secretary of State to suggest to the German Government that it should give evidence of a desire to co-operate and work with France in an endeavor to break down the bitter antagonism which had been raised by the proposed German-Austrian Customs Union. In consequence the German Chancellor delivered a radio speech of conciliatory character which was well received in France.

June 24, 1931: The Ministry of Czechoslovakia expressed the opinion that the moratorium had saved a world catastrophe. Also the Austrian Government said: "It has given the people of Europe a new hope."

The Creditanstalt in Vienna was able to make financial arrangements to keep open, instead of closing as had been contemplated.

The difficulties became acute when the French Government definitely stated that it would not surrender the "unconditional" reparations and counter proposals to us were made which protected the payment of reparations to France. Secretary Mellon advised from Paris that the prospect of the French acceptance of the moratorium was hopeless. The President refused to proceed if any country were to have a preferential position.

June 25, 1931: Secretary Stimson, believing that the situation was in process of settlement, left for Italy.

June 26, 1931: The British, Italian, Rumanian, German, Japanese, Polish, Czech, Finnish, New Zealand, Hungarian, Austrian, Norwegian, Swedish, Canadian, and Greek governments had now accepted the moratorium.

June 26, 1931: President Hoover made reply to France that he proposed "a strictly economic remedy to meet the most serious crisis, the

THE GERMAN MORATORIUM 97

threatened complete financial collapse in Central Europe with all the serious economic and social consequences entailed for the entire world. . . . The American people thereby accept a budget deficit of $250,000,000. . . . [He] is acting for the benefit of France as well as our own. . . . The American Government cannot admit any connection between proposal and European political problems. . . . Impossible . . . [to] make concessions as to principle of total suspension. Any concession to one country necessitated concessions to others until project would be whittled away. . . . American people will never consent unless sacrifice mutual. . . . At the end of last week Germany was on the verge of collapse, and was saved by the announcement . . . delay or refusal to go along will result in confronting us with the conditions which existed last week. . . . The delay already renewing drains on Germany while the situation in Austria and Hungary is desperate. . . . All other important nations except Belgium are now in agreement."

The President renewed a suggestion for overcoming the technical difficulties raised for purposes of obstruction by the French Government on a basis which would bring the same result that he originally had proposed.

July 1, 1931: Individuals in the French Senate attacked both the proposal and the President. Jacob Gould Schurman, a former American ambassador to Germany now in London, stated that Germany was in peril of a complete collapse unless the plan were adopted.

July 2, 1931: The President was advised by our representatives abroad that it was evident that the delays of the French were breaking down confidence and that again drains had begun on Germany and other Central European countries.

July 3, 1931: The President, through the State Department, sent a long dispatch to the French Government. He urged action, reviewed their contentions, pointed out that they were unacceptable, and endeavored to find a basis on which to meet French opposition. The President directed that the dispatch be made public. Meanwhile, the German financial crisis continued. The Reichsbank had exhausted the proceeds of a temporary loan of $100,000,000 made to it by the central banks of other countries.

July 4, 1931: There were further runs on the Reichsbank to the amount of $14,000,000 in one day.

A joint loan of $20,000,000 by our Federal Reserve Banks, the Bank for International Settlements, and the Bank of England was made to the Hungarian National Bank to prevent its collapse.

July 5, 1931: The French replied to the President at great length, raising no less than eight new difficulties not hitherto mentioned by them.

President Hoover, after conferences with Acting Secretaries Mills and Castle, and Senators Reed and Morrow, discussed the situation with our representatives abroad by means of the trans-Atlantic telephone. He instructed them to state to the French Government that we saw no alternative to their latest proposal but to withdraw our proposal. The obvious result would be default of Germany on the "conditional" reparations. Then the President would renew his proposal to all other governments except France, leaving her way clear to collect her share of the "unconditional" reparations but at the same time obligated to pay the sums due from her to other governments. He regretted the isolation of France in this effort but already many of the world benefits of reviving confidence were being lost by her delays. In a final effort to find a basis, he proposed a joint statement by the American and French governments which should merely say that the principles had been agreed upon, and that the details would be referred to a technical commission which would settle them "within the spirit of the President's proposal."

July 6, 1931: The President directed Acting Secretary Castle to give to the press the gist of this final proposal. At his suggestion, Mr. Castle also informed by trans-Atlantic telephone Arthur Henderson, the British Foreign Minister, that we were transmitting our final suggestion to the French; that we did not expect its acceptance; that we had done all we could; that we felt that if the French did refuse, the British should be forewarned to call the heads of European states instantly to a conference and to warn them to look out for themselves. The President anticipated the worst of effects from a failure of the plan and felt that we should have all we could do to prevent a financial panic in the United States.

The French authorities were indignant at this pressure and after a "final" refusal in the morning, in the afternoon, under Foreign Minister Briand's insistence, suddenly recalled their last action and paraphrased the President's formula into a "proposal" of their own which amounted to complete acceptance.

President Hoover announced accordingly that all the governments concerned had approved the moratorium. "While the plan is particularly aimed at economic relief, yet economic relief means the swinging of men's minds from fear to confidence. . . . It means tangible aid to unemployment and agriculture."

July 7, 1931: In accordance with understandings arrived at, the British Government today issued a call for the technical representatives of the powers concerned under the plan to meet in London on July 17th. This was the conference which settled the technical details "within the spirit of President Hoover's proposal."

The President had spoken with our representatives in London, Paris and Berlin more than twenty times over the trans-Atlantic telephone during the negotiations and had been in contact every hour of the day for over two weeks. The long public and business experience of Ambassador Walter E. Edge particularly fitted him for these difficult negotiations. The successful results were greatly due to his tact and influence. Moreover, the President had been assisted greatly and unfailingly at all hours of the day by Acting Secretary of the Treasury Ogden Mills, Acting Secretary of State William R. Castle, Senators Dwight Morrow of New Jersey, and David A. Reed of Pennsylvania, and by Ambassador Charles G. Dawes who was, during part of the time, in Washington, staying at the White House.

In many of the various actions proposed to meet the depression time was an important element. This was especially true with regard to the German moratorium. The mere announcement gave a great impetus to recovery. Every hour taken in inducing other nations to join in this action was vital. Otherwise impetus was lost and we should slip back.

July 7, 1931: The President was advised that the situation in Europe, which again had been growing worse under French delay, now was rising to a renewed panic through continual demands on Germany for payment of short-term banking bills, and through the flight of capital from Central Europe. The $100,000,000 advanced to the Reichsbank had been exhausted. Today one thousand German commercial firms guaranteed the Reichsbank $120,000,000 of foreign exchange.

On *July 8th*, the German Government announced that it would seek a great international loan.

July 9, 1931: President Luther of the Reichsbank flew to London to seek a loan of $400,000,000; $12,000,000 gold was withdrawn from the Reichsbank during the day. Herr Luther proceeded the same day to Paris and interviewed French officials, pressing for an international loan of $400,000,000 to $600,000,000. He was told by the French that a condition precedent to negotiations was "substantial political guarantees," which further alarmed the world.

July 10, 1931: Meanwhile the home situation demanded attention. President Hoover said: [7]

It has come to my knowledge that certain persons are selling short in our commodity markets, particularly in wheat. These transactions have

[7] State Papers, Vol. I, p. 596.

been continuous over the past month. I do not refer to the ordinary hedging transactions, which are a sound part of our marketing system. I do not refer to the legitimate grain trade. I refer to a limited number of speculators. I am not expressing any views upon economics of short selling in normal times.

But in these times this activity has a public interest. It has but one purpose and that is to depress prices. It tends to destroy returning public confidence. The intent is to take a profit from the losses of other people. Even though the effect may be temporary it deprives many farmers of their rightful income.

If these gentlemen have that sense of patriotism, which outruns immediate profit, and a desire to see the country recover, they will close up these transactions and desist from their manipulations. The confidence imposed upon me by law as a public official does not permit me to expose their names to the public.

Three months later, on October 17th, definite reforms were adopted by the exchanges.

July 11, 1931: The Reichsbank lost another $25,000,000 through demands for payment of bank bills and flight of capital. There also were considerable gold withdrawals from London to Paris. The British dispatches stated that when earlier the French withdrew gold from Germany in payment of demand bills they deposited it in London. Chancellor Bruening appealed to Ambassador Sackett for further aid.

Press dispatches from Berlin said that President Hoover had agreed to a loan to Germany, which the President promptly denied through Under Secretary Castle. The President advised our representatives abroad that this was now a banking matter and that the European banks should get together and find a solution.

July 12, 1931: President Hoover asked Secretary Stimson to proceed to Paris from Italy where he had just arrived. Also the President directed Under Secretaries Castle and Mills to make statements clarifying the American position that this was now a banking proposition between bankers. Mr. Castle said:

The heads of the principal European central banks including the Bank of England and the Bank of France are meeting tomorrow morning in Basel with the Bank for International Settlements. They will no doubt consider the German banking crisis. Obviously any plan for a banking solution of the situation must originate from these banks which are on the ground, and it is my understanding that our bankers are prepared to consider assistance in any effective plan of relief that they shall evolve.

July 14, 1931: All Hungarian banks were closed for three days by government order. German banks were held closed except for payrolls.

The German Government declared a moratorium for a further period. A statement from Berlin showed that withdrawals from Germany on short-term notes, and the flight of capital, had amounted to nearly $800,000,000 since the end of March, and to $500,000,000 in the last ten weeks.

Today the American press stated that there was held in the United States between $500,000,000 and $700,000,000 of German short-term trade paper and between $200,000,000 and $300,000,000 German bank acceptances. The President, not being satisfied that the reports to the Federal Reserve officials were correct as to the volume of foreign short-term bills held by American banks, directed an independent survey to be made. In a few hours a partial canvass disclosed over $1,000,000,000 of these German bills alone.

The price of wheat dropped in Canada and the Argentine.

July 15, 1931: The flight of capital throughout the world to the United States and France upset all foreign exchanges. The German Government imposed restrictions on exchange and the Reichsbank raised the discount rate to ten per cent.

President Hoover feared that, much against his will, the United States again might have to intervene, as European countries seemed unable to work together. He requested Secretary Mellon to return to Paris from the south of France to co-operate with Secretary Stimson and Ambassador Edge. The European governments had arranged that the German, British, French, Italian, Belgian, and Japanese premiers, finance ministers, or ambassadors should meet in London on the twentieth.

July 16, 1931: In preliminary discussions between representatives of the various governments in Paris the French proposed a loan to the Germans of $500,000,000 equally from the governments of the United States, France and England, to be secured by customs control and also to be conditional upon political consideration.

The President advised our representatives that the United States Government would lend no money to Germany; that he did not approve of any more private loans to Germany; that it was no use to pour water into a bucket with a hole in the bottom; that the hole was Germany's short-term obligations of unknown and huge amounts. He saw no reason why the American public directly or indirectly should pay off these bills. The holders of them must stand the brunt.

July 17, 1931: President Hoover concluded that the new crisis which had developed could be handled only on an entirely new and drastic basis; that Europe was failing utterly to show co-operation; that this crisis again threatened the United States; that the bankers showed no leadership and the governments would need to tell them what to do. He cabled to Secretaries Stimson and Mellon in Paris a definite plan for their presentation at the forthcoming conference in London on the twentieth. This was subsequently called the "standstill" proposal by which all the banks in the nine or ten nations who held the mass of German short-term bills should agree not to present them for payment for a stipulated time.

This "standstill" proposal from the President was as follows:

The essence of the problem is the restoration of confidence in Germany's economic life, both in Germany and abroad.

1. On the political side, the United States hopes that, through mutual good will and understanding, the European nations may eliminate all friction, so that the world may rely upon the political stability of Europe.

2. On the economic side, the present emergency is strictly a short-term credit crisis. Fundamental pressure on German economy during the period of depression has been relieved by the joint action of the creditor powers in suspending all payments upon governmental debts during the period of one year. But Germany has financed her economic activities to a very great extent through the medium of short-term foreign credits. There is no reason to doubt the soundness of the basis upon which these credits rest, but the general uncertainty which has prevailed for the last few weeks resulted in such a loss of confidence that the German banking and credit structure was subjected to a very severe strain. This strain took two very definite forms, both of which resulted in a drain of banking resources and the depletion of German gold and foreign exchange holdings.

In the first place there was a flight from the mark within Germany. In the second place there was a withdrawal of foreign deposits and a curtailment on the part of foreign banks of outstanding lines of credit.

Fundamentally there is nothing to justify these movements and if, through co-operative action they can be arrested, there is no reason why the present emergency cannot be immediately and definitely surmounted.

(a) As to the first, namely, the internal flight from the mark, this can be and is being successfully combated by the vigorous action of the German Government and the Reichsbank. Once unreasonable fear has been eliminated, it is certain that the patriotism of the German people can be relied on to prevent the destruction of the credit of their own country.

(b) As to the external credits, we believe that the first approach to this problem is the development of a program that will permit the maintenance for an adequate period of time of the present outstanding lines of credit. In this connection it is our understanding that this volume of credit, together with the freed reparations and the natural gain from the allayment of the panic, should be adequate to meet the needs of German economic life for the immediate moment.

On the other hand, it must be apparent that, unless provision is made for the maintenance of these credits, an attempt to provide new ones, whether of a short- or long-term character, would be ineffective. In the development of such a program the governments of the countries having principal banking centers, including the United States, Belgium, France,

Great Britain, Holland, Italy, Japan and Switzerland, and other important banking centers, might well undertake to encourage their bankers so to organize as to permit the maintenance for an adequate period of time of present-day outstanding lines of credit to Germany.

The responsibility for working out the details of such a program and the methods of making it effective with due regard to the protection of the banks and the needs of German economy should be left to the banking communities of the respective countries and the central banks could, we believe, be relied on to furnish the necessary leadership, co-operation and direction.

Such voluntary arrangements should be supplemented, for the time being, by strict control of all foreign exchange transactions by the Reichsbank so that the integrity of the program can be maintained and the banks that are participating can be assured that there would be no arbitrary withdrawal either from within or without Germany.

3. It is our belief that if such a program could be made promptly effective it would result in an immediate restoration of confidence and that in a comparatively short time the necessity for restrictions of this character would disappear and normal conditions would once more prevail. There is all the more ground for faith in such a result in view of the fact that the United States debt suspension program has not become effective and that the events which succeeded the announcement of that program clearly demonstrate that relief from payment of inter-governmental debts established in the minds of the business world the basis for renewed confidence.

4. A committee should be selected by the Bank for International Settlements or created by some other appropriate method to secure co-operation on the following question:

(a) In consultation with the banking interests in the different countries to provide for the renewal of the present volume of outstanding short-term credits from those countries.

(b) In making an inquiry into the immediate further needs in credit of Germany.

(c) In the development during the course of the next six or eight months of plans for a conversion of some proportion of the short-term credits to long-term credits.

Again it was proposed that the governments should lend to Germany. Again President Hoover declined, knowing that loans would be but a drop in the bucket; that it simply meant that the American public would be relieving the banks of nine countries from their follies. If the object was to get additional money to spend in Germany, he was of the opinion that, in the present state of the world, Germany should be grateful for the respite already provided without asking for more.

July 18, 1931: The German Chancellor Bruening and Premier Laval of France met in Paris. The French continued their loan proposal, which was largely political. The President again informed our representatives that positively we would take no part whatever in any fresh loans to Germany.

July 19, 1931: The French press attacked us for not being "co-operative." The President instructed our delegates to present the "standstill" plan as the American proposal to the London Conference about to meet.

July 21, 1931: The results of the London Conference meetings on Monday and Tuesday were reported in detail by telephone to President Hoover. The French and British had reverted to a loan plan again. The President did not believe that, in view of the already developing difficulties of the Bank of England or the political objectives of the French, there was any genuine basis to these discussions. He did not believe they would join in such a loan. He felt that the conference was milling around hopelessly, with jockeying for political position, while the world was swiftly moving into chaos. His "standstill" proposal had not been presented formally to the conference by the American delegates who feared it would arouse antagonism as being "American dictation," although the idea had been mentioned privately. The President therefore determined to release the plan to the press and to force the issue by bringing the whole thing into the open. This was done.

July 22, 1931: Certain Wall Street bankers attacked the "standstill" plan.

July 23, 1931: The Hoover Plan was adopted by the London Conference, which issued the following statement:

The recent excessive withdrawals of capital from Germany have created an acute financial crisis. These withdrawals have been caused by a lack of confidence which is not justified by the economic and budgetary situation of the country.

In order to insure maintenance of the financial stability of Germany, which is essential in the interests of the whole world, the governments represented at the conference are ready to co-operate so far as lies within their power to restore confidence.

The governments represented at the conference are ready to recommend for the consideration of the financial institutions in their respective countries the following proposals for relieving the present situation:

First, that the central bank credit of $100,000,000 recently granted to the Reichsbank under the auspices of the Bank for International Settlements be renewed at maturity for a period of three months.

Second, that concerted measures should be taken by the financial institutions in the different countries, with a view to maintaining the volume of credits they have already extended to Germany.

The conference recommends that the Bank for International Settlements should be invited to set up without delay a committee of representatives nominated by the governors of the central banks interested to inquire into the immediate further credit needs of Germany and to study the possibilities of converting a portion of the short-term credits into long-term credits.

The conference noted with interest a communication from Dr. Bruening relative to the joint guarantee recently placed by German industry at the disposal of the Gold Discount Bank. The conference is of the opinion a guarantee of this description should make it possible to provide a sound basis for the resumption of normal operations of international credit.

The conference considers that if these measures are carried through they will form a basis for more permanent action to follow.

The conference also decided that a committee should proceed with an elaboration of the detailed measures required for giving effect to President Hoover's proposal for a year's suspension of inter-governmental debts.

July 23, 1931: The President said:[8]

The London conference has laid sound foundations for the establishment of stability in Germany.

The major problem is one affecting primarily the banking and credit conditions and can best be solved by the voluntary co-operation of the bankers of the world rather than by governments with their conflicting interests. Such a basis of co-operation is assured.

The program supplements the suspension of inter-governmental debts already in effect. The combined effect should enable the German people with their resources, industry and courage, to overcome the temporary difficulties and restore their credit.

The program contributes to expedite recovery from world-wide depression through the overcoming of the most important elements in the crisis affecting Central Europe.

The world is indebted to Premiers MacDonald, Laval, and Bruening, to Messrs. Stimson, Mellon, Grandi, Francqui and other governmental representatives in this conference. The conference has demonstrated a fine spirit of conciliation and consideration amongst nations that will have lasting benefits in establishment of stability.

July 23, 1931: During the negotiations protracted through more than forty days, after the declaration of the moratorium on inter-governmental debts, American information became more and more clear as to the real situation in Central Europe. It was found that short-term and demand obligations had been piled up by these governments, their banks and business houses, to a sum then estimated at more than five billion dollars. This was subsequently found to be under-estimated. And more billions were found to have been put afloat by other governments. Germany alone had outstanding in March, 1931, probably $4,000,000,000. This money had been spent in factories, improvements and reckless government expendi-

[8] State Papers, Vol. I, p. 600.

tures. It had been loaned by the banks of a dozen nations, each banker anxious for the high rates of interest offered and without proper precautionary inquiry as to the economic condition of these countries. France alone had withdrawn her loans. Scores of banks throughout the world held large amounts of these short-term bills. If Germany had been allowed to collapse it would have produced a universal panic.

July 24, 1931: The French now began withdrawing their gold deposits from England. President Hoover asked Secretary Stimson by trans-Atlantic telephone if it were not possible to suggest to the French that they cease these withdrawals, which were being interpreted here as foreboding a collapse in England, and everybody's nerves were on edge after the Central European experience. He suggested that if the French Government needed gold, the Bank of France had $800,000,000 of it in the United States which was subject to demand.

Through the courteous assistance of General Dawes, we are enabled to quote the following from his unpublished diary as a sidelight on the times, which gives a vivid picture of President Hoover during these trying negotiations. It should be remembered that General Dawes not only had been Vice President of the United States, but also had wide experience and reputation as soldier, banker, and diplomat.

"My brother Henry's Home,
"Evanston [Illinois]   Thursday June 11, 1931.

"I left Monday night for Marion, Ohio, to attend the dedication of the Harding Memorial by President Hoover at exercises presided over by ex-President Coolidge. I had received a telegram from President Hoover asking me to go with him from Marion to Springfield, Ill., as he had important matters to talk over with me. . . .

"On the train going to Columbus, Hoover went over the financial situation in Europe which is critical. At that time, he expected the State Bank in Austria to fail, as the relief measures under negotiation seemed likely to fall through. We were reassured on this point, however, by a telephone from Stimson which was received at the State Capital. If the Austrian bank failed, it was expected that the Reichsbank would be compelled to take a moratorium. This would precipitate a world financial crisis, affecting our own country materially. . . . His [President Hoover's] present thought was to suggest a reparations moratorium all around for one or two years, funding the payment due to the United States for that time. France in this case would have to forego receiving reparations, at present amounting to more than she is paying the United States. Hoover could not propose such a plan without being assured by the leaders of the opposition in the Senate that his proposal would be ratified by the Senate next December.

"He asked my opinion on this course, and if he took it said he wished to call me to Washington to help in securing senatorial agreement. I approved the tentative plan, but urged that the period be made two years instead of one.

"European finance is tottering, but this plan might help in tiding things over. . . .

"In our own country banks are closing every day, and money is being hoarded in safe deposit boxes. Conditions here approximate those of 1873 and 1893.

"White House, Washington, July 21, 1931.
"Monday night.

"So much has happened this busy day that, despite its great importance, I can but note the salient things. . . .

"Continuously the telephone rang.

"Mills carried on conversations with Harrison, President [Governor] of the Federal Reserve Bank in New York, and with Secretary Mellon at London. The President talked with Stimson at London at one time for an hour. Harrison, at New York, was in direct communication with Norman, President [Governor] of the Bank of England, and would report from him.

"Direct word was had through these sources from Luther, President of the Reichsbank.

"Only first authority was consulted by the President and his immediate staff as affording proper information to justify his own conclusions. The President had with him in his office, Ogden Mills, Under Secretary of the Treasury, Castle, Under Secretary of State, Eugene Meyer, Chairman [Governor] of the Federal Reserve Board, Senator Morrow and myself.

"When he would finish a telephone conversation, he would summarize it to us for our observation. All information that he received only strengthened him in his original position.

"I believe no one concerned with the whole situation in Europe had at his command more authoritative information than did our President. He had not an idle moment during the day except for lunch. His clearness and quickness of comprehension—his equipoise and calmness—and his command of knowledge of every element in this diversified world-important problem, were remarkable. He was always the alert, competent, and compelling Executive, and at the end of the day nothing had shaken his confidence in the soundness of his original position and views. . . .

"I leave tomorrow morning for New York, sailing from there at 5 P.M. My stay here with the President has been an experience, and I leave with increased admiration for his genius.

"At Sea, S.S. *Mauretania,*
"Thursday, July 23, 1931.
"It is interesting this evening to read the condensed radiogram of the meeting of the London Conference, after having sat by the side of the President at the White House for two days while his guiding hand was steering a dangerous situation to a safe conclusion. The President never lost sight of the fact that he was dealing primarily with a financial crisis in Germany; that such a crisis demands immediate decisions and that delay to render them only intensifies that crisis.

"The interjection of a loan discussion meant the interjection of political discussion and delay.

"As hoped for, the [British] Prime Minister and other dignitaries in their speeches confined themselves to generalities, adopted the President's suggestions in toto, and adjourned.

"Now there is time to work out other help if such is feasible, since Germany's further financial pressure from abroad is stayed. I expressed my ideas of his accomplishment to the President in the following radiogram.

"Herbert Hoover,
"White House,
"Washington, D. C.
"Have just received word of the London outcome. Congratulations. By your recent statement from Washington you again assumed leadership and announced in advance of the Conference the only way out in a way which reassured the financial and business world and preserved confidence. Not only this, but the statement determined the nature of a prompt report of the Conference and compelled its speedy adjournment, thus preventing an otherwise inevitable debate over vital national differences which would have undermined world business confidence and largely if not entirely destroyed the present value of anything the Conference would have reported. Your intervention was necessary to preserve the full benefits of your reparations moratorium arrangement. In financial crises nothing is more important than central leadership, with definite opinions, and which acts without delay. This Conference could not have furnished it, and you alone were in a position to do so."

CHAPTER VII

THE AMERICAN DEPRESSION RELIEVED

JULY–SEPTEMBER, 1931

July 24, 1931: The President was furnished with a summary of the national finances for the fiscal year ending July 1st.

(In order that they may be more useful for comparison, they have been recast as described under the date of July 1, 1930.)

	1930	1931
General Expenditures	$ 2,740,011,582	$ 2,724,293,879
Emergency Expenditures:		
Agriculture	10,958,911	48,255,674
Public Works, other construction and relief items	410,420,141	574,874,107
Provisions for loans to veterans on bonus certificates in excess of trust funds		112,000,000
Emergency loans to farm cooperatives through Farm Board, etc.	148,591,009	191,506,622
[Total Emergency]	$569,970,061	$926,636,403
Total Expenditures	$ 3,309,891,643	$ 3,650,930,282
Total National Debt at end of period:	$16,185,308,000	$16,801,485,000
Increase in the debt, being practically the deficit		$ 616,177,000

The government revenues were largely dependent upon income taxes which now were falling rapidly. It was obvious that the Administration must seek new revenues and further drastic reductions in such expenditures as could be postponed to better times in order that the budget might be balanced.

The loss in revenues during the past year, due to the depression, was $860,709,000, which more than accounted for the increase in the debt.

At a Cabinet meeting President Hoover stated that the situation was "extremely dangerous; that the prairie fire now put out on the continent may have caught in England; that we must again pull in our belts." He strongly urged the departmental heads to review every part of the government and prepare further reductions in all expenditures except for relief. This was in view of the prospect of a further budget deficit for the current fiscal year. He issued the following directions to all officials:

... In view of the fact that our receipts are falling off materially from the amount estimated at the time of the preparation of the budget for 1932, and the consequent large deficit indicated for the current fiscal year, I wish again to bring to your attention the seriousness of our financial situation and desire that you assure yourself that all those in your department are impressed with the urgent need for economies and postponements in view of this emergency.

The situation is a serious one and demands that we all make the most earnest efforts to eliminate or postpone all such activities as may be so treated without serious detriment to the public welfare. . . .

. . . I wish that you refrain from actually obligating money available for expenditure during the current fiscal year, except in those cases where such postponement or elimination will clearly be to the detriment of the public welfare.

Today (July 24th) the press stated that French gold withdrawals from London amounted to $125,000,000. "If France continues withdrawing the remainder of their gold holdings in London, the Bank of England will admittedly be placed in a serious position." French denied political aims in their withdrawals.

July 26, 1931: A revolution in Chile. Many killed in riots.

July 27, 1931: A conference of British and French was held in Paris on the subject of relieving the French drain on British gold.

Germany prepared to re-open her banks.

July 28, 1931: Bankers the world over accepted the "standstill" agreement.

July 30, 1931: The Bank of England raised the discount rate to four and one-half per cent.

President Hoover moved for reorganization of unemployment relief for the next year. He must anticipate developments and provide for the necessary public co-operation.

The month ended gloomily and the impulse given by the moratorium was being rapidly lost. Although the fire had been put out in Central Europe by great efforts, it plainly was threatening to spring up again in England. All European nations were busily restricting imports. In the United States, the price of wheat fell below any record of the Chicago market. The price of cotton collapsed to 6.70 cents per pound. The price of livestock was the lowest in years. Unemployment had increased since March by an additional 500,000 to about 7,000,000, instead of there being a seasonal decrease. A movement had started to reduce wages by an amount equal to the reduction of the cost of living (ten to fifteen per cent). The prices of industrial stocks had fallen fifteen points from their moratorium recovery.

But beyond all this were the waves of fear which, created by the events in Europe and the alarming daily headlines, had swept through the American people. One of its visible evidences was the hoarding of currency. According to estimates given to the President from the Federal Reserve Board, this rose to $40,000,000 per week in early June. It was reversed to a return of currency at the time of the moratorium, but again rose with the new German difficulties to $80,000,000 a week. With the settlement of these difficulties currency again began to return to the banks at the rate of $20,000,000 a week during the last half of July. This currency movement merely was the surface result of the fear that had gripped our people. A much deeper result was the paralyzing effect upon all business and upon new enterprises.

August 1, 1931: The Bank of England negotiated a short-term loan of $250,000,000 from American and French banks. The French had withdrawn $160,000,000 in gold from London during the last twenty days. The Reichsbank raised its discount rate to fifteen per cent.

August 3, 1931: The President engaged in a series of conferences to overhaul relief agencies in preparation for the winter. John Alpine, assistant to the Secretary of Labor in charge of the new Federal Employment Agencies, reported that 332 such agencies now were established and that in sixty days 630,000 persons had been placed in employment by them with the assistance of other co-operating agencies.

August 4, 1931: Germany imposed additional embargoes and quotas on imports in order to balance her trade.

August 5, 1931: A further break in British exchange occurred, judged to be due to French and other withdrawals of gold from London.

August 7, 1931: Hungary imposed more restriction on imports and exchange. Germany and Austria already had done so.

The President announced a nation-wide survey of the employment and relief situation. The object was to determine what relief measures were needed to meet the situation. He stated to the press:[1]

> During the past three weeks I have been engaged . . . in a study of the problems of unemployment and relief likely to confront us over the coming winter. . . . The problem, whatever it may be will be met . . . [through] co-operation of local and State and Federal authorities, and . . . private organizations. . . . We are making a survey of the organization over the past year . . . a survey to determine the probable load next winter. . . . We are appraising the machinery now in operation. . . . We are obtaining recommendations of governors, mayors, business and labor leaders, and relief heads. . . . Survey and new organization . . . [will be] completed in a month.

[1] State Papers, Vol. I, p. 602.

The primary object of the President's inquiry was to make certain whether or not the States, municipalities, and voluntary agencies would be able to prevent distress without Federal contributions, beyond the indirect aid from the Federal public works program and other such measures. He was unalterably opposed to the Federal Government undertaking to organize direct relief to individuals. He again insisted that such administration must be done by State and local committees, and that if Federal help became necessary, it must be supplementary to State and local resources. President Hoover was resolved to delay such Federal support to the States until it was absolutely necessary, not only because of the immediate drain on the Federal Treasury, but also and of much more importance, because he was convinced that, once committed to Federal contributions, he would be confronted by Congressional manipulation for political purposes, and that once on this course much of the State and local responsibility would be undermined. On the other hand, he was prepared to face the giving of supplementary aid by the Federal Government if it were necessary to prevent distress. Eight months later he did propose and secure from Congress Federal aid to the States, but only after waging a vigorous and successful fight against pork-barrel methods which the Democratic Congress sought to impose.

August 12, 1931: The President gave to the press the results of the survey of the relief situation. That survey was made both through the Federal agencies and through the State and local organizations which now covered every State. Administrative organizations were functioning in nearly every State, in 227 large cities, and in nearly one thousand smaller towns and counties. These local committees, who had to deal directly with the problem, reported that, in co-operation with existing national and State agencies, they believed they could cope with the situation during the coming winter and within the resources available to them. The President considered that the devotion of the thousands of men and women who had voluntarily undertaken the burden of administering relief was one of the finest developments of American life. Particularly the women were carrying on with a determination and courage that had never been surpassed.

August 17, 1931: Important banks in Toledo, Ohio, failed.

August 19, 1931: President Hoover announced that Walter S. Gifford, president of the American Telephone and Telegraph Company, had been appointed head of "The President's Unemployment Relief Organization" to succeed Colonel Arthur Woods, whose private business prevented his longer continuance in service. In his letter of appointment the President said to Mr. Gifford: "It is clear . . . the United States will be faced

... with a heavy relief load. ... I am asking you to set up such organization as may be desirable. ... This care of misfortune is our first duty to the Nation. ... The whole forces of the Administration are at your disposal."

Fred C. Croxton, who had served as chief assistant to Colonel Woods, continued as chief assistant to Mr. Gifford.

Among the surveys of the efficiency of relief measures undertaken was an estimate of the state of the health of the nation. The many years of his experience in such matters had demonstrated to President Hoover that the public health was most sensitive to a shortage of food and shelter, and that it offered an almost infallible index to the efficiency of relief measures. Surgeon-General Hugh S. Cumming, head of the Public Health Service, reported:[2]

[We have surveyed] ... the comparative state of the public health during the period of maximum burden of distress and relief, that is, in the early months of 1931, as compared with similar months in 1928, a period of full employment. ...

... A compilation ... during the first five months of 1931 shows that the death rate was 12.0 per 1,000 as compared with 13.7 for the same period in 1928. ...

... industrial insurance companies [have] ... 70,000,000 policies in force. For the first six months of 1931 the death rate among these policy-holders was 10.5 per 1,000; in 1928, the rate was 10.6 per 1,000 for the six months. ...

Infant mortality is a rather sensitive index of health conditions. It is computed as the number of deaths under one year of age per 1,000 live births. Such rates ... show that the rate (71.4) in the first five months of 1931 was less than for 1928 (75.6).

... death rate from tuberculosis has continued to decline, the rate for the first five months of 1931 being only 63.4 per 100,000 against 77.5 for 1928.

... illness among a group of wage-earner members of sick benefit associations [is as follows]. Sickness rates for the first half of 1931 are 104.2 per 1,000, and for 1928, 117.9, or 71.2 and 82.8, respectively. ...

These results were conclusive proof that the people in a large sense had been protected from hunger and cold during the past year by the relief organization of the country. Any failure in relief at once lowers vitality and increases sickness and mortality, especially among children. The actual improvement was due to the greater public solicitude for the unemployed.

This day (August 19th) there was a revolution in Ecuador.

August 21, 1931: In co-operation with Mr. Gifford the President ex-

[2] State Papers, Vol. I, p. 607.

panded the membership of the Advisory Committee of the President's Unemployment Relief Organization to sixty members. The purpose was to include influential men and women who at once were assigned to report upon plans and proposals. This committee also included the men and women who acted as liaison officers between Mr. Gifford's office and the State and local committees. Three sub-committees also were appointed, the first under Fred C. Croxton upon Administration of Relief, the second under Harry A. Wheeler upon Expansion of Federal Public Works, and the third under Owen D. Young upon Co-ordination of Private Charity. The National Committee consisted of the following men and women: Richard H. Aishton, W. Rufus Abbott, Bernard M. Baruch, Clarence E. Bookman, Newton D. Baker, Reese Blizzard, J. Herbert Case, Martin H. Carmody, Harvey C. Couch, Fred C. Croxton, James A. Drain, Edward D. Duffield, Pierre S. Dupont, John E. Edgerton, William Ellis, Milton H. Esberg, Warren Fairbanks, Harold P. Fabian, Fred Fisher, Homer L. Ferguson, Mrs. John M. Glenn, Dr. Lillian Gilbreth, William Green, Carl E. Grunsky, Edward N. Hurley, E. Johnston, H. C. Knight, H. G. Lloyd, Alexander Legge, J. F. Lucey, Alvan Macaulay, Samuel L. Mather, Wesley C. Mitchell, John R. Mott, Charles Nagel, Cleveland A. Newton, John K. Ottley, John Barton Payne, Frank M. Phillips, William Proctor, Raymond Robins, Henry M. Robinson, John D. Ryan, Edward L. Ryerson, Mrs. John F. Sipple, Rabbi Abba H. Silver, A. O. Smith, George Sloan, Matthew S. Sloan, Silas H. Strawn, Louis J. Taber, Walter C. Teagle, Myron C. Taylor, George E. Vincent, Daniel Willard, Colonel Arthur Woods, Matthew Woll, William Allen White, Oscar Wells.

Later were added Harry H. Rogers, George E. Brimmer, Thomas H. West, Jr., Colonel Edward Underwood, George Whitney, Atholl McBean, John F. Tinsley, William Foster, Henry Merrill, John W. Davis, Jacob H. Hollander, Eliot Wadsworth, W. S. Sterrett, Harry Chandler, Will H. Hays, M. H. Aylesworth, W. S. Paley, and Paul A. Schoellkopf.

August 22, 1931: The President made public the results of a survey of Federal public works activities in aid to employment.[3]

The number of persons directly or indirectly employed by the Federal Government in construction and maintenance of public works at the opening of the depression was 180,000. This time last year the number was increased to 430,000. The number was 760,000, on the first of August. That number will probably increase some in the autumn. . . .

The President informed the press that a preliminary canvass by Mr. Gifford showed that the organization for relief, established the

[3] State Papers, Vol. I, p. 611.

previous year in co-operation with governors, was functioning well. Also that active reorganization by the strengthened committee was in progress, with "widespread resolution to meet the situation again."

August 24, 1931: The Labor-Socialist Government of Great Britain fell and was replaced by a Nationalist Ministry, the majority of which was from the Conservative Party.

August 26, 1931: The new British Ministry informed our government that the recent British loan of $250,000,000, placed equally in the United States and France to support its currency, was about exhausted. It asked if the President would view sympathetically an effort to place a new loan of $400,000,000 jointly with banks in the United States and France. The ministers were told to go ahead. These loans were repaid.

August 30, 1931: The battle in Central Europe seemed to be won. Banks re-opened. There was no longer fear of Communist revolutions. But the restrictions on imports through quotas and embargoes, in an effort to create favorable exchange, were seriously affecting our agricultural exports and prices. Our economic situation had continued to deteriorate during the month, under foreign trade restrictions and the cloud of a possible British financial collapse. The only hope for improvement lay in the success of the British to prevent such a collapse. The large flight of capital from Great Britain to the United States did not look encouraging. The return from hoarding of our own currency which marked the latter part of July, upon the improvement in the Central European situation, began again in the early part of August, from the apprehension over the British situation. Hoarding no doubt was caused by bank failures and the fear of further failures, but the failures also were in part the effect of withdrawals due to the apprehension created by the world situation. It was estimated by the Federal Reserve Board that withdrawals for hoarding amounted to nearly $50,000,000 a week during this month.

September 1, 1931: The situation in Germany was somewhat improved by the reduction of the Reichsbank discount rate of eight per cent and the re-opening of the public exchanges without further panic. The situation in England became decidedly worse.

In the United States, Mr. Gifford announced the inauguration of a consolidated national drive for funds for all private relief agencies under the direction of Owen D. Young. Speaking to the press upon the governmental side of relief, the President said:

One of the primary problems is the maintenance of the social obligations of the government to a population that are in difficulties; no government of substantial character and of any humanity will see its people starve or go cold, and every agency of a government whether Federal,

State, or local must be implemented to that end. . . . We have another problem which bears indirectly on the same purpose. . . . We must maintain the complete (financial) stability and confidence in our government . . . upon that . . . depends the maintenance of employment . . . and recovery.

September 4, 1931: In reply to persistent criticism in Europe that we were draining the world's gold, the President made a public statement to the effect that while there had been no great increase in our own monetary gold stocks in nine years, yet about $3,000,000,000 of gold or foreign deposits were here. Part of this was the result of flight of capital for refuge to the United States from all over the world and part was on deposit here by foreign banks and governments seeking interest upon their reserves, which they should keep at home. Were it not for this phenomenon we should hold less gold by that amount. The President further stated that the French Government alone had nearly $800,000,000 here. The solution of the world distribution of gold, he explained, lay in the re-establishment of confidence in other countries. He expressed the view that this increase was not a healthy financial situation. In fact, it could be of harm to us, as the funds were a demand deposit which instantly could be withdrawn, and thereby the amount of credit extended by our banks to our citizens would be dislocated.

The Farm Board today announced a large wheat sale to China by farm co-operatives.

September 5, 1931: The World Court held that the Austrian-German Customs Union was a violation of treaties. The question was thus disposed of. Like the assassination of the Austrian Grand Duke, the incident was not a major calamity—it merely caused a calamity.

September 7, 1931: The agitation for increased governmental expenditures for relief continued. Senator Wagner of New York (Dem.), in a speech at the New York State Fair, denounced the President for not having spent another two billions on Federal relief.

September 8, 1931: President Hoover today addressed the following letter to Governor Meyer of the Federal Reserve Board:

Honorable Eugene Meyer,
Governor, Federal Reserve Board,
Washington, D. C.
MY DEAR MR. MEYER:
I wish again to refer to a subject which I have mentioned on several occasions to yourself and to the New York and other bankers. I feel strongly that our banking community must now organize itself to a renewed and stronger effort in solution of the problem of frozen deposits in our closed banks.

It appears that since the depression began, state and national banks holding over $1,500,000,000 of deposits have suspended, in the larger part of which there has been no liquidation payment to depositors. It is obvious that in every one of these closed banks there are some valuable assets, and in fact experience over years shows that depositors realize an average of about 70 per cent. A huge sum of resources and credit is therefore immobilized which can and should be, at least in part, released as a vital measure of relief in our national emergency.

Apparently a million people have resources tied up in this situation, and many of them are thrust upon public relief in consequence.

Certainly safe loans can be made upon some portion of the value of these assets and promptly distributed to the depositors. The method of effecting this relief seems to me a problem which this country has a right to expect that the banking community can solve. I am not unmindful of the difficulties, but there are times when obstacles must be overcome. I am not unmindful of the many instances where the banks have cooperated in courageous manner to prevent failures, and of the isolated instances where depositors in closed banks have been assisted by some advance payments. The very success of these measures leads me to the conviction that there is the energy, courage, and resourcefulness in our bankers to go still farther.

My belief is that if the Federal Reserve Bank officials in each district would call their leading bankers together, they would find a solution to this problem in their respective districts.

The effort I suggest does not lie within the required activities of either the President, the Federal Reserve Board, or the Federal Reserve Banks. But the Federal Reserve Board, the Federal Reserve Banks and the member banks constitute our banking system, and the nation expects leadership from this system in solution of such questions. What I am suggesting is a vigorous effort at voluntary organization under the leadership of the institution to which the nation naturally looks for assistance.

Our banks have shown capacity and courage to solve the banking situation of Germany and England. These efforts in these directions have been of profound importance to the American people. But I feel it is necessary for me to say that it seems to me that an equal effort to serve our own people in the matter of closed banks to that which has been given to foreign banks is now required, or we shall have failed in our duty to our own people, and that further credits extended abroad are likely to be denied or curtailed by our people until the credit agencies of the United States can solve so obvious a credit question as this.

Yours faithfully,
(Signed) HERBERT HOOVER.

September 10, 1931: The farm co-operatives, acting with the authority of the Farm Board, sold a large quantity of wheat to Germany on secured credit.

September 14, 1931: There was a mutiny in the British Navy over governmental attempts to reduce its pay, in the campaign to balance the British budget.

CHAPTER VIII

BRITISH DIFFICULTIES AND THE AMERICAN
REPERCUSSION

SEPTEMBER–NOVEMBER, 1931

September 15, 1931: President Hoover asked Mr. Henry M. Robinson, who was in Washington at the President's request, to advise him upon the financial situation, to invite the Federal Reserve Advisory Council to meet at the White House. This council was comprised of representatives from each Federal Reserve District and met the President at dinner. There were present: Eugene Meyer, Governor of the Federal Reserve Board; John Poole (Washington), and Herbert K. Hallett (Boston), Robert H. Treman (Ithaca), Howard A. Loeb (Philadelphia), J. A. House (Cleveland), John K. Ottley (Atlanta), Melvin A. Traylor (Chicago), W. W. Smith (St. Louis), George H. Prince (St. Paul), Walter McLucas (Kansas City), Henry M. Robinson (Los Angeles), and Walter Lichtenstein (Chicago).

After a discussion of the general situation, the President sought their views upon the possibility of creating a temporary pool of $500,000,000 to be subscribed by the banks. This fund was to be used in loans to banks under pressure from depositors, such loans to be upon securities which were not eligible for loans from the Federal Reserve Banks. The purpose was to stop the many bank closings now going on because of unliquid assets. Melvin Traylor insisted that the job was too great for the banks; that they could not find such a sum of money; that, in any event, there was not sufficient co-operative spirit among them. Some of the others agreed with the President that it was feasible. After the conference the President requested Mr. Robinson to make a special study of the possibilities of such action by the banks and, alternatively, the possibilities of the government's creating some such institution with government guarantee of its loans which might cover a wider field of loans for the purpose of industrial and agricultural recovery.

After the conference some of these gentlemen present, probably with the idea of not disclosing the real subject under consideration, when under questioning by representatives of the press as to the matter discussed, hinted that it was war-debts. While this subject had been scarcely mentioned, it was featured in the press with much speculation and in large headlines.

September 16, 1931: The British Government met in part the demands of the navy mutineers. The incident had caused world-wide apprehension.

September 17, 1931: There were heavy withdrawals of gold from the Bank of England. Practical panic on continental security and commodity markets was reflected in the United States.

Gerard Swope, President of the General Electric Company, today published a "plan" for the reorganization of American industry. The President's office memorandum written at the time was as follows:

This plan provides for the consolidation of all industries into trade associations, which are legalized by the government and authorized to "stabilize prices." There is no stabilization of prices without price-fixing, and this feature at once becomes the organization of gigantic trusts such as have never been dreamed of in the history of the world. This is the creation of a series of complete monopolies over the American people. It means the repeal of the entire Sherman and Clayton Acts, and all other restrictions on combinations and monopoly. In fact, if such a thing were ever done, it means the decay of American industry from the day this scheme is born, because one cannot stabilize prices without protecting obsolete plants and inferior managements. It is the most gigantic proposal of monopoly ever made in history.

This was the real genesis of the NRA.

The President also sought the opinion of the Attorney-General and others upon it. The Attorney-General reported it to be wholly unconstitutional.

September 18, 1931: Japan took possession of Manchuria, which further multiplied world fears. Our markets continued to reflect these situations.

September 21, 1931: The Bank of England defaulted on gold payments. The commodity and security markets over the most of Europe were closed. All prices dropped in the United States. The British governmental statement said that one billion in gold and foreign exchange had been withdrawn since July; that they could not longer stand the pressure.

September 21, 1931: In the midst of the general conflagration some members of the American Legion, led by Congressman Wright Patman of Texas, Democrat, proposed to push the cash payment of the remaining half of the bonus at their annual meeting at Detroit. Three or four days before the convention met, the President determined to address the Legion directly in an effort to stop it. He went by special train to Detroit, remained there less than an hour, and returned immediately to Washington. In his speech he said:[1]

. . . The world is passing through a great depression fraught with gruelling daily emergencies alike to men and to governments. This depression today flows largely from Europe through fundamental dislocations of economic and political forces caused by the Great War. . . . We would have recovered long since but for these forces from abroad. . . . Some individuals may have lost their nerve and faith. . . . You of the Legion have a peculiarly sacred stake in the future of the country which you fought to preserve. . . . During the past year our expenses have exceeded our income. . . . Today we face . . . large deficit . . . decrease . . . of yield of income taxes alone by . . . $1,200,000,000 . . . simultaneously we are carrying a huge and necessary extra burden of the unemployed . . . agriculture . . . and the veterans themselves. . . . Drastic economy [is needed] in every non-vital branch of government . . . the imperative moment has come when increased expenditure of the government must be avoided. . . . Any alternative will strike down the earnest efforts of the citizenry of our nation. . . . Your National Commander . . . came to me and offered your strength . . . to help in relief over [the] winter . . . an even greater service [is needed] today . . . [a] determined opposition by you to additional demands upon the nation. . . . I am speaking not alone of veterans' legislation . . . [but] equally of demands . . . which would require increased . . . expenditures. . . . The first stone in the foundation of recovery and stability . . . in the world is the stability of the Government of the United States. It is my purpose to maintain that stability and I invite you to enlist in that service. . . .

You would not have the President of the United States plead with . . . any group of citizens. . . . I make no plea to you. . . . But you would have your President point out the path of service in this nation. . . . My mind goes back to the days of the war . . . at the end of those years of heartsickness over the misery of it all, when peace came you and I knew that the wounds of the world were unhealed and that there would be further emergencies still before our country when self-denial and courageous service must be given. This is an emergency and these are the times for service. . . .

The Bonus resolution was voted down in the Legion. It did not prevent the Democratic-controlled House from passing it later on, but it did create a public opinion which caused its defeat in the Senate.

September 22, 1931: In an extended "off the record" press conference, and in view of the hoarding then in progress, the President asked the press to use its utmost exertion to keep the country "steady in the boat," to which the press responded helpfully. He gave an outline of the situation, both its dangers and the tendency of news statements to over-

[1] State Papers, Vol. I, p. 618.

estimate these dangers and to make the situation worse, also, some of the effects. He stated that the world again was faced with a crisis as great as that of June, but with the difference that the economic situation in Great Britain was fundamentally stronger than had been that of Central Europe. No doubt the British crisis seriously weakened the whole economic fabric of the world. All now depended upon the United States. We now were the Verdun of world stability.

September 22, 1931: France withdrew $120,000,000 of gold from New York.

September 23, 1931: Industry in the United States generally began a ten per cent to fifteen per cent wage cut. The cost of living had fallen fifteen per cent. There were no labor disturbances. The maintenance of wage standards for the past two years had created a favorable relationship between employers and employees that had eased for both sides this necessary adjustment. In fact, no important labor disturbance occurred during the whole of President Hoover's Administration.

The President spent considerable time in conference with Professor E. W. Kemmerer, of Princeton University, upon the situation now developing through abandonment of the gold standard by many foreign countries. Professor Kemmerer, an outstanding authority upon finance, approved the steps being considered by the President to strengthen our situation.

September 24, 1931: Europe drew more gold from the United States. France "earmarked" more gold in New York for future withdrawal.

President Hoover invited Premier Laval of France to Washington to discuss the world economic situation.

September 25, 1931: Italy raised all tariffs fifteen per cent to block what was claimed to be British dumping as the result of the recent British action in depreciating currency. This prompted many other countries to follow with similar action, and further it affected seriously many American exports.

In view of depreciating revenues and the prospect of added tax burdens upon the people, the necessity for economy caused President Hoover to scrutinize most carefully and in most instances to cut the recommendations for appropriations coming from the various departments for the ensuing year, and it was necessary to pare down the recommendations of the Navy Department for increased expenditures. Despite the support of the President by senior officers, some subordinate officers, lacking the broader knowledge and vision coming with added years of service, were very critical. Not content with submitting their views in the department and to the committees of Congress when called upon, they transgressed professional ethics by lending themselves to attack upon the President. This caused him to say, publicly, "That was not a question for subordinates who have no appreciation of national necessities to determine. If I see more of it there will be changes in the Navy." At the same time he took occasion to denounce the Navy League for issuing misleading statements and for their collusion with these few naval officers in creating and spreading false and misleading propaganda.

September 30, 1931: The ordeal through which the nation had passed since the beginning of the European crisis is indicated by prices and commercial index numbers from the summary of current business of the United States Department of Commerce:

	Existing as of April 1931	*Existing in late September 1931*
Price of wheat	74c. per bu.	55c. per bu.
Price of cotton	10c. per lb.	6c. per lb.
Bank debits to industrial accounts (141 cities)	46 billion	36 billion
Index numbers:		
Common stocks	121	70
All commodities	76	70
Farm products	70	60
Industrial production	88	74
Construction contracts	77	55
Factory employment	78	70
Factory payrolls	73	59

Banks suspended:
April to October, 1931, in deposits (Federal Reserve Board Bulletin, 1931):
    National Banks.......................... $202,373,000
    State Banks............................ $569,570,000

The apprehension over the British situation, which began in the latter part of July, cancelled many of the results of the victory over the panic from Central Europe. With the crisis in Great Britain on September 21st, an increased feeling of apprehension swept over the entire United States. It was accelerated by the abandonment of the gold standard by Denmark, Sweden, Norway, Columbia, Bolivia, and India; by exchange restrictions in Greece, Italy, Germany, Austria, Hungary, and Chile; and by various accompanying import restrictions on trade. Discount rates were raised sharply in all these countries. The stability of the United States, hitherto the refuge of capital from all over the world, was called into question abroad, from a suspicion that, as England had gotten into difficulties, the United States would be the next to fall a victim. A heavy drain of gold and exchange set in which made it necessary for banks to call in their loans, and for the Federal Reserve System to increase credits. Hoarding of currency jumped to an estimated rate of $100,000,000 a week. Bank failures increased. The effect of the European panic was well shown by the fact that cotton exports to those countries, as compared with the year before, dropped nearly a million bales in the three months prior to October 1st. Again, as in November, 1929, and in June, 1931, our citizens were everywhere on the verge of panic. An entirely new and much more dangerous situation now confronted the President.

October 1, 1931: European cotton associations practically suspended purchase of cotton due to agitation for an American export bounty by a group of senators. The President announced he would oppose the passage of any such bounty. In the meantime the sudden drop in price had cost the farmers about five dollars per bale.

On this same date the President received the reports of various agencies as to the probable financial relief load during the next winter.

From an investigation made by the Census Bureau of a test period of the first three months of 1931, it was shown that in eighty-five per cent of the country the expenditure upon direct family relief and homeless men by State, city, and county authorities, together with private agencies, had for the whole three months been about $75,000,000. The normal expenditures of these agencies was about $25,000,000 as shown by an examination of the first three months of 1929, a non-depression year. In the areas tested the number of families receiving direct relief in the first three months of 1931 (the peak load of the year) was 1,287,000. Checks through other agencies confirmed the general conclusion that the direct relief load during the calendar year so far had been a whole or partial support of about 1,500,000 families. Taking into account the lesser burden in some months and the area not covered by the survey, the cost of direct emergency relief (excluding the normal load of indigents) was at the rate of about $300,000,000 for the calendar year of 1931, including State, county, municipal, and charitable relief. These actual sums, however, did not represent the vast amount of personal relief extended through the stimulative effects of the vast network of voluntary effort which had been created. The burden of help to specific neighbors through monetary aid and through employment, undertaken by a multitude of families, must be added to the vast amount of corporate aid to employees which had provided against an immense amount of distress. A portion of the load also was carried as a result of the stimulation of utility and other construction work.

The inquiry into indirect relief through public works—Federal, State, county, and municipal—made by the new Federal Stabilization Board, showed that the States and subdivisions were spending during the year 1931 somewhat less than normal, while the Federal Government was spending $500,000,000 more than normal. The cost of relief, direct and indirect, was, therefore, about $800,000,000 for the year 1931, of which the Federal Government was doing indirectly more than one-half. It was anticipated that the load would increase materially over the next winter, but that it was not likely to exceed 2,000,000 families. The direct relief was not likely to cost more than $500,000,000.

The President also announced the results of the relief survey undertaken as the result of a direct communication from himself to the governors, together with the canvass made by Walter S. Gifford through the State relief committees and the Advisory Committee which was appointed on August 21st. All the States except one reported that with the aid of the Federal and local public works then in progress added to the resources of State, local, and private agencies, they would be able to carry the burdens of direct relief through the next year. The one exception was the State of Pennsylvania, with its great wealth and vast resources. Governor Pinchot demanded direct Federal aid. At the same time he refused to favor increased State taxes or otherwise to make suitable provisions for relief by his own State.

From these evidences, and from the high state of public health which indicated that up to the present distress had been provided for, the President determined that the responsibility for direct relief during the winter again should be continued by the States and other agencies. Also he decided that the Federal Government should confine itself to public works, together with national drives to support private agencies, the stimulation of State and local action, and the encouragement of private construction and employment. A staff was appointed to check local results to see that there was no failure in relief.

October 3, 1931: During the entire week the President had been engaged night and day in canvassing the financial, employment, and agricultural situation both at home and abroad. He had held interviews with departmental heads in Washington. By long distance telephone and through Under Secretary Mills, Henry M. Robinson, and others, he had consulted with leaders of banking, agriculture, and labor, and with leading economists in every part of the country. He had made this use of the telephone and of outside agents in order to avoid exciting fear through bringing many men to Washington, with the natural press speculation which might increase an already growing panic.

President Hoover now was confronted with a third great crisis. The first was the stock crash of 1929. The second was the Central European collapse of June and July, 1931. This new situation may be summarized:

(a) He was faced with renewed financial collapse abroad, following the British crisis, which again was breaking down our export markets and causing a domestic fall of prices and increased unemployment. It was placing decided strains on our security markets and our financial system. It was radiating fear and panic in the country.

(b) He was faced with the inadequacy of a badly organized banking system which already was weakened by the collapse of our own boom and that of Central Europe. As stated before, our system consisted of thousands of separate banks operating under different and uncorrelated State systems of supervision, with a superimposed Federal system. Our Federal Reserve System was not sufficiently flexible to meet the situation.

(c) He was faced with a fall of over $2,000,000,000 in government revenues from the pre-depression normal, which forecast a budget deficit of over $1,500,000,000 at a time when expenditures on relief must be increased.

(d) He was faced with a Democratic-controlled House and an opposition Senate.

(e) Finally, a general calling of loans by the banks, under the pressure of the foreign situation and domestic hoarding, would mean the collapse of the banking and business system with the possibility of our being forced off the gold standard. He now had two alternatives: first, the one advocated by orthodox economists and bankers, of allowing unrestrained liquidation; second, that of adopting unprecedented measures. Many counselled the former course. The President realized that would mean infinite hardship through a general foreclosure of mortgages on homes and farms, through widespread receiverships for railways and industries, through the collapse of securities which would draw in its train the insurance companies and savings banks with a possibility of general repudiation, through enormously extended unemployment, with all the social consequences of these great dangers to the entire nation. His view was that if America failed, the whole of modern civilization might be paralyzed.

Together with his Cabinet members and other advisers, he determined upon a broad program both of defense and offense to meet the new situation. His first move to inaugurate these measures was to summon the heads of the Clearing House banks in New York and the heads of the leading insurance companies within reach, to meet with him confidentially at Secretary Mellon's apartment in Washington on Sunday evening, the 4th of October. A conference of that size could not have met at the White House without the press discovering it. The mere knowledge by the public, while an acute crisis was on, of such a conference would have caused wild rumors and increased the existing apprehension and possibly interfered with the making of plans.

At the same time, the President requested the ranking members of the banking, finance, and other committees in both Houses of Congress, including members of both political parties, to meet him at the White House the evening of the 6th.

October 4, 1931: The President, Secretary Mellon, Under Secretary Mills, and Governor Meyer of the Federal Reserve Board met tonight at Secretary Mellon's apartment with thirty financial leaders. The President prepared in advance of the conference a note on the situation. It said:

> . . . the situation since the British collapse ten days ago is approaching disaster at an accelerated speed until it has reached a panic condition. . . . That while a similar situation due to the economic breakdown in Central Europe in the spring . . . had been overcome by the action of the Government . . . the rise of recovery therefrom had been again stifled by the . . . fears over the British situation, those fears had been realized . . . we are again faced with a new and even worse emergency. . . . A survey shows . . . at least twenty other countries will be forced off the gold standard with Great Britain . . . inevitably they would increase tariffs, quotas and other restrictions on their imports . . . their depreciated currencies make further barriers to our exports . . . our prices of agricultural commodities are again further demoralized . . . current European attitude is that we will collapse next . . . a drain of at least one billion of the gold, hitherto here for refuge, by export and earmarking is in progress . . . [causing] the greatest withdrawal of all time. . . . The Federal Reserve system is expanding credit by every device to meet the sapping of our credit foundations . . . the fears of the people were, since the British failed ten days ago, expressed in unprecedented hoarding of currency . . . the volume of hoarding has reached $150,000,000 a week . . . it totalled over $500,000,000 since the middle of August and $900,000,000 over May 1st. . . . Security prices were demoralized by European selling and forced liquidations. . . . This with hoarding is breaking down an already weak banking system by compelling a sacrifice of their assets to meet withdrawals. . . . Bank failures in the twelve days since the British collapse already exceeded $500,000,000. . . . But beyond this, the banks in the large centers are calling interior loans to fortify themselves against foreign drains . . . the secondary banking centers being drained are fortifying themselves against it by calling loans from country banks and customers . . . the imminent collapse of banks threatens in many interior centers particularly in the south and mid-west . . . [and] the inability of farmers and home owners to meet mortgage requirements. . . . In all, a senseless "bankers' panic" and public fears are contributing to dragging the country down.

The President then stated his plan:

The bankers were to create a national credit association with $500,-

000,000 capital to support the financial structure, to be subscribed by all the banks in a ratio of two per cent of their deposits.

The insurance companies, with the Federal Farm Loan Banks, were to announce to the farmers and home-owners that no mortgages would be foreclosed so long as the borrowers made an honest effort to repay. He proposed that the institutions join in forming a national mortgage discount system to relieve permanently the "frozen" mortgage capital and the assets of financial institutions.

Under Secretary Mills earnestly supported the President's proposal, as did Governor Meyer, who considered it the only alternative. As for the others, there was enthusiasm from some of those present. The representatives of the insurance companies refused to act upon the suggested plan. The President stated that he had called the Congressional leaders for forty-eight hours later. If the banks could not organize for financial protection of the country in an emergency, his purpose was to propose a legislative program that would do it and to call Congress immediately into session. He pointed out that he wanted to give the banks a chance; if they would not take it, the government must protect the people. If the effort were made and if it did not succeed, he would bring in government support.

The bankers agreed to appoint a committee to meet in New York the next morning in order to see if they could not work out a plan, and they asked for the President's proposal in writing. The insurance companies agreed not to press mortgage foreclosures and to join with a committee the President would appoint to consider the whole situation of mortgage banking. The meeting adjourned early in the morning.

October 5, 1931: At daybreak the President sent for a stenographer and dictated the first draft of the letter given below. He left on that same morning to attend the World Series baseball game at Philadelphia. Mr. Hoover enjoyed a good baseball game. Furthermore, he felt that his attendance might be taken as an indication of a lack of alarm. He perfected the letter on the train and sent it on to New York for the meeting of the bankers, to be held at the Federal Reserve Bank that day.

October 5, 1931

HONORABLE GEORGE HARRISON,
Federal Reserve Bank,
New York City.

DEAR MR. HARRISON:

The request which I laid before the leading New York bankers last night for cooperation in unity of national action to assure credit security can, in the light of our discussion, be simplified to the following concrete measures:

1. They are to take the lead in immediate formulation of a national institution with a capital of $500,000,000. The function of this institution to be:

(a) The rediscount of bank assets not now eligible in the Federal Reserve System in order to assure the stability of banks throughout the country from attack by unreasoning depositors. That is to prevent bank failures.

(b) Loans against the assets of closed banks to enable them to pay some early dividend to depositors and thus revive many business activities and relieve families from destitution.

2. It is proposed that the capital be underwritten by the banks of the United States as a national effort, possibly with the support of the industrials. New York being the financial center of the nation must of necessity assume both the initiative and the major burden. The effort should be participated in by the country at large by appropriate organization.

3. As I said last night, we are in a degenerating vicious cycle. Economic events of Europe have demoralized our farm produce and security prices. This has given rise to an unsettlement of public mind. There have been in some localities foolish alarm over the stability of our credit structure and considerable withdrawals of currency. In consequence, bankers in many other parts of the country in fear of the possibility of such unreasoning demands of depositors have deemed it necessary to place their assets in such liquid form as to enable them to meet drains and runs. To do this they sell securities and restrict credit. The sale of securities demoralizes their price and jeopardizes other banks. The restriction on credit has grown greatly in the past few weeks. There are a multitude of complaints that farmers cannot secure loans for their livestock feeding or to carry their commodities until the markets improve. There are a multitude of complaints of business men that they cannot secure the usual credit to carry their operations on a normal basis and must discharge labor. There are complaints of manufacturers who use agricultural and other raw materials that they cannot secure credits beyond day to day needs with which to lay in their customary seasonal supplies. The effect of this is to thrust on the back of the farmer the load of carrying the nation's stocks. The whole cumulative effect is today to decrease prices of commodities and securities and to spread the relations of the debtor and creditor.

4. The only real way to break this cycle is to restore confidence in the people at large. To do this requires major unified action that will give confidence to the country. It is this that I have asked of the New York bankers.

5. I stated that if the New York banks will undertake to comply with this request, I will seek to secure assurance from the leaders of appropriate committees in Congress of both political parties to support my recommendation at the next session for

(a) The extension of rediscount eligibility in the Federal Reserve System.

(b) If necessity requires to recreate the War Finance Corporation with available funds sufficient for any emergency in our credit system.

(c) To strengthen the Federal Farm Loan Bank System.

Yours faithfully,
HERBERT HOOVER.

The bankers during Monday night (October 5th) sent word that they would form the National Credit Association as requested.

At the close of the game at Philadelphia, the President received word of the death of Senator Dwight Morrow of New Jersey. He was greatly affected. He now had lost a fourth national leader: the first was Secretary James W. Good, then Senator Theodore E. Burton of Ohio, then Speaker Longworth, and now Senator Morrow. The wide business experience of Senator Morrow, and his zeal in the public service, made him invaluable in such a time of need. The country could ill afford to lose such men.

October 6, 1931: The President settled with Paul Bestor, the chairman of the Federal Farm Loan Board, the question of Federal Land Bank foreclosures on farm mortgages. The President gave Mr. Bestor his ideas as to the foreclosure policy that should be used by the Federal Land Banks in view of the existing conditions. He emphasized that "every man who in fact was doing his best to meet his obligations should be aided in every possible way." A form of suggestions from the Board to the officers of the banks was agreed upon, under which foreclosures would be limited to those who wished to or already had abandoned their farms; the banks should function in a thoroughly humane way in respect to their own loans; and they would make every effort where feasible to assume the loans of others in danger of foreclosure, so as to prevent such dispossession. After going over the question thoroughly with Mr. Bestor, the President decided to recommend to Congress an appropriation of $125,000,000 to strengthen the land banks, to make possible such a program, and thus prevent loss of confidence by their own security holders. This additional capital was to be used to enable the banks to grant extensions to worthy borrowers; to enable them to provide legal collateral for their outstanding bonds sold to the public, and to provide new funds to loan to new borrowers who wished to avail themselves of the Farm Loan Act. This sum was to be used as a revolving fund and it was thought that it would furnish capital sufficient to meet the demand until new bonds could be sold by the banks.

October 6, 1931: The President met with some thirty Congressional leaders, members of the committees involved, in his study at the White

House in the evening. Among those present were Senators Watson, Borah, Walcott, Bingham, Reed, Glenn, Carey, Vandenberg, Townsend, Republicans; Senators Robinson (Arkansas), Pat Harrison, Swanson, Wagner, Walsh (Montana), Glass, and King, Democrats; Representatives Tilson, Snell, Bacharach, Aldrich, McFadden, Treadway, Luce, Crowther, and Davenport, Republicans; and Representatives Garner, Crisp, Byrns, Brand, McDuffie, Stevenson, and Goldsborough, Democrats. Also Secretary Mellon, Under Secretary Mills and Governor Meyer.

President Hoover reviewed the whole economic situation very fully. He stated that we were faced with another crisis as great as that of the previous June, with the world much weaker to withstand the shock and with a banking system defective in organization. He announced that the time had come when national unity and the abandonment of political opposition were imperative. He recounted the agreement with the bankers and added that he had invited the Premier of France to visit the United States to discuss the world situation. He assured those present that he had a program for the immediate moment; that he would have further proposals when Congress met; that whether the Congress would be called earlier than its regular session on December 2nd would depend upon the development of the crisis. He had prepared a memorandum of his proposals in the form of a joint public statement to be issued on the part of all present if they felt they could agree with it or with modifications of it.

A frank discussion followed, in which practically all present took part. Generally speaking, both Republicans and Democrats alike expressed apprehension about the proposal to set up another governmental financial agency similar to the old War Finance Corporation, and hoped it would not be necessary and only a last resort. The desire not to project the government into the business of lending money was quite generally expressed. When Congress convened about two months later, the situation in this respect had so changed that practically no opposition of this character developed. The foreclosure policy of the Federal Land Banks came in for some criticism. In the course of the discussion it developed that the specific instances cited arose out of action by the Joint Stock Land Banks and their foreclosure policies. Some of those present appeared not to know the very substantial distinction between the two systems. In the supervision of the Joint Stock Land Banks the Federal Farm Loan Board had no jurisdiction which would permit it to interfere in the foreclosure policies.

The discussion lasted until one o'clock in the morning. Congressman Garner was outspoken in his lack of sympathy with the program, but the others present were helpful and co-operative. Senator Borah questioned the reference in the proposed statement to the Laval visit. To obviate any possible objection the Laval paragraph was phrased so that the President took the entire responsibility for its implications. The statement was finally agreed upon.

This agreement in peace time between the President and Congressional leaders representing both parties was a substantial achievement. Later on we shall see the extent of the performance. The text appeared in the press the same morning. Because of its historic importance the memorandum is given in full:[2]

The prolongation of the depression by the succession of events in Europe, affecting as they have both commodity and security prices, has produced in some localities in the United States an apprehension wholly unjustified in view of the thousand-fold resources we have for meeting any demand. Foolish alarm in these sections has been accompanied by wholly unjustifiable withdrawal of currency from the banks. Such action results in limiting the ability of the banks in these localities to extend credit to business men and farmers for the normal conduct of business, but beyond this to be prepared to meet the possibility of unreasoning demands of depositors the banks are compelled to place their assets in liquid form by sales of securities and restriction of credits, so as to enable them to meet unnecessary and unjustified drains. This affects the conduct of banking further afield. It is unnecessary to specify the unfortunate consequences of such a situation in the districts affected both in its further effect on national prices of agricultural products, upon securities and upon the normal conduct of business and employment of labor. It is a deflationary factor and a definite impediment to agricultural and business recovery.

There is no justification for any such situation in view of the strength of our banking system, and the strong position of our Federal Reserve System. Our difficulty is a diffusion of resources and the primary need is to mobilize them in such a way as to restore in a number of localities the confidence of the banker in his ability to continue normal business and to dispel any conceivable doubt in the mind of those who do business with him.

In order to deal with this wholly abnormal situation and to bring about an early restoration of confidence, unity of action on the part of our bankers and co-operative action on the part of the government is essential. Therefore, I propose the following definite program of action, to which I ask our citizens to give their full co-operation.

1. To mobilize the banking resources of the country to meet these conditions, I request the bankers of the nation to form a national institution of at least $500,000,000. The purpose of this institution to be the rediscount of banking assets not now eligible for rediscount at the Federal Reserve Banks in order to assure our banks, being sound, that they may attain liquidity in case of necessity, and thereby enable them to continue

[2] State Papers, Vol. II, p. 4.

their business without the restriction of credits or the sacrifice of their assets. I have submitted my proposal to the leading bankers of New York. I have been advised by them that it will receive their support, and that at my request they will assume the leadership in the formulation of such an organization. The members of the New York City Clearing House Association have unanimously agreed to contribute their share by pledging $150,000,000, which is two per cent of their net demand and time deposits. I have been assured from other large centers, as far as I have been able to reach, of their support also. I consider that it is in the national interest, including the interest of all individual banks and depositors, that all the banks of the country should support this movement to their full responsibility. It is a movement of national assurance and of unity of action in an American way to assist business, employment, and agriculture.

2. On September 8th, I requested the governors of the Federal Reserve Banks to endeavor to secure the co-operation of the bankers of their territory to make some advances on the security of the assets of closed banks or to take over some of these assets in order that the receivers of those banks may pay some dividends to their depositors in advance of what would otherwise be the case pending liquidation. Such a measure will contribute to free many business activities and to relieve many families from hardship over the forthcoming winter, and in a measure reverse the process of deflation involved in the tying up of deposits. Several of the districts have already made considerable progress to this end, and I request that it should be taken up vigorously as a community responsibility.

3. In order that the above program of unification and solidarity of action may be carried out and that all parts of the country be enlisted, I request the governors of the Federal Reserve Banks in each district to secure the appointment of working committees of bankers for each Reserve district to co-operate with the New York group and in carrying out the other activities which I have mentioned.

4. I shall propose to the Congress that the eligibility provisions of the Federal Reserve Act should be broadened in order to give greater liquidity to the assets of the banks, and thus a greater assurance to the bankers in the granting of credits by enabling them to obtain legitimate accommodation on sound security in times of stress. Such measures are already under consideration by the Senate Committee upon Currency and Banking.

5. Furthermore, if necessity requires, I will recommend the creation of a finance corporation similar in character and purpose to the War Finance Corporation, with available funds sufficient for any legitimate call in support of credit.

6. I shall recommend to Congress the subscription of further capital stock by the government to the Federal Land Banks (as was done at their founding) to strengthen their resources so that, on the one hand, the farmer may be assured of such accommodation as he may require and, on the other hand, their credit may be of such high character that they may obtain their funds at low rates of interest.

7. I have submitted the above-mentioned proposals which require legislation to the members of Congress, whose attendance I was able to secure on short notice at the evening's meeting—being largely the members of committees particularly concerned—and they approve of them in principle.

8. Premier Laval of France is visiting the United States. It is my purpose to discuss with him the question of such further arrangements as are imperative during the period of the depression in respect of intergovernmental debts. The policy of the American Government in this matter is well known, and was set out by me in public statement on June 20th in announcing the American proposal for a year's postponement of debt payments. Our problem in this respect is one of such adjustment during the period of depression as will at the same time aid our own and world recovery. This being a subject first of negotiation with foreign governments was not submitted for determination at this evening's conference.

9. The times call for unity of action on the part of our people. We have met with great difficulties not of our own making. It requires determination to overcome these difficulties and above all to restore and maintain confidence. Our people owe it not only to themselves and in their own interest, but they can by such an example of stability and purpose give hope and confidence in our own country and to the rest of the world.

October 7, 1931: The President called to the White House a committee which he had appointed from important insurance, mortgage, building and loan, and construction interests. These included James L. Madden, William E. Best, Hiram S. Cody, Clarence Dillon, Harry Kahler, Harry S. Kissell, Samuel N. Reep, W. A. Starrett, and Clarence M. Woolley. Also Secretary of Commerce Lamont was present. President Hoover laid before them his proposal to establish a national system of mortgage discount banks, somewhat comparable with the Federal Reserve System. As in that system, the government was to provide for the initial capital, but in this case the capital should be absorbed by the members, who were to embrace all kinds of institutions making real estate mortgages. He proposed that the mortgage banks thus created should issue debentures for funds and that mortgages should be available at all times for discount up to ninety per cent of any "live" mortgage, so long as the ninety per cent did not exceed fifty per cent of the reasonable value of the property in normal times. He urged that this would thaw out billions of frozen assets. It would relieve the pressure of foreclosure upon millions of farmers and home-owners. It was a much-needed institution on the road toward the separation of long-time and short-time credit systems in our national economy. It would pave the way to taking the demand-deposit banks out of the mortgage business.

The representatives present from the building and loan associations and some of the mortgage companies favored it strongly. The representatives of the insurance companies opposed it on the ground that ultimately it would affect their earnings by lowering mortgage interest rates. They claimed that there was no necessity for it, and that there were ample mortgage lending facilities. The President pointed out the obvious facts. The conference then adjourned, to meet again.

This was no new interest of the President. While Secretary of Commerce, he had established a division for study and development of home building, and had taken a large part in the organization of "Better Homes in America." The former developed the whole question of inadequate finance, construction and design for home building, and the latter conducted a nation-wide campaign for better housing.

At Mr. Hoover's suggestion, some years before, Julius Rosenwald had supported a financial institution in Chicago in trying out the methods of financial aid which he had in mind. This institution functioned successfully for a number of years and greatly reduced interest charges on mortgages.

October 8, 1931: The President addressed the Pan-American Commercial Conference, which represented the governments of the Western Hemisphere, upon his views as to foreign loans. The most important paragraphs were: [3]

. . . There is one lesson from this depression to which I wish to refer, and I can present it no more forcibly than by repeating a statement which I made to this conference just four years ago, when we were in the heyday of foreign loans. I stated, in respect to such loans, that they are helpful in world development "provided always one essential principle dominates the character of these transactions. That is, that no nation as a government should borrow or no government lend, and nations should discourage their citizens from borrowing or lending unless this money is to be devoted to productive enterprise.

"Out of the wealth and the higher standards of living created from enterprise itself must come to the borrowing country the ability to repay the capital. Any other course of action creates obligations impossible of repayment except by a direct subtraction from the standards of living of the borrowing country and the impoverishment of its people.

"In fact, if this principle could be adopted between nations of the world—that is, if nations would do away with the lending of money for the balancing of budgets, for purposes of military equipment or war purposes, or even that type of public works which does not bring some direct or indirect productive return—a great number of blessings would follow to the entire world.

"There could be no question as to the ability to repay; with this

[3] State Papers, Vol. II, p. 7.

increasing security capital would become steadily cheaper, the dangers to national and individual independence in attempts of the lender to collect his defaulted debts would be avoided; there would be definite increase in the standards of living and the comfort and prosperity of the borrower. . . ."

The response of the whole country to the President's action of the 6th was instantaneous. In twenty-four hours the impending panic was dissipated. The prices of wheat and cotton, and of all securities generally, rose at once. Hoarding diminished rapidly. By the end of the month currency was returning to the banks.

Pursuant to the suggestions made by the President, the bankers incorporated the National Credit Corporation and started business at once by coming to the assistance of certain banks in South Carolina and Louisiana and preventing their collapse.

October 9, 1931: Taking advantage of the President's announced conference with Premier Laval of France, certain Democratic newspapers claimed a concealed intention to cancel the war-debts, rather than merely to postpone their payment for a limited period during the world-wide depression. The President told the Washington representatives "that as to cancellation, the position was exactly as stated on June 20th." As to the extension of the moratorium: "It is not customary among decent individuals or amongst nations to insist upon a debtor making payments beyond the capacity of the individual or nation to pay, but that does not imply that they shall not pay to the full extent of their capacity. In fact, it is one of the foundations of moral and economic life."

October 9, 1931: The world-wide influence of the depression was becoming more and more apparent. Uruguay abandoned the gold standard, practically suspended her foreign obligations and, in effect, followed Europe in raising tariffs and in control of exchange.

October 13, 1931: This evening the President was in conference with Chairman Bestor of the Farm Loan Board and Secretary Hyde in going over the farm loan problem.

October 17, 1931: Brazil suspended foreign payments, went off the gold standard, increased tariffs to protect exchange.

The railroads had been suffering from substantial loss in tonnage and consequent loss in revenue. It was feared that a number of them would be forced to default on their bonds. Involved was not only the question of freight rates as between shipper and carrier, there was also a larger question. These bonds were widely distributed. They were held by savings banks, life insurance companies and fiduciary institutions. The President conferred with representatives of the Interstate Commerce

Commission. The Commission made an investigation which resulted in an authorization for an increase in certain rates. None were on the products of agriculture. The increase was conditioned upon the additional revenue obtained being paid into a pool, where it would be available for loan purposes to railroads requiring assistance.

The President, following up his warning of July 10th to the Chicago commodity markets, interested Silas H. Strawn in revising the rules of the Chicago Board of Trade and the administration of them. Mr. Strawn secured the co-operation of the exchange and the evils complained of were materially lessened.

October 18, 1931: The President was en route to Yorktown, Va., where he was to speak at the 150th anniversary of the victory at Yorktown. He stopped off at Fortress Monroe to make a radio address.[4] The President spoke to the entire nation, urging support to the national drive for funds for private relief organization which had been organized by Mr. Gifford. He said:

> This broadcast tonight marks the beginning of the mobilization of the nation for a great undertaking to provide security for those of our citizens and their families who, through no fault of their own, face unemployment and privation during the coming winter. . . . No one with a spark of human sympathy can contemplate unmoved the possibilities of suffering that can crush many of our unfortunate fellow Americans if we fail them.
>
> The depression has been deepened by events from abroad which are beyond the control either of our citizens or our government. . . . We must meet the consequences in unemployment which arise from it with that completeness of effort and that courage and spirit for which citizenship in this nation always has and always must stand.
>
> As . . . part of our plans for national unity of action in this emergency I have created a national organization under the leadership of Mr. Walter Gifford to co-operate with the governors, the State and local agencies, and with the many national organizations of business, labor, and welfare, with the churches and other societies so that the countless streams of human helpfulness which have been the mainstay of our country in all emergencies may be directed wisely and effectively.
>
> Over a thousand towns and cities have well organized and experienced unemployment relief committees . . . to meet their task over the forthcoming winter . . . to lighten the burden of the heavy laden and to cast sunshine into the habitation of despair. . . .
>
> The Federal Government is taking its part in aid to unemployment through . . . enlargement of public works in all parts of the nation. All immigration has been stopped. . . . Measures have been adopted which will assure normal credits and thus stimulate employment in industry, commerce, and agriculture. The employers in national industries have

[4] State Papers, Vol. II, p. 12.

spread work amongst their employees so that the maximum number may participate in the wages that are available. Our States, counties, and municipalities, through the expansion of their public works and through tax-supporting relief activities, are doing their part. Yet beyond all this, there is a margin of relief which must be provided by voluntary action. . . .

Similar organization and generous support were provided during the past winter. . . . We succeeded in the task. . . . We demonstrated that it could be done . . . our need will be greater this winter. . . .

The possible misery of helpless people gives me more concern than any other trouble this depression has brought us. . . .

The maintenance of a spirit of mutual self-help through voluntary giving, through the responsibility of local government, is of infinite importance to the future of America. . . .

I would that I possessed the art of words to fix the real issue with which the troubled world is faced into the mind and heart of every American man and woman. Our country and the world are today involved in more than a financial crisis. We are faced with the primary question of human relations, which reaches to the very depth of organized society and to the very depth of human conscience. This civilization and this great complex, which we call American life, is builded and can alone survive upon the translation into individual action of that fundamental philosophy announced by the Savior nineteen centuries ago. Part of our national suffering today is from failure to observe these primary yet inexorable laws of human relationship. Modern society cannot survive with the defense of Cain, "Am I my brother's keeper?"

No governmental action, no economic doctrine, no economic plan or project can replace that God-imposed responsibility of the individual man and woman to their neighbors. That is a vital part of the very soul of the people. If we shall gain in this spirit from this painful time, we shall have created a greater and more glorious America. The trial of it is here now. It is a trial of the heart and conscience of individual men and women. . . .

I am on my way to participate in the commemoration of the Victory of Yorktown. It is a name which brings a glow of pride to every American. It recalls the final victory of our people after years of sacrifice and privation. This nation passed through Valley Forge and came to Yorktown.

Shortly after this Mr. Gifford reported to the President that the response to the appeal for private relief for the unemployed had been fifty per cent greater than in the drive a year ago.

October 23, 1931: Premier Laval arrived in Washington. Certain of the press seemed to have a desire to interpret the conference as having a bearing upon the "political" situation in Europe. The President and the Premier issued a joint statement, again repeating the facts:[5]

Both the President and Premier Laval wish it made clear that the conversations upon which they are engaged are solely in respect of such

[5] State Papers, Vol. II, p. 18.

policies as each of the two governments can develop to expedite recovery from the world economic depression. There is no remote basis whatever for statements as to "demands," "terms of settlement" or any other like discussions. Happily there are no controversies to be settled between France and America. None such exist. The sole purpose of these conversations is the earnest, frank exchange of views with view to finding common ground for helpful action in the promotion of constructive progress in the world.

October 24, 25, 1931: The President and Premier Laval were in constant conference, the former accompanied by Secretaries Stimson and Mills, the latter by the French Ambassador and by his own economic experts. A great number of proposals were discussed and discarded. Among them was the immediate calling of a conference on currency stabilization. It was not thought possible to secure adherence of the "off-gold" countries to any constructive steps in this direction for the next few months.

The points of agreement are set out in the joint statement issued at the time:[6]

The traditional friendship between the United States and France, the absence of all controversy between our two governments, a record of many events in collaboration toward peace of the world, embracing among its recent phases the adoption of the Kellogg-Briand Pact, render it possible and opportune for the representatives of our governments to explore every aspect of the many problems in which we are mutually interested.

Indeed the duty of statesmen is not to overlook any means of practical co-operation for the common good. This is particularly true at a time when the world looks for leadership in relief from a depression which reaches into countless homes in every land. Relations of mutual confidence between governments have the most important bearing upon speeding the recovery which we seek. We have engaged upon that mission with entire frankness. We have made real progress.

We canvassed the economic situation in the world, the trends in international relations bearing upon it; the problems of the forthcoming conference for limitation and reduction of armaments; the effect of the depression on payments under inter-governmental debts; the stabilization of international exchanges and other financial and economic subjects.

An informal and cordial discussion has served to outline with greater precision the nature of the problems. It has not been the purpose of either of us to engage in commitments binding our governments, but rather, through development of fact, to enable each country to act more effectively in its own field.

It is our joint purpose that the conference for limitation of armaments

[6] State Papers, Vol. II, p. 19.

will not fail to take advantage of the great opportunity which presents itself and that it will be capable of meeting what is in reality its true mission, that is the organization on a firm foundation of permanent peace. Insofar as inter-governmental obligations are concerned we recognize that prior to the expiration of the Hoover year of postponement, some agreement regarding them may be necessary covering the period of business depression, as to the terms and conditions of which the two governments make all reservations. The initiative in this matter should be taken at an early date by the European powers principally concerned within the framework of the agreements existing prior to July 1, 1931.

Our especial emphasis has been upon the more important means through which the efforts of our governments could be exerted toward restoration of economic stability and confidence. Particularly we are convinced of the importance of monetary stability as an essential factor in the restoration of normal economic life in the world in which the maintenance of the gold standard in France and the United States will serve as a major influence.

It is our intent to continue to study methods for the maintenance of stability in international exchange.

While in the short time at our disposal it has not been possible to formulate definite programs, we find that we view the nature of these financial and economic problems in the same light and that this understanding on our part should serve to pave the way for helpful action by our respective governments.

It should be stated that, in accordance with these declarations on debts, the Germans acted under the terms of the reparation agreements on November 19th and the Lausanne Conference followed in May, 1932. The President in December proposed to Congress a temporary readjustment during the depression, but Congress refused all concession. The ultimate effect of this attitude and the further action of the following year was the practical repudiation of the debts by the debtor nations and a consequent loss of any payment, with a resultant loss to the American taxpayers.

October 25, 1931: The President met with the chairman, George M. Reynolds, and President Mortimer Buckner of the National Credit Association. They reported that the Association had completed its organization throughout the country, was actively making loans and participating with other groups to help out banks which were under pressure. The President urged that they should consider means for the reorganization and opening of closed banks. The full board of the Association was: George M. Reynolds, Chicago, chairman; Mortimer Buckner, New York, president; Daniel Wing, Boston; Livingston Jones, Philadelphia; Arthur Braun, Pittsburgh; John M. Miller, Jr., Richmond; John K. Ottley,

Atlanta; Walter W. Smith, St. Louis; Edward W. Decker, Minneapolis; W. S. McLucas, Kansas City; Nathan Adams, Dallas; and Frank Anderson, San Francisco. The Association made over 750 loans and prevented failures in many instances.

October 27, 1931: The Conservative landslide in the Parliamentary elections in Great Britain today meant an extension of the tariff and trade quotas and the reduction of imports as measures for currency stabilization. All of this reduced our markets.

The committee of business, agricultural and labor leaders, and economists appointed by the President in conjunction with Mr. Gifford, to recommend methods of economic recovery and relief, made its report. The committee was composed of Harry A. Wheeler of Chicago, W. Rufus Abbott of Chicago, Leonard Ayres of Cleveland, T. H. Bonfield of Portland, Frederick C. Croxton of Columbus, S. P. Bush of Columbus, Homer L. Ferguson of Newport News, Virginia, Charles G. Gates of Denver, William Green of Washington, E. N. Hurley of Chicago, A. Johnston of Cleveland, H. C. Knight of New Haven, Alexander Legge of Chicago, Wesley C. Mitchell of New York, Matthew S. Sloan of New York, L. R. Smith of Milwaukee, W. A. Starett of New York, and Daniel E. Willard of Baltimore. The report endorsed the already existing program. The main points were "united national action of confidence in the future . . . expansion of credit . . . continued spreading of available work including public employees and private office employees . . . preference in employment to persons with dependents . . . public works . . . community surveys of work available . . . a survey to be made of possibility to transfer excessive city population to argriculture. . . ."

October 30, 1931: The President concluded his conferences for the time being with Chairman Bestor of the Farm Loan Board. As a result of these conferences still further ameliorating amendments to the Farm Loan Act were agreed upon. Later, and following the convening of Congress, these suggestions were drafted into amendments and were introduced in the Senate by Senator Fletcher of the Committee on Banking. They passed the Senate, but consideration and passage were delayed in the House for many months.

November 1, 1931: The "Progressive" group in the Senate again demanded large Federal expenditures as a remedy for the depression.

November 6, 1931: At his press conference the President announced that direct cuts of $350,000,000 in expenditures would be proposed in the budget and that authority from Congress would be sought which would result in further reductions. Many proposals were being made by minority groups and sectional interests to increase governmental expenditures. To these proposals, some of which might have been meritorious under different circumstances, the President stated his opposition. His thought was that additional appropriations should be confined to whatever might become necessary for the Federal Government to do by way of relief in meeting the problem of unemployment and the distress in agriculture.

CHAPTER IX

THE OPENING OF CONGRESS AND THE CLOSE OF THE YEAR

NOVEMBER–DECEMBER, 1931

November 10, 1931: As a result largely of the President's leadership the third great crisis appeared to have been weathered. Each of the three crises—of the stock markets in October-November, 1929, the collapse of Central Europe in June, 1931, and the British difficulties in September of this year—seemed now to have been safely overcome. The United States again was showing signs of recovery. The spirit of the nation was hopeful. The press everywhere carried news of re-awakening industry and employment. Since early October the price of wheat had increased by fifty per cent, cotton by fifteen per cent, industrial stocks by nearly forty per cent. Not only had hoarding ceased but also currency was returning to the banks at the estimated rate of $25,000,000 a week. Debits to individual accounts in the banks had increased markedly. Bank failures had almost ceased. Discount rates had been lowered by many foreign banks. The flow of gold was returning. Unemployment was decreasing.

To meet the proposed reduction in government expenditures from the discharge of a large number of individuals from the government service, thereby adding to the existing number of unemployed, the President announced his plan for the sharing of work among these Federal employees. This would avoid actual discharges as the result of the proposed reductions.

November 13, 1931: President Hoover, finding that opposition in Congress and in the banking and insurance world would greatly delay, if not defeat, a system of permanent and complete mortgage discount banks, determined to confine his proposal to a system for home and farm mortgages. He planned to do so prior to the National Conference on Home Ownership so as to have it before that body. Selfish interests were active in delaying consideration. The Presidential campaign was in the offing. There were those who for purely partisan reasons did not want the bill to pass so that the President would be credited with a major accomplishment. So that notwithstanding the urgency, the quiet but effective influence of these elements delayed its adoption for nine months, cut out the farm mortgage feature, and greatly restricted its effectiveness in home ownership. However, the foundations for future development were laid. The President's announcement read as follows:[1]

I shall propose to Congress the establishment of a system of Home Loan Discount Banks for four purposes:

1. For the present emergency purpose of relieving the financial strains upon sound building and loan associations, savings banks, deposit banks, and farm loan banks that have been giving credit through the medium of small mortgage loans upon urban and farm properties used for homes. Thereby to relieve pressures upon home and farm owners.

2. To put the various types of institutions loaning on mortgage in a position to assist in the revival of home construction in many parts of the country and with its resultant increase in employment.

3. To safeguard against the repetition of such experiences in the future.

4. For the long view purpose of strengthening such institutions in the promotion of home ownership particularly through the financial strength thus made available to building and loan associations. . . . I propose the following general principles. . . .

(a) That there be established twelve Home Loan Discount Banks . . . under the direction of a Federal Home Loan Board.

(b) The capital of these discount banks shall be initially of minimum of five to thirty million as may be determined by the Federal Board. . . .

(c) The proposed discount banks to make no initial or direct mortgages but to loan only upon the obligations of the loaning institutions secured by the mortgage loans as collateral so as to assure and expand the functioning of such institutions.

(d) Building and loan associations, savings banks, deposit banks, farm loan banks, etc., may become members of the system. . . .

(e) The mortgage loans eligible for collateral shall not exceed $15,000 each and shall be limited to urban and farm property used for home purposes.

(f) The maximum amount to be advanced against the mortgage collateral not to exceed more than fifty per cent of the unpaid balance on un-amortized or short-term mortgage loans and not more than sixty per cent of the unpaid balance of amortized long-term mortgages. . . .

(g) The discount banks as their needs require from time to time to issue bonds or short-term notes to investors to an amount not to exceed in the aggregate twelve times the capital of the issuing bank. . . .

(h) If the aggregate initial capital of the discount banks should in the beginning be fixed at $150,000,000, it would be possible for the twelve banks to finance approximately something over $1,800,000,000 of advance to the borrowing institutions which could be further expanded by increase in their capital.

(i) It is proposed to find the initial capital stock for the discount banks in much the same way, in so far as is applicable, as the capital was found for the Federal Reserve Banks . . . first offer the capital to the

[1] State Papers, Vol. II, p. 31.

institutions which would participate in the service. . . . And as was provided in respect to the Federal Reserve Banks, if the initial capital is not wholly thus provided, it should be subscribed by the Federal Government; and, further, somewhat as was provided in the case of the Federal Land Banks, other institutions using the facilities of the discount banks should be required to purchase from time to time from the government some proportionate amount of its holdings of stock if there be any. In this manner any government capital will gradually pass over to private ownership as was the case in the Federal Land Banks. . . .

There is no element of inflation in the plan but simply a better organization of credit for these purposes. . . .

November 16, 1931: The President conferred with Congressional leaders Watson, McNary, Snell, Hawley and others, upon an increase in taxation. He had determined that at least $1,200,000,000 increase in revenues must be found to balance the budget.

November 19, 1931: The German Government, in preparation for the expiration of the moratorium, asked the former Allies for an investigation of its capacity to pay, as provided in the reparations agreements with the European powers.

November 20, 1931: The British, as the result of agitation which was begun as early as 1926, enacted a general tariff. The purpose was to increase revenues, protect home production, and to reduce imports as an aid to their financial situation. This was at great cost to us. Their depreciated currency also was in itself a barrier to our exports.

November 22, 1931: The British established a wheat "quota" to force the use of domestic wheat as against foreign grain.

November 30, 1931: The rapidly improving situation early in the month had slowed down sharply and a new wave of fear was again sweeping the country. Prices of wheat had fallen ten cents a bushel and cotton had fallen ten per cent, hoarding had begun again, bank failures increased, industrial stocks had fallen twenty per cent. The impacts upon us of the European hurricane still continued. The National Credit Association had proved unable to stop the financial pressure. The President determined that the national measures which he had forecast on October 6th must all be brought into action and more be done, if we were to be saved from another crisis. Here also he was compelled to set aside certain measures of sound social and economic reform which he long had hoped to complete in his administration. His view was that recovery must come before reform; that jobs must be restored, that the country must be saved and reconstruction must be under way before these long-view questions were advanced.

December 1, 1931: Senator Glass had sent a questionnaire to the

Federal Reserve Banks upon the President's recent proposal to increase the range of eligibility of bank loans for Reserve re-discount. He now announced that they and he were opposed to it. It may be noted that Senator Glass himself later introduced the bill providing for this.

Bertrand Snell of New York, with the convening of the Seventy-second Congress, replaced John Q. Tilson of Connecticut as Republican floor-leader. Mr. Tilson ably and devotedly had co-operated with the President. Mr. Snell likewise carried on the best traditions of party organization and in the difficult rôle of minority leader established a fine record.

December 2, 1931: The President opened the National Housing Conference, the preparations for which had been in progress for more than a year. This conference is dealt with elsewhere, but should be mentioned here since in his recovery plans the President used the conference to secure backing for the Home Loan Discount Banks which were partly for emergency purposes but in the main comprised a long-time program.

December 3, 1931: The Governor of the Federal Reserve Board having indicated his lack of sympathy with the President's program for extending the authority of the Federal Reserve Banks, the President addressed him the following letter:

HON. EUGENE MEYER,
Federal Reserve Board,
Washington, D. C.
MY DEAR MR. MEYER:

Apropos of our conversation yesterday I think it is desirable that you should re-read the statement I put out on October 6th as to the eligibility provisions of the Federal Reserve Banks. This statement you will recollect was approved by yourself, Messrs. Mellon, Mills and Harrison. It was also approved by all the Congressional gentlemen present at the meeting on October 6th. I do not believe, therefore, that we should retreat from that position but that our administration should be prepared to follow up our promise by some constructively formulated ideas.

There is no doubt that the mortgage discount banks which I proposed would relieve a very great segment of stress in this direction but it would not cover the entire field of assurances which we gave to the public at that time.

Yours faithfully,

HERBERT HOOVER.

December 6, 1931: A committee was appointed by the former Allies in response to Germany's request that an investigation be made of her capacity to pay at the expiration of the moratorium.

December 7, 1931: The first session of the Seventy-second Congress convened. The Senate comprised what might be termed thirty-six Regular Republicans, twelve "Progressives," forty-seven Democrats, and one Farmer-Labor. The Republicans with the aid of the Progressives organized the Senate. However, so far as the President was concerned, the organization was only nominally Republican. In practice, as in the preceding session, a coalition of Democrats and certain "Progressives" would number from fifty to sixty, a clear majority. The House of Representatives comprised 219 Democrats, 15 "Progressives," and 192 Republicans. The Democrats organized the House with Mr. John N. Garner as Speaker. Two days before (December 5th), Mr. Garner had set forth the duty of the Democratic majority in a public statement:

My idea of the duty of the Democratic majority of the House of Representatives is to offer such measures as we believe will best advance the return of our country to prosperity and to enhance the comfort, security and the contentment of our people.

The extent and character of the various measures offered and their effect upon recovery will appear as we examine their detailed provisions.

The Seventy-second Congress was to exhibit extremely partisan action in a time of national emergency. President Hoover, confronted with this legislative opposition, appealed again and again for national unity, but obtained only a most sparing co-operation from an opposition intent on playing politics even at the expense of national recovery, in order to assure its party success in the coming election. The President, by persistence and by patiently working with various groups, managed to secure a large amount of vitally needed legislation.

December 7, 1931: The President requested Senator Watson and Representative Snell, the Republican leaders of the Senate and the House, to canvass the Democratic leaders of the assembling Congress to learn if the Democratic Party really intended to propose a recovery program for this session in accordance with the public statement of their leaders given a year ago upon the election of the Congress now about to assemble. The President suggested that if the Democrats had any program in mind it was urgent that "we all get together with our ideas and have unified action." These Republican leaders reported that the Democrats stated that they had no program, that the responsibility was that of the President, and that they would "scrutinize" anything he had to offer. They said that it was obvious that the Democrats would use the destructive power they now possessed through the control of Congress for political purposes just as far as they thought that destruction would not discredit them, and that they were resolved to defeat the President in the next election regardless of what delay in recovery might cost the country.

December 8, 1931: The President's annual message on that occasion was the most important economic message he delivered to Congress. He necessarily was under great restraint because of the current panicky situation. He said: [2]

. . . The chief influence affecting the state of the Union during the past year has been the continued world-wide economic disturbance. Our national concern has been to meet the emergencies it has created for us and to lay the foundations for recovery. . . .

The economic depression has . . . deepened in every part of the world. . . . In many countries political instability, excessive armaments, debts, governmental expenditures, and taxes have resulted in revolutions, in unbalanced budgets and monetary collapse and financial panics, in dumping of goods upon world markets, and in diminished consumption of commodities.

Within two years there have been revolutions or acute social disorders in nineteen countries, embracing more than half the population of the world. Ten countries have been unable to meet their external obligations. In fourteen countries, embracing a quarter of the world's population, former monetary standards have been temporarily abandoned. In a number of countries there have been acute financial panics or compulsory restraints upon banking. These disturbances have many roots in the dislocations from the World War. Every one of them has reacted upon us. They have sharply affected the markets and prices of our agricultural and industrial products. They have increased unemployment and greatly embarrassed our financial and credit system.

As our difficulties during the past year have plainly originated in large degree from these sources, any effort to bring about our own recuperation has dictated the necessity of co-operation by us with other nations in reasonable effort to restore world confidence and economic stability. . . .

Many undertakings have been organized and forwarded during the past year to meet the new and changing emergencies which have constantly confronted us . . . to meet the needs of honest distress, and to take such emergency measures as would sustain confidence in our financial system and would cushion the violence of liquidation in industry and commerce, thus giving time for orderly readjustment of costs, inventories, and credits without panic and widespread bankruptcy. These measures have served those purposes and will promote recovery.

. . . continued speeding up of the great Federal construction program has provided direct and indirect aid to employment . . . the States and municipalities have also maintained large programs of public improvement . . . employers have been organized to spread available work amongst all their employees, instead of discharging a portion of them.

[2] State Papers, Vol. II, p. 41.

A large majority have maintained wages at as high levels as the safe conduct of their business would permit. . . . Immigration has been curtailed by administrative action . . . the decrease amounts to about 300,000 individuals who otherwise would have been added to our unemployment. The expansion of Federal employment agencies . . . has proved most effective. Through the President's organization for unemployment relief, public and private agencies were successfully mobilized last winter to provide employment and other measures against distress. Similar organization gives assurance against suffering during the coming winter . . . they have been assured the funds necessary which, together with local government aids, will meet the situation. . . . The evidence of the Public Health Service shows an actual decrease of sickness and infant and general mortality below normal years. No greater proof could be adduced that our people have been protected from hunger and cold. . . .

. . . the loans authorized for the drought area have enabled farmers to produce abundant crops. . . . The Red Cross . . . administered relief for over 2,500,000 drought sufferers. . . . It has undertaken . . . relief to 100,000 sufferers in the new drought area. . . . The action of the Federal Farm Board . . . to farm co-operatives saved many of them from bankruptcy. . . . By enabling farm co-operatives to cushion the fall in prices of farm products in 1930 and 1931 the Board secured higher prices than would have been obtained otherwise, although the benefits of this action were partially defeated by continued world overproduction. . . . The failure of a large number of farmers and of country banks was averted. . . .

To meet . . . domestic emergencies in credit and banking arising from the reaction to acute crises abroad the National Credit Association was set up by the banks with resources of $500,000,000 to support sound banks against the frightened withdrawals and hoarding. . . . Federal officials have brought about many beneficial unions of banks and have employed other means which have prevented many bank closings. . . .

Although some of the causes of our depression are due to speculation, inflation of securities and real estate, unsound foreign investments, and mismanagement of financial institutions, yet our self-contained national economy, with its matchless strength and resources, would have enabled us to recover long since but for the continued dislocations, shocks, and setbacks from abroad. . . .

After an outline of the present situation, the President laid out the following economic program (the numbers are ours).

. . . We must put some steel beams in the foundations of our credit structure. It is our duty to apply the full strength of our government not only to the immediate phases, but to provide security against shocks and the repetition of the weaknesses which have been proven. . . .

1. The first requirement of confidence and of economic recovery is financial stability of the United States Government . . . call attention to the magnitude of the deficits . . . and . . . for determined and courage-

ous policies. These deficits arise in the main from the heavy decrease in tax receipts due to the depression and to the increase in expenditure on construction in aid to unemployment, aids to agriculture, and upon services to veterans. . . .

The budget for the fiscal year beginning July 1st next . . . after allowing for drastic reduction in expenditures, still indicates a deficit of $1,417,000,000. . . .

Several conclusions are inevitable. We must have insistent and determined reduction in government expenses. We must face a temporary increase in taxes. . . .

2. I recommend that the Congress authorize the subscription by the Treasury of further capital to the Federal Land Banks. . . . It is urgent . . . that they may continue their services to agriculture and that they may meet the present situation with consideration to the farmers.

3. A method . . . to make available quickly to depositors some portion of their deposits in closed banks as the assets of such banks may warrant. Such provision would go far to relieve distress in a multitude of families. . . .

4. I recommend the establishment of a system of home-loan discount banks as the necessary companion in our financial structure of the Federal Reserve Banks and our Federal Land Banks. Such action will relieve present distressing pressures against home and farm property owners. It will relieve pressures upon and give added strength to building and loan associations, savings banks and deposit banks, engaged in extending such credits. Such action would further decentralize our credit structure. It would revive residential construction and employment. It would enable such loaning institutions more effectually to promote home ownership. I discussed this plan at some length in a statement made public November 14th, last. This plan has been warmly indorsed by the recent National Conference upon Home Ownership and Housing, whose members were designated by the governors of the States and the groups interested.

5. In order that the public may be absolutely assured and that the government may be in position to meet any public necessity, I recommend that an emergency reconstruction corporation of the nature of the former War Finance Corporation should be established. It may not be necessary to use such an instrumentality very extensively. The very existence of such a bulwark will strengthen confidence. The Treasury should be authorized to subscribe a reasonable capital to it, and it should be given authority to issue its own debentures. It should be placed in liquidation at the end of two years. Its purpose is by strengthening the weak spots to thus liberate the full strength of the nation's resources. It should be in position to facilitate exports by American agencies; make advances to agricultural credit agencies where necessary to protect and aid the agricultural industry; to make temporary advances upon proper securities to establish industries, railways, and financial institutions which cannot otherwise secure credit, and where such advances will protect the credit structure and stimulate employment. Its functions would not overlap those of the National Credit Corporation.

6. On October 6th I issued a statement that I should recommend to the Congress an extension during emergencies of the eligibility provisions in the Federal Reserve Act. This statement was approved by a representative gathering of the members of both Houses of Congress, including members of the appropriate committees. It was approved by the officials of the Treasury Department, and I understand such an extension has been approved by a majority of the governors of the Federal Reserve Banks.

7. The Postal Savings deposits have increased from about $200,000,000 to about $550,000,000 during the past year. This experience has raised important practical questions in relation to deposits and investments which should receive the attention of the Congress.

8. Our people have a right to a banking system in which their deposits shall be safeguarded and the flow of credit less subject to storms. The need of a sounder system is plainly shown by the extent of bank failures. I recommend the prompt improvement of the banking laws. Changed financial conditions and commercial practices must be met. . . .

9. The railways present one of our immediate and pressing problems. They are and must remain the backbone of our transportation system. Their prosperity is interrelated with the prosperity of all industries . . . the enormous investment in their securities . . . by insurance companies, savings banks, benevolent and other trusts. . . . Through these institutions the railway bonds are in a large sense the investment of every family. . . . The Interstate Commerce Commission has made important and far-reaching recommendations upon the whole subject. . . .

10. In my message of a year ago I commented on the necessity of congressional inquiry into the economic action of the anti-trust laws. . . . I do not favor their repeal. Such action would open wide the door to price fixing, monopoly, and destruction of healthy competition. Particular attention should be given to the industries founded upon natural resources, especially where destructive competition produces great wastes of these resources and brings great hardships upon operators, employees, and the public. . . .

11. As an aid to unemployment the Federal Government is engaged in the greatest program of public-building, harbor, flood-control, highway, waterway, aviation, merchant and naval ship construction in all history. Our expenditures on these works during this calendar year will reach about $780,000,000 compared with $260,000,000 in 1928. . . .

We must avoid burdens upon the government which will create more unemployment in private industry than can be gained by further expansion of employment by the Federal Government. . . . We can now stimulate employment and agriculture more effectually and speedily through the voluntary measures in progress, through the thawing out of credit, through the building up of stability abroad, through the Home Loan Discount Banks, through an emergency finance corporation and the rehabilitation of the railways and other such directions. . . .

12. I have recommended in previous messages the effective regulation of interstate electrical power as the essential function of the reorganized

Federal Power Commission. I renew the recommendation. It is urgently needed in public protection. . . .

13. I have referred in previous messages to the profound need of further reorganization and consolidation of Federal administrative functions to eliminate overlap and waste. . . . I shall lay before the Congress further recommendations upon this subject. . . .

14. At present the Shipping Board exercises large administrative functions independent of the Executive. These administrative functions should be transferred to the Department of Commerce, in keeping with that single responsibility which has been the basis of our governmental structure since its foundation. . . .

The Shipping Board should be made a regulatory body acting also in advisory capacity on loans and policies, in keeping with its original conception. Its regulatory powers should be amended to include regulation of coastwise shipping. . . .

15. I recommend that all building and construction activities of the government now carried on by many departments be consolidated into an independent establishment under the President to be known as the "Public Works Administration" directed by a public works administrator. This agency should undertake all construction work in service to the different departments of the government (except naval and military work). . . . Great economies, sounder policies, more effective co-ordination to employment, and expedition in all construction work would result from this consolidation. . . .

16. These improvements are now proceeding upon an unprecedented scale. Some indication of the volume of work in progress is conveyed by the fact that during the current year over 380,000,000 cubic yards of material have been moved—an amount equal to the entire removal in the construction of the Panama Canal. . . .

Negotiations are now in progress with Canada for the construction of the St. Lawrence Waterway. . . .

17. I recommend that immigration restriction now in force under administrative action be placed upon a more definite basis by law. The deportation laws should be strengthened. Aliens lawfully in the country should be protected by the issuance of a certificate of residence.

Many vital changes and movements of vast proportions are taking place in the economic world. The effect of these changes upon the future cannot be seen clearly as yet. Of this, however, we are sure: Our system, based upon the ideals of individual initiative and of equality of opportunity, is not an artificial thing. . . . It has carried us in a century and a half to leadership of the economic world. If our economic system does not match our highest expectations at all times, it does not require revolutionary action to bring it into accord with any necessity that experience may prove. . . .

Later, as the session progressed and as the situation developed, the President added further recommendations, which can be summarized as follows:

1. He proposed to make government bonds eligible for coverage of the currency in the Federal Reserve System to prevent our being forced off the gold standard.

2. In consequence of congressional refusal of parts of the original program, he subsequently returned to the charge, asking Congress to authorize the Reconstruction Finance Corporation to lend up to $1,800,000,000 for reproductive public and semi-public and industrial works, slum clearance, etc., to States, municipalities, etc.

3. He asked authority for the Reconstruction Finance Corporation to establish a system of Agricultural Credit Banks.

4. He asked for a reform of the bankruptcy laws to facilitate re-organization and settlement of overwhelming debt.

5. He proposed to lend $300,000,000 to the States for direct relief of distress.

December 9, 1931: The Democratic leaders attacked the President's program, but offered nothing themselves despite their public assurances of doing so when they won control of the Congress the year before.

The President's budget message for the fiscal year beginning July 1st was forwarded to Congress. It recommended $369,000,000 decrease in appropriations, together with a request for legislation repealing or modifying provisions of existing law authorizing further appropriations. The granting of this legislation would result in further reductions. The President urged an increase of $1,300,000,000 in tax revenues by taxes on amusements, automobiles and conveyances, and a substantial increase in the income and estate taxes rising up to fifty per cent in the upper brackets. The other proposals were approximately the taxes of the Revenue Act of 1924. Experience with that act had proved them successful.

December 10, 1931: In a message to Congress submitting the Moratorium Agreement for formal approval, the President, after setting out the agreement, stated:[3]

The effect of this agreement was instantaneous in reversing the drift toward general economic panic and has served to give time to the peoples of those countries to readjust their economic life. The action taken was necessary. . . . As we approach the new year it is clear that a number of the governments indebted to us will be unable to meet further payments to us in full *pending recovery of their economic life*. . . . Therefore it will be necessary in some cases to make still further temporary adjustments. . . . The Congress has shared with the Executive in the past the consideration of . . . these debts . . . the legislative branch . . . should continue to share this responsibility. . . .

I recommend the re-creation of the World War Foreign Debt Com-

[3] State Papers, Vol. II, p. 74.

mission, with authority to examine such problems as may arise . . . during the present economic emergency, and to report to Congress. . . .

December 11, 1931: The President issued a public statement reviewing the twelve parts of a non-partisan program for recovery:[a]

In my recommendations to Congress and in the organizations created during the past few months, there is a definite program for turning the tide of deflation and starting the country upon the road to recovery. . . . A considerable part of it depends on voluntary organization in the country. This is already in action. A part of it requires legislation. It is a non-partisan program. I am interested in its principles rather than its details. I appeal for unity of action for its consummation.

The major steps that we must take are domestic. The action needed is in the home field, and it is urgent. While re-establishment of stability abroad is helpful to us and to the world, and I am confident that it is in progress, yet we must depend upon ourselves. If we devote ourselves to these urgent domestic questions we can make a very large measure of recovery irrespective of foreign influence.

That the country may get this program thoroughly in mind, I review its major parts:

1. Provision for distress among the unemployed by voluntary organization and united action of local authorities in co-operation with the President's Unemployment Relief Organization, whose appeal for organization and funds has met with a response unparalleled since the war. Almost every locality in the country has reported that it "will take care of its own." In order to assure that there will be no failure to meet problems as they arise, the organization will continue through the winter.

2. Our employers are organized and will continue to give part-time work instead of discharging a portion of their employees. This plan is affording help to several million people who otherwise would have no resources. The government will continue to aid unemployment over the winter through the large program of Federal construction now in progress. This program represents an expenditure at the rate of over $60,000,000 a month.

3. The strengthening of the Federal Land Bank System in the interest of the farmer.

4. Assistance to home owners, both agricultural and urban, who are in difficulties in securing renewals of mortgages by strengthening the country banks, savings banks, and building and loan associations through the creation of a system of Home Loan Discount Banks. By restoring these institutions to normal functioning, we will see a revival in employment in new construction.

5. Development of a plan to assure early distribution to depositors in closed banks, and thus relieve distress amongst millions of smaller depositors and smaller businesses.

6. The enlargement under full safeguards of the discount facilities of

---

[a] State Papers, Vol. II, p. 82.

the Federal Reserve Banks in the interest of a more adequate credit system.

7. The creation for the period of the emergency of a Reconstruction Finance Corporation to furnish necessary credit otherwise unobtainable under existing circumstances, and so give confidence to agriculture, to industry and to labor against further paralyzing influences and shocks, but more especially by the re-opening of credit channels which will assure the maintenance and normal working of the commercial fabric.

8. Assistance to all railroads by protection from unregulated competition, and to the weaker ones by the formation of a credit pool, as authorized by the Interstate Commerce Commission, and by other measures, thus affording security to the bonds held by our insurance companies, our savings banks, and other benevolent trusts, thereby protecting the interest of every family and promoting the recuperation of the railways.

9. The revision of our banking laws so as better to safeguard the depositors.

10. The safeguarding and support of banks through the National Credit Association, which has already given great confidence to bankers and extended their ability to make loans to commerce and industry.

11. The maintenance of the public finance on a sound basis.

   (a) By drastic economy.
   (b) Resolute opposition to the enlargement of Federal expenditure until recovery.
   (c) A temporary increase in taxation, so distributed that the burden may be borne in proportion to ability to pay amongst all groups and in such a fashion as not to retard recovery.

12. The maintenance of the American system of individual initiative and individual and community responsibility.

The broad purpose of this program is to restore the old job instead of creating a made job, to help the worker at the desk as well as the bench, to restore their buying power for the farmer's products—in fact, turn the processes of liquidation and deflation and start the country forward all along the line.

This program will affect favorably every man, woman and child—not a special class or any group. One of its purposes is to start the flow of credit now impeded by fear and uncertainty, to the detriment of every manufacturer, business man and farmer. To re-establish normal functioning is the need of the hour.

December 13, 1931: The country was advised through the press that Japan went off the gold standard.

December 14, 1931: Senator Wagner of New York (Democrat) demanded $2,000,000,000 additional expenditure on public works.

December 18, 1931: The Committee on Ways and Means of the House, controlled by Democrats, refused to report out the legislation requested by the President, creating a new World War Debt Commission for the purpose of temporary adjustment of the war-debts during the depression to capacity to pay. On the contrary, they adopted an amendment to the act which ratified the one year moratorium as follows:

It is hereby expressly declared to be against the policy of Congress that any of the indebtedness of foreign countries should be *in any manner* cancelled or *reduced*.

It again may be observed that this refusal of the Democratic-controlled Congress to give temporary relief to our debtors together with its subsequent action probably has cost the United States the whole war debt. The President repeatedly impressed upon the members individually that once the foreign governments defaulted there would be the greatest difficulty in getting them to resume payments again and, unless they could be given some ease during the depression, they would default. It also may be noted that the President at the next session again endeavored to secure authority for this policy and to secure the co-operation of President-elect Roosevelt to influence the Democratic Congress, but was refused. Later, these debtor nations did default and since have made no effort to resume payments.

December 19, 1931: The Chamber of Commerce of the United States reported the results of a referendum to its members, the more important points of which were that (a) the anti-trust laws should be modified to permit combinations to keep "production related to consumption"; (b) there should be governmental supervision and enforcement of such processes; (c) each representative trade association should perform the functions of an economic council to bring about these agreements, the whole to be governed by a superior economic council; (d) there should be curtailment of production in natural resource industries wherever there was overproduction. The general plan was a modification of that proposed by Gerard Swope some months previously.

The President's opinion was that this plan if carried into practice would, through the creation of monopolies, drive the country toward the Fascism of which it was a pattern, or toward Socialism as the result of public exasperation. He would be unable to support the Chamber's recommendation. The President stated to its representatives that a modification of the anti-trust laws to permit co-operation when it was clearly in public interest in his view would be of value. He pointed out that the elimination of waste, the advancement of business ethics, and many other similar avenues of collective action did not make for monopoly. The merit of such action should be determined by the Federal Trade Commission in open hearings, provided always that the commission had the right to stop any such action when it proved to be against public interest.

Mr. Hoover, when Secretary of Commerce, often had opposed all suggestions of price-fixing, restraint on production, and other monopoly practices but he had carried forward a large amount of co-operative action in business and industry which had proved to be in the public interest. The advancement of these measures, on the lines then laid down by him, had been the object of his frequent recommendations to Congress to review this subject.

December 21, 1931: The President had appointed at the end of September a committee of leading men to consider the desirability of the further expansion of public works as an aid to recovery. The committee was composed of the following: James R. Garfield, former Secretary of the Interior; W. Rufus Abbott, utility operator; Leonard P. Ayres, economist; Milton H. Esberg, manufacturer; Homer L. Ferguson, manufacturer; Jacob H. Hollander, economist; William Cooper Procter, manufacturer; Raymond Robins, publicist; John D. Ryan, mining man; John F. Tinsley, manufacturer; Matthew Woll, labor; George E. Vincent, former university president. The committee now strongly condemned any further expansion of expenditures on public works as a contribution to recovery with the statement:

The proposals favoring a great public works program are usually discussed in terms . . . of three, five or seven billions to be raised by Federal bond issues. . . . The Committee is of the opinion that borrowing of large sums for public works emergency construction cannot be justified as a measure for the aiding in restoration of normal business activity. . . . Whatever may have been the causes of the present condition, the common sense remedy is to stop borrowing except to meet unavoidable deficits, balance the budget and live in our income. . . . In the long run the real problem of unemployment must be met by private business interests if it is to be permanent. Problems of unemployment cannot be solved by any magic of appropriation from the public treasury. . . . Hardships of the depression are in reality the readjustments being made in the endeavor to meet new and changing conditions. It does not appear reasonable to believe that a construction program financed by public funds in this country could greatly hasten or alter this process of economic adjustment, for fundamentally the general levels of commodity prices are international and alterations in them result from interchange of trade between countries. Experience of England and Germany substantiates this.

There was actually expended each year for public works, including all kinds of public construction during the Hoover Administration, the following:

1930 (fiscal year) $412,420,000
1931   "   "   574,874,000
1932   "   "   670,299,000
1933   "   "   727,844,000
(estimated on Feb. 15, 1933)

December 22, 1931: In spite of the supreme importance of the time element, the President in vain had endeavored to persuade Congress to remain in session over the holidays in order that the emergency legislation might be enacted. He informed the press:

I had urged that the proposed Congressional holidays should be shortened but leaders have informed me that they do not believe it is possible to secure a quorum before January 4th.

December 23, 1931: Upon signing the legislation formally approving the moratorium, the President said:[5]

... our government ... averted a catastrophe the effects of which ... would have caused the American people a loss of many times the amount involved. ... In saving the collapse of Germany ... the American people have done something greater than ... the prevention of panic and unlimited losses. ... They have contributed to maintain courage and hope in the German nation ... to give opportunity for other nations to work out their problems.

The committee established by the Allies and meeting at Basel reported that in its opinion Germany could not pay reparations at least for another two years.

December 26, 1931: The Allies, having called a conference on German reparations to meet at Lausanne on January 18th, intimated that the United States should attend. The President intimated in return that Europe, having now the time and opportunity due to the moratorium, should take initiative in making its own readjustments.

December 29, 1931: The President, by means of public statements and interviews with Congressional leaders, had started a drive for the amendment of numerous laws, which would permit of great economies in government through consolidation of the functions of departments and the reduction in compulsory expenditures. This movement became known as the "Legislative" Economy Program as distinguished from the Budget Economy Program. The latter comprised those expenditures subject to ordinary annual appropriation.

December 31, 1931: During the month President Hoover had conferred personally with over one hundred and fifty members of Congress

[5] State Papers, Vol. II, p. 96.

in explaining and urging his program. There was great opposition, especially in the Senate, to his Reconstruction Finance Corporation legislation. The President wished to have included the authority to make loans to public bodies and industries as well as banks in order to stimulate construction and further to have provision for setting up a series of agricultural credit institutions to give the farmers "production and livestock" credits, the capital of these corporations to be gradually transferred to the farmers themselves through a small premium on loans. As will be seen later, it required eight months to secure these proposals at an inestimable loss of their influence in stimulating recovery when the time element still was of first importance.

CHAPTER X

REMEDIES FOR THE DRAIN UPON GOLD AND THE CONTRACTION OF CREDIT

JANUARY–FEBRUARY, 1932

THE new year opened under great economic strain. The procession of countries which had followed Great Britain off the gold standard and had joined the "sterling bloc" was a blow to us. With their currencies fluctuating and depreciated, with the new trade barriers they erected to protect their exchange, their purchases from the United States decreased rapidly and our prices were falling accordingly. The drain on our gold and the withdrawal of foreign deposits resulted in constant calling of loans by our domestic banks which greatly stifled industry and affected prices. The Federal Reserve System was striving to expand credit to meet these curtailments, but its powers were limited. Bank failures and hoarding were increasing. The National Credit Association was reaching the end of its resources. Unemployment had risen to approximately 10,000,000.

The Democratic leadership in Congress was following a policy of obstruction. The plan for winning the Presidential election ten months hence seemed to be: to offer no program, although the Democrats were in the majority in the House, and for all practical purposes were in control of the Senate; to stir up popular discontent and create dissatisfaction with the President; to obstruct and cripple his measures; to pass enormous and extravagant appropriation bills which would frighten business and appeal to local cupidity; all with the anticipation that recovery would be delayed until after the election. It was only a step from this obstructive policy to an invidious attempt to fasten the whole depression on the President. A phrase—"the Hoover depression"—was injected into the campaign and studiedly reiterated. The poison of this artful phrase gradually seeped into a public mind rendered susceptible to propaganda of this character by the hardships of the depression.

January 1, 1932: Legislation for additional revenue was imperative. Again time was the essential thing. The balancing of outgo with income was a major feature of the President's program. This required not only a cutting down of expenditures wherever possible, but also the levy of additional revenue. Notwithstanding these facts, Speaker Garner announced that the Committee on Ways and Means of the House would first consider tariff legislation. It was obvious that months would elapse before any tariff legislation could pass both Houses of Congress. The purpose undoubtedly was to delay the enactment of the President's recovery program, especially a new revenue bill.

January 2, 1932: The President received from Surgeon-General Cumming a survey of the effectiveness of relief measures in the country at the end of the year. The report stated:

. . . Mortality in the United States during the year . . . [was] definitely lower than in the two previous years. . . .

Records for this last quarter . . . indicate that the mortality at the beginning of the winter of 1931-32 has continued on a very favorable level, the rate being only 10.7 per 1,000 as compared to 11.4, 12.0 and 13.2 in the last quarters of 1930, 1929 and 1928, respectively. . . .

Infant mortality during the past year . . . was definitely lower than in any preceding year on record, the rate being 55.8 against 58.1 for 1930. . . . This . . . showing has persisted during the last weeks of the year, the rate for the final quarter being 46.6 against an average of 56.9 for the corresponding period in the three preceding years and against 51.9 for the same period of 1929, the lowest previous rate.

Many more people are asking for charity medical services and this gives the impression at first that there is an increase in sickness, but to counterbalance this there are many reports of decreases in paid medical practice. . . .

January 4, 1932: Congress giving added evidence of its partisanship and dilatory tactics, the President this day sent to them an emphatic message designed to expedite action and to awaken public support:[1]

At the convening of the Congress on December 7th I laid proposals before it designed to check the further degeneration in prices and values, to fortify us against continued shocks from world instability and to unshackle the forces of recovery. The need is manifestly even more evident than at the date of my message a month ago. I should be derelict in my duty if I did not at this time emphasize the paramount importance to the nation of constructive action upon these questions at the earliest possible moment. These recommendations have been largely developed in consultation with leading men of both parties, of agriculture, of labor, of banking and of industry. They furnish the bases for full collaboration to effect these purposes. They have no partisan character. We can and must replace the unjustifiable fear in the country by confidence.

[1] State Papers, Vol. II, p. 102.

The principal subjects requiring immediate action are:

1. The strengthening of the Federal Land Bank System to aid the farmer. . . .

2. The creation of a Reconstruction Finance Corporation to furnish during the period of the depression credits otherwise unobtainable under existing circumstances in order to give confidence to agriculture, industry and labor against further paralyzing influences. . . .

3. The creation of a system of Home Loan Discount banks in order to revive employment by new construction and to mitigate the difficulties of many of our citizens in securing renewals of mortgages on their homes and farms. It has the further purpose of permanent encouragement of home ownership. To accomplish these purposes we must so liberate the resources of the country banks, the savings banks and the building and loan associations as to restore these institutions to normal functioning. . . .

4. The discount facilities of our Federal Reserve banks are restricted by law more than that of the central banks in other countries. This restriction in times such as these limits the liquidity of the banks and tends to increase the forces of deflation, cripples the smaller businesses, stifles new enterprise and thus limits employment. . . .

5. The development of a plan to assure early distribution to depositors in closed banks is necessary to relieve distress among millions. . . .

6. Revision of the laws relating to transportation in the direction recommended by the Interstate Commerce Commission would strengthen our principal transportation systems and restore confidence. . . .

7. Revision of banking laws in order to better safeguard depositors.

8. The country must have confidence that the credit and stability of the Federal Government will be maintained by drastic economy in expenditure, by adequate increase of taxes; and by restriction of issues of Federal securities. The recent depreciation in prices of government securities is a serious warning which reflects the fear of further large and unnecessary issues of such securities. Promptness in adopting an adequate budget relief to taxpayers by resolute economy and restriction in security issues is essential to remove this uncertainty.

Combating a depression is indeed like a great war, in that it is not a battle upon a single front but upon many fronts. These measures are all a necessary addition to the efficient and courageous efforts of our citizens throughout the nation. . . .

. . . Our internal economy is our primary concern and we must fortify our economic structure in order to meet any situation that may arise. . . .

This does not mean that we are insensible to the welfare of other nations or that our own self-interest is not involved in economic rehabilitation abroad. . . .

Action in these matters by the Congress will go far to re-establish confidence, to restore the functioning of our economic system, and to rebuilding of prices and values and to quickening employment. . . .

January 7, 1932: A deputation of unemployed called at the White House. The President said:

. . . I have an intense sympathy for your difficulties.

. . . the vital function of the President and of the Federal Government is to exert every effort and every power to the restoration of stability and employment in our country. . . . World wide depressions and their result in unemployment are like great wars. They must be fought continuously, not on one front, but upon many fronts. It cannot be won by any single skirmish or any panacea. . . . The real victory is to restore men to employment through their regular jobs. That is our object. We are giving this question our undivided attention.

January 8, 1932: The President issued through his press conference a public appeal for co-operation and economy in government, and informed the country that "we cannot squander ourselves into prosperity." [2]

I wish to emphasize to the full extent of my ability the necessity, as a fundamental to recovery, for the utmost economy of governmental expenditures . . . [with a] determination . . . to assure the country of the balancing of the Federal expenditures and income. . . . The amount of taxes we will need to impose . . . will depend entirely upon . . . further cuts . . . in government expenditures. The budget before Congress represents a reduction of $360,000,000 . . . we should also at last be able to bring about the wholesale elimination of overlapping in the Federal Government bureaus and agencies which will also contribute materially to the program of economy. . . .

The balancing of next year's expenditure and receipts and the limitation of borrowing implies the resolute opposition to any new or enlarged activities of the government. . . . The flood of extravagant proposals . . . would imply an increase of government expenditure during the next five years of over forty billions of dollars or more than eight billions per annum. The great majority of these bills have been advanced by some organization or some sectional interest. . . . They . . . represent a spirit of spending in the country which must be abandoned . . . drastic economy requires sacrifice. . . .

Rigid economy is a real road to relief, to home owners, farmers, workers, and every element of our population. The proposed budget . . . amounts to about four billion dollars of which over $2,800,000,000 is for debt, military and veterans' services, and nearly half the balance is for aid to employment in construction works and as aids to agriculture. . . .

Our first duty as a nation is to put our governmental house in order, national, State and local. With the return of prosperity the government can undertake constructive projects both of social character and in public improvement. We cannot squander ourselves into prosperity. The people will, of course, provide against distress, but the purpose of the nation must be to restore employment by economic recovery. The reduction in gov-

[2] State Papers, Vol. II, p. 104.

ernmental expenditures and the stability of government finance is the most fundamental step towards this end. . . . That must be our concentrated purpose.

General Dawes resigned as Ambassador to Great Britain.

January 13, 1932: In reply to various inquiries the President directed Secretary Stimson to state that if for no other reason—and there were many—we could not participate in the Lausanne Reparations Conference owing to the action of Congress.

January 16, 1932: The Reconstruction Finance Corporation Bill passed both Houses. The President made an earnest effort with the members of the Conference Committee to secure the restoration of the loan powers contained in his original recommendations and which had been greatly curtailed. But Democratic obstruction prevailed. These powers were partially but not wholly restored in a vigorous contest later on. However some of them never were given until they were also requested by the succeeding administration.

January 18, 1932: The Lausanne Conference was postponed.

January 19, 1932: France withdraws $125,000,000 in gold from the United States.

January 20, 1932: The President announced the selection of Eugene Meyer for chairman, and General Charles G. Dawes for president of the Reconstruction Finance Corporation. Time again was an important factor. It had been six or seven weeks since he had recommended its creation. Now that the bill had passed both Houses, the President was anxious to get that great agency to work. It was a foregone conclusion that the bill would become law in a day or two. After the bill had passed both Houses, but before the bill had been signed by him, he announced these appointments. The partisan and captious character of the opposition is shown by the criticism by certain Democratic leaders for this expeditious action.

January 22, 1932: The President signed the act creating the Reconstruction Finance Corporation. This provided $500,000,000 capital to be advanced by the government, and authorized the Corporation to borrow up to $1,500,000,000. The President, while disappointed by the failure of Congress to grant all of the powers he had requested for the Corporation, said: [3]

It brings into being a powerful organization with adequate resources, able to strengthen weaknesses that may develop in our credit, banking and railway structure, in order to permit business and industry to carry on

---
[3] State Papers, Vol. II, p. 106.

normal activities free from the fear of unexpected shocks and retarding influences.

Its purpose is to stop deflation in agriculture and industry and thus to increase employment by the restoration of men to their normal jobs. It is not created for the aid of big industries or big banks. Such institutions are amply able to take care of themselves. It is created for the support of the smaller banks and financial institutions, and through rendering their resources liquid to give renewed support to business, industry, and agriculture. It should give opportunity to mobilize the gigantic strength of our country for recovery.

January 22, 1932: Largely because of the President's efforts following the crash in 1929 in his conference with leaders of labor and industry, and the earnest and sincere efforts later by these leaders to avoid labor troubles, the country had been practically free from such disturbances. But today a long-drawn-out dispute between the railways and their employees over wages threatened to culminate in a strike. The President intervened by telephone to Chicago, talking with leaders on both sides and finally secured an agreement. This was done without accompanying publicity which might have interfered with securing a settlement.

January 23, 1932: The President signed the act providing additional capital to the Federal Land Banks. He said:

It should (a) reinforce the credit of the Federal Land Bank system and reassure investors in land bank bonds; (b) thus enable the banks to obtain capital for farmers at reasonable rates; and (c) above all bring relief and hope to many borrowers from the banks who have done their honest best but, because of circumstances beyond their control, have been unable temporarily to make the grade.

Certain other necessary amendments to the Farm Loan Act had not been acted upon by Congress. They were delayed in the House until March, 1933. In fact, one of the last official acts of President Hoover was to approve a bill (S. 5337) containing these liberalizing amendments. An analysis of the bill is contained in a letter from Chairman Bestor of the Farm Loan Board.

Section 1 permitted the Federal Land Banks to make direct loans to farmers where the Farm Loan Association was not functioning.

Section 2 enlarged the purposes for which loans might be made by the Federal Land Banks.

Section 3 granted authority to Federal Land Banks to carry real estate for five years at its normal value. This was to relieve the situation as regards the collateral which Banks placed back of their bonds.

Section 4 provided three things. First, it permitted Federal Land

Banks to postpone payment of delinquent instalments for a period of ten years. Second, it changed the Act itself so that farmers would not be compelled to pay penalty interest. Third, it permitted the Banks to amortize delinquent items over a period of forty years. . . .

Section 6 further liberalized the collection policy of the Banks and permitted them to substitute purchase money mortgages as collateral in place of amortized mortgages provided under the original Act.

Section 7 was one of the most important Sections in the Bill and is the basis for the present 4% rate quoted by the Federal Land Banks in that it cleared up the faulty provisions of the Act of 1923 permitting Land Banks to issue consolidated bonds.

In brief, it may be said that this legislation made possible later a substantial portion of the activities of the Farm Credit Administration.

The President had now completed the appointment of the directors of the Reconstruction Finance Corporation. They comprised Eugene Meyer, chairman; Charles G. Dawes, president; Ogden L. Mills, Under Secretary of the Treasury; Harvey C. Couch, Jesse H. Jones, Gardner Cowles and Wilson McCarthy.

January 24, 1932: The Board met with the President. He stated that the first object of the Board must be to stop bank failures wherever the assets with reasonable valuation would protect the depositors. It also must place every credit allowable under the law which would aid agriculture and expand employment.

January 26, 1932: The President addressed a letter to the Speaker of the House recommending that all departments of the government should be authorized to give preference to American goods in the purchase of supplies except where it would result in unreasonable cost. This authority already had been granted to the War and Navy departments upon the President's recommendation. The existing law required the acceptance of the lowest bidder from wherever it might come.

January 27, 1932: The President today in conference with Senator Glass, who naturally dominated the Senate Banking and Currency Committee, urged that he should introduce the legislation temporarily to expand the eligibility provisions in the Federal Reserve Act; to place temporarily the whole of the assets of the Reserve banks behind the currency and to provide an immediate system of loans to expedite the partial liquidation of closed banks. The senator was not in agreement. He was desirous, however, of expediting the Banking Reform Bill.

January 28, 1932: The President today informed Senators Watson and Reed that he would not approve of the proposal made by Senator Walsh (Democrat) of Massachusetts, to issue $1,000,000,000 fiat money.

He also conferred with the Republican members of the Senate Committee on Banking and Currency with the hope of expediting consideration and passage of the emergency banking measure and also the Banking Reform Bill. His view was that the major features of the Reform Bill should contain the following:

(a) to compel every commercial bank to join the Reserve System;
(b) to establish inspection of all commercial banks by the System;
(c) to attain gradual separation of promotion affiliates;
(d) to exclude long-term credits from demand deposit banks;
(e) to separate savings and long-term loan institutions from demand deposit institutions;
(f) to establish State-wide branch banking by national banks under suitable regulations with provision that no new branches be established where there were adequate facilities, except by purchase of an existing bank;
(g) to create a system of mortgage discount banks.

He strongly urged action and expressed himself hopeful that some progress had been made with the Senate.

January 31, 1932: The economic situation again deteriorated during the month. Hoarding continued even more than was indicated by the estimates because the usual outpouring of Christmas money did not fully return to the banks. The gold drain continued. Bank failures reached $219,-000,000 during the month. Business loans and credit were shrinking. Unemployment increased. The President had been unceasing in his conferences with members of the Senate and House in forwarding his program. He had, during the month, conferred with over forty members of both parties in the Senate and sixty members of the House, some of them many times.

February 1, 1932: The whole world was greatly disturbed by the news of the Japanese attack on Shanghai. The President directed our fleet to land 1600 men to protect Americans. The British and other nations landed troops.

February 3, 1932: After a conference with savings banks, building and loan associations, insurance companies and with the principal Federal officials, also despite some opposition from certain banking interests, President Hoover now determined to make an open attack upon the evil of hoarding and that coincident with the opening of the R.F.C. The opponents of his proposal asserted that to bring such a condition into the open would only stimulate it. The situation had, however, become most dangerous. Runs were causing many failures of solvent banks. Credit was restricted because bankers were compelled, in order to protect their reserves, to reduce loans in even larger proportion than the withdrawal of deposits. Furthermore, since all the currency was covered by about seventy per cent of gold, hoarding of currency was immobilizing an enormous sum of that metal from the credit base just as surely as if it were drawn away by foreigners.

The President persuaded Colonel Frank Knox of Chicago to lead the drive against hoarding, and invited the representatives of various national patriotic and civic organizations to meet with him at the White House on February 6th. In his announcement of the opening of the drive, the President said:[4]

> There is now a patriotic opportunity for our citizens unitedly to join in this campaign against depression. . . . That service is to secure the return of hoarded money back into the channels of industry. During the past year and with an accelerated rate during the last few months a total of over a billion three hundred millions of money has been hoarded. That sum is still outstanding . . . citizens hoarding money do not realize its serious effect. . . . Every dollar hoarded means a destruction of from five to ten dollars of credit. Credit is the bloodstream of our economic life. Restriction . . . cripples the revival and expansion of agriculture, industry, commerce and employment. Every dollar returned from hoarding to circulation means putting men to work. It means help to agriculture and business. . . . A prime need today is the extension and liberalization of credit facilities to farmers and small business men. The credit institutions are greatly crippled in furnishing these needed credits, unless the hoarded money is returned. I urge all those persons to put their dollars to work—either by conservative investment, or by deposit in sound institutions. . . .
>
> During the Great War our people gave their undivided energies to the national purpose. Today we are engaged in a war against depression . . . [with] the same service and the same confidence to our government and our institutions, the same unity and solidarity of courageous action . . . we can overcome this situation. . . .
>
> In order that we may have definite organization for this service, I am today calling upon the heads of the leading civil organizations to meet with me on Saturday next for the creation of a national organization to further this campaign. . . .

The President nominated Andrew W. Mellon to be Ambassador to Great Britain.

February 4, 1932: Substantial opposition was arising against the passage of the Banking Reform Bill. The New York State Chamber of Commerce passed resolutions opposing it.

The President asked Republican Senate and House leaders to amend

[4] State Papers, Vol. II, p. 108.

the Agricultural Marketing Act so as to authorize the Federal Farm Board to transfer 40,000,000 bushels of wheat to the Red Cross for domestic relief purposes.

February 5, 1932: Mr. Mellon having resigned the Secretaryship of the Treasury to accept the post of Ambassador to Great Britain, the President appointed Under Secretary Mills to that Cabinet post. Mr. Mellon had given ten years of devoted and able service to the country. Mr. Mills had the youth, ability and experience which the tremendous problems of the Treasury demanded. His service during the year which followed comprises one of the most brilliant administrations of that office.

February 6, 1932: A number of leaders of patriotic and civic organizations, who had been invited to consider the "means and measures of organization to meet the problem of hoarding," met at the White House. Among those present were: President Dawes of the Reconstruction Finance Corporation, Secretaries Lamont and Mills, Assistant Secretary Julius Klein of the Department of Commerce, Governor Meyer of the Federal Reserve Board, Messrs. Couch and McCarthy of the Reconstruction Finance Corporation, Paul Bestor of the Farm Loan Board, William Green, Warner Hayes, A. C. Pearson, Harold Devoe, Vincent Hitsitt, Gilbert Hodges, J. E. Spingarn, D. J. Woodlock, A. F. Whitney, Gerrish Gassaway, Warren Platt, Mrs. John Sippel, A. Johnston, Melvin Jones, James A. Emery, Michael J. Ready, Allan A. Pope, Henry Heimanon, Reuben Bogley, Harry Haas, Magnus Alexander, Emily Kneubuhl, Samuel McCreavert, Rush Holland, George B. Cutler, Frederick W. Parton, Edith Salisbury, Harold S. Bettelheim, H. C. Knight, Leon J. Obermayer, John Poole, Colonel James Walsh, Julius Barnes, J. W. Crabtree, Chester Berry, L. W. Wallace, Morton Bodfish, Arthur East, James MacLean, William Best, and Harold Tschudi. The President presided and said: "Hoarding of currency had accumulated to the extent of $1,250,000,000 to $1,500,000,000. Its results had been to immobilize a large portion of the national gold supply, to cause drastic deflation and credit contraction, seriously to restrict business expansion and maintenance of employment and affect commodity prices. A large portion of the hoarding was due to misunderstanding of the national effect of such acts. It arose out of unnecessary fears and apprehension. Nothing could contribute more to the resumption of employment, to the stability of agricultural and other commodity prices, than to restore this money to work."

The leaders gave assurance that all of the 20,000,000 members of the organizations they represented would take it as their special mission to

REMEDIES FOR THE DRAIN UPON GOLD

organize and carry forward this campaign of appeal to reason, to patriotism, and to action. Methods of organization were agreed upon.

February 8, 1932: The Reconstruction Finance Corporation now began to make loans.

February 9, 1932: The British again raised their tariffs.

Messrs. Meyer and Harrison of the Federal Reserve System, General Dawes from the Reconstruction Finance Corporation, and Secretary Mills called at the White House to report the peril into which the country's gold supply had fallen and also the imminent dangers to the gold standard. They reviewed the situation, saying that under the law the Federal Reserve banks must hold forty per cent of gold against currency issued and thirty-five per cent against their deposits, and in addition a minor gold fund must be held with the Treasury for redemption purposes. The coverage of the remaining sixty per cent of the Federal Reserve currency was by "eligible" securities (mostly commercial bills) held by the Federal Reserve banks. Various factors had come into play. Due to the foreign drain, over $1,000,000,000 of gold had been withdrawn from the monetary gold stock. Due to hoarding, the Reserve currency issued had swollen by $1,500,000,000 above normal, against which gold and eligible paper must be held. Due to slackness of business the Federal Reserve banks did not have the "eligible" paper to cover the sixty per cent with such paper and therefore had to increase the gold percentage of the Reserve by the amount of this deficiency. A memorandum was presented to the President which showed that through the interplay of these factors the "free" gold—that is to say the amount of gold which could be paid out to foreigners—had been reduced to $433,000,000.

The Board further furnished a list of foreign governments and citizens of other nations who held $1,393,500,000 on deposit or invested in short-term bills within the United States. They could take out about $900,000,000 of it on demand and the balance in less than ninety days. Of this, France alone held nearly $500,000,000. Under the prevailing conditions the free gold was being drawn down at the rate of $150,000,000 a week through hoarding and foreign demands, and a more rapid drain was threatened. On that basis we should be compelled to place an international embargo on gold or on the convertibility of the currency within two to three weeks. The memorandum, at the President's request given subsequently in more detail by the Reserve officials, showed that the amounts of deposits for account of the following countries or the holdings of short-term bills which were subject to demand or very short notice, were:

England	$142,533,000
France	491,740,000
Germany	38,158,000
Italy	30,616,000
Netherlands	41,042,000
Canada	136,712,000
Latin America	105,548,000
Far East	46,647,000
All others	195,545,000
Total	$1,228,541,000

Reports of member banks of the Federal Reserve System showed that, on December 31, 1931, there was due from banks outside New York to banks in foreign countries, an additional $65,000,000. This probably was somewhat less on the current date.

The amount of monetary gold stock in the United States was shown to be as follows:

Held by the U. S. Treasury

(a) Against gold certificates	$1,675,000,000
(b) Reserve against U. S. Notes and Treasury Notes	156,000,000
(c) In general fund	37,000,000
(d) For Reserve Banks and agents	1,628,000,000
Held in Reserve Banks	500,000,000
Coin in circulation	407,000,000
Total	$4,403,000,000

If commercial bills were available to the Reserve banks or other coverage were made available, so that the gold reserve against Federal Reserve notes needed to be only the legal reserve of forty per cent, then the necessary gold to hold for this purpose would be $1,169,836,200, or would "free" from this source $902,144,000. It was stated by the Reserve officials that to attempt to call in gold or gold certificates and publicly to substitute Federal Reserve currency, would project a general panic. If this were done privately and when opportunity offered, it would be of no avail, as months would be required to get in even a few hundred million. In any event, the gold certificates now were being tightly hoarded.

The situation was rendered more imperative by the conviction in many circles both at home and abroad that, owing to the steady drain, we were on the same route to gold currency embarrassment that had been witnessed in Austria, Hungary, Germany, Great Britain, and other countries. In consequence, and aside from foreigners withdrawing their funds with increasing rapidity, a flight of capital from the United States had been started by some of our own citizens.

The President already had sought to fortify this situation by his proposal of October 6, 1931, at the joint conference of political leaders, to make other types of loans discountable by the Federal Reserve System. This was to enlarge the amount of "eligibles" available in the System, thus at the same time expanding the amount of credit available to business, and it had been agreed to at that time. He had recommended it in his message of December 6th. The Democratic members of the Senate committee would not act.

As a result of this conference (February 9th), it was decided that in order to relieve the situation, another effort must be made to enlarge temporarily the "eligibility" of commercial paper, and to make government bonds held by the Reserve banks temporarily legal as coverage of the currency above the forty per cent gold reserve. Such action would "free" over $1,000,000,000 of gold and thus allow full payment of foreign demands without endangering the gold standard. The President held that this must be for the emergency only. He at once requested Senators Watson and Robinson, the Republican and Democratic floor-leaders, together with Senators Glass, Bulkley, Walcott, and Townsend (the subcommittee of the Banking and Currency Committee), Secretary Mills, President Dawes of the Reconstruction Finance Corporation, and Governor Meyer of the Federal Reserve Board, to meet him at breakfast the following morning.

February 10, 1932: At this breakfast the President stated the danger to the gold standard, gave the figures and urged immediate action. He also took occasion to urge the immediate legislation he had asked for in respect to authorizing loans from the Reconstruction Finance Corporation or from Federal Reserve banks to closed banks upon their assets, in order that they might make earlier distribution to their depositors. General Dawes urged also a system of joint guarantees by banks eligible for loans from the Federal Reserve. A program was agreed upon after three hours of discussion. In the program, aside from extending "eligibility" and making "governments" a coverage to the currency, a provision was added for joint loans to not less than five banks. Senator Glass agreed to introduce a special bill covering these emergency points, but on condition that the provision for loans to closed banks should be omitted as he wanted to reserve this "attractive" feature to help carry along the general Banking Reform Bill.

The President agreed that if a good Banking Reform Bill could thus be quickly passed, it was worth yielding this point for the time being.

Having this agreement, the President at once called to the White House Speaker Garner, House Floor Leader Rainey, Minority Leader Snell, and Congressmen Steagall, Luce, Strong, and Beedy of the House Committee on Banking and Currency. The same ground was again gone over and an approval was given. The approval of the measure by Senator Glass very largely determined the action of the Democratic members, and they were frank to say so. In order to expedite passage through the House, inasmuch as the Democrats were in control and as he wanted to avoid any partisanship in its consideration, the President suggested that Mr. Steagall (Democrat), chairman of the committee, should introduce it there. It became known as the Glass-Steagall Bill. The market at once reacted to the removal of the fear. Wheat, cotton, and the securities markets commenced to move upward.

As it was impossible to disclose the actual situation in its entirety without creating senseless fears and a further rush for gold, the explanations given for the bills in Congress and elsewhere necessarily were rather inadequate. Due in part at least to this, the legislation was denounced by certain bankers and other persons uninformed as to the underlying circumstances prompting the legislation.

It is important to note that on a later occasion, at Des Moines, Iowa, on October 4, 1932, when the danger was past, the President referred to the narrow margin by which we had escaped being forced off the gold standard and the provisions which had been devised to save us. Senator Glass, in a campaign speech on October 7, 1932, denied that the country had been in such danger.

Upon Senator Glass's campaign statement being made, Senator Watson promptly issued the following reply on October 10, 1932:

I notice by the press that Senator Glass has made the statement that he had no record of having been presented with the facts as to the gold crisis in the United States. . . . The Senator will perhaps remember the two-hour confidential conference of Senate leaders, including Senator Glass, called in February of last winter by the President, together with officials of the Treasury, the Federal Reserve System and the Reconstruction Finance Corporation. In that conference the President and these gentlemen urged the great gravity of the situation and the necessity for the immediate enactment of the legislation recommended by the President for extension of authority to the Federal Reserve System to enable them to prevent imminent jeopardy to the gold standard in the United States.

I well recall that it was pointed out by these officials that under the foreign drains of gold and the hoarding then current, together with the inflexibility of the Federal Reserve laws, and despite our nominal gold holdings, we had at that time only about $350,000,000 of free gold and that losses to foreigners and hoarders were going on at a rate of $150,000,000 a week.

Although Senator Glass had been opposed to these proposed measures, in the face of the evidence presented he patriotically agreed to proceed with the increased authority asked for, and to introduce them in the Congress, where they were enacted and the dangers from this quarter were finally and completely averted.

CHAPTER XI

PRESIDENT HOOVER AND CONGRESS
THE STRUGGLE OVER TAXATION AND ECONOMY

FEBRUARY–APRIL, 1932

February 12, 1932: Leaders of the House Ways and Means Committee inquired if the President would approve a manufacturers' sales tax in substitution for some of the taxes proposed by the administration. The President replied that he would, provided there was no tax on staple food and cheaper clothing.

In a Lincoln Day radio address the President, speaking from the Lincoln study, said:[1]

This room in the White House . . . was the room in which a long line of Presidents have labored for the single purpose of their country's welfare. It was in this room . . . that Lincoln labored incessantly day and night for the preservation of the Union. No one can enter here without being sensitive to those invisible influences of the men who have gone. . . . It was from this window that for five years Lincoln looked across the Potomac upon a flag under which embattled forces threatened our national unity. Unafraid, he toiled here with patience, with understanding, with steadfastness, with genius and courage that those wounds of a distraught nation might be healed and that the flag which waved over this house might be restored as the symbol of a united country. . . . Its wounds have long since healed and its memories are of the glorious valor and courage of our race. . . .

. . . We may well entertain the feeling that history will record this period as one of the most difficult in its strains and stresses upon the timbers of the Republic that has been experienced since Lincoln's time. There are enduring principles and national ideals to be preserved against the pressures of today.

The forces with which we are contending are far less tangible than those of Lincoln's time. They are invisible forces, yet potent in their powers of destruction. We are engaged in a fight . . . requiring just as greatly the moral courage, the organized action, the unity of strength and the sense of devotion in every community as in war.

February 16, 1932: The Costigan-LaFollette Bill appropriating $375,-000,000 of Federal money for direct relief was defeated in the Senate, mostly by Democratic votes. Later on they revealed that their opposition was caused in large part by pork-barrel considerations, for they intro-

[1] State Papers, Vol. II, p. 111.

duced and passed such an appropriation to the States, based not upon need, but on a per capita basis. This later bill was vetoed by the President.

The President today stated to the press: [2]

I am glad to report that since February 4th when I took action on hoarding, there has been an entire turn in the tide. Up to a few days previous to that time hoarding was greatly on the increase. Since that time it has not only stopped, but it is estimated that $34,000,000 has been returned to circulation from hoarding.

The President had several conferences with members of the New York Stock Exchange upon the question of amendments to the rules by which they controlled bear and pool operations. He pointed out that the bear raids by certain groups in anticipation of gold difficulties had contributed to the general discouragement and had accentuated the situation. He again warned that unless they took stronger measures against such practices the government would ultimately have to regulate the Exchange.

February 17, 1932: President Hoover long had been an advocate of the reorganization of the executive branch of the government, as a matter of economy and efficiency. At the request of President Harding some years before he had served upon a committee on reorganization composed of representatives from both the executive and legislative branches of the government. It had been impossible to get action through Congress. With the growing appreciation of the necessity for economy, President Hoover saw an opportunity to obtain Congressional approval. In a special message to Congress, on economy through departmental and independent agency reorganization, the President said: [3]

Because of its direct relation to the cost of government, I desire again to bring to the attention of the Congress the necessity of more effective organization of the Executive branch of the government. . . .

The need . . . is obvious. . . . A gradual growth of the government by the accretion in its departments and by . . . boards, and commissions as problems requiring solution confront the President and the Congress. Today the government embraces from 150 to 200 separate units . . . [which] when once set up grow independently . . . [with] marked tendency to find new occupations when the initial duties are completed . . . [they] overlap and [the] number of agencies can be reduced.

A few consolidations . . . have been effected. . . . [They] have been able to discharge the very greatly increased burdens imposed upon them without . . . increase in administrative expense. . . .

In the present crisis the absolute necessity for the most drastic economy makes the problem . . . one of paramount importance. . . .

[I] . . . frankly admit the practical difficulties . . . different frac-

[2] State Papers, Vol. II, p. 113.   [3] State Papers, Vol. II, p. 113.

tions of the government fear such reorganization . . . associations and agencies throughout the country will be alarmed . . . a signal for the mobilization of opposition . . . [with] little hope for success . . . unless it is placed in the hands of some one responsible for it. . . .

I recommend. . . .

(a) Consolidation and grouping of the various executive and administrative activities according to their major purposes. . . .

(b) . . . the general principle that executive and administrative functions should have single-headed responsibility and that advisory, regulatory and quasi-judicial functions should be performed by boards and commissions. . . .

(c) Authority under proper safeguards to be lodged in the President to effect these transfers and consolidations . . . by Executive order, such Executive order to lie before the Congress for sixty days . . . before becoming effective. . . .

It is an essential part of a sound reconstruction and economy program. A patchwork organization compels inefficiency, waste, and extravagance. Economy and efficiency can come only through modernization . . . [with] saving of many millions of dollars now extracted annually from our overburdened taxpayers.

February 18, 1932: The Democrats continued their attacks upon the bureau consolidation proposal. The House Democratic leaders introduced a proposal to consolidate the army and navy into a Department of National Defense. This soon was buried.

February 19, 1932: The Stock Exchange put in a new rule expected to control bear raids. The President was not satisfied that the rule meant much. He stated publicly through a press conference:[4]

. . . as to conferences held with officials of the New York Stock Exchange. There have been discussions, as is reported, between myself and other officials of the Administration with officials of the New York Stock Exchange on the question of bear raids. Stock Exchange officials have, during the past eight months, from time to time taken steps to restrain bear raiding with a degree of success, but during the latter part of January, despite these steps, there was a large increase in the short account which unquestionably affected the price of securities and brought discouragement to the country as a whole. I, and other administration officials, again expressed our views to the managers of the Exchange that they should take adequate measures to protect investors from artificial depression of the price of securities for speculative profit. Individuals who use the facilities of the Exchange for such purposes are not contributing to recovery of the United States.

February 20-25, 1932: The President conferred with a number of the members of the Senate and the House upon additional Federal meas-

[4] State Papers, Vol. II, p. 118.

ures in relief of distress. He stated that any further expansion of Federal public works programs was inadvisable for many reasons. One was that it was already apparent that, even counting all the indirect labor, it was costing over $1,200 a year to give relief to one family in that fashion. To reach 6,000,000 would cost $7,200,000,000 per annum. It was two to four times as expensive as direct family relief. It had proved unavailable as relief to regions removed from such works and to great groups who could not do such work. Moreover, the opportunity for economically sound direct Federal public works was being rapidly exhausted. Were the program of Federal works to be expanded it must be mostly by "made work" and therefore of little moral value as distinguished from direct relief. Direct Federal relief to the individual citizen also had vital objections. If it were once started, States and subdivisions would at once shirk their own local obligations. The devotion of local committees, responsible to their own municipalities and counties, would be lost. If Federal money were disbursed directly to individuals by the Federal Government it would be impossible to set up in an emergency such organization as would keep it free of politics and corruption. The President believed that some localities, especially in Illinois, Ohio, and Michigan, were beginning to show strain in their available resources and would require help from the Federal Government sooner or later, and if the depression lasted, other localities would need help. That help must be given to the State for administration, and not by direct Federal relation to the individual citizen.

The President was convinced that some action must be provided before the Congressional session was over. He believed that it should be done by loans to the States at a percentage of their own expenditures for this purpose, and that the States in turn must require some percentage contribution from local authorities. In any event, Federal funds should not be loaned to any States or subdivisions unless they could show that they unquestionably required such aid in order to prevent hunger and cold, and that they themselves were contributing something. Such a method was the least likely to undermine State responsibility and would avoid vast possibilities of corruption and fraud. It was agreed that if a proposal strictly along these lines were introduced into Congress at this time, the Democrats would, at the expense of the country, by constantly proposing higher and higher sums, substantially raise the amount and, of course, inevitably try to picture the President as being inhuman. Since the need was not immediate, it was decided to delay until a favorable opportunity offered for a safe proposal.

February 23, 1932: Under the leadership of Speaker Garner, the House passed a resolution, no doubt in response to the President's public statement. A special economy committee was created, consisting of seven members, to undertake bureau reorganization and other economies. Speaker Garner said the House would not stand any "suggestion that Congress abdicate its prerogatives and give the President blanket power." The committee made a modest effort toward economy, most of which the House eliminated as we shall see later. During the succeeding administration a much wider power for this purpose was granted to the Executive with no word of protest.

February 24, 1932: The President preserved his equanimity and complimented the House of Representatives:[5]

I am delighted that the Congress is earnestly taking up the reorganization of the Federal machinery. I will be entirely happy if my repeated messages to the Congress on the subject succeed in securing action in an effective fashion.

It is a most unpleasant task to abolish boards and bureaus and to consolidate others, and at the same time it is a difficult job to do it so wisely as not to injure the efficiency and morale of our army and navy and other essential government services. Congress has attempted repeatedly in the last twenty-five years to effect reorganizations and had always abandoned the efforts under a multitude of oppositions. . . .

The President sent the following to Colonel Frank Knox, chairman of the national campaign to combat hoarding:

. . . from the first of the year up to my announcement of your organization and its program, the amount of hoarding estimated by the Federal Reserve Board, after making allowance for seasonal changes, was two hundred ninety-five millions, and that since that date until February twenty-third there has been a return of sixty millions to circulation, likewise after making allowance for seasonal changes.

The President in a letter to Dr. M. C. Potter of the National Educational Association expressed opposition to cuts in expenditures for education:

. . . However national economy may vary or whatever fiscal adjustments may need be made, the very first obligation upon the national resources is the undiminished financial support of the Public Schools. . . .

February 26, 1932: No adequate action for self-regulation having been taken by the stock exchanges, the President requested Senators Norbeck and Walcott of the Senate Banking and Currency Committee to initiate a Senatorial investigation into the practices, by a minority of the New York Stock Exchange, which were against public interest.

February 27, 1932: There were more Democratic attacks on the Presi-

[5] State Papers, Vol. II, p. 125.

dent. Senator Thomas (Democrat) of Oklahoma, said that the Reconstruction Finance Corporation was a failure. It has been functioning for only two weeks. Setting up the far-flung organization of the Corporation and its prompt functioning had been an extraordinary performance, for which the President gave great credit to Governor Meyer and General Dawes. It was necessary to assemble not only an expert staff in Washington to consider the merits of every application for help, but to create an advisory committee of volunteer business men in every locality, who could pass upon the loans.

From the first, every taint of mere politics in appointments was rigidly excluded, and it is worth noting that no charge of corruption or favoritism has ever been successfully leveled at the corporation with respect to its work during the Hoover Administration. The work of considering thousands of loans was immense, appeals and visits to the White House by borrowers were incessant, and consultation with the directors and the President were daily necessary.

The President upon signing the Glass-Steagall Bill,[6] said:

. . . I desire to express my appreciation to the leaders and members of both Senate and House of both parties, who have co-operated in its enactment. The fine spirit of patriotic non-partisanship shown in carrying out the emergency program is, I know, appreciated by the whole country.

The bill should accomplish two major purposes.

First. In a sense this bill is a national defense measure. By freeing the vast amounts of gold in our Federal Reserve System (in excess of the gold reserve required by law), it so increases the already large available resources of the Federal Reserve Banks as to enable them beyond question to meet any conceivable demands that might be made on them at home or from abroad.

Second. It liberalizes existing provisions with regard to eligibility of collateral, and thereby enables the Federal Reserve Banks to furnish accommodations to many banks on sound assets heretofore unavailable for rediscount purposes.

The gradual credit contraction during the past eight months, arising indirectly from causes originating in foreign countries and continued domestic deflation, but more directly from hoarding, has been unquestionably the major factor in depressing prices and delaying business recovery.

This measure I am signing today, together with the additional capital provided for the Federal Land Banks and the creation of the Reconstruction Finance Corporation, will so strengthen our whole credit structure and open the channels of credit as now to permit our banks more adequately to serve the needs of agriculture, industry and commerce.

[6] See preceding chapter; also State Papers, Vol. II, p. 128.

I trust that our banks, with the assurances and facilities now provided, will reach out to aid business and industry in such fashion as to increase employment and aid agriculture.

One result of the Glass-Steagall Act of 1932 was to enable the Federal Reserve System to embark upon a much more extensive campaign of credit expansion through "open market" operations. After the British crisis the Federal Reserve System had expanded its "bills bought" by considerable amounts to adjust gold withdrawals, but it now could undertake a definite program of credit expansion through the purchase of "governments." After consultation with the President, such a policy was inaugurated at once upon a large scale. About $1,000,000,000 of "governments" were bought in the open market between March and July, and in the usual ratios would make available five to ten billions of dollars of credit to the ultimate borrower. Without this expansion to meet the credit contraction due to withdrawals of gold and currency, there would have been widespread bankruptcy.

February 29, 1932: In a special message to Congress the President urged an immediate and entire reform of the bankruptcy laws. He said in part:[7]

A sound bankruptcy system should operate:
First, to relieve honest but unfortunate debtors of an overwhelming burden of debt;
Second, to effect a prompt and economical liquidation and distribution of insolvent estates; and
Third, to discourage fraud and needless waste of assets by withholding relief from debts in proper cases.
. . . our present Bankruptcy Act has failed in its purpose and needs thorough revision. During the past year the Department of Justice, with my approval, has conducted investigation into the administration of bankrupt estates in the Federal courts. Nation-wide in its scope, the inquiry has involved intensive study of the practical operation of the Bankruptcy Act under varying local conditions throughout the United States. Court records and special reports of referees have been analyzed. Organizations of business men and lawyers have assisted in gathering information not available through official channels. Judges, prosecuting officers, referees, merchants, bankers, and others have made available their experience. Data gathered by the Department of Commerce relating to causes of failure and the effect of bad debts upon business have been studied. The history of bankruptcy legislation and administration in this country, and in Great Britain, Canada, and other countries, has been reviewed. . . .
The Bankruptcy Act should be amended to provide remedial processes in voluntary proceedings under which debtors, unable to pay their debts in due course, may have the protection of the court without being ad-

[7] State Papers, Vol. II, p. 134.

judged bankrupt, for the purpose of composing or extending the maturity of their debts, or amortizing the payment of their debts out of future earnings, of procuring the liquidation of their property under voluntary assignment to a trustee; or, in the cases of corporations, for the purpose of reorganization.

His broad object was to facilitate the readjustment downward of private debt. Debts which were the result of inflated values of property were, many of them, impossible of payment without complete bankruptcy and foreclosures to the detriment of both lenders and borrowers. In spite of constant urging, Congress took no action during the session.

March 3, 1932: The Democratic National Committee continued its attack upon the President for doing nothing and now claimed that the Democratic Party had originated such recovery measures as has been passed.

March 4, 1932: The Senate, following the President's suggestion, authorized an investigation of the stock exchanges.

March 6, 1932: The President broadcast an address to the country upon the subject of the hoarding of money.[8]

> For more than two years our people have paid the penalty of over-speculation, but far greater than that, they have suffered from economic forces from abroad that fundamentally are the reflexes of the Great War, a situation for which our people had no blame. They have stood their ground with grim courage and resolution.
> But this is no occasion to discuss the origins or the character of the economic forces. . . . We must meet these destructive forces by mobilizing our resources and our people against them. . . .
> . . . The battle front today is against the hoarding of currency, which began about ten months ago, and with its growing intensity became a national danger during the last four months. It has sprung from fears and apprehensions largely the reflex of foreign and domestic causes which now no longer maintain. But it has grown to enormous dimensions and has contributed greatly to restrict the credit facilities of our country, and thus directly to increase unemployment and depreciate prices to our farmers.
> I believe that the individual American has not realized the harm he has done. . . . It strangles our daily life, increases unemployment and sorely afflicts our farmers. No one will deny that if the vast sums of money hoarded in the country today could be brought into active circulation there would be a great lift to the whole of our economic progress. . . .

March 7, 1932: The President signed the bill appropriating 40,000,000 bushels of Farm Board wheat for relief, this to be distributed through the Red Cross. It amounted to about 10,000,000 barrels of flour.

[8] State Papers, Vol. II, p. 137.

The Committee on Ways and Means of the House, through its acting-chairman, Charles R. Crisp of Georgia, by a vote of twenty-four to one reported out a new revenue bill. The committee consisted of fifteen Democrats and ten Republicans.

The committee set out to obtain sufficient revenue to balance the budget and maintain the credit of the government. As reported, the bill was estimated to raise additional revenue of $1,246,000,000, which would balance the budget. A manufacturers' excise or sales tax of two and one-quarter per cent was relied upon to raise one-half of that amount. Increases in income taxes, corporate and individual, estate taxes and new excise and stamp taxes took care of the balance. It was an example of what could be accomplished through united bi-partisan effort, and the country was encouraged.

March 8, 1932: In their report the Ways and Means Committee had counted upon a further reduction in expenditures of $125,000,000 if the budget was to be balanced. The President, intent on balancing the budget, seized the opportunity to make a public statement through the press conference in which he urged a reduction of appropriations by Congress.[9]

. . . It is necessary that further cuts be made. There is very little room left for reductions by administrative action, and the House Appropriations Committee has passed upon the major supply bills except the army and navy. Further economies must be brought about by authorization of Congress, either by reorganization of the Federal machinery or change in the legal requirements as to expenditure by the various services.

The director of Veterans' Affairs has proposed to the Special House Committee on Economy some changes in the laws relating to pensions and other allowances, which would produce economies of between fifty and sixty millions per annum. The Postmaster-General is placing before the committee changes in the legal requirements of postoffice expenditures. The Secretary of Agriculture has suggested changes in the law requiring expenditures in the Department of Agriculture, and the other departments are engaged in preparation of similar drastic recommendations.

I believe the Committee on Economy, through administrative reorganization and such methods as I have mentioned, will be able to find a large area of economy.

Nothing is more important than balancing the budget with the least increase in taxes. The Federal Government should be in such position that it will need issue no securities which increase the public debt after the beginning of the next fiscal year, July 1st. That is vital to the still further promotion of employment and agriculture. . . .

March 9, 1932: Certain Democratic members of Congress engaged in

[9] State Papers, Vol. II, p. 140.

an attack upon the economy statement of the day before. The following reply was issued from the White House:[10]

Congressman Byrns [floor-leader of the majority] seems to be under some misimpression. The President, in view of the twenty years of failure of every effort by Congress to eliminate overlapping and useless functions in the Federal Government for purposes of economy, asked, in a message on February 17th, that authority should be given to him to execute definite projects of reorganization and economy subject to the opportunity to the Congress to express its views upon each action. . . .

The House recognized the importance of the matter, but felt that it should be again undertaken directly by the Congress instead of by the President. They set up the Economy Committee for this purpose. The President has been glad that this committee should undertake this great task. He at once instructed all officials of the government to co-operate in full with the committee. . . .

. . . every avenue of saving will be laid before the committee. . . . The President's desire is for action at this session of Congress. . . . What the country wants and needs is real results.

March 10, 1932: The House of Representatives began consideration of the new revenue bill.

March 11, 1932: The President's economy measure was defeated in the Senate.

Today the President stated in respect to the hoarding campaign:

The campaign has already produced positive and useful results, as reflected in the increase of currency returned to circulation, the increase of bank deposits. . . .

Their work has just one final objective—that is, the restoration of employment and aid to agriculture.[11]

[10] State Papers, Vol. II, p. 141.

[11] That this anti-hoarding campaign initiated by President Hoover met with almost instant success is illustrated by the following extract from the Republican National Committee weekly letter, issued March 31, 1932:

"In a radio address Colonel Frank Knox, Chairman of the Citizens Reconstruction Organization, as the anti-hoarding undertaking is called, declares that the campaign has been an unqualified success. From under carpets, between mattresses, from cans, trunks, coffee pots, pockets and safety deposit boxes, Colonel Knox declared the dollars are rolling back into employment. In New York City one business man is cited who took $380,000 in gold and gold certificates from a safety deposit box and placed it in his checking account. In Atlanta, Georgia, one bank has had a $200,000 increase in deposits since February 1. In New Mexico a man emptied his safety deposit box and placed the $5,000 in currency it contained in a savings account.

"And so it seems to be going all over the country,"

and by the following quotation from an editorial in the *Chicago Evening Post:*

"Some rather extraordinary local evidence is offered that confidence is returning among investors and depositors.

"One of the larger brokerage houses was paid $7,000 in gold by a customer who completed some odd-lot purchases of high grade common stocks for investment purposes. Two other customers paid for several small blocks of stock in gold coin. In one of the outlying

March 12, 1932: Ivor Kreuger, a Swedish promoter, committed suicide during the exposure of enormous fraud. The Democratic opposition endeavored to reproach the President as being a "friend" of Kreuger. As a matter of fact, the President knew nothing of him until Kreuger had, on an American visit, through intermediaries, endeavored to reach the President for an invitation to the White House. This had been refused. Finally, the Swedish Minister had requested the State Department to arrange that he might formally present Kreuger to the President. This was done at the public reception hour at noon at the Executive Offices, the Minister and Kreuger being with the President less than five minutes.

March 15, 1932: The situation in the country had again begun to turn from the upward course of the middle of February. By now the Reconstruction Finance Corporation had gotten well under way. The gold standard appeared secure by the agreement on the Glass-Steagall Bill. The anti-hoarding campaign was launched. The expansion of credit by the Federal Reserve System was proceeding. These activities greatly relieved the economic strain. More banks, measured in deposits, were reopened than closed. Gold drains of any consequence ceased. Hoarded currency returned to the banks. The prices of wheat and cotton stiffened. The price of industrial stocks rose about ten per cent. The increase in unemployment ceased. The whole country breathed easier, as another crisis had been passed. However, it was not to be for long, for the moment that the fright was removed the Democratic leaders in Congress again began to play politics. They proceeded to sabotage the remainder of the President's recovery program. They introduced a multitude of demagogic measures of pork-barrel and inflationary varieties, and defeated every economy and tax program until the country was steadily driven again into despair. This did not find its bottom until the middle of July when, with the adjournment of Congress, the country was assured the defeat of these demagogic measures.

March 16, 1932: It was repeatedly charged in the Senate that the States and localities were failing in their relief work, this resulting in widespread distress. The information coming to the President was to the contrary. An independent canvass was made of the governors of the States, asking if there were any starvation or privation in their areas. Thirty-nine emphatically replied no, eight made no reply, one replied in

---

sound banks, a super-wary depositor recovered enough courage to deposit $30,000 in gold for safekeeping and borrowed $27,000 in currency against it, with the understanding that the bank was to keep the precious collateral intact until the loan was paid.

"In all four cases the gold had been withdrawn from circulation and hoarded. Little by little these hidden reserves are returning to circulation as the nervousness of the public wanes."

the affirmative. Relief committee leaders in that particular State denied this and accused the governor of sabotaging the efforts they were making to get that State to do its obvious duty.

March 17, 1932: The President arranged with Judge Payne, head of the Red Cross, the method by which the Red Cross would manage and distribute to the needy the ten million barrels of flour ground from Farm Board wheat, which had been appropriated in accordance with his recommendations to Congress.

March 19, 1932: Conflicts having arisen between the various government agencies concerning possible financial assistance to the railways, the President called together in conference the directors of the Reconstruction Finance Corporation, the members of the Interstate Commerce Commission, and representatives of the Department of Commerce, together with the executive committee of the Association of Railway Executives. As a result of the meeting he stated: [12]

> Examination of the financial problem confronting the railroads shows that it is of smaller dimensions than has been generally believed or reported. It is estimated that the financial necessities of the important railways of the country which are likely to require aid in meeting the interest and renewal of their maturing securities, and in meeting their other obligations during 1932, will be from $300,000,000 to $400,000,000. Of this amount the Railway Credit Corporation will provide a minimum of from $50,000,000 to $60,000,000, and it is assumed that many bank loans will be continued in the normal way. Therefore recourse to the Reconstruction Corporation by the railroads will be much less than was originally thought, and even the mentioned amounts could be diminished by revival of the bond market and the placing of bond renewals in normal fashion. . . .
>
> The co-ordination of programs and policies has been arrived at by the government and the railway agencies to effect these results.

March 10 to 25, 1932: The new revenue bill, notwithstanding its bipartisan and almost unanimous committee report, ran into serious difficulty from the start. With its large membership, for years it has been the practice of the House of Representatives to consider its revenue legislation under a special rule, limiting the number of hours that the bill could be considered under general debate. No such rule preceded the consideration of this extremely important and urgent measure. Time again was an important element. Early in December the President had urged the necessity for additional revenue and had submitted recommendations. The committee had given several weeks' consideration to the measure. No committee could have been more representative of the House. A minimum of

[12] State Papers, Vol. II, p. 143.

partisanship had prevailed in the consideration of the measure in committee. Twenty-four out of the twenty-five members, including both Democrats and Republicans, had joined in the report. The remaining and only dissenting member did not submit a minority report. There was every reason for expediting consideration of the detailed provisions of the bill through the House and practically none for delaying it. But no special rule to accomplish this by limiting general debate was presented.

This failure to limit debate was brought to the attention of the Republican floor-leader, Mr. Snell. The latter at once saw the possible danger and endeavored to have it corrected. He took the matter up with Speaker Garner, but to no avail. The attitude of the Speaker was to "Let them talk." This same thought was expressed by other leaders of the majority. General debate was permitted to run from March 10th to 18th, inclusive. By a teller vote in committee of the whole on March 24th, of 211 to 178, the manufacturers' sales tax, carrying $600,000,000 of revenue, was stricken from the bill despite the efforts of Majority Leader Rainey and Acting Chairman Crisp to prevent it. The manufacturers' excise tax had literally been talked to death. A sub-committee of the Ways and Means Committee was appointed to submit to the House at a later date and as promptly as possible, other tax provisions in lieu thereof. Having been turned down decisively on a major policy, Acting Chairman Crisp offered to turn his position over to the opposition, but the opposition did not care to assume this responsibility and turned the offer down. The effect upon the country, when it was commencing to show substantial signs of improvement, was most disturbing. Hope again gave way to despair. In commenting publicly upon the gravity of the situation, Jouett Shouse, chairman of the executive committee of the Democratic National Committee, said:

> The House has wrecked the Committee bill and the legislative situation has been thrown into a state of such confusion *and even chaos* that the outcome is difficult to predict.

While the sub-committee was at work again upon the President's original tax proposals, the House continued its consideration of the remaining provisions of the revenue bill.

It had now been four months since the legislation was urged by the President, and constant delay was visibly discouraging the country. In an appeal to the public for support in his efforts to balance the budget, the President said (March 25th): [13]

I have received many hundred inquiries from different parts of the

[13] State Papers, Vol. II, p. 147.

country as to the prospects of balancing the budget. . . .

. . . the undertaking of the representatives of both political parties to balance the budget remains . . . it is the very keystone of recovery. It must be done. Without it the several measures for restoration of public confidence and reconstruction which we have already undertaken will be incomplete and the depression prolonged indefinitely. . . .

We must eliminate this deficit for next year by the further reduction of governmental expenditures and by increases in taxation. . . . But when all this is done the balancing of the budget must in the main be accomplished by an increase in taxation, which will restore government revenues.

Economies in expenditure or increase in taxes alike call for sacrifices —sacrifices which are a part of the country's war on depression. The government no more than individual families can continue to expend more than it receives without inviting serious consequences. . . .

The American people are no less courageous and no less wise than the people of other nations. All other great nations of the world have been faced with even greater necessity during the past year. In order to preserve their national credit these countries have increased their taxes far more severely than our deficit demands of the American people. . . .

It must not be forgotten that the needs of the government are inseparable from the welfare of the people. Those most vitally concerned in recovery are the ones whose margins of savings are the smallest. They are affected by the depression more seriously than any others; ultimately they will pay the biggest price for any failure on our part of the government to take the necessary action at this time. . . .

The President gave out a statement of the work of the Reconstruction Finance Corporation to date. This showed that of over 600 institutions which had been assisted, spread over forty-five States, ninety-eight per cent of the aid had been extended to small institutions.

March 26, 1923: The Democratic National Committee charged the President with responsibility for the upset of the Democratic tax bill, notwithstanding the fact that the Republican leaders were supporting it, while the Democratic leaders were divided.

March 29, 1932: The President said: [14]

Informal polls of the House of Representatives have created apprehension in the country that a further bonus bill of $2,000,000,000 or thereabouts for World War veterans will be passed.

I wish to state again that I am absolutely opposed to any such legislation. I made this position clear at the meeting of the American Legion in Detroit last September 21st, and the Legion has consistently supported that position. I do not believe any such legislation can become law.

Such action would undo every effort that is being made to reduce government expenditures and balance the budget. The first duty of every

[14] State Papers, Vol. II, p. 151.

citizen of the United States is to build up and sustain the credit of the United States Government. Such an action would irretrievably undermine it.

March 30, 1932: During the month the Glass Banking Reform Bill was reported out of committee. The bill as reported did not reach the full extent of needed reform except in the separation of affiliates and in liquidation of closed banks and correction of certain abuses. Yet it was instantly attacked by certain banking interests and was recommitted to the Senate committee.

April 1, 1932: The House finally passed a patchwork revenue bill. The Committee on Ways and Means submitted to the House its substitute tax provisions for the stricken manufacturers' sales tax. Speaker Garner took the floor and urged its adoption. He had remained silent during the fight on the manufacturers' excise tax. Four months had elapsed since the President made his urgent and specific recommendations. The presented bill was three to four hundred millions short of the revenue required to balance the budget, even if a saving of six hundred millions were made. The amendment striking out the manufacturers' sales tax came up for a yea and nay vote in the House. This was accomplished by a vote of 236 to 106. About seventy-five per cent of those voting in the affirmative and against the manufacturers' sales tax were Democrats. Of the negative and in support of the tax about seventy-five per cent were Republicans.

The President signed the act extending the time for payments to settlers on irrigation projects which he had agreed upon with the members of Congress from the arid States.

The President announced: [15]

> I do not propose to fill the vacancy on the Shipping Board, created by the death of Mr. Plummer, for the present. I am in hopes that Congress will pass the legislation necessary to reorganize the whole of our merchant marine activities in order that we may make drastic reduction of expenditures in this session. . . .
>
> I have pointed out in messages and elsewhere on several occasions. . . . We have merchant marine activities in many different departments and independent establishments. We now expend in aid and loans to the merchant marine services, directly and indirectly, about $100,000,000 per annum. We cannot remedy the situation without legislation. The present Shipping Board should be abolished. Its administrative functions should be transferred to the departments. . . . The Board was designed originally for regulatory purposes . . . subsequently given enormous administrative and financial functions. The President has no authority or con-

[15] State Papers, Vol. II, p. 152.

trol over its activities . . . independence from all control except the indirect pressures of Congress . . . the Board's authority in certain matters is divided with the Postmaster General. . . . There can be no adequate check or co-ordinated direction of expenditure or commitments. . . .

The Democratic Congress refused to take action.

April 2, 1932: The President, having received a protest from a group of New York bankers upon his criticism of market raids and the effects, replied as follows:

My Dear Mr. ————:

I am greatly obliged for your memorandum of April 1st. It seems to me, however, that some other factors enter into this consideration.

The first is that prices today [of securities] do not truly represent the values of American enterprise and property. To base the prices on earnings either at top of a boom or at bottom of a depression is not correct interpretation of values.

The second point at which I find myself in disagreement is that the pounding down of prices to a basis of earnings by obvious manipulation of the market and propaganda that values should be based on earnings at the bottom of a depression is an injury to the country and to the investing public; just as is also an interpretation of values on the basis of earnings in a boom.

My third point is that so long as these processes continue, the public which is willing to invest on the basis of the future of the United States rather than upon immediate bear coloring of earnings is driven from the market.

My fourth point is that these operations destroy public confidence and induce a slowing down of business and a fall in prices.

My fifth point is that men are not justified in deliberately making a profit from the losses of other people.

I recognize that these points of view are irreconcilable, but I hope you will agree with me that there is here an element of public interest.

Yours faithfully,

Herbert Hoover.

April 4, 1932: There had been pending before the House a bill granting independence to the Philippine Islands. The bill was popular with the sentimentalists and the sugar growers. As an evidence of how the House can expedite the passage of legislation, when the party in control desires to do so, the following is an example. It is in striking contrast to the delay accompanying the consideration of the Revenue Bill. The Philippines Bill was considered by the House with no privilege of amendment and with debate limited to forty minutes. By these forty minutes the fate of 13,000,000 people was to be determined. If there had been anything approaching this in expeditious consideration of the President's recovery program that program would have passed the House months before.

As Congress was taking no serious action with regard to the reduction of expenditures, the President determined upon an even more vigorous drive to arouse public opinion. He opened with a special message to Congress, stating:[16]

> I have in various messages to the Congress over the past three years referred to the necessity of organized effort to effect far-reaching reduction of governmental expenditures.
>
> To balance the budget for the year beginning July 1st next, the Revenue Bill passed by the House of Representatives on April 1st necessitates that there shall be a further reduction of expenditures for the next year of about $200,000,000 in addition to the reduction of $369,000,000 in expenditures already made in the budget recommendations which I transmitted to the Congress on December 9th.
>
> It is essential in the interest of the taxpayer and the country that it should be done. It is my belief that still more drastic economy than this additional $200,000,000 can be accomplished. Such a sum can only be obtained, however, by a definite national legislative program of economy. . . .
>
> These objects cannot be accomplished without far-reaching amendment to the laws. The Executive is bound to recommend appropriations adequate to provide for the functions and activities of the government as now established by law. This is mandatory, and the opportunity for administrative savings is limited . . . it is necessary to enter upon other fields by amending existing laws . . . we should undertake a definite, separate and co-ordinated program of economy legislation. . . .
>
> . . . the latitude necessary for real reduction of expenses can only be secured by a thoroughgoing renovation of the law to bring about a real national economy program. . . .
>
> It appears to me that with four different agencies of the Congress at work on the problem, operating independently with the different departments, the time which has already elapsed and the short time available to us before the beginning of the new fiscal year, all point to the absolute necessity of better organized unity of effort in all the branches of the government primarily concerned with the problem.
>
> Therefore, I recommend to the Congress that in order to secure this unity of effort and prompt action, and thus insure the relief of the taxpayer and a balanced budget, at the same time protecting vital service of the government, that representatives be delegated by the two Houses, who, together with representatives of the Executive, should be authorized to frame for action by the present Congress a complete national program of economy and to recommend the legislation necessary to make it possible and effective. Such a course would expedite rather than delay the passage of appropriations bills.

[16] State Papers, Vol. II, p. 153.

I am convinced that only by such unified non-partisan effort, and by a willingness on the part of all to share the difficulties and problems of this essential task, can we attain the success so manifestly necessary in public interest.

April 5, 1932: Senator Robinson and other Democratic leaders attacked this message, the main line of attack being that it was "another commission," and demanded that specific recommendations be sent to Congress. In response, the President made the following press conference statement: [17]

What I asked for in my message today was organized, non-partisan co-operation by all forces to reduce government expenses in the national emergency, which insistently demands relief for the taxpayer.

There are three general directions in which expenses can be reduced:

First: The direct reduction of appropriations, within the authority of existing laws creating and specifying various activities of the government.

A definite program to this end was placed before Congress in the Executive budget proposals, in which there was a reduction of $369,000,000 for the forthcoming year. I welcome and hope for further cuts by the Congress. . . .

Second: There are a large number of expenditures within the bureaus and departments which cannot be reduced without a change in the laws so that the Executive or the Appropriations committees can reduce such expenditures.

In this direction the department heads have appeared before many different committees in Congress in the last months, and have pointed out a multitude of directions which could be considered by these committees for a reduction of expenditures, but most of them require repeal or amendment of the laws which compel expenditures. Seven departments alone have pointed out over eighty-five such different directions for consideration of those committees and which offer a possibility of very large reductions. There are still other areas which could no doubt be developed.

Third: Those directions of economy which can only be accomplished by reorganization and consolidation of government functions so as to eliminate overlap, useless bureaus and commissions, and waste.

Seven years ago, five years ago, as a member of a Cabinet committee on the subject, and again three years ago, . . . I recommended authorization to the Executive to make a wholesale reorganization of government functions. . . .

A dominant consideration is that all these items, methods, and programs concern a great number of committees in the Congress. They concern a great number of departments and bureaus. If we take the eleven principal spending branches of the government, each of them working independently with some part of over thirty different Congressional committees which are concerned in these ideas and proposals, then even if we have the very best will in the world, without an atom of partisanship,

[17] State Papers, Vol. II, p. 155.

the mere diffusion of effort seemingly makes effective progress on important items impossible.

What I have asked for is not a commission but merely that the Senate and the House should each delegate representatives to sit down with representatives from the administration and endeavor to draft a comprehensive, general, national economy bill. . . . Without such action, I see no way by which there can be a maximum reduction in expenditures.

April 6, 1932: Congressman McDuffie, Democratic chairman of the House Economy Committee, addressed a letter to the President asking "that you participate in the task of the House committee by sending your representative to present specific recommendations." The President wanted results, so he replied as follows:[18]

THE WHITE HOUSE

Washington,
April 7, 1932.

Hon. John McDuffie, Chairman
Economy Committee,
House of Representatives,
Washington, D.C.

My Dear Mr. Chairman:

I am in receipt of your letter of April 6th. I greatly welcome the response of your committee to my suggestion that the fiscal situation necessitates honest, courageous and non-partisan action in the development of a national economy program and the preparation of a definite comprehensive bill that will assure its accomplishment. With this purpose in mind I would be glad if your committee would meet with me at this office at 11 o'clock on Saturday morning, April 9th, with a view to taking stock of the progress made by your committee in the development of a program of economy, and affording the Executive an opportunity to make suggestions. Through the interchange of ideas we can thus lay the foundation for the development of such national program.

It is my understanding that your suggestion carries with it the thought that in such development the representatives whom I may appoint from the Executive branches of the Government will sit in and co-operate with your committee. I shall continue to urge that a similar committee be appointed by the Senate in order that we shall not need to traverse the whole subject again.

Yours faithfully,

Herbert Hoover.

April 7, 1932: It was evident that certain speculators were at work endeavoring to stifle the Senate investigation of the New York Stock Exchange. The President requested Senator Frederic C. Walcott of

[18] State Papers, Vol. II, p. 159, for this and subsequent letters.

Connecticut to interest the other Republican senators in it. The President was determined that the methods used by certain members of this institution should be thoroughly reviewed, first with the view to determining if the authorities of the Exchange were doing their part to bring certain immediate practices to an end; and second, to determine if the New York State authorities could any longer be entrusted with protection of the public interest under their power to regulate it. The bear raids and pools formed in anticipation of the German collapse, in anticipation of the British crisis, and in anticipation of the gold crisis, all of them greatly had increased public apprehension at the time and had caused hoarding, flights of capital, and bank failures. Every occasion was to be "the last." Since the New York State authorities, who had primary responsibility, would not intervene, the President had determined that the information must be secured upon which action could be founded that would protect the public interest.

Senator Walcott, who was familiar with the Exchange, was equally earnest in the belief that self-government of the Exchange had failed and that the New York State authorities would do nothing, although the need was as great as in the similar case of some years before, when the State authorities set an example in the control of insurance practices under the leadership of Charles E. Hughes. The President informed the Senator that he was confident from many communications that a majority of the members of the Stock Exchange would like to see these practices cleaned up, but that they would not come forward voluntarily against their colleagues. The truth could be brought out only under the compulsion that a Senate committee could exert. His hope was that such important institutions could govern themselves, or at least the States would recognize their fundamental responsibility. In any event, he was tired of having reform promises broken.

April 9, 1932: The President met with the House Economy Committee in the Cabinet room at the White House, there also being present Secretaries Mills and Wilbur, and Postmaster-General Brown, together with Director of the Budget Roop. The members of the House committee were: John McDuffie, chairman, Will R. Wood, William Ramseyer, Joseph Byrns, John Cochran, Lewis Douglas, and William Williamson. A statement was issued to the press:

As a result of mutual exchange of views by the Administration and the Economy Committee the following was tentatively agreed upon as a national economy program.

The total of the savings so far arrived at would amount to somewhere from $160,000,000 to $210,000,000. This does not include the savings to be made from consolidation (Group II), nor from reductions in appropriations (Group III).

The conferences will continue.

Reductions in expenses require action in three directions:

Class 1. The amendment or repeal of existing laws which would prevent the realization of savings.

Class 2. Legislation for the reorganization and consolidation of government functions so as to eliminate overlap, unnecessary bureaus and commissions, and waste.

Class 3. Reduction of appropriations which are within the authority of the existing laws creating and specifying various activities of the government. This class being under consideration by the Appropriations Committee of Congress, was not dealt with in the conference.

There then followed a detailed list of proposals including a five-day week for government employees.

April 12, 1932: The President called a further session with the House Economy Committee. He stated to the press conference:[19]

> The joint conference of the administrative officials and the Economy Committee of the House on Saturday resulted in most encouraging progress.
>
> Any program of legislation for fundamental changes in the laws affecting reduction of government expenditure involves a very large amount of detailed research and detailed consideration. I have felt that we would make most distinct progress by continuing these conferences and I have asked the Economy Committee to meet with me again tomorrow.
>
> The businesslike and effective way to handle the whole question of reduction of governmental expenditures where it requires legislative action as distinguished from action by appropriation committees is to work out a definite national economy bill which can be presented to Congress and to the country as a completed whole. Obviously it requires effort, but I do not believe it will consume a large amount of time.
>
> The development of such a program requires the closest co-operation between the executive and the legislative branches of the government. It is most desirable that such a program shall be presented on an entirely non-partisan basis on which we all take our measure of responsibility.

April 14, 1932: The House Economy Committee announced that it preferred direct salary cuts. The President insisted that the five-day week for five days pay (the furlough system) had the same result with the further advantage that it would enable the government to absorb employees who otherwise would be discharged as a result of other cuts in governmental expenditures.

[19] State Papers, Vol. II, p. 164.

April 15, 1932: The President discussed the economic situation at length with the press representatives. He said in part:

... The economic situation in the country ... has reached that stage where the great economic forces of liquidation have ... gone in fact entirely too far. In the middle of March we had a very distinct re-establishment ... of courage throughout the country. We have had during the last three weeks a considerable set-back. It has arisen from a number of apprehensions. ... These are times, of course, when sentiment is easily influenced, and it is time when we peculiarly need the courage and confidence of the business world ... there are a good many causes which have discouraged them. ...

The tax bill ... contains items which are discouraging and its passage was delayed ... the tendency of any action by the Congress on commodities—irrespective of what the nature of the action may be—tends to slow up business in those particular lines of activity. ...

Another one of the contributions to the set-back ... had been the agitation of the bonus. ...

And another apprehension ... is ... the banking situation. The results attained by the Reconstruction Corporation ... clearly indicate that the last major banking crisis ... is now past ... in the nine weeks prior to the time when the corporation came into action we had a net number of 655 banks closed. That is net after deducting the number that were reopened in the same period. And the net amount of deposits in those banks that were closed was $478,000,000. Taking the average size of deposits in the United States, that means that something over 1,200,000 people were deprived of their immediate resources in that period of nine weeks. ... In the nine weeks since the corporation has been operating, after we deduct banks reopened, there were only 77 banks closed, and total deposits of $25,000,000. In other words, there has been a reversal of the situation by 95 per cent. Another indication of the passage of the banking crisis is the fact that in the nine weeks before the anti-hoarding campaign, which coincided with the Reconstruction Corporation, we had about $400,000,000 of currency withdrawn from the banks, whereas in the nine weeks since we not only have had no withdrawals of balance, but have $250,000,000 of returned currency. ...

... Another fundamental contribution to the stability of the situation is that the budget must be balanced. ... Sentiment has grown definitely in the last two weeks for the acceptance of a drastic ... economy bill which will attack that quarter of expenditure which cannot be reached except by amendment and alteration of the existing laws. In other words, outside of the field that can be reached by appropriations. ... The economies that can be reached in that direction are apparently close to $300,000,000, and that, added to the $369,000,000 already cut from the budget before it was sent to Congress ... [will make] an aggregate from all of over $650,000,000. ...

... Nearly 60 per cent of the expenditures of the Federal Government are fixed commitments of the government in the shape of debts and obligations for pensions and subsidies to the States, outstanding contracts, etc., etc. We have only 40 per cent of the Federal expenditure to attack, and out of that area of 40 per cent we are securing a reduction of nearly 40 per cent. That is the most drastic reduction of governmental expenses that has been undertaken by any government in any time in any one year.

. . . The fixed expenditures are somewhat between $2,500,000,000 and $2,600,000,000 out of the $4,300,000,000 budget.

. . . That the government is facing the reduction of expenditures . . . ought to contribute to confidence. . . .

. . . Another phase of the general situation is the general impression of the public that the government has been extravagantly run and that the cause of our difficulties is that. . . . The financial difficulties of the government are due to the drop in income receipts. One figure illustrates that the income tax has averaged in a normal year somewhere about $2,400,000,000, and we are budgeting only for $860,000,000 for next year. In other words, we are anticipating a drop in all our calculations of approximately $1,600,000,000 in one category of tax receipts alone. The total drop in government income . . . is about $2,000,000,000. . . . The necessity of increase in taxes to reduce expenses does not arise from our extravagances. The proposed increase of tax is somewhere about $1,200,000,000. . . . We are not asking the taxpayer to make up the whole deficit—a considerable degree by cutting expenses. . . .

April 16, 1932: After several meetings with the Economy Committee, Director of the Budget Roop was requested to prepare for it a draft of an omnibus economy bill. The President's statement to the press upon the dispatch of the bill was: [20]

The omnibus bill for amendment to the various laws so as to permit reduction of government expenses beyond those which can be effected by the executive and the appropriations committees, should ultimately reduce expenditures by upwards of $225,000,000 and possibly $250,000,000.

The bill represents the drafting of matters discussed by the joint sessions of the administration representatives and the House Economy Committee. . . .

The President then went on to describe the working of the five-day week in government without interruption of service. The economies here proposed were in addition to the economies of $360,000,000 heretofore proposed in the President's budget.

April 16-25, 1932: While these efforts were under way and progress was being made with the House Committee on Economy, certain Democratic senators proposed and finally secured the passage of a resolution in the Senate pertaining to the annual appropriation bills. This resolution

[20] State Papers, Vol. II, p. 165.

provided for a horizontal or flat cut of ten per cent from each departmental appropriation. If adhered to there is no question that it would have reduced appropriations. It was a simple, rough and unscientific method of cutting down expenditures. As to some departments and agencies, it would have been quite impracticable. Some of its supporters thought it sufficiently objectionable from the standpoint of efficient administration as to invite Presidential criticism. This, if forthcoming, could then be used as a basis for claiming that the President was really opposed to reducing governmental expenditures. The President took this philosophically, knowing that any such method would be abandoned when the bill came into conference between the Houses, and realizing they would hardly dare to cut appropriations ten per cent from Federal courts, the jails, the postoffices, lighthouses, etc.

April 18, 1932: Many important business men and bankers objected to an increase in taxation at this time. They insisted that the budget could be balanced by a simple reduction of governmental expenses. The President was of course between two fires—those who opposed reducing expenses and those who wanted more reductions than were possible. As indicating the situation, we introduce the following letter:

MY DEAR MR. ———

I have your letter of April 16th. I am afraid the problems confronting us are not so simple as to permit of the action you suggest.

As to cutting government expenses, approximately $2,500,000,000 of the federal budget, out of a total of $4,400,000,000, are fixed charges of the government and cannot be reduced. Of the remainder, the budget which I sent to Congress proposed direct cuts of $369,000,000, and as you may have seen in the Press, I have asked for changes in the laws to permit cuts of $250,000,000, and in addition Congress, with its larger authorities, may be able to cut the budget another hundred million. No such drastic cut has ever been made by any government at any time in one year.

It is often overlooked that our financial difficulties are largely due to the fact that our tax income has decreased by over $2,000,000,000 from the normal of about $4,000,000,000. We are proposing new taxes for $1,250,000,000 and propose to cover the balance of the situation by reduction of expenses.

As to balancing the budget itself, you are aware that if we do not balance the budget we must continually issue government securities for the difference. Every security we issue depletes the capital available to industry and commerce by just that amount. . . .

Your thesis is that the government expenses can be reduced by $2,000,000,000—the amount of the tax decrease. This is utterly and wholly impossible. It would mean cutting off every solitary government service except the fixed commitments of the government. It would mean we must give up the postal service, the Merchant Marine, protection of life and property and public health. We would have to turn 40,000 prisoners loose in the country; we would have to stop the maintenance of rivers and harbors; we would have to stop all construction work going on in aid of unemployment; it would mean abolishment of the Army and Navy. In other words it means complete chaos.

As concerns the relative expenditure of the government in 1926 the proposals now before Congress, except for two items, cut government expenditures far below that year or any other year since the War. Those two items are the increased expenditure imposed by Veterans' legislation and increased expenditure on public works being conducted in aid to unemployment.

Yours faithfully,
HERBERT HOOVER.

April 23, 1932: For some days the Senate committee, which had been set up at the President's instigation, diligently exposed stock manipulations of large dimensions.

April 25, 1932: The House Economy Committee reported the Omnibus Economy Bill, which contained a part of the President's proposals, but omitted items amounting to $135,000,000.

April 27, 1932: The President vetoed a special veterans' pension bill, stating:[21]

I must withhold approval of the bill because of the number of cases which I do not deem worthy of public bounty. Most of these undeserving cases have been previously rejected by the Pension Bureau as having no sound basis upon which to construe any obligation in equity for the granting of special benefits.

. . . I cite some instances in the bill without mentioning names. . . . Such instances comprise:

. . . pension for a man who was courtmartialled for drunkenness . . . sentenced to six months confinement. . . .

. . . to a man who was discharged without honor because of chronic alcoholism. . . .

. . . to a man guilty of desertion and dishonorably discharged. . . .

. . . to a man shown to have been a deserter. . . .

. . . to a man for self-inflicted injuries incurred in attempted suicide. . . .

. . . a widow whose husband gave eight days service, with no disability. . . .

. . . for loss of a leg as the result of being struck by the fender of a streetcar while claimant was lying on the track in a completely intoxicated condition. . . .

Many other instances were given.

April 27, 1932: State and local taxes make up a substantial portion

[21] State Papers, Vol. II, p. 167.

of the taxes that the average citizen must pay. These taxes were constantly increasing and becoming very burdensome. They constituted a real problem. With this in mind the President addressed the Governors' Conference at Richmond, Virginia, urging drastic economy in all government.[22]

Our tax revenues have all greatly diminished. We must find new tax revenues to supplement those sources which have been dried up by the depression. . . . We must resolutely balance our budgets.

The economic safety of the Republic depends upon the joint financial stability of all our governments . . . not alone the Federal Government —equally State, county, and municipal government. . . .

A few figures will assist . . . for purpose of illustration. . . .

	1913	1924	1930
Expenditures:			
Federal	$ 700,000,000	$4,100,000,000	$4,200,000,000
State	400,000,000	1,400,000,000	2,300,000,000
Local	1,800,000,000	5,400,000,000	7,500,000,000
Total	$2,900,000,000	$10,900,000,000	$14,000,000,000
Our outstanding debt was approximately:			
Federal	$1,000,000,000	$21,300,000,000	$16,200,000,000
State	300,000,000	1,100,000,000	1,800,000,000
Local	3,500,000,000	8,000,000,000	12,600,000,000
Total	$4,800,000,000	$30,400,000,000	$30,600,000,000

. . . Today we are clearly absorbing too great a portion of the national income for the conduct of our various branches of government . . . before the war the total cost of . . . governments represented only about 8 per cent of our national income. In boom times . . . the cost of government actually increased to . . . 15 per cent of the national income, of which less than 3 per cent was directly due to the war. Today, with the falling off of business, the aggregate expenditures [are] . . . more than 20 per cent of the national income.

Before the war theoretically every man worked twenty-five days a year for the national, State and local governments combined. In 1924 he worked forty-six days a year. Today he works for the support of all forms of government sixty-one days out of a year. Continued progress on this road is the way to national impoverishment. . . .

. . . Nor can we hide our heads in the sand by borrowing to cover current government expenses, for thus we drain the capital of the country into public securities and draft it away from industry and commerce . . . dominant national necessity is to reduce the expenditures. . . .

. . . every dollar of decrease . . . touches some sensitive spot where it causes pain and resentment . . . people demand and applaud . . . economy, in the large, [but] . . . threats of sections and groups greatly impede. . . .

[22] State Papers, Vol. II, p. 169.

. . . The taxes upon real property . . . are the least flexible of all taxes . . . an increasing burden upon property owners both in rural and urban communities . . . almost unbearable. Tax . . . upon real estate is wholly out of proportion to that upon other forms of property and income. There is no farm relief more needed today than tax relief for I believe it can be demonstrated that the tax burdens upon the farmer today exceed the burden upon other groups. . . .

May 2, 1932: The President was in conference with Republican and Democratic leaders on the speeding up of the recovery program.

The Democratic House passed a pension bill involving additional annual appropriations of $100,000,000. This was done in the face of their previous assurance that they would co-operate with the President in reducing expenses.

The House passed the Goldsborough Bill, which directed the Federal Reserve to inflate credit—the rubber dollar—until prices returned to the 1921-1929 levels. It was an indication of the Democratic determination to appeal to the inflation sentiment in the country.

May 3, 1932: After days devoted to rejection of one item of economy after another, the House finally passed the Omnibus Economy Bill, with only $30,000,000 left of the $250,000,000 savings which had been recommended by the President.

May 3, 1932: Under the guise of excise duties, Democratic senators were instrumental in putting tariff duties on lumber, coal, oil and copper into the Revenue Bill in the Senate.

CHAPTER XII

PRESIDENT HOOVER AND CONGRESS—THE STRUGGLE TO BALANCE THE BUDGET

MAY–JULY, 1932

May 5, 1932: It became quite clear now that certain Democratic leaders were delaying the whole recovery program in the hope of lessening the fortunes of the President and his party in the fall election. Five months had elapsed since the opening of the session. In this time every recommendation of the President could have been enacted into law and with due legislative deliberation. The country was exceedingly apprehensive that Congress was incapable of action. After long delay, the House at last had sent to the Senate the Revenue and Economy bills. The scene of the struggle for budget balancing now was shifted to the Senate. The President therefore transferred his attention more particularly to that body. As an initial step he sent a pointed message to Congress: [1]

I should not be discharging my Constitutional responsibility to give to the Congress information on the state of the Union and to recommend for its consideration such measures as may be necessary and expedient, if I did not report to the Congress the situation which has arisen in the country in large degree as the result of incidents of legislation during the past six weeks.

The most essential factor to economic recovery today is the restoration of confidence. In spite of the unquestioned beneficial effect of the remedial measures already taken and the gradual improvement in fundamental conditions, fear and alarm prevail in the country because of events in Washington which have greatly disturbed the public mind.

The manner in which the House of Representatives rejected both the revenue program proposed by the Treasury and the program unanimously reported by the Committee on Ways and Means; the character of the tax measures passed; the action of the House which would increase governmental expenditure by $132,000,000 for road building; the action further to enlarge expenditures in non-service connected benefits from the Veterans' Bureau at the very time when the House was refusing to remedy abuse in these same services; the virtual destruction of both the national economy program proposed by the executive officials and the program of the Special House Committee on Economy; the failure of the House to

[1] State Papers, Vol. II, p. 175.

give adequate authority for early reduction of government bureaus and commissions; the passage of legislation by the House placing burdens of impossible execution upon the Federal Reserve System over the protest of the Federal Reserve Board; the threat of further legislation looking to uncontrolled inflation—have all resulted in diminishing public confidence and offsetting the constructive, unified efforts of the Executive and the Congress undertaken earlier in the year for recovery of employment and agriculture.

I need not recount . . . revenues show . . . decrease of . . . $1,700,000,000 and inexorably require . . . taxation and a drastic reduction of expenditures. . . . Nothing is more necessary at this time than balancing the budget. Nothing will put more heart into the country than prompt and courageous and united action. . . .

The details and requirements of the situation are now well known to the Congress and plainly require:

1. The prompt enactment of a revenue bill. . . .
2. A drastic program of economy which, including the savings already made in the Executive budget of $369,000,000, can be increased to exceed $700,000,000 per annum. . . .

With the . . . reductions . . . proposed, it will be necessary to discharge 50,000 to 100,000 employees, unless we divide the remaining work of the government amongst the whole of its employees just as has been done in industry. I know of nothing more inhuman in the present situation than for the government to add to the pool of unemployment and destitution when it is entirely unnecessary and can be provided against by the same measures which were undertaken by industry at the request of the government itself nearly three years ago.

. . . Less than $30,000,000 direct and definite savings were covered in the bill which finally passed the House. . . .

In the category of economies that can be made by consolidation, reorganization, and elimination of the less necessary bureaus, commissions, etc., the authority given in the measure passed by the House of Representatives is so restricted that it cannot be made effective until late in the next fiscal year. . . .

The imperative need of the nation today is a definite and conclusive program for balancing the budget. Uncertainty is disastrous. . . . I refuse to believe that the country is unable to reflect its will in legislation.

In conclusion, let me urge the national necessity for prompt and resolute and unified action keeping constantly in mind the larger aspects of the problem and that the necessity for these measures is born of a great national emergency. If such a program should be agreed to by the leaders and members of both Houses it would go far to restore business, employment, and agriculture alike. It would have a most reassuring effect on the country.

May 6, 1932: After a storm of attack from the Democratic side, the President issued a public statement supporting his message.[2]

[2] State Papers, Vol. II, p. 180.

The issue before the country is the re-establishment of confidence and speed toward recovery by ending these delays in balancing the budget through immediate passage of revenue measures and reduction of government expenditures. It is not a partisan issue. This was one of the most important steps of the non-partisan program for restoring stability proposed by me and patriotically accepted by the leaders of both political parties last December. Effective programs, projects, estimates, and possibilities for both economy and revenue have been presented and are known in every detail.

This is not a controversy between the President and Congress or its members. It is an issue of the people against delays and destructive legislation which impair the credit of the United States. It is also an issue between the people and the locust swarm of lobbyists who haunt the halls of Congress seeking selfish privilege for special groups and sections of the country, misleading members as to the real views of the people by showers of propaganda.

What is urgently required is immediate action upon and conclusion of these questions. This is a serious hour which demands that all elements of the government and the people rise with stern courage above partisanship to meet the needs of our national life.

On the other side, the following editorial comments are impressive:
The Baltimore Sun (Democratic):

Congress deserves what it has been given. It asked for all it has been given. Mr. Hoover's message is an unanswerable indictment. Bitter and savage as it is, in substance it is no more than a summary of the proceedings of Congress in the last two months. Any bare recital of those proceedings would inevitably give forth the bitter and savage tone of this presidential message. Congress has flagrantly and disgracefully deserted its own standards. . . . Congress has missed no opportunity to disembowel the policy of orthodox finance.

The New York Times:

A Democratic senator, Mr. Harrison, calls upon the President to bring order out of chaos. The budget is not balanced. Tax plans have gone astray. "If ever there was a time," he says, "when the President ought to speak out to his leaders in Congress, it is now." But the President has been speaking out to his leaders and appealing to his adversaries, vigorously and consistently since Congress convened five months ago. On the importance of Federal retrenchment and the necessity of balancing the budget he has spoken in no less than 21 messages, statements and addresses. . . . Responsibility for the chaos which now exists in Washington rests upon those members of Congress who have blocked the President at every turn and bolted their own party leadership.

May 7, 1932: The President began a series of conferences with members of Congress upon the possibilities of securing legislation which would grant the full powers originally asked for the Reconstruction Finance Corporation. His idea was that through those powers four major things could be accomplished which now were more demonstrable than when the idea of the Reconstruction Finance Corporation was first launched. First, the Corporation should make loans to public and semi-public institutions for construction of reproductive works such as toll bridges, waterworks, clearance of slums; second, to industry for modernization of plant and housing; third, to agriculture to create a real system of "production credits"; fourth, to the creation of emergency export credits. His view was that this form of recovery measure could be carried on without cost to the taxpayer by the temporary use of government credit, and would greatly aid agriculture and employment. In order that he might more fully make his case, he directed a survey be made by the departments to determine what volume of these activities could be stimulated.

The press of the country had supported the President warmly in his vigorous message to Congress on the 5th. He began today with the Republican leaders of both Houses a series of night conferences on the completion of the recovery program, especially for the immediate balancing of the budget.

May 10, 1932: The Senate in reaction to the President's conferences set up a special economy committee of its own and promised a *real* economy bill of $300,000,000.

May 11, 1932: The Democratic majority in the House and the coalition majority in the Senate passed a tariff bill which the President vetoed.

The President's discussion of the granting of the authority originally sought for the Reconstruction Finance Corporation had become a matter of public knowledge. The Democratic leaders in the Senate, seeing an opportunity to secure political advantage, hastily proposed some portions of the plan as a new idea of their own. Their proposal was cumbered with certain unworkable provisions. The President, in the hope of expediting matters, determined to take advantage of the situation at once by requesting Senator Robinson, Democratic Senate leader, to confer with him on the whole subject.

May 12, 1932: After his conference with Senator Robinson, of Arkansas, in which the Senator agreed to accept certain changes by the President in the legislation proposed, the President said:

At a conference this morning, the President and Senator Robinson canvassed the plan of Senator Robinson and the plans of the President to provide for relief and to stimulate and enlarge employment. Methods were considered for combining, simplifying and putting into concrete form the different proposals so as to secure united non-partisan and immediate action and not to delay completion of the work at this session.

The President expressed his high appreciation of Senator Robinson's action in opening the way for unified action and his confidence that a solution will be found. It was agreed that the prerequisite of any plan is the balancing of the budget.

Later in the day, after conferring with Republican leaders, the President thus expanded this statement: [3]

The program for united action discussed by the President with Senators Robinson and Watson is as follows:

1. The policy steadfastly adhered to up to the present time has been that responsibility for relief to distress belongs to private organizations, local communities, and the States. That fundamental policy is not to be changed. But since the fear has arisen that existing relief measures and resources may prove inadequate in certain localities and to insure against any possible breakdown in those localities it is proposed that authority be granted to the Reconstruction Finance Corporation to assist such States as may need it by underwriting only State bonds or by loaning directly to such States as may not be in position temporarily to sell securities in the market. The funds so obtained to be used for relief purposes and the total limited to $250,000,000 or $300,000,000.

The second part of the program contemplates providing the machinery whereby employment may be increased through restoring normal occupations rather than works of artificial character. Without entering the field of industrial or public expansion, there are a large number of economically sound and self-supporting projects of a constructive replacement character that would unquestionably be carried forward were it not for the present situation existing in the capital markets and the inadequate functioning of the credit machinery of the country. They exist both in the field of public bodies and of industry. There is no dearth of capital, and on the other hand there is a real demand for capital for productive purposes that have been held in abeyance. The problem is to make the existing capital available and to stimulate its use in constructive capital activities. This involves under existing conditions resort to special machinery which is adapted to furnish the necessary element of confidence.

It is proposed to use the instrumentality of the Reconstruction Finance Corporation which has a nation-wide organization by authorizing the corporation either to underwrite or make loans for income-producing and self-sustaining enterprises which will increase employment whether undertaken by public bodies or by private enterprises.

In order to safeguard the program beyond all question, it is proposed that there must be proper security for the loans, that as said projects must be income-producing, that borrowers must have sufficient confidence to furnish part of the capital, and that the project must contribute to early and substantial employment.

It is proposed to provide the necessary funds as they are required by

[3] State Papers, Vol. II, p. 187.

the sale of securities of the Reconstruction Corporation and its total borrowing powers to be increased up to $3,000,000,000. It is not proposed to issue government bonds. It is hoped that this further process of speeding up the economic machine will not involve any such sum. But in view of the early adjournment of Congress it is desirable to provide an ample margin.

It is necessary to sharply distinguish between the use of capital for the above purposes and its use for unproductive public works. This proposal represents a flow of funds into productive enterprises, which is not taking place today because of abnormal conditions. These being loans on security and being self-liquidating, in character, do not constitute a charge against the taxpayer or the public credit. The issue of bonds for public works, non-productive of revenue, is a direct charge either upon the taxpayer or upon the public credit, the interest on which and the ultimate redemption of which must be met from taxation.

An examination shows that to increase Federal Government construction work during the next year beyond the amounts already provided for would be to undertake works of largely artificial character far in advance of public return and would represent a wasteful use of capital and public credit.

May 13, 1932: The proposals for loans from the Reconstruction Finance Corporation for "income-producing works" having met some criticism which might delay action, the President stated at the press conference: [4]

Our job in the government is unity of action to do our part in an unceasing campaign to re-establish public confidence. That is fundamental to recovery. The imperative and immediate step is to balance the budget and I am sure the government will stay at this job until it is accomplished.

When our people recover from frozen confidence then our credit machinery will begin to function once more on a normal basis and there will be no need to exercise the emergency powers already vested in any of our governmental agencies or the further extensions we are proposing for the Reconstruction Corporation. If by unity of action these extensions of powers are kept within the limits I have proposed they do not affect the budget. They do not constitute a drain on the taxpayer. They constitute temporary mobilization of timid capital for positive and definite purpose of speeding the recovery of business, agriculture, and employment.

I have, however, no taste for any such emergency powers in the government. But we are fighting the economic consequences of over-liquidation and unjustified fear as to the future of the United States. The battle to set our economic machine in motion in this emergency takes new forms and requires new tactics from time to time. We used such emergency powers to win the war; we can use them to fight the depression, the misery and suffering from which are equally great.

[4] State Papers, Vol. II, p. 188.

May 13, 1932: A drive against increasing taxes and in favor of reducing government expenses as a method of balancing the budget was in motion, having been started by Democratic business men and bankers. To one of their letters addressed to the President, he again made the following reply:

MY DEAR MR.————:

I have your letter. The only trouble with your plan is that it goes beyond the limits of possibility in reduction of government expenses. Over $2,500,000,000 of our federal expenditure is in fixed or contractual obligations and your plan would leave only $500,00,000 with which to conduct the Army and Navy at one-half their present strength; it would necessitate turning our prisoners out of jails, a reduction in the fundamental services to public health and other activities that just simply cannot be abandoned.

I have hopes that if Congress will co-operate we can get within $250,000,000 of your ideal, but closer than that we cannot go and maintain a government.

Yours faithfully,

HERBERT HOOVER.

May 19, 1932: The President requested Secretary Mills to undertake the organization of banks and business men to secure the public use of the surplus credit now available from the open market operations of the Federal Reserve System. A committee for this purpose was announced today from New York City as the result of this effort. This committee was composed of Owen D. Young, chairman, Mortimer Buckner, Floyd L. Carlisle, Walter S. Gifford, Charles E. Mitchell, William C. Potter, Jackson E. Reynolds, Alfred P. Sloan, Jr., Walter C. Teagle, A. A. Tilney, Albert H. Wiggin, and Clarence M. Woolley.

May 20, 1932: The President made a statement to the press in support of the committee.

I am much gratified at the action taken in New York by which a joint committee has been appointed representing financial and industrial leaders of that city for the purpose, amongst other things, of securing that the expansion of credit facilities made available through the Federal Reserve Banks and the Reconstruction Finance Corporation shall be translated into industry, employment, and agriculture. I am in hopes that similar action may be taken in other Federal Reserve districts. It would seem desirable that the governors of the different Federal Reserve banks should proceed in a similar manner and as soon as the chairmen of such committees are known, I shall be glad to invite them to Washington in order that the whole program may be set up on a national basis.

The committees were formed and an organization was set up in Washington under the chairmanship of Henry M. Robinson. The conference later was called by the President in August.

May 21, 1932: Various drives had been launched over the country to encourage large issues of Federal bonds to promote relief through direct public works. The President sent a letter in reply to a query, again setting out his views. It was addressed to Herbert S. Crocker, of the American Society of Civil Engineers. The President said:[5]

. . . I have . . . the presentation . . . suggesting that the depression can be broken by a large issue of Federal Government bonds to finance a new program of huge expansion of "public works" construction, in addition to the already large programs now provided for in the current budgets. The same proposals have been made from other quarters, and have been given serious consideration during the past few days. . . .

1. The vice in that segment of the proposal made by your society and others for further expansion of "public works" is that they include public works of remote usefulness; they impose unbearable burdens upon the taxpayer; they unbalance the budget and demoralize government credit. A larger and far more effective relief to unemployment at this stage can be secured by increased aid to "income-producing works." I wish to emphasize this distinction between what . . . we may term "income-producing works" (also referred to as "self-liquidating works") on the one hand and non-productive "public works" on the other. By "income-producing works" I mean such projects of States, counties and other subdivisions as waterworks, toll bridges, toll tunnels, docks and any other such activities which charge for their service and whose earning capacity provides a return upon the investment. With the return of normal times, the bonds of such official bodies based upon such projects can be disposed of to the investing public and thus make the intervention of the Reconstruction Corporation purely an emergency activity. I include in this class aid to established industry where it would sustain and increase employment with the safeguard that loans for these purposes should be made on sound security and the proprietors of such industries should provide a portion of the capital. Non-productive "public works" in the sense of the term here used include public buildings, highways, streets, river and harbor improvement, military and navy construction, etc., which bring no direct income and comparatively little relief to unemployment.

2. I can perhaps make this distinction clear by citing the example of the recent action of the Reconstruction Finance Corporation in the matter of the Pennsylvania Railroad Company on one hand, and the recent bill passed by the House of Representatives for increased road building on the other. The railroad company applied to the Reconstruction Corporation for a loan of $55,000,000 to help finance a fund of over $68,000,000 needed to electrify certain of its lines. By so doing it would employ directly and indirectly for one year more than 28,000 men distributed over

[5] State Papers, Vol. II, p. 189.

twenty different States. An arrangement was concluded by which the Reconstruction Corporation undertook to stand behind the plan to the extent of $27,000,000, the railway company finding the balance. This $27,000,000 is to be loaned on sound securities and will be returned, capital and interest, to the Corporation. The Reconstruction Corporation is acting as agent to make available otherwise timid capital for the Pennsylvania Railroad in providing employment. There is no charge upon the taxpayer. On the other hand the proposal of the House of Representatives is to spend $132,000,000 for subsidies to the States for construction of highways. This would be a direct charge on the taxpayer. The total number of men to be directly employed is estimated at 35,000 and indirectly 20,000 more. In other words, by this action we would give employment to only 55,000 men at the expense by the government of $132,000,000, which will never be recovered. In the one instance we recover the money advanced through the Reconstruction Corporation, we issue no government bonds, we have no charge on the taxpayer. In the other instance, we have not only a direct cost to the taxpayer but also a continuing maintenance charge, and furthermore, the highways in many sections have now been expanded beyond immediate public need.

3. These proposals of huge expansion of "public works" have a vital relation to balancing the Federal budget and to the stabilizing of national credit. The financing of "income-producing works" by the Reconstruction Corporation is an investment operation, requires no Congressional appropriation, does not unbalance the budget, is not a drain upon the Treasury, does not involve the direct issue of government bonds, does not involve added burdens upon the taxpayer either now or in the future. It is an emergency operation which will liquidate itself with the return of the investor to the money markets.

The proposal to build non-productive "public works" of the category I have described necessitates making increased appropriations by the Congress. These appropriations must be financed by immediate increased taxation or by the issuance of government bonds. Whatever the method employed, they are inescapably a burden upon the taxpayer. If such a course is adopted beyond the amounts already provided in the budget now before Congress for the next fiscal year, it will upset all possibility of balancing the budget; it will destroy confidence in government securities and make for the instability of the government which in result will deprive more people of employment than will be gained.

4. I have for many years advocated the speeding up of public works in times of depression as an aid to business and unemployment. That has been done upon a huge scale and is proceeding at as great a pace as fiscal stability will warrant. All branches of government—Federal, State, and municipal—have greatly expanded their "public works" and have now reached a stage where they have anticipated the need for many such works for a long time to come. Therefore, the new projects which might be undertaken are of ever more remote usefulness. From January, 1930, to July 1, 1932, the Federal Government will have expended $1,500,000,000 on "public works." The budget for the next fiscal year carries a further

$575,000,000 of such expenditures (compared with about $250,000,000 normal) and includes all the items I have felt are justified by sound engineering and sound finance. Thus by the end of next year the Federal Government will have expended over $2,000,000,000 on public works, which represents an increase over normal of perhaps $1,200,000,000. Thus we have largely anticipated the future and have rendered further expansion beyond our present program of very remote usefulness and certainly not justified for some time to come, even were there no fiscal difficulties. They represent building of a community beyond its necessities. We cannot thus squander ourselves into prosperity.

5. A still further and over-riding reason for not undertaking such programs of further expansions of Federal "public works" is evident if we examine the individual projects which might be undertaken from an engineering and economic point of view. The Federal "public works" now authorized by law cover works which it was intended to construct over a long term of years and embrace several projects which were not of immediate public usefulness. In any event, the total of such authorized projects still incomplete on the 1st of July will amount to perhaps $1,300,000,000. If we deduct from this at once the budgeted program for the next fiscal year—$575,000,000—we leave roughly $725,000,000 of such authorized works which would be open for action. If we examine these projects in detail, we find great deductions must be made from this sum. Construction of many projects physically requires years for completion such as naval vessels, buildings, canalization of rivers, etc., and therefore as an engineering necessity this sum could only be expended over four or five years; a portion of the projects not already started will require legal and technical preparation and therefore could not be brought to the point of employment of labor during the next year; a portion of these authorized projects are outside continental United States and do not contribute to the solution of our problem; a portion are in localities where there is little unemployment; a portion are in the District of Columbia where we already have a large increase in program for the next fiscal year and where no additional work could be justified. A portion are of remote utility and are not justified, such as extension of agricultural acreage at the present time. Deducting all these cases from the actual list of authorized Federal public works, it will be found that there is less than $100,000,000 (and this is doubtful) which could be expended during the next fiscal year beyond the program in the budget. That means the employment of say less than 40,000 men. Thus the whole of these grandiose contentions of possible expansion of Federal "public works" fall absolutely to the ground for these reasons if there were no other.

If it is contemplated that we legislate more authorization of new and unconsidered projects by Congress we shall find ourselves confronted by a logrolling process which will include dredging of mud creeks, building of unwarranted postoffices, unprofitable irrigation projects, duplicate highways and a score of other unjustifiable activities.

6. There is still another phase of this matter to which I would like to call attention. Employment in "public works" is largely transitory. It does

not have a follow-up of continued employment as is the case with "income-producing works." But of even more importance than this, the program I have proposed gives people employment in all parts of the country in their normal jobs under normal conditions at the normal place of abode, tends to re-establish normal processes in business and industry and will do so on a much larger scale than the projects proposed in the so-called "public works" program.

7. To sum up. It is generally agreed that the balancing of the Federal budget and unimpaired national credit is indispensable to the restoration of confidence and to the very start of economic recovery. The administration and Congress have pledged themselves to this end. A "public works" program such as is suggested by your committee and by others, through the issuance of Federal bonds creates at once an enormous further deficit.

What is needed is the return of confidence and a capital market through which credit will flow in the thousand rills with its result of employment and increased prices. That confidence will be only destroyed by action in these directions. These channels will continue clogged by fears if we continue attempts to issue large amounts of government bonds for purposes of non-productive works.

Such a program as these huge Federal loans for "public works" is a fearful price to pay in putting a few thousand men temporarily at work and dismissing many more thousands from their present employment. . . .

It will serve no good purpose and will fool no one to try to cover appearances by resorting to a so-called "extraordinary budget." That device is well known. It brought the governments of certain foreign countries to the brink of financial disaster. It means a breach of faith to holders of all government securities, an unsound financial program, and a severe blow to returning confidence and further contraction of economic activities in the country. . . .

The prophetic character of the above statement is remarkable.

May 24, 1932: The President authorized Secretary of State Stimson to open conversations with Premier MacDonald of Great Britain upon the subject of summoning an international monetary and economic conference. The purpose of this was to be stabilization of currencies, exchanges, monetary standards, and the removal of trade interferences. The financial and currency collapse in the world, beginning with the German crisis a year before, gradually was being transformed into an actual trade war between nations in which depreciated currencies, quotas, embargoes, and emergency tariffs were the weapons. The results everywhere were seen in the gradual paralysis of exports and the constant fall in commodity prices. The creditor-debtor relationships both in the domestic and the international fields were becoming intolerable. The whole economic fabric again was endangered. The President last October had discussed with Premier

Laval the question of a conference but it then was considered too early to launch a proposal for a joint discussion of the subject with any hope of success, as Great Britain probably would not be prepared for any conclusions as to her currency base.

Secretary Stimson, while in Europe in April, had some discussions of the subject with Premier MacDonald and with the French, but reached no final conclusions. On May 13th, the British Ambassador asked if we had any views upon the subject. It apparently was the idea of the British to attach such a project to the forthcoming Lausanne Conference which was called for a consideration of German reparations. The President did not believe anything could be accomplished if the two subjects were mixed. He concluded now that the time had arrived when genuine and determined action should be taken. If the British were in a receptive mood, we should move to arrange an independent world conference and to get the British to call it.

May 25, 1932: The publishers of a number of leading papers, meeting in Washington, sought an interview with the President. The President spent four hours in continuous discussion of the general situation with them.

Secretary Stimson called Premier MacDonald on the trans-Atlantic telephone and presented to him the President's views: The time now was favorable for calling an economic conference. It should be separate from German reparations questions. It was urgent to give the world some encouragement in a fast deteriorating situation. Since the British were off the gold standard, it would be much more desirable that they should call the conference than we, who had a stable currency and no import quotas. The conference should not be merely a meeting of experts, but Premier MacDonald personally should head it and it should be constituted of the ablest men of each nation. Mr. MacDonald approved. Ambassador Mellon now was requested to place these views formally before the British Government.

May 27, 1932: There were introduced into the House of Representatives bills which were clearly presented for the purpose of making political capital and jeopardizing the proposals of the President. He responded with a clear statement to the public through the press conference.[6]

The urgent question today is the prompt balancing of the budget. When that is accomplished I propose to support adequate measures for relief of distress and unemployment. In the meantime, it is essential that there should be an understanding of the character of the draft bill made public yesterday in the House of Representatives for this purpose. That

[6] State Papers, Vol. II, p. 195.

draft bill supports some proposals we have already made in aid to unemployment through the use of the Reconstruction Finance Corporation to make loans for projects which have been in abeyance and which proposal makes no drain on the taxpayer. But in addition it proposes to expend about $900,000,000 for Federal public works.

I believe the American people will grasp the economic fact that such action would require appropriations to be made to the Federal departments, thus creating a deficit in the budget that could only be met with more taxes and more Federal bond issues. That makes balancing of the budget hopeless. The country also understands that an unbalanced budget means the loss of confidence of our own people and of other nations in the credit and stability of the government and that the consequences are national demoralization and the loss of ten times as many jobs as would be created by this program even if it could be physically put into action.

An examination of only one group of these proposals—that is, proposed authorizations for new postoffices—shows a list of about 2,300 such buildings, at a total cost of about $150,000,000. The Post Office Department informs me that the interest and upkeep of these buildings would amount to $14,000,000 per annum, whereas the upkeep and rent of buildings at present in use amounts to less than $3,000,000. Many of the other groups in this bill will no more stand the light of day than this example.

A total of over 3,500 projects of various kinds are proposed in this bill, scattered into every quarter of the United States. Many of these projects have heretofore been discredited by Congress because of useless extravagance involved. Many were originally authorized as justified only in the long distant future. I do not believe that twenty per cent could be brought to the stage of employment for a year. I am advised by the engineers that the amount of labor required to complete a group of $400,000,000 of these works would amount to only 100,000 men for one year, because they are in large degree mechanical jobs.

This is not unemployment relief. It is the most gigantic pork barrel ever proposed to the American Congress. It is an unexampled raid on the public treasury.

Detailed lists of all these projects have been broadcast to every part of the country during the past twenty-four hours, to the cities, towns, villages and sections who would receive a portion of this pork barrel. It is apparently expected that the cupidity of these towns and sections will demand that their congressmen and senators vote for this bill or threaten to penalize them if they fail to join in this squandering of money.

I just do not believe that such lack of intelligence or cupidity exists amongst the people of our United States. . . . Our nation was not founded on the pork barrel, and it has not become great by political logrolling. I hope that those many members of Congress of both parties who I know will oppose this bill will receive the definite support of the people in their districts in resisting it.

May 30, 1932: The situation again was approaching a panic character. The hopefulness of security inspired by the Reconstruction Finance Corporation and by measures for the protection of the gold standard had been dissipated by the total failure of Congress to take the next step in the recovery program and balance the budget. Six months now had passed since the opening of Congress. No real measures for economy or for new revenue had been enacted. Other important recovery measures had been delayed or left untouched. The introduction of other measures, such as bills for inflation, tariff and "pork barrel" had contributed much to the discouragement. A new flight of capital began and a new period of gold drafts by foreign nations. While the number of bank failures had been less than the number of closed banks re-opened, yet the hoarding of currency again had returned. The prices of wheat and cotton were falling. The prices of industrial stocks had dropped over fifty per cent from March. The dollar went to a seven and one-half per cent discount in Paris. The foreign press considered it was but a matter of days until we should be compelled to abandon the gold standard.

May 31, 1932: The President determined to address the Senate in person in the hope of saving the situation. Omitting the detailed discussion, the President in part said:[7]

An emergency has developed in the last few days which it is my duty to lay before the Senate.

The continued downward movement in the economic life of the country has been particularly accelerated during the past few days and it relates in part definitely to the financial program of the government. There can be no doubt that superimposed upon other causes the long-continued delays in the passage of legislation providing for such reduction in expenses and such addition to revenues as would balance the budget, together with proposals of projects which would greatly increase governmental expenditures, have given rise to doubt and anxiety as to the ability of our government to meet its responsibilities. These fears and doubts have been foolishly exaggerated in foreign countries. They know from bitter experience that the course of unbalanced budgets is the road of ruin. They do not realize that slow as our processes may be we are determined and have the resources to place the finances of the United States on an unassailable basis.

The immediate result has been to create an entirely unjustified run upon the American dollar from foreign countries and within the past few days, despite our national wealth and resources and our unparalleled gold reserves, our dollar stands at a serious discount in the markets of the world for the first time in half a century. This can be and must be immediately corrected or the reaction upon our economic situation will be such

[7] State Papers, Vol. II, p. 197.

as to cause great losses to our people and will still further retard recovery. Nor is the confusion in public mind and the rising feeling of doubt and fear confined to foreign countries. It reflects itself directly in diminished economic activity and increased unemployment within our own borders and among our own citizens. There is thus further stress upon already diminished and strained economic life of the country.

No one has a more sympathetic realization than I of the difficulties and complexities of the problem with which the Congress is confronted. . . . The time has come when we must all make sacrifice of some parts of our particular views and bring these dangers and degenerations to halt by expeditious action. . . .

We have three major duties in legislation in order to accomplish our fundamental purposes.

1. Drastic reduction of expenditures.
2. Passage of adequate revenue legislation, the combination of which with reductions will unquestionably beyond all manner of doubt declare to the world the balancing of the Federal budget and the stabilizing of the American dollar.
3. Passage of adequate relief legislation to assure the country against distress and to aid in employment pending the next session of Congress.

It is essential that when we ask our citizens to undertake the burdens of increased taxation we must give to them evidence of reduction of every expenditure not absolutely vital to the immediate conduct of the government. . . .

. . . Non-partisan effort . . . in the House . . . largely failed. . . .

In the matter of tax legislation, we must face the plain and unpalatable fact that due to the degeneration in the economic situation during the past month the estimates of fertility of taxes which have been made from time to time based upon the then current prospects of business must be readjusted to take account of the decreasing business activity and shrinking values. . . .

I recognize the complaint that estimates of the taxes required and reductions of expenses needed have been repeatedly increased, but on the other hand it should be borne in mind that if tax and economy legislation recommended from time to time since last December had been promptly enacted there would have been less degeneration and stagnation in the country. But it is unprofitable to argue any such questions. We must face the situation as it exists today. . . .

Our third problem is that of relief. The sharp degeneration has its many reflexes in distress and hardship upon our people. I hold that the maintenance of the sense of individual and personal responsibility of men to their neighbors and the proper separation of functions of the Federal and local governments requires the maintenance of the fundamental principle that the obligation of distress rests upon the individuals, upon the communities and upon the States. In order, however, that there may be no failure on the part of any State to meet its obligation in this direction I have, after consultation with some of the party leaders on both sides, favored authorization to the Reconstruction Finance Corporation to loan up to $300,000,000 to State governments where they are unable to finance themselves in provision of relief to distress. Such loans should be made by purchase of State bonds by the corporation, but where States are unable to issue bonds then loans should be made upon application of State authorities, and if they are not regularized by the issuance of bonds within a period of twelve to eighteen months they should become a charge upon the Federal aid funds to which such States may be entitled.

In order to aid unemployment and to avoid wasteful expansion of public works I have favored an authority to the Reconstruction Corporation to increase its issues of its securities to the maximum of $3,000,000,000 in order that it may extend its services both in aid to employment and agriculture on a wide scale. . . .

I have not been able to favor the expansion of public works beyond the program already proposed in the budget. . . . We have already forced every project for which we have justification. . . . We are indeed all desirous of serving our fellow citizens who are in difficulty and we must serve them in such a fashion that we do not increase the ranks of unemployed. . . . If we are to balance our budget and balance it in such fashion that our people and the world may know it is balanced, we cannot make further appropriations in any direction beyond the amounts now before the Congress. . . .

The natural wealth of this country is unimpaired and the inherent abilities of our people to meet their problems are being restrained by failure of the government to act. Time is of the essence. Every day's delay makes new wounds and extends them. I come before you in sympathy with the difficulties which the problem presents and in a sincere spirit of helpfulness. I ask of you to accept such a basis of practical adjustment essential to the welfare of our people. In your hands at this moment is the answer to the question whether democracy has the capacity to act speedily enough to save itself in emergency. The nation urgently needs unity. It needs solidarity before the world in demonstrating that America has the courage to look its difficulties in the face and the capacity and resolution to meet them.

The personal address of President Hoover to the Senate proved effective. That body remained in session all day and at midnight passed the revenue bill. During the day the President, in response to an inquiry from Senate leaders, urged them to support an increase of income tax rates up to fifty-five per cent in the upper brackets, being an increase from twenty-four per cent in the Coolidge base, and from forty per cent in the original Administration proposal in December. It also was recommended that estate taxes be increased to fifty-five per cent in the upper brackets.

The President authorized the Secretary of State to announce that the United States would support the British proposal for a world conference on monetary and trade questions with a view to raising world price levels. It was understood that the conference should assemble after the American elections in the fall, and that in the meantime experts from the different nations should meet and formulate programs and proposals for consideration. All questions of reparations and inter-governmental debts were to be excluded from the discussions of the conference. It was expected that solutions as to reparations would be reached by the forthcoming Lausanne Conference. The President considered that we must do our negotiating of foreign debt questions individually with the debtor nations.

June 1, 1932: Several senators attacked the President over the announcement of an international monetary conference. Apparently they had not carefully read the statement, and thought that it was the Lausanne Conference on German reparations which was under consideration. The administration again affirmed that we were not to be represented at the Lausanne Conference, as German reparations were solely a European question.

Senator Glass introduced a bill to expand the national bank currency by one billion dollars. While technically the bill was inflationary yet the Senator's purpose apparently was to head off the fiat money expansionists. The bill was safeguarded, for it contained many references to conditioning clauses in former monetary legislation. In his familiarity with the past legislation on this subject, Senator Glass was an expert. The country had ample currency. Later, on motion of Senator Borah, the proposal was offered as an amendment to the Federal Home Loan Bank Bill. The amendment subsequently passed (July 12th) over the President's protest. But the limitations introduced by Senator Glass resulted in less than $200,000,000 ever being issued.

June 3, 1932: The Young committee in New York had organized a pool to support the bond market and, consequently, the assets of all public institutions. Certain interests, asked to join in this endeavor, made it a condition that President Hoover should agree to take no action in respect to short selling in the stock market. The President informed the Federal official who brought him this report that he declined to be under any such restraints.

June 5, 1932: The President, in conference at the Rapidan Camp with the directors of the Reconstruction Finance Corporation and others, settled the plans for obtaining a legislative grant of the full powers for the Corporation originally recommended by him the preceding December. The President issued a statement thereon:[8]

[8] State Papers, Vol. II, p. 203.

The following are the conclusions of the Rapidan conference between President Hoover and the directors, Governor Meyer, General Dawes, Messrs. Jones, Couch, McCarthy, Bestor, and Ballantine, of the Reconstruction Finance Corporation. . . . Of nearly 3,000 borrowing banks more than seventy per cent are located in towns of 5,000 in population or less; while eighty-four per cent are located in towns of 25,000 in population or less; . . . only 4.5 per cent of money loaned to banks has gone to institutions in cities of over one million in population . . . banks have been able to meet the demands of their depositors and to minimize the necessity of forced collections, foreclosures and sales of securities and have thus contributed to protect community values. One hundred and twenty-five closed banks have either been re-opened or their depositors paid out. And bank failures which amounted to nearly 100 a week when the Corporation began are now down to about the casualties of normal times . . . over ten million individual depositors and borrowers have been benefited. . . . Over 250 building and loan associations have borrowed from the Corporation to make their routine payments to their depositors and participants to avoid the foreclosures of mortgages . . . benefits to hundreds of thousands of individuals. . . .

In the agricultural field the Corporation has . . . placed $68,000,000 of the Federal Intermediate Credit Bank debentures . . . which sums are loaned directly to farmers . . . to agricultural, market and livestock finance corporations . . . enabled loans upon livestock . . . loans to about 45,000 farmers for seed purposes . . . one million individual farmers have been directly or indirectly helped . . . approximately $170,000,000 authorized loans to railroads . . . repayment of loans has begun . . . $30,000,000 repaid.

The conference conclusions as to immediate policies necessary to speed economic recovery embrace four principal items affecting the Reconstruction Finance Corporation.

1. In order . . . to stimulate employment and to stiffen the whole agricultural situation, to extend the authority . . . to issue $3,000,000,000 . . . (a) to buy bonds from political subdivisions or public bodies or corporations so as to start construction of income-producing or self-liquidating projects which will increase employment; (b) to make loans upon security of agricultural commodities . . . and thus by stabilizing their loan value at once to steady their price levels; (c) to make loans to the Federal Farm Board to enable extension of loans to farm co-operatives and loans for export of agricultural commodities to quarters unable otherwise to purchase them; (d) the authority to loan up to 300 million dollars to such States as are unable to finance themselves for distress. . . .

2. Creating the system of Home Loan Discount Banks . . . these institutions would protect great numbers of homes from foreclosure [and] stimulate construction.

3. Joint committee of industry and finance . . . in each district . . . application of the credit facilities now available . . . co-ordinated with the work of the Reconstruction Corporation.

4. That government expenditures must be held . . . within the tax

income . . . no programs of expenditures should be undertaken which cannot be paid for from current tax incomes. . . .

June 6, 1932: The President signed the revenue bill, stating: [9]

The willingness of our people to accept this added burden in these times in order impregnably to establish the credit of the Federal Government is a great tribute to their wisdom and courage. While many of the taxes are not as I desired, the bill will effect the great major purpose of assurance to the country and the world of the determination of the American people to maintain their finances and their currency on a sound basis.

General Dawes resigned from the Reconstruction Finance Corporation. His reason was the difficulties into which the Central Republic Bank and Trust Co. in Chicago had fallen. Although General Dawes had not been actively an officer of the bank for many years, he originally had organized it, and his genius had built it. He felt that he must go to its rescue.

June 7, 1932: The House of Representatives passed the Garner Bill appropriating $2,300,000,000 to be expended largely upon "pork-barrel" projects and loans to individuals.

June 8, 1932: The Senate passed the Omnibus Economy Bill, having trimmed it from the $300,000,000 originally proposed by the President down to $134,000,000, but it included the President's plan for a five-day week for Federal employees which, while reducing their pay 8¼ per cent, avoided the discharge of over 50,000 employees.

June 10, 1932: A committee of business men addressed the President with a publicized request that he reconstitute the Council of National Defense. He stated to the press:

The resurrection of the old Council of National Defense is being advocated . . . the Council of National Defense is a statutory body comprised of five members of the Cabinet and an advisory body comprised of civilians. The duties . . . are absolutely war duties. . . . The old advisory body . . . recently [was] canvassed to see what its opinion would be on the subject. Several of the members have written . . . that they would not serve on such a body . . . they do not believe anything could be accomplished by it . . . we already have a Cabinet in which there are eminent representatives of agriculture and labor and finance and industry . . . the Reconstruction Corporation with seven directors who represent directly industry and finance and agriculture . . . the Federal Reserve Board, which represents finance and industry and agriculture

[9] State Papers, Vol. II, p. 206.

... the Federal Farm Board which represents seven different branches of agriculture ... the Farm Loan Board with representatives of both agriculture and finance; the President's Organization for Unemployment Relief which is an advisory body of one hundred leading citizens of the United States ... [the] recently formed joint committee of industry and finance in leading centers to co-ordinate the credit facilities; and back of all these organizations we have the bureaus of the government with their mass of information and all of their expert advice; all of these bodies are co-operating closely. ... Comprised of men of both political parties ... they constitute the most effective economic council that could be devised because they have behind them both authority and cooperation. The creation of any more commissions or committees is not needed. I am a strong exponent of the desirability of committees of leading men which are created for some specific purpose or some specific duty where there is some definite and positive goal that can be set and methods by which it can be arrived at.

June 11, 1932: The President called members of the House and Senate Economy Committees into conference, urging that the original $300,000,000 of economies be enacted.

June 15, 1932: The House passed the Patman Bonus Bill of $2,400,000,000 to be paid with fiat money. This inflation measure backed largely by Democratic votes gave a greater shock to the country than the proposed payment of the bonus, and even more stimulated the flight of capital. The President indicated that he would veto it should it pass the Senate.

The House passed the Federal Home Loan Bank Bill. It was somewhat different from the original draft and was substantially crippled in its effectiveness. This bill had been delayed for months.

The generally destructive action by Congress and the prospect of inflationary legislation had started again the flight of gold and of capital from the United States. In view of the renewed heavy withdrawals of gold during the past few days, the President secured from the Federal Reserve authorities the following information upon the gold situation. Since the British defaulted on gold in September, 1931, $1,130,000,000 of gold had been withdrawn from the United States by Europe and $377,000,000 more had been earmarked. Some of this had been replaced by imports from other parts of the world. France had withdrawn her entire holdings in the United States of $790,000,000. In all, through gold and exchange operations, over $3,000,000,000 of foreign short-term deposits had been withdrawn from the United States since the depression began. This sum represented the substratum of several times this amount of credit to American business and agriculture. Practically all gold and exchange which foreigners held in the United States had been withdrawn.

June 17, 1932: The House and Senate having sent the Economy Bill to conference, the President urged in a press conference statement:[10]

I am in hopes that the conferees . . . will find it possible to accept the so-called furlough plan for dealing with Federal employees. It is in reality the five-day week applied to the government. It will produce a larger saving in expenditure in Federal employment than any other plan which is likely to pass Congress. . . . It avoids discharges and enables some increase in the number of people employed by the government through the necessity of some substitutions. . . .

. . . It shows a willingness of the government itself to co-operate with the country in a movement for shortening the hours of labor with view to increasing the number of people employed. . . .

I am also in hopes that the emergency powers to the President . . . for immediate reorganization of government departments . . . will be restored by the conference. It is one of the most important avenues for economy in government that has been proposed. . . . Under the terms of the bill as it left the Senate no reorganization of any great consequence could be made effective until next March. The economies are needed now more than a year hence. The emergency powers left in the bill by the Senate reduced the bureaus and commissions which can be immediately dealt with to those expending only $25,000,000 a year. . . .

June 18, 1932: The Senate defeated the Patman Bonus Bill.

June 19, 1932: The President called further conferences of Republican and Democratic leaders in an effort to eliminate the pork-barrel features which had been attached to the bills providing for new powers to the Reconstruction Finance Corporation.

June 24, 1932: The Senate and House each passed the "relief" bill which embraced some of the President's ideas for granting of the originally proposed powers for the Reconstruction Finance Corporation. In addition it contained much that he considered to be against public interest. The President made an effort with the Senate and House conferees to secure a revision of the bill so that he could avoid a veto and delay. He stated:[11]

I am glad to see the adoption by the Senate and House of the principle of generous relief to unemployment. They have adopted the major provision for which I have been contending. . . . While these features in the Wagner and Garner bills are not in the form and are not as well safeguarded as they should be, they are in line with major objectives I have been advocating.

On the other hand, I intensely regret that these major provisions for relief of unemployment in both the Garner and the Wagner bills should have been made the vehicle for committing the Federal Treasury to the

[10] State Papers, Vol. II, p. 210.   [11] State Papers, Vol. II, p. 214.

expenditure of from $600,000,000 to $1,200,000,000 for non-productive public works because these provisions have the triple vice of being a charge on the taxpayer, of unbalancing the budget, and of providing only a small amount of employment and that to a large extent in localities where it is not needed.

Any study of many of these public works provisions will indicate plainly their pork-barrel characteristics. A large part of the expenditures proposed are wasteful in the present times. They impose tremendous future costs on the people for maintenance; they are not economically needed. Much of it represents a squandering of public money. Much of it is mechanized work. The report of the different technical bureaus of the government show that they would produce direct employment during the next year to an average of less than one hundred thousand men out of the many millions unemployed.

These expenditures cannot be recovered; they must be met by the taxpayer now or in the future. . . . We have worked for four months in heart-breaking struggle to bring about a balanced budget. We have imposed $1,100,000,000 in taxes upon the people; we have reduced government expenditure by $600,000,000 or $700,000,000 through which many government employees will have lost employment all in order that we might maintain the integrity of Federal credit. To start now to break down that credit and stability will result in the eventual unemployment of far more men than this comparatively few who are benefited. We cannot restore employment in the United States by these methods.

It would be far better to increase the authorizations to the Reconstruction Corporation to make loans for reproductive works which will be repaid by the additional amounts proposed for non-productive public works than to resort to these dangerous courses. It would also give more actual and continued employment.

There is another phase of the bill as passed which is disheartening. The $300,000,000 which I recommended should be loaned to such States as are unable to finance care of their own distress were to be made on proper loan terms, and the whole sum was to be available for application to the points of need. It has been transformed into a pork-barrel operation by being apportioned amongst all States according to population, irrespective of their needs. The amounts assignable to States which have major burdens of unemployment are insufficient for their purpose, and the great majority of States which have the ability and will to take care of their own are now invited to dip into the Federal Treasury.

It was unfortunate also that the provision for agricultural relief through the Reconstruction Corporation was omitted. The authority is needed to assure term credit for storage and carrying of these commodities so as to restore orderly marketing in the normal way. That proposal is the most fundamental of all in agricultural relief, and could stop the débâcle in agricultural prices. . . .

There is, however, a possibility of immediately rectifying these destructive factors and delinquencies of the bill. The Senate bill and the House bill differ totally in text. I am advised that it is within the power of the conferees to rewrite the bill perfecting the fine constructive provisions and eliminating these wholly destructive proposals. I earnestly hope that this may be done.

June 27, 1932 (Saturday). The President was at the Rapidan Camp for a week-end respite from Washington heat. Secretary Mills was on Long Island, Governor Meyer in upstate New York for the same purpose. For a similar reason the directors of the Reconstruction Finance Corporation were scattered. During the afternoon before (Friday) runs had started upon the principal banks in Chicago, which became even more intense on the next day (the 27th). Their origins were uncertain, but investigation indicated a systematic alarming telephone propaganda. During Saturday afternoon the President was advised that unless large Reconstruction Finance Corporation aid could be extended before Monday morning, the Central Republic Bank and Trust Company must suspend, and that the closing of other large banks would be inevitable. The President by telephone brought the various agencies of the government into touch with one another. An examination of the situation was undertaken by the government agencies. Fortunately, Directors Jones and McCarthy were in Chicago. They were attending the Democratic National Convention. They gave immediate attention to the situation, following it up with a recommendation to the Reconstruction Finance Corporation for advances which if granted would keep open the Dawes bank and a whole affiliated group of Illinois country banks. The Reconstruction Finance Corporation acted favorably on the recommendation and the advances were made which enabled all the banks to keep open. Otherwise a national panic would have been inevitable. The advances to the Dawes bank subsquently were much used against Mr. Hoover in the campaign by the Democrats, who entirely ignored the fact that one-half of the board of the Reconstruction Finance Corporation were Democrats of high standing in their party; that the loans were made upon their unqualified recommendation; and that these recommendations had the support of Melvin A. Traylor, whose name at that moment was being mentioned as a possible candidate for President in the Democratic National Convention.

June 30, 1932: The President today signed the Omnibus Economy Bill. It was a disappointment. The total savings were less than $130,000,000. The President had pointed out and recommended to Congress how $300,000,000 could be saved. The requested authority to consolidate certain government bureaus, departments and agencies had been partially granted but under limitations causing months of needless delay and ultimate defeat by Congress. In signing the measure he said: [12]

[12] State Papers, Vol. II, p. 216.

I have signed the Economy Bill with but limited satisfaction.

First. It falls far short of the economies proposed by the Cabinet and other executive officers of the government; many items of their proposals which were in turn recommended by committees on economy of the two Houses failed of passage. Also, the bill is so framed as to render abolition or consolidation of the most consequential commissions and bureaus impossible of consummation until some months after the next session of Congress.

Second. It imposes unnecessary hardship on government employees in minor matters of little consequence economically. Some of these hardships should be remedied at the next session of Congress. I believe we can administratively alleviate some of these difficulties and hardships. Every effort will be made to do so.

July 3, 1932: The receipts and expenditures of the government for the fiscal year ending June 30th, when cast into the form introduced by the Roosevelt Administration were as follows (the statutory retirement of the debt is excluded as the debt situation reflects in the total):

	1931	1932
General Expenditures	$2,724,293,879	$2,673,572,614
Emergency Expenditures:		
Agriculture	48,255,674	12,358,208
Public Works, other construction and relief items	574,874,107	670,299,878
Provision for loans to veterans on bonus certificates in excess of trust funds	112,000,000	88,000,000
Emergency loans to farm co-operatives, building and loan associations, banks, etc., through Farm Board, Farm Loan Banks, and R.F.C. after deducting collections	191,506,622	1,029,254,650
[Total Emergency Expenditures]	926,636,403	1,799,912,736
Grand Total	$3,650,930,282	$4,473,485,350
Total National Debt at end of period	$16,801,485,000	$19,487,449,766

The increase in National Debt of $2,685,000,000 was caused by a fall of over $2,000,000,000 in revenues below normal and the emergency expenditures of nearly $2,000,000,000 above normal. Of the debt increase, however, about one billion was in the form of recoverable loans.

July 5, 1932: The President signed the act which appropriated to the Red Cross a further 45,000,000 bushels of wheat, and 500,000 bales of cotton from the Farm Board stocks. The President had requested the appropriation.

July 5, 1932: In a special message to Congress, the President requested administrative funds for the President's Unemployment Relief Organization, of which Mr. Gifford was chairman. The Democratic leaders had struck the appropriation out of the departmental bills. The message was:[13]

> The second Deficiency Bill just passed omitted an appropriation for continuance of the activities of the President's Organization on Unemployment Relief. I urgently request that Congress make a special appropriation of $120,000, to continue this work over the next fiscal year.
> This organization, of which Mr. Walter S. Gifford is director, is comprised of leading men and women throughout every State in the Union and has served to establish and co-ordinate State and local volunteer effort in relief of distress throughout the nation. . . .
> . . . serving without pay or expense. It is non-partisan and representative of various economic and social groups. To function successfully it must have funds to employ a relatively small number of trained personnel, together with necessary office help.
> The appropriation requested for continuance of this organization is infinitesimal in its ratio to the large resources which are put at the command of those in distress.

Despite this message, the Democratic leaders refused to pass the appropriation.

Congress having agreed in conference to the very objectionable provisions in the Relief Bill, the President called a meeting at the White House of the Senate and House leaders, the conferees, and administrative officers. Senators Robinson, Wagner, Norbeck, Speaker Garner, Democratic Floor-leader Rainey, Republican Floor-leader Snell, Representatives Hawley and Treadway, Secretary Mills, Governor Meyer, and Director Jesse Jones of the Reconstruction Finance Corporation, were called. No agreement having been reached that night, the conference was adjourned until the next morning.

July 6, 1932: Further conferences failed to eliminate the objectionable provisions in the Relief Bill. The discussions largely were caused by the insistence of Speaker Garner that loans should be made to individuals or corporations or municipalities. He also insisted upon the dangerous provision that recipients of the Reconstruction Finance Corporation loans should be published. The President made a statement on the questions at issue. The points he urged were repeated in his veto message of July 11th.

July 8, 1932: The Lausanne Conference ended the payment of reparations from the former enemy powers, except for a payment of $714,-

[13] State Papers, Vol. II, p. 220.

000,000 in bonds. The Conference passed a resolution which urged the convocation of the World Economic Conference and outlined the monetary and trade subjects to be dealt with.

July 9, 1932: It now developed that the Lausanne settlement was conditional upon the consummation of a secret "gentleman's agreement" that the United States should cancel the war-debts. Although our government was not represented at Lausanne in any way, directly or indirectly, to avoid any possible misunderstanding the President directed Under Secretary Castle, in Secretary Stimson's absence,to issue the following statement:

The American Government is pleased that in reaching an agreement on the question of reparations, the nations assembled at Lausanne have made a great step forward in stabilization of the economic situation in Europe.

On the question of war debts to the United States by European Governments there is no change in the attitude of the American Government which was clearly expressed in the President's statement concerning the proposed moratorium on inter-governmental debts on June 20th of last year.

July 11, 1932: The President vetoed the Relief Bill, saying:[14]

I am returning herewith, without my approval, H.R. 12445, Emergency Relief and Construction Act of 1932.

On the 31st of May last I addressed the Senate recommending further definite and large-scale measures to aid in relief of distress and unemployment imposed upon us by the continued degeneration in the world economic situation. These proposals were made after discussion with leaders of both political parties in Congress and in endeavor to secure united non-partisan action. . . .

. . . I have expressed myself at various times upon the extreme undesirability of increasing expenditure on non-productive public works beyond the $500,000,000 of construction already in the budget. It is an ultimate burden upon the taxpayer. It unbalances the budget after all our efforts to attain that object. It does not accomplish the purpose in creating employment for which it is designed, as is shown by the reports of the technical heads of the bureaus concerned that the total annual direct employment under this program would be less than 100,000 out of the 8,000,000 unemployed. Strongly as I feel that this departs from sound public finance, and that it does not accomplish the purpose for which it is instituted, I am not prepared for this reason alone to withhold my assent to the bill provided there is a proper provision that . . . these works should not be initiated except on certificate of the Secretary of the

[14] State Papers, Vol. II, p. 228.

Treasury that the moneys necessary for such expenditures are available or can be obtained. . . .

This title is the major extension of the authority of the Reconstruction Finance Corporation. The creation of the Reconstruction Finance Corporation itself was warranted only as a temporary measure to safely pass a grave national emergency which would otherwise have plunged us into destructive panic in consequence of the financial collapse in Europe. Its purpose was to preserve the credit structure of the nation and thereby protect every individual in his employment, his farm, his bank deposits, his insurance policy, and his other savings, all of which are directly or indirectly in the safekeeping of the great fiduciary institutions. Its authority was limited practically to loans to institutions which are under Federal or State control or regulation and affected with public interest. These functions were and are in the interest of the whole people.

Our problem now is to further widen the activities of the Reconstruction Corporation in the field of employment and to further strengthen agriculture in such a practical fashion as will benefit the whole people, as will not damage any part of the people and confer no special privileges upon any of the people.

So far as those portions of the proposed extension of authority to the corporation provide authorization temporarily to finance self-liquidating works up to the sum of $1,500,000,000, it is in accord with my recommendations. The section dealing with agricultural relief does not provide for loans to sound institutions upon the security of agricultural products in order to assist in production and finance of normal holdings and stocks of those commodities and thus aid in the orderly marketing of agricultural products so sorely needed at the present time. Such action would contribute to improve price levels of farm products.

. . . my major objection to the measure, as now formulated, lies in the inclusion of an extraordinary extension of authority to the Reconstruction Corporation to make loans to "individuals, to trusts, estates, partnerships, corporations (public or quasi-public or private), to associations, joint-stock companies, States, political subdivisions of States, municipalities, or political subdivisions thereof." The following objections are directed to this particular provision:

1st. This expansion of authority of the Reconstruction Corporation would mean loans against security for any conceivable purpose on any conceivable security for anybody who wants money. It would place the government in private business in such fashion as to violate the very principle of public relations upon which we have builded our nation, and render insecure its very foundations. Such action would make the Reconstruction Corporation the greatest banking and money-lending institution of all history. It would constitute a gigantic centralization of banking and finance to which the American people have been properly opposed for the past one hundred years. The purpose of the expansion is no longer in the spirit of solving a great major emergency but to establish a privilege whether it serves a great national end or not.

2nd. One of the most serious objections is that under the provisions of this bill those amongst 16,000 municipalities and the different States that have failed courageously to meet their responsibilities and to balance their own budgets would dump their financial liabilities and problems upon the Federal Government. All proper and insuperable difficulties they may confront in providing relief for distress are fully and carefully met under other provisions in the bill.

3rd. The Board of Directors of the Reconstruction Corporation inform me unanimously that miscellaneous loans under this provision are totally impracticable and unworkable. It would be necessary to set up a huge bureaucracy, to establish branches in every county and town in the United States. The task of organization, of finding competent personnel, would not be a matter of months but of years. Hundreds of thousands of applications representing every diversity of business and interest in the country would immediately flood the Board, all of which must be passed upon by seven men. The directors would be dependent upon the ability and integrity of local committees and branch managers. Every political pressure would be assembled for particular persons. It would be within the power of these agencies to dictate the welfare of millions of people, to discriminate between competitive business at will, and to deal favor and disaster amongst them. If it be contended that these hundreds of thousands of miscellaneous loans will be used to increase employment, then an additional bureaucracy for espionage must follow up each case and assure that these funds be used for such purpose.

4th. The sole limitation under the bill is that loans shall be secured and that the borrowers shall not have been able to obtain loans from private institutions upon acceptable terms. This at once throws upon the corporation all the doubtful loans in the United States. It would result in every financial institution calling upon their customers whom they regard as less adequately secured to discharge their loans and to demand the money from the government through the Reconstruction Corporation. The organization would be constantly subjected to conspiracies and raids of predatory interests, individuals and private corporations. Huge losses and great scandals must inevitably result. It would mean the squandering of hundreds of millions of public funds to be ultimately borne by the taxpayer.

5th. The bill provides only the funds to the corporation which the Senate with reason deemed the minimum necessary to aid construction projects and to cover loans to the States in aid of distress. There is, therefore, no provision in the bill for any sum of money for the purpose of these miscellaneous loans. The corporation would thereby be charged with a duty impossible to carry out in practice with no additional funds with which to make loans unless the unemployment projects and the loans to the States are abandoned or seriously curtailed and the fundamental purpose of the legislation defeated.

6th. Under the new obligations upon the Reconstruction Corporation to finance the additional construction activities and loans to the States in addition to its present activities it will be necessary for the corporation to place over $3,000,000,000 of securities. It can place these securities only because the credit of the United States is pledged to secure these obligations. To sell any such vast amount of securities at a time like this is a difficult enough task, strong as is the credit of the United States, without having the credit of the government undermined by the character of use to which it is directed that these moneys should be applied. As long as obligations of the corporation are based on wholly sound securities for self-liquidating purposes, of which early repayment is assured, there is no burden upon the taxpayer. There is an assurance of a strengthening of the economic situation. But if the funds of the corporation are to be squandered by making loans for the purpose here referred to, it will be at once evident that the credit of the government is being misused and it is not too much to say that if such a measure should become law it further weakens the whole economic situation by threatening the credit of the United States Government with grave consequences of disaster to our people.

This proposal violates every sound principle of public finance and of government. Never before has so dangerous a suggestion been seriously made to our country. Never before has so much power for evil been placed at the unlimited discretion of seven individuals.

In view of the short time left to the Congress for consideration of this legislation and of the urgent need for sound relief measures, the necessity of which I have on several occasions urged upon the Congress, I recommend that a compromise should be reached upon terms suggested by members of both Houses and both parties, and that the Congress should not adjourn until this is accomplished. Such compromise proposal should embrace:

. . . provisions for loans to States in amount of $300,000,000 for the care of distress in States where needed.

. . . that such works shall not be initiated except on certificate of the Secretary of the Treasury. . . .

. . . provide not only loans for construction work of projects of self-liquidating character but also essential aids to agriculture.

That the corporation be authorized to increase its issues of capital by $1,800,000,000 for these purposes.

With the utmost seriousness I urge the Congress to enact a relief measure, but I cannot approve the measure before me, fraught as it is with possibilities of misfeasance and special privileges, so impracticable of administration, so dangerous to public credit and so damaging to our whole conception of governmental relations to the people as to bring far more distress than it will cure.

July 11, 1932: Neville Chamberlain, British Chancellor of the Exchequer, stated in the House of Commons that we had taken part in the conclusions of the Lausanne Conference. The President immediately asked of the State Department whether his instructions to keep our representatives from the conference had been violated. The President's desire was that we should be free to deal with our war debts separately with each nation on our own terms and without implications of connection with German reparations. He resented efforts to "gang up" against us.

July 12, 1932: Premier MacDonald of Great Britain stated that we had taken no part at Lausanne, directly or indirectly. Secretary Stimson made a public statement to that effect.

On motion of Senator Borah the Senate passed the $1,000,000,000 currency bill of Senator Glass as an amendment to the Federal Home Loan Bank Bill.

The Senate also had passed the amendment to the Federal Home Loan Bank Bill, introduced by Senator Couzens, which made basic changes in the legislation and which, if enacted into law, would have prevented the development of a permanent and sound home financing system. The President spent a large part of the day interviewing and telephoning senators, and prevailed against it. Senator Carey of Wyoming moved for a reconsideration, which was carried. The amendment was then rejected.

July 14, 1932: The British announced an agreement with France as to a "solid front" on war debts. In answer to an inquiry the President wrote the following letter to Senator Borah:[15]

MY DEAR MR. SENATOR:

I have your inquiry this morning, through Secretary Stimson, as to the effect on the United States of recent agreements in Europe.

Our people are, of course, gratified at the settlement of the strictly European problem of reparations or any of the other political or economic questions that have impeded European recovery. Such action, together with the real progress in disarmament, will contribute greatly to world stability.

I wish to make it absolutely clear, however, that the United States has not been consulted regarding any of the agreements reported by the press to have been concluded recently at Lausanne and that of course it is not a party to, nor in any way committed, to any such agreements.

While I do not assume it to be the purpose of any of these agreements to effect combined action of our debtors, if it shall be so interpreted then I do not propose that the American people shall be pressed into any line of action or that our policies shall be in any way influenced by such a combination either open or implied.

Yours faithfully,

HERBERT HOOVER.

This letter resulted in an immediate statement from Europe that the pact was not directed against us and did not affect debts to us.

The President announced the conclusion of a treaty with Canada, after years of negotiation, for the construction of a St. Lawrence seaway.

[15] State Papers, Vol. II, p. 235.

THE STRUGGLE TO BALANCE THE BUDGET

July 15, 1932: In reply to a question by Senator Steiwer of Oregon on the attitude of the Administration on foreclosure on farms by the Federal Land Banks, the President forwarded to him the instructions sent to the Federal Land Banks on October 6, 1931, and stated that those instructions had been sent at the President's own request "in a desire to have the banks function in a thoroughly humane and constructive way."

In the efforts to reduce appropriations the salaries of Federal officials and employees had been cut. Naturally, the pay of the officials whose compensation under the Constitution could not be diminished was not affected, but the President, although according to the Constitution his salary could "neither be increased nor diminished during the period for which he may have been elected," informed the Economy Committee that he would voluntarily remit back to the Treasury twenty per cent of his salary if Congress would pass the necessary legislation authorizing its acceptance by the Treasury. Such a provision was included in the 1932 Economy Act. In this way President Hoover cut his own salary twenty per cent. At or about the same time and upon the request of his Cabinet officers their salaries were reduced fifteen per cent, so that there could be no complaint of unfairness by other governmental officials, whose salaries had been cut by 8¼ per cent. As a matter of general interest the fact here may be mentioned that Mr. Hoover throughout his public career never used any of the salary paid him as a public official for his personal purposes, but always applied such money to public service or to charity.

July 16, 1932: Congress passed the Federal Home Loan Bank Bill. Although the House of Representatives twice had refused to accept it, the Borah inflation amendment was included. In no other way could the bill have been passed. The Controller of the Currency now informed the President that as it would work out, there would be little use made of the provision. The House and Senate did not come to an agreement on the Federal Home Loan Bank Bill until an hour or two before Congress adjourned the session *sine die*. However, the opposition to putting the legislation into effect still continued. The bill carried an authorization for an appropriation but no appropriation. An appropriation resolution had been introduced but it would have to go over, under the rules, until the next day unless unanimous consent were obtained. By the next day Congress would have been adjourned. When this appropriation resolution was presented Senator Couzens said he would insist on the rules being rigidly followed. But in an unguarded moment, Senators Moses and Jones offered the Federal Home Loan Bank appropriation as an amendment to one of the minor House bills that was awaiting Senate consideration. This amendment was carried and the appropriation was made and became immediately available.

Also the extension of powers to the Reconstruction Finance Corporation (the so-called Relief Bill) was passed, mainly in the form insisted upon by the President. The House bill had contained Speaker Garner's provisions for publication of the Reconstruction Finance Corporation loans. The President appealed to the Senate to eliminate this as it would cause runs upon banks, and affect adversely insurance companies, and building and loan associations. The Senate modified the provision slightly and both Democratic and Republican senators made a public statement that as amended it would necessitate only a confidential communication to the House and Senate.

Congress adjourned.

July 17, 1932: The President made the following statement as to the Relief Bill:[10]

I expect to sign the Relief Bill on Tuesday. . . .
Its three major features are:
First—Through provision of $300,000,000 of temporary loans by the Reconstruction Corporation to such States as are absolutely unable to finance the relief of distress, we have a solid back log of assurance that there need be no hunger and cold in the United States. These loans are to be based upon absolute need and evidence of financial exhaustion. I do not expect any State to resort to it except as a last extremity.

Second—Through the provision for $1,500,000,000 of loans by the Reconstruction Corporation for reproductive construction work of public character, on terms which will be repaid, we should ultimately be able to find employment for hundreds of thousands of people without drain on the taxpayer.

Third—Through the broadening of the powers of the Corporation in the character of loans it can make to assist agriculture, we should materially improve the position of the farmer.

The obnoxious features which had been injected into the legislation from time to time by members of the House of Representatives and had so long delayed action, have been eliminated. The $100,000,000 charity feature has been abandoned. The pork-barrel infection that the loans to the States for relief of distress should be based upon population instead of need has been eliminated and also the sum of $1,300,000,000 nonproductive public works ultimately payable by the taxpayer has been reduced to $322,000,000, of which about $210,000,000 are advances to the States for highways and most of the balance is not to be expended if the necessities of the Federal Treasury prevent it.

[10] State Papers, Vol. II, p. 235.

The provisions for the establishment of a gigantic centralized banking business have been removed.

The possible destructive effect upon credit institutions by the so-called publicity clause has been neutralized by the declaration of the Senate leaders of all parties that this provision is not to be retroactive and that the required monthly reports of future transactions are of confidential nature and must be so held by the Clerks of the Senate and House of Representatives unless otherwise ordered by the Congress when in session.

While there are some secondary features of the measure to which I have objection, they are not so great as to warrant refusal to approve the measure in the face of the great service that the major provisions will be to the nation. It is a strong step toward recovery.

This measure gave effect to the powers, originally asked for eight months before, to make loans for construction work to public and private agencies and to establish wider credit for agriculture.

But these were secondary features to which the President objected. While the bill established the agricultural credit banks which he desired, it did so without including the method by which the capital of these banks would be gradually absorbed and the banks themselves ultimately managed by their customers, thus retiring the government from private business. Also, the provisions for slum clearance were not as effective as he had wished.

The President approved the Federal Home Loan Bank Bill. His statement issued some days later said: [17]

I have today signed the Home Loan Bank Bill. This institution has been created on the general lines advocated by me in a statement to the press on November 13th last. . . . Its purpose is . . . a function for home owners somewhat similar to that performed in the commercial field by the Federal Reserve banks through their discount facilities.

There are to be eight to twelve such banks established in different parts of the country with a total capital of $125,000,000 to be initially subscribed by the Reconstruction Finance Corporation. Building and loan associations, savings banks, insurance companies, etc., are to be eligible for membership in the system. Member institutions are required to subscribe for stock of the Home Loan Banks and to absorb gradually the capital and they may borrow from the banks upon their notes to be secured by the collateral of sound home mortgages.

The Home Loan Banks are in turn to obtain the resources required by them through the issue of debentures and notes. These notes have back of them the obligation of the members, the mortgages pledged as securities of such obligations and the capital of the Home Loan Banks themselves. The debentures and notes thus have a triple security.

[17] State Papers, Vol. II, p. 238.

The creation of these institutions does not involve the government in business except in the initial work of the Reconstruction Corporation.

The purpose of the system is both to meet the present emergency and to build up home ownership on more favorable terms than exist today . . . to renew existing mortgages with resultant foreclosures and great hardships.

. . . Thus the institution should serve to immediately increase employment.

In the long view we need at all times to encourage home ownership and for such encouragement it must be possible for home owners to obtain long-term loans payable in installments. . . .

There was attached to the bill by the Congress a rider for the limited extension of the old national bank currency. I am advised by the Treasury that in the practical working of this provision it will not result in inflation. . . .

I do not, therefore, feel that the amendment is such as would warrant refusal to approve the measure which means so much to hundreds of thousands of home owners, is such a contribution to their relief; such a contribution to establishment of home ownership; and such an aid to immediate increase of employment.

The delay in this bill was simply to prevent its influence upon recovery until after the election. The persistence of the President had finally prevailed. Mortgages upon thousands of homes had been foreclosed which might have been saved if his suggestion had been promptly enacted into law. The President, however, was pleased that the foundations had been laid for an institution of great and lasting importance to the American people.

July 18, 1932: The work of this session of Congress now can be appraised.

The President had secured, of emergency legislation:

(1) The ratification of the moratorium.
(2) The Reconstruction Finance Corporation with resources up to $3,500,000,000 and the authority to (a) support banks, insurance companies, building and loan associations, railways; (b) to make large loans for productive works and for employment relief; (c) to establish the Agricultural Credit Banks; (d) to make loans to States which were unable to care for distress; (e) to create the great program of credit expansion which compensated for the withdrawals of gold and credit by foreigners.
(3) The expansion of the Federal Land Banks.

THE STRUGGLE TO BALANCE THE BUDGET

(4) The Glass-Steagall Bill expanding eligibility in the Federal Reserve System; the protecting of the gold standard; and the making flexible of the Reserve System.
(5) The Federal Home Loan Banks.
(6) An increase in Federal revenues by about $1,000,000,000.
(7) A reduction in expenditures of about $300,000,000 out of the $700,000,000 he had proposed.
(8) A restricted authority to reorganize government departments in the interest of economy.
(9) The appropriation of 85,000,000 bushels of wheat and 350,000 bales of cotton to the Red Cross for the relief of distress. This averaged about three barrels of flour and many yards of cotton cloth (less the cost of distribution) to every unemployed family.
(10) Various measures of continued public works employment, at the rate of $700,000,000 a year.

In addition there were also a number of constructive pieces of legislation not connected with the emergency. These are dealt with in another place. They embraced the limitations of the use of injunctions in labor disputes, the reorganization of procedure in juvenile cases in the Federal courts; and the making of kidnaping a Federal crime.

The President and his associates also prevented evils by bringing about the defeat of unsound legislative proposals.

(1) The bonus, including the Patman fiat money provisions;
(2) The "pork-barrel" bill
(3) The "universal loan" bill;
(4) The attempted raid on the Treasury under the guise of loans to States for relief;
(5) The Goldsborough credit inflation bill;
(6) The omnibus pension bill.

On the other side of the ledger, Congress had failed to provide:

(1) Banking reform;
(2) Authority to make loans to liquidate closed banks;
(3) Reform of the bankruptcy laws;
(4) Regulation of interstate transmission of electrical power;
(5) Revision of railway consolidation laws;

(6) Revision of the anti-trust laws with respect to natural resource industries;
(7) Authority to create a new World War Debt Commission to revise the war debts during the depression;
(8) An increase in revenues by about $400,000,000 and a reduction of expenditures by $300,000,000.

The adjournment of Congress coincided with the bottom of the depression. As soon as it became evident, early in this month of July, 1932, that the President would secure a large part of his major program and that he would be able to defeat the unsound measures, the whole country began to breathe easier.

The period from the middle of March, when the new crisis began to develop, until the middle of July, when Congress adjourned, had been one of continuous economic deterioration which was largely due to the influence of this Congress. From mid-March to mid-July, cotton had dropped by over sixteen per cent, wheat by twenty-five per cent, and industrial stocks had fallen in price by nearly fifty-four per cent. During approximately the same period, Europe had drawn from us $550,000,000 in gold and large amounts in exchange, which were partially made good from other parts of the world. Hoarding of currency again increased during this period by $500,000,000. But for the activities of the Reconstruction Finance Corporation, the expansion of Federal Reserve activities and the evidence of resolution in balancing the budget, conditions woud have been even more serious. We had been saved for a fifth time from acute crisis.

The first was caused by the stock market débâcle in the fall of 1929; the second by the Austrian and German banking difficulties beginning in June, 1931; the third by the departure of the British from the gold standard in September, 1931; the fourth by the flight from the dollar in February, 1932; and the fifth was brought about by the refusal of the Democratic Party in Congress in the spring of 1932 to co-operate with the administration in patriotic action.

The world was ready for a turn to the better. The forces of liquidation induced by the European crisis, both at home and abroad, in large part had exhausted themselves. The Lausanne Conference, the stiffening of the European economic situation by balanced budgets and strengthened currencies, the successful battle which proved the stability of the United States through holding to the gold standard, a free credit market, a resolution to balance the budget, the constructive measures of the President's recovery program—all began to have their effect. History now records that the Great Depression reached its low point in June and July, 1932. Recovery began all over the world and has continued in greater or less measure in other countries until today. And President Hoover was the world leader who had contributed most to this victory over chaos. The battle against the depression had been won.

CHAPTER XIII

THE THIRD STAGE OF THE DEPRESSION
A PERIOD OF ECONOMIC RECOVERY

JULY–NOVEMBER, 1932

IN late June and July, 1932, economic life definitely turned for the better the world over. Since that time recovery in most of the world has moved forward, but to a less degree in the United States, where a setback began with the change of policies at the election in November, 1932.

The Presidential campaign engrossed much of the President's attention during this period from July to November, but he gave first place to the administration of his office and to measures of recovery. We shall indicate the major activities in this direction and shall review the economic progress up to the election. The campaign addresses will be treated separately.

July 23, 1932: The President made the following announcement: [1]

I have been requested by Governor Winant of New Hampshire to receive the representatives of the recent conference in New England to discuss their conclusions upon the five-day week or shorter week hours as a means of wider distribution of employment. I welcome the opportunity to do so. In the meantime I have instructed the departments of Labor and Commerce immediately to resurvey the present situation and experience of the industries now using such plans.

At the White House conferences with employers and labor over two years ago, the general policy of spreading available work over the largest number was adopted and has been consistently followed by a great many industries. The same action was further spread by the President's Employment Committee Conference held last fall. We have, therefore, a large amount of actual experience. There are many different methods in different industries to spread work through shorter hours. Some of them have adopted the five-day, the four-day or three-day week; some have adopted six-hour shifts; some are staggering employment; some are using the furlough plan for salaried employees; some of them have suspended night shifts; some are using the flexible week, depending on the volume of business. In fact, many varieties of attaining the same end have now been developed, and I welcome the opportunity to review the situation and see what further co-ordinated steps can be taken.

The New England conference has made constructive suggestions, and

[1] State Papers, Vol. II, p. 241.

with our accumulated experience we should be in position for a new stage for action by further conference between employers and labor representatives.

July 26, 1932: For some months Chairman Meyer of the Reconstruction Finance Corporation had been working on double shift. Carrying on duties as governor of the Federal Reserve Board and chairman of the Reconstruction Finance Corporation proved to be too great a burden. He was compelled to relinquish his duties as chairman of the Corporation. The President announced today the appointment of former United States Senator Atlee Pomerene of Ohio as chairman of the Reconstruction Finance Corporation to fill the vacancy caused by his resignation. Senator Pomerene was a Democrat. The result of this appointment was to make the majority of that board Democratic. Aside from Senator Pomerene's wide experience, fine standing and excellent qualifications for the position, the President had an added reason for making the appointment. He was interested in the Reconstruction Finance Corporation attaining maximum results. The Presidential campaign was under way. His opponents would attack the Reconstruction Finance Corporation and charge it with playing politics and otherwise try to impair its usefulness before the eyes of the country. This would retard recovery, and recovery was at all times the objective of the President. He desired the country to know beyond any question that he was not playing politics with the miseries of the people.

July 28, 1932: The President announced the appointment of Charles A. Miller of Utica, New York, lawyer and president of the Utica Savings Bank, and one time president of the New York Savings Bank Association, to be president of the Reconstruction Finance Corporation to succeed General Dawes.

July 29, 1932: The President outlined further recovery moves: [2]

Some erroneous speculation has taken place with regard to conferences which have been held during the past two weeks in respect to organizing concerted action along the front of economic recovery. Such conferences have been held by myself, the Secretaries of the Treasury and of Commerce, the heads of the Reconstruction Corporation, Federal Reserve Board, and other government officials, together with representative groups in the country. The activities comprise:

1. The organization of the new powers granted the Reconstruction Finance Corporation in respect to self-liquidating works, for which $1,500,000,000 is available, is being co-ordinated with other government agencies. An engineer of standing will be delegated by the Army Engineer Corps as Chairman of the Board of outstanding engineers to advise the

[2] State Papers, Vol. II, p. 245.

Corporation . . . in stimulating employment by starting of the work and the placing of orders for material.

2. Stimulation of a movement for slum clearance and replacement under the Reconstruction Act is being given immediate examination, with view to early expansion of employment through such programs of modernization.

3. In order effectively to make adequate provision for livestock and feeder loans, I have requested Commissioner Bestor of the Farm Loan Board . . . the Secretary of Agriculture . . . and the Federal Farm Board . . . to place themselves at the disposal of the Reconstruction Corporation, so as to develop a co-ordinated program to solve these and other agricultural questions under the leadership of the Corporation.

4. The Reconstruction Corporation is devoting particular attention under its new powers to the possibilities of financing the movement of agricultural commodities into consumption, with view to stimulating demands through restoration of orderly marketing. We are discussing the possible supplement of such efforts by private agencies.

5. We have also taken up the subject of organized co-ordination of the wider expansion of credit facilities to business and industry through business, . . . and thus materially expand employment, which has been hampered by dislocation of the credit machinery.

6. Preliminary conferences have taken place with some of the railway leaders, with a view to their developing programs for increased repair and maintenance in co-operation with the agencies of the government for the purpose of expanding railway employment and for expansion in orders . . . which would also be immediately reflected in increased employment in the supply and steel industries.

7. I am proceeding as rapidly as possible with the selection of the directors of the Home Loan Bank Board, and have already under discussion methods . . . to secure the fullest effect in assistance to home owners under mortgage duress and expansion of home building in localities where there is a present shortage.

8. I have under discussion with various agencies the question of a movement to further spread existing employment through reduction of work hours.

9. Other avenues of co-operation between the government in aid to private and public agencies are under preliminary consideration.

When this program is more fully developed I shall confer with the "Business and Industrial" committees created in each Federal Reserve district and other groups . . . with view to establishing united and concerted action on a broad front throughout the country.

August 3, 1932: Robert P. Lamont resigned as Secretary of Commerce to re-enter private business. Secretary Lamont had conducted the affairs of the department on the high plane of national service upon which it had been placed by Mr. Hoover when he had occupied the same position. And besides their regular duties, Secretary Lamont and Assistant Secretary Julius Klein had performed yeoman service to the country during the depression, and had given able and devoted support and advice to the President in these trying times. Roy D. Chapin of Detroit was appointed Mr. Lamont's successor. His service was to be no less distinguished.

August 5, 1932: After a year of devoted and successful service, Walter S. Gifford resigned as director of the President's organization for Unemployment Relief, owing to the press of private business. The President promoted Mr. Gifford's chief assistant, Fred C. Croxton of Ohio, to head the organization and attached him to the Reconstruction Finance Corporation to administer the $300,000,000 distress fund. The President separated the function of co-ordinating the annual drive for private relief funds from the rest of the activities. Subsequently Newton D. Baker of Cleveland was to take over this latter job, with Mrs. Nicholas Brady heading the woman's committee. Mr. Baker had served as Secretary of War in the cabinet of President Wilson.

Mr. Gifford, in relinquishing his office, said that "to centralize the responsibility either for providing or expending the relief funds needed in the emergency, would demoralize the greatest voluntary decentralized organization ever assembled in peace times in this country."

August 6, 1932: The President announced the appointments to the Federal Home Loan Bank Board. They were: Franklin W. Fort, member of the Sixty-ninth, Seventieth, and Seventy-first Congresses, and president of the Lincoln National Bank of Newark, New Jersey; Nathan Adams, president of the First National Bank of Dallas, Texas; William E. Best, an attorney of Pittsburgh, Pennsylvania, who had been closely identified with building and loan associations; H. Morton Bodfish, executive manager, United States Building and Loan League, Chicago, Illinois, and Dr. John M. Gries of Ohio, economist. Had Congress promptly enacted this measure as requested, the Board could have functioned six months earlier, and a vast amount of misery and loss have been prevented.

August 12, 1932: The President arranged with the Reconstruction Finance Corporation, through one of its directors, Harvey Couch, for the appointment of a board of engineers to pass upon and facilitate loans for "self-liquidating works." The engineers selected by the President were Charles D. Marx of Palo Alto, California; Major-General Lytle Brown, chief of engineers, United States Army; John L. Harrington of Kansas City, Missouri; John F. Coleman of New Orleans, Louisiana, and John H. Gregory of Baltimore, Maryland. The wide engineering experience of Mr. Couch, his ability and industry, quickly sped these measures for the relief of unemployment.

Several great projects, in which the President long had been interested, were made possible by this legislation and were quickly set in motion by the Board of Engineers. Among them was the San Francisco Bay Bridge which, without the President's interest, would not have been possible for many years. Another great project was the aqueduct for bringing water from the Colorado River to Southern California—the final step in making use of the Colorado River Dam, a project which in itself owed much to his energies over a long period of years. Also other important projects in many parts of the country were started. These necessarily required a large amount of engineering preparation, and the actual relief of unemployment operated only in the administration of Mr. Hoover's successor.

August 14, 1932: President Hoover made the following press statement:[3]

I have called a national conference for August 26th of the Business and Industrial Committees of the twelve Federal Reserve districts for the purpose of organizing a concerted program of action along the whole economic front. The conference will deal with specific projects where definite accomplishments in business, agriculture, and employment can be attained, and will co-ordinate the mobilization of private and governmental instrumentalities to that end.

On July 29th I announced that preliminary conversations were in progress between responsible heads of the government instrumentalities and private groups in business and industry as to such a program, and that at a later time I would announce the date of a conference for a more definite development of these ideas. . . .

Among the subjects which will be considered and definitely formulated are:

A canvass of the means, methods, agencies and powers available in the country for general advancement; wider expansion of credit facilities to business and industry where consumption of goods is assured; co-ordination and expansion of livestock and agricultural credit facilities; co-ordination and expansion of financial facilities for the movement of commodities into consumption; expansion of programs for repairs and maintenance of the railways; and creation of organization for further spread of existing employment and expansion of employment.

A number of other possible questions such as the forthcoming world economic conference; protection of bondholders and mortgage renewals, co-ordination with trade groups and other subjects will be explored. It is expected to outline a basis for public, commercial and trade group co-operation in the execution of the purposes of the conference. . . .

August 25, 1932: Chairman Fort, of the Federal Home Loan Bank Board, reported that it had set up banks in twelve districts, with a minimum capital of five million dollars, and was now commencing to

[3] State Papers, Vol. II, p. 266.

operate in the release of hundreds of millions of dollars in frozen mortgages.

August 26, 1932: The newly created organization of the Business and Industrial Committees, under the chairmanship of Henry M. Robinson, was addressed by the President as follows:[4]

We have asked you, the members of the twelve Federal Reserve district Banking and Industrial Committees, to confer together and with the officials of the government agencies which are engaged in the problems of the depression. The purpose of the conference is to better organize private initiative and to co-ordinate it with governmental activities, so as to further aid in the progress of recovery of business, agriculture, and employment. . . . This is a meeting not to pass resolutions on economic questions but to give you the opportunity to organize for action. It is not proposed that you shall have authority from the Government, but that you should join in stimulation of the organized private initiative of America.

The reason for calling this conference at this particular moment is that we are convinced that we have overcome the major financial crisis—a crisis in severity unparalleled in the history of the world—and that with its relaxation confidence and hope have reappeared in the world. We are now able to take further steps in solution of the industrial and agricultural problems with which we are still confronted.

To have overcome this stupendous crisis is not alone a tribute to the courage of American people but a proof of our resources. . . .

It is not proposed to engage in artificialities. Nor is it proposed that you attempt to settle here in a day great economic problems of the future. It is simply proposed that you organize for action in the problems immediately before us. Great future problems will occur to you as they are in the minds of all of us. You will no doubt seek the co-operation of national groups of business, agriculture, and labor to put such questions on the road to investigation and consideration.

I should like to suggest to you some general directions of thought.

We have a powerful governmental program in action for aid to recovery formulated and organized upon a non-partisan basis. I am in hopes you will familiarize yourselves with its possibilities so as to co-ordinate your activities with it.

We need a better distribution of credit. . . .

In the furtherance of business recovery it is clearly necessary that there be co-ordination of effort in hastening the return of unemployed to employment in their natural industries. . . .

I do not need to remind you that the distressing problems of agriculture are not alone the problems of the farmer and the government. Its relief is one of the primary foundations of all progress in our country, and upon it does the progress of your business depend. It is as much your problem as it is the problem of the farmer, and co-operation of your committees with the leaders of agriculture and the agencies which affect their welfare cannot but be helpful. . . .

[4] State Papers, Vol. II, p. 268.

... Now as always recuperation of the country will be the result of the multitude of activities of our citizens and the sustained confidence of our people in its great future. The problem before this conference is not to settle great questions of the future, or to establish artificialities, but rather by practical steps today or organization contribute to make more effective the activities of every agency which can promote the recovery of the nation. ...

On the 31st of October Mr. Robinson was able to report that these committees were working in each district to aid local distressed mortgagees; to make capital available to small business; to encourage rehabilitation in industrial plants and sharing the work; and by personal contact to integrate the new Federal Home Loan Banking System with the local situation.

September 9, 1932: The President announced through the press: [5]

In order further to aid employment, I have instructed the various departments to undertake the speeding up of the Federal construction program by the amount of slightly less than $200,000,000, being the contingent appropriation in the 1932 Relief and Construction Act. The Secretary of the Treasury has notified me that the necessary funds can now be ... applied from this fund, the total Federal construction work during this present fiscal year of all kinds will exceed $750,000,000. ...

The expenditure on all classes of construction since the depression began, and up to next July will total about $2,300,000,000. This sum is more than double the normal pace and the enlarged work has, of course, been undertaken solely in aid of employment. ...

September 13, 1932: The President asked the new Business and Industrial Committees to arrange temporary livestock loans pending completion of the set-up of the new Agricultural Credit Banks which comprised a part of the enlarged Reconstruction Finance Corporation authority.

The President instructed the Director of the Budget to prepare executive orders containing a plan for a complete reorganization of the Federal Government, such plan to be submitted to Congress at the next session.

September 15, 1932: President Hoover presented Newton D. Baker as the head of "The Mobilization of Private Charities for Human Need," at an opening meeting of the organization, at the White House. The President stated: [6]

For the third time representatives of the great voluntary relief agencies of this country are here assembled to consider, with earnestness and sympathy, what measures may be undertaken for the relief of those in distress among our people.

[5] State Papers, Vol. II, p. 274.   [6] State Papers, Vol. II, p. 281.

To that great work, two years ago, Colonel Arthur Woods gave devoted effort. When Colonel Woods was reluctantly obliged to return to other commitments, Mr. Walter Gifford assumed command for the winter of 1932. Unable, because of other great responsibilities, to continue the work this year, Mr. Gifford leaves the chairmanship to another man of leadership and proved ability, Mr. Newton Baker.

You are here again to discuss ways and means, to estimate resources and needs. Our tasks are definite.

The first is to see that no man, woman or child shall go hungry or unsheltered through the approaching winter.

The second is to see that our great benevolent agencies for character building, for hospitalization, for care of children and all their vast number of agencies of voluntary solicitude for the less fortunate, are maintained in full strength.

The third is to maintain the bedrock principle of our liberties by the full mobilization of individual and local resources and responsibilities.

The fourth is that we may maintain the spiritual impulses in our people for generous giving and generous service—in the spirit that each is his brother's keeper. Personal feeling and personal responsibility of men to their neighbors is the soul of genuine good will; it is the essential foundation of modern society. A cold and distant charity which puts out its sympathy only through the tax collector, yields a very meager dole of unloving and perfunctory relief.

With each succeeding winter in this period of great distress our problem has become larger and more difficult. Yet the American people have responded to meet it. . . .

September 18, 1932: The President, in conference with Chairman Pomerene, arranged to set up a committee of leading architects to consider and forward plans for slum clearance, which the Reconstruction Finance Corporation now had authority to inaugurate by "self-liquidating" loans. Such a double service to public health and welfare, and to employment, was a part of the President's original reconstruction proposals of the year before, but it was delayed until the authority of the Corporation was expanded in July. The plan did not place the Federal Government in the housing business, but permitted it to make loans at low rates upon proper security and for sound enterprises.

September 20, 1932: The Insull utility interests in Chicago and other parts of the country had crashed. Federal investigation by postal inspectors and Department of Justice investigators was at once begun, to see whether or not irregularity by use of the mails, or by income tax evasion, was involved.

September 23, 1932: Henry I. Harriman, president of the United States Chamber of Commerce, called upon the President to urge that he pledge himself to support the Chamber's recommendations of December,

1931, to set up what subsequently became the NRA. The President, not having changed his point of view, again refused to accept it.

September 27, 1932: The President had conferred with leading railway presidents and labor representatives to urge them to postpone discussion of further wage cuts till the end of the present year. The current agreement was to expire on February 1st next. The President hoped that the general economic situation would be much clearer at that time, and more favorable for further negotiations.

September 28, 1932: In reply to an inquiry from Governor Dan W. Turner of Iowa on the farm mortgage question, the President said:[7]

> You will be glad to know that I have secured a preliminary discussion amongst eastern mortgage concerns and governmental agencies upon the question of farm mortgages. As a result, Mr. Henry M. Robinson, chairman of the Executive Committee of the Federal Reserve Banking and Industrial Committees, has arranged for a further meeting of members of those committees for the mid-west districts, together with representatives of mortgage agencies in Chicago. . . . In order that we may have full co-ordination of governmental agencies the Secretary of Agriculture and representatives of the Reconstruction Corporation and the Federal Farm Loan Banks will participate in these meetings with other mortgage agencies. I am very hopeful that constructive steps will follow from these conferences.

October 24, 1932: Complaints were frequently coming in from certain manufacturers and the workmen in their plants and their representatives, of increased importations of foreign-made goods due to the more recent devaluation of their currencies by certain foreign countries. The President gave the following instructions to the chairman of the Tariff Commission, Robert L. O'Brien:[8]

> In extension of my recent verbal instruction as to the necessity for investigation of certain tariff schedules due to depreciation of currencies in foreign countries, I enclose herewith a list furnished me by the Department of Commerce of industries and localities where there has been actual increase of unemployment, or alternatively where it is inevitable that it will increase from importations arising out of this cause unless they be halted. . . .
> . . . If it shall prove that the differences in cost of production between here and abroad in these industries have altered the basis of the tariff duties, I wish to receive recommendations of the Tariff Commission at the earliest possible moment.

[7] State Papers, Vol. II, p. 288.   [8] State Papers, Vol. II, p. 384.

October 28, 1932: President Green of the American Federation of Labor announced that 560,000 men had returned to work during September, a gain for the third consecutive month.

October 30, 1932: Under the able direction of Fred C. Croxton, the disposition of the Federal relief fund was organized. It provided for loans to the States in supplement to State and local resources for direct relief, but only such supplement as was shown upon Federal investigation to be actually needed, and also upon a showing that the States and local divisions themselves were providing a proper share of the burden. These funds were administered through the committees which had been established in 1930. The program was held to the President's conception of a non-political, decentralized administration under the control of leading citizens who volunteered in a national service.

The amounts allocated during President Hoover's Administration were as follows:

July, 1932	$ 3,000,000
August, 1932	13,931,669
September, 1932	18,523,502
October, 1932	22,594,762
November, 1932	18,484,823
December, 1932	35,958,117
January, 1933	49,435,416
February, 1933	48,187,271

These amounts covered the demonstrated need for efficient relief at a tense period of unemployment.

A review of the period from June to the November election shows that the movement upward from the bottom of the depression was evident in every part of the economic structure.

While in other leading commercial nations improvement was more or less general, conditions in the United States became worse, in spite of the fact that it was economically stronger and more resilient than any other country. The only satisfactory explanation for this situation is to be found in the results of the November election and the disastrous interim between the election and the inauguration of the new administration.

CHAPTER XIV

EXTRACTS FROM THE SPEECHES OF MR. HOOVER IN THE PRESIDENTIAL CAMPAIGN, 1932

PRESIDENT HOOVER took an active part in the campaign during the two months preceding the election. There is nothing one can add to his able discussion of the issues. In order to give a comprehensive view, in as limited space as may be possible, we have chosen certain paragraphs from President Hoover's speeches, which bear upon his emergency policies, and which show his uncanny foresight and anticipation of exactly what since has happened. They are arranged according to subject matter under the following headings:

1. Economic review of the period;
2. Summary of the measures adopted to meet the emergency;
3. Relief of distress;
4. Agricultural relief;
5. Responsibility for the depression;
6. Private foreign loans;
7. The Reconstruction Finance Corporation;
8. Balancing the budget;
9. The bonus;
10. War-debts;
11. Relief to depositors of closed banks;
12. Tinkering with the currency;
13. The turn in the depression;
14. A summary of the Democratic proposals.

I

ECONOMIC REVIEW OF THE PERIOD

In his acceptance address in Washington on August 11, 1932, the President briefly reviewed the economic history of the past three years:[1]

Before the storm broke we were steadily gaining in prosperity. Our wounds from the war were rapidly healing. Advances in science and invention had opened vast vistas of new progress. Being prosperous, we became optimistic—all of us. From optimism some of us went to over-expansion in anticipation of the future and from over-expansion to reckless speculation. In this soil poisoned by speculation grew those ugly weeds of waste, exploitation, and abuse of financial power. In this over-

[1] State Papers, Vol. II, p. 247.

production and speculative mania we marched with the rest of the world. Then three years ago came retribution by the inevitable world-wide slump in consumption of goods, in prices, and employment. At that juncture it was the normal penalty for a reckless boom such as we have witnessed a score of times in our history. Through such depressions we have always passed safely after a relatively short period of losses, of hardship and adjustment. We adopted policies in the government which were fitting to the situation. Gradually the country began to right itself. Eighteen months ago there was a solid basis for hope that recovery was in sight. . . .

Then there came on us a new calamity, a blow from abroad of such dangerous character as to strike at the very safety of the Republic. The countries of Europe proved unable to withstand the stress of the depression. . . .

New blows from decreasing world consumption of goods and from failing financial systems rained upon us. We are part of a world, the disturbance of whose remotest population affects our financial system, our employment, our markets, and prices of our farm products. Thus beginning eighteen months ago the world-wide storm rapidly grew to hurricane force and the greatest economic emergency of all history. Unexpected, unforeseen and violent shocks with every month brought new dangers and new emergencies. Fear and apprehension gripped the heart of our people in every village and city. . . .

Two courses were open. We might have done nothing. That would have been utter ruin. Instead, we met the situation with proposals to private business and the Congress of the most gigantic program of economic defense and counterattack ever evolved in the history of the Republic. We put it into action.

Our measures have repelled these attacks of fear and panic. We have maintained the financial integrity of our government. We have co-operated to restore and stabilize the situation abroad. As a nation we have paid every dollar demanded of us. We have used the credit of the government to aid and protect our institutions, public and private. We have provided methods and assurances that there shall be none to suffer from hunger and cold. We have instituted measures to assist farmers and home owners. . . . We have created vast agencies for employment. Above all, we have maintained the sanctity of the principles upon which this Republic has grown great. . . .

The function of the Federal Government is in these times to use its reserve powers and its strength for the protection of citizens and local governments by support to our institutions against forces beyond their control. It is not the function of the government to relieve individuals of their responsibilities to their neighbors, or to relieve private institutions of their responsibilities to the public, or of local government to the States, or of State governments to the Federal Government. In giving that protection and that aid the Federal Government must insist that all of them assert their responsibilities in full. It is vital that the programs of the government shall not compete with or replace any of them, but shall add to their initiative and strength. It is vital that by the use of public revenues and public credit in emergency the nation shall be strengthened and not weakened. . . .

. . . It does not follow, because our difficulties are stupendous, because there are some souls timorous enough to doubt the validity and effectiveness of our ideals and our system, that we must turn to a state-controlled or state-directed social or economic system in order to cure our troubles. That is not liberalism; it is tyranny. It is the regimentation of men under autocratic bureaucracy with all its extinction of liberty, of hope and of opportunity. Of course no man of understanding says that our system works perfectly. It does not. The human race is not perfect. Nevertheless, the movement of a true civilization is toward freedom rather than regimentation. This is our ideal.

Ofttimes the tendency of democracy in presence of national danger is to strike blindly, to listen to demagogues, and slogans, all of which would destroy and would not save. We have refused to be stampeded into such courses. . . .

Our emergency measures of the past three years form a definite strategy dominated in the background by these American principles and ideals, forming a continuous campaign waged against the forces of destruction on an ever-widening or constantly shifting front. . . .

We have not feared boldly to adopt unprecedented measures to meet the unprecedented violence of this storm. But because we have ever kept before us these eternal principles of our nation, the American Government in its ideals is the same as it was when the people gave the Presidency into my trust. We shall keep it so. We have resolutely rejected the temptation, under pressure of immediate events, to resort to those panaceas and short cuts which, even if temporarily successful, would ultimately undermine and weaken what has been slowly built and molded by experience and effort throughout these hundred and fifty years. . . .

No government in Washington has hitherto considered that it held so broad a responsibility for leadership in such times. Despite hardships, the devotion of our men and women to those in distress is demonstrated by the national averages of infant mortality, general mortality, and sickness, which are less today than in times of prosperity. For the first time in the history of depression, dividends, profits, and the cost of living have been reduced before wages have suffered. We have been more free from industrial conflicts through strikes and lockouts and all forms of social disorder than even in normal times. The nation is building the initiative of men toward new fields of social co-operation and endeavor.

2

SUMMARY OF MEASURES ADOPTED TO MEET THE EMERGENCY

In speaking at St. Paul on November 5, 1932, three days before the election, the President summarized the measures taken during the four years to combat the depression:[2]

[2] State Papers, Vol. II, p. 449.

... I have enumerated at various times ... the measures adopted ... to meet this emergency. ...

1. The first of our measures, which subsequently proved of great emergency service, was the revision of the tariff. By this act we gave protection to our agriculture, from a world demoralization which would have been far worse than anything we have suffered and we prevented unemployment to millions of workmen.

2. We have secured extension of authority to the Tariff Commission by which the adjustments can be made to correct inequities in the tariff, and to make changes to meet economic tides, thereby avoiding the national disturbance of general revision of the tariff with all its greed and logrolling. That authority becomes of vital importance today in the face of depreciated currencies abroad.

3. At the outset of the depression we brought about an understanding between employers and employees that wages should be maintained. They were maintained until the cost of living had decreased and the profits had practically vanished. They are now the highest real wages in the world.

With the concurrent agreement of labor leaders at that time to minimize strikes, we have had a degree of social stability hitherto unknown in the history of any depression in our country. ...

4. An agreement to a spread of work where employers were compelled to reduce production was brought about in order that none might be deprived of all their living and all might participate in the existing jobs and thus give real aid to millions of families.

5. We have mobilized throughout the country private charity and local and State support for the care of distress under which our women and men have given such devoted service that the health of our country has actually improved.

6. By the expansion of State, municipal, and private construction work as an aid to employment, and by the development of an enlarged program of Federal construction which has been maintained at the rate of $600,000,000 a year throughout the depression, we have given support to hundreds of thousands of families.

7. By the negotiation of the German moratorium and the standstill agreements upon external debts of that country we saved their people from a collapse that would have set a prairie afire and possibly have involved all civilization itself.

8. We created the National Credit Association by co-operation of the bankers of the country, with a capital of $500,000,000 which prevented the failure of a thousand banks with all the tragedies to their depositors and borrowers.

9. By drastic reduction in the ordinary operating expenses of the Federal Government, together with the increasing of the revenues in the year 1932, we contributed to balancing the Federal Budget, and thus held impregnable the credit of the United States.

10. We created the Reconstruction Finance Corporation originally, with $2,000,000,000, of resources, in order that, having maintained na-

tional credit we should thrust the full resources of public credit behind private credit of the country and thus re-establish and maintain private enterprise in an unassailable position that with this backing of the Federal credit, acting through existing institutions, we might protect depositors in savings banks, insurance policyholders, lenders and borrowers in building and loan associations; through banking institutions expand the funds available for loans to merchants, manufacturers, farmers, and marketing associations; that we should protect the railways from receiverships in order that in turn railway securities in the great fiduciary institutions such as insurance companies and savings banks might be protected and a score of other services performed.

11. In addition to strengthening the capital of the Federal Land Banks by $125,000,000, we have, through the Reconstruction Corporation, made large loans to mortgage associations for the same purpose, and lately we have organized all lending agencies into co-operative action to give the farmer who wants to make a fight for his home a chance to hold it from foreclosure.

12. We extended authorities under the Federal Reserve Act to protect beyond all question the gold standard of the United States and at the same time expand the credit in counter action to the strangulation due to hoarding and foreign withdrawals of gold.

13. We created the Home Loan Discount Banks with direct and indirect resources of several hundred millions also acting through existing institutions in such fashion as to mobilize the resources of building and loan associations and savings banks and other institutions, furnishing to them cheaper and longer-term capital, to give them the ability to save homes from foreclosure, to furnish credit to create new homes, and expand employment.

14. We secured further authorities to the Reconstruction Corporation to assist in the earlier liquidation of deposits in closed banks in order that we might relieve distress to millions of depositors. Through Democratic opposition we failed to secure authority from Congress to carry this on a scale the country so sorely needs.

15. We secured increased authorities to the Reconstruction Corporation to loan up to $300,000,000 to the States whose resources had been exhausted, to enable them to extend full relief to distress and to prevent any hunger and cold in the United States.

16. We increased the resources to the Reconstruction Corporation by a further $1,500,000,000 to reinforce the undertaking of great public works which otherwise would have to await finance, due to the stringency of credit. These works are of a character which by their own earnings will enable disposal of the repayment of these loans without charge upon the taxpayer.

17. We have erected a new system of agricultural credit banks with indirect resources of $300,000,000 to reinforce the work of the intermediate credit banks in the financing of production and livestock loans to farmers.

18. We have extended the authority to the Reconstruction Corpora-

tion to make loans for financing the normal movement of agricultural commodities to markets both at home and abroad.

19. We have systematically mobilized banking and industry and business with the co-operation of labor and agricultural leaders to attack the depression on every front. . . .

20. We have developed, together with European nations, a worldwide economic conference with view to relieving pressure upon us from foreign countries, to increase their stability to deal with silver, and to prevent recurrence of these calamities for the future.

21. We have given American leadership in development of drastic reductions of armament in order to reduce our own expenditures by $200,000,000 a year and to increase the financial stability of foreign nations and to relieve the world of fear and political friction.

These are a part of the great and effective weapons with which we have fought the battle that has saved the American people from disaster and chaos. They are still in action and advancing along the whole front to the restoration of recovery.

3
RELIEF OF DISTRESS

Cleveland, October 15, 1932.[3]

My first concern in dealing with the problems of these times, while fighting to save our people from chaos and to restore order in our economic life, has been to avert hunger or cold amongst those upon whom these blows have fallen with heartbreaking severity—that is the unemployed workers.

. . . the President's Organization for Unemployment Relief . . . [enlisted the] co-operation of every State, town and village . . . fearing that the resources of individuals of the local communities and States were being exhausted, I settled with the Congress an authority to be given to the Reconstruction Corporation to loan a total of $300,000,000 to those States whose needs might be found greater than the voluntary associations and local authorities could provide. . . . We have provided, in addition, large quantities of wheat and cotton for their aid. There should be no fear or apprehension at any deserving American fireside that starvation or cold will creep within their doors to menace families and loved ones over the forthcoming winter. . . .

With these three years of unceasing effort in relief and by the patriotic service of our citizens and local communities and public officials, the stimulus and mobilization that we have been able to give through the use of the Presidential office, we present to the world a record unparalleled in any other nation. That is a record expressed in technical terms yet interpretable in sheer human sympathy. That record is the information furnished to me constantly by the Surgeon General of the Public Health Service, which shows, down to this latest moment, that the adult mor-

[3] State Papers, Vol. II, p. 337.

tality and infant mortality are at the lowest rate on record, and the general health of the American people is at a higher level today than ever before in the history of our country. I know that there are exceptions and that there is suffering which always arises in communities where their organization is less efficient than it should be. Even so, no such record could be established if the nation's unemployed were starving and without shelter.

... I may reiterate that the only method by which we can stop suffering and unemployment is by returning people to their normal jobs in their normal homes, carrying on their normal functions of life. This can only be done by sound processes of protecting and stimulating the existing economic system which we have in action today.

Fort Wayne, October 5, 1932.[4]

I wish to take occasion of this meeting to say a word to you and to all the people of the great Midwest.

During my public life, I have believed that sportsmanship and statesmanship called for the elimination of harsh personalities between opponents. On this journey, however, I have received a multitude of reports as to the widespread personal misrepresentations which have been promulgated in the Midwest in the past few weeks. I regret that the character of these personalities necessitates a direct word from me.

I shall say now the only harsh word that I have uttered in public office. I hope it will be the last I shall have to say. When you are told that the President of the United States, who by the most sacred trust of our nation is the President of all the people, a man of your own blood and upbringing, has sat in the White House for the last three years of your misfortune without troubling to know your burdens, without heartaches over your miseries and casualties, without summoning every avenue of skillful assistance irrespective of party or view, without using every ounce of his strength and straining his every nerve to protect and help, without using every possible agency of democracy that would bring aid, without putting aside personal ambition and humbling his pride of opinion, if that would serve—then I say to you that such statements are deliberate, intolerable falsehoods.

4

Agricultural Relief

Des Moines, October 4, 1932:[5]

... That agriculture is prostrate needs no proof. You have saved and economized and worked to reduce costs, but with all this, yours is a story of distress and suffering.

What the farmer wants and needs is higher prices, and in the meantime to keep from being dispossessed from his farm, to have a fighting chance to keep his home. ... Every decent citizen wants to see the farmer

[4] State Papers, Vol. II, p. 319.   [5] State Papers, Vol. II, p. 308.

receive higher prices and wants to see him hold his home. Every citizen realizes that the general recovery of the country cannot be attained unless these things are secured to the farmer.

. . . I come to you with no economic patent medicine especially compounded for farmers. I refuse to offer counterfeit currency or false hopes. I will not make any pledge to you which I cannot fulfil.

As I have stated before, in the shifting battle against depression, we shall need to adopt new measures and new tactics as the battle moves on. The essential thing is that we should build soundly and solidly for the future.

Washington, August 11, 1932: [6]

. . . There is no relief to the farmer by extending government bureaucracy to control his production and thus curtail his liberties, nor by subsidies that bring only more bureaucracy and ultimate collapse. I shall oppose them.

Des Moines, October 4, 1932:

I wish to speak directly to those of my hearers who are farmers of what is on my mind, of what is in my heart, to tell you the conclusions I have reached from this bitter experience of the years in dealing with these problems which affect agriculture at home and their relations to foreign countries. . . .

Every thinking citizen knows that most of these low price levels and most of this distress, except in one or two commodities where there is an unwieldy surplus, are due to the decreased demand for farm products by our millions of unemployed and by foreign countries. Every citizen knows that part of this unemployment is due to the inability of the farmer to buy the products of the factory. Every thinking citizen knows that the farmer, the worker, and the business man are in the same boat and must all come to shore together.

Every citizen who stretches his vision across the United States realizes that for the last three years we have been on this downward spiral owing to the destructive forces which I have already described. If he has this vision, he today takes courage and hope because he also knows that these destructive forces have been stopped; that the spiral is moving upward; that more men are being employed and are able to consume more agricultural products.

The policies of the Republican Party and the unprecedented instrumentalities and measures which we have put in motion, many of which are designed directly for agriculture—they are winning out. If we continue to fight along these lines we shall win.

1. The very basis of safety to American agriculture is the protective tariff on farm products.

The Republican Party originated and proposes to maintain the protective tariff on agricultural products. We will even widen that tariff further where necessary to protect agriculture. Ninety per cent of your

[6] State Papers, Vol. II, p. 247.

market is at home, and I propose to reserve this market to the American farmer. . . .

Bad as our prices are, if we take comparable prices of farm products today in the United States and abroad, I am informed by the Department of Agriculture that you will find that except for the guardianship of the tariff, butter could be imported for 25 per cent below your prices, pork products for 30 per cent below your prices, lamb and beef products from 30 to 50 per cent below your prices, flaxseed for 35 per cent below your prices, beans for 40 per cent below your prices, and wool 30 per cent below your prices. Both corn and wheat could be sold in New York from the Argentine at prices below yours at this moment were it not for the tariff. I suppose these are ghastly jests.

The removal of or reduction of the tariff on farm products means a flood of them into the United States from every direction, and either you would be forced to still further reduce your prices, or your products would rot on your farms. . . .

What the Democratic Party proposes is to reduce your farm tariffs. Aside from ruin to agriculture, such an undertaking in the midst of this depression will disturb every possibility of recovery.

2. Four years ago organized agriculture requested the passage of an agricultural marketing act. I called a special session of Congress to pass such an act and increase tariffs on farm products. A distinguished board of men recommended by organized agriculture was appointed to administer the act. Those portions of the board's activities which directed themselves to the support and expansion of co-operative marketing organizations have proved of great benefit to the farmer. Today over a million farm families participate in the benefits which flow from it.

I wish to state frankly the difficulties that have arisen under some other portions of the act. They arise mostly from the so-called stabilization provisions, which never were and are not now the major purpose of the Farm Board. Even indirect purchase and sale of commodities is absolutely opposed to my theory of government.

When the panic struck agricultural prices the Board determined that unless the markets were supported hundreds of thousands of farmers would be bankrupt by the sale of their products at less than the money they had already borrowed upon them, that a thousand country banks would likely be closed, and that a general panic was possible.

As a result of these emergency purchases the prices of farm commodities were temporarily held and their fall cushioned. The farmers secured hundreds of millions of dollars of income which they would not otherwise have received.

Experience has shown that the patent weakness of such actions is the damaging aftermath which accompanies disposal of these products. I am convinced that the act should be revised in the interest of the farmer, in the light of our three years of experience, and this proposal should be repealed.

3. For several years the United States Department of Agriculture has studied the complex social and economic problems which lie embedded in

the general problem of land use. About a year ago these studies had reached such a point that the Secretary of Agriculture felt justified in calling a conference of economists, farm leaders, agricultural college authorities, to formulate practical means of action. The broad objective of such a program is to promote the reorganization of agriculture so as to divert lands from unprofitable to profitable use and to avoid the cultivation of lands the chief return of which is the poverty and misery of those who live upon them. The Republican platform contains a plank which constitutes the first declaration upon this subject. I shall be happy to support a sound program.

4. Four years ago, in this State, I gave assurance to the farmers that one of the first policies of my administration would be the vigorous prosecution and completion of the inland waterway system and advancement of the Great Lakes–St. Lawrence seaway as a fundamental relief to agriculture by cheaper transportation. I am glad to report to you that more than twice the amount of work has been done on the waterways in the last three years than in any similar period in the history of the United States. I am also glad to report that after twenty years of discussion, examination, and intermittent negotiation a treaty has been signed with Canada which only awaits ratification by the United States Senate and the Dominion Parliament for us to undertake that great contribution to the strengthening of Mid-west agriculture in reaching out to world markets. . . .

5. We have suffered from unprecedented droughts both to the north and to the south of you. Some other sections were unable to obtain credit for seed and feed for livestock. Through various government agencies loans to the amount of $120,000,000 have been made to 900,000 of our families to rehabilitate their production and ameliorate these conditions. Some of these families are in difficulties in making immediate repayment because of demoralized prices. I have seen to it that they are not unduly pressed.

6. . . . I stated in effect that the most inflexible tax in our country is the tax on land and on real property. It is the least adaptable to the varying income of the taxpayers. I stated that in the present situation the taxes upon farms and homes have become almost unbearable, that such taxes are wholly out of proportion to other forms of taxes.

I stated then emphatically that there is no farm relief more needed today than readjustment of land taxes.

Such readjustments should be found which would enable the States to find other sources of tax revenue and would more equitably distribute the burden over the whole people. I announced last April that I would call tax experts of the nation together to determine methods we should pursue. I shall do so as soon as the national election is out of the way, and I shall then recommend methods to Congress.

7. The very first necessity to prevent collapse and secure recovery in agriculture has been to keep open to the farmer the banking and other sources from which to make short-term loans for planting, harvesting, feeding livestock, and other production necessities. That has been accom-

plished indirectly in a large measure through the increased authority to the Federal Reserve System and its expansion of credits, and indirectly through the Reconstruction Corporation loans to your banks. It has been aided directly through the Intermediate Credit banks and through the ten new Agricultural Credit institutions which alone can command over $300,000,000 credit and which are now being erected in all parts of the country.

We are thus rapidly everywhere restoring normal short-term credits to agriculture.

8. In another direction upon my recommendation the Reconstruction Corporation has been authorized to make credit available to processors to purchase and carry their usual stocks of agricultural products and thus relieve a burden which was resting upon farm prices because the farmer was forced to carry these stocks. But even more important than this, at my recommendation the Reconstruction Corporation has been authorized to make credits available for sales of farm products in new markets abroad. This is today and will, with increasing activity, extend immediate markets in relief of farmers and the prices of products.

9. The mortgage situation—that is, long-term credits—is one of our most difficult problems. On October 6th a year ago, I secured and published an undertaking from the leaders of both political parties that we should extend aid to this situation. In December we appropriated $125,000,000 directly to increase the capital of the Federal Land Banks, and we provided further capital through authority that the Reconstruction Corporation should purchase the bonds of these banks. The purpose was to enable the Federal Land Banks to expand their activities and to give humane and constructive consideration to those indebted to them who were in difficulties. In the large sense it has pursued this policy. A little over one per cent of the farms held under mortgage by the Federal Land Bank system today are under foreclosure, and these are mostly cases where men wished to give up.

The character of the organization of the Joint Stock Land Banks whose business methods are not controlled by the Federal Farm Loan Board has resulted in disastrous and unjust pressure for payments in some of these banks. The basis of that organization should be remedied. We have sought to further aid the whole mortgage situation by loans from the Reconstruction Corporation to banks, mortgage companies, and insurance companies to enable them to show consideration to their farmer borrowers. As a result of these actions hundreds of thousands of foreclosures have been prevented.

But despite the relief afforded by these measures, the mortgage situation has become more acute. There must be more effective relief. In it lies a primary social problem.

I conceive that in this civilization of ours, and more particularly under our distinctive American system, there is one primary necessity to its permanent success. That is, we must build up men and women in their own homes, on their own farms, where they may find their own security and express their own individuality.

A nation on such foundations is a nation where the real satisfactions of life and happiness thrive, and where real freedom of mind and aspiration secure that individual progress in morals, in spirit and accomplishment, the sum of which makes up the greatness of America. Some will say this is a mere ideal. I am not ashamed of ideals. America was founded upon them, but they must be the premise for practical action.

And for prompt and practical action I have, during the last month, secured definite and positive steps in co-ordination of the policies not only of the Federal agencies but of the important private mortgage agencies as well. These agencies have undertaken to give their help.

But further and more definitely than this I shall propose to Congress at the next session that we further reorganize the Federal Land Banks and give to them the resources and liberty of action necessary to enable them definitely and positively to expand in the refinancing of the farm-mortgage situation where it is necessary to give men who want to fight for it a chance to hold their homes.

10. I cannot over-emphasize the importance of the element of world stability in the recovery and expansion of our agricultural markets. This involves the promotion of good will, of disarmament, and of maintained peace. It requires the rebuilding of the credit structure within nations which have been forced off the gold standard or compelled to restrict exchange. Until that is done there is a definite blockade upon the movement of commodities and upon the market for your products. We have given aid in these things. That we may get to grips with these questions in the interest of world progress, I am participating in the organization of a world economic conference to be held late this year. Every intelligence the world can command will be concentrated on the rehabilitation of economic stability. . . .

11. In the advancement of agricultural prices from the depression the first fortress to take and to hold was the increased tariffs on farm products. There will be an immediate decrease in prices if these tariffs are reduced as our opponents propose. The next move in the battle for improved prices was to stop the general deflation. By deflation I mean the lessening of market values and prices for land, products of the land, manufactures, and all securities. That battle has been won. The next attack on this front is to reverse these processes of deflation and bring things back to their real values. That battle is in progress.

The government is giving aid by its vast constructive program for agriculture, for commerce, and for industry. Through the renewed flow of credit for industry and by direct measures of employment, by the great co-operative movements which we have instituted in commerce and industry for attacks all along the line, we are returning men to work. Every new man re-employed is a greater purchaser of farm products. Wherever we properly can, without entangling ourselves in political difficulties abroad, we are joining for the rehabilitation of the world and thereby the foreign markets for agricultural products. . . .

. . . my solicitude and willingness to advance and protect the interests of agriculture is shown by the record. Protection and advancement of this industry will have my continued deepest concern, for in it lies the progress of all America. It was in this industry that I was born.

5

Responsibility for the Depression

Cleveland, October 15, 1932:[7]

Our opponents have been going up and down the land repeating the statement that the sole or major origins of this disruption and this worldwide hurricane came from the United States through the wild flotation of securities and the stock market speculation in New York three years ago, together with the passage of the Smoot-Hawley Tariff Bill, which took place nine months after the storm broke.

I propose to discuss this assertion. . . .

This thesis of the opposition as to the origin of our troubles is a wonderful explanation for political purposes. I would be glad indeed, if all the enormous problems in the world could be simplified in such a fashion. If that were all that has been the matter with us, we could have recovered from this depression two years ago instead of fighting ever since that time against the most destructive forces which we have ever met in the whole history of the United States—and I am glad to say fighting victoriously.

Nowhere do I find the slightest reference in all the statements of the opposition party to the part played by the greatest war in history, the inheritances from it, the fears and panics and dreadful economic catastrophes which have developed from these causes in foreign countries, or the idea that they may have had the remotest thing to do with the calamity against which this administration is fighting day and night. . . .

The leaders of the Democratic Party appear to be entirely in ignorance of the effect of the killing or incapacitating of 40,000,000 of the best youth of the earth, or of the stupendous cost of war—a sum of $300,-000,000,000, or a sum nearly equal to the value of all the property in the United States—or the stupendous inheritance of debt, with its consequent burden of taxes on scores of nations, with their stifling effect upon recuperation of industry and commerce or paralyzing effect upon world commerce by the continued instability of currencies and budgets.

Democratic leaders have apparently not yet learned of the political instability that arose all over Europe from the harsh treaties which ended the war and the constant continuing political agitation and creation of fear which from time to time paralyzed confidence. They have apparently never heard of the continuing economic dislocation from the transfer on every frontier of great masses of people from their former economic setting.

They apparently have not heard of the continuing dislocation of the

[7] State Papers, Vol. II, p. 337.

stream of economic life which has been caused by the carving of twelve new nations from three old empires. These nations have a rightful aspiration to build their own separate economic systems; they naturally have surrounded themselves with tariffs and other national protections and have thereby diverted the long-established currents of trade. I presume however, that if our Democratic leaders should hear of these nine new tariff walls introduced into the world some fourteen years ago they would lay them at the door of the Smoot-Hawley Bill passed twelve years later.

They apparently have not heard of the increase of standing armies of the world from two to five million men, with consequent burdens upon the taxpayer and the constant threat to the peace of the world.

Democratic leaders apparently ignore the effect upon us of the revolution among 300,000,000 people in China or the agitations among 300,000,000 in India or the Bolshevist revolution amongst 160,000,000 people in Russia. They have ignored the effect of Russia's dumping into the world the commodities taken from its necessitous people in a desperate effort to secure money with which to carry on—shall I call it—a new deal.

The Democratic leaders apparently have never heard that there has been gigantic overproduction of rubber in the Indies, of sugar in Cuba, of coffee in Brazil, of cocoa in Ecuador, of copper in the Congo, or lead in Burma, overproduction of zinc in Australia, overproduction of oil from new discoveries in the United States, Russia, Sumatra, and Venezuela; and likewise the effect of the introduction into the world of gigantic areas of new wheatlands in the Argentine and in Canada; new cotton lands in Egypt. In each and every case these enormous overproductions, far beyond consumption even in boom times, have crashed into the immutable law of supply and demand and brought inevitable collapse in prices and with it a train of bankruptcies and destruction of buying power for American goods.

They appear not to recognize that these forces finally generated economic strangulations, fears, and panic, the streams of which precipitated another long series of world-wide disasters. . . .

They seem not to know that the further accumulation of all these causes and dislocations finally placed a strain upon the weakened economic systems of Europe until one by one they collapsed in failure of their gold standards and the partial or total repudiation of debts. They would hold the American people ignorant that every one of these nations in their financial crises imposed direct or indirect restrictions on the import of goods in order to reduce expenditures of their people. They call these "reprisals" against the Smoot-Hawley Tariff Bill.

They apparently have never heard of the succeeding jeopardy in which our nation was put through these destructions of world commerce, or the persistent dumping of securities into the American market from these panic-stricken countries; the gigantic drains upon our gold and exchange; or the consequent fear that swept over our people, causing them to draw from our bank resources $1,500,000,000, all of which contracted credit, resulted in demand for payment of debts right and left, and thwarted our every effort for industrial recovery.

Yet in the face of all these tremendous facts, our Democratic friends leave the impression with the American people that the prime cause of this disaster was the boom in flotations and stock prices and a small increase in American tariffs.

Such an impression is unquestionably sought by the Democratic candidate when he says:

"That bubble burst first in the land of its origin—the United States. The major collapse abroad followed. It was not simultaneous with ours."

I do not under-rate the distressing losses to millions of our people or the weakening of our strength from the mania of speculation and flotation of securities, but I may incidentally remark that the State governments have the primary responsibility to protect their citizens in these matters and that the vast majority of such transactions originated or took place in the State of New York.

But as to the accuracy of the statement I have quoted I may call your attention to a recent bulletin of the highly respected National Bureau of Economic Research, in which it is shown that this depression in the world began in eleven countries, having a population of 600,000,000 people, before it even appeared in our country, instead of the bubble having "first burst in the United States." Their report shows that the depression in eight other countries with a population of another 600,000,000 people, started at the same time with ours. In fact, the shocks from the continued economic earthquakes in these other countries carried our prices far below the values they would otherwise have sunk to, with all its train of greatly increased losses, perils, and unemployment.

Our opponents demand to know why the governmental leaders or business men over the world did not foresee the approach of these disintegrating forces. That answer is simple. The whole world was striving to overcome them, but finally they accumulated until certain countries could no longer stand the strain, and their people, suddenly overtaken by fear and panic, through hoarding and exporting their capital for safety, brought down their own houses and these disasters spread like a prairie fire through the world. No man can foresee the coming fear or panic, or the extent of its effect. I did not notice any Democratic Jeremiahs.

So much for the beginnings and forces moving in this calamity.

I now come to the amazing statements that the tariff bill of 1930 has borne a major influence in this débâcle.

I quote from the Democratic candidate.

"The Hawley-Smoot Tariff is one of the most important factors in the present world-wide depression."

"It has destroyed international commerce."

"The tariff has done so much to destroy foreign trade as to make foreign trade virtually impossible."

I shall analyze the accuracy of these statements not only because I should like to get before my countrymen a picture of the lack of understanding which the Democratic Party has of world trade, but also for the further reason that it is of vital importance to labor that, as our opponents have this obsession, it means that if they are intrusted with control of our government they intend to break down the protective tariff which is the very first line of defense of the American standard of living against these new forces.

It requires a collection of dull facts to demonstrate the errors in these bald assertions by Democratic leaders.

. . . this tariff bill was not passed until nine months after the economic depression began. . . .

. . . 66 per cent of our imports are free of duty . . . two-thirds of the trade of the world is in non-dutiable goods. . . .

But this decrease is almost exactly the same in the free goods everywhere as in the dutiable goods. . . .

. . . the new tariff shows an increase of 2.2 per cent. This is the margin with which they say we have pulled down foreign governments, created tyrannies, financial shocks, and revolutions.

I may mention that upon the same basis the Dingley duties were 25.8 per cent; the McKinley duties were 23 per cent; the Payne-Aldrich duties were 19.3 per cent of the whole of our imports—all compared with the 16 per cent of the present tariff—and yet they produced in foreign countries no revolutions, no financial crises, and did not destroy the whole world, nor destroy American foreign trade.

. . . the import trade of the United States . . . was about 12 per cent of the whole import trade. Thus they would say that 2.2 per cent increase applied to one-eighth of the world's imports has produced this catastrophe.

. . . Thus this world catastrophe and this destruction of foreign trade happened because the United States increased tariff on one-fourth of one-third of one-eighth of the world's imports. Thus we pulled down the world, by increases on less than one per cent of the goods being imported by the world.

And I may explore the responsibility of the tariffs still further. My opponent has said that it——

"Started such a drain on the gold reserves of the principal countries as to force practically all of them off the gold standard."

At Des Moines I defended the American people from this guilt. I pointed out that it happens there had been no drain of gold from Europe, which is the center of this disturbance, but on the contrary that Europe's gold holdings have increased every year since the Smoot-Hawley Tariff was passed.

My fellow citizens, I could continue for hours in an analysis of mistaken statements and misinformation from the opposition. . . . We did not inaugurate the Great War or the panics in Europe.

St. Louis, November 4, 1932: [8]

Of more importance, the Governor in his speeches conveys the impression that as President I should have stopped the boom. . . . Of course there is no constitutional or statutory authority to Presidents to stop booms. If the President should have attempted to stop the boom one of

[8] State Papers, Vol. II, p. 431.

the persons he would have needed to warn is the present Democratic candidate.

The only way . . . a President could even tilt with a boom would be to turn himself personally into a blue sky law and go on the stump analyzing balance sheets and stock market prices and proving to the people that their investments were overvalued. I have little taste for this proposal that the White House should be turned into a stock tipster's office. I earnestly object to the idea that such a form of dictatorship should ever be set up over the American people even if they do get over-optimistic. The Democratic platform does not seem to accord with the Governor for it says: "We condemn the actions of high public officials designed to influence stock-market prices." . . .

I could go further with this argument of futility by pointing out that the leading Democrats did not discover the Republican responsibility of this depression until it reached a vote-getting stage. . . .

Governor Roosevelt also in a recent speech in defending his boom argument said that when our boom collapsed all but 20 per cent of the people of the world were in a state of prosperity. If he will examine carefully a statement of the National Bureau of Economic Research, whose authority no one denies, . . . he will find he has been misinformed about 300 per cent.

. . . if the Democratic candidate actually wants to put the true causes of this situation before the American people, he should withdraw all this multitude of conflicting, confusing, and misleading statements and disclose to the American people that the most tremendous fact in modern history was the Great War and its aftermath . . . even domestically in the United States . . . the tremendous increase in public debt . . . a larger army and navy . . . in a greatly disturbed world. . . . A Democratic administration . . . having spent the money should not have forgotten. . . . They ought frankly to recognize the problem with which the American people are faced. They should not be appealing to discontent on a basis that ignores their full participation in the real causes. . . .

Now all of this statement . . . has importance . . . because it proves the falsity . . . of their campaign . . . their utter confusion of mind . . . their insincerity or their utter lack of grasp of the forces loose in the world . . . the continuous broadcasting of misinformation . . . indicates an irresponsibility which does not promise well . . . a responsible political party [should] cease to appeal to unthinking people for votes based upon their suffering by misleading them as to its causes.

6

PRIVATE FOREIGN LOANS

Indianapolis, October 28, 1932: [9]

During the past few weeks the Democratic candidate has had a great deal to say in endeavoring to establish the idea in the minds of the

[9] State Papers, Vol. II, p. 402.

American people that I am responsible for bad loans by American bankers and investors in foreign countries. He says:

"This is an unsavory chapter in American finance. These bonds in large part are the fruit of distressing policies pursued by the present Administration in Washington. None other, if you please, than the ability of lending to backward and crippled countries."

The Governor does not inform the American people that there is no Federal law of regulation of the sale of securities and that there is doubtful constitutional authority for such law; that most of these bonds are issued from New York State, which has such authority; and that the Governor has done nothing to reform that evil, if it be one. I recollect a Republican governor of New York who, believing wrong was being done to citizens of his own and other States on their life insurance found a man in Charles Evans Hughes who cleaned it up once and for all.

The Governor has not stated to the American people my oft-repeated warnings that American loans made in foreign countries should be on sound security and confined to reproductive purposes. I have defined these as being loans for creative enterprises which of their own earnings would repay interest and capital. . . . I will say at once that when we have surplus capital, properly secured loans for reproductive purposes abroad are an advantage to the American people. They furnish work to American labor in the manufacture of plants and equipments; they furnish continuing demand for American labor in supplies and replacements. The effect of such creative enterprise is to increase the standards of living amongst the people in those localities and enable them to buy more American products and furnish additional work for American labor.

I have no apologies to make for that statement. It is sound; it makes for the upbuilding of the world; it makes for employment of American workmen and profit to American investors. If it be followed there will be no losses. In these statements the Governor entirely omits the conditions and warnings with which I have always pointedly surrounded the statements on the subject. Although no Federal official has the authority to control the security offered on these loans, none have defaulted where my proposed safeguards have been followed.

7

The Reconstruction Finance Corporation

Detroit, October 22, 1932: [10]

Practically the only evidence of the attitude of the Democratic candidate upon this program is the sneer that it has been designed to help banks and corporations, that it has not helped the common man.

[10] State Papers, Vol. II, p. 364.

He knows full well that the only purpose of helping an insurance company is to protect the policyholder. He knows full well that the only purpose in helping a bank is to protect the depositor and the borrower. He knows full well that the only purpose of helping a farm-mortgage company is to enable the farmer to hold his farm. He knows full well that the only purpose of helping the building and loan associations is to protect savings and homes. He knows full well that in sustaining the business man it maintains the worker in his job. He knows full well that in loans to the States it protects the families in distress.

Millions of men and women are employed today because there has been restored to his employer the ability to borrow the money to buy raw materials and pay labor and thus keep his job. If he be a farmer, it has restored his ability to secure credit upon which to produce his crops and livestock. If he be a home owner or a farm owner in jeopardy of foreclosure of his mortgage, it now gives him a chance. If he had borrowed for any purpose, he has not been forced to the wall by bankruptcy through inability to instantly meet his debt. If he has savings in the bank, it has protected him and removed his anxieties. If he has an insurance policy, it has preserved the validity of that policy. If he be a merchant, it has stopped the calling of his loans and today enables him again to borrow to purchase his stock and thus start employment. If he be unemployed, it is making hundreds of thousands of jobs. If he be in distress it enables his State or city to secure the money which assures him that he will not suffer hunger and cold. Those who are in distress in this city are today receiving their bread and their rent from the result of these measures. But beyond this it is today creating new jobs and giving to the whole system a new breath of life. Nothing has ever been devised in our history which has done more for those whom Mr. Coolidge has aptly called the common run of men and women.

8

BALANCING THE BUDGET

Washington, August 11, 1932: [11]

I have insisted upon a balanced budget as the foundation of all public and private financial stability and of all public confidence. I shall insist on the maintenance of that policy. Recent increases in revenues, while temporary, should be again examined, and if they tend to sap the vitality of industry, and thus retard employment, they must be revised.

The first necessity of the nation, the wealth and income of whose citizens have been reduced, is to reduce expenditures on government, national, State, and local. It is the relief of taxes from the backs of men which liberates their powers. It is through lower expenditures that we get lower taxes. This must be done. Considerable reduction in Federal expenditures has been attained. If we except those extraordinary

[11] State Papers, Vol. II, p. 247.

expenditures imposed upon us by the depression, it will be found that the Federal Government is operating for $200,000,000 less annually today than four years ago. The Congress rejected recommendations from the administration which would have saved an additional $150,000,000 this fiscal year. The opposition leadership insisted, as the price of vital reconstruction legislation and over my protest, upon adding $300,000,000 of costs to the taxpayer through public works inadvisable at this time. I shall repeat my proposals for economy. The opposition leadership in the House of Representatives in the past four months secured passage of $3,000,000,000 in such raids by the House. They have been stopped. I shall continue to oppose raids upon the Federal Treasury.

I have repeatedly for seven years urged the Congress either themselves to abolish obsolete bureaus and commissions and to reorganize the whole government structure in the interest of economy, or to give some one the authority to do so. I have succeeded partially in securing authority, but I regret that no act under it is to be effective until approved by the next Congress.

9

THE BONUS

September 14, 1932. Stated to the Press: [12]

It is due to the country and to the veterans that there should be no misunderstanding of my position upon payment of the face value of the adjusted service certificates prior to maturity, as recommended in the resolution pending before the convention at Portland. I have consistently opposed it. In public interest I must continue to oppose it.

I have the duty not alone to see that justice and a sympathetic attitude is taken by this nation toward the four million veterans and their families but also to exert myself for justice to the other 21,000,000 families to whom consummation of this proposal at this time would be a calamity. Cash payment of face value of certificates today would require an appropriation from the Treasury of about $2,300,000,000. No matter how or in what form the payment to the veterans is imposed it will come out of all these families, but of more importance it will indefinitely set back any hope of recovery for employment, agriculture or business and will impose infinite distress upon the whole country. We owe justice and generosity to the men who have served under our flag. Our people have tried to discharge that obligation. Regular expenditures on account of the veterans already constitute nearly a billion a year or almost one-fourth of our whole Federal Budget.

Every right-thinking man has the deepest sympathy for the veteran suffering from disability for those out of work or for veterans on farms struggling with the adversities of the depression. No one who began life

[12] State Papers, Vol II, p. 278.

in the humble circumstances that I did, and who at the earliest and most impressionable age learned the meaning of poverty from actual experience, can be lacking in feeling and understanding of the problems and sufferings of these men and their families. I have seen war at first hand. I know the courage, the sacrifice of our soldiers.

But there are many million others in the same circumstances. They too must be entitled to consideration. Their employment and their farm recovery, as well as that of the veterans, can be secured only by the restoration of the normal economic life of the nation. To that end we have been and are devoting our best efforts. Anything that stands in the way must be opposed. The welfare of the nation as a whole must take precedence over the demands of any particular group.

10

WAR DEBTS

Cleveland, October 15, 1932: [13]

In this connection, with all these problems, the European war debts to the United States constantly arise. I have consistently opposed cancellation of these debts. The Democratic candidate, to use his own words, proposes to reduce our tariffs so that out of Europe's profits through the increased trade they would obtain from us Europe would pay us these debt annuities. That is vastly worse than cancellation. This would take money out of the pockets of the farmer, laborer, and business man to pay Europe's debts.

In the constructive handling of this question I have said that I would favor the utilization of war debts to advantage agriculture and labor. Such action has received support of many leaders of labor and agriculture.

I am confident that if these policies which we are proposing in building up in these three directions—that is, disarmament, economic stabilization of the world, and the proposed use of these debts to secure the ends I have mentioned—I believe we can confidently hope to promote more rapid recovery, and that we can greatly safeguard ourselves from future economic shocks.

Des Moines, October 4, 1932: [14]

In my acceptance address I stated. . . .

"If for some particular annual payment we are offered some other tangible form of compensation, such as the expansion of markets for American agriculture and labor and the restoration and maintenance of our prosperity, then I am sure our citizens would consider such a proposal."

I am prepared to go farther. I am prepared to recommend that any annual payment on the foreign debt be used for the specific purpose of

[13] State Papers, Vol. II, p. 337.   [14] State Papers, Vol. II, p. 293.

securing an expansion of the foreign markets for American agricultural products. There is justice in that for the difficulties inherited from the war are part of your difficulties today. That is a proposal of more importance to the farmer than any panacea.

11
Relief to Depositors in Closed Banks

Indianapolis, October 28, 1932: [15]

I recommended to the Congress an emergency relief to our depositors in closed banks that through the temporary use of the credit of the Federal Government a substantial part of their assets should be forthwith distributed in order to relieve distress and enable depositors to re-establish their business. The Democratic Congress refused to pass such legislation in the last session, except for a minor provision of authority to the Reconstruction Finance Corporation which does not reach to the heart of the question at all.

12
Tinkering with the Currency

Washington, August 11, 1932: [16]

Our views upon sound currency require no elucidation. They are indelibly a part of Republican history and policies. We have affirmed them by preventing the Democratic majority in the House from effecting wild schemes of uncontrolled inflation.

Des Moines, October 4, 1932: [17]

They [the Democrats] passed a price-fixing bill which might be colloquially called the rubber dollar. . . .

. . . Worse still the bill they passed provided . . . the creation of sheer fiat money. That would have made our currency a football of every speculator and every vicious element in the financial world at the very time when we were fighting for the honesty of the American dollar. I can do no better than quote Daniel Webster, who, one hundred years ago, made one of the most prophetic statements ever made when he said:

"He who tampers with the currency robs labor of its bread. He panders, indeed, to greedy capital, which is keen-sighted and may shift for itself, but he beggars labor, which is unsuspecting and too busy with the present to calculate for the future. The prosperity of the work-people lives, moves and has its being in established credit and steady medium of payment."

The experience of scores of governments in the world since that day has confirmed Webster's statement, and yet the dominant leadership of

[15] State Papers, Vol. II, p. 400.   [16] State Papers, Vol. II, p. 247.
[17] State Papers, Vol. II, p. 293.

the Democratic Party passed that measure, to issue paper money, through the House of Representatives.

Indianapolis, October 28, 1932: [18]

One of the most important issues of this campaign arises from the fact that the Democratic candidate has not yet disavowed the bill passed by the Democratic House of Representatives under the leadership of the Democratic candidate for Vice President to issue $2,300,000,000 of greenback currency—that is, unconvertible paper money. That is money purporting to come from the horn of plenty but with the death's-head engraved upon it. Tampering with the currency has been a perennial policy of the Democratic Party. The Republican Party has had to repel that before now. In the absence of any declaration by the Democratic candidate on this subject for seven weeks of his campaign no delayed promise now can effectually disavow that policy. The taint of it is firmly embedded in the Democratic Party. The dangers of it are embedded in this election. If you want to know what this "new deal" and this sort of money does to the people, ask any of your neighbors who have relatives in Europe, especially as to German marks.

New York, October 31, 1932: [19]

. . . No candidate and no speaker in this campaign has disavowed this action. . . . The use of this expedient by nations in difficulty since the war in Europe has been one of the most tragic disasters. . . .

13
The Turn in the Depression

Detroit, October 22, 1932: [20]

I wish to present to you the evidence that the measures and policies of the Republican Administration are winning this major battle for recovery. They are taking care of distress in the meantime. It can be demonstrated that the tide has turned and the gigantic forces of depression are in retreat. Our measures and policies have demonstrated their effectiveness. They have preserved the American people from certain chaos and have preserved a final fortress of stability in the world. Recovery would have been faster but for four months of paralysis during the spring months while we were defeating proposals of the Democratic House of Representatives to increase governmental expenses by $3,500,000,000, the issue of fiat money and other destructive legislation.

The battle must be continued. We have yet to go a long way and capture many positions to restore agriculture and employment. But it can be made plain that if the strategy we have established is maintained, and the battle not halted by change in the midst of action, we shall win.

If we examine but a few indications, we find that since it was known

[18] State Papers, Vol. II, p. 401.   [19] State Papers, Vol. II, p. 408.
[20] State Papers, Vol. II, p. 364.

that the destructive proposals of the Democratic House were stopped, over $300,000,000 of gold has flowed into our country through restored confidence abroad; $250,000,000 of currency has returned from hoarding through restoration of confidence at home; the values of bonds have increased by twenty per cent, thus safeguarding every depositor in a savings bank and every policyholder in an insurance company. Manufacturing production has increased by ten per cent. Some groups, such as textiles, have increased over fifty per cent in activity.

Contrary to the usual seasonal trend, building contracts have steadily increased. The Department of Commerce shows that over 180,000 workers returned to the manufacturing industry in August, 360,000 more in September, and there is evidence of even a still larger number in October. Car loadings have increased from 490,000 per week to 650,000 per week, showing the increased volume of materials moving. Exports and imports have increased nearly twenty-three per cent. Agricultural prices, always the last to move, have improved from their low points, although they are still hideously low. Bank failures have almost ceased; credit has begun to expand. Every week some improvement is recorded somewhere.

As I have said, improvement would have begun four months earlier but for the fear of the destructive Democratic program. Today we would be moving faster in the restoration of farm prices and employment but for the threat that these destructive measures will be revived by change at this election.

St. Paul, November 5, 1932: [21]

I recently enumerated at Detroit, some of the evidences of recuperation of the country under these measures in so short a period as four months since the destruction of public confidence by the Democratic House of Representatives ceased.

. . . over a million men have now returned to work in these four months . . . we are now gaining a half-million a month.

Production of boots and shoes . . . higher than the same month of the previous year.

Hoarded currency continues to return; imports of gold withdrawn by frightened European holders have continued to increase; deposits of banks continue to show steady expansion. In four months they have increased by nearly a billion dollars. This is money being put to work and an evidence of renewed confidence.

[There is increased] . . . demand for electrical power, which has increased by over eight per cent in the last four months. Every business index shows some progress somewhere in the nation.

Detroit, October 22, 1932: [22]

I can well understand that my countrymen are weary and sore and tired. I can well understand that part of this weariness comes from the exhaustion of a long battle. But in the battle we have carried the first-line trenches. It is of transcendent importance that there shall be no interrup-

[21] State Papers, Vol. II, p. 449.   [22] State Papers, Vol. II, p. 383.

tion; that there shall be no change in the strategy and tactics used in the midst of victorious movement. The essentials of American life must not be broken down in chaos and in peril.

14

SUMMARY OF THE DEMOCRATIC PROPOSALS

St. Paul, November 5, 1932: [23]

And now in contrast with this constructive program of the Republican Party I wish to develop for you the Democratic program to meet this depression as far as we have been able to find any definition to it. I would again call your attention to the fact that with the Democratic victory in Congressional elections of 1930 their leaders promised to produce a program which would redeem this country from the depression. No such program was produced until we were well into the winter of 1932. Their program as developed under the leadership of Mr. Garner by the Democratic House of Representatives was:

1. They passed the Collier Bill, providing for destruction of the Tariff Commission by reducing it again to a mere statistical body controlled by the Congress. Had they succeeded, the relief which you so sorely require from competition from countries of depreciated currencies would now be impossible.

2. They attempted to instruct me by legislation to call an international conference through which the aid of foreign nations was requested to lower American tariffs, by which the independence of the United States in control of its domestic policies was to be placed in the hands of an international body.

3. They passed an act instructing me to negotiate reciprocal tariffs, the result of which could only be to deprive some locality of its tariff protection for the benefit of another, and by which the only possible agreements would involve the reduction of farm tariffs in order to build up markets for other goods.

4. They passed an omnibus pension bill with unworthy payments as an indication of their economical temper.

5. They passed an inadequate, patchwork revenue bill, the injustice of which to different industries and groups must yet be remedied.

6. They passed Indian claims bills to re-open settlements of seventy-five years ago in order to favor certain localities at the expense of the public treasury.

7. They passed a bill instructing the Federal Reserve System and the Treasury to fix prices at averages prevailing during the years 1921 to 1929 by constantly shifting the volume of currency and credit and thus creation of every uncertainty to business and industry by a rubber dollar. This bill was stopped, but it has not been removed from their political calendar.

[23] State Papers, Vol. II, p. 440.

8. They defeated a large part of the national economy measure proposed by the Administration, by reduction of ordinary expenditures from $250,000,000 to less than $50,000,000, a part of which was subsequently rescued in the Senate.

9. They passed the Garner-Rainey pork-barrel bill, increasing expenditures by $1,200,000,000 for unnecessary, non-productive public works, purely for the benefit of favored localities. We stopped this bill, but it is still on their political calendar.

10. They passed the cash pre-payment of the bonus calling for immediate expenditure of $2,300,000,000 and for actual increase in liabilities of the Federal Government over the original Act of $1,300,000,000. We stopped this bill, but it is still on their political calendar.

11. They passed the provision for the issuance of over $2,200,000,000 of greenback currency, a reversion to vicious practices already demonstrated in the last hundred years as the most destructive to labor, agriculture and business. We stopped this bill and even as late as last night the Democratic candidate failed to frankly disavow it.

12. They passed the Rainey Bill providing for direct personal banking for any conceivable purpose on every conceivable security to every one who wants money, and thus the most destructive entry of the government into private business in a fashion that violates every principle of our nation. I vetoed this bill—but Mr. Garner still advocates it, and it has not been removed from their political promises.

13. They injected an expenditure of $322,000,000 for entirely unnecessary purposes in time of great emergency. They complain daily that we do not spend it fast enough.

14. The Congress passed proper authority to the Executive for reorganization and elimination of useless government commissions and bureaus, but by refusing my recommendations for immediate action they destroyed its usefulness for a long time to come and probably destroyed its consummation.

15. The Democratic candidate eloquently urges the balancing of the budget, but nowhere disavows these gigantic raids on the Treasury, under which a budget cannot be balanced.

Thus far is the program of the Democratic House under the leadership of Mr. Garner whose policies the Democratic Party ratified by nominating him Vice-President.

16. The Democratic candidate adds to this program the proposal to plant a billion trees and thereby immediately employ a million men, but the Secretary of Agriculture has shown that the trees available to plant will give them a total of less than three days' work.

17. The candidate promises to relieve agriculture with the six-point program which amounts to envisaging to distressed farmers a great structure of agricultural relief, but he has refused to submit it to debate. He disclosed no details of the plan except six methods by which he can escape from the promise.

18. The candidate has promised the immediate inauguration of a program of self-liquidating public works such as utilization of our water-

resources, flood control and land reclamation, to provide "employment for all surplus labor at all times." It would exceed in cost $9,000,000,000 a year. The works are unavailable, the cost would destroy the credit of the government, deprive vast numbers of the men working of their jobs and thus destroy the remedy itself. This fantasy is a cruel promise to these suffering men and women that they will be given jobs by the government which no government could fulfill.

19. The Democratic Party makes its contribution to the emergency by proposing to reduce that tariff to a "competitive tariff for revenue." Their candidate states that he supports this promise 100 per cent. A competitive tariff today would be ruinous to American agriculture and industry.

It is important to mention one further incident of the campaign. Governor Roosevelt, in his speech at Baltimore, Maryland, on October 25th, made the following portentous statement: "After March 4, 1929, the Republican party was in complete control of all branches of the government—the legislature, with the Senate and Congress, and the executive departments, and I may add for full measure to make it complete, the United States Supreme Court as well." President Hoover replied to this in his speech at Indianapolis, on October 28, 1932, as follows: [24]

> I invite your attention to that statement about the Supreme Court. There are many things revealed by the campaign of our opponents which should give American citizens concern about the future. One of the gravest is the state of mind revealed by my opponent in that statement. He implies that it is the function of the party in power to control the Supreme Court. For generations Republican and Democratic Presidents alike have made it their most sacred duty to respect and maintain the independence of America's greatest tribunal. . . . All appointees to the Supreme Court have been chosen solely on the basis of character and mental power. Not since the Civil War have the members of the court divided on political lines.
>
> Aside from the fact that the charge that the Supreme Court has been controlled by any political party is an atrocious one, there is a deeper implication in that statement. Does it disclose the Democratic candidate's conception of the functions of the Supreme Court? Does he expect the Supreme Court to be subservient to him and his party? Does that statement express his intention by his appointment or otherwise to attempt to reduce that tribunal to an instrument of party policy and political action for sustaining such doctrines as he may bring with him?
>
> My countrymen, I repeat to you, the fundamental issue in this campaign, the decision that will fix the national direction for a hundred years to come, is whether we shall go on in fidelity to the American traditions or whether we shall turn to innovations, the spirit of which is disclosed to us by many sinister revelations and veiled promises.

[24] State Papers, Vol. II, p. 407.

CHAPTER XV

WORLD ECONOMIC STABILIZATION AND WAR DEBTS

MR. ROOSEVELT carried the election on November 8th by a vote of fifty-seven per cent of the people. It was a certainty that this result would cause some hesitation in the general recovery from the depression which had begun in the previous June-July (1932). President Hoover had pointed this out in his speech at St. Paul on November 5th.

There is no one more devoted to our form of government than myself, but there is one unfortunate incident in our system and that is that a change of parties in power at the national election may come at a difficult time. A change at this election must mean four whole months in which there can be no definition of national policy, during which time not only the commander of the forces in battle for economic recovery must be changed but the subordinate commanders as well. . . . The battle must stagnate at a time of its height and recovery must be delayed. . . .

For one reason alone, if no other untoward developments occurred, there would be hesitation in recovery. Governor Roosevelt in his campaign repeatedly had promised immediate and drastic reductions in the tariff. Following the election, merchants and manufacturers at once cancelled orders, expecting lower-priced imports, and thus created an increase in unemployment in the manufacturing trades.

The Hoover Administration, with regard to its positive influence on recovery, was over on November 9th. From that moment the people naturally looked to Mr. Roosevelt for the nation's future policies. These policies controlled any constructive action of the government, for the Democratic House of Representatives and the opposition Senate would take no action without regard to Mr. Roosevelt's views. Any legislation in advancement of the Hoover policies, which were in conflict with Roosevelt policies, was impossible.

Congress soon was to meet in short session, in which some program must be presented. The President had gone to Palo Alto to vote. The day after the election he communicated with his Cabinet by telephone "to explore the avenues of constructive action which might be pursued within the area apparently outside of conflict between the incoming and outgoing administrations." The country and the whole world was emerging from the world-wide depression, and it was vital to the public interest that this progress should be maintained if possible.

It was quickly determined that in major foreign affairs there had been no divergent Democratic policies advanced in the campaign. Aside from routine relations, President Hoover was conducting two international negotiations, one for further disarmament, and the other for the stabilization of world currencies and the mitigation of foreign trade barriers against our exports.

In domestic policies it seemed obvious that the incoming Administration would want continued economic recovery. There could be no conflict with regard to continued relief to the destitute. Governor Roosevelt had promised a great reduction in expenditures and a balanced budget. Congress would need to pass at the short session the appropriations and any new revenue bills prior to the inauguration for use in Mr. Roosevelt's first fiscal year. Banking and bankruptcy reform also had been advocated by him. He had pledged himself to maintain sound money.

Also it was obvious that in the national interest there must be immediate co-operation between the outgoing and incoming administrations upon these questions if economic recovery was to proceed. President Hoover, of course, abandoned any thought of advancing his ideas of agricultural or social legislation which differed from Mr. Roosevelt's policies. Therefore, on November 11th, in a short speech at Glendale, California, while en route to Washington, President Hoover said:

The majority of the people have decided to entrust the government to a new administration. The political campaign is over. I asked for unity of national action in the constructive measures which have been initiated during the past three years for care of distress, to protect the nation from imminent dangers, and to promote economic recovery. If we are to continue the recovery so evidently in progress during the last few months by overcoming the many difficulties which still confront us, we must have continued unity in constructive action all along the economic front. I shall work for that unity during the remaining four months of this administration. . . .

The first consideration today of every American citizen is the continued recovery of the country—a consideration far above partisanship.

To that end President Hoover worked unceasingly, as these chapters will show. He was, however, not to receive co-operation—far from it. Within thirty days policies were adopted by the incoming Administration and its adherents in Congress, which totally reversed the economic recovery then in progress and, through a complete breakdown of confidence, drove the country into a banking panic by the day of the inauguration.

President Hoover, some six months before the election of November, 1932, had actively participated in the calling of a World Economic Conference. The major purpose of the conference was to stabilize world currencies and get relief from trade barriers. The announcement of the determination of the important commercial countries to join in the conference, together with the progress made by the preliminary meetings of experts, had contributed materially to revive hope for the future and to develop world confidence during the summer and fall. The purpose of the World Economic Conference was stated by President Hoover in a message to Congress on December 19, 1932. He said, in part:[1]

. . . While it is difficult in any analysis of world economic forces to separate the cause from the effect or the symptom from the disease, or to separate one segment of a vicious cycle from another, we must begin somewhere by determination of our objectives.

It is certain the most urgent economic effort still before the world is the restoration of price levels. The undue and continued fall in prices and trade obviously has many origins. One dangerous consequence, however, is visible enough in the increased difficulties which are arising between many debtors and creditors. The values behind a multitude of securities are lessened, the income of debtors is insufficient to meet their obligations, creditors are unable to undertake new commitments for fear of the safety of present undertakings.

It is not enough to say that the fall in prices is due to decreased consumption, and thus the sole remedy is the adjustment by reduced production. That is in part true, but decreased consumption is brought about by certain economic forces which, if overcome, would result in a great measure of recovery of consumption and thus recovery from the depression. Any competent study of the causes of continued abnormal levels of prices would at once establish the fact that the general price movement is world-wide in character, and international influences therefore have a part in them. Further exploration in this field brings us at once to the fact that price levels have been seriously affected by abandonment of the gold standard by many countries and the consequent instability and depreciation of foreign currencies. These fluctuations in themselves, through the uncertainties they create, stifle trade, cause invasions of unnatural marketing territory, result in arbitrary trade restrictions and ultimate diminished consumption of goods, followed by a further fall in prices.

. . . Restrictions have not alone been put upon the movement of gold and exchange, but they have been imposed upon imports of goods in endeavor to prevent the spending of undue sums abroad by their nationals, as a further precaution to prevent the outflow of gold reserves and thus undermining of currency. These steps have again reduced consumption and diminished prices, and are but parts of the vicious cycles which must be broken at some point if we are to assure economic recovery.

[1] State Papers, Vol. II, p. 547, *et seq.*

... Prices of agricultural and other commodities in the United States are being seriously affected and thousands of our workers are today being thrown out of employment through the invasion of such goods.

I concur in the conclusions of many thoughtful persons that one of the first and most fundamental points of attack is to re-establish stability of currencies and foreign exchange, and thereby release an infinite number of barriers against the movement of commodities, the general effect of which would be to raise the price of commodities throughout the world. ...

I am well aware that many factors which bear upon the problem are purely domestic in many countries, but the time has come when concerted action between nations should be taken in an endeavor to meet these primary questions. While the gold standard has worked badly since the war, due to the huge economic dislocations of the war, yet it is still the only practicable basis of international settlements and monetary stability so far as the more advanced industrial nations are concerned. The larger use of silver as a supplementary currency would aid to stability in many quarters of the world. In any event it is a certainty that trade and prices must be disorganized until some method of monetary and exchange stability is attained. It seems impossible to secure such result by the individual and separate action of different countries, each striving for separate defense.

It is for the purpose of discussing these and other matters most vital to us and the rest of the world that we have joined in the World Economic Conference, where ... measures for the turning of the tide of business and price levels ... can be fully and effectively considered, and if possible undertaken simultaneously between nations.

The reduction of world armament also has a bearing upon these questions. The stupendous increase in military expenditures since before the war is a large factor in world-wide unbalanced national budgets, with that consequent contribution to instable credit and currencies and to the loss of world confidence in political stability. While these questions are not a part of the work proposed for the economic conference, cognizance of its progress and possibilities must be ever in the minds of those dealing with the other questions.

The problem of the war-debts to the United States has entered into this world situation. It is my belief that their importance, relative to the other world economic forces in action, is exaggerated. Nevertheless, in times of deep depression some nations are unable to pay and in some cases payments do weigh heavily upon foreign exchange and currency stability. In dealing with an economically sick world many factors become distorted in their relative importance, and the emotions of peoples must be taken into account. ...

President Hoover consistently had urged that the war debts must be temporarily readjusted during the depression to the capacity of the debtors to pay. If any long-distance concessions were to be made, they should be only in return for definite advantages to the American people.

All the world, including our own business public, looked anxiously for the attitude of the incoming administration toward these objectives. It was important that they should be pursued without interruption, and that the conference should be convened at the earliest moment. Its objectives were wholly non-political, and it seemed possible that the incoming administration would be anxious to proceed. It had been expected that the conference would convene early in the new year of 1933.

President Hoover practically had determined upon the men whom he would send as American delegates, although he had deferred communicating with them on the subject and had made no public announcement concerning the conference until the results of the approaching election might be known. The intended list embraced the names of Secretary of the Treasury Mills; Senators David A. Reed and Carter Glass; Congressmen Robert Luce and Charles R. Crisp; Silas H. Strawn, of Chicago; Henry M. Robinson, of Los Angeles; Colonel Edward M. House; William Green, president of the American Federation of Labor; Louis J. Taber, master of the National Grange, and yet another which remained to be selected. It was necessary that our delegates should get to work immediately after the election, to be ready for the conference, if it were not to be long postponed and discouragement created thereby.

The conclusions of the conference in any event would fall in the new administration, and President Hoover recognized that Mr. Roosevelt would wish to appoint a different delegation. But also he assumed that the new President would wish to proceed at the earliest possible moment, since a successful and early consummation of the conference would give further impulse to the world recovery already in progress. At this time, the urgent thing was to secure the appointment of an American delegation, for it was expected the conference would meet early in the new year. Two months' preparation would be required for the thorough equipment of such a body. Furthermore, of still greater importance was the fact that, as long experience had shown, no international conference could be successful unless the result were assured by advance negotiations among the leading powers involved.

On November 10th, two days after the election, a disturbing element was thrown into the entire situation by some of the debtor governments, seeking to take prompt advantage of any chance of division in our national leadership pending the inauguration of the new President. They demanded immediate readjustment of their debts prior to the December 15th payments. The demand of these governments, which obviously were acting in concert, was followed by a flood of propaganda in this country, in which, evidently, they were aided by certain New York City banking groups and others. Much of this propaganda was designed to discredit President Hoover's Administration in the hope of luring Mr. Roosevelt to their side. It was imperative that this attempt to outwit the United States should be broken up, and that the United States should preserve its freedom of separate action with each debtor; also that the debts should be preserved as a weapon to influence the negotiations in the economic conference and for other like legitimate advantages. It further was imperative that at once there should be a solidarity upon the American front.

It was while the President still was in the West that this new complication arose. Immediately he conferred with the State Department in Washington by telephone and, on the train crossing the Mojave Desert during his trip East, he wrote the following telegram to President-elect Roosevelt. He desired at once to enlist the co-operation of the latter. The following is the text of the comprehensive telegram:

Yuma, Arizona,
November 12, 1932.

GOVERNOR FRANKLIN D. ROOSEVELT,
Albany, New York.

The Secretary of State has informed me that the British Ambassador, on behalf of his government, has handed him a note stating that "They believe that the régime of inter-governmental financial obligations as now existing must be reviewed; that they are profoundly impressed with the importance of acting quickly and that they earnestly hope that the United States Government will see its way clear to enter into an exchange of views at the earliest possible moment."

The British Ambassador further asks for a suspension of the payments due by the British Government to our government for the period of the discussion suggested or for any other period that may be agreed upon. This last suggestion clearly relates to the payment of $95,000,000 which will fall due on December 15, 1932. I have requested the Secretary of State to transmit to you a full copy of that note.

The Secretary of State has also just been informed that similar requests are to be made by other debtor governments which likewise are obligated to make payments to the United States on December 15th next. One debtor nation has defaulted on a payment due November 10th and another debtor nation has served notice on our government of its incapacity to make a payment due in December. Thus our government is now confronted with a world problem of major importance to this nation.

The moratorium which I proposed a year ago in June—that is, the year's postponement of inter-governmental debts and the spread of the deferred payment over ten years—was approved by the Congress. It served a great purpose in staying destruction in every direction and giving to Europe a year in which to realize and so modify their attitude on solely

[2] State Papers, Vol. II, p. 483.

European questions, as to support their credit structure from a great deal of further destruction. They have made very substantial progress during that year in financial adjustments among themselves and toward armament reduction.

Practically all of our World War debt settlements were made not by the Executive, but by the commission created by act of Congress, and all were approved in the form of legislation enacted by both Houses. A year ago, in recommending to the Congress the ratification of the moratorium, I presented a statement of my views as to the whole of the relationship of ourselves to our debtor countries, and pointed out that debts to us bore no relationship to debts between other nations which grew out of the war.

At the same time I recommended to the Congress that a new debt commission be created to deal with situations that might arise, owing to the temporary incapacity of any individual debtor to meet its obligations to our country during the period of world depression. Congress declined to accede to this latter recommendation; it passed a joint resolution reading in part as follows:

"It is hereby expressly declared to be against the policy of the Congress that any of the indebtedness of foreign countries to the United States should be in any manner cancelled or reduced; and nothing in this Joint Resolution shall be construed as indicating a contrary policy or as implying that favorable consideration will be given at any time to a change in the policy hereby declared."

The limitation to purely temporary individual action as to those incapable of payment during the depression, expressed in the "Communiqué" referred to in the British note, and in my recommendation to the Congress, was evident in these documents. The refusal of the Congress to authorize even the examination of this limited question, together with the above resolution, gave notice to all debtor governments of the attitude of this government toward either cancellation or reduction of existing obligations. Therefore any commitments which European governments may have made between themselves could not be based upon any assurances of the United States. Moreover, the tenor of negotiations asked for by the debtor governments goes beyond the terms of the Congressional resolution referred to.

I have publicly stated my position as to these questions, including that I do not favor cancellation in any form, but that we should be receptive to proposals from our debtors of tangible compensation in other forms than direct payment in expansion of markets for the products of our labor and our farms. And I have stated further that substantial reduction of world armament, which will relieve our own and world burdens and dangers, has a bearing upon this question.

Furthermore, President Hoover pointed to the fact that any negotiations now begun would be protracted beyond the remaining period of his own administration, and suggested that he confer personally with Mr. Roosevelt at some convenient date, as the policies must be settled before

December 15th. Time, of course, was of great importance. The President closed by suggesting that the President-elect, who was reported to be contemplating a trip to the South, might stop in Washington some time during the latter part of the ensuing week, for the purposes of this conference. President Hoover also stated his willingness to have Mr. Roosevelt bring to the conference any Democratic Congressional leaders, or other advisers, as he might wish.

This frank and friendly offer brought the following reply from Mr. Roosevelt. The delay of two days was explained by the fact that he was suffering from a slight cold. *The New York Times* said that "the care with which this message was drafted, after telephone talks with Colonel Louis McHenry Howe, Colonel Edward M. House, and Bernard M. Baruch, indicated that Mr. Roosevelt thought he should make clear his own relation to the problem before entering such a parley."

November 14, 1932.

THE PRESIDENT:

I appreciate your cordial telegram. On the subjects to which you refer, as in all matters relating to the welfare of the country, I am glad to cooperate in every appropriate way, subject, of course, to the requirements of my present duties as Governor of this State.

I shall be delighted to confer with you in Washington, but I have been confined to the house with a slight cold and I am, therefore, not able to suggest a definite date. I shall call you on the telephone as soon as the time of my departure for the South has been determined.

May I take the liberty of suggesting that we make this meeting wholly informal and personal. You and I can go over the entire situation.

I had already arranged to meet a number of the Democratic leaders of the present Congress late this month at Warm Springs. It will be helpful for me to have your views and all pertinent information when I meet with them. I hope that you also will see them at the earliest opportunity because, in the last analysis, the immediate question raised by the British, French and other notes creates a responsibility which rests upon those now vested with executive and legislative authority. My kindest regards.

(signed) FRANKLIN D. ROOSEVELT.

A conference was arranged for November 22nd at the White House, to which Professor Raymond Moley accompanied Governor Roosevelt, and Secretary Mills was present with President Hoover. President Hoover presented his view that the December 15th payments should be insisted upon; also that if they were paid then, the subject would be reviewed with each government, but that the whole question must be dealt with in the light of the forthcoming monetary and trade conference. He urged that the practical thing to do was at once to appoint the delegates to the World Economic Conference, and that the same men should deal with the war debts. Such a program required Congressional authority, but Mr. Roosevelt already was actively consulting the Democratic majority in Congress on the policies of the Hoover Administration pending before that body, which soon was to be convened. They thus would be in a position to negotiate all along the line. Congress should be represented in the delegation, which should begin discussions with the leading powers immediately after the December 15th installments were paid.

President Hoover had called a conference of Congressional leaders for the following morning. He therefore proposed to the President-elect that if the two of them agreed on a policy, they should jointly meet the Congressional leaders. Governor Roosevelt appeared to agree with the program, but he felt that he would rather not attend the White House meeting with the Congressional leaders; that he himself would see the Democratic members at once.

It was decided that the President should issue a memorandum of principles and methods in accord with their discussion and the President-elect also should issue a statement. It was agreed that the President prepare his memorandum for issue the following day, and that Secretary of the Treasury Mills and Professor Moley should meet finally to settle the two memoranda.

On the morning of November 23rd, the President met with the Congressional leaders of both parties and reviewed the entire war-debt situation with them and the necessity for national solidarity. The Democratic members, however, opposed the whole program and stated that they would not co-operate with it. When Secretary Mills called upon Mr. Roosevelt to settle the promised statements, it was suggested that President Hoover should issue his own memorandum and that the President-elect would comment upon it afterward. The President's statement of November 23rd thereupon was issued to the press. It went fully into the whole question, partially for a better public understanding of the problem. The most important parts of the statement were:[3]

The communications submitted by a number of governments in substance request that their war debts to the United States should be again reviewed; that our government should enter into an exchange of views on this subject, and that during the period of such a conference there should be a suspension of the payments due to the United States on December 15th next.

This presents a problem which merits thoughtful consideration of the American people. To avoid misunderstanding it seems desirable to sum-

[3] State Papers, Vol. II, p. 487.

marize briefly the complex questions and the policies consistently followed by the United States. . . .

1. These debts were created, and were undoubtedly based, on the proposal of the borrowers, no doubt in good faith, and the assumption of the Government of the United States, that they were actual loans which would be repaid. Had it not been for this assumption, it is hardly to be supposed that this government would have been so largely involved. We have held at all times that these agreements voluntarily entered upon must be maintained in their full integrity except as adjusted by mutual consent. This is fundamental to upholding the whole structure of obligations between nations and beyond this is basic to the very structure of credit and confidence upon which the modern economic life depends.

2. The United States Government from the beginning has taken the position that it would deal with each of the debtor governments separately, as separate and distinct circumstances surrounded each case. Both in the making of the loans and in the subsequent settlements with the different debtors, this policy has been repeatedly made clear to every foreign government concerned.

3. Debt settlements made in each case took into consideration the economic conditions and the capacity to pay of the individual debtor nation. The present worth of the payments to be received under the terms of the settlements at the time they were made, on the five per cent interest basis, provided in the original agreements, show concessions ranging from thirty per cent to eighty per cent of the total amounts that were due.

As indicating the consistent policy of adjustment to ability of the debtor to pay I may cite (Here follow the views of previous administrations).

4. From the time of the creation of these debts to the United States, this government has uniformly insisted that they must be treated as entirely separate from reparation claims arising out of the war. The reasons for adherence to this position are plain. After the war we refused to accept general reparations or any compensation in territory, economic privileges, or government indemnity.

Moreover, in the matter of reparations and other inter-governmental debts arising from the war, our position is entirely different from that of governments that are both creditors and debtors. Since we owe no obligation of any kind to others, no concession made in respect of a payment owed to us could either in whole or in part be set off or balanced against claims owed by us to any other creditor of our country. On the contrary, every such concession would result in the inevitable transfer of a tax burden from the taxpayers of some other country to the taxpayers in our own, without the possibility of any compensating set-off. . . .

In my statement of June 20, 1931, proposing that one year's payment of all inter-governmental debts should be distributed over a term of years, and again to the Congress on December 10th last, submitting the agreements thereon, I said:

"I wish to take this occasion also to frankly state my views upon our relations to German reparations and the debts owed to us by the Allied governments of Europe. Our government has not been a party to, or exerted any voice in determination of reparation obligations. We purposely did not participate in either general reparations or the division of colonies or property. The repayment of debts due to us from the Allies for the advance for war and reconstruction was settled upon a basis not contingent upon German reparations or related thereto. Therefore reparations is necessarily wholly a European problem with which we have no relation."

5. The debt agreements are, through force of law, unalterable save by Congressional action. Without entering into legalistic consideration of the respective powers of the Executive and the Congress, it may be said at once that, based upon the relation of these debts to revenue, the Congress has insisted upon participation in initiation of negotiations and in any ultimate decisions in respect to the war debts. . . . (Here are cited previous actions of the government.)

Believing that emergencies of temporary character might arise in some cases during the depression—which has already proved the case—on December 10, 1931, I sent a recommendation to the Congress that the commission should be reconstituted to consider such emergency cases. The Congress refused to take such action, and adopted a joint resolution which read in part as follows:

"Section 5: It is hereby expressly declared to be against the policy of Congress that any indebtedness of foreign countries to the United States should be in any way cancelled or reduced, and nothing in this Joint Resolution should be construed as indicating a contrary policy or as indicating that favorable consideration will be given for change in the policy hereby declared."

It must be obvious, therefore, from a practical point of view, that no progress is possible without active co-operation of the Congress.

6. The necessity of this authority does not, however, relieve me of the responsibilities of this office, and I therefore shall state my own views.

The world-wide crisis has at least temporarily increased the weight of all debts throughout the world. Tremendous disparity in price levels, contraction in markets, depreciation in currency, stagnation of trade and industry—are all part of this world-wide depression which is not only increasing the weight of these debts and has made their payment more difficult to some nations, but has thrust them as well into the problem of world recovery and its effect upon our own farmers, workers, and business. These are realities. We cannot blind ourselves to their existence. They are vital factors in the problem now before us for consideration.

At the same time, it must be emphatically recalled that the aftermath of the Great War and these incidents of the depression have also fallen with great weight on the American people, and the effect upon them directly as taxpayers, of any modification with respect to the debts due this country, must not be disregarded. Other nations have their budgetary problems. So have we. Other people are heavily burdened with taxes. So are our people.

I have stated on many occasions my opposition to cancellation. Furthermore, I do not feel that the American people should be called upon to make further sacrifices. I have held, however, that advantages to us could be found by other forms of tangible compensation than cash, such as expansion of markets for products of American agriculture and labor. There are other possible compensations in economic relations which might be developed on study which would contribute to recovery of prices and trade. Such compensations could be made mutually advantageous. These things might serve to overcome difficulties of exchange in some countries and to meet the question of inability of some of them otherwise to pay.

The World Economic Conference will convene in a few months to deal with matters of the deepest import to economic recovery of the world and of ourselves as well. A world disarmament conference is now in progress. And I must reiterate that the problem of foreign debts has in the American mind very definite relationship to the problem of disarmaments and the continuing burden which competitive armaments impose upon us and the rest of the world. There are, therefore, important avenues of mutual advantage which should be genuinely explored.

It is unthinkable that, within the comity of nations and the maintenance of international good will, our people should refuse to consider the request of friendly people to discuss an important question in which they and we both have a vital interest, irrespective of what conclusions might arise from such a discussion. This is particularly true in a world greatly afflicted, where co-operation and good will are essential to the welfare of all.

I believe, therefore, that Congress in view of the requests made by these governments should authorize the creation of an agency to exchange views with those governments, enlarging the field of discussion as above indicated, and to report to Congress such recommendations as they deem desirable. Furthermore, such agency should be so constituted through complete or partial identity of membership with the delegations to the World Economic Conference and to the General Disarmament Conference, that under the direction of the President and with the final decision in the Congress, we may take the strongest possible co-ordinated steps toward the solution of the many underlying causes of the present calamity. . . .

There is a larger aspect to this question of responding to an invitation from a friendly nation to discuss, through effectively authorized agents, a problem of deep concern to both. Discussion does not involve abandonment on our part of what we believe to be sound and right. On the other hand, a refusal to afford others the opportunity to present in conference their views and to hear ours upon a question in which we are both concerned, and an insistence upon dealing with our neighbors at arm's length, would be the negation of the very principles upon which rests the hope of rebuilding a new and better world from the shattered remnants of the old.

If our civilization is to be perpetuated, the great causes of world peace, world disarmament and world recovery must prevail. They cannot prevail until a path to their attainment is built upon honest friendship, mutual confidence, and proper co-operation among the nations.

These immense objectives upon which the future and welfare of all mankind depend must be ever in our thought in dealing with immediate and difficult problems. The solution of each one of these, upon the basis of an understanding reached after frank and fair discussion, in and of itself strengthens the foundation of the edifice of world progress we seek to erect; whereas our failure to approach difficulties and differences among nations in such a spirit serves but to undermine constructive effort.

Governor Roosevelt issued the following separate statement on November 23rd:

My conferences with the President and with leaders of my party have been most illuminating and useful. I wish to express my appreciation of the opportunity thus afforded me.

At this time I wish to reaffirm my position on the questions that have been the principal subjects of our discussions.

As to the debt payments due December 15th, I find no justification for modifying my statement to the President on November 14th when I pointed out that "the immediate questions raised by the British, French and other notes create a responsibility which rests upon those now vested with executive and legislative authority."

With regard to general policies respecting these debts I firmly believe in the principle that an individual debtor should at all times have access to the creditor; that he should have opportunity to lay facts and representations before the creditor and that the creditor always should give courteous, sympathetic and thoughtful consideration to such facts and representations.

This is a rule essential to the preservation of the ordinary relationships of life. It is a basic obligation of civilization. It applies to nations as well as to individuals.

The principle calls for free access by the debtor to the creditor. Each case should be considered in the light of the conditions and necessities peculiar to the case of each nation concerned.

I find myself in complete accord with four principles discussed in the conference between the President and myself yesterday and set forth in a statement which the President has issued today.

These debts were actual loans made under the distinct understanding and with the intention that they would be repaid.

In dealing with the debts each government has been and is to be considered individually, and all dealings with each government are independent of dealings with any other debtor government. In no case should we deal with the debtor governments collectively.

Debt settlements made in each case take into consideration the capacity to pay of the individual debtor nations.

The indebtedness of the various European nations to our government has no relation whatsoever to reparations payments made or owed to them.

Once these principles of the debt relationships are established and recognized, the methods by which contacts between our government and the debtor nations may be provided are matters of secondary importance. My view is that the most convenient and effective contacts can be made through the existing agencies and constituted channels of diplomatic intercourse.

No action by the Congress has limited or can limit the constitutional power of the President to carry on diplomatic contacts or conversations with foreign governments. The advantage of this method of maintaining contacts with foreign governments is that any one of the debtor nations may at any time bring to the attention of the Government of the United States new conditions and facts affecting any phase of its indebtedness.

It is equally true that existing debt agreements are unalterable save by Congressional action.

This was very disappointing. Obviously, unless there was full co-operation both in debts and stabilization, President Hoover could not proceed. He had less than ninety days to remain in office, and not even the machinery for negotiations could be set up without the approval of the Democratic majority in Congress, who would not act without Mr. Roosevelt's approval.

The importance of this to the later banking crisis was simply that it caused discouragement in the country and apprehension as to delay in stabilization of debts and currencies. Disappointment in Mr. Roosevelt's attitude was quick to appear in the press.

Said the *Detroit Free Press:*

It is highly unfortunate that Governor Roosevelt was unable to bring himself to meet the President half way. The refusal of the governor to co-operate actively with Mr. Hoover and his subsequent statement that the matter at issue was "not his baby," are indicative of the lack of largeness and vision more disquieting in a person about to become the Chief Executive of the nation. . . . Mr. Roosevelt had an opportunity unique in the history of the American presidency, and he failed to grasp it.

The New York Herald Tribune stated (November 24, 1932):

Americans are so accustomed to having Mr. Hoover do the right and courageous thing that his admirable statement on the debts will hardly occasion surprise. It covers a complex issue, endlessly bedeviled by national prejudices and selfishness, clearly, fairly, and with a minimum of words. . . .

It may be recalled that during the campaign there was heat and resentment in Democratic quarters when it was argued that a change of administration inevitably meant marking time for a number of months. Mr.

Hoover has now done his utmost to prevent such a delay in respect to the debt issue. Mr. Roosevelt has felt unable to aid him. The delay must ensue.

The Baltimore Sun said (November 24th) that the debts

may not be legally his baby until the fourth of March, but it seems to us that Mr. Roosevelt might wisely have given thought to the possibility that this baby, which is not now his, may soon develop into an unruly stepchild, permanently lodged under his roof, and disposed to play with matches.

However, Mr. Roosevelt agreed on the secondary question as to insisting upon the December 15th payments, and also that in this event our government would negotiate for the future. President Hoover then proceeded upon this line.

On December 6th, the President, in his message to Congress,[*] again urged:

Our major difficulties during the past two years find their origins in the shocks from economic collapse abroad, which in turn are the aftermath of the Great War. If we are to secure rapid and assured recovery and protection for the future we must co-operate with foreign nations in many measures. . . . We are participating in the formulation of a World Economic Conference, successful results from which would contribute much to advance in agricultural prices, employment, and business. Currency depreciation and correlated forces have contributed greatly to decrease in price levels. Moreover, from these origins rise most of the destructive trade barriers now stifling the commerce of the world. We could by successful action increase security and expand trade through stability in international exchange and monetary values. By such action world confidence could be restored. . . .

Again he recommended that these measures should be considered in conjunction with settlement of the debts. He was convinced that we must insist upon the December 15th payments to us, in view of the fact that the debtor governments were trying to establish the contention that the debts were no longer a real obligation.

After many attempts at negotiation, the principal debtors, with the exception of France, met their December 15th payments. The French were being pressed by our government and might have met the payment had not an unfortunate press dispatch appeared from Warm Springs, Georgia, where the President-elect was resting. It purported to express the view of Mr. Roosevelt that he did not regard payment of the December 15th installment to be a necessary condition for the opening of nego-

[*] State Papers, Vol. II, p. 494, *et seq.*

tiations for debt adjustment. The French Government and the French press received the dispatch with joy, applauding Mr. Roosevelt and condemning the President. The French authorities declined to make the December 15th payment. Mr. Roosevelt denied that the statement had any authority from him.

The failure to proceed to the settlement of these questions, and especially to the monetary conference, had its ill effect upon the domestic situation. The necessity for quickly ending the world trade war was imperative. Therefore, on December 17th the President re-opened the subject in a telegram to Governor Roosevelt at Hyde Park, New York.[5]

Washington, 5:35 P.M.

My dear Governor:

As you have seen from the press the position of the debtor governments in respect to the December 15th payments is now largely determined. In accord with both your expressions and my own statements it is the duty of the United States to survey and exchange views on these questions individually with some of the debtor governments. It is necessary to consider the character of machinery to be erected for this purpose.

These problems cannot be disassociated from the problems which will come before the World Economic Conference and to some degree from those before the Conference on World Disarmament. As the economic situation in foreign countries is one of the dominant depressants of prices and employment in the United States it is urgent that the World Economic Conference should assemble at as early a date as possible. The United States should be represented by a strong and effective delegation. This delegation should be chosen at an early moment in order that it may give necessary consideration and familiarize itself with the problems, and secure that such investigation and study are made as will be necessary for its use at the conference. . . .

While we must not change our established policy of dealing with each debtor separately, and indeed no other course could be entertained in view of the widely divergent conditions which exist in the different countries and the very different situations in which they find themselves, and while the decision heretofore reached not to consider the debt question at the coming World Economic Conference is a wise one, it seems clear that the successful outcome of the World Economic Conference will be greatly furthered if the debt problems can be satisfactorily advanced before that conference although final agreement in some cases may be contingent upon the satisfactory solution of certain economic questions in which our country has a direct interest and the final determination of which may well form a part of the matters coming before the Economic Conference.

It is desirable that such delegation should include members of the Congress in order that such intricate facts and circumstances can be effectively presented to the Congress. . . .

[5] This, and the following exchange of telegrams, in State Papers, Vol. II, p. 554 *et seq.*

If it were not for the urgency of the situation both at home and abroad and the possible great helpfulness to employment and agricultural prices and general restoration of confidence which could be brought about by successful issue of all these questions and the corresponding great dangers of inaction, it would be normal to allow the whole matter to rest until after the change of administration, but in the emergency such as exists at the moment I would be neglectful of my duty if I did not facilitate in every way the earliest possible dealing with these questions. It is obvious that no conclusions would be reached from such discussions prior to March 4th, but a great deal of time could be saved if the machinery could be created at once by the appointment of the delegates as I have mentioned. . . .

I should be glad to know if you could join with me in the selection of such delegation at the present time or if you feel that the whole matter should be deferred until after March 4th. I believe that there would be no difficulty in agreeing upon an adequate representation for the purpose. In such selection the first concern would be the selection of a chairman for the delegation.

Herbert Hoover.

The message to Congress of December 19th embraced the statement as to currency stabilization and ending the trade war already given early in this chapter. The remaining portions of the message devoted to the debt questions were as follows:

As Congress is aware the principle debtor nations recently requested that the December payments on those debts should be postponed and that we should undertake an exchange of views upon possible revision in the light of altered world conditions.

We have declined to postpone this payment as we considered that such action (a) would amount to practical breakdown of the integrity of these agreements, (b) would impose an abandonment of the national policies of dealing with these obligations separately with each nation, (c) would create a situation without consideration of the destructive forces militating against economic recovery, (d) would not be a proper call upon the American people to further sacrifices unless there were definite compensations. It is essential in our national interest that we accept none of these implications and undertake no commitments before these economic and other problems are canvassed and so far as possible are solved.

Of the total of about $125,000,000 due, Czechoslovakia, Finland, Great Britain, Italy, Latvia, and Lithuania have met payments amounting to $98,685,910, despite the difficulties inherent in the times. Austria, Belgium, Esthonia, France, Greece, Hungary and Poland have not made their payments. In the case of some of these countries such failure was unquestionably due to inability in the present situation to make the payments contemplated by the agreements.

Certain nations have specifically stated that they do not see their way clear to make payments under these agreements for the future. Thus our government and our people are confronted with the realities of a situation in connection with the debts not heretofore contemplated.

It is not necessary for me at this time to enter upon the subject of the origins of these debts, the sacrifices clearly made by the American people, the respective capacities of other governments to pay, or to answer the arguments put forward which look toward cancellation of these obligations. I may, however, point out that except in one country the taxation required for the payments upon the debts owing to our government does not exceed one-quarter of the amounts now being imposed to support their military establishments. As their maintained armaments call for a large increase in expenditures on our defensive forces beyond those before the war, the American people naturally feel that cancellation of these debts would give us no relief from arms but only free large sums for further military preparations abroad. Further it is not amiss to note that the contention that payment of these debts is confined to direct shipment of goods or payment in gold is not a proper representation, since in normal times triangular trade is a very large factor in world exchanges, nor is any presentation of the trade balance situation complete without taking into account services as for instance American tourist expenditure and emigrant remittances alone to most of the debtor countries exceed the amount of payments. I may also mention that our country made double the total sacrifice of any other nation in bringing about the moratorium which served to prevent the collapse of many nations of Europe with its reaction upon the world. This act of good will on our part must not now be made either the excuse or opportunity for demanding still larger sacrifices.

My views are well known; I will not entertain the thought of cancellation. I believe that whatever further sacrifices the American people might make by way of adjustment of cash payments must be compensated by definite benefits in markets and otherwise.

In any event in protection to our own vital interests, as good neighbors and in accord with our traditional duty as wise and fair creditors whether to individuals or nations, we must honor the request for discussion of these questions by nations who have sought to maintain their obligations to us.

The decision heretofore reached to exclude debt questions from the coming World Economic Conference or from any collective conference with our debtors is wise, as there are obligations subject only to discussion with individual nations and should not form part of a collective discussion or of discussion among many nations not affected, yet it seems clear that successful outcome of the Economic Conference would be greatly furthered if the debt problem were explored in advance, even though final agreement might well be contingent on the satisfactory solution of economic and armament questions in which our country has direct interest.

Thus from this present complex situation certain definite conclusions are unavoidable:

1. A number of the most serious problems have now arisen and we are bound to recognize and deal with them.

2. It is of great importance that the preparatory action should be taken at once, otherwise time will be lost while destructive forces are continuing against our agriculture, employment, and business.

3. Adequate and proper machinery for dealing with them must be created. It is clear that ordinary diplomatic agencies and facilities are not suitable for the conduct of negotiations which can best be carried on across the table by specially qualified representatives.

4. As I have pointed out, the discussion of debts is necessarily connected with the solution of major problems at the World Economic Conference and the Arms Conference. The ideal way would therefore seem to be that some of our representatives in these matters should be selected at once who can perform both these functions of preparing for the World Economic Conference, and should exchange views upon the debt questions with certain nations at once and to advise upon the course to be pursued as to others. It would be an advantage for some of them to be associated with the Arms Conference. Some part of the delegates appointed for this purpose could well be selected from the members of the Congress. On the side of the Executive this is no derogation of either Executive authority or independence; on the side of the Congress it is no commitment but provides for the subsequent presentation to the Congress of the deliberations, intricacies, reasoning and facts upon which recommendations have been based and is of first importance in enabling the Congress to give adequate consideration to such conclusions.

5. Discussions in respect to both debt questions and the World Economic Conference cannot be concluded during my administration, yet the economic situation in the world necessitates the preliminary work essential to its success. The undertaking of these preliminary questions should not be delayed until after March 4th.

I propose, therefore, to seek the co-operation of President-elect Roosevelt in the organization of machinery for advancement of consideration of these problems.

A year ago I requested that the Congress should authorize the creation of a debt commission to deal with situations which were bound to arise. The Congress did not consider this wise. In the situation as it has developed it appears necessary for the Executive to proceed. Obviously any conclusions would be subject to approval by the Congress.

On the other hand should the Congress prefer to authorize by legislative enactment a commission set up along the lines above indicated it would meet my hearty approval. . . .

The situation is one of such urgency that we require national solidarity and national co-operation if we are to serve the welfare of the American people and indeed if we are to conquer the forces which today threaten the very foundations of civilization.

Governor Roosevelt replied to the telegram of the 17th as follows:

Albany, N. Y., 8:50 P.M.,
December 19, 1932.

THE PRESIDENT:
The White House.

DEAR MR. PRESIDENT:

I have given earnest consideration to your courteous telegram of December 17 and I want to assure you that I seek in every proper way to be of help. It is my view that the questions of disarmament, intergovernmental debts and permanent economic arrangements will be found to require selective treatment even though this be with full recognition of the possibility that in the ultimate outcome a relationship of any two or of all three may become clear.

(1) As to Disarmament: Your policy is clear and satisfactory. Some time, however, is required to bring it to fruition. Success in a practical program limiting armaments abolishing certain instruments of warfare, and decreasing the offensive or attack power of all nations will in my judgment have a very positive and salutary influence on debt and economic discussions.

(2) As to the Debts: If any debtor nation desires to approach us such nation should be given the earliest opportunity so to do. Certainly in the preliminary conversations the Chief Executive has full authority either through the existing machinery of the Diplomatic service or by supplementing it with specially appointed agents of the President himself, to conduct such preliminary investigations or inquiries without in any way seeking formal Congressional action. I am impelled to suggest however that these surveys should be limited to determining facts, and exploring possibilities rather than fixing policies binding on the incoming administration. I wholly approve and would in no way hinder such surveys.

(3) As to the Economic Conference: I am clear that a permanent economic program for the world should not be submerged in conversations relating to disarmament or debts. I recognize of course a relationship, but not an identity. Therefore I cannot go along with the thought that the personnel conducting the conversations should be identical.

By reason of the fact that under the constitution I am unable to assume the authority in the matter of the agenda of the economic conference until after March fourth next, and by reason of the fact that there appears to be a divergence of opinion between us in respect to the scope of the conference and further by reason of the fact that time is required to conduct conversations relating to debts and disarmaments, I must respectfully suggest that the appointing of the permanent delegates and the final determination of the program of the economic conference be held in abeyance until after March fourth. In the meantime I can see no objection to further informal conferences with the agenda committee, or to the carrying on of preliminary economic studies which would serve an undoubtedly useful purpose.

I feel that it would be both improper for me and inadvisable for you, however much I appreciate the courtesy of your suggestion, for me to take part in naming representatives. From the necessity of the case, they could be responsible only and properly to you as President for the effective performance of their assignments particularly in matters calling for almost daily touch with and direction of the Executive. I would be in no position prior to March fourth to have this constant contact.

I think you will realize that it would be unwise for me to accept an apparent joint responsibility with you when, as a matter of constitutional fact, I would be wholly lacking in any attendant authority.

FRANKLIN D. ROOSEVELT.

President Hoover promptly replied to the President-elect by telegram as follows:

December 20, 1932, 2:30 P.M.

GOVERNOR FRANKLIN D. ROOSEVELT,
Albany, New York.

MY DEAR GOVERNOR:

I have your telegram expressing the difficulties which you find in cooperation at the present time. In the face of foreign conditions which are continually degenerating agricultural prices, increasing unemployment and creating economic difficulties for our people, I am unwilling to admit that co-operation cannot be established between the outgoing and incoming administrations which will give earlier solution and recovery from these difficulties.

If you will review my previous communications and conversations I think you will agree that while outlining the nature of the problems my proposals to you have been directed to the setting up not of solutions but of the machinery through which by preparedness the ultimate solution of these questions can be expedited and co-ordinated to the end that many months of delay and increasing losses to our people may be avoided.

I fully recognize that your solution of these questions of debt, the world economic problems and disarmament might vary from my own. These conclusions obviously cannot be attained in my administration and will lie entirely within your administration. I wish especially to avoid any embarrassment to your work and thus have no intention of committing the incoming administration to any particular policy prior to March 4th. Even the exploratory work you suggest should be participated in by men in whom you have confidence, and I wish to facilitate it. What I deem of the utmost importance is that when you assume responsibility on March 4th machinery of your approval will be here, fully informed and ready to function according to the policies you may determine.

My frequent statements indicate agreement with you that debts, world economic problems and disarmament require selective treatment, but you will agree with me that they also require co-ordination and preparation either in the individual hands of the then President or in the hands of men selected to deal with them and advise him. There is thus no thought of submerging the World Economic Conference with other questions, but rather to remove the barriers from successful issue of that conference.

With view to again making an effort to secure co-operation and that solidarity of national action which the situation needs, I would be glad if you could designate Mr. Owen D. Young, Colonel House, or any other men of your party possessed of your views and your confidence and at the same time familiar with these problems, to sit with the principal officers of this administration, in endeavor to see what steps can be taken to avoid delays of precious time and inevitable losses that will ensue from such delays.

HERBERT HOOVER.

On December 21st the Governor again replied as follows:

Albany, N. Y.,
9:45 P.M., December 21, 1932.

THE PRESIDENT,
The White House.
DEAR MR. PRESIDENT:

I think perhaps the difficulties to which you refer are not in finding the means or the willingness for co-operation but, rather, in defining clearly those things concerning which co-operation between us is possible.

We are agreed that commitments to any particular policy prior to March fourth are for many reasons inadvisable and indeed impossible. There remains therefore before that date only the possibility of exploratory work and preliminary surveys.

Please let me reiterate not only that I am glad to avoid the loss of precious time through delay in starting these preliminaries but also that I shall gladly receive such information and expression of opinion concerning all of those international questions which because of existing economic and other conditions must and will be among the first concerns of my administration.

However, for me to accept any joint responsibility in the work of exploration might well be construed by the debtor or other nations, collectively or individually, as a commitment—moral even though not legal, as to policies and courses of action.

The designation of a man or men of such eminence as your telegram suggests would not imply mere fact-findings; it would suggest the presumption that such representatives were empowered to exchange views on matters of large and binding policy.

Current press dispatches from abroad already indicate that the joint action which you propose would most certainly be interpreted there as much more of a policy commitment than either you or I actually contemplate.

May I respectfully suggest that you proceed with the selection of your representatives to conduct the preliminary exploration necessary with individual debtor nations and representatives to discuss the agenda of the World Economic Conference, making it clear that none of these representatives is authorized to bind this government as to any ultimate policy.

If this be done, let me repeat that I shall be happy to receive their information and their expressions of opinion.

To that I add the thought that between now and March fourth I shall be very glad if you will keep me advised as to the progress of the preliminary discussions, and I also shall be happy to consult with you freely during this period.

FRANKLIN D. ROOSEVELT.

It was manifestly illogical that the President should appoint a delegation to present policies that might be entirely repudiated within two months. No foreign government would take such a delegation seriously. President Hoover in the meantime conveyed to the Governor that he would appoint any experienced men to the delegation whom the Governor would suggest.

As distorted versions of the discussions were appearing daily in the press, the President considered less harm would be done by full publication and gave out the complete correspondence to the press representatives at Washington on December 22nd, with the statement:

Governor Roosevelt considers that it is undesirable for him to accede to my suggestions for co-operative action in the foreign proposals outlined in my recent message to Congress. I will respect his wishes. . . .

There can be no question that the failure to move promptly upon a united front with the object of currency stabilization and adjustment of the war debts impeded the whole world recovery. It also hampered a return by the world to stable money standards. Of like importance is the fact that it encouraged default and resistance to adequate compensation for any adjustment we might make in the war debts.

At the end of January, President-elect Roosevelt asked that the British Government should be requested to send a delegate to the United States after the fourth of March. From this point forward the President-elect set up his own relations with the British Ambassador and carried forward his negotiations directly with the British Government.

The World Economic Conference was postponed until July, 1933, and subsequent installments on the war debts have been defaulted.

By mid-February the President determined to lay before the country his views on the subject of international currency relations, as well as upon the necessity of maintaining the gold standard. He did so in a Lincoln Day address delivered in New York City on the thirteenth of that month. It was a report upon the danger which, as he knew, then was facing the American people: [6]

[6] State Papers, Vol. II, p. 587, *et seq.*

. . . While we have many concerns in the domestic field we must realize that so long as we engage in the export and import of goods and in financial activities abroad our price levels and credit system, our employment, and above all our fears will be greatly affected by foreign influences. During the past two years the crash of one foreign nation after another under direct and indirect war inheritances has dominated our whole economic life. The time has now come when nations must accept, in self interest no less than in altruism, the obligations to co-operate in achieving world stability so mankind may again resume the march of progress. Daily it becomes more certain that the next great constructive step in remedy of the illimitable human suffering from this depression lies in the international field. It is in that field where the tide of prices can be most surely and quickly turned and the tragic despair of unemployment, agriculture and business transformed to hope and confidence.

. . . Many countries in addition to the other pressures of the depression were overburdened with debt and obligations from the World War or from excessive borrowing from abroad for rehabilitation or expansion. Many created or added to their difficulties through unbalanced budgets due to vast social programs or armament, finally reaching the point where collapse in governmental credit was inevitable. Foreigners in fear withdrew their deposits in such countries. Citizens in fright exported their capital. The result was a large movement of gold from such a country followed by the immediate undermining of confidence in its currency and its credit system. Runs on its banks ensued. Restrictions were imposed upon exchange to stop the flight of capital. Barriers were erected against the imports of commodities in endeavor to reduce the spending of her citizens for foreign goods and in an effort to establish equilibrium in exchange and retention of their industries, increase in their unemployment and further shrinkage in consumption of world goods, again and again affecting all other nations. Depreciated currencies gave some nations the hope to manufacture goods more cheaply than their neighbors and thus to rehabilitate their financial position by invasion of the markets of other nations. Those nations in turn have sought to protect themselves by erecting barriers, until today as the result of such financial breakdown we are in the presence of an incipient outbreak of economic war in the world with the weapons of depreciated currencies, artificial barriers to trade by quotas, reciprocal trade agreements, discriminations, nationalistic campaigns to consume home-made goods, and a score of tactics each of which can be justified for the moment, but each of which adds to world confusion and dangers.

Out of the storm center of Europe this devastation has spread until, if we survey the world situation at the present moment, we find some forty-four countries which have placed restrictions upon the movement of gold and exchange or are otherwise definitely off of the gold standard. In practically all of them these actions have within the past twelve months been accompanied by new restrictions upon imports in an endeavor to hold or attract gold or to give some stability to currencies. . . .

A new phase is now developing among these nations that is the rapid degeneration into economic war which threatens to engulf the world. The imperative call to the world today is to prevent this war.

Ever since the storm began in Europe the United States has held staunchly to the gold standard. In the present setting of depreciated currencies and in the light of differences in costs of production our tariffs are below those of most countries; we have held free from quotas, preferences, discriminations among nations. We have thereby maintained one Gibraltar of stability in the world and contributed to check the movement of chaos.

We are ourselves now confronted with an unnatural movement of goods from the lowered costs and standards of countries of depreciated currencies, which daily increase our unemployment and our difficulties. We are confronted with discriminatory actions and barriers stifling our agricultural and other markets. We will be ourselves forced to defensive action to protect ourselves unless this mad race is stopped. We must not be the major victim of it all. . . .

Another phenomenon of the gold situation has increased disturbance and wrought havoc. That is the effect of waves of fear and apprehension. We have a parallel in nations to an unreasoning panic run on a bank. The fears and apprehensions directed in turn to the stability of first one nation and then another have caused the withdrawal of foreign balances from a particular nation, followed by flights of capital, through purchases of exchange by its own citizens seeking refuge and security for their property. These movements are followed by large flows of gold to meet exchange demands, thus undermining the domestic currency and credit system of the victim nation and leading to an unnatural piling up of gold in some nation temporarily considered safe. These movements, themselves in large degree unwarranted, have forced some nations off the gold standard that could otherwise have maintained their position. We ourselves a year ago suffered from the effects of such a movement. Thus a mass of the gold dashing hither and yon from one nation to another, seeking maximum safety, has acted like a cannon loose on the deck of the world in a storm.

In the meantime the currencies of the world are fluctuating spasmodically. Countries off of the gold standard are in reality suffering from their managed paper currencies by reason of the fact that men are unable to make contracts for the future with security, and that insecurity itself again dries up enterprise, business, employments, consumption of goods, and further causes reductions of prices. Other nations to hold their own are attempting to compete in destruction.

Broadly, the solution lies in the re-establishment of confidence. That confidence cannot be re-established by the abandonment of gold as a standard in the world. So far as the human race has yet developed and established its methods and systems of stable exchange, that solution can only be found now and found quickly through the re-establishment of gold standards among important nations. The huge gold reserves of the world can be made to function in relation to currencies, standards of value, and exchange. And I say with emphasis that I am not proposing this as a favor to the United States. It is the need of the whole world. The United

States is so situated that it can protect itself better than almost any country on earth.

Nor is it necessary from an international point of view that those nations who have been forced off the gold standard shall be again restored to former gold values. It will suffice if it only is fixed. From this source are the principal hopes for restoring world confidence and reversing the growing barriers to the movement of goods and making possible the security in trade which will again revive a demand for such goods. To do this it is necessary to have strong and courageous action on the part of the leading commercial nations. If some sort of international financial action is necessary to enable central banks to co-operate for the purpose of stabilizing currencies, nations should have no hesitation in joining in such an operation under proper safeguards. If some part of the debt payments to us could be set aside for temporary use for this purpose, we should not hesitate to do so. At the same time the world should endeavor to find a place for silver, at least in enlarged subsidiary coinage. . . .

If the major nations will enter the road leading to the early re-establishment of the gold standard, then and then only can the abnormal barriers to trade, the quotas, preferences, discriminatory agreements, and tariffs which exceed the differences in cost of production between nations be removed, uniform trade privileges among all nations be re-established and the threat of economic war averted. A reasonable period of comparative stability in the world's currencies would repay the cost of such effort a hundred times over in the increase of consumption, the increase of employment, the lessening of the difficulties of debtors throughout the land, with the avoidance of millions of tragedies. The world would quickly see a renewed movement of goods and would have an immediate rise in prices everywhere, thereby bringing immediate relief to the whole economic system. . . .

I do not underestimate the difficulties nor the vast fiscal and financial problems which lie behind the restoration of stability and economic peace. Bold action alone can succeed. The alternative to such constructive action is a condition too grave to be contemplated in passive acceptance.

The American people will soon be at the fork of three roads. The first is the highway of co-operation among nations, thereby to remove the obstructions to world consumption and rising prices. This road leads to real stability, to expanding standards of living, to a resumption of the march of progress by all peoples. It is today the immediate road to relief of agriculture and unemployment, not alone for us but the entire world.

The second road is to rely upon our high degree of national self-containment, to increase our tariffs, to create quotas and discriminations, and to engage in definite methods of curtailment of production of agricultural and other products and thus to secure a larger measure of economic isolation from world influences. It would be a long road to readjustments into unknown and uncertain fields. But it may be necessary if the first way out is closed to us. Some measures may be necessary pending co-operative conclusions with other nations.

The third road is that we inflate our currency, consequently abandon the gold standard, and with our depreciated currency attempt to enter a world economic war, with the certainty that it leads to complete destruction, both at home and abroad. . . .

The first road can only be undertaken by the co-operation among all important nations. Last April, in conjunction with the leaders of Europe our government developed the idea of a World Economic Conference to deal with these questions. It is unfortunate that the delay of events in Europe and the election in the United States necessarily postponed the convening of that conference. It has been further delayed by the change of our administrations.

The question naturally arises whether other nations will co-operate to restore world confidence, stability, and economic peace. In this connection, I trust the American people will not be misled or influenced by the ceaseless stream of foreign propaganda that cancellation of war-debts would give this international relief and remedy. That is not true. These debts are but a segment of the problem. Their world trade importance is being exaggerated. In this respect I stated some months ago, the American people can well contend that most of the debtor countries have the capacity to raise these annual amounts from their taxpayers, as witness the fact that in most cases the payments to us amount to less than one-third of the military expenditures of each country. But at the same time we can well realize that in some instances the transfer of these sums may gravely disturb their currency or international exchanges. But if we are asked for sacrifices because of such injury we should have assurances of co-operation that will positively result in monetary stability and the restoration of world prosperity. If we are asked for sacrifices because of incapacity to pay we should have tangible compensation in restoration of our proportion of their agricultural and other imports. The world should have relief from the sore burden of armaments. If they are unwilling to meet us in these fields, this nation, whether you or I like it or not, will be driven by our own internal forces more and more to its own self-containment and isolation, as harmful to the world and as little satisfactory to us as this course may be.

But this is the counsel of despair. The full need of prosperity among nations can not be builded upon mutual impoverishment. It is to the interest of the world to join in bold and courageous action which will bring about economic peace. . . .

On our side this problem is not to be solved by partisan action but by national duty. Whatever our differences of view may be on domestic policies, the welfare of the American people rests upon solidarity before the world, not merely in resisting proposals which would weaken the United States and the world, but solidarity in co-operation with other nations in strengthening the whole economic fabric of the world. These problems are not insoluble. There is a latent, earnest, and underlying purpose on the part of all nations to find their solution. Of our own determination there should be no question.

The problem before the world is to restore confidence and hope by the release of the strong, natural forces of recovery which are inherent in this civilization. They passed through most terrible conflicts. They met many great depressions. They created a state of human well-being in normal times such as the world has never seen. The next step is as great as any in history. It is that we perpetuate the welfare of mankind through the immense objectives of world recovery and world peace.

We need not underscore here the prophetic character of these utterances.

There can be no question as to the influence of the delays in the world-currency-stabilization conference, upon a public confidence already shaken. They were a direct contribution to the subsequent bank panic. And the world currency situation did indeed steadily deteriorate.

CHAPTER XVI

PREVENTING A BALANCED BUDGET

FOLLOWING the November election President Hoover recognized that many of his policies of agricultural and social betterment must be laid aside on account of lack of support, but he also felt that, in view of the promises made by Governor Roosevelt during the campaign, upon certain subjects it might be possible to secure an adjournment of partisan politics. In addition to war debt and stabilization these subjects related to balancing the budget, banking reform and the reorganization of the bankruptcy laws, which were urgent for recovery. He supposed that the Democratic leadership even would be glad to have him take the onus of unpopular actions, such as increased taxes and reduced expenditures. And the Democratic leaders in Congress appeared willing to support such a program.

One of the first of these important projects was balancing the budget. Any country in the world which has continued for any length of time upon an unbalanced budget has known the bitter experience of increased economic instability, a constant danger of forced inflation and at all times a lack of confidence, both at home and abroad, paralyzing to economic recovery.

The Democratic majority in the previous session of Congress had defeated President Hoover's proposals of reduction of expenses and increase of revenues. The Democratic platform of June 30, 1932, however, had stated: "The Democratic Party solemnly promises . . . an immediate and drastic reduction of governmental expenditures . . . to accomplish a saving of not less than twenty-five per cent in the cost of the Federal Government. . . . We favor maintenance of the national credit by a Federal budget annually balanced. . . ." On July 30, 1932, Governor Roosevelt had repeated this economy pledge and charged that the Republican Administration had "become sponsor for deficits which, at the end of this fiscal year, will add $5,000,000,000 to the national debt. . . . We must have the courage to stop borrowing to meet the crisis. . . . Let us have the courage to stop borrowing to meet continuing deficits. Stop the deficits. . . . Any government, like any family, can for a year spend a little more than it earns. But you and I know that a continuation of that habit means the poorhouse."

During the campaign, Governor Roosevelt had promised to reduce Federal expenses by $1,000,000,000. In so doing he ignored the conduct of the Democratic majority in the last Congress.

In any event, President Hoover thought that the incoming administration would welcome his lifting from their backs the political unpopularity of retrenchment and new taxes. By assuming this liability he would give a new impetus to recovery, although he realized that the Democrats would secure the political credit. He felt strongly that this policy would be the means greatly to benefit the country. He had been denounced in the campaign by substantial groups of veterans, government employees, and other groups which had resented his reduction of payments, and that despite the justice of his actions. Disappointed bonus seekers, together with the vast number of taxpayers who had resented the tax increases, further added to the opposition. At his urging, revenues had been increased in the previous session, but many people had believed the Democratic propaganda that taxes could have been avoided by means of "economy" in government. Even the increase in postage had been used as an issue in the campaign. Veterans had been told that they would receive the bonus as soon as funds were available. Thus the promises of economy made by Governor Roosevelt and the chance to place the responsibility upon the outgoing administration for further taxes and for reductions in government pay and allowances, seemed to warrant President Hoover's expectations of co-operation.

The course of events was as follows:

On November 18, 1932, the President directed a downward revision by all departments of the tentative budget expenditures for the next year. On December 6, 1932, in the annual message to Congress, he laid especial emphasis upon the need and opportunity to balance the budget:[1]

I shall in due course present the Executive budget to the Congress. It will show proposed reductions in appropriations below those enacted by the last session of the Congress by over $830,000,000. In addition, I shall present the necessary Executive Orders under the recent act authorizing the re-organization of the Federal Government which, if permitted to go into force, will produce still further substantial economies. . . .

After discussion of various items of public works and payments to government employees and veterans, President Hoover continued:

Many of the economies recommended in the budget were presented at the last session of the Congress, but failed of adoption. . . .

[1] State Papers, Vol. II, p. 494, *et seq.*

Some of the older revenues and some of the revenues provided under the act passed during the last session of the Congress, particularly those generally referred to as the nuisance taxes, have not been as prolific of income as had been hoped. Further revenue is necessary in addition to the amount of reductions in expenditures recommended. Many of the manufacturers' excise taxes upon selected industries not only failed to produce satisfactory revenue but they are in many ways unjust and discriminatory. The time has come when, if the Government is to have an adequate basis of revenue to assure a balanced budget, this system of special manufacturers' excise taxes should be extended to cover practically all manufactures at a uniform rate, except necessary food and possibly some grades of clothing. . . .

The budget estimates immediately showed the effect of these recommendations. A threatened deficit of nearly two billions would be reduced to only $300,000,000. That is, the first full fiscal year of the Roosevelt Administration,—between July 1, 1933 and June 30, 1934—would see the nation back on a practically balanced budget, which also could have been the case the year before if the Democratic Congress had been willing to co-operate.

As an additional step in the same direction, the President sent to Congress on December 9th a complete series of executive orders reorganizing the entire administrative structure of the government.[2]

This was in fulfillment of the promise contained in his annual message of three days previous, in which he had spoken of the authorization by Congress in the Economy Act of 1932 of proposals for government reorganization by the President. Such proposals were to be transmitted to Congress and not become effective for sixty days unless sooner approved by Congress.

Mr. Hoover continued:

I shall issue such Executive orders within a few days, grouping or consolidating over fifty executive and administrative agencies, including a large number of commissions and "independent" agencies.

The second step, of course, remains that after these various bureaus and agencies are placed cheek by jowl into such groups, the administrative officers in charge of the groups shall eliminate their overlap and still further consolidate these activities. Therein lie large economies.

The Congress must be warned that a host of interested persons inside and outside the government, whose vision is concentrated on some particular function, will at once protest against these proposals. These same sorts of activities have prevented reorganization of the government for over a quarter of a century. They must be disregarded if the task is to be accomplished.

[2] State Papers, Vol. II, p. 532 *et seq.*

December 23, 1932: The Republican leaders reported to the President that in discussions with Democratic leaders of the House, the latter had agreed to support a general revenue bill this session which, with reductions of expenditures, would practically balance the budget; also that they would support a manufacturers' sales tax. This, although it had been proposed during the previous session by the Democrats, now would have to be a "Republican" proposal. This major item alone was estimated to raise $500,000,000. Other items of increased revenues also were to be included.

December 27, 1932: Chairman Collier (Democrat) of the House Ways and Means Committee, quoted in *The New York Times,* after expressing his dislike of the manufacturers' sales tax as a basis of the balancing of the budget, said:

I have been looking the field over very carefully and I am afraid that I do not see any other possible tax. But we are going to balance the budget in fairness to the country and to the incoming administration by whatever means is possible.

According to *The New York Times* dispatch, Speaker Garner, now Vice-President-elect, taking the 1932 platform of his party seriously, "reiterated his desire to balance the budget in the present session of Congress and his willingness to use his influence for the adoption of the sales tax if that should be necessary to accomplish his purpose. . . ." Mr. Garner stated:

We must balance the budget and carry out what appeared to be the mandate of the people in November. . . . I feel we must carry out our promises.

According to the same journal, Senator Pat Harrison gave similar assurances.

Governor Roosevelt the next day announced in Albany, through the press, that he was "amazed" and "horrified" at the action of the Democratic leaders in agreeing to a manufacturers' sales tax. It is to be noted that the manufacturers' sales tax of two per cent, as proposed by President Hoover, excluded food and the cheaper forms of clothing. There could have been no principle here involved, for President Roosevelt, within ninety days thereafter, advocated and imposed a form of manufacturers' sales tax—under the term "processing tax"—exclusively upon foods and cheaper clothing, which amounted to from twenty to forty per cent.

December 28, 1932: The New York Times dispatch from Washington stated:

> The Democratic framers of revenue measures were in a state of confusion today over the tax situation. Speaker Garner again reiterated his desire to balance the budget, but indicated unmistakably a feeling of perplexity since the revelation of Governor Roosevelt's opposition. . . . The quick rebound from Albany occasioned by the support of Speaker Garner and Chairman Collier of the sales tax as a last resort was declared by a member of the committee to have "taken the heart out of the boys!" . . . House leaders declared it extremely doubtful that any general revenue bill would be reported in the short session.

December 29, 1932: The press carried the report that Governor Roosevelt had instructed the Democratic leaders to defeat the President's proposals for re-organization of government bureaus and commissions.

Governor Roosevelt had discussed a method of budget-balancing by separating expenditure into ordinary and "emergency" items, balancing the former to revenues and borrowing for the latter. *The New York Times,* commenting on this today, said:

> The proposal of Governor Roosevelt to bond permanent government improvements and certain fixed charges through a special budget to be paid off by regular sinking funds was being talked of more and more today as one of the methods for balancing the Treasury accounts. This idea received no special favor from Speaker Garner however. He said that such a plan would be "simply a matter of book keeping" and in the end would avail little toward solving the fiscal problems of the government.

The extent to which Governor Roosevelt assumed the direction of the Democratic Congress is indicated by the further statement in *The Times:*

> With the proposed general manufacturers' sales tax killed by his opposition Governor Roosevelt will turn next week, after he relinquishes the governorship, to consideration of methods for balancing the Federal Budget and bringing about economy in government expenditures. During this period the President-elect expects to confer with leading Democratic members of Congress and obtain their advice on the Federal fiscal problems.

December 31, 1932: A new aspect appeared upon the face of affairs when Governor Roosevelt announced that he had called a conference of Democratic Congressional leaders to meet him at New York on January 5, 1933. It was announced that policies as to legislation then pending before Congress would be considered.

It must here be noted that this action of an incoming President, in dictating the policies of Congress during the remaining term of an outgoing President, was unprecedented. As the Democrats were in a majority in the House and in effectual control of the Senate, the President-elect thereby undertook the responsibility of determining legislative policies. Thereafter the Democratic majority publicly and privately consulted his wishes. This should be considered not only in the light of the failure in co-operation, but also in the light of the denial of responsibility before taking office in other matters of even more vital import.

January 3, 1933: It was announced by the Democratic leaders that they had suspended action upon the bills intended to balance the budget until after the conference called by President-elect Roosevelt for January 5th. President Hoover stated the same day in a press conference that——[3]

The proposals of Democratic leaders in Congress to stop the reorganization of government functions which I have made is a backward step. . . .

Any real re-organization sensibly carried out will sooner or later embrace the very orders I have issued. . . . Every other advanced government on earth has a definite public works department or division. . . . It is only by consolidation that duplication and waste of a multitude of offices and officials can be eliminated. . . . They can only be brought under the limelight if they are concentrated in one place. It is the only way to further reduce logrolling and personal politics in these appropriations.

No other government and no good government would tolerate merchant marine activities separated over seven departments or independent establishments. The same can be said as to Public Health, Education, Land Utilization, etc. . . . The financial and economic functions relating to agriculture should be consolidated. The major departments should be changed.

January 5, 1933: President-elect Roosevelt held his conference in New York with the Democratic Congressional leaders. According to the press statements, they apparently came to an agreement upon an increased tax on incomes in the lower brackets "to balance the budget," in substitution for the manufacturers' sales tax. Speaker Garner and other leaders gave out a statement.

January 6, 1933: In the face of immediate nation-wide protest, the Democratic leaders abandoned the proposal to increase the lower brackets of the income tax. They further declared that no revenue bill would be undertaken during the session of Congress.

January 17, 1933: President Hoover returned to the attack and sent

[3] State Papers, Vol. II, p. 561.

to Congress a special message in which again he stressed the urgent necessity for balancing the budget by a reduction in expenditures and an increase in the revenues. He again recommended a general sales tax at a low rate upon all manufactures except food and the cheaper grades of clothing. He said:[4]

In my Budget Message of December 5th I laid before the Congress the financial situation of the government together with proposals for the next fiscal year. . . . I urged upon the Congress the necessity for further drastic reduction in expenditures and increase in revenues.

I now approach the Congress again upon this subject, knowing that the members are fully possessed of the complete necessity of a balanced budget as the foundation of economic recovery and to urge that action should be taken during the present session to bring this about.

The great problem before the world today is a restoration and maintenance of confidence. I need scarcely repeat that the maintenance of confidence in the financial stability of the United States Government is the first contribution to all financial stability within our borders, and in fact in the world as a whole. Upon that confidence rests the credit of the States, the municipalities, all our financial institutions and industry—it is the basis of recovered employment and agriculture.

The increases in revenues enacted at the last session have not had the results hoped for because of continued economic stagnation. The income of the government for the next fiscal year nominally estimated at $2,950,-000,000 is likely to fall short under present world conditions by anywhere from $100,000,000 to $300,000,000.

Expenditures (and I speak in terms of expenditures rather than appropriations because of the confusion caused by carry-over of appropriations for the present fiscal year) including postoffice deficit but excluding debt redemption, are estimated at about $3,771,000,000. If expenditures are continued during the next fiscal year at the present rate there would thus be a deficit of from $920,000,000 to $1,120,000,000 in the next fiscal year exclusive of sinking fund charges.

Obviously the first necessity of a nation of decreasing income is reduction in expenditures. . . .

. . . Certainly with the general economic outlook in respect to income and the legislative outlook in respect to recommended economies the latter figure is the most likely of realization.

The first essential is that the maximum appropriations and economies set out in the budget message as supplemented should be adhered to. The second is that there should be no new authorizations or appropriations brought forward. The third is that even the appropriations recommended should be reduced at every point the Congress is able to find an avenue therefor. So far as appropriation bills as dealt with by the House of Representatives or the committees thereof, the results have been disappointing. Maximum appropriations for the different departments which

[4] State Papers, Vol. II, p. 576 *et seq.*

were recommended in the Executive budget have not been adhered to. My Executive Orders to consolidate some fifty-eight government functions into a few divisions with resulting economies appear likely of refusal by the Congress with resultant continuing waste. I regret to say that the same forces are at work which thwarted the savings of several hundred millions we sought to effect at the last session of Congress. We are during the current year and even in the next fiscal year suffering from that failure. . . .

. . . I also recognize many . . . do not fully understand the limitations under which the Congress works in reduction of expenditures. In order to clarify this I may classify the government expenditures proposed for the next fiscal year into six groups (excluding debt redemption but including postoffice deficit):

1. Interest on the public debt which cannot be reduced $725,000,000
2. Trust funds, tax refunds, D. C. budget, contributions to Civil Service pensions, Post Office subsidies to air and foreign mail which are represented by fixed obligations and other similar items on which there is no opportunity to reduce 310,900,000
3. Public works and their maintenance (excluding military, naval, and veterans' construction which are in following items) have been reduced practically to commitments and contracts outstanding 305,000,000
4. Expenditures on military establishments 612,700,000
5. Expenditures on veterans have been reduced in the Executive proposals by $121,000,000 818,400,000
6. All other expenditures of the government including the legislative, the judiciary, law enforcement, prisons, foreign affairs, fiscal and tax-service, public health, education, forests, fisheries, aids to agriculture, labor, commerce, safety of life at sea, inspection of food products and a multitude of vital services including the Post Office as represented by the remaining deficiency and all other independent establishments except the veterans' bureau 461,000,000

$3,223,000,000

It will be seen that about eighty-six per cent of the whole expenditure of the Government lies in the first five items. . . .

In canvassing the three major fields of possible income—that is income taxes, custom and excise taxes—I believe that inquiry by the Congress will develop that income taxes under the Act of 1932 have been developed to the point of maximum productivity unless we are prepared to abandon our American system of fairly high exemption and reasonably low rates applicable to the smaller incomes and in any event by keeping to these principles no further burdens in this direction would substantially increase revenues and solve the questions. One of the first economic effects of the increases already made is the retreat of capital into tax exempt securities and the denudation of industry and commerce of that much available capital.

The customs revenues and other miscellaneous revenues are not likely to be increased except through recovery in trade. In my view, therefore, the field for substantial increase in Federal Government revenues resolves itself in the exploration of the possibilities of so-called excise taxes or sales taxes. In the estimated revenues for the next fiscal year, nearly $700,000,000 is comprised of so-called excise taxes which are levied on a few score different manufactured commodities. These taxes are in fact manufacturers' sales taxes. Any attempted distinction between "excise" taxes on manufactured commodities, or "sales" taxes on manufactured commodities is mere juggling with words. Of the taxes now levied nearly $200,000,000 are upon essentials as distinguished from so-called non-essentials. The Congress has thus already established a "sales tax" as the basis of one quarter of the whole public revenues, and has already adopted "sales" taxes upon essentials as distinguished from non-essentials. To extend this form of taxation is neither new nor revolutionary. Instead of spreading it over a few scores of commodities and services at irregular rates which cause discrimination and hardship between industries, it would seem the essence of good statesmanship to apply such a tax generally at a low rate upon all manufactures except upon food and cheaper grades of clothing, and thereby give to the Federal Government a stable basis of income during the period of depression.

The balancing of the budget is one of the essential steps in strengthening the foundations for recovery. Capital expenditures are a very important item in our economic life. There can be no doubt that there is an enormous accumulated demand for capital funds that would be expended for equipment and replacements of all kinds if long-time funds could be obtained cheaply and if confidence were restored. For some time now long-time funds have not been available to the public at reasonable rates. The retirement of the Federal Treasury from the market as a constant borrower, the balancing of the Federal Budget and the refunding operations necessary to bring the government debt into better balance would have a stimulating effect, would vitalize our entire credit structure and produce one of the conditions essential to continued recovery.

It is essential that the Government undertake at an early moment the refunding of outstanding high interest bearing Liberty bonds into bonds bearing a lower rate of interest. It is essential, too, that a portion of our short-term borrowing should be converted into longer term issues. A balanced budget would greatly facilitate such an operation.

Every principle of sound governmental management and wise economic policy call for the prompt balancing of the Federal budget. This all-important objective is definitely within reach, and more determined effort will bring us to the goal we have been striving to reach in the face of unparalleled difficulties.

One of the most helpful contributions which the Congress and this administration would give to the next administration would be to enable them to start with the Federal budget in balance and the Federal finances in order.

This action failed to have any effect.

January 19, 1933: The Democratic majority of the House defeated the President's plan for the reorganization of government bureaus. The next day—January 20th—the President made a public statement through a press conference in which he said:[5]

> The estimates which I gave in my recent message to Congress as to the probable size of the deficit will depend, of course, upon how far the Congress adopts economies which I have recommended. . . .
> I stated the other day that the five appropriation bills so far dealt with by the House or committees of the House showed an actual increase of about $35,000,000 instead of a decrease. . . .
> I regret, of course, that the consolidation of fifty-eight bureaus and commissions into a few divisions, which I had directed by Executive Orders, has been nullified by the action of the House of Representatives. There was apparently no examination of the merits of the different Executive Orders by the House or the House committees. . . .

Thus, not content with defeating the President's proposals to increase the revenues, the Democratic majority also undertook to defeat his reductions in expenditures.

January 30, 1933: The following statement was issued from the White House:[6]

> The appropriation bills for the next fiscal year for the State, Justice, Commerce, and Labor departments—together with the Independent Offices Bill, have now been reported out from the House Appropriations Committee. The President recommended total appropriations for these services of $977,637,002, excluding permanent appropriations. The House Committee recommended $1,106,172,812 . . . or $128,535,810 increase over the President's recommendations. To this should be added $1,268,480 for deferments which will be required in the fiscal year, making a total increase for these services of $129,804,290.
> The totals of the increases over the President's recommendations to date are . . . $163,319,642 and, if finally adopted by the Congress, will make an increase in the estimated deficit by that amount.

From December to March, President Hoover incessantly urged individual members of Congress to take action necessary to balance the budget. All this failed of result. Fighting to the last to keep down appropriations, on March 4, 1933, the President issued this statement upon a pocket veto of the Independent Offices Appropriation Bill:[7]

> The appropriation bills passed by the Congress when taking into account mere postponements to later deficiency bills show that the total appropriations for the next fiscal year were approximately $161,000,000 above the President's recommendations. Of this increase, $130,900,000

[5] State Papers, Vol. II, p. 582.   [6] State Papers, Vol. II, p. 584.
[7] State Papers, Vol. II, p. 602.

is in the Independent Offices Bill. The President is not signing this bill, in order that it may be reviewed in the next session.

It is a reasonable assumption that the immediate purpose of all this partisan political activity and the interference by the President-elect was to give to the incoming administration the prestige of balancing the budget. Had the budget been balanced during the session, the message to Congress of President Roosevelt on March 10th, six days after the inauguration, would scarcely have been possible.

Mr. Roosevelt stated:

For three long years the Federal Government has been on the road toward bankruptcy. . . .
With the utmost seriousness I point out to the Congress the profound effect of this fact upon our national economy. It has contributed to the recent collapse of our banking structure. It has accentuated the stagnation of the economic life of our people. It has added to the ranks of the unemployed. Our Government's house is not in order, and for many reasons no effective action has been taken to restore it to order.
Upon the unimpaired credit of the United States Government rest the safety of deposits, the security of insurance policies, the activity of industrial enterprises, the value of our agricultural products, and the availability of employment. . . . National recovery depends upon it.
The effect of the failure to balance the budget upon the growth of the banking crisis is undoubted. The responsibility for this dates back to December 27, 1932, when the events began that prevented budget balancing.

In view of Governor Roosevelt's insistence during the campaign upon the necessity of a balanced budget, it is interesting to observe subsequent history. Governor Roosevelt contended that the final test of governmental expenditures is the increase in the national debt. We may put to test both administrations on this simple basis.

TOTAL NATIONAL DEBT

March 5, 1929	$17,343,850,202
March 13, 1933	20,937,350,964
Increase during President Hoover's four years of administration	3,593,500,762

This increase, however, was to the amount of over $2,500,000,000 due to secured loans made by the Federal Government through the Reconstruction Finance Corporation and other agencies of the government, the greater part of which was subsequently repaid. In other words, the net increase in the national debt was about $1,000,000,000.

The debt on June 30, 1935, plus the estimated increase by December 31, 1936, will be at least $32,000,000,000 and may be larger. This is an increase, during the three years and nine months of the Roosevelt Administration, of about $11,000,000,000 if we take the smaller figure. To realize the real situation, there should be added the losses on the Roosevelt system of bonds and securities of government—guaranteed corporations, which will not appear in the budget for some years.

As against this, on the other side, again must be deducted the collectible loans on security made directly by the government during the Roosevelt Administration through the Reconstruction Finance Corporation, etc. They may somewhat exceed the above deductions.

Also, it should be repeated that it later became customary for the Roosevelt Administration, when discussing fiscal matters, to announce separately the "emergency" expenditures. It should be noted that a similar classification of "emergency" expenditures, if applied to the Hoover Administration, would show in the "emergency" column a total of nearly $4,000,000,000 during four years. The Hoover budget would have been balanced if the Democratic Congress of 1931-1932-1933 had accepted his recommendations of reduced expenditures and increased revenues.

CHAPTER XVII

BREAKING DOWN CONFIDENCE BY DELAY IN BANKING AND BANKRUPTCY REFORM, AND BY THE PUBLICATION OF R.F.C. LOANS

THE second project undertaken by President Hoover to secure constructive action was that of banking reform.

For three years, in various messages, conferences and interviews, the President had been urging reform in the whole banking system. This had been held up in the earlier stages of the depression by the difficulties of evolving a workable plan and by the opposition of many of the banks, and in the later stages by the refusal of the Democratic majority of the House of Representatives to act. Senator Glass, as the author of the bill finally worked out for this purpose, had given conscientious and patient service to it. President Hoover resolved to make every effort to drive reform of banking through this last session of Congress, as both sides had professed to welcome it. His ideas of the nature of banking reform have already been given.

A part of the reforms required the setting up of a system of mortgage banks. In order to lay the foundation for such a system, he already had secured the creation of the Home Loan Banks. In his annual message to Congress of December 6, 1932, the President had said:[1]

> The basis of every . . . effort toward recovery is to reorganize at once our banking system. The shocks to our economic system have undoubtedly multiplied by the weakness of our financial system. I first called attention of the Congress in 1929 to this condition, and I have unceasingly recommended remedy since that time. The subject has been exhaustively investigated both by the committees of the Congress and the officers of the Federal Reserve System. . . .
> The banking and financial system is presumed to serve in furnishing the essential lubricant to the wheels of industry, agriculture, and commerce, that is, credit. Its diversion from proper use, its improper use, or its insufficiency instantly brings hardship and dislocation in economic life. As a system our banking has failed to meet this great emergency. It can be said without question of doubt that our losses and distress have been greatly augmented by its wholly inadequate organization. Its inability as a system to respond to our needs is today a constant drain upon progress toward recovery. In this statement I am not referring to indi-

[1] State Papers, Vol. II, p. 500, *et seq.*

vidual banks or bankers. Thousands of them have shown distinguished courage and ability. On the contrary, I am referring to the system itself, which is so organized, or so lacking in organization, that in an emergency its very mechanism jeopardizes or paralyzes the action of sound banks and its instability is responsible for periodic dangers to our whole economic system.

Bank failures rose in 1931 to 10½ per cent of all the banks as compared to 1½ per cent of the failures of all other types of enterprise. Since January 1, 1930, we have had 4,665 banks suspend, with $3,300,000,000 in deposits. Partly from fears and drains from abroad, partly from these failures themselves (which indeed often caused closing of sound banks), we have witnessed hoarding of the currency to an enormous sum, rising during the height of the crisis to over $1,600,000,000. The results from inter-reaction of cause and effect have expressed themselves in the strangulation of credit which at times has almost stifled the nation's business and agriculture. The losses, suffering and tragedies of our people are incalculable. Not alone do they lie in the losses of savings to millions of homes, injury by deprival of working capital to thousands of small businesses, but also, in the frantic pressure to recall loans to meet pressures of hoarding and in liquidation of failed banks, millions of other people have suffered in the loss of their homes and farms, businesses have been ruined, unemployment increased, and farmers' prices diminished.

That this failure to function is unnecessary and is the fault of our particular system is plainly indicated by the fact that in Great Britain, where the economic mechanism has suffered far greater shocks than our own, there has not been a single bank failure during the depression. Again in Canada, where the economic situation has been in large degree identical with our own, there have not been substantial bank failures.

The creation of the Reconstruction Finance Corporation and the amendments to the Federal Reserve Act served to defend the nation in a great crisis. They are not remedies; they are relief. It is inconceivable that the Reconstruction Corporation, which has extended aid to nearly 6,000 institutions and is manifestly but a temporary device, can go on indefinitely. . . .

There is no reason now why solution should not be found at the present session of the Congress. Inflation of currency or governmental conduct of banking can have no part in these reforms. The Government must abide within the field of constructive organization, regulation, and the enforcement of safe practices only. . . .

Parallel with reform in the banking laws must be changes in the Federal Farm Loan Banking System and in the Joint Stock Land Banks. Some of these changes should be directed to permanent improvement and some to emergency aid to our people where they wish to fight to save their farms and homes.

I wish again to emphasize this view—that these widespread banking reforms are a national necessity and are the first requisites for further recovery in agriculture and business. They should have immediate consideration as steps greatly needed to further recovery.

BANKING AND BANKRUPTCY REFORM

During the session President Hoover continued to press for action. Senator Glass re-introduced his bill, which cured part of the current evils. That it did not extend more deeply was through no fault of the Senator. The President, nevertheless, urged its passage. Senator Huey Long, of Louisiana, undertook a filibuster against the bill, delaying its passage in the Senate until January 26, 1933. It was promptly refused a hearing by the House leaders, who stated that President-elect Roosevelt did not wish them to deal with the subject.

President Hoover had intended to deliver an address upon the whole banking situation on Lincoln's Birthday in New York City, but the panic situation in the country made it undesirable to discuss this in the terms the subject required. Instead, he discussed there the gold standard. Having shown to a friend some of the deleted paragraphs in relation to banking, he complied with that friend's request for the preservation of their content by addressing to him the following letter:

February 17, 1933.

Mr. Arch W. Shaw,
Chicago, Illinois.
Dear Mr. Shaw:

I have your request that I should state in writing what I said to you a few days ago as to the broad conclusions I have formed from experience of the last four years as to the functioning of our economic system. It is, of course, impossible in the time I have left at my disposal or within the reach of a short statement, to cover all phases of the problem.

Our whole economic system naturally divides itself into production, distribution, and finance. By finance I mean every phase of investment, banking and credit. And at once I may say that the major fault in the system as it stands is in the financial system.

As to production, our system of stimulated individual effort, by its creation of enterprise, development of skill and discoveries in science and invention, has resulted in production of the greatest quantity of commodities and services of the most infinite variety that were ever known in the history of man. Our production in 1924-28, for instance, in the flow of commodities, service and leisure, resulted in the highest standard of living of any group of humanity in the history of the world. Even in these years, with our machinery and equipment and labor and business organizations, we could have produced more and could have enjoyed an even higher standard of living if all the adjustments of economic mechanism had been more perfect. We can say, however, without qualification, that the motivation of production based on private initiative has proved the very mother of plenty. It has faults, for humanity is not without faults. Difficulties arise from overexpansion and adjustment to the march of labor-saving devices, but in broad result it stands in sharp contrast with the failure of the system of production as in its greater exemplar—Russia—where after 15 years of trial, in a land of as great natural resources as ours, that system has never produced in a single year an adequate supply of even the barest necessities in food and clothing for its people.

In the larger sense our system of distribution in normal times is sufficient and effective. Our transportation and communication is rapid and universal. The trades distribute the necessities of life at profits which represent a remarkably small percentage of their value.

The system moves supplies of everything into remotest villages and crossroads; it feeds and clothes great cities each day with the regularity and assurance which causes never a thought or anxiety. The diffusion of commodities and services in a social sense has faults. In normal times out of our 120,000,000 people there are a few millions who conscientiously work and strive, yet do not receive that minimum of commodities and services to which they have a just right as earnest members of the community. The system does not give to them that assurance of security and living which frees them from fear for the future.

There is another fringe of a few hundred thousand who receive more than they deserve for the effort they make. But taxes are furnishing rapid correction in this quarter. The great mass of people enjoy in normal times a broader diffusion of our wealth, commodities and services than ever before in history. The enlarging social sense of our people is furnishing the impulse to correction of faults. That correction is to be brought about by diffusion of property through constructive development within the system itself, with social vision as well as economic vision. It is not to be brought about by destruction of the system.

The last four years have shown unquestionably that it is mainly the third element of our system—that is, finance—which has failed and produced by far the largest part of the demoralization of our systems of production and distribution with its thousand tragedies which wring the heart of the nation. I am not insensible to the disturbing war inheritances, of our expansion of production in certain branches, nor to the effect of increased labor-saving devices on employment, but these are minor notes of discord compared to that arising from failure of the financial system. This failure has been evidenced in two directions: That is, the lack of organization for domestic purposes and the weakness presented by a disintegrated front to the world through which we have been infinitely more demoralized by repeated shocks from abroad.

The credit system in all its phases should be merely a lubricant to the systems of production and distribution. It is not its function to control these systems. That it should be so badly organized, that the volume of currency and credit, whether long or short term, should expand and shrink irrespective of the needs of production and distribution; that its stability should be the particular creature of emotional fear or optimism; that it should be insecure; that it should dominate and not be subordinate to production and distribution—all this is intolerable if we are to maintain our civilization. Yet these things have happened on a gigantic scale. We could have weathered through these failures with some losses and could have secured reorganization as we went along, planing out failures in the fundamental organization of the financial system. The rain of blows from abroad, however, on the system of such weakness has wholly prostrated us by a second phase of this depression which came from a collapse of the financial systems in Europe.

In this system I am not referring to individual banks or financial institutions. Many of them have shown distinguished courage and ability. On the contrary I am referring to the system itself, which is so organized, or so lacking in organization, that it fails in its primary function of stable and steady service to the production and distribution system. In an emergency its very mechanism increases the jeopardy and paralyzes action of the community.

Clearly we must secure sound organization of our financial system as a prerequisite of the functioning of the whole economic system. The first steps in that system are sound currency, economy in government, balanced governmental budgets, whether national or local. The second step is an adequate separation of commercial banking from investment banking, whether in mortgages, bonds or other forms of long-term securities. The next step is to secure effective co-ordination between national and state systems. We cannot endure 49 separate regulatory systems which are both conflicting and weakening. We must accept the large view that the mismanagement, instability and bad functioning of any single institution affects the stability of some part of production and distribution and a multitude of other financial institutions. Therefore there must be co-operation within the financial system enforced by control and regulation by the Government, that will assure that this segment of our economic system does not, through faulty organization and action, bring our people again to these tragedies of unemployment and loss of homes which are today a stigma upon national life. We cannot endure that enormous sums of the people's savings shall be poured out either at home or abroad without making the promoter responsible for his every statement. We cannot endure that men will either manipulate the savings of the people so abundantly evidenced in recent exposures.

That it has been necessary for the Government, through emergency action, to protect us while holding a wealth of gold from being taken off the gold standard, to erect gigantic credit institutions with the full pledge of Government credit to save the nation from chaos through this failure of the financial system, that it is necessary for us to devise schemes of clearing-house protections and to install such temporary devices throughout the nation, is full proof of all I have said. That is the big question. If we can solve this, then we must take in hand the faults of the production and distribution systems—and many problems in the social and political system. But this financial system simply must be made to function first.

There is a phase of all this that must cause anxiety to every American. Democracy cannot survive unless it is master in its own house. The economic system cannot survive unless there are real restraints upon unbridled greed or dishonest reach for power. Greed and dishonesty are not attributes solely of our system—they are human and will infect socialism or any ism. But if our production and distribution systems are to function we must have effective restraints on manipulation, greed and dishonesty. Our Democracy has proved its ability to put its unruly occupants under control but never until their conduct has been a public scandal and a stench. For instance, you will recollect my own opposition to Government operation of electric power, for that is a violation of the very fundamentals of our system; but parallel with it I asked and preached for regulation of it to protect the public from its financial manipulation. We gained the Power Commission but Congress refused it the regulatory authority we asked. I have time and again warned, asked and urged the reorganization of the banking system. The inertia of the Democracy is never more marked than in promotion of what seems abstract or indirect ideas. The recent scandals are the result. Democracy, always lagging, will no doubt now act and may act destructively to the system, for it is mad. It is this lag, the failure to act in time for prevention which I fear most in the sane advancement of economic life. For an outraged people may destroy the whole economic system rather than reconstruct and control the segment which has failed in its function. I trust the new Administration will recognize the difference between crime and economic functioning; between constructive prevention and organization as contrasted with destruction.

During these four years I have been fighting to preserve this fundamental system of production and distribution from destruction through collapse and bad functioning of the financial system. Time can only tell if we have succeeded. Success means higher and higher standards of living, greater comfort, more opportunity for intellectual, moral and spiritual development. Failure means a new form of the Middle Ages.

If we succeed in the job of preservation, certainly the next effort before the country is to reorganize the financial system so that all this will not happen again. We must organize for advance in the other directions, but that is another subject.

Yours faithfully,

HERBERT HOOVER.

In a final effort to persuade the Democratic majority to act, President Hoover, on February 20, 1933, addressed Congress upon banking:[2]

There are certain measures looking to the promotion of economic recovery which have been under consideration by the Congress and are so advanced toward completion or understanding as to seem possible of enactment during the present session. . . .

The enactment by the House of the general principles embodied in the Glass Banking Bill, which has already passed the Senate, will greatly contribute to re-establish confidence. It is the first constructive step to remedy the prime weakness of our whole economic life—that is, organization of our credit system. . . .

[2] State Papers, Vol. II, p. 597.

While the Congress could not enact such a law during this session I recommend that it should institute an inquiry with view to the early expansion of the Home Loan Discount Banks into a general mortgage discount system to be owned co-operatively by banks and mortgage companies (with adequate encouragement of the special activities of building and loan associations) and thus to parallel in the field of long-time credit the service of the Federal Reserve System for short-time credit. Such a system would relieve the Reconstruction Finance Corporation of many of its functions, would assist in the orderly readjustment of the present situation, and through private initiative would serve many purposes for which the Congress is striving through direct action by the government. . . .

An altered Glass Banking Bill subsequently was enacted—after March 4th—but the long delay added to the economic disaster.

President Hoover was firmly of the opinion that one of the essentials to recovery from the depression was the readjustment of inflated and unbearable debt. For this reason he urged upon Congress the reform of the bankruptcy laws to facilitate the adjustment of such debt. While it is certain that the processes of war and of booms build up inflated debts, the processes of depression, in turn, correct this ill balance between the debtor and the creditor. This latter step is always delayed by the considerable lapse of time necessary to bring the creditor to a realization that the debtor cannot meet his entire obligation. It is one of the inexorable delays to recovery. But this stage had been reached in 1931.

President Hoover urged that "debtors should not be sacrificed for causes beyond their control and to an advantage of the creditor." "Sacrifices must be mutual." But he likewise insisted that "debts are individual, not collective." "It must be a process of individual adjustment." And he believed that these adjustments could be greatly facilitated by taking advantage of the constitutional control of bankruptcy vested in the Federal Government to provide a more workable method of mutual readjustment between debtors and creditors. By reform of the bankruptcy acts, facilities might be provided by which the reorganization of corporate and private debts could take place swiftly and under the protection of the courts, with a proper check upon rapacity and a recognition of realities.

The President regarded this reform as one of the most important policies of the administration. He was convinced that it would make a valuable contribution to the necessary readjustments, and in accordance with the mutual interests of both creditors and debtors. Moreover, there was a vast amount of graft and plunder current in old bankruptcy practices, in certain localities, which required immediate reform.

Early in the depression Attorney-General Mitchell, at the request of the President, had undertaken a thorough investigation of the whole subject. His report was published in December, 1931, and on February 29, 1932, President Hoover recommended to Congress far-reaching reforms based upon it. In the message he stated:[3]

> A sound bankruptcy system should operate——
> First, to relieve honest but unfortunate debtors of an overwhelming burden of debt;
> Second, to effect a prompt and economical liquidation and distribution of insolvent estates;
> Third, to discourage fraud and needless waste of assets by withholding relief from debtors in proper cases.

The Democratic majority which controlled that session of Congress refused to allow action. On January 11, 1933, the President returned to the question in a special message to Congress which he closed by saying:[4]

> On February 29th last I addressed the Congress on the urgent necessity for revision of the bankruptcy laws, and presented detailed proposals to that end. These proposals were based upon most searching inquiry into the whole subject which had been undertaken by the Attorney-General at my direction. While it is desirable that the whole matter should be dealt with, some portions of these proposals as an amelioration of the present situation are proving more urgent every day. With view to early action, the department, committees and members of the Congress, have been collaborating in further development of such parts of these proposals as have, out of the present situation, become of most pressing need. I urge that the matter be given attention in this session, for effective legislation would have most helpful economic and social results in the welfare and recovery of the nation.
> The process of forced liquidation through foreclosure and bankruptcy sale of the assets of individual and corporate debtors who through no fault of their own are unable in the present emergency to provide for the payment of their debts in ordinary course as they mature, is utterly destructive of the interests of debtor and creditor alike, and if this process is allowed to take its usual course misery will be suffered by thousands without substantial gain in their creditors, who insist upon liquidation and foreclosure in the vain hope of collecting their claims. In the great majority of cases such liquidation under present conditions is so futile and destructive that voluntary readjustments through the extension or composition of individual debts and the reorganization of corporations must be desirable to a large majority of the creditors.
> Under existing law, even where majorities of the creditors desire to arrange fair and equitable readjustments with their debtors, their plans may not be consummated without prohibitive delay and expense, usually

[3] State Papers, Vol. II, p. 134.   [4] State Papers, Vol. II, p. 567.

attended by the obstruction of minority creditors who oppose such settlements in the hope that the fear of ruinous liquidation will induce the immediate settlement of their claims.

The proposals to amend the Bankruptcy Acts by providing for relief of debtors who seek the protection of the court for the purpose of readjusting their affairs with their creditors carry no stigma of an adjudication in bankruptcy and are designed to extend the protection of the court to the debtor and his property, while an opportunity is afforded the debtor and a majority of creditors to arrange an equitable settlement of his affairs, which upon approval of the court will become binding upon minority creditors. Under such process it should be possible to avoid destructive liquidation through the composition and extension of individual indebtedness and the reorganization of corporations with the full protection of the court extended to the rights and interests of creditors and debtors alike. The law should encourage and facilitate such readjustments, in proceedings which do not consume the estate in long and wasteful receiverships.

In the case of individual and corporate debtors all creditors should be stayed from the enforcement of their debts pending the judicial process of readjustment. The provisions dealing with corporate reorganizations should be applicable to railroads, and in such cases the plan of reorganization should not become effective until it has been approved by the Interstate Commerce Commission.

I wish again to emphasize that the passage of legislation for this relief of individual and corporate debtors at this session of Congress is a matter of the most vital importance. It has a major bearing upon the whole economic situation in the adjustment of the relation of debtors and creditors. I therefore recommend its immediate consideration as an emergency action.

The House passed a bill, but it was held up in the Senate. President Hoover addressed yet another message to Congress on February 20, 1933, in which he said:[5]

It is most necessary that the principles of the Bankruptcy Bill which has already been acted upon by the House should be passed by the Senate. The whole object of the bill is to secure orderly co-operation between creditors and debtors, whether farmers, individuals, general corporations or railroads, for mutual adjustment which will preserve the integrity and continuous operation of business, save the values of good will and the continuation of people in their occupations and thus avoid destruction of the interest of both parties. This legislation is of the most critical importance in this period of readjustment. Incidentally such a workable system is highly necessary in order to permit a certain minority of railroads to be so reorganized as to reduce fixed charges and thus relieve the Reconstruction Finance Corporation of drains in prevention of destructive receiverships.

[5] State Papers, Vol. II, p. 597.

Congress ultimately passed a bill, but the Senate had excluded the provisions for corporation reorganization, retaining the provision for individual adjustment and railway reorganization. In the previous October the President had canvassed many leading insurance and mortgage companies and received assurance that if such a bill were passed, they would immediately undertake co-operation with their debtors for wide-scale and rapid readjustments. Had the bill been passed promptly and completely the year before, it would greatly have alleviated human hardship by the readjustment of the oppressive debts of the farm and home owners. It would have offered a method for the readjustment of the impossible corporation and railway debts. It would have saved much fraud and waste current under the old bankruptcy processes, and thousands of concerns from bankruptcy, and also have prevented much of that spread of fear which is so destructive to public confidence when large and continuous closures of business and dispossession of home owners are in process. Even had it been promptly passed after the election, it would have contributed greatly to stability. The deletion of the corporation feature and this delay in passage have prevented the use of it to the extent it would have been, had it been made a feature of the original legislation as recommended.

The destructive attitude of the Democratic majority toward this legislation, and the delays in its passage, only added to the general discouragement of the country. It is interesting to note that the incoming Administration caused Congress to pass the clauses which had been deleted from the President's bill and announced it as part of the New Deal.

Another step in the breakdown of confidence was the publication of Reconstruction Finance Corporation loans.

Just before the adjournment of Congress on the 16th of July, 1932, an amendment was introduced, under the leadership of Speaker Garner, to the Unemployment Relief Act which provided for the future monthly publication of the names of all borrowers from the Reconstruction Finance Corporation. A "rumor" was in circulation that preferences were being given to Republicans in the making of loans by the Corporation. It was precisely to assure complete freedom of the country from partisanship in the conduct of the Corporation and to protect it from such demagogic and cheap political attack, that President Hoover had appointed former Senator Atlee Pomerene, of Ohio, a Democrat, as Chairman of the Board, which resulted in a majority of the Board being Democratic members. Among them was one specifically recommended by Mr. Garner as his lifelong friend.

The directors of the Corporation at once protested that this publicity provision, if enacted into law, would undo a large part of the work already accomplished by the Corporation in preserving the credit structure of the nation. They also pointed out that advances already had been made to more than 3,600 insurance companies, savings banks, building and loan associations, and commercial banks. Most of the institutions that borrowed from the Corporation had done so in order to secure further capital for the people of their locality, to enable them to meet the demands of their depositors or policyholders. With the nervous public temper of the time, the publication of their borrowings would be apt to subject these institutions to the suspicion that their borrowing was because they were weak when, as a matter of fact, they were not. Runs and other disastrous effects on them would result.

The President and the directors insisted that the real protection of public interest could be fully obtained through the provision requiring reports to the appropriate committees of the Senate and the House. Public reports already had been made regularly as to the totals, number of institutions, and States served. The House amendment was modified by the Senate, and a public declaration was made by the Democratic and Republican leaders of the Senate to the effect that under the changes made, the disclosure extended only to confidential filing with the clerks of the Houses of Congress. The President made the public press statement, on signing the bill on July 17, 1932, that "the possible destructive effect on credit institutions by the so-called publicity clause has been neutralized by the declaration of the Senate leaders of all parties that this provision is not retroactive, and that the required monthly reports of future transactions are all of a confidential nature, and must be so held by the clerks of the Senate and House of Representatives unless otherwise ordered by the Congress when in session."

The detailed reports were thereafter duly made by the Reconstruction Finance Corporation officials to the Senate and House authorities, and no questions arose over the matter until after the election in November, 1932, when, at Speaker Garner's insistence, the Clerk of the House gave out the current monthly reports to the public.

On January 4, 1933, the House, under Speaker Garner, passed a resolution commanding that all loans prior to July 21, 1932, should also be made public. This resolution was passed despite the emphatic protest of the administration and the Democratic directors of the Reconstruction Finance Corporation Board.

Chairman Pomerene and Democratic members Jones, Couch, and McCarthy personally urged its dangers upon Speaker Garner. Numerous public leaders also protested, including William Green, of the American Federation of Labor, but, nevertheless, the loans were given to the press. Already the monthly publications of current loans had induced runs on banks, and now the publicity of nearly 4,000 institutions, made all at once, had an extremely serious effect.

President Hoover attempted to prevent the disaster by a public statement commending the institutions for their action in borrowing, as it represented an effort on their part to aid their communities. He showed that in many cases there had been previous panic runs on these same institutions which had been stopped by their ability to meet these demands through the loans from the Reconstruction Finance Corporation.

On January 14, 1933, Senator Couzens' special committee, after many months investigation into the early loans of the Reconstruction Finance Corporation, said in its report: "Your committee does not recommend that loans be made public in view of the fact that when the loans were made the act did not require that they be made public." On January 26, 1933, Jesse Jones, director of the Corporation, called personally on Representative Howard (Nebraska) and made a plea for suppression of the "new list of loans sent to the Congress today for publication tomorrow." These were the retroactive-list names of the first five months of Reconstruction Finance Corporation activities. On February 2, 1933, Governor A. Harry Moore of New Jersey joined with leading New Jersey bankers in a telegram of protest to President-elect Roosevelt on the publication of loans made by the Reconstruction Finance Corporation, as being harmful to smaller banks.

But all this urging was in vain. Reports promptly came in of runs on several hundred banks, savings banks, building and loan associations, and insurance companies, in consequence of the publication of their borrowings. A sample list furnished by one of the directors to the President showed sixty-two banks, holding $70,000,000 of deposits, which were closed by runs within thirty days after publication of the Reconstruction Finance Corporation loans.

Another list showed forty banks, holding $42,000,000 of deposits, which had managed to linger for sixty days after publication, but finally closed under runs. These banks were mainly in the agricultural sections. They were inherently solvent, or the Reconstruction Finance Corporation loans would not have been made.

On February 18, 1933, Senator Robinson of Arkansas, with a vigorous speech of support, introduced a bill in the Senate to stop the publication. The bill was suddenly dropped.

In one last hope of appealing to the Democratic majority even at a date desperately late, President Hoover, on February 20th, addressed that body:[*]

> I earnestly recommend repeal of the procedure of the House of Representatives in publishing loans made by the R.F.C. These transactions should be open to the fullest degree to the representatives of Congress, but their publication in the last few months has led to widespread, mostly innocent, misinterpretations, vicious in effect, by depositors and alarmists who do not recognize that such borrowings represent an endeavor of the institutions to provide funds needed in service of their respective communities. This publication is destroying the usefulness and effectiveness of the R.F.C., is exaggerating fears, and is introducing a new element of great danger. It is drying up the very sources of credit. The effect of such publication is forcing payment by distressed debtors to replenish bank funds. It is causing the hoarding of currency.

It was an extremely moderate statement of the effect of this outrage. The public apprehension, fanned by the closing of these banks, affected in turn other banks. The fear of currency devaluation already was weakening the financial structure. It particularly affected the State of Michigan, where the banking situation now was very weak.

Chairman Pomerene, of the Reconstruction Finance Corporation, later made a statement to the press, saying:

> The banks which got R.F.C. loans were good banks. The loans were amply secured as the law required. Request for loans did not mean that applicant banks were unsound, but some silly persons construed them that way. It was the most damnable and vicious thing that was ever done. It almost counteracted all the good that we had been able to do.

That the President-elect and his Democratic followers had no definite principle which required newspaper publication of the government's business was to be demonstrated by the later suppression of the publication of Reconstruction Finance Corporation loans when they came into power. It further was demonstrated by the secrecy placed by them around the government's new $2,000,000,000 Treasury fund for stabilization in foreign exchange, where even Congress is precluded from knowing the facts.

It is interesting to note a protest which appeared in the *Congressional Record* after Mr. Hoover had retired from the Presidency. It came from a prominent Democrat at present a United States senator.

[*] State Papers, Vol. II, p. 598.

Jersey City, N. J.
April 5, 1933.

Hon. W. Warren Barbour,
United States Senate,
Washington, D. C.

The last publication of Reconstruction Finance loans to banks did incalculable harm. To continue these publications will mean further runs on banks and ruin to many. Again I vehemently repeat my protest as Governor of New Jersey to the publication of the names of banks. Such publication can serve no purpose and only serves to undo the good work which the President has accomplished in restoring confidence. Senator Robinson deserves support and co-operation in his effort to remedy this situation.

A. Harry Moore,
Governor of New Jersey.

The publication of these loans, and the consequent destruction and fear, were definitely contributing elements to the banking panic. On March 5th, 1933, *The New York Herald Tribune* said that Congress "virtually sealed the fate of the Corporation and of the banks by insisting on including in the relief bill of last July the indefensibly vicious provision of detailed publicity of all loans."

CHAPTER XVIII

FEAR OF CURRENCY TINKERING STOPS RECOVERY

IN order to reconstruct the monetary situation at the time of the election, November 8, 1932, it is necessary to recall that the Democratic Party had at various times in the past advocated inflation and defended monetary instability. All the fears in this respect which it might have inspired in some of the electorate were revived by the bills for monetary change which had been passed by the Democratic majority of the House of Representatives under the leadership of Speaker Garner in the spring of 1932. Mr. Garner now was Vice President-elect, and occupied a conspicuous place in the counsels of the new Administration.

The questions of devaluation and inflation had been raised in the public mind during the election campaign. Many Democratic candidates for the House and Senate had been advocating various forms of inflation and rubber dollars and did so unceasingly. The fact that President-elect Roosevelt was closely associated with many well-known exponents of currency manipulation such as Professors James Harvey Rogers, of Yale University, and George F. Warren, of Cornell University, and prospective Secretary of Agriculture Henry A. Wallace, together with Senators Burton K. Wheeler, of Montana, Elmer Thomas, of Oklahoma, and others, gave much satisfaction to the inflationists. President Hoover and the Republican leaders repeatedly charged Governor Roosevelt with intention to tinker with the currency.

At the late date in the campaign of November 2nd, Senator Glass was requested by Governor Roosevelt to refute these charges, which the Senator attempted to do. Finally, upon a charge by the Republicans that no one could speak for the President-elect except Mr. Roosevelt himself, on November 4th, four days before the election, he made a vigorous statement:

. . . It is worthy of note that no adequate answer has been made to the magnificent philippic of Senator Glass the other night, in which he showed how unsound this assertion was. I might add, Senator Glass made a devastating challenge that no responsible government would have sold to the country securities payable in gold if it knew that the promise —yes, the covenant—embodied in these securities was as dubious as the President of the United States claims it was. Why, of course, the assertion was unsound. . . .

One of the most commonly repeated misrepresentations by Republican speakers, including the President, has been the claim that the Democratic position with regard to money has not been made sufficiently clear. The President is seeing visions of rubber dollars. But that is only a part of his campaign of fear. I am not going to characterize these statements. I merely present the facts.

The Democratic platform specifically declares, "we advocate a sound currency to be preserved at all hazards." That, I take it, is plain English.

In discussing this platform on July 30, I said, "Sound money is an international necessity; not a domestic consideration for one nation alone." In other words, I want to see sound money in all the world.

Far up in the Northwest at Butte I repeated the pledge of the platform, saying "sound money must be maintained at all regards."

In Seattle I reaffirmed my attitude on this question. The thing has been said, therefore, in plain English three times in my speeches. It is stated without qualification in the platform and I have announced my unqualified acceptance of that platform in every plank.

The expressive term "the covenant" was no doubt intended to convince the public that the gold clause on government bonds and currency embodied in these obligations was more than an ordinary contract, that it had moral bindings. The "covenant" on the currency is "Redeemable in gold at the United States Treasury"; upon the gold certificates it says, "This certifies that there has been deposited in the Treasury of the United States .... dollars in gold coin payable to the bearer on demand"; upon the United States Government bonds is: "The principal and interest hereof are payable in United States gold coin of the present standard of value."

It would have been easy for the President-elect to answer directly that he would allow no tinkering with the currency. But the continued assertions of men around the Governor that implied inflation and tinkering, caused many people still to be unconvinced. Immediately after the election they became apprehensive of the whole monetary policies of the new administration. That apprehension was quickly increased by the actions of Mr. Roosevelt and various Democratic leaders.

Mr. Roosevelt's friends frequently have since stated that in his repeated use of the term "sound money" he did not imply the old gold dollar or even the gold standard. Mr. Ernest K. Lindley, a long-time associate and intimate friend of Mr. Roosevelt, when discussing, in his book *The Roosevelt Revolution* (pages 37-38, 64-65), the Governor's currency stand during the campaign, has said:

The points on which Mr. Roosevelt specifically strove to reassure conservatives were the balancing of the budget by drastic governmental economies and the preservation of sound money. Yet, adhering to the pattern of the Democratic platform, Mr. Roosevelt at no time said that by sound money he meant the existing gold standard or the existing gold content of the dollar. . . . The conservatives naturally assumed he meant a dollar of the existing gold content, and Mr. Roosevelt undoubtedly was glad to have them think so without completely quashing the hopes of the inflationists of various schools. . . . Mr. Roosevelt, as we have seen, had at least a mental reservation as to the possibility or desirability of maintaining the gold standard. But he could not admit it or even hint at it except in the most intimate circle of tight-lipped friends. Only a hint that he contemplated departure from the gold standard or inflation and he would have instantly caused the catastrophe that everyone wished to avoid. . . .

This was the situation at the time of the election. There soon were to be added rumors that the President-elect was discussing methods of devaluation, inflation or "reflation" of the currency. From these, and from his refusals to disavow such intentions, apprehension arose and quickly spread.

Whether it was advisable or inadvisable to revalue the currency is not a part of this discussion. But it is a fair statement that no change in the value of the currency could be noised about with the banks still open, and not produce a panic. The reason is that the American people do not dumbly wait for an event; they act in anticipation of it. At once people who "knew" sought to protect themselves. Some of the knowing ones bought foreign currencies or securities—that is, exported their capital. Other knowing ones bought real estate, and still others bought gold bullion and secreted it; less-knowing ones drew gold coin; still less-knowing ones drew currency from the banks under their belief in the assurance printed upon its face that it was redeemable in gold. Of course, during this period, these knowing ones imparted their information to their friends.

That the banking system had been weakened by the depression, the effects of which made it more difficult to meet such shocks, may be accepted without argument. But it is a fact that, largely by the efforts of President Hoover and his administration, the American people had been brought through several crises of greater possibility of damage than the crisis that was to come in February, 1933, and without a general panic. The banks were, in fact, stronger than they had been at the time of the previous crisis in June, 1932. There had been no serious hoarding or runs upon the banks between July and December, 1932. Gold was coming to the country from abroad, deposits were increasing, and generally a much sounder situation had been built up. The following indications of this increasing strength are taken from the Federal Reserve Board reports of improvement over the low of the spring of 1932. They give the situation as of January 1, 1933:

Increase in monetary gold stock	$580,000,000
Returned to the banks from hoarding	150,000,000
Increase in member-bank Reserve balances	500,000,000
Deposits in member banks subject to Reserve showed an increase of	700,000,000
Borrowing from Federal Reserve Banks had decreased	137,000,000
The volume of check transactions as shown by debits to individual accounts in 141 cities had increased	1,500,000,000

The value of bonds had increased by nearly fifteen per cent. The value of industrial stocks had increased by thirty per cent. The withdrawal of foreign deposits during the previous year had removed this disturbing element from the banking system.

It is obvious that not only were the banks stronger but also that by the end of the year public confidence in them was greatly increased over that of the preceding spring. Had not new factors, apart from the situation of the banks, entered upon the scene, there would have been no panic.

A statement of day-to-day events clearly shows how the conviction gradually spread that there was to be devaluation or monetary change, and the effect which this had upon the banking situation.

December 17, 1932: At about this time Mr. Roosevelt discussed devaluation with persons of wide influence in the American financial world.

January 2, 1933: That thoughtful people became uneasy is indicated by the issue of an open letter from twenty leading economists, who, in an appeal to Mr. Roosevelt, urged a settlement of the debt question and lower tariffs, but laid especial emphasis upon the maintenance of the gold standard:

> The gold standard of the present weight and fineness should be unflinchingly maintained . . . agitation for experiments would impair confidence and retard recovery.

The public conclusion was that unless there was reason to be disturbed, these economists would not have written this letter.

January 4, 1933: Senators Burton K. Wheeler, of Montana; Tom Connally, of Texas; Elmer Thomas, of Oklahoma; and others close to the President-elect, began, in and out of the Senate, the support of devaluation and inflation. Likewise, some ten or twelve Democratic congressmen of prominence advocated it in the House of Representatives.

An informal committee was organized at about this time to support devaluation of the currency. This committee sprang from various groups who had for some time been advocating devaluation, and included Professor George F. Warren, of Cornell University, General R. E. Wood, and Messrs. James H. Rand, Jr., Frank A. Vanderlip, Samuel Fels, John Henry Hammond, E. L. Cord, Vincent Bendix, Ed. A. O'Neal, and several scores of others. They ultimately came out into the open as the Committee for the Nation, with an enlarged membership. The discussions of the members with Mr. Roosevelt and throughout the banking world increased the public fears, especially since Professor Warren was known to be close to the President-elect and, furthermore, many of the members of this enlarged group had supported Mr. Roosevelt's election.

January 5, 1933: Mr. Roosevelt held his third conference with René Léon, a banker, upon the monetary policies. Mr. Léon was an ardent advocate of currency tinkering (see *The New York Times,* May 16, 1935).

January 21, 1933: President Hoover and Secretary of the Treasury Mills, sensing the effect of these fears upon the public mind, determined that the theory of devaluation and inflation should be answered. Secretary Mills issued a most able statement in explanation and refutation. It was hoped that such a statement would be supported by the President-elect or by his advisers. There was no such response.

January 23, 1933: The increasing public uneasiness was indicated by a strong statement by Alexander Dana Noyes, the financial editor of *The New York Times,* who urged the necessity of an affirmation by the President-elect as to his intentions not to tinker with the currency:

It is probable enough that the present spirit of hesitancy, not only in financial markets but in general trade is more or less influenced by lack of such reassurance. . . .

In numerous older similar occasions doubt and mistrust prevailed with exceedingly bad effect on financial sentiment, until the President-elect took matters into his own hands and publicly avowed his purposes. This was notably true in the pre-inauguration period of 1885 and 1893, at both of which junctures the maintenance of gold payments was being discussed uneasily and at both of which Mr. Cleveland stated so positively and so courageously his own views of the general problem as to remove at once all apprehension.

During the week of January 18th, physical results of fright became apparent. It was accompanied by two phenomena—the hoarding of currency and "flight of the dollar."

During the period prior to the week of January 18th, gold had been flowing heavily to the United States from abroad.

The usual holiday increase of currency had been steadily returning to the banks. The movement suddenly reversed. Hoarding appeared, and by February 1st, $64,000,000 of currency was withdrawn for that purpose.

Furthermore, in the period from January 18th to February 1st, $38,000,000 of gold was marked for export. This gold movement was but a part of the real flight of the dollar. While European payments to us in trade and in obligations normally would have caused exchange or gold to flow to the United States, the natural current was reversed. This reversal could not be attributed to withdrawals by foreign countries, which had been the cause of the crisis the year before, for they had already withdrawn all but an inconsequential amount of their gold deposits. The volume of flight of the dollar far exceeded the $38,000,000 of gold exports, for, in order to check an inward tide and to turn it outward, the volume also must necessarily equal the normal balance payable to us for goods and other services. Moreover, it was known that the British Stabilization Fund was buying dollars, for the British had increased their American balances by between $50,000,000 and $75,000,000. This sum must be equaled by the flight from this side. Also, the simple purchase of foreign securities dealt in upon the American markets effected the same result in the flight of the dollar. The financial world at once recognized that this purchase of gold, foreign currencies, securities, or shipment of gold, was due to American capital rushing to a refuge abroad.

The movement was accelerated by speculative activities. What were the profits in the flight from the dollar is indicated by the fact that a person who exchanged $1,000,000 worth of English sterling at the average price in January, 1933, and returned it home in July, only six months later, would have profited by $390,000. If he held it for eleven months he would have profited by nearly $550,000. All of this abnormal condition made exports of American commodities more difficult, and tended to stifle business.

January 27, 1933: The public concern over the situation had grown so great that the Federal Reserve Bank of New York considered it necessary to prepare a memorandum for its members upon the effect of devaluation. This memorandum pointed out both the futility and the danger of such a course.

TINKERING WITH THE CURRENCY

January 30, 1933: The monetary intention of the incoming administration appeared in public print in a press dispatch of this date, and this was promptly emphasized by being read before the Senate by Senator Thomas, of Oklahoma, who said:

I desire at this point to call the attention of the Senate to a news item that appears in today's *Washington Herald* under the following heading:
"Roosevelt tells advisers he'll o.k. reflation. Reported prepared to accept some change in currency. By Fraser Edwards.
"President-elect Roosevelt has assured advisers he will sign a measure for controlled currency reflation, it was learned yesterday by Universal Service.
"While the President-elect was represented as being open-minded on the proper plans to adopt, he was said to be prepared to accept some form of currency inflation in order to raise commodity prices and ease the financial stringency of the nation. He still is studying the question.
"As a consequence of this commitment, Senator Carter Glass, of Virginia, according to his friends, is hesitating about accepting the post of Secretary of the Treasury, which, they say, has been offered to him by Roosevelt.
"This issue has been dinned into the ears of Roosevelt by both Democratic and Progressive partisans. They say they have his promise to accept some plan worked out by the new Democratic Congress."
Mr. President [of the Senate], inasmuch as apparently the responsible leader of the United States, soon to be, is now convinced that something must be done to cheapen the dollar, I desire to make plain, if I may, my position upon this question.
Mr. President, I am in favor of cheapening the buying power of the American dollar. If this can be done, to the extent that the dollar is cheapened to the same extent will commodity prices be increased.

President Hoover, and also a large part of the country, hoped that, in accordance with President-elect Roosevelt's sound money assurances in the campaign, he would at once issue a denial. But no denial was forthcoming.

January 31, 1933: Henry A. Wallace, who was known to be an intimate friend of the President-elect, in repeated conference with him, and probably already chosen for the Cabinet, stated: "The smart thing would be to go off the gold standard a little farther than England has. The British debtor has paid off his debts 50 per cent easier than the United States."

The New York Herald Tribune, commenting on this statement, said:

Misleading statements such as these of Mr. Wallace are unfortunate under any circumstances where honesty and adherence to facts are as urgent requirements as they are at present; they are more than unfortunate—they are profoundly disturbing—when they emanate from a man whose name has been conspicuously mentioned as a probable Cabinet member in the new administration.

February 4, 1933: President-elect Roosevelt left for a cruise on Vincent Astor's yacht, and remained at sea until February 14th.

February 13, 1933: Alexander Dana Noyes, the financial editor of *The New York Times,* returned to the subject:

However ill-grounded may be the fear of dangerous experiment with the currency, the mere fact that such things are publicly talked about by their promoters has necessarily thrown a shadow over financial confidence at a time when mental influences are of paramount importance and when confidence is needed urgently. The Federal Reserve gold holdings ... never [were] equaled in its history except one period of a few months.

February 14, 1933: During the month of February, a Senate committee had undertaken an inquiry into possible methods of recovery. The committee called a large number of economists and business men. Their almost universal recommendation was to maintain the gold standard, to balance the budget, to negotiate the debt, and to stabilize world currencies. Apprehension in the country caused the press to attach unusual importance to each recommendation for the maintenance of the gold standard, and the discussion filled columns. Its indirect result was further to stimulate fear.

This day, Bernard M. Baruch, before the Senate committee, stated:

I regard the condition of this country the most serious in its history ... inflation ... is the road to ruin.... The mere talk of inflation retards business. If you start talking about that [devaluation] you would not have a nickel's worth of gold in the Reserve System day after tomorrow.

Mr. Baruch's vigorous statement attracted a great deal of attention because of his influence in the Democratic Party, and it was assumed it would not have been made but for his personal knowledge of imminent danger.

The developments during the first two weeks of February had transformed mere apprehension into fear all over the country. The withdrawal of currency and gold for hoarding had increased from about $5,000,000 a day at the first of February to $15,000,000 a day by the middle of the month. All the phenomena so well-known in European experience antecedent to an abandonment of, or change in, the gold standard both appeared and grew. It should be stressed again that there was no pressure from abroad to withdraw gold from the United States. All consequential foreign gold deposits had been withdrawn during the previous year and the current then normally should have been inward. It was solely the domestic financial situation that was pressing it outward.

During the first fourteen days of February the flight of the dollar had enormously increased the movement of gold outward. During this period the exports of gold reached $114,000,000 and, as explained above, the open export movement by no means represented the full volume of flight. In the week ending February 11th, domestic hoarding had arisen to $149,000,000, of which $24,000,000 was in gold and gold certificates. An effect which possibly was of even greater danger to the country was that the banks in central cities and national business concerns were withdrawing their balances from the interior of the country and from their correspondent banks, and thus were debilitating the whole banking situation the country over. Michigan, being one of the weakest banking States, due to the rapid growth of the motor industry and the depth of the depression in this same industry, was visibly tottering. The Governor of that State, on the 14th, had declared a banking holiday.

As the situation, from fear of impending currency change and other like acts of the new Administration, now was visibly rising to an actual panic, President Hoover determined that there could be no effective remedy for the fears which caused it except a statement from the President-elect. Obviously, any assurance from the outgoing Administration could not allay fears as to the policies of the incoming Administration.

February 15, 1933: The effect of the constantly increasing public anxiety reached the United States Senate, as indicated by the following dispatch, which appeared in *The New York Herald Tribune:*

> Democratic conservatives are prepared to urge an immediate offensive by President-elect Roosevelt against currency inflation sentiment in Congress. . . . Among Democratic conservatives the belief is strong that this is the time for the incoming President to strike a telling blow in support of the Democratic platform pledge to preserve a sound currency "at all hazards." . . . Certain of the Democratic leaders apprehend that the absence of any supporting word from him when leaders of both parties are on the firing line may be construed as confirming a current rumor. . . .
> Senator Carter Glass, of Virginia, author of the sound-money plank in the party platform, is represented in responsible Democratic circles as prepared to seek a satisfactory understanding with President-elect Roosevelt on this subject. . . . It is certain that the Virginian would decline to

assume this responsibility [Secretary of the Treasury] in the absence of positive assurance. . . .

February 17, 1933: The President had been expecting to communicate directly with Mr. Roosevelt upon his return from the Florida fishing trip. Immediately upon Mr. Roosevelt's arrival the President appealed to him for co-operation in the impending danger:

My dear Mr. President-elect:

A most critical situation has arisen in the country of which I feel it is my duty to advise you confidentially. I am therefore taking this course of writing you myself and sending it to you through the Secret Service for your hand direct as obviously its misplacement would only feed the fire and increase the dangers.

The major difficulty is the state of the public mind, for there is a steadily degenerating confidence in the future which has reached the height of general alarm. I am convinced that a very early statement by you upon two or three policies of your Administration would serve greatly to restore confidence and cause a resumption of the march of recovery.

The large part which fear and apprehension play in the situation can well be demonstrated by repeated experience in the past few years and the tremendous lift which has come at times by the removal of fear can be easily demonstrated.

One of the major underlying elements in the broad problem of recovery is the re-expansion of credit so critically and abruptly deflated by the shocks from Europe during the last half of 1931. The visible results were public fear, hoarding, bank failures, withdrawal of gold, flight of capital, falling prices, increased unemployment, etc. Early in 1932 we created the agencies which have steadily expanded available credit ever since that time and continue to expand it today. But confidence must run parallel with expanding credit and the instances where confidence has been injured run precisely with the lagging or halting of recovery. There are, of course, other facts but I am only illustrating certain high lights.

Within the last twelve months we have had two profound examples of the effect of restoration of confidence. Immediately after the passage of the measures for credit expansion act early in 1932, there was a prompt response in public confidence with expression in rising prices, employment, decrease in bank failures, hoarding, etc., even before the actual agencies were in action. This continued until it was interrupted by the aggregate of actions starting in the House of Representatives last spring [which] again spread fear and practical panic across the country. This interruption brought back all the disastrous phenomena that I have mentioned, but near the end of the session, when it became clear to the country that the revenue bill would be passed, that inflation of the currency and bonus were defeated, that the government credit would be maintained, that the gold standard would be held, etc., promptly for a second time confidence returned and ran parallel with the expansion and reconstruction measures. The country resumed the march of recovery. At once there was a rise in farm, commodity and security prices, production, industry and employment. There was a practical cessation of bank failures and hoarding, and gold returned from abroad.

This continued during the summer and fall when again there began another era of interruptions to public confidence which have finally culminated in the present state of alarm and it has transformed an upward movement into a distinct downward movement.

The facts about this last interruption are simple and they are pertinent to the action needed. With the election there came the natural and inevitable hesitation all along the economic line, pending the demonstration of the policies of the new administration. But a number of very discouraging things have happened on top of this natural hesitation. The breakdown in balancing the budget by the House of Representatives; the proposals for inflation of the currency and the widespread discussion of it; the publication of the R.F.C. loans and the bank runs, hoarding and bank failures from this cause; increase in unemployment due to imports from depreciated currency countries; failure of the Congress to enact banking, bankruptcy and other vital legislation; unwillingness of the Congress to face reduction in expenditures; proposals to abrogate constitutional responsibility by the Congress, with all the chatter about dictatorship, and other discouraging effects upon the public mind. They have now culminated to a state of alarm which is rapidly reaching the dimensions of a crisis. Hoarding has risen to a new high level; the bank structure is weakened as witness Detroit and increased failures in other localities. There are evidences of flight of capital and foreign withdrawals of gold. In other words, we are confronted with precisely the same phenomena we experienced late in 1931 and again in the spring of 1932. The whole has its final expression in the increase of unemployment, suffering and general alarm.

During all this time the means of credit expansion has been available, but neither borrowers nor lenders are willing to act in the situation of business. While the financial agencies of the government can do much to stem the tide and to localize fires, and while there are institutions and situations that must be liquidated, these things can only be successfully attained in an atmosphere of general confidence. Otherwise the fire will spread.

I therefore return to my suggestion at the beginning as to the desirability of clarifying the public mind on certain essentials which will give renewed confidence. It is obvious that as you will shortly be in a position to make whatever policies you wish effective, you are the only one who can give these assurances. Both the nature of the cause of public alarm and experience give such an action the prospect of success in turning the tide. I do not refer to action on all the causes of alarm, but it would steady the country greatly if there could be prompt assurance that there will be no tampering or inflation of the currency; that the budget will be unquestionably balanced, even if further taxation is necessary; that the Government credit will be maintained by refusal to exhaust it in the issue of securities. The course you have adopted in inquiring into the problems of world stabilization are already known and helpful. It would be of further help if the leaders could be advised to cease publication of R.F.C. business.

I am taking the liberty of addressing you because both in my anxiety over the situation and my confidence from four years of experience that such tides as are now running can be moderated and the processes of regeneration which are always running can be released.

Incidentally, I will welcome the announcement of the new Secretary of the Treasury, as that would enable us to direct activities to one point of action and communication with your good self.

I wish again to express my satisfaction at your escape and to wish you good health.

Yours sincerely,
(Signed) HERBERT HOOVER.

February 19, 1933: Senator Glass had been tendered the Secretaryship of the Treasury by the incoming Administration. It was reported to the White House that Senator Glass had had an interview with the President-elect and had decided to decline the Cabinet position because either he had learned of the intention of Mr. Roosevelt to go off the gold standard or at least he had been unable to secure satisfactory assurances upon that subject. The President concluded from this that his request to Mr. Roosevelt for public assurances would not be complied with.

The financial editor of *The New York Times* urged that "a clear and positive declaration of the incoming Government's attitude toward the currency will be imperative. . . ."

February 20, 1933: Senator David A. Reed, of Pennsylvania, called upon the President to inform him that certain Democratic leaders in the Senate had assured him that if the President would make a declaration suspending the convertibility of the currency into gold they would secure legislation ratifying it. He further informed the President that, appearing before an executive session in the Banking and Finance Committee, Melvin A. Traylor, an important Chicago banker who had been a backer of Mr. Roosevelt's campaign, had informed the committee that nothing but a declaration by Mr. Roosevelt that there would be no inflation or devaluation would save the situation from general panic.

The President then informed Senator Reed of his appeal to President-elect Roosevelt and requested that he should use his influence with the Democratic senators to have them urge such an immediate public declaration upon the President-elect. He gave the following memorandum to Senator Reed on the subject:

Confidential

My dear Senator:

I have now given thought to the assurance of the Democratic Senate leaders through you to me that they would undertake to secure Congressional ratification if I determined it was necessary and would first act to suspend the convertibility of currency into gold and stop gold shipments abroad. . . .

These movements [of gold currency and flight of capital] are, however, symptomatic and very disturbing. Considered with the very much larger question of currency hoarding they show an alarming state of public mind. That state of mind is simple. It is the breakdown of public confidence in the new administration now coming in. The American people do not wait for a known business event; they act to protect themselves individually in advance.

The things they fear the most are inflation, an unbalanced budget, and governmental projects which will surtax the borrowing power of the Government. The way to stem the tide is that assurance should be at once given by the new administration that they have rigidly opposed such policies. That is the only way to re-establish confidence. And therefore, my suggestion is that you should transmit to the Democratic leaders this fundamental necessity, that they may urge it upon the President-elect. These may or may not be "new deal," but the actions of the majority party in Congress, the measures proposed by its members, the failure of the President-elect to disavow them, and the fact that they constitute Republican policies of which there is constant promise of reversal,—all serve to confirm public beliefs. . . .

I realize that if these declarations be made by the President-elect, he will have ratified the whole major program of the Republican Administration; that is, it means the abandonment of 90% of the so-called new deal. But unless this is done, they run a grave danger of precipitating a complete financial debacle. If it is precipitated, the responsibility lies squarely with them for they have had ample warning—unless, of course, such a debacle is part of the "new deal."

Yours faithfully,

HERBERT HOOVER.

Senator David A. Reed,
Washington, D. C.

February 21, 1933: The Baltimore Sun stated:

Word reached New York this afternoon that Senator Glass had taken himself out of the Cabinet situation and had so advised Mr. Roosevelt. The latter smilingly declined to confirm this, but did admit that he had been in communication with the senator not once but several times that day. As a matter of fact, terrific last-minute pressure seems to have been brought to bear upon Mr. Glass to take the place, some of this pressure proceeding directly from the President-elect himself, and it is firmly believed in quarters very close to both men that if satisfactory assurances had been given the senator that the new administration under no circumstances would accept inflation as a policy, his answer would have been different. On the other side of the picture—the Roosevelt side—he cannot at this stage absolutely close the doors of his administration on any possible proposals that might lead to inflation. One or more such measures may be found to have merit and entitled to a trial as he sees it. For that reason he refused to bind himself to any rigid line of action, even though it cost him Mr. Glass' services.

The New York Times stated:

Part of this conviction [of Senator Glass against acceptance of the Treasuryship] arises, perhaps, from his uncertainty as to the degree to which the incoming administration will support his view on currency and the banking questions. It is not believed that in the three brief conferences Mr. Glass has had with Mr. Roosevelt, Senator Glass received the assurances he required on controversial parts of financial economies.

The same day—February 21st—at the monthly meeting of the Federal Reserve Advisory Council, where there were present leading bankers from each of the twelve Federal Reserve Districts, the following views were formulated:

The Federal Reserve Advisory Council expresses the view that there is considerable unrest in the country due to the uncertainty as to what the policy of the incoming administration is in respect (1) to the necessity of balancing the Federal budget largely by reduction of expenditures, (2) the dangers inherent in the various proposals to inflate the currency, and (3) the desirability of preventing the undue expansion of Government credit which, if continued, will be a menace to the credit of the Government.

In view of the situation, the Federal Advisory Council believes that the President-elect should issue a statement of his policy in reference to the above problems as promptly as possible.

The chairman of the Advisory Committee transmitted its views to the President-elect, and received only a secretarial acknowledgment.

Also on this day—February 21st—Senator Simeon D. Fess, of Ohio, made an appeal in the Senate that the President-elect make an immediate statement:

There could be no statement issued that would have such an ameliorating effect and such a salutary result as a statement from the incoming President that there will be no tampering with sound money in his administration.

Upon press application to the President-elect for a statement he refused to comment.

The morning papers—February 21st—carried the news that William H. Woodin had been selected as Secretary of the Treasury for the new administration. Secretary Mills having arranged to meet with Mr. Woodin that evening in New York City, the President sent to Mills the following note:

My dear Mr. Secretary:

You are about to meet Mr. Woodin to discuss with him the financial crisis which has developed since the election and the measures which must be taken to prevent its further development.

I know it is your intention to offer him every assistance. I would be glad if you would assure him also that I join in a desire to co-operate in every possible way.

The causes of this sudden critical development are simple enough. The public is filled with fear and apprehension over the policies of the new Administration. People are acting now in individual self-protection, and unless it is checked, it jeopardizes every bank deposit, every saving, every insurance policy, and the very ability of the Federal Government to pay its way. The indices of fear are hoarding and flight of capital. The drain of gold is not yet alarming, yet its wide spread is symptomatic. The hoarding of currency, however, has arisen to enormous dimensions and cannot go on at this rate without creating panic. There is obvious flight of capital to foreign countries in progress. The weakness of the Government bond market despite the support of the Federal Reserve Banks is but a further symptom.

The policies of which the public are mainly alarmed are, first, inflation of the currency, second, failure to balance the budget, third, prospective projects which will overtax the borrowing power of the Government. These may or may not be the policies of the new Administration, but the actions of the majority party in Congress, the measures proposed by its members, and the failure of the President-elect to disavow them, and constant assurance of reversal of administration policies serve to confirm such public beliefs. The people do not wait to see these new policies developed after the administration comes into power. They are acting in self-protection before March 4th.

The way to stem the tide is that assurances should at once be given by the new Administration that they rigidly oppose such policies. They alone can establish confidence. This should be made clear and it should be made clear where the responsibility will be if the crisis shall develop to extremes.

There are, of course, other fundamental policies needed. First, determination to settle no war debts until foreign currency is stabilized and other problems of the World Economic Conference and compensations brought to fruition; and second, such moderate palliatives in banking, agriculture, readjustment of debts, as will not overstrain the government and will carry the situation until the turn in the tide of prices which can come with world stability.

I trust, Mr. Woodin will realize that, because a Republican Administration has stood stanchly for these principles and policies, it is no reason for their abandonment, for they are fundamental.

Yours faithfully,

HERBERT HOOVER.

Hon. Ogden Mills,
Secretary of the Treasury,
Washington, D. C.

February 23, 1933: On his return from New York, Secretary Mills advised the President that Mr. Woodin had informed him that positively no statement would be made.

Up to the end of the week of February 25th the situation could have been saved if the President-elect had been willing to co-operate and in some way to repeat the assurances which he had given in a public address four days before the election. Then he had emphasized the sanctity of "the covenant" of the government to pay in gold. The panic now was under way. Mr. Roosevelt had not responded to the President's appeal and to the urging of many others. Should the panic reach the stage of general bank closings, it meant enormous injury to the country, the increase of unemployment and the collapse of farm prices. In the face of the situation, President Hoover's policies, therefore, shifted to devising methods of controlling the panic. That is to say he and his associates worked to keep the banks wholly or partially open and functioning, through various devices, until Mr. Roosevelt, in power and with a Congress the majority of whom were at his bidding, could take such emergency measures as he might have in mind. The first-aid policy of President Hoover is described elsewhere in the narrative.

February 27, 1933: New York Times dispatches from abroad described the European view that the situation was due to "lack of information regarding the definite intentions of the new American Government. A declaration by Mr. Roosevelt . . . to maintain sound currency would have an extremely reassuring effect." Apparently the foreigners appreciated that this was largely a gold panic.

March 1, 1933: President-elect Roosevelt's reply to President Hoover's appeal of February 17th arrived at the White House today, after an elapse of twelve days.

DEAR MR. PRESIDENT:

I am dismayed to find that the inclosed which I wrote in New York a week ago did not go to you, through an assumption by my secretary that it was only a draft of a letter.

Now I have yours of yesterday and can only tell you that I appreciate your fine spirit of co-operation and that I am in constant touch with the situation through Mr. Woodin, who is conferring with Ogden and with various people in N. Y. I am inclined to agree that a very early special session will be necessary—and by tonight or tomorrow I hope to settle on a definite time—I will let you know—you doubtless know of the proposal to give authority to the Treasury to deposit funds directly in any bank.

I get to Washington late tomorrow night and will look forward to seeing you on Friday.

Sincerely yours,
(Signed) FRANKLIN D. ROOSEVELT.

The President,
The White House.

(*Inclosure*)

DEAR MR. PRESIDENT:

I am equally concerned with you in regard to the gravity of the present banking situation—but my thought is that it is so very deep-seated that the fire is bound to spread in spite of anything that is done by way of mere statements. The real trouble is that on present values very few financial institutions anywhere in the country are actually able to pay off their deposits in full, and the knowledge of this fact is widely held. Bankers with the narrower viewpoint have urged me to make a general statement, but even they seriously doubt if it would have a definite effect.

I had hoped to have Senator Glass' acceptance of the Treasury post—but he has definitely said no this afternoon—I am asking Mr. Woodin tomorrow—if he accepts I propose to announce it tomorrow together with Senator Hull for the State Department. These announcements may have some effect on the banking situation, but frankly I doubt if anything short of a fairly general withdrawal of deposits can be prevented now.

In any event, Mr. Woodin, if he accepts, will get into immediate touch with Mills and the bankers.

Very sincerely yours,
(Signed) FRANKLIN D. ROOSEVELT.

The President,
The White House.

Mr. Roosevelt's statement in the above letter that "the real trouble is that on present values very few financial institutions anywhere in the country are actually able to pay off their depositors," he obviously learned later to be untrue. When, after a few days, the banks were all closed by him, and then, within another few days, re-opened, there had been no essential addition to their assets. Banks holding ninety-two per cent of the country's deposits were so re-opened and Mr. Roosevelt himself publicly declared that they were sound, and that he would open only those that were sound. The reports of the Comptroller of the Currency show several per cent of the remainder subsequently were opened without loss to the depositors.

It was not primarily a bank scare that induced a flight of capital abroad estimated by some at exceeding a billion dollars, or the purchase of large quantities of gold bullion, or the withdrawal of gold coin for hoarding. Even many of the hoarders of currency believed in the faith of the government to convert it into gold. It is obvious that the fear of the prospective change in monetary policies, since justified, contributed to the general breakdown of confidence.

CHAPTER XIX

THE GOLD PANIC

THE New Deal, so far as the economic situation was concerned, began its influence immediately on the winning of the election on November 8, 1932. The country turned to examine the reality of the policies of the new administration, and acted accordingly. Both the political parties in their platforms, and the candidates by their assurances, had pledged themselves to recovery, to stability, to maintain sound money, to balance the budget, to reduce expenditures, and to set up banking reform. We have seen the gradual destruction of confidence by the unwillingness of the incoming administration to co-operate on the question of war debts and stabilization of world currencies, in balancing the budget, in banking reform, and the publication of Reconstruction Finance Corporation loans, and by the intent to tinker with the currency, and to attempt some form of inflation.

In this chapter we shall tell of the growth of the banking storm and the efforts of President Hoover to check and overcome it. Under the forces we have mentioned, the movement toward world recovery quickly turned in America to hesitation, then to apprehension, then to fear, and finally to panic. These stages were quite clearly defined.

THE SEVENTY DAYS OF HESITATION

November 8, 1932, to January 18, 1933: In the first seventy days after the election, there was a marked let-down in the steady upward swing of economic recovery which generally had characterized the period since mid-summer of 1932.

The first banking difficulties after the election were shown in the closing of banks under runs, many of them directly induced by the publication of the Reconstruction Finance Corporation loans. During the recovery months from September to November, 1932, the Reconstruction Finance Corporation had been authorizing, in loans to banks and trust companies, only about $30,000,000 per month, as compared with $220,-000,000 per month during the previous crisis in June. But the increase in demands for help began to show in December, when these loans ran up to $50,000,000. New strains were developing during the same month in the country banks and the building and loan associations, especially in the mid-West and Pennsylvania. In early January, 1933, larger banks in interior cities began to need more help from the Reconstruction Finance Corporation. Despite these difficulties, there still was, up to mid-January, no panic in the public mind.

We may recall the figures as to this period of hesitation, from November, 1932, to the week ending January 18, 1933:

Net additions to the gold stock	$322,000,000
Return of currency from hoarding	40,000,000
Net bank closings (in deposits)	118,000,000
R.F.C. loans	121,000,000

The Twenty-six Days of Apprehension

January 18 to February 13, 1933: During the latter part of January, the discussion and rumors of inflation and devaluation, the failure to secure co-operation in world currency stabilization, the wrecking of the budget, the whisperings as to the intentions of the President-elect to tamper with our currency, and the publication of the Reconstruction Finance Corporation loans, all began to have effect. Fear grew more acute after the press confirmation on January 30th of the intention of the President-elect to devalue or inflate.

The hoarding of currency, practically non-existent for many months, began again in mid-January, partly on account of isolated bank failures, but in large part from fear of the policies to be undertaken by the incoming administration. Hoarding, which was at the daily rate of $2,000,000 in the last twelve days of January, rose to $5,000,000 a day by the first of February, and, by the end of the week of the eleventh of the month, had grown to more than $15,000,000 a day. These were the current estimates reported to the President by Federal Reserve officials. Of even more significance was the movement abroad of gold. This was the flight of the dollar. Beginning in mid-January at the rate of about $2,000,000 per day, it rose by February 15th to the rate of $18,000,000 per day. The actual gold movement abroad, however, as we have discussed in previous chapters, represented but a small part of the volume of the flight of the dollar. The purchases of gold bullion, of foreign exchange, of foreign securities have been estimated as rising even into billions. No one ever can determine their full volume.

Early in February further acute banking situations developed in interior cities, and in San Francisco, and Boston. President Hoover was called upon personally to help in mobilizing assistance in these difficulties. He and his associates often worked far into the night in conference and by telephone, and each crisis was overcome in turn.

A serious difficulty in the Detroit banks developed on Friday, the tenth of February. The situation required a co-ordination of many forces. A legal holiday on Monday, February 13th—for Lincoln's Birthday—gave an extra day for negotiations, and by that evening some progress had been made. The Governor of Michigan, however, under local advice and to meet upstate difficulties, during the night declared an eight-day bank holiday.

The details of the continuous day and night leadership of President Hoover to re-open the Michigan banks from this time forward are not pertinent to this story. In this he was ably and devotedly assisted by Secretary Mills, Chairman Pomerene, and President Miller of the Reconstruction Finance Corporation, and especially by Henry M. Robinson of Los Angeles, whom he had asked to co-ordinate all the financial forces that could help. These efforts comprised a series of successive attempts by the President, as one method after another broke down, first to mobilize industrial and banking support to co-operate with the Reconstruction Finance Corporation; then to act through the State Legislature with the Federal support from the Reconstruction Finance Corporation; then to install a clearing-house scrip system with the Reconstruction Finance Corporation support; then to re-open the banks with partial payment to depositors with Reconstruction Finance Corporation and other banking support. The size of the situation made it impossible for the Reconstruction Finance Corporation to assume the whole burden under the limitations imposed upon it by law, without the co-operation of other forces. One plan after another disintegrated after it was thought a remedy had been found. Had the situation been isolated from the atmosphere of fear throughout the country, these actions would have been successful, as they had been in even more difficult cases which had arisen during the previous two years. There were political and community questions which added to the difficulties. It is an interesting commentary that apparently the two Detroit institutions which were the scene of the major difficulty, even under the destruction of forced liquidation, now probably will meet their depositor liabilities. The story is a long one, the details of which, perhaps, will not be known for years, but one thing is certain, and that is that no more sincere and substantial effort under more difficult circumstances ever was made.

We may review the critical figures for this twenty-six-day period of apprehension from mid-January to mid-February.

Decrease in monetary gold stocks	$75,000,000
Hoarding of currency, gold coin and gold certificates (estimated)	256,000,000
Bank failures, in deposits (to February eleventh)	129,000,000
R.F.C. loans	92,000,000

The situation, though now distressing enough, was hardly comparable to the five previous crises out of which the President had led the country in November, 1929; in June, 1931; in October, 1931; in February, 1932, and again in June, 1932. President Hoover still considered that, with necessary co-operation from the other side, this crisis also could be overcome. But the forces needed to turn the tide now in motion could be had only by a co-operation which was refused.

THE TWELVE DAYS OF FEAR

The period from February 13th to 25th was ushered in by the critical situation in Michigan. It now became clear that nothing would halt a general panic unless the forces of disintegration could be stopped, and public confidence restored by declaration from President-elect Roosevelt that there would be no tampering with the currency, that the budget would be balanced, and that no unbearable expenditures would be undertaken by the government.

February 13, 1933: During a conference upon the Michigan situation, the President asked Chairman Pomerene, of the Reconstruction Finance Corporation, who for twelve years had represented Ohio Democracy in the Senate, if he could help to secure such a statement from the President-elect. Chairman Pomerene was in full accord with its necessity. With a continuation of national fear, the Michigan situation would be beyond remedy. Mr. Roosevelt was due to land in Florida from his sea trip with Vincent Astor on the next day—February 14th. The incidents of communications with the President-elect up to February 25th have been given. They need only be summarized here.

February 14, 1933: The President conferred with Democratic leaders upon the necessity for this statement of reassurance upon currency questions from Mr. Roosevelt, in accordance with his public statement made before the election. These leaders believed there would be no difficulty in securing it at once upon Mr. Roosevelt's return from Florida. As stated in previous chapters, they gave some indications of their views to the press.

February 17, 1933: The President dispatched his urgent letter to Mr. Roosevelt, given in full in the preceding chapter. In view of the critical situation, the President counted upon Mr. Roosevelt's co-operation at least to the extent of a statement which would dissipate currency fears. This was essential if the Michigan and other difficulties were to be remedied.

February 19, 1933: Senator Glass was reported to have declined the Treasury portfolio upon his inability to secure a declaration from Mr.

Roosevelt that he would adhere to the gold standard. As already shown, news to this effect appeared in the press within the next two or three days and carried immediate repercussion in the banking situation.

Time was an important element. The President, being concerned as to the lack of reply from the President-elect, requested a confirmation from the Secret Service officials as to the actual delivery of his letter. They immediately sent to the White House a full report which contained all the details of the delivery of the letter into Mr. Roosevelt's own hand. No reply was, in fact, received by President Hoover until nearly two weeks later, on March 1st.

February 21, 1933: The Federal Reserve Advisory Board formulated its views—given in the preceding chapter—urging Mr. Roosevelt to relieve the pressing anxieties of the situation. No comment was made by the President-elect. The President now requested Secertary Mills the next day—February 22nd—to take up with Mr. Woodin, who had been announced as the next Secretary of the Treasury, the question of a statement from Mr. Roosevelt. President Hoover's instructions to the Secretary also have been given in the preceding chapter.

During the day, Senator Fess, of Ohio, had called upon the President in order to discuss the situation, and he requested the President to give him a memorandum upon the present situation, including past and present developments of the banking and financial phases of the depression. The President dictated the following:

February 21, 1933.

HON. SIMEON D. FESS,
United States Senate,
Washington, D. C.

MY DEAR MR. SENATOR:

I am glad to respond to your request that I put in writing for your records the statement I made to you yesterday as to the economic situation at the moment, and the causes thereof.

Today we are on the verge of financial panic and chaos. Fear for the policies of the new administration has gripped the country. People do not await events, they act. Hoarding of currency, and of gold, has risen to a point never before known; banks are suspending not only in isolated instances, but in one case in an entire state. Prices have fallen since last autumn below the levels which debtors and creditors can meet. Men over large areas are unable or are refusing to pay their debts. Hundreds of millions of orders placed before election have been cancelled. Unemployment is increasing, there are evidences of the flight of capital from the United States to foreign countries, men have abandoned all sense of new enterprises and are striving to put their affairs in defense against disaster.

Some days before election the whole economic machine began to hesitate from the upward movement of last summer and fall. For some time after election it continued to hesitate but hoped for the best. As time has gone on, however, every development has stirred the fear and apprehension of the people. They have begun to realize what the abandonment of a successful program of this administration, which was bringing rapid recovery last summer and fall, now means and they are alarmed at possible new deal policies indicated by the current events. It is this fear that now dominates the national situation. It is not lack of resources, currency, or credit.

The incidents which have produced this fear are clear. There was a delay by the President-elect of over two months in willingness to cooperate with us to bring about order from confusion in our foreign economic relations. There have been a multitude of speeches, bills, and statements of Democratic members of Congress and others proposing inflation or tinkering with the currency. My proposals for reduction of expenditures have been ignored to the extent of over $200,000,000 by the Democratic House of Representatives. The differences between Democratic leaders and the President-elect over the basis of taxation with which to balance the budget caused them to reject the balancing of the budget. The publication by Democratic leaders of the House of the Reconstruction Corporation loans has caused runs on hundreds of banks, failures of many of them and hoarding on a wide scale.

There have been proposed in the Congress by Democratic leaders, and publicly even by the President-elect, projects involving Federal expenditures of tremendous dimensions which would obviously lie beyond the capacity of the Federal Government to borrow without tremendous depreciation in government securities. Such proposals as the bills to assume Federal responsibility for billions of mortgages, loans to municipalities for public works, the Tennessee improvements and Muscle Shoals, are all of this order. The proposals of Speaker Garner that constitutional government should be abandoned because the Congress, in which there will be an overwhelming majority, is unable to face reduction of expenses, has started a chatter of dictatorship. The President-elect has done nothing publicly to disavow any of these proposals.

The Democratic House has defeated a measure to increase tariffs, so as to prevent invasion of goods from depreciated currency countries [and] thus stopping increased unemployment from this source. There have been interminable delays and threatened defeat of the Glass Banking Bill, and the Bankruptcy Bill.

How much this whole situation is the result of fear of the policies of the new administration is further indicated by a short review of the five distinct periods in recent economic history.

The first period began with the financial and monetary collapse of Europe in the last half of 1931 culminating in October, bringing contraction of credit and reduction of exports, falling prices of both commodities and securities, followed by great fear and apprehension in the people which was promptly represented by hoarding, bank failures, flight of capital, withdrawal of foreign gold balances, with final interpretation in decreased employment, demoralization of agriculture and general stagnation.

The second period following the approval by Congress of our measure of reconstruction in early February, 1932, was a period of sharp recovery over a period between 60 and 90 days; during this period confidence was restored, currency began to return from hoarding, gold shipments abroad were greatly lessened, and bank failures ceased and the whole country moved upward.

The third period began in April and continued through July. This was a period of a sharp débâcle which was brought about in the Democratic House by the same character of proposals we now see again, that is by the original failure of the revenue bill, the failure to reduce expenditures recommended by the Executive with consequent fear that the movement toward balancing the budget would not be successful; the passage of a group of inflationary measures including the Patman Bill, the Goldsborough Bill, etc. The passage of a series of projects which would have required greater issues of government securities than the Treasury could support including the Garner Bills, for gigantic public works and unlimited loans by the Reconstruction Corporation, etc. Public confidence was destroyed; hoarding, withdrawal of foreign gold, decrease in employment, falling prices and general economic demoralization took place.

The fourth period began about the adjournment of Congress when it was assured that these destructive measures were defeated and that constructive measures would be held. This period extended from July until October and was a period of even more definite march out of the depression. Employment was increasing at the rate of half a million men a month, bank failures ceased, hoarded currency was flowing back steadily and gold was returning from abroad, car loadings, commodity and security prices and all the other proofs of emergence from the depression were visible to everyone. Fear and despair had again been replaced by hope and confidence.

The fifth period began shortly before election when the outcome became evident and has lasted until today. I have already recited its events.

The causes of this terrible retrogression and fear in this fifth period have an exact parallel in the third period of last spring. The fact that there was no disavowal of the actions of last spring by the Democratic candidates during the campaign lends added color and alarm that the same actions and proposals which are now repeated in this period positively represent the policies of the new administration—and the people are seeking to protect themselves individually but with national damage. The movement forward in recovery of our people is again defeated by precisely the same factors as last spring and again emanating from the Democratic leaders.

In the interest of every man, woman, and child, the President-elect has, during the past week, been urged by the saner leaders of his own party, such as Senator Glass and others, by myself and by Democratic bankers and economists whom he has called on for advice, to stop the conflagration before it becomes uncontrollable, by announcing firmly and at once that (a) the budget will be balanced even if it means increased taxation; (b) new projects will be so restricted that government bond issues will not in any way endanger stability of government finances; (c) there will be no inflation or tampering with the currency; to which some have added that as the Democratic party is coming in with an overwhelming majority in both houses, there can be no excuse for abandonment of Constitutional process.

The President-elect is the only man who has the power to give assurances which will stabilize the public mind, as he alone can execute them. Those assurances should have been given before now but must be given at once if the situation is to be greatly helped. It would allay some fear and panic whereas delay will make the situation more acute.

The present administration is devoting its days and nights to put out the fires or to localize them. I have scrupulously refrained from criticism which is well merited, but have instead been giving repeated assurances to the country of our desire to co-operate and help the new administration.

What is needed, if the country is not to drift into great grief, is the immediate and emphatic restoration of confidence in the future. The resources of our country are incalculable, the available credit is ample but bankers will not lend, and men will not borrow unless they have confidence. Instead they are withdrawing their resources and their energies. The courage and enterprise of the people still exist and only await release from fears and apprehension.

The day will come when the Democratic party will endeavor to place the responsibility for the events of this fifth period on the Republican Party. When that day comes I hope you will invite the attention of the American people to the actual truth.

Yours faithfully,

HERBERT HOOVER.

Tuesday, February 22, 1933: The Federal Reserve System functioned automatically in the crisis to supply gold and currency against eligible paper and from its own coverage. But eligible paper was a minor part of bank assets and if the public over the country were going to demand all their bank deposits, obviously the Reserve System could not supply it. Action in such case would be necessarily outside the Reserve System. Aside from the recommendation of a gold statement by Mr. Roosevelt as indicated by the views of the Federal Advisory Council, the Federal Reserve Board and the directors of the Federal Reserve banks were loth to take definite action. Numerous conferences had been held upon possible courses of action, but the Board was greatly divided. Finally, the

President in an endeavor to secure conclusions from them addressed the following letter to the Board:

February 22, 1933.

GENTLEMEN:

I wish to leave no stone unturned for constructive action during the present crisis. Without being technical in regard to the provisions of the law, it is obvious that the Federal Reserve Board has a great responsibility in the control and management of the currency. It is obvious that hoarding of currency, and to some minor extent of gold, has now risen to unprecedented dimensions, and this, together with a disposition to export their capital, has become a threat to public interest.

I should like to be advised by the Board as to whether the Board considers that the situation is one that has reached a public danger and whether the Board considers the Federal Reserve system can protect the public interest, or whether the Board considers any measures should be undertaken at this juncture and especially what, if any, further authority should be obtained.

Yours faithfully,
HERBERT HOOVER.

To the Governor and Members
Federal Reserve Board
Washington, D. C.

February 23, 1933: Financial interests in the city of Cleveland called the President by telephone and asked for more assistance. He arranged for it at once through Chairman Miller of the Reconstruction Finance Corporation.

February 24, 1933: Secretary Mills returned from his interview in New York with Mr. Woodin and reported that Mr. Woodin had definitely informed him that no statement on policy would be made by Mr. Roosevelt.

Out of the President's efforts to re-open the Michigan banks, Henry Ford undertook to co-operate with the Reconstruction Finance Corporation in the establishment of a new union bank in Detroit. This progressed to the extent that Mr. Ford sent a proposed public statement on his part to the President for approval. With the announcement of this arrangement it appeared that the solution to the Michigan situation was making real progress.

February 25, 1933: Governor Albert C. Ritchie closed the banks of Maryland for a three-day banking holiday.

The President sent for Chairman Pomerene, of the Reconstruction Finance Corporation, and requested that he again should communicate to the President-elect and the Democratic leaders the gravity of the immediate situation and urge upon them the absolute necessity for a statement that there would be no tinkering with the currency. Mr. Pomerene agreed that such action was of vital importance if panic were to be arrested, and no doubt he used his influence for that purpose.

An incident of an illuminating character arose this day—February 25th, 1933. A nationally prominent manufacturer telephoned a message to the President, the purport of which is clear from a self-explanatory note the President sent in a reply a day or two later:

My dear Mr. ———:

I beg to acknowledge your telephone message received through Mr. Joslin, as follows:

"Professor Tugwell, adviser to Franklin D. Roosevelt, had lunch with me. He said they were fully aware of the bank situation and that it would undoubtedly collapse in a few days, which would place the responsibility in the lap of President Hoover. He said, 'We should worry about anything except rehabilitating the country after March 4th. Then there would be several moves; first, an embargo on exportation of yellow chips; second, suspension of specie payments; third, reflation if necessary, after one and two, and after that arrangements would be made for the so-called business men's committee of 60 prominent manufacturers who have been invited to spend a half day with Mr. Woodin on Tuesday in an attempt to again support the business interests for a program.'"

I also have your suggestion that in consequence of this attitude I should at once demand of Congress a general guarantee of bank deposits.

When I consider this statement of Professor Tugwell's in connection with the recommendations we have made to the incoming administration, I can say emphatically that he breathes with infamous politics devoid of every atom of patriotism. Mr. Tugwell would project millions of people into hideous losses for a Roman holiday.

Yours faithfully,

Herbert Hoover.

February 25, 1933: Secretary Mills, in communication with Mr. Woodin, again urged that it was not too late for a statement from the President-elect, in accordance with the President's letter of eight days before—not yet answered—to turn the tide now approaching the whirlpool of panic. Mr. Mills reported to the President that Mr. Woodin had informed him again that not only would no statement be made but that they had no part in the government nor any responsibility to the country until March 4th.

The Federal Reserve Board replied to the President's letter of the 22nd as follows:

FEDERAL RESERVE BOARD
WASHINGTON

Office of Governor February 25, 1933.

THE PRESIDENT,
The White House.

DEAR MR. PRESIDENT:

The Board has requested me to acknowledge the receipt of your letter of February 22, 1933 addressed to the Governor and Members of the Federal Reserve Board.

The Board has been keeping in close touch with the important changes that are taking place in the situation and the matters to which you refer have received, and are receiving, its constant attention. No definite information is available as to the amount of capital that has been exported, but so far as the Board is advised, it appears to be a relatively small item so far. As you say, however, withdrawals of currency have reached large proportions, and gold withdrawals have increased to some extent.

While some of the recent developments are disturbing, and many proposals as to ways and means of dealing with them are being made, the Board feels it is essential in times like these that every suggestion be carefully weighed and considered from the point of view of whether it would be likely to bring even greater disturbance and make worse the situation that it is designed to correct.

Recently the Board, after giving the matter careful thought with these considerations in mind, approved the joint resolution regarding the powers of the Comptroller of the Currency introduced by Senator Couzens, which has passed the Senate and which has been favorably reported by the Committee on Banking and Currency of the House. It felt that such a measure would be helpful in facilitating the working out of existing situations in various communities without erecting undue disturbance. The Board also from time to time, has expressed its views regarding other legislative proposal which would affect the exercise of its functions or the operations of the Federal Reserve System, and is continually studying the various problems that are presented as the picture changes, with the view of developing concrete suggestions for appropriate action if and when the need should arise.

At the moment the Board does not desire to make any specific proposals for additional measures or authority but it will continue to give all aspects of the situation its most careful consideration.

Respectfully yours,

EUGENE MEYER, *Governor.*

Sunday, February 26, 1933: The solution of the Michigan situation failed again. It was reported that certain New York banks refused to continue the secured loans which they had made prior to the closure of the

Detroit banks—if they should open. This would diminish the amounts which would be credited to each depositor and transferred to a new union bank. Thereupon, Mr. Ford refused to go on.

As indicative of the acceleration of the movement during these past ten days of fear, it may be noted that the monetary gold stocks decreased by $114,000,000, while hoarding of currency, gold coin and certificates was reported to the President by Federal Reserve officials to be increased by $290,000,000. The actual decrease in gold stocks, of course, represented only a part of the flight of capital abroad. Despite the closing of Michigan and Maryland banks and of some others, in minor localities, by governors' holidays, more than ninety-five per cent of the banks, measured in deposits, were functioning. The flight from the dollar, also a steady seepage from hoarding and the strain of inter-city withdrawals, however, were growing daily. The banks were selling government bonds in order to meet withdrawals.

THE PANIC WEEK

The accelerating fears now were drifting steadily to the panic stage. The President's campaign of economic defense had to be shifted, due to the exclusion of any hope of re-establishing confidence through the co-operation of the President-elect.

Monday, February 27, 1933: The President reviewed the situation at a meeting of his advisers at the White House late tonight. He stated to them that while we were in a wholly unnecessary panic effort must be unremitting to check its growth during the five days of his administration which remained. The President-elect had not even replied to the President's appeal of ten days ago. It was obvious from Senator Glass' action that the President-elect would make no favorable reply to the President's appeal, that he should confirm his pledge to the "covenant." It was proposed by one of the President's advisers that the whole question should be brought to a head by a public statement by President Hoover, calling for a public reply. The purpose was, that if Mr. Roosevelt denied any intention to repudiate the covenant, that would stop the panic. If he refused to reply, or quibbled, then the responsibility was clearly Mr. Roosevelt's and the people would know it. Unless this was done Mr. Hoover would rest under an unfair and false imputation in the public mind. The President said that he would play no politics with national welfare, that the only question was, what course would best protect the public; that he would continue the fight to control the situation, and that some other basis of co-operation with the incoming President might be found. Although no co-operation appeared possible to remove the causes of the panic, yet, perhaps, the incoming administration even now might co-operate to control it, so that it might do as little damage to the people as possible. The record of many of the efforts made and the details of those here mentioned must be left to future historians. Here will be recorded merely the story in its major outlines.

Tuesday, February 28, 1933: The President again addressed the Federal Reserve Board:

February 28, 1933.

To the Governor and Members
of the Federal Reserve Board.

GENTLEMEN:

Since my letter of a few days ago the banking situation has obviously become one of even greater gravity. I naturally wish to be properly advised as to such measures as can be taken to prevent the hardships to millions of people which are now going on. Although the Board is not the technical adviser of the President, yet it appears to me that in the large sense it should be prepared to advise me as to the measures necessary for the protection of the banking and currency system in times of emergency. I would, therefore, be glad to know whether the Board considers it desirable:

(a) To establish some form of Federal guarantee of banking deposits; or
(b) To establish clearing house systems in the affected areas; or
(c) To allow the situation to drift along under the sporadic State and community solutions now in progress.

Yours faithfully,
(Signed) HERBERT HOOVER.

The outline of the legislative plan of bank guarantees referred to in the President's note to the Federal Reserve Board provided for a temporary Federal guarantee of each bank depositor's account in all banks up to the ratio of the assets of the bank. If the assets were 100 per cent of the depositor's liability, the deposits would have been guaranteed in full. If the assets were equal to eighty per cent of the deposits, then the depositor would have been guaranteed that far, and his further claims suspended, pending reorganization of that bank. The plan would have kept all banks open and functioning. As was confirmed subsequently only a small per cent of the banks measured in deposits were partially deficient of sufficient assets to meet their deposit liabilities. It was designed to protect the government from losses in a small minority of banks, especially of State banks, known to be weak, yet possible of reorganization, and at the same time keep them all going. The relative merits of this plan and that subsequently adopted by the new administration by which six or seven per cent—measured in deposits—were closed absolutely until they could be reorganized, are not here under discussion.

Only the then President could issue a call for a meeting of the new Congress. President Hoover, therefore, wrote to the President-elect offering to issue such a call, so as to bring Congress into session as quickly as possible after the fourth of March in order that Mr. Roosevelt could at once take measures to advance his banking and currency policies.

THE WHITE HOUSE

February 28, 1933.

DEAR MR. PRESIDENT-ELECT:

It is my duty to inform you that the financial situation has become even more grave and the lack of confidence extended further than when I wrote to you on February 17th. I am confident that a declaration even now on the line I suggested at that time would contribute greatly to restore confidence and would save losses and hardships to millions of people.

My purpose, however, is to urge you—upon the basis of evident facts—that the gravity of the situation is such that it is desirable that the coordinate arm of the government should be in session quickly after March 4th. There is much legislation urgently needed but will not be completed by the present session. The new Congress being in majority with the administration is capable of expeditious action.

But beyond that, it would make for stability in public mind and there are contingencies in which immediate action may be absolutely essential in the next few days.

I am at your disposal to discuss the situation upon your arrival here or otherwise. I wish to assure you of the deep desire of my colleagues and myself to co-operate with you in every way.

Yours sincerely,

(Signed) HERBERT HOOVER.

The President-elect,
Franklin D. Roosevelt,
New York.

Wednesday, March 1, 1933: President Hoover today received from the President-elect the reply to his letter of February 17th already given in the preceding chapter. Certainly, the elapsed eleven days robbed the reply of any pertinence and possible application to the situation.

Obviously a legislative program was now necessary if any adequate handling of the situation was to be effective. There was still time for emergency legislation if there was a will to do it. But without the co-operation of the President-elect and, through him, of the Democratic majority in Congress, no such program would be possible of consummation. The President and Secretary Mills determined to open up again conferences with Mr. Woodin, whom the President-elect had designated to represent him, and see if the incoming administration would agree upon any legislative plan to be presented to Congress to control temporarily the situation. Mr. Woodin was called up and said that he would be glad to see Secretary Mills in New York.

The President gave the following letter to Secretary Mills:

March 1, 1933.

HONORABLE OGDEN L. MILLS,
Secretary of the Treasury,
Washington, D. C.

MY DEAR MR. SECRETARY:

The appointment you have made with Mr. Woodin is to again offer the full co-operation of the administration to the President-elect in any line of sensible action which will meet the present banking situation. If he or his advisers will indicate to us what they wish to have done to meet the present emergency, and if it is of a nature that will serve the purpose, I shall be glad to present it to the Congress, but it would be futile to present anything unless the President-elect will publicly declare that it is his desire that it should be undertaken. It is obvious to anybody that the majority of the Congress during this session have acted, and will continue to act, only with his indicated approval. In view of our repeated offers to co-operate, this very fact assesses him with responsibilities for the present situation which no amount of declamation can postpone until after March 4.

Yours faithfully,
(Signed) HERBERT HOOVER.

Secretary Mills, after conferring with Mr. Woodin, called up the President that same evening from New York to say that Mr. Woodin had repeated the statement that his "instructions" were not to agree to anything.

Thursday, March 2, 1933: During the previous day and evening, the governors of a few Western and Southern States had declared bank holidays or restricted withdrawals. Even with these depletions of banking strength, eighty-five per cent of the banks measured in deposits were still open and functioning, although under increasing pressure from the flight of capital to foreign countries and domestic runs upon gold and currency.

The Federal Reserve Board replied to the President's note as follows:

FEDERAL RESERVE BOARD
WASHINGTON

Office of the Governor March 2, 1933.

THE PRESIDENT,
The White House,
Washington, D. C.

DEAR MR. PRESIDENT:

The Board has received and carefully considered your letter of February 28, 1933.

In response to your first inquiry, the Board has requested me to advise you that it is not at this time prepared to recommend any form of Federal guarantee of banking deposits. You are, of course, thoroughly familiar with the history of such experiments in some of the States and the inherent dangers in a proposal of this kind.

With respect to your second inquiry, it is understood that, in referring to the establishment of clearing house systems, you have in mind the possibility of the issuance of clearing house certificates or scrip in different communities throughout the country. This, of course, would require the voluntary and wholehearted co-operation of the bankers in particular areas, and, under conditions like these, the matter is one that presents a number of complications from the standpoint of practical operation. The possibility of issuing such certificates has been discussed with some of the leaders of several important communities where critical situations have developed, including Detroit, Cleveland, and Baltimore, and information regarding mechanics and procedure has been furnished to them. Similar information also has been transmitted to the chairmen and governors of all Federal Reserve banks. In addition, we are advised that the Finance Department of the United States Chamber of Commerce recently sent to the presidents of clearing houses, the governors of the Federal Reserve banks, and to some individual bankers, considerable material relating to clearing house certificates and other substitutes for cash, with the statement, however, that the Chamber is not urging the adoption of particular devices to meet current situations which necessarily change from day to day.

We know that the question of issuing clearing house certificates has been or is being considered in the communities named and others, including the District of Columbia, but, for a number of reasons, many of which relate directly to their local situations, they have not felt, up to this time, that it would be feasible or desirable for them to resort to such a device. In Cleveland, it is our understanding that a committee has been appointed by the Clearing House Association for the purpose of canvassing all aspects of the matter in the light of the situation there.

Answering your third inquiry, the Board has requested me to point out that the question is not whether the situation should be allowed to drift along under the sporadic state and community solutions now in progress, but whether any other step can properly be taken now which would produce better results and which at the same time would not create greater difficulty or alarm. All sorts of proposals and possibilities for dealing with the general situation with which we are confronted have been and are being canvassed and discussed, but so far no additional measures or authority have developed in concrete form, which at the moment, the Board feels it would be justified in urging.

I may add that these matters are dealt with here only in summary form, because it is understood that you are familiar with the results of the discussions that have taken place recently including the conference that was held Tuesday evening.

Respectfully yours,
(Signed) EUGENE MEYER,
Governor.

The President was resolved that no stone should remain unturned to end the panic, although there were but forty-eight hours left of his own responsibilities. During the day he invited Senator Robinson, the Democratic leader of the Senate, and Senator Glass to the White House to consider any remaining possibilities of action.

The various steps and actions in the crisis were canvassed and the various proposals were discussed. These proposals included deposit guarantees, control of withdrawals, clearing-house scrip, and so on. The Glass Banking Bill had passed the Senate and was being held up in the House Committee. The President suggested that if there were a will so to do, some form of Congressional action for the emergency could be tacked on to, or substituted for, this bill in the House Committee. Upon its being passed by the House, it could go to conference and all that would be required was the agreement of the Senate to a conference report. This could be done quickly if the Democratic side would co-operate. The conclusion of the two senators, after long discussion and a manifestly earnest desire to co-operate, was that it was hopeless to attempt anything in Congress independently of the President-elect.

After banking hours—March 2nd—one of the members of the Federal Reserve Board called upon the President to inform him that since its letter of that morning the Board took a much more serious view of the situation and that a special meeting had been called for eight o'clock to consider it. The Reserve official raised the question whether or not the President would declare, under certain old war powers, a general banking holiday, to run for at least thirty-six hours until President-elect Roosevelt should be inaugurated.

The use of these powers had been considered by the President during the crisis of February, 1932, in the event that it then should become necessary to limit withdrawals from the banks pending emergency action by Congress. Following this request the President told the representative of the Federal Reserve Board that he would not close the banks, since that was wholly unnecessary if other steps of co-operation could be undertaken. To bring this about he was prepared to use these war powers to control exchange and thus stop the flight of the dollar. He would also use them to direct the banks not to pay withdrawals of currency and gold, except for manifest positive commercial needs, in order to stop hoarding and the drawing of funds from the country banks into the city centers. The President insisted that if hoarding and exchange were controlled, it would not be necessary to close the banks and cause the incalculable inconvenience or even injury that this action would bring down on the nation.

Probably eighty-five per cent of the banks, measured in deposits, were still open, and it was not only unnecessary but also would injure the people greatly thus even temporarily to paralyze agriculture and business, and largely increase unemployment.

During the consideration of this question, Attorney-General Mitchell was called in. He advised that these war powers were so doubtful that they could safely be used only if it were certain that Congress would ratify the action. The President-elect was the only person who could assure this. Otherwise their use and disavowal would create an involved mass of litigation and entanglement. To this end, President Hoover informed the Board that approval from the President-elect should be secured.

As the Federal Reserve Board was meeting that evening, the President sent them the following note:

March 2, 1933.

To the Governor and Directors
of the Federal Reserve Board,
Washington, D. C.

GENTLEMEN:

I understand that the Board is meeting this evening to consider recommending to me the use of the emergency powers under Section 5 of the Enemy Trading Act as amended, *for the purpose of limiting the use of coin and currency to necessary purposes.* I shall be glad to have the advice of the Board. If it is the view of the Board that these powers should be exerted I would be glad to have your recommendation accompanied by a form of proclamation, as it would seem to me it should be issued by me before banking hours tomorrow morning.

I also take this occasion to acknowledge the receipt of your letter of February 28. I am familiar with the inherent dangers in any form of federal guarantee of banking deposits, but I am wondering whether or not the situation has reached the time when the Board should give further consideration to this possibility. I am enclosing herewith a rough outline of a method upon which I should like to have the Board advise me.

Yours faithfully,
(Signed) HERBERT HOOVER.

The majority of the Federal Reserve Board apparently decided in favor of absolute closing of the banks for a holiday for the ensuing thirty-six hours, rejecting President Hoover's proposal. Representatives of the Board and of the Treasury communicated with Mr. Woodin, urging him to secure Mr. Roosevelt's approval of the issue of a proclamation closing all the banks. At about eleven o'clock that night Mr. Woodin reported that the President-elect would not approve such a proclamation. Upon this interchange being reported to President Hoover, he insisted that this was not his proposal, that a proclamation controlling exchange and hoarding was all that was necessary, and that thus the banks could be kept open for all serious business purposes until Mr. Roosevelt could develop his currency and other policies in legislation. He insisted that his proposal should be placed before the incoming administration. This was done, and it was reported to President Hoover that Mr. Woodin replied that the President-elect would not approve of this proclamation.

The President ended the day at two o'clock in the morning.

Friday, March 3, 1933: Secretary Mills reported to President Hoover that the banks in the larger centers had taken various measures which he felt would prevent any general closing over the inauguration and that the President-elect's inaugural address might give the necessary assurances to stop the monetary panic.

In the afternoon, however, the situation took another turn for the worse, partly due to further withdrawal of balances held from one bank to another; Chicago institutions in particular drawing their balances from New York. During the day, New York had lost $110,000,000 to foreigners and $200,000,000 to the interior.

In consequence of this new situation, during the late afternoon President Hoover arranged a conference at the White House with Mr. Roosevelt, Secretary Mills, Governor Eugene Meyer and Professor Moley, the latter at Mr. Roosevelt's request. Mr. Meyer felt that a bank-closing proclamation should be issued prior to the opening of the banks the next morning. President Hoover's view was that there was no such necessity as eighty per cent of the banks measured in deposits were still functioning and that they could be kept open by a national proclamation controlling foreign exchange and withdrawals such as he had previously proposed. They thereby would be able to continue doing business until the new administration's plans were formulated. The possible action of State governors was discussed. Mr. Roosevelt wished to discuss the situation with his advisers.

A good deal of discussion took place between representatives of the two administrations and a great amount of telephoning was done around the country. Finally, at 11:30 that night, from a conference meeting in the White House, President Hoover telephoned to President-elect Roosevelt, who was in conference with his advisers at his hotel in Washington, and asked for their conclusions. Mr. Roosevelt stated that Senator Glass, with whom he was conferring, was opposed to national closing, that the Senator believed the country should go temporarily onto a clearing-house scrip basis. Mr. Roosevelt believed that the governors of the States would take care of the closing situation where it was necessary. He said he did not want any kind of proclamation issued. The President asked if he could repeat Mr. Roosevelt's statement to the men assembled with him at the White House, and did so.

March 4, 1933: The President was up at six o'clock after having had less than four hours' rest—in fact he had not had five hours' sleep any night for the past ten days—and was engaged in cleaning up the accumulation of the formal business of the White House. His only remark to his staff, relating to the crisis was: "If I can keep awake through these ceremonies today and get to New York, I shall go to bed for forty-eight hours and don't any of you dare call me up!"

President Hoover realized the fact, which since has become known, that failure of co-operation and interference by the incoming Executive and Congress caused the crisis. When the crisis arrived, inexcusable as it was, no general closing of the banks was necessary if the policy of controlling hoarding and withdrawals had been adopted and a proclamation to that effect had been issued with the approval of the incoming administration.

History will record that the depression was overcome during the last year of Mr. Hoover's Administration; that the march of recovery which began in the late spring of 1932 was continuous in the rest of the world but was interrupted here by the Presidential campaign and the results of the election in November; that the banking panic of 1933 was the result of fears concerning the monetary and other policies of the incoming administration, which fears were subsequently justified.

The panic can now be viewed in its proper perspective. It did not represent, except in a minor way, any change in basic economic forces or change in fundamental conditions. It was only an interruption in the progress of the country. In other words, spectacular as was this bank

THE GOLD PANIC 367

panic, it was not in reality an economic crisis except in a restricted sense. It came home to the daily life of each and every citizen. The country was in a highly emotional state. But its real underlying importance may be gauged by the fact that ninety-two per cent of the banks were re-opened in a short time as solvent. The country was not in ruins, or it could not have weathered what has happened to it since.

CHAPTER XX

CONCLUSION

Now that the world-wide depression can be viewed in the light of the clearer perspective that only comes with lapse of time and accumulating data, distinguished economists throughout the world are convinced that the depression reached its lowest point in June-July of 1932. In the months following, business activity quickened and confidence in the future was revived.

Production in the United States turned decidedly upward along with a similar turn in production in the major countries of the world. In the United States increased production was followed by increased employment and larger payrolls which, together with more satisfactory farm incomes, brought about increased retail buying. The Federal Reserve index of industrial production increased over fifteen per cent. Unemployment declined by nearly 1,000,000. The adjusted index of department store sales rose almost six per cent. Wheat prices rose ten per cent, cotton prices rose nearly fifty per cent, and the combined index of farm prices rose seven per cent.

Bond prices were up twenty per cent, and stock prices increased over seventy per cent. A return of confidence on the part of the public was evidenced by a termination of the long decline in the awarding of residential contracts, and in the stopping of gold exports and the release of gold hoards. In four months gold stocks increased $350,000,000 and deposits rose by nearly $1,000,000,000. More banks, measured in deposits, were re-opened than were closed.

The upward surge in the United States was destined to be of short duration, however, and was first checked by the Maine election in September. The rest of the world continued to move forward, but in this country an increasing realization, following the Maine election, of the dangers inherent in a change of administration retarded the gains in industrial activity, and with the Presidential election in November a new decline set in.

It would be possible to quote from a large number of economic reviews of the period showing that people of diverse political and economic views all believed that the depression had been overcome by the middle of 1932. It is sufficient to cite three such expressions of opinion as typical of many others.

CONCLUSION

Colonel Leonard P. Ayres, Vice President of the Cleveland Trust Company, writes in his book, *The Economics of Recovery* (p. 137):

It seems probable that when the passage of time allows us to consider the events and developments of the great depression in proper perspective, we shall agree that the corner was turned even in this country in the summer of 1932 rather than after the bank crisis in the spring of 1933. . . . Probably the most important factor in preventing our incipient recovery of 1932 from developing into a continuing improvement, as did those that began abroad at the same time, was political in nature.

The National Industrial Conference Board stated in a bulletin dated November 10, 1934:

The dramatic events of March, 1933, made so vivid an impression upon the public mind that that month is widely associated with the lowest depths of the depression. However, a close inspection of the accompanying chart should dispel that impression . . . The facts presented in the chart bring out clearly that the first steps toward recovery . . . were taken in the year 1932.

According to the *New York Times* of June 16, 1935:

The change for the better in the last half of 1932 is beyond dispute. . . . That this evident revival of confidence was suddenly reversed in February of 1933 is equally true. . . .

It may be well in conclusion to summarize the policies by which these results were attained. The President rightly held that time was required for liquidation of the destructive forces of inflation and World War inheritance; that the problem was to cushion these impacts; to protect the country against panic; to prevent destructive bankruptcy; to care for those in distress; and continually to mobilize the people to fight the depression. In these policies his actions varied with the time, and with each new emergency.

He rigidly maintained a stable currency. Its integrity was protected by holding to the gold standard without changing in any way the gold content of the dollar and by continuing to meet all international obligations by permitting the export of gold. He maintained the credit of the Federal Government by faithfully carrying out all government obligations and by striving unceasingly to balance the budget.

He maintained the credit functions and the financial structure of the country by eliminating as far as possible all shocks through expansion of Federal Reserve credits; through the creation of the National Credit Association, the Reconstruction Finance Corporation and the Federal

Home Loan banks—all of them emergency "steel beams" under the banks, building and loan associations, savings banks and insurance companies.

He upheld the credit structure of agriculture and cushioned the collapse of prices of farm products through the Federal Farm Board, drought relief, expansion of the Land Banks, and the creation of the Agricultural Credit Banks.

Through these policies and actions he maintained the United States as "a Gibraltar of financial strength in a crumbling world." But his policies extended further. By co-operation with foreign nations through the moratorium, the standstill agreement, the preparation for the world conference on stabilization of currencies, and the removal of trade barriers, he protected the United States and further contributed to world recovery.

By promoting co-operation in industry he upheld real wages during the worst period of the depression and avoided industrial strife. He relieved unemployment by inducing employers to stagger work. He urged private industry to undertake and continue construction and conducted a program of public works so far as these would add to national wealth. He organized relief, but in such fashion that State and local responsibility was maintained unimpaired.

By reduction of the ordinary functions of government he was able to conduct all the emergency activities of the government with an actual decrease in government employees.

And all these policies and actions were carried on rigidly within the framework of the Constitution; his measures have not been challenged in the courts. Above all, no attempt was made to have the government take over the functions of the citizen. Emergency institutions set up were to be but temporary. The functions to be performed were to be returned to the people when the emergency was ended. What was done was to assist the citizen in such fashion that he could work himself out of a great emergency by his own efforts. In other words, there was no regimentation, but complete individual initiative of the people was maintained. The forces of depression were definitely checked and the road to full recovery was freed from obstacles during the Hoover Administration.

PART II
THE NORMAL TASKS OF ADMINISTRATION

PART II
THE NORMAL TASKS OF ADMINISTRATION

INTRODUCTION

PART I described the activities of the Hoover Administration in combating the depression. This part deals with the normal day-to-day activities of the Administration which were of necessity carried forward simultaneously with those described in Part I. Generally speaking, they have not the same dramatic interest as those which have been related in the earlier part of the book, but, nevertheless, they are frequently of permanent importance and significance. In many respects, new and advanced methods were employed.

If the depression itself had not overshadowed everything the public would unquestionably have realized more than it did the greatness of Mr. Hoover as an administrator. To be sure, after the European collapse and the intense deepening of the economic disaster which overtook this country, followed by the election of a Democratic House and the continuation of a Senate in opposition, the possibilities of developing improved methods of government were greatly diminished. Many economic and social programs had to be set aside lest the readjustments required in all substantial reform, should delay the essential need of the nation—to return the people to work.

Nevertheless, the President persisted with tireless energy in such economic fields as the reform of banking, the regulation of electric power, railways, and natural resources, and the tariff; in such social fields as public health, child health and protection, and housing and industrial relations; in such governmental fields as the civil service, the reform in the administration and enforcement of law, the prisons, and in governmental reorganization. In all of these fields there was great accomplishment. But, most important of all, he laid the foundations for a public understanding of economic and social problems which yet will be returned to as the basis of any effective building. One characteristic of all his efforts was the insistence upon determination of fact before action.

To those who wish to pursue further a study of Mr. Hoover's concepts of Government, a reading of his speeches and state papers, the more important of which are reproduced in Parts I and II, is suggested. A still further presentation of his ideas is to be found in his recent book, *The Challenge to Liberty*.

CHAPTER I

LAUNCHING THE ADMINISTRATION. THE SPECIAL SESSION OF THE SEVENTY-FIRST CONGRESS. FARM LEGISLATION, AND THE STRUGGLE OVER THE TARIFF.

APRIL–NOVEMBER, 1929

March 4, 1929: The President's first official declaration of his social and economic policies was in his Inaugural Address: [1]

Confidence in rigid and speedy justice is decreasing. I am not prepared to believe that this indicates any decay in the moral fiber of the American people. I am not prepared to believe that it indicates an impotence of the Federal Government to enforce its laws.

It is only in part due to the additional burdens imposed upon our judicial system by the 18th Amendment. The problem is much wider than that . . . re-establish the vigor and effectiveness of law enforcement . . . that justice may be sure and that it may be swift. . . . There is a belief abroad that . . . justice may be thwarted by those who can pay the cost. . . .

Reforms have been advocated for years. . . . Rigid and expeditious justice is the first safeguard of freedom, the basis of all ordered liberty, the vital force of progress. . . .

But a large responsibility rests directly upon our citizens. . . . If citizens do not like a law, their duty is to discourage its violation; their right is openly to work for its repeal. . . .

The election has again confirmed the determination of the American people that regulation of private enterprise and not government ownership or operation is the course rightly to be pursued in our relation to business. In recent years we have established a differentiation in the whole method of business regulation between the industries which produce and distribute commodities on the one hand, and public utilities on the other. In the former, our laws insist upon effective competition; in the latter, because we substantially confer a monopoly by limiting competition, we must regulate their services and rates. Rigid enforcement of the laws applicable to both groups is the very base of equal opportunity and freedom. Such regulation should be extended by the Federal Government within the limitations of the Constitution and only when the individual States are without the power to protect their citizens through their own authority. . . . The larger purpose of our economic thought should be to establish more firmly stability and security of business and thereby remove poverty still further from our borders. Our people have

[1] State Papers, Vol. I, p. 3.

in recent years developed a new-found capacity for co-operation among themselves to effect high purposes in public welfare. It is an advance toward the highest conception of self-government. Self-government does not and should not imply the use of political agencies alone. Progress is born of co-operation in the community—not from governmental restraints. The government should assist and encourage business. There is an equally important field of co-operation by the Federal Government with the multitude of agencies, State, municipal, and private, development of those processes to perfect the means by which government can be adapted to human service. . . .

We cannot hope to succeed unless we can draw all the talent of leadership. One civilization after another has been wrecked upon the attempt to secure sufficient leadership from a single group or class. The full opportunity for every boy and girl to rise to this leadership. . . . Ideals and aspirations are the touchstones upon which the day-to-day administration and legislative acts of government must be tested. . . . These ideals should be: the preservation of self-government and its full foundations in local government; the perfection of justice whether in economic or in social fields; the maintenance of ordered liberty; the denial of domination by any group or class; the building up and preservation of equality of opportunity; the stimulation of initiative and individuality; absolute integrity in public affairs; the choice of officials for fitness to office; the direction of economic progress toward prosperity and the further lessening of poverty; the freedom of public opinion; the sustaining of education and of the advancement of knowledge; the growth of religious spirit and the tolerance of all faiths; the strengthening of the home; the advancement of peace.

There is no short road to the realization of these aspirations. Ill-considered remedies for our faults bring only penalties after them. But if we hold the faith of the men in our mighty past who created these ideals, we shall leave them heightened and strengthened for our children.

March 8, 1929: The President took his stand upon the entire question of "to the victor belong the spoils" by announcing definitely [2] that "he proposed to adhere to the principle of retaining as many as possible of those public servants who have given honest and zealous public service." He indicated that appointment by merit through the Civil Service Commission would be maintained and extended. This was a great disappointment to certain groups.

March 12, 1929: In order to bring every part of the government into the light of day, the President today issued an Executive order [3] ending a policy of secrecy by the government in the making of substantial tax refunds.

It is hereby ordered that decisions of the Commissioner of Internal Revenue allowing a refund, abatement of income, . . . etc. . . . taxes in

[2] State Papers, Vol. I, p. 15.   [3] State Papers, Vol. I, p. 16.

excess of $20,000 shall be open to inspection in accordance and upon compliance with regulations.

March 12, 1929: At a general press conference in response to a question, the President stated [4] that there "will be no leases or disposal of government oil lands no matter what the emergency they may be in," except those mandatory by Congress or the courts. "In other words, there will be complete conservation of government oil in this administration." The announcement of this policy stirred up considerable criticism in some of the Western States that possessed great natural resources. This was followed by pressure to change or modify the policy.

March 19, 1929: Walter Strong, publisher of *The Chicago Daily News,* called upon the President and stated that Chicago had so fallen into the hands of the gangsters that the courts and police were impotent to act, and that some outside force must intervene if the city's ability to protect itself was to be restored. The President directed that the various government law-enforcement agencies at once and without publicity should combine and, regardless of expense, send these gangsters to jail if they had violated Federal laws.

The only Federal criminal statutes to invoke were the Prohibition Act and the income tax laws. The grip of the gangs was broken up with the conviction of Al Capone and others in the Federal courts during the succeeding two years.

March 22, 1929: The President had been an advocate and supporter of the plan to make the 1890 census the basis for fixing immigration restriction quotas as opposed to the so-called "national origins" plan. His view was that the number of foreign-born in this country, as found by the 1890 census, would most nearly approximate the restriction objective. During the previous administration Congress had passed an act requiring the national origins plan and had created a commission to establish the quotas. As Secretary of Commerce, Mr. Hoover had served upon the commission. He knew the difficulties of determining national origins with any reasonable degree of accuracy or of convincing any one aside from its proponents that it could be done with fairness and satisfaction. But under the law as it stood he was required by April 1st to issue the proclamation making the plan effective on July 1st. In issuing the proclamation under these circumstances, he said: [5]

While I am strongly in favor of restricted and selected immigration, I have opposed the national origins basis. I therefore dislike the duty of issuing this proclamation . . . but the President of the United States must be the first to obey the law.

[4] State Papers, Vol. I, p. 15.   [5] State Papers, Vol. I, pp. 17 and 21.

March 25, 1929: The President issued a proclamation [6] designating May 1st as "Child Health Day":

Whereas the future of the nation rests with the children of today . . . the march forward of our country must be upon the feet of our children. . . .

March 26, 1929: Every Republican President has had his difficulties in the appointment of Federal officials in the South. Mr. Hoover was a firm believer in party organization. In common with other Republican Presidents he wanted to build up an effective and creditable organization in these States. At times, certain leaders in some of these organizations had made poor recommendations for Federal office. Very early in his administration, therefore, the President made a public statement reviewing the question of party organization and patronage in the Southern States and stating his policies: [7]

It has been the aspiration of Republican Presidents over many years to build up sound Republican organization in the Southern States, of such character as would commend itself to the citizens of those States.

This aspiration has arisen out of no narrow sense of partisanship, but from the conviction shared in equally by the leaders of all parties that the basis of sound government must rest upon strong two-party representation and organization; that the voice of all States in the councils of the government can be assured by no other means; that the welfare of the nation at large requires the breaking down of sectionalism in politics; that the public service can be assured only by responsible organization. Furthermore, it has been the belief of these leaders, whose views I share, that the building up of such organizations must in every conception of our foundations of local self-government evolve from those States themselves. . . .

Recent exposures of abuse in recommendations for Federal office, particularly in some parts of the States of South Carolina, Georgia, and Mississippi, under which some of the Federal departments, mainly the postoffice, were misled in appointments, obviously render it impossible for the old organizations in those States to command the confidence of the Administration, although many members of these organizations are not subject to criticism. But such conditions are intolerable to public service, are repugnant to the ideals and purposes of the Republican Party, are unjust to the people of the South and must be ended. The duty of reorganization so as to correct these conditions rests with the people of those States, and all efforts to that end will receive the hearty co-operation of the Administration. If these three States are unable to initiate such organization through the leadership of men who will command confidence and protect the public service, the different Federal departments will be compelled to adopt other methods to secure advice as to the selection of Federal employees.

[6] State Papers, Vol. I, p. 21.   [7] State Papers, Vol. I, p. 22.

The President subsequently appointed committees of leading citizens, independent of the political organizations, in Georgia, Mississippi, and South Carolina, to advise him upon public appointments.

April 2, 1929: The President in conference with Attorney-General Mitchell and Secretary of the Interior Wilbur determined that the Federal Oil Conservation Board had no authority to sanction any agreement proposing immunity from the anti-trust laws for the oil companies, in a desire to restrict production in order to maintain or increase prices. The entire industry was so notified. The President stated to the representatives of the press that action was urgently needed in the oil industry to stop the waste of this great natural resource, and to give stability to the industry by regulating the periodic overproduction from newly discovered pools. He suggested that agreements by the States through their conservation officials, which would control activities upon these questions, was the way out rather than attempts at Federal regulation. Subsequently, the President proposed interstate compacts for this purpose in order to avoid extensions of Federal authority over the States.

April 5, 1929: In reply to a press question as to Federal income taxes, the President stated that he strongly favored a much wider distinction between "earned" and "unearned" incomes, to use terms that are not so accurate as they should be, by taxing the former less than the latter.

April 9, 1929: Representatives of the New York Bar Association called in reference to the filling of Federal judicial vacancies. The President informed them that he would be glad to have Bar recommendations. In response to an inquiry he said that appointments to the Federal bench would be based upon merit as distinguished from mere political endorsements.

April 12, 1929: The President reviewed the proposed Agricultural Marketing Bill with the sub-committee of the Committee on Agriculture of the House. Among other suggestions he urged that a provision authorizing co-operative action between farm-operatives and processors or individual shippers in perishable produce should be made effective, in order that ruinous market surpluses and shortages, due to irregular shipments, could be controlled with benefit to both producer and consumer.

April 15, 1929: During the latter part of the campaign, Mr. Hoover had issued a statement on October 27, 1928, as follows:

The question of a special session of Congress after March 4th in the event of the return of the Republican Party has been under discussion for some time. There are a number of questions, particularly agricultural relief, which urgently require solution and should not be delayed for a whole year. It is our most urgent economical problem. I should hope it can be dealt with at the regular session this fall and thus a special session avoided. . . . I would if necessary call an extra session so as to secure early constructive action.

Today Congress convened in extraordinary session following the call of the President.

April 16, 1929: The President sent a special message to Congress devoted almost entirely to farm relief and to limited changes in the tariff.[8]

I have called this special session of Congress to redeem two pledges given in the last election—farm relief and limited changes in the tariff.

The difficulties of the agricultural industry arise out of a multitude of causes. A heavy indebtedness was inherited by the industry from the deflation processes of 1920. Disorderly and wasteful methods of marketing have developed. The growing specialization in the industry has for years been increasing the proportion of products that now leave the farm and, in consequence, prices have been unduly depressed by congested marketing at the harvest or by the occasional climatic surpluses. Railway rates have necessarily increased. There has been a growth of competition in the world markets from countries that enjoy cheaper labor or more nearly virgin soils. There was a great expansion of production from our marginal lands during the war, and upon these profitable enterprise under normal conditions cannot be maintained. Meanwhile their continued output tends to aggravate the situation. Local taxes have doubled and in some cases trebled. Work animals have been steadily replaced by mechanical appliances, thereby decreasing the consumption of farm products. There are many other contributing causes.

The general result has been that our agricultural industry has not kept pace in prosperity or standards of living with other lines of industry.

There being no disagreement as to the need of farm relief, the problem before us becomes one of method by which relief may be most successfully brought about. Because of the multitude of causes and because agriculture is not one industry but a score of industries, we are confronted not with a single problem alone but a great number of problems. Therefore there is no single plan or principle that can be generally applied. Some of the forces working to the detriment of agriculture can be greatly mitigated by improving our waterway transportation; some of them by readjustment of the tariff; some by better understanding and adjustment of production needs; and some by improvement in the methods of marketing.

An effective tariff upon agricultural products . . . has a dual purpose. Such a tariff only protects the farmer in our domestic market, but it also stimulates him to diversify his crops and to grow products that he could not otherwise produce, and thus lessens his dependence upon exports to foreign markets. . . .

[8] State Papers, Vol. I, p. 31.

The government has a special mandate from the recent election . . . to extend systematic relief. . . .

I have long held that the multiplicity of causes of agricultural depression could only be met by the creation of a great instrumentality, clothed with sufficient authority and resources to assist our farmers to meet these problems, each upon its own merits. . . .

Certain safeguards must naturally surround these activities and the instrumentalities that are created. Certain vital principles must be adhered to in order that we may not undermine the freedom of our farmers and of our people, as a whole, by bureaucratic and governmental domination and interference. We must not undermine initiative. There should be no fee or tax imposed upon the farmer. No governmental agency should engage in the buying and selling and price fixing of products, for such courses can lead only to bureaucracy and domination. Government funds should not be loaned or facilities duplicated where other services of credit and facilities are available at reasonable rates. No activities should be set in motion that will result in increasing the surplus production, as such will defeat any plans of relief.

The most progressive movement in all agriculture has been the upbuilding of the farmer's own marketing organizations, which now embrace nearly two million farmers in membership, and annually distribute nearly $2,500,000,000 worth of farm products. These organizations have acquired experience in virtually every branch of their industry, and furnish a substantial basis upon which to build further organization. . . .

The difficulties of agriculture can not be cured in a day; they can not all be cured by legislation; they can not be cured by the Federal Government alone. But farmers and their organizations can be assisted to overcome these inequalities. . . .

In considering the tariff for other industries than agriculture, we find that there have been economic shifts necessitating a readjustment of some of the tariff schedules. . . .

It would seem to me that the test of necessity for revision is, in the main, whether there has been a substantial slackening of activity in an industry during the past few years, and a consequent decrease of employment due to insurmountable competition in the products of that industry. . . .

In determining changes in our tariff, we must not fail to take into account the broad interests of the country as a whole, and such interests include our trade relations with other countries. . . .

. . . Seven years of experience have proved the principle of flexible tariff to be practical . . . the basis upon which the Tariff Commission makes its recommendations . . . should be made more automatic and more comprehensive. . . . With such strengthening of the Tariff Commission and of its basis for action, many secondary changes in tariff can well be left to action by the commission, which at the same time will give complete security to industry for the future. . . .

There are . . . certain matters of emergency legislation . . . the decennial census, the reapportionment of congressional representation, and the suspension of the national-origins clause of the Immigration Act of

1924. . . . I recommended their consummation as being in the public interest.

April 17, 1929: The first bill introduced in the House (H. R. 1.) was the Agricultural Marketing Bill creating a Federal Farm Board. It was favorably reported by the Committee on Agriculture to the House.

April 19, 1929: Certain farm organizations having come forward with other farm relief plans, which were not included in the party platform, the President said:[9]

I regret to see that some farm organizations are again divided on measures of agricultural relief. One primary difficulty in the whole of this last eight years has been the conflict in point of view in the ranks of the agricultural organizations and the farmers themselves.

A definite plan of principles for farm relief was adopted by the Republican Convention at Kansas City. It was the plan of the party; it was not then or now the plan of any individual or group; it was necessarily the result of compromise; it represented an effort to get together and secure fundamental beginnings and necessitated the yielding of views by all of us; it was supported by all elements of the party in the campaign and upon it we have a clear mandate. . . . We have need of unity in the ranks of the farmers themselves and the different groups which reflect their views on Congress. No great step in public action can ever succeed without some compromise of views and some sacrifice of opinion.

The President came to the conclusion that the public interest would be served if the names of people recommending candidates for Federal judgeships were published. It had become a habit of many members of the bar to endorse any or every candidate or to recommend candidates under pressure. The habit had grown to the point where, in many instances, recommendations had become of little value. The President published all the recommendations for eleven judges appointed by him. At the same time it was announced at the White House that this practice would be followed in the future as to all nominations to the Federal judiciary.

April 20, 1929: Certain farm organizations and certain progressive senators urged upon the President the "Export Debenture Plan." This "plan" had not even been mentioned in the campaign of 1928. It was simply an export subsidy upon agricultural products. That the purpose of its introduction was largely obstructive is indicated by the fact that four years later, when every conceivable "plan" for agriculture was being advocated and adopted, it was not even mentioned. The President's views upon it were promptly expressed at its first appearance, in a letter addressed to

[9] State Papers, Vol. I, p. 38.

Senator McNary, chairman of the Senate Committee on Agriculture, who opposed it:[10]

MY DEAR MR. SENATOR:

On April 12th I received a call . . . requesting my opinion on the "Export Debenture Plan" for agricultural relief, since it is a complete departure from the principles already debated during the campaign. . . . The principle of this plan . . . is to issue a government debenture to merchants exporting agricultural products in amount of one-half of the tariff on such products—such debentures to be redeemed by presentation for payment of import duties. The assumption is that by creating a scarcity through stimulating exports that the domestic price will rise above world prices to the amount of the debenture—that is, if the debenture on wheat exports is twenty-one cents a bushel, the price of wheat will be twenty-one cents higher in the domestic market than in the world market.

. . . I am convinced that it would bring disaster to the American farmer.

The weaknesses of the plan as set forth in the Senate bill may be summarized as follows:

1. The issue of debentures amounts to a direct subsidy from the United States Treasury. . . .

2. The first result of the plan, if put into operation, would be a gigantic gift from the government and the public to the dealers and manufacturers and speculators in these commodities. For instance, in the principal export commodities the value of the present volume of stocks in possession of these trades would, if the plan worked, rise by from $200,000,000 to $400,000,000, according to different calculations, without a cent return to the farmer or consumer. Every speculator for a rise in our public markets would receive enormous profits. . . .

3. If the increased price did reflect to the farmer, the plan would stimulate overproduction, and thereby increase world supply which would in turn depreciate world prices and consequently decrease the price which the farmer would receive, and thereby defeat the plan. Stimulation of production has been the outstanding experience abroad where export subsidy has been applied. . . .

4. The stimulation of production of certain commodities would disturb the whole basis of diversification in American agriculture. . . .

5. Although it is proposed that the plan should only be installed at the discretion of the Farm Board, yet the tendency of all boards is to use the whole of their authority. . . .

6. It is not proposed to pay the debentures of subsidies to the farmers, but to the export merchants, and it seems certain that a large part of it would not be reflected back to the farmer. It offers opportunity for manipulation in the export market, none of which would be of advantage to the farmer. . . .

7. The provision of such an export subsidy would necessitate a revision of the import tariffs. For instance, an export subsidy of two cents

[10] State Papers, Vol. I, p. 39.

a pound on raw cotton would mean the foreign manufacturers would be receiving cotton at two cents a pound less than the American manufacturer, and the foreigner could ship his manufactured goods back into the American market with this advantage. . . .

8. Export bounties are recognized by many nations as one form of dumping. I am advised that a similar action by another nation would be construed as a violation of our own laws. . . .

9. A further serious question arises again (if the plan did have the effect intended), where the foreign producer of animals would be enabled to purchase feed for less than the American farmer producing the same animals. For instance, the swine growers in Ontario would be able to purchase American corn for less than the American farmers across the border, and it would tend to transfer the production of pork products for export to Europe from the United States to Canada. It would have the same and probably even more disastrous effect in dairy products.

10. The plan would require a substantial increase in taxes. . . .

The theoretical benefits would not be reflected to the American farmer; it would create profiteering; it contains elements which would bring American agriculture to disaster.

Yours faithfully,

HERBERT HOOVER.

April 22, 1929: The Associated Press was holding its annual meeting in New York City. The President had been invited to address it. With a keen appreciation of the necessity for law observance and enforcement in a country where popular government prevailed, he used the occasion to speak on that subject and of his own responsibilities under the Constitution, saying:[11]

I have accepted this occasion for a frank statement. . . . That is the enforcement and obedience to the laws of the United States, both Federal and State.

I ask only that you weigh this for yourselves, and if my position is right, that you support it—not to support me but to support something infinitely more precious—the one force that holds our civilization together—law. And I wish to discuss it as law, not as to the merits or demerits of a particular law, but all law, Federal and State, for ours is a government of laws made by the people themselves.

A surprising number of our people, otherwise of responsibility in the community, have drifted into the extraordinary notion that laws are made for those who choose to obey them. And in addition, our law-enforcement machinery is suffering from many infirmities arising out of its technicalities, its circumlocutions, its involved procedures, and too often, I regret, from inefficient and delinquent officials.

We are reaping the harvest of these defects. More than 9,000 human beings are lawlessly killed every year in the United States. Little more than half as many arrests follow. Less than one-sixth of these slayers are

[11] State Papers, Vol. I, p. 42.

convicted, and but a scandalously small percentage are adequately punished. Twenty times as many people in proportion to population are lawlessly killed in the United States as in Great Britain. In many of our great cities murder can apparently be committed with impunity. At least fifty times as many robberies in proportion to population are committed in the United States as in Great Britain, and three times as many burglaries.

Even in such premeditated crimes as embezzlement and forgery our record stands no comparison with stable nations. No part of the country, rural or urban, is immune. . . .

In order to dispel certain illusion in the public mind on this subject, let me say at once that while violations of law have been increased by inclusion of crimes under the Eighteenth Amendment, and by the vast sums that are poured into the hands of the criminal classes by the patronage of illicit liquor by otherwise responsible citizens, yet this is but one segment of our problem. I have purposely cited the extent of murder, burglary, robbery, forgery, and embezzlement, for but a small percentage of these can be attributed to the Eighteenth Amendment. In fact, of the total number of convictions for felony last year, less than eight per cent came from that source. It is therefore but a sector of the invasion of lawlessness.

What we are facing today is something far larger and more fundamental, the possibility that respect for law as law is fading from the sensibilities of our people. Whatever the value of any law may be, the enforcement of that law written in plain terms upon our statute books is not, in my mind, a debatable question. Law should be observed and must be enforced until it is repealed by the proper processes of our democracy. The duty to enforce the laws rests upon every public official, and the duty to obey it rests upon every citizen.

No individual has the right to determine what law shall be obeyed and what law shall not be enforced. If a law is wrong, its rigid enforcement is the surest guaranty of its repeal. If it is right, its enforcement is the quickest method of compelling respect for it. . . .

In my position, with my obligations, there can be no argument on these points. There is no citizen who would approve of the President of the United States assuming any other attitude. . . .

Every student of our law-enforcement mechanism knows full well that it is in need of vigorous reorganization; that its procedure unduly favors the criminal; that our judiciary needs to be strengthened; that the method of assembling our juries needs revision; that justice must be more swift and sure. In our desire to be merciful the pendulum has swung in favor of the prisoner and far away from the protection of society. The sympathetic mind of the American people in its over-concern about those who are in difficulties has swung too far from the family of the murdered to the family of the murderer. . . .

Finally, I wish to again reiterate that the problem of law enforcement is not alone a function or business of government. . . . Every citizen has a personal duty in it—the duty to order his own actions, to so weigh the effect of his example, that his conduct shall be a positive force in his community with respect to the law.

It is unnecessary for me to argue the fact that the very essence of freedom is obedience to law; that liberty itself has but one foundation, and that is in the law.

April 23, 1929: "Sen. 1.," a bill introduced by Senator McNary creating a Federal Farm Board was favorably reported from the Senate Committee on Agriculture.

April 25, 1929: The first President of the United States, George Washington, was an engineer. Under his immediate supervision the District of Columbia was laid out and the Capitol, the President's House, and other public buildings were planned and construction started. In Washington's day the Federal employees in the district numbered less than 150. Since then had come a great increase in the activities of the Federal Government, especially following the Civil War and the World War. By March of 1929 another engineer was President. What Washington so well and nobly had initiated President Hoover wanted appropriately continued, for the government needed additional buildings. At a meeting of the American Institute of Architects on the development and improvement of the City of Washington, which was attended by a large group of government officials, the President said: [12]

I am glad that the opportunity has come to me as President to contribute to impulse and leadership in the improvement of the national capital. This is more than merely the making of a beautiful city. Washington is not only the nation's capital, it is the symbol of America. By its dignity and architectural inspiration we stimulate pride in our country, we encourage that elevation of thought and character which comes from great architecture.

. . . We must fit that program into the traditions and the symbolism of the capital. Our forefathers had a great vision of the capital for America, unique from its birth in its inspired conception, flexibility, and wonderful beauty. No one in 150 years has been able to improve upon it.

It is the wish and the demand of the American people that our new buildings shall comport with the dignity of the capital of America, that they shall meet modern requirements of utility, that they shall be a lasting inspiration. In architecture it is the spiritual impulse that counts. These buildings should express the ideals and standards of our times; they will be the measure of our skill and taste by which we will be judged by our children's children.

It is on this national stage that the great drama of our political life has been played. Here were fought the political battles that tested the foundations of our government. We face similar problems of our time, and here centuries hence some other Americans will face the great problems of their

[12] State Papers, Vol. I, p. 47.

time. For our tasks and their tasks there is need of a daily inspiration of surroundings that suggest not only the traditions of the past but the greatness of the future.

In laying the cornerstone of the Department of Commerce building, the first of the several buildings to be constructed, Mr. Hoover, the thirty-first President of the United States, used the trowel with which George Washington, the first President, had laid the cornerstone of the Capitol in 1793. That trowel was loaned for the occasion by the Masonic Lodge in Alexandria, Virginia, of which Washington was a member.

This program envisaged a beautification of the city approaches, in the parking of the Potomac River side from Great Falls to Mount Vernon, with the new Arlington Memorial Bridge, and the landscaping of Capitol Hill from the Union Station. The new Supreme Court building, additions to the House and Senate Office building, an extension of the Congressional Library, a new civic center for the Washington municipal government, were completed or under way during the Administration. Of the beautiful buildings in the Great Triangle, the Department of Commerce, Labor, Post Office, Justice, Interstate Commerce Commission, and Archives buildings had their cornerstones laid during this administration.

April 25, 1929: The House passed the Agricultural Marketing Bill and sent it to the Senate. While both bills provided for a Farm Board, there were material differences between them.

May 1, 1929: Following an investigation and report by the Department of Justice, the President today summarily removed William A. DeGroot, the United States District Attorney for the Eastern District of New York, for failure to enforce the laws.

Congress had for years failed to pass legislation placing first-, second-, and third-class postmasters within the merit system of Civil Service. These positions were held by the only large group of government officials not under Civil Service. In order to remove them from the spoils system to a merit system, as far as could be accomplished without the legislation which Congress had for years failed to grant, the President today issued an Executive Order revising the existing method by which the Civil Service Commission was to examine such applicants, and thus approximated the merit service in the Post Office. The order said:[13]

When a vacancy exists or occurs in the position of postmaster of an office of the first, second, or third class, if such vacancy is not filled by nomination of some qualified person within the competitive classified Civil Service, the Postmaster-General shall certify the fact to the commission,

[13] State Papers, Vol. I, p. 49.

which shall forthwith hold an open competitive examination to test the fitness of applicants to fill such vacancy, and when such examination has been held and the papers submitted therewith have been rated, the commission shall furnish a certificate of not less than three eligibles for appointment to fill such vacancy . . . (certain requirements as to residence, age, and character). . . . If pursuant to this order it is desired to submit to the President for nomination the name of a person in the competitive classified service, such person must first be found by the Civil Service Commission to possess the requisite qualifications.

May 2, 1929: Eugene Meyer resigned from the Federal Farm Loan Board, and the President appointed H. Paul Bestor as a member of that board.

At the President's request and in conjunction with the Interstate Commerce Commission, the railways reduced the rail-rate on export wheat and flour, for a temporary period. The purpose was to stimulate the movement of exports before the harvest. The President felt that in addition to relieving congestion, this concession of several cents per bushel might be a test whether a subsidy on exports would stimulate such exports. No particular increase in exports developed, and no particular change in price of wheat at the mid-West markets resulted either from the concession or later from its withdrawal.

May 4, 1929: The Democratic and Progressive leaders in the Senate agreed to adopt the "Export Debenture Plan" and make it a part of the Agricultural Marketing Bill.

May 9, 1929: The Committee on Ways and Means reported the new Tariff Bill (H. R. 2667) today. The committee, under Chairman Hawley, had concluded its hearings during the preceding short session of Congress. The tariff plank of the Republican platform had promised a revision restricted to giving agriculture full benefit of the American market and affording needed protection to those other industries which were finding it impossible successfully to compete with foreign producers. The plank was as follows:

> While certain provisions of the present law require revision in the light of changes in the world competitive situation, since its enactment. . . . However, we realize that there are certain industries which cannot now successfully compete with foreign producers because of lower foreign wages and a lower cost of living abroad, and we pledge the next Republican Congress to an examination, and where necessary to a revision of these schedules, to the end that American labor in these industries may again command the home market, may maintain its standard of living, and may count upon steady employment in its accustomed field. . . . The home market . . . belongs to the American farmer, and it [the party]

pledges its support of legislation which will give this market to him to the full extent of his ability to supply it. . . .

In his message to the new Congress, the President had urged a limited revision in accordance with the platform. However, in the meantime the Committee on Ways and Means was having its difficulties. Changes were made in from fifteen to twenty per cent of the items in the existing tariff law. Many of these changes in existing schedules and rates could have been better considered by the new Tariff Commission, acting through the revised flexible provisions and its added responsibility in their application.

May 12, 1929: The President requested several members of the Ways and Means Committee to meet with him at the White House to discuss the pending Tariff Bill. He reminded them that only a limited revision had been promised, that the revision was approaching a wider scope and that complaints were coming in that some of the proposed rates were too high.

May 13, 1929: As the coalition of Progressive and Democratic senators was able to vote the "Export Debenture Plan" into the Agricultural Marketing Bill the President in conference with Republican senators expressed the opinion that the passage of the bill could be expedited if the opponents of the plan would cease temporarily any opposition to it in the Senate, for it could easily be eliminated in the House. The Senate bill did not embody the ideas of the President in some other particulars, but the Committee on Agriculture of the House generally shared the President's views and could be depended upon to "go the limit" in standing by the House bill.

The Senate passed the Agricultural Marketing Bill H. R. 1 after striking out the House bill provisions and inserting the text of S. 1. The House bill had been drawn substantially in accordance with the principles set forth in the platform adopted by the Republican National Convention at Kansas City, and as had been previously recommended by President Coolidge. In brief, the House bill emphasized the farm co-operatives, requiring the Farm Board to work largely through them and upon their initiative. In substance, the Senate amendment was the McNary Equalization Fee Bill of the preceding Congress, with the equalization fee section eliminated and the Export Debenture Plan inserted. The Senate bill utilized the co-operatives, but the emphasis was placed on the Farm Board and the stabilization corporation, and their activities.

The Committee on Recent Economic Changes brought in its report today. It was a study of technical and cyclical unemployment. It warned against waste of national resources and the transfer of credit from production to speculation.

The Committee on Recent Economic Changes, a continuing Committee of the Conference on Unemployment appointed by the President of the United States in 1921, was brought together in 1927 under the chairmanship of Herbert Hoover, the Secretary of Commerce, its purpose being to make a comprehensive fact-and-figure picture of the results of the working of economic forces during a major business cycle. Early in 1929 the Committee's first report was published, intended as a record, partly statistical and partly descriptive, of the ascending curve of the major cycle which started after the depression of 1921 and carried into 1929.

Arch W. Shaw of Chicago succeeded Mr. Hoover as chairman of the Committee, the other members being: Walter F. Brown, Assistant Secretary of Commerce; Renick W. Dunlap, Assistant Secretary of Agriculture; William Green, President of the American Federation of Labor; Julius Klein, Director of the Bureau of Foreign and Domestic Commerce; John S. Lawrence, merchant; Max Mason, President of the Rockefeller Foundation; George McFadden, merchant; Adolph C. Miller, member of the Federal Reserve Board; Lewis E. Pierson, Chairman of the Board, Irving Trust Company; John J. Raskob, member of Finance Committee, General Motors Corporation; Louis J. Taber, Master of the National Grange; Daniel Willard, President, Baltimore & Ohio Railroad; Clarence M. Woolley, Chairman of the Board, American Radiator and Standard Sanitary Corporation; and Owen D. Young, Chairman of the Board, General Electric Company. Edward Eyre Hunt was appointed secretary of the Committee.

May 17, 1929: The House received the Agricultural Marketing Bill as it had been amended in the Senate, including the "Export Debenture Plan." By a substantial majority it determined to send the bill to conference.

May 20, 1929: During the campaign the President had said that if elected he would appoint a Law Enforcement Commission. He named this commission, which consisted of former Attorney-General George W. Wickersham; former Secretary of War Newton D. Baker, of Ohio; United States Circuit Judge William S. Kenyon, of Iowa; United States District Judges, Paul J. McCormick, and William I. Grubb; former Chief Justice Kenneth Mackintosh of the Supreme Court of the State of Washington; Dean Roscoe Pound of the Harvard Law School; President Ada L. Comstock of Radcliffe College, and three practicing lawyers, Henry W. Anderson, Esq., of Virginia; Monte M. Leman, Esq., of New

Orleans, and Frank J. Loesch, Esq., of Chicago. This commission was exhaustively to examine and report upon the broad question of law enforcement and the organization of the machinery of justice. It is to be regretted that much of its work and some of its recommendations were lost sight of because of the impression by the public that it was to deal almost entirely with the "wet and dry" question and the Eighteenth Amendment.

May 22, 1929: The President, in conference at the White House, urged House leaders, in considering the Tariff Bill, to agree to necessary increases on farm products and to resist certain increases on industrial products, and expedite the bill through the House. He stated that if the bill embraced a flexible provision, the mistakes and later injustices could be worked out, and that such a provision was absolutely essential.

May 23, 1929: House leaders announced certain reductions of the proposed rates in the Tariff Bill.

May 28, 1929: At the initial meeting of the National Law Enforcement Commission usually known as Wickersham Commission, at the White House, the President said:[14]

> The American people are deeply concerned over the alarming disobedience of law, the abuses in law enforcement and the growth of organized crime, which has spread in every field of evil-doing and in every part of our country. A nation does not fail from its growth of wealth or power. But no nation can for long survive the failure of its citizens to respect and obey the laws which they themselves make. Nor can it survive a decadence of the moral and spiritual concepts that are the basis of respect for law, nor from neglect to organize itself to defeat crime and the corruption that flows from it. Nor is this a problem confined to the enforcement and obedience of one law or the laws of the Federal or State governments separately. The problem is partly the attitude toward all law.
>
> It is my hope that the commission shall secure an accurate determination of fact and cause, following them with constructive, courageous conclusions which will bring public understanding and command public support of its solutions. . . . I do pray for the success of your endeavors, for by such success you will have performed one of the greatest services to our generation.

Mr. Wickersham, in reply, said:

> We are under no illusions as to the difficulty of our task. We know there is no short cut to the millennium. But we have confidence in the fundamental honesty and right-mindedness of the American people, and their readiness to support sound methods of reform when the existence of evils is exposed and practical methods for their eradication submitted to popular judgment. . . .

[14] State Papers, Vol. I, p. 63.

The Tariff Bill passed the House. The President was of the opinion that it contained rates that were too high.

May 29, 1929: The Senate passed a bill (S. 312) to provide for the fifteenth and subsequent decennial censuses, and also to provide for the apportionment of representatives in Congress following those censuses. This census was due to be taken in 1930. Ever since the taking of the census of 1920, Congress had first neglected, then later refused, to carry out the Constitutional mandate and reapportion the representatives in Congress.

June 1, 1929: Congressman Byrns of Tennessee, ranking member of the Committee on Appropriations, issued a statement blaming the Republican Administration for a fall in the price of wheat.

June 3, 1929: The President again indicated that some of the proposed industrial tariff rates were too high.

June 4, 1929: The President and Postmaster-General Brown desired to make the Post Office Department self-supporting. To accomplish this, a different and more businesslike system of accounting was essential. The President appointed Frederic A. Tilton, a partner in a leading national firm of accountants, Third Assistant Postmaster-General. His duties included the installation of a new system of accounting.

June 5, 1929: After having been deadlocked for some days the Senate and House conferees today eliminated the "Export Debenture Plan" from the Agricultural Marketing Bill.

June 7, 1929: The House passed the Agricultural Marketing Bill as reported by the conferees.

June 10, 1929: A conference of representatives of the oil States and of the industry was called by the President to meet at Colorado Springs. Secretary of the Interior Wilbur laid before them the President's plan of regional interstate compacts, which was based on his experience in settling the Colorado River improvement program. It called for a compact for control of physical and economic waste in the oil industry, as the only sound basis of conservation and stability. Secretary Wilbur urged the necessity of action and stated: "The position of the Federal Government is not to interfere with the rights and duties of the States, but to lend such aid as it can. . . . This administration has no desire to concentrate the forces of government in Washington. It has every desire to co-operate with the States."

Mark Requa of California was chosen chairman of the meeting.

After several days of debate the President's plan for stabilizing the industry was practically rejected in favor of Federal control. It is of interest to note that after Federal control was adopted in the next administration and tried out for eighteen months, the same men who led the opposition to the proposal of the President and Secretary Wilbur, advanced the "interstate compact proposal" based on the Hoover principle, and it was almost unanimously supported by the industry.

June 11, 1929: The Democratic and Progressive coalition in the Senate again insisted upon the inclusion of the "Export Debenture Plan" in the Agricultural Marketing Bill. As a result, the Senate disagreed with the conference report requesting a further conference. The President made a public statement regretting this action and deploring the consequent delay. He said:

> The vote in the Senate today at best adds further delay to farm relief and may gravely jeopardize the enactment of legislation. . . . The Senate has in effect rejected a bill which provides for the creation of the most important agency ever set up in the government to assist an industry—the Federal Farm Board. . . .
> The conferees bill carried out the plan advanced in the campaign in every particular. Every other plan of agricultural relief was rejected in that campaign, and this plan was one of the most important issues in the principal agricultural states, and was given as a mandate by an impressive majority in these states. Subsidies were condemned in the course of the campaign and the so-called debenture plan—that is, the giving of subsidies on exports—was not raised by either party, nor by its proponents.
> . . . No matter what the theory of the export subsidy may be, in the practical world we live in, it will not bring equality but will bring further disparity to agriculture. It will bring immediate profits to some speculators and disaster to the farmer. . . .

June 13, 1929: The new tariff bill had been referred to the Committee on Finance of the Senate. We have seen that the House Committee had become involved in extensive hearings covering every schedule, and including hundreds of items. Today Senator Borah introduced a resolution to limit the committee hearings of the Senate to the taking of testimony, consideration, recommendation and reporting on only the rates and schedules of agricultural products and those directly related thereto. The terms of this resolution were, of course, more restrictive than the party platform and the recommendations of the President. Designed to meet a difficult situation, it went too far. In an effort to assist in remedying the situation Senator Jones, of Washington, moved to amend the resolution by broadening the limitation so as to include the products of those industries which had experienced a substantial slackening of business, with consequent decrease of employment due to insurmountable competition. This was in line with the views of the President and in accordance with the party platform. Senator Borah opposed the Jones amendment and it was lost by a vote of thirty-eight to thirty-nine. On June 18th the Borah resolution also failed of adoption, by a vote of thirty-eight to thirty-nine.

The Senate agreed to the conference report on the Census and Reapportionment Bill. The House having agreed to the report two days previously, the bill soon would be presented to the President for his approval.

Today the Senate ended any chance of favorable action on the recommendation of the President for the repeal of the national origins provision of the Immigration Restriction Act of 1924. The Committee on Immigration and Naturalization, which had been considering this question since the commencement of the session, had taken no action whatever upon it and apparently was so closely divided that favorable action in the immediate future was out of the question. Unless repealed or further postponed by legislation the new quotas would become affective July 1st. Senator Nye, of North Dakota, introduced a resolution to discharge the committee from further consideration. Following debate it was defeated by a vote of 37 to 43. It was the first definite setback that the President had received.

By a vote of 250 to 113 the House again refused to yield to the Senate and accept the "Export Debenture Plan."

June 14, 1929: In a vote which was seventy-four to eight the Senate finally gave way on including the "Export Debenture Plan" and passed the Agricultural Marketing Act, which created the Federal Farm Board.

Some of the provisions pertaining to the stabilization corporations, their operations in the control of surpluses, were substantially different from that in the House bill and were far from satisfactory, including a particular provision reading as follows: "Sec. 9 (d) . . . all losses of the corporation from such operations shall be paid from such reserves, or if such reserves are inadequate, then such losses shall be paid by the Board as a loan from the revolving fund . . ." That changes of this character were embodied in the bill as agreed to by the conferees was not known until they had reported. In view of the difficulties which the conferees had had in reconciling their differences, it was deemed inadvisable to have the House reject the report and ask for a further conference. It was felt that the Board that would be appointed could control the situation. However, at that time no one knew that the Board would have to meet great problems incident to the depression.

June 15, 1929: The President in signing the bill made the following statement:

After many years of contention we have at last made a constructive start at agricultural relief with the most important measure ever passed by Congress in aid of a single industry. . . . I am asking for a preliminary appropriation of $150,000,000 at once out of the $500,000,000 that has been authorized, and as Congress will be in session except for short periods, the Board will be able to present its further requirements at almost any time.

The President announced that he would canvass the several hundred farmers' organizations and agricultural colleges to get their views: first, on whether some outstanding business man should be placed upon the Board; second, on the persons whom these organizations favored for appointment to the Board to represent the major branches of agriculture. These were to be men of actual experience in agriculture. As a result of this canvass, carried out through Secretary of Agriculture Hyde, the several hundred farm organizations recommended that a business man of wide experience should be appointed chairman. They recommended a list of names for other members of the Board from which the President during the next few days appointed

- Alexander Legge of Chicago, president of the International Harvester Company, chairman;
- James C. Stone, Kentucky, founder and former president of the Burley Tobacco Growers' Co-operative Association;
- Carl Williams, Oklahoma, of the Farmers' Co-operative Marketing Association;
- C. B. Denman, Missouri, of the National Livestock Producers' Association;
- Charles S. Wilson, New York, professor of agriculture, Cornell University;
- William F. Schilling, Minnesota, of the National Dairy Association;
- Ex-Governor Samuel McKelvie, Nebraska, publisher of the *Nebraska Farmer*; and
- C. C. Teague, California, of the California Fruit Growers' Exchange.

June 18, 1929: The President signed the Reapportionment Bill, thereby ending the legislative deadlock of nearly ten years. It was so drawn as to provide for the taking of a census every ten years and a reapportionment following that census without the necessity for further legislation. This was a permanent census and reapportionment act as distinguished from hitherto temporary legislation.

June 18, 1929: The Senate changed one of its long-established rules and courses of procedure which would materially affect its future deliberations in reference to nominations. Heretofore nominations from the Executive were considered in executive session. Under the new rule the nominations would be considered in open executive session, unless the Senate should otherwise determine in a closed executive session and by a majority vote. The fight to prevent the confirmation of Chief Justice Hughes would not have been made without the opportunity for publicity which it afforded. Likewise the fight preventing the confirmation of Judge Parker would not have succeeded without the publicity accompanying the extended open executive session.

June 23, 1929: After conference with the President, Secretary of War Good appointed a committee of army staff officers to study the entire problem of army equipment in view of the improvement in mechanization of transport, etc.

June 25, 1929: Owen D. Young, J. P. Morgan, Thomas N. Perkins, and Thomas W. Lamont, who at the request of foreign governments, had participated in the "Young Plan" of German reparations, came to the White House to urge that the United States directly or indirectly should join in the formation of the Bank for International Settlements (the World Bank) which had been proposed under the reparation settlements. The President declined to allow such participation as he felt that it was likely to result in European influence upon American finance, of which we had had sufficient experience in 1927-1929.

June 25, 1929: The President announced the signing of a proclamation, making effective the compact between six of the seven States in the Colorado River Basin. This agreement rendered possible the construction of the Boulder Dam. The compact had been consummated after seven years of constant effort of Mr. Hoover while Secretary of Commerce. The President said:[15]

> I have particular interest in its consummation not only because of its great intrinsic importance but because I was the chairman of the Colorado River Commission that formulated the Compact. The Compact itself relates entirely to the distribution of water rights between the seven States in the Basin. . . . It is the final settlement of disputes that have extended over twenty-five years, and which have estopped the development of the river. The difficulties over the respective water rights of the different States have served to prevent development in a large way for nearly a quarter of a century. And it has an interest also in that it is the most extensive action ever taken by a group of States under the provisions of the Constitution permitting compacts between States. . . . It opens the avenue for some hope of the settlement of other regional questions as between the States rather than the imposition of these problems on the Federal Government.

The Compact was originally signed five years ago by the seven States

[15] State Papers, Vol. I, p. 71.

subject to ratification by their legislatures ... for the first time in history a compact involving so many interests has been made effective.

There is only one point still left open, and that is the relation of Arizona to the Compact. I am in hopes that Arizona and California may compose their mutual problems which have hitherto prevented Arizona from joining in the Compact.

July 2, 1929: Senators Reed, Smoot, and Edge, in conference with the President, agreed upon plans to reduce in the Senate some of the tariff rates set forth in the House Bill.

Intensely interested in children and in promoting their development, especially the under-privileged ones, and having spent some years as the head of two national organizations for the promotion of their welfare, the President had determined to advance their interests by calling a national conference on Child Health and Protection.[16]

I have decided to call a White House conference on the health and protection of children. This conference will be comprised of representatives of the great voluntary associations, together with the Federal and State and municipal authorities interested in these questions. Its purpose will be to determine the facts as to our present progress and our future needs in this great field and to make recommendations for such measures for more effective official and voluntary action and their co-ordination as will further develop the care and protection of children. ...

To cover the expenses of the preliminary committees and the conference and follow-up work which will be required to carry out the conclusions of the conference, a sum of $500,000 has been placed at my disposal from private sources.

This will be the first national conference held in review of this subject since the conference called by President Roosevelt in 1909. That conference resulted in a great impulse to social and protective activities in behalf of children. ...

The work of the conference will be under the direction of Secretary of the Interior, Dr. Ray Lyman Wilbur, with the co-operation of the Secretary of Labor, James J. Davis. Dr. Harry E. Barnard, formerly State Health Commissioner of Indiana, has been selected as executive secretary of the conference. ...

July 11, 1929: Still disturbed by some of the tariff rates in the House Bill, the President again conferred with Senators Smoot, Watson, Reed and others as to the necessity for a most careful scrutiny for unjust rates and their elimination.

July 15, 1929: With a keen appreciation of the tremendous task con-

[16] State Papers, Vol. I, p. 73.

fronting the newly appointed Federal Farm Board, the President decided to meet with them at their initial meeting and generally to outline the objectives of the Board as he saw them. This was not planned for relief measures, but as a "long-view" effort to build agriculture on a more sound foundation. He said: [17]

... I am deeply impressed with the responsibilities which lie before you. Your fundamental purpose must be to determine the fact and to find solution to a multitude of agricultural problems, among them to more nearly adjust production to need; to create permanent business institutions for marketing which, owned and controlled by the farmers shall be so wisely devised and soundly founded and well managed, that they by effecting economies and giving such stability will grow in strength over the years to come. Through these efforts we may establish to the farmer an equal opportunity in our economic system with other industry.

I know there is not a thinking farmer who does not realize that all this cannot be accomplished by a magic wand or an overnight action. Real institutions are not built in that way. If we are to succeed it will be by strengthening the foundations and the initiative which we already have in farm organizations, and building steadily upon them with the constant thought that we are building not for the present only but for next year and the next decade.

July 23, 1929: The President was convinced that the so-called flexible tariff provisions were absolutely essential. If they could be provided upon a broad basis, then extensive alterations in Congress would be unnecessary. While Secretary of Commerce he had witnessed two years of struggle over the passage of a general tariff bill. Obviously the country ought not to go through such another ordeal if it could be avoided. A tariff bill limited to a few articles could be put through the House. An adhesive, compact majority of this House could provide for that with a special rule to meet the occasion. As a practical proposition such a bill could not be so restricted while under consideration in the Senate. The general rules of the Upper House are not drawn with the idea of limiting debate. Senatorial courtesy often permits violations of the rule that discussion must be germane. The President was very earnest in his desire for a workable flexible tariff in order to avoid the necessity for constant legislative revision, and promptly to correct injustices. With this thought in mind he conferred with Senator Borah, in order to enlist his support. The Senator, however, was unconvinced and publicly announced his opposition.

July 26, 1929: The Federal Farm Board, in a meeting with repre-

[17] State Papers, Vol. I, p. 75.

sentatives of farmers and grain co-operatives, agreed to lend a working capital of $20,000,000 to finance a consolidation of farmer-owned, farmer-controlled grain co-operatives.

July 29, 1929: A national meeting of farm co-operatives at Baton Rouge strongly upheld the President's program for the solution of the agricultural marketing problem.

The first meeting of the Planning Committee for the White House Conference on Child Health and Protection under Secretary Wilbur was held at the White House. The President said:[18]

> ... We should take national stock of the progress and the present situation in the health and protection of childhood; that out of this investigation we should also develop common sense plans for the further advancement in these directions. ... We realize that major progress in this direction must be made by voluntary action and by activities of local government. The Federal Government has some important functions to perform in these particulars, all of which will need to be considered, but we may save years in national progress if we can secure some measure of unity as to view and unity as to program, more especially as these views and programs are to be based on searching examination of fact and experience. ... I need not urge upon you the fundamental importance of this undertaking. The greatest assets of a race are its children, that their bodily strength and development should prepare them to receive the heritage which each generation should bequeath to the next. These questions have the widest of social importance, that reaches to the roots of democracy itself. By the safeguard of health and protection of childhood we further contribute to that equality of opportunity which is the unique basis of American civilization.

The committee which directed the White House Child Conference and later was engaged in activities in child health and protection, was made up of the following: Secretary of the Interior Wilbur, chairman; Secretary of Labor Davis, vice chairman; H. E. Barnard, director; Edgar Rickard, treasurer; Grace Abbott, Washington, D. C.; Henry Breckenridge, New York; Frederick Cabot, Boston; Frank Cody, Detroit; Senator James Couzens, of Michigan; S. J. Crumbine, New York City; Hugh S. Cummings, Washington, D. C.; Lee Frankel, New York; William Green, Washington, D. C.; Samuel McHammill, Philadelphia; William King, Indianapolis; Gertrude Lane, New York City; Julia C. Lathrop, Washington, D. C.; Mrs. William B. Meloney, New York City; Mrs. Bina West Miller, Port Huron, Michigan; Mrs. Raymond Robins, Florida; Mrs. F. Louis Slade, New York; Louise Stanley, Washington, D. C.; and French Strother, Administrative Assistant to the

[18] State Papers, Vol. I, p. 83.

President. The expenditures for the work were met out of the Children's Fund of the American Relief Association.

August 6, 1929: The increase in the jurisdiction of the Federal Government in preventing crime and punishing wrongdoers had gradually increased the number of prisoners in our Federal prisons far beyond their capacity. Conditions in some of the over-crowded Federal penitentiaries were subject to criticism. The President, commenting upon the prison riot at the non-military Federal prison at Leavenworth, Kansas, said:[19]

I have had an opportunity for lengthy discussions with the Attorney-General, and I have the recommendations of Mr. Bates, who is the new Director of Prisons, and I have accepted their view that further Federal accommodations for prisoners cannot be any longer delayed. We will ask Congress at the regular session to give us the necessary authority and appropriations to revise the system.

The increased number of prisoners is due to the general increase in crime, the largest item in our Federal prisoners being the violators of the Narcotics Act. They comprise now about thirty-three per cent of the inmates at Leavenworth and Atlanta. Prohibition contributes about fourteen per cent. The balance is made up of increases all along the line.

Our plans necessitate an expenditure of about five millions of dollars, and will comprise some additions and revisions of the old prisons, and probably a new prison somewhere in the northeastern States. . . .

August 10, 1929: The House had increased the tariff duties on sugar. While this was done to protect domestic sugar producers, it was important to prevent that increase from being used unduly to advance prices to the consumer. A substantial percentage of the sugar consumed in this country must come from Cuba or elsewhere abroad. The President had proposed a sliding scale of sugar tariff, lowering the tariff with any increase of price so as to protect the consumer against undue price exactions if the producer already was receiving an adequate return. The Senate committee today declined to accept this method, but they did reduce the rates on sugar in the House Bill.

August 11, 1929: The Federal Farm Board moved to consolidate the marketing facilities of the farmers' co-operatives in both fruit and vegetables.

August 13, 1929: The President announced the appointment of a committee to solve the problem of locating a bridge across San Francisco Bay which would not interfere with navigation and national defense. This much needed project had been held up for ten years through disagreement between the Federal and local authorities. The President had promised to find a solution for the problem. He said:[20]

[19] State Papers, Vol. I, p. 89.   [20] State Papers, Vol. I, p. 90.

There can be no question as to the necessity for such a bridge for the economic development of these communities. In addition to the cities of San Francisco, Oakland, and Alameda the Governer of California through recent legislation has recently taken an interest in this problem. In order that we may have an exhaustive investigation with a view to final determination which I hope will be acceptable to all parties, I have consulted the Secretary of War and the Secretary of the Navy, as well as Mr. Meek, the representative of Governor Young, and I shall appoint a commission comprising two representatives from the Navy, two from the Army, and I shall ask the authorities of the east side of the bay to appoint another member. I shall ask the Governor to appoint one or two members and I shall appoint a leading citizen, Mr. Mark Requa, if he will undertake it, in the hope that we may arrive at a determination of the common interest.

The President announced joint action between himself and the Governor of California in the creation of a plan for the development of the water resources of California. He said:[21]

Some years ago I advocated the co-ordination of the multitude of activities, governmental and otherwise, engaged in direct and indirect control and development of California water supply and the provision of some definite policies instead of the haphazard and often conflicting action of different agencies. Governor Young had forwarded this idea by enactment of certain State legislation which now enables us to bring about a larger measure of such co-ordination. The first step is the creation of a commission to supervise an exhaustive investigation of the engineering facts and to determine the policies which should be pursued in the long view development of the State, as to irrigation, flood control, navigation and power.

In order that all of the commission should embrace all agencies, I have requested the War Department which controls the navigation channels and flood control, the Power Commission which controls water-power permits, and the Interior Department which is interested in irrigation, each to designate a member of the commission which the Governor is now appointing. The Governor's representatives will embrace the State agencies and leading citizens.

The commission members were Lt. Colonel Thomas M. Robins, U. S. A., Frank E. Bonner, Federal Power Commission, and Dr. Elwood Mead of the Interior Department, for the Federal Government; and for the State, George Pardee, William Durbrow, B. A. Etcheverry, Alfred Harrell, W. B. Mathews, Judge Warren Olney, Jr., Frank E. Weymouth, B. B. Meek and W. J. Carr. Its report was brought in on December 27, 1930.

[21] State Papers, Vol. I, p. 90.

August 20, 1929: The Committee on Finance of the Senate reported the House tariff bill with the Senate amendments which were substantial. The general result was to decrease the House rates on many commodities. In the bill, as amended, the agricultural duties were increased by forty-three per cent, and industrial commodities were increased over the existing law by about eight per cent. The President considered some rates too high and insisted that his proposal for adequate powers to a tariff commission for a flexible tariff must be included.

The bill was under consideration in the Senate for many months. During this time it was daily being misrepresented to the public by its opponents as involving tremendous increases. Those in charge of the bill were desirous of expediting its passage, thereby putting an end to the uncertainty as to rates so harmful to business. As a result they did not take the time to expose the many misrepresentations and misstatements. They let the opposition do most of the talking without putting up an adequate defence. This permitted an erroneous impression to be created throughout the country.

August 23, 1929: The President transferred the almost unoccupied army prison at Leavenworth, Kansas, to the Department of Justice, thus relieving the pressure on Federal criminal prisons.

August 26, 1929: The President submitted, through Assistant Secretary of the Interior Dixon, a plan for proper conservation of public lands and for reorganization of the Reclamation Service, to a meeting of Western governors at Salt Lake City. He said: [22]

I have for some years given thought to the necessity and desirability for a further step in development of the relations between the Federal and State governments in respect to the Public Lands and the Reclamation Service. . . .

. . . The time has come when we should determine the facts in the present situation, should consider the policies now being pursued and the changes which I might recommend to Congress. . . .

PUBLIC LANDS

The most vital question in respect to the remaining free public lands . . . is the preservation of their most important value—that is grazing. The remaining free lands of the public domain (that is, not including lands reserved for parks, forests, Indians, minerals, power sites and other minor reserves), are valuable in the main only for that purpose.

The first of the tentative suggestions, therefore, is that the surface rights of the remaining unappropriated, unreserved public lands should, subject to certain details for protection of homesteaders and the smaller

[22] State Papers, Vol. I, p. 91.

stockmen, be transferred to the State governments for public school purposes and thus be placed under State administration.

At the present time these unappropriated lands aggregate in the neighborhood of 190,000,000 acres. . . .

RECLAMATION SERVICE

The Reclamation Fund and the Reclamation Service were created in 1902 and the situation has since changed materially. The present plan as you are aware is that receipts from sale of public lands, mineral royalties and repayments by the beneficiaries for expenditure upon projects all accrue to this fund. The Reclamation Service undertakes special projects upon the authorization of Congress, which are financed from the fund on the basis of return by the landowners or purchasers of the cost of the project but without interest for a term of years. A total of approximately $182,000,000 has been expended from the fund. . . .

. . . the Reclamation Service for all new projects might well be confined to the construction of permanent works, that is dams and such construction as results in water storage—and at the completion of such construction the entire works be handed over to the States with no obligation for repayment to the Reclamation Fund except such revenues as might arise from electrical power and possibly in some cases from the sale of water until the outlay has been repaid or in any event for not longer than, say fifty years.

. . . there are certain instances of insufficiently capitalized community-owned irrigation projects which are at the point of failure, for whom the Reclamation Fund might be made a proper vehicle to rescue homes that are now in jeopardy.

A further activity which might be considered for incorporation in the Reclamation Service would be the authorization to join with the States and local communities or private individuals for the creation of water storage for irrigation purposes. The primary purpose of these suggestions is thus to devote the Federal Government activities to the creation of water storage and a reduction of other activities within the States.

Under such arrangements the States would have the entire management of all new reclamation projects and would themselves deal with the irrigation land questions and land settlements. . . .

MINERAL RESOURCES

. . . Because of such abuse and waste I recently instituted measures to suspend further issue of oil-prospecting permits on public lands and to clean up the misuse of outstanding permits, and thereby to clear the way for constructive conservation. . . .

. . . It is my desire . . . to check the growth of Federal bureaucracy, reduce Federal interference in affairs of essentially local interest and thereby increase the opportunity of the States to govern themselves. . . .

August 27, 1929: The governors of the Western States telegraphed their approval of the appointment of a joint commission with the President to study the problems of public lands and reclamations outlined in the President's message to them of the 26th, and to advise policies.

September 6, 1929: The attitude of the President to those persons who seek to destroy efforts toward limitation of armament is reflected in his statement to the press of this date, as follows: [23]

I have been a great deal interested in the disclosures in respect to the relations of a naval expert, Mr. William Shearer, with three important shipbuilding companies, as disclosed in a suit filed in the New York State Supreme Court. That suit calls for payment for services which are described in the complaint, and acknowledges receipt of $50,000 in payment. That particular propagandist in the past few years organized very zealous support for increased armament and has been a very severe critic of all efforts of our government to secure international agreement for the reduction of naval arms, including not only the attendance at the Geneva conference but also continued propaganda against the movement that I have launched in the last three months. And a considerable part of that propaganda is devoted to creation of international distrust and international hate. . . . I have directed the Attorney-General to determine what action he can take, . . .

Now every American has a right to express his opinions and to engage in open propaganda on any subject that he sees fit, but to secretly undertake such propaganda for persons who have a definite interest—who are engaged in the undertaking of naval contracts with the American Government to secure international agreement for the limitation of armament, or to employ persons for that purpose, is not a fitting thing. And I am making that statement publicly, so that there will be no misapprehension of my determination that our present international negotiations shall not be interfered with by any such activities or by any such methods.

September 13, 1929: The President had appointed, on June 1st, an interdepartmental committee consisting of Postmaster-General Brown, Secretary of Commerce Lamont, Secretary of the Navy Adams, and Chairman O'Connor of the Shipping Board, to determine the character of ocean-mail contracts to be let under the Merchant Marine Act (Jones-White Law) of 1928. A conflict was reported between the purpose of the Act of building up the merchant marine through new construction and of absorbing the Shipping Board's vessels, and the law for accepting the lowest responsible bid. It requested clarifying legislation from Congress. A few months later Congress passed a bill awarding contracts to purchasers of Shipping Board lines.

[23] See State Papers, Vol. I, p. 98.

September 24, 1929: The flexible tariff provisions were meeting with increasing difficulties in the Senate. In a statement to the public through the press the President said: [24]

In my message to Congress of April 16th at the opening of the Special Session I ... presented the importance of ... the flexible tariff...,

The essential of the flexible tariff is that with respect to a particular commodity, after exhaustive determination of the facts as to differences of cost of production at home and abroad by a tariff commission, comprised of one-half of its members from each political party, whose selection is approved by the Senate, then the President should, upon recommendation of the commission, promulgate changes in the tariff on that commodity not to exceed fifty per cent of the rates fixed by Congress. ...

The reasons for the continued incorporation of such provisions are even more cogent today than ever before. No tariff bill ever enacted has been or ever will be perfect. It will contain injustices. ... It could not be otherwise. Furthermore, if a perfect tariff bill were enacted the rapidity of our changing economic conditions and the constant shifting of our relations with economic life abroad would render some items in such an act imperfect in some particular within a year.

... It is only a destruction of the principle of the flexible tariff to provide that the Tariff Commission recommendations should be made to Congress for action instead of the Executive. Any person of experience in tariff legislation in the last half-century knows perfectly well that Congress cannot re-open single items of the tariff without importing discussion all along the line. ...

... The flexible provision is one of the most progressive steps taken in tariff making in all our history. It is entirely wrong that there shall be no remedy to isolated cases of injustice ... through the failure to adequately protect certain industries, or to destroy the opportunity to revise duties which may prove higher than necessary to protect some industries and, therefore, become onerous upon the public. ...

... I regard it as of the utmost importance in justice to the public; as a protection for the sound progress in our economic system, and for the future protection of our farmers and our industries and consumers. ...

September 26, 1929: There was a vacancy in the position of United States Attorney for the Southern District of Florida. After advising locally, the President decided to appoint W. P. Hughes. Mr. Hughes had been a special assistant in the Department of Justice and had been assigned to the Southern District of Florida. His work was being done to the satisfaction of the department but he lacked local party organization support. Certain members of the Republican organization in Florida wrote the President protesting his making appointments in that State without their approval. He replied as follows: [25]

[24] State Papers, Vol. I, p. 102.   [25] State Papers, Vol. I, p. 105.

DEAR SIR:

I have your letter of September 21st.

I cannot believe that you and the many . . . who have protested the appointment of Mr. Hughes (United States Attorney), overlook the primary responsibility which rests upon the President of the United States. That responsibility is one of the most sacred which he assumes upon his oath of office. It is that he shall, to his utmost capacity, appoint men to public office who will execute the laws of the United States with integrity and without fear, favor, or political collusion. The appointive responsibility rests in the President, not in any organization. . . .

The success of the Republican Party rests upon good government, not on patronage, and Florida will have good government so far as it is within my powers to give it. . . . I note your demands that the organization shall dictate appointments . . . and that you appeal to the opponents of the administration to attack me. I enclose a statement which I issued last March. That statement was no idle gesture.

September 26, 1929: The President invited the Executive Committee of the National Association of Life Insurance Underwriters to lunch at the White House. Those present were Paul F. Clark, Julian S. Myrick, Seaborn T. Whatley, John H. Russell, Ernest J. Clark, Frederick H. Ecker, Thomas I. Parkinson, Walter L. Crocker, Harold A. Ley, Dr. S. S. Huebner, and William M. Duff.

At this meeting the President asked their opinion as to the ability of the life insurance companies to write an old age pension policy differing entirely from the usual "annuity." They agreed that it was feasible.

On September 28th the President addressed to the heads of certain mutual life insurance companies the following letter:

I am wondering whether it would be too much trouble for you to have your actuaries prepare a table for me, indicating what the cost of an old age pension would be, assuming that there are no repayments of any kind except the pension itself—that is, take some basis, say $1200 a year payable in two cases, one at 60 years of age and another at 70, and tabulate the annual payments the policy holders of different ages must make, say from 21 years onward.

It would also be of great interest to know what sort of *lump sum payment* would need to be made at 21 and other ages in order to secure such pension.

The response showed that for a pension of $50 per month, beginning at sixty-five years, the following approximate lump sum payments would be required.

Age at which lump sum payment is made:

21	$ 775.00
31	1,010.00
41	1,540.00
51	2,450.00

If the payments were made annual, the yearly payment for persons of different ages would be:

Age 21	$39.00
Age 31	58.00
Age 41	110.00
Age 51	250.00

The President followed this up and found that a lump payment of $300 at one year of age would secure $50.00 per month after sixty-five, until death. He then proposed to some of the leading companies that they should issue such a policy to the public, also that the industrial and commercial groups in the country should be organized to push it. His purpose was to build old age insurance through the normal insurance channels of the country and at some stage, after it was developed, to determine what steps might be necessary for the government to supplement it or to assist the companies to care for certain groups. He succeeded in getting Mr. Samuel Crowther to interest himself in obtaining endorsement from commercial organizations to make the plan widely known. An interview with a prominent insurance president upon the plan was published in the *Ladies' Home Journal* in March, 1930.

It was the President's thought that with public attention and experience it might be possible to build up the whole question of old age pensions through the natural channels of insurance by individual initiative. If desirable, the States and Federal governments could work out some form of contribution to assist. However, with the economic crash every effort had to be concentrated on restoring jobs. The matter was deferred until times improved.

September 27, 1929: "Progressive" senators attacked the flexible tariff provision in the Senate. Many of the regulars also were opposed to it. The Democrats likewise assailed it. The President sent word, "no provision for flexible tariff, then no tariff bill." He was convinced that there was little hope of securing a just and equitable bill out of the sectional and group conflicts which had arisen and that any mistakes and injustices would have to be corrected later by a tariff commission.

October 2, 1929: The Senate, by a coalition vote of forty-seven to forty-two, defeated the flexible tariff provisions. In view of the determined attitude of the President, this looked like a deadlock and no tariff legislation. The President was not greatly disturbed as he had been advised that some of the Democrats and Progressives wanted the Tariff Bill to pass despite their outward attitude to the contrary.

October 5, 1929: The Progressives in the Senate now proposed various forms of flexible tariff, just short of the President's requirements, as a "try-out." The President advised certain Republican leaders to allow them to put anything in the bill that they liked, but he also gave them to understand that when the bill was in conference they would write an adequate and reasonable flexible tariff provision such as he had proposed, or he would veto the bill. At the same time certain Old Guard "Republicans" urged that he drop the flexible provision altogether.

October 16, 1929: Intensely interested in the work carried on by the government through the Children's Bureau and the Women's Bureau, in the Department of Labor, the President addressed the following letter to J. Clawson Roop, director of the budget:

I would be obliged if you would treat with as liberal a hand as possible the applications of Miss Abbott and Miss Anderson of the Children's and Women's bureaus respectively. I have a great deal of sympathy for the tasks they are undertaking.

Yours faithfully,

HERBERT HOOVER.

October 17, 1929: The President during the day sent for various senators. He urged that a workable flexible tariff provision was essential, especially in view of the increases in rates which were being voted in on the floor by Democratic-Republican-Progressive logrolling, and that the only way out was a subsequent corrective revision by the commission through the flexible provision.

Progressive senators had been unsuccessful in having an export bonus included in the Agricultural Marketing Act. They were now to attempt to have it included in the pending tariff bill.

October 18, 1929: The President announced appointments to the Commission on Conservation and Administration of the Public Domain, which he had discussed with the governors of several Western States on August 27th, saying: [26]

In co-operation with Secretary Wilbur, I have now made a start at the selection of this commission. In order that each of the all-important Public Land States may be represented and that there may be representatives from other sections of the country, I have decided to make the commission approximately twenty in number, of whom two will be women. The following have accepted the invitation so far sent out:

[26] State Papers, Vol. I, p. 109.

Mr. James R. Garfield, Secretary of the Interior during Mr. [Theodore] Roosevelt's Administration, who is to be the chairman.

Of the general representatives, Mr. George Horace Lorimer of Philadelphia, ex-Governor James P. Goodrich of Indiana, Col. W. B. Greeley, former head of the Forestry Service and Mr. Gardiner Cowles of Des Moines, Iowa, have so far accepted invitations to serve. . . .

The purpose of the commission is to study the whole question of the public domain, particularly the unreserved lands. We have within it three outstanding problems.

First, there has been overgrazing throughout these lands, the value of the ranges having diminished as much as eighty to ninety per cent in some localities. The major disaster, however, is that destruction of the natural cover of the land imperils the water supply. The problem therefore in this sense is really a problem of water conservation.

Second, the question as to what is the best method of applying a reclamation service to the West in order to gain real and enlarged conservation of water resources.

Third, the commission is free to consider the questions of conservation of oil, coal, and other problems that arise in connection with the domain.

The full commission added Messrs. Perry Jenkins, Wyoming; Huntley Spaulding, New Hampshire; E. C. Van Petten, Oregon; Wallace Townsend, Arkansas; Francis Wilson, New Mexico; and Mrs. Mary Roberts Rinehart, Washington, D. C.

October 19, 1929: Secretary of Agriculture Hyde called a conference to discuss trade practises in the meat-packing and wholesale meat business:

To bring about by voluntary act of the industry elimination of wasteful, unfair, and uneconomic practises and to agree upon a code of sound practises that will tend to decrease costs of business, insure fair competition and be generally beneficial to the industry and to the public. . . . The participation of the Department of Agriculture in the conference is occasioned by its administration of the Packers and Stockyards Act which covers many of the operations and practises of the meat-packing industry.

The Progressive-Democratic coalition voted the "Export Debenture Plan" into the tariff bill. It was suggested to the President that by agreeing to it as a *quid pro quo* for their accepting the flexible tariff he could secure the latter. The President's attitude was that they could do so in the Senate if they wished, but that it would come out in conference, because the House would not accept it.

October 21, 1929: Speaking at a gathering at Detroit in honor of Thomas A. Edison, the President paid the following tribute:[27]

. . . I may emphasize that both scientific discovery and its practical application are the products of long and arduous research. Discovery and

[27] State Papers, Vol. I, p. 112.

invention do not spring full grown from the brains of men. The labor of a host of men, great laboratories, long, patient, scientific experiment build up the structure of knowledge, not stone by stone, but particle by particle. This adding of fact to fact some days brings forth a revolutionary discovery, an illuminating hypothesis, a great generalization, or a practical invention.

Research both in pure science and in its application to the arts is one of the most potent impulses to progress. For it is organized research that gives daily improvement in machines and processes, in methods of agriculture, in the protection of health, and in understanding. From these we gain constantly in better standards of living, more stability of employment, lessened toil, lengthened human life, and decreased suffering. In the end our leisure expands, our interest in life enlarges, our vision stretches. There is more joy in life. . . .

Mr. Edison has given a long life to such service. Every American owes a debt to him. It is not alone a debt for great benefactions he has brought to mankind, but also a debt for the honor he has brought to our country. Mr. Edison by his own genius and effort rose from modest beginnings to membership among the leaders of men. His life gives renewed confidence that our institutions hold open the door of opportunity to all those who would enter.

Our civilization is much like a garden. It is to be appraised by the quality of its blooms. In degree as we fertilize its soil with liberty, as we maintain diligence in cultivation and guardianship against destructive forces, do we then produce those blossoms, the fragrance of whose lives stimulate renewed endeavor, give to us the courage to renewed effort and confidence of the future.

October 23, 1929: The President during his entire term as Secretary of Commerce had devoted much time and energy to the planning and promotion of waterway development. He today attended the opening of the nine-foot canalization of the Ohio River, and reviewed his policies in this direction.[28] He said:

I am speaking tonight from the deck of the steamboat at the Louisville Levee. . . .

The river has now been formally opened to traffic from above Pittsburgh, 1,000 miles to Cairo, on the Mississippi, from which point another 1,000 miles of modernized waterway leads to the sea at New Orleans. By dams and locks, by dredging and revetments, we have transformed the Ohio River from a stream of shallows, oft-times dangerous even to rafts, into a canalized waterway of an assured nine feet of depth at all seasons. This transformation will not revive the romantic steamboatin' days of Mark Twain, but it will move more goods. . . .

And while we celebrate the completion and connection of a great waterway 2,000 miles, from Pittsburgh to New Orleans, we have still

[28] State Papers, Vol. I, p. 116.

unfinished tasks in improvement of our other great waterways up to the standards we have established upon the Ohio. . . .

Five or six years ago I . . . suggested that all these tributaries of the Mississippi and the Great Lakes comprised a single great transportation system. That it must be developed in vision of the whole and not in parts.

Without delaying to traverse the detailed ramifications of these great natural waterways, I may well summarize their present condition and enunciate the policies of my administration in respect to them:

1. As a general and broad policy I favor modernization of every part of our waterways which will show economic justification in aid of our farmers and industries.

2. The Mississippi system comprises over 9,000 miles of navigable streams. I find that about 2,200 miles have not been modernized to nine feet in depth, and about 1,400 miles have been modernized to at least six feet in depth. Therefore some 5,000 miles are yet to be connected or completed so as to be of purpose to modern commerce. . . .

This administration will insist upon building these waterways as we would build any other transportation system—that is, by extending its ramifications solidly outward from the main trunk lines. Substantial traffic or public service can not be developed upon a patchwork of disconnected local improvements and intermediate segments. Such patchwork has in past years been the sink of hundreds of millions of public money.

3. We must design our policies so as to establish private enterprise in substitution for government operation of the barges and craft upon these waterways. We must continue government barge lines through the pioneering stages, but we must look forward to private initiative not only as the cheapest method of operation but as the only way to assured and adequate public service.

4. We should complete the entire Mississippi system within the next five years. . . .

5. At the present time we have completed 746 miles of intracoastal canals. We still have approximately 1,000 miles to build. We should complete this program over a period of less than ten years.

6. We should continue improvement of the channels in the Great Lakes; we should determine and construct those works necessary for stabilizing the lake levels.

7. One of the most vital improvements to transportation on the North American Continent is the removal of the obstacles in the St. Lawrence River to ocean-going vessels inward to the Great Lakes. . . .

9. With the increasing size of ocean-going vessels and the constantly expanding volume of our commerce, we must maintain unceasing development of our harbors and the littoral waterways which extend inland from them.

10. The total construction of these works which I have mentioned amounts to projects three and four times as great as the Panama Canal. In order that there may be no failure in administration, and as an indication of our determination to pursue these works with resolution, we have

in the past month entirely recast the organization of this executive staff in the government. With the approval of the Secretary of War, and under the newly appointed Chief of Engineers, we have assigned to each of these major projects a single responsible engineer. We thus secure a modern business organization, direct responsibility, and continuous administration. We wish to see these projects completed with all the expedition which sound engineering will permit. . . .

. . . To complete these programs within the periods I have mentioned will require an [annual] increase equal to . . . the cost of one-half of one battleship. If we are so fortunate as to save this annual outlay on naval construction as the result of the forthcoming naval conference in London, nothing could be a finer or more vivid conversion of swords to plowshares.

To carry forward all these great works is not a dream of the visionaries—it is the march of the nation. We are re-opening the great trade routes upon which our continent developed. This development is but an interpretation of the needs and pressures of population, of industry, and civilization. They are threads in that invisible web which knits our national life. They are not local in their benefits. They are universal in promoting the prosperity of the nation. It is our duty as statesmen to respond to these needs, to direct them with intelligence, with skill, with economy, with courage.

A nation makes no loss by devotion of some of its current income to the improvement of its estate. This is an obligation we owe to our children and our grandchildren. I do not measure the future of America in terms of our lifetime. . . .

October 27, 1929: The tariff bill was having a difficult time. With all the trouble in reference to individual rates, there was also substantial disagreement upon the flexible provisions, and the "Export Debenture Plan" had just been included in the bill. Senator Reed of Pennsylvania stated in the Senate that in his opinion the tariff bill was dead. On the other hand, Senator Borah denied this, and stated "it is going to be made into a good bill and passed."

October 29, 1929: The Republican regulars, having practically given up the tariff bill in the Senate, the Progressive-Democratic coalition now insisted on passing it.

October 31, 1929: The following statement in reference to the pending tariff bill was issued from the White House.

The President was visited yesterday by a number of senators, all of whom called at their own suggestions, and presented to him the grave situation that had arisen by delays in tariff legislation. They called attention to the fact that the Senate has had the Tariff Bill since June, with 15 schedules to work out, and has not yet completed Schedule 1. It was pointed out that a large amount of important legislation must be undertaken at the regular session which would be prevented by carrying the debate into the next session. Some of the senators considered progress hopeless as it appeared to them that the coalition intended to delay or defeat legislation, or did not intend to give adequate protection to industry.

The President said ... that campaign promises should be carried out by which adequate protection should be given to agriculture and to the industries where the changes in economic situation demand their assistance. He would not admit that the United States Senate was unable to legislate and the interests of the country required that legislation should be completed during the special session.

... he pointed out that the wide differences of opinion and the length of the discussions in the Senate were themselves ample demonstration of the desirability of a real flexible clause in order that injustice in rates could be promptly corrected by scientific and impartial investigation and put in action without such delays as the present discussions give proof.

November 17, 1929: President Hoover sanctioned an advisory committee on national illiteracy which Secretary Wilbur directed in a campaign to gather facts on illiteracy in the United States. It was the first extensive study made since the World War, and its findings included the percentage by States and by races of illiteracy through lack of opportunity as well as through mental handicaps. It was privately financed through the devoted efforts, over many years, of Mrs. Cora Wilson Stewart. Local campaigns of publicity and schools for adult illiterates were a result of this committee's work. It consisted of Secretary Wilbur and Dr. William Cooper for the Administration; Senator Henry J. Allen, Kansas; Dr. J. A. C. Chandler, Virginia; Dr. Caswell Ellis, Ohio; Mrs. Cora Wilson Stewart, Kentucky; T. H. Harris, Louisiana; Raymond Fosdick, New York; R. H. Edmonds, Maryland; Dr. Glenn Frank, Wisconsin; Dr. John H. Finley, New York; Dr. C. R. Mann, Dr. A. E. Winship, Lorado Taft, Illinois; John Abercrombie, Alabama; M. L. Brittain, Georgia; Mrs. A. H. Reeve, Pennsylvania; Herbert Houston, New York; Henry Goddard Leach, New York; Dr. Rufus Weaver, North Carolina; Dr. Frank Cody, Michigan; R. A. Nestos, North Dakota; and Mrs. Marvin Rosenberry, Wisconsin.

The Secretary of War, James W. Good, died today. Mr. Good was one of the strong men in the Cabinet. His death was a great personal grief to the President, who made the following public statement:

The passing of Secretary Good removes a devoted public official. For most of his mature life he served the nation, earning the highest esteem for his abilities, his fine integrity, and his courageous spirit. But the first thoughts of those who knew and loved him are not of his public service. It is for his loyal and self-effacing friendship that thousands remember him; and that affectionate association is now broken.

Patrick J. Hurley, Assistant Secretary of War, was later appointed to succeed Secretary Good.

November 22, 1929: Congress concluded its special session, which began April 19th, but without finishing its work. The regular session would convene the first Monday in December.

CHAPTER II

THE FIRST REGULAR SESSION OF THE SEVENTY-FIRST CONGRESS. THE DEVELOPMENT OF ADMINISTRATIVE POLICY. THE CHILDREN'S CHARTER

DECEMBER, 1929–DECEMBER, 1930

THE first regular session of the Seventy-first Congress opened with the tariff legislation still uncompleted. The pall of the collapse of the eighteen months of wild credit inflation, with its orgy of stock speculation, and the beginning of the Great Depression hung over the country. The political situation in Congress, as has been said, showed a minority of administration senators but a staunch administration majority in the House of Representatives.

December 3, 1929: The President's first message on "the state of the Nation" dealt largely with depression questions. Nevertheless he presented a strong program of constructive action. Upon economic questions the President in summary urged:[1]

Public Buildings

... insufficient for most pressing governmental needs ... inadequate facilities are an extravagance, consideration should be given to extension of authorizations ... over a term of years. It would be helpful to the present economic situation ... in the National Capital. ... The Fine Arts Commission should be required to pass upon private buildings proposed for sites facing on public buildings and parks.

Waterways

The development of inland waterways ... the Mississippi System should be expedited ... expansion of our intracoastal waterways ... is well warranted. ... We are awaiting Canada upon the St. Lawrence waterway project.

Highways

There are over 3,000,000 miles of legally established highways ... 626,000 miles have been improved ... 102,000 miles are hard-surfaced ... proper planning ... give consideration to increase of our contribution ... to stimulating the improvement of farm-to-market roads.

Aviation

Government improved airways now exceed 25,000 miles ... 6,400 planes in commercial use ... 9,400 pilots licensed ... manufacturing

[1] State Papers, Vol. I, p. 138 *et seq.*

414

capacity, 7,500 planes per annum . . . the revision of airmail rates . . . is necessary . . . further expansion of South American services.

Railways

Not yet assured . . . adequate transportation . . . consolidations . . . to secure well-balanced systems with more uniform and satisfactory rate structure, a better assurance of service, more stable financial structure . . . greater efficiency . . . lower and more even rates. . . . Legislation . . . to protect public interest should be enacted.

Merchant Marine

. . . the necessity of securing much larger undertakings as to service and new construction in future contracts (for mail subsidy).

The Banking System

. . . Congress should consider the revision of some portions of the banking laws. . . . The development of "group" and "chain" banking presents many new problems . . . without restraint these methods would dangerously concentrate control of credit . . . to some degree . . . a groping for more secure basis.

. . . the trend in country districts with many failures and losses . . . upon the agricultural community.

. . . national banks unable to compete with State banks, and their withdrawal (of charters) results in weakening our national banking system . . . permission to engage in branch banking . . . within limited regions . . . requires careful investigation . . . advantageous to create joint commission embracing members of Congress and . . . Federal officials for subsequent reports.

The Radio Commission

I recommend the reorganization of the Radio Commission . . . requirement . . . that the commissioners shall be appointed from specific zones should be abolished . . . there is danger that the system will degenerate from a national system into five regional agencies . . . consequent failure to attain . . . service to the people as a whole.

Muscle Shoals

. . . this question should be disposed of. . . . Under present conditions the income . . . is less than could . . . be secured . . . public is not securing the full benefits . . . should be dedicated for all time to the farmers of the United States . . . experimentation on commercial scale in agricultural chemistry. . . . I do not favor the operation by the government of either power or manufacturing business except as an unavoidable by-product of some other major purpose . . . lease of the plants either as a whole or in parts and the reservation of facilities, products or income for agricultural purposes. . . .

Electrical Power Regulation

The Federal Power Commission is now comprised of three Cabinet officers and the duties involved in the competent conduct of the growing responsibilities of this commission far exceed the time and attention which these officials can properly afford from other important duties. I recommend that authority be given for the appointment of full-time commissioners to replace them.

It is also desirable that the authority of the commission should be extended to certain phases of power regulation. The nature of the electric utilities industry is such that about ninety per cent of all power generation and distribution is intra-state in character, and most of the States have developed their own regulatory systems as to certificates of convenience, rates, and profits of such utilities. To encroach upon their authorities and responsibilities would be an encroachment upon the rights of the States. There are cases, however, of inter-state character beyond the jurisdiction of the States. To meet these cases it would be most desirable if a method could be worked out by which the initial action may be taken between the commissions of the States whose joint action should be made effective by the Federal Power Commission with a reserve to act on its own motion in case of disagreement or non-action by the States.

Conservation

Conservation of national resources is a fixed policy of the government. Three important questions. . . . Conservation of our oil and gas resources against future need is a national necessity. The working of the oil permit system in development of oil and gas resources on the public domain has been subject to great abuse. I considered it necessary to suspend the issuance of such permits and to direct the review of all outstanding permits as to compliance of the holders with the law. The purpose was not only to end such abuse but to place the government in position to review the entire subject.

We are also confronted with a major problem in conservation due to the over-grazing on public lands. The effect of over-grazing (which has now become general) is not only to destroy the ranges but by impairing the ground coverage seriously to menace the water supply in many parts of the West through quick run-off, spring floods, and autumn drought.

We have a third problem of major dimensions in the reconsideration of our reclamation policy. The inclusion of most of the available lands of the public domain in existing reclamation projects . . . completes the original purpose of the Reclamation Service. There still remains the necessity for extensive storage of water in arid States. . . . I have appointed a Commission on Conservation of the Public Domain.

Upon governmental and social questions the President recommended:

The Federal Government provides for an extensive and valuable program of constructive social service, in education, home building, protection to women and children, employment, public health, recreation and in many other directions. . . . Federal activity in these directions has been confined to research and dissemination of information and experience, and at most to temporary subsidies to the States in order to secure uniform advancement in practice and methods. Any other attitude by the Federal Government will undermine one of the most precious possessions of the American people; that is, local and individual responsibility. We should adhere to this policy. . . . I have recently in co-operation with the Secretaries of Interior and of Labor, laid the foundations of an exhaustive inquiry into the facts precedent to a nation-wide White House conference on child health and protection. This co-operative movement among interested agencies will impose no expense upon the government. Similar nation-wide conferences will be called in connection with better housing and recreation at a later date.

In view of the considerable difference of opinion as to the policies which should be pursued by the Federal Government with respect to education, I have appointed a committee representative of the important educational associations and others to investigate and present recommendations. In co-operation with the Secretary of the Interior I have also appointed a voluntary committee of distinguished membership to assist in a nation-wide movement for the abolition of illiteracy.

I have recommended additional appropriations for the Federal Employment Service in order that it may more fully cover its co-operative work with State and local services. I have also recommended additional appropriations for the Women's and Children's Bureaus for much-needed research as to facts which I feel will prove most helpful.

Public Health

The advance in scientific discovery as to disease and health imposes new considerations upon us. The nation as a whole is vitally interested in the health of all the people; in protection from spread of contagious disease; in the relation of physical and mental disabilities to criminality; and in the economic and moral advancement which is fundamentally associated with sound body and mind. . . . Such organization should be as universal as public education. Its support is a proper burden upon the taxpayer. It can not be organized with success, either in its sanitary or educational phases, except under public authority. It should be based upon local and State responsibility, but I consider that the Federal Government has an obligation of contribution to the establishment of such agencies.

In the practical working out of organization, exhaustive experiment and trial have demonstrated that the base should be competent organization of the municipality, county, or other local unit. . . .

I recommend to the Congress that the purpose of the Sheppard-Towner Act should be continued through the Children's Bureau for a limited period of years; and that the Congress should consider the desirability of confining the use of Federal funds by the States to the building up of such county or other local units, and that such outlay should be positively co-ordinated with the funds expended through the United States Public Health Service directed to other phases of the same county

Federal Prisons

... Our Federal penal institutions are overcrowded. ... The parole and probation systems are inadequate. These conditions make it impossible to perform the work of personal reconstruction of prisoners so as to prepare them for return to the duties of citizenship. ...

Civil Service

Approximately four-fifths of all the employees in the executive civil service now occupy positions subject to competitive examination under the civil service law.

There are, however, still commanding opportunities for extending the system. These opportunities lie within the province of Congress and not the President. I recommend that a further step be taken by authorization that appointments of third-class postmasters be made under the civil service law.

Prohibition

The first duty of the President under his oath of office is to secure the enforcement of the laws. The enforcement of the laws enacted to give effect to the Eighteenth Amendment is far from satisfactory and this is in part due to the inadequate organization of the administrative agencies ... there should be an immediate concentration of responsibility and strengthening of enforcement agencies of the Federal Government by transfer to the Department of Justice of the Federal functions of detection and to a considerable degree of prosecution, which are now lodged in the Prohibition Bureau in the Treasury ... provision should be made for relief of congestion in the Federal courts. ...

Law Enforcement and Observance

No one will look with satisfaction upon the volume of crime of all kinds and the growth of organized crime in our country. We have pressing need so to organize our system of administering criminal justice as to establish full vigor and effectiveness. We need to re-establish faith—the swift and even-handed administration of justice to all offenders, whether they be rich or poor. ...

Law cannot rise above its source in good citizenship—in what right-minded men most earnestly believe and desire. If the law is upheld only by government officials, then all law is at an end. Our laws are made by the people themselves; theirs is the right to work for their repeal; but until repeal it is an equal duty to observe them and demand their enforcement.

December 5, 1929: In transmitting to Congress the Annual Report of the National Advisory Committee on Aeronautics, the President said: [2]

[2] State Papers, Vol. I, p. 184.

... progress on the two outstanding problems of increased safety and decreased costs necessitates continuous scientific research on the fundamental problems of flight. To this end enlarged facilities are being provided. ...

December 13, 1929: The President requested the American Child Health Association, of which he was the founder, to investigate the condition of children in Puerto Rico.

December 14, 1929: One of the partisan criticisms of the President from time to time was his appointment of commissions and committees. It was a basis for one or more of the stunts incident to the December dinner of the Gridiron Club. In his remarks at the conclusion of the evening, the President referred to his commissions and committees, as follows: [3]

The President of the United States is obliged to determine a multitude of questions and policies. By the Constitution he must recommend to Congress such measures as he shall deem necessary and expedient, and he is required to finally pass upon every act of Congress. He is the Chief Executive of the greatest business in the world, which at some point touches upon every single activity of our people.

By his position he must, within his capacities, give leadership to the development of moral, social and economic forces outside of government which make for betterment of our country. ...

The committees of Congress are themselves commissions for the investigation and the determination of legislative policies. But Congress cannot longer encompass the entire human field. Congress cannot determine administrative policies; it cannot inspire or lead voluntary forces.

The most dangerous animal in the United States is the man with an emotion and a desire to pass a new law. He is prolific with drama and the headlines. His is not the road to the fundamental advance of the liberty and the progress of the American people at this time in our history. The greatest antidote for him is to set him upon a committee with a dozen people whose appetite is for facts. The greatest catastrophe that could come to our country is that administration policies or legislation or voluntary movements shall be encouraged or enacted upon the basis of emotion, not upon facts or reason.

The President has open to him many governmental agencies in search for fact and for the determination of conclusion from them. He receives the largest measure of assistance from executive departments and Congressional committees. But over and beyond all these agencies there are a thousand problems where the truth must be searched from a multitude of facts; where individuals and regional experience must be had; where new ideas must be recruited from the kaleidoscope of a great shifting mass of humanity; where judgment must be distilled from many minds; where common agreement must be secured from conflicting forces; where

[3] State Papers, Vol. I, p. 189.

assurance must be given to the people of the correctness of conclusions; and where their exposition must be secured.

These subjects cover the whole range of human thought and I do not arrogate to myself the combined knowledge or judgment of the technologists, the philosophers, the scientists, the social thinkers, the economists, and the thousand callings of our people.

In these matters commissions and committees of our citizens can be made to add to the security of our steps and the certainty of acceptance of our policies. There is no worse agency of government than commissions and committees for executive action. Action requires undivided mind and undivided responsibility. But for the purpose of these special determinations I shall need more and more commissions and more and more conferences, and I am grateful for the willingness our citizens have shown to give their time and service upon them.

And it is my belief that this is a vital means of government by the people and for the people now that the people have ceased to live the simple life.

December 19, 1929: The President announced his plan for a searching inquiry into the broad social needs of the nation through the appointment of a Research Committee on Social Trends. He placed great importance upon this study, and was convinced that vital changes had taken place during the past two decades which must be constructively recognized by the country. He believed that for clarity of action by associations, by local, State and Federal governments there must be accurate, unbiased determination of fact. For illustration, public health measures had increased the span of life and the number of the aged. He wanted to know the social and economic implications of that fact and the governmental obligations. He likewise wanted to know what the effect had been of rapid technical advances in their relation to employment. It was necessary to determine the facts of unemployment, of housing, and of recreation; the problems raised by the changes in rural life and by rural migration to the cities, slums and other conditions of city life; and a score of other subjects. The inquiry was to be exhaustive, conducted by experts, and the results to be boldly given. The directing members of the inquiry were Wesley C. Mitchell, Charles E. Merriam, Dr. Alice Hamilton, William F. Ogburn, Howard W. Odum, and Shelby M. Harrison, with Edward Eyre Hunt, as secretary, and French Strother as the liaison with the President. This survey required three years. The report was issued January 1, 1933, and it forms the first foundation for national social fact ever presented as a guide to public action. It has had a profound effect upon the whole thinking of the nation. The loss of the election prevented the President offering his program of practical application. The report covered several volumes devoted to special subjects, and over 300 specialists were employed in research. The cost was borne by private benevolent agencies. In this connection extracts from a letter of December 30, 1929, from the President to President W. O. Thompson of Ohio State University are of interest:[4]

> The solicitude and philosophic ripeness of your letter of December 28th requires more than reciprocation of kindly holiday greetings. . . .
>
> You aptly penetrate the vital question of public action—the discovery and promulgation of truth. No real believer in democracy questions the sureness of public judgment—if the public is given the truth, but there is a time element in the triumph of truth. When we look back over history we see the period of either moral, social, economic, or political stagnation while the truth was en route and some variety of untruth occupied the scene. We can and must, however, greatly increase the production of truth and we must know the truth before the grave interest of 120,000,000 people is involved in government policies. We can sometimes speed up production before the ill-informed awakes to his opportunities. Facts are bad for his digestion and the truth makes misrepresentation uncomfortable. And the truth, as you say, is hard to discover; it must be distilled through the common judgment of skilled men and women from accurately and patiently collected facts and knowledge of forces before the extraction of the essence of wisdom. The materials themselves are also hard to come by; it takes time and patience, especially as our many inventions have forever banished the simple life. In the meantime, a vast clamor of half-truths and untruths and injured facts will always fill the air and intoxicate people's emotions. The President himself cannot pretend to know or to have the time for detailed investigation into every one of the hundreds of subjects in a great people. But the fine minds of our citizens are available and can be utilized for the search.
>
> . . . We get . . . the fundamental confusion that government, since it can correct much abuse, can also create righteousness.
>
> . . . My resolutions for the new year include a continued effort to keep pure the wells of wisdom, and to reassure you that I have faith that the people want the truth determined even if it takes time and patience.

December 22, 1929: The purely destructive criticism by the Democratic National Committee still was continuing. It had been characterized by Frank R. Kent, a nationally prominent Washington newspaper correspondent, as a "smearing" campaign. Today the committee, utilizing Speaker Garner as the spokesman, charged the President with being connected with sugar tariff lobbyists and beneficiaries.

December 24, 1929: An earnest and sincere effort was being put forth by the Administration to enforce the prohibition laws as was its sworn duty. On the other hand, in increasing measure the States and localities whose duties were primary in handling a problem of this character were

[4] State Papers, Vol. I, p. 196.

leaving the entire field of enforcement to the Federal Government. Additional legislation had been requested from Congress. Senator Borah criticized the President for not making the prohibition law effective.

December 26, 1929: The Attorney-General replied to Senator Borah, saying: "when Congress is ready to consider and adopt legislation to carry out the Administration's recommendations, those whose duty it is to enforce the law will be able to accomplish more."

The President, in conference with Senator Borah suggested that prohibition enforcement in part depended upon Congress passing his recommendations for the reorganization and merger of the several Federal bureaus having to do with enforcement. He pointed out, more especially, that many of the States had almost abdicated their powers of enforcement, and without them prohibition would necessarily fail.

January 3, 1930: In a statement to the press, the President said:[5]

I have emphasized the necessity for the reorganization of the Indian Bureau by the appointment of Mr. Rhoads as the head of the Bureau and of Mr. Scattergood as his assistant, and Secretary Wilbur is giving it his very special attention.

We have presented to Congress a request for an increased appropriation of some $3,000,000 for next year's budget, and in the meantime we have submitted an estimate in the Deficiency Bill for some increase for the balance of this year. The purposes of these increases are mainly to build up the education and health facilities, to change the direction of educational work and to develop the industrial improvement of the Indians. . . . We have 338,000 Indians. The broad problem is to better train the Indian youth to take care of themselves and their property. It is the only course by which we can ultimately discharge this problem from the nation, and blend them as a self-supporting people into the nation as a whole.

The Indian Bureau is recommending to the Congress a number of changes in the laws bearing on Indian affairs. The recommendations are designed to secure better administration of the very large properties owned by the Indians and to correct many things in the administration of these properties that will make for citizenship.

January 8, 1930: Democratic members of the Senate Tariff Lobby Investigating Committee again endeavored to imply that the President's name, in some manner or other, was entangled with the sugar tariff lobby. On January 14, 1930, the Committee finally reported: "There is no impropriety nor anything open to criticism upon the President's part."

January 13, 1930: The President sent a special message to Congress urging immediate changes in law enforcement machinery:[6]

[5] State Papers, Vol. I, p. 201.   [6] State Papers, Vol. I, p. 203.

In my previous messages I have requested the attention of the Congress to the urgent situation which has grown up in the matter of enforcement of Federal criminal laws. . . .

The development of the facts shows the necessity for certain important and evident administrative reforms in the enforcement and judicial machinery, concrete proposals for which are available from government departments. They are in the main:

1. Reorganization of the Federal court structure so as to give relief from congestion.
2. Concentration of responsibility in detection and prosecution of prohibition violations.
3. Consolidation of the various agencies engaged in prevention of smuggling of liquor, narcotics, other merchandise, and aliens over our frontiers.
4. Provision of adequate court and prosecuting officials.
5. Expansion of Federal prisons and reorganization of parole and other practices.
6. Specific legislation for the District of Columbia.

I believe the administrative changes mentioned above will contribute to cure many abuses. . . .

January 31, 1930: While the President had his difficulties with some of the Progressives of his own party, he likewise had his troubles from time to time with some of the so-called "Old Guard." A vacancy occurring in the Senate from Pennsylvania, Governor Fisher had appointed Joseph W. Grundy. Senator Grundy was universally known as an extreme protectionist. During the 1928 campaign Mr. Hoover, not sharing Mr. Grundy's extreme protection views, had disagreed with him. Shortly after his appointment and in the midst of the tariff discussion in the Senate, the senator criticized the President's views severely.

February 3, 1930: The President announced the nomination of Charles Evans Hughes as Chief Justice. William Howard Taft had resigned on account of ill health. This nomination met with great approval all over the country, but a group of Democrats and Progressives endeavored to defeat confirmation. They were unsuccessful. Mr. Hughes was finally confirmed by fifty-two votes to twenty-six.

February 5, 1930: Speaking in the East Room of the White House to a group of Community Chest workers, the President said:[7]

Community Chests in our cities have demonstrated their value and importance for effective conduct in administration of the multitude of charities necessary within our great municipalities. They represent our greatest advance in the administration of charity. Their great purpose is

[7] State Papers, Vol. I, p. 211.

the handling with large vision of the obligations of a whole city to its less fortunate residents. They guarantee integrity and efficient conduct of charitable administration. They assure skill in administration, freedom from prejudice; they give support to charities of vital necessity yet of less emotional appeal; they free the administrators of our charitable institutions from anxiety and the diversion of their time from primary duties to the constant collection of funds. They give assurance of continuity; they make for the relief of the residents of a community from constant supplication and uncertainty.

. . . At this time when we attach too much importance to material and economic success, we place great emphasis on the idea of greater comfort, the possession of riches, and we too often overlook the necessity for stimulated spiritual development. The Community Chest has come to stand for this spiritual development of a community.

The relief organizations set up by the President, in the winters of 1930, 1931 and 1932, were assisted by the co-operation of these Community Chest workers.

February 18, 1930: The President prepared to issue a public protest at the dilatory tactics of the Senate in the failure to pass any of the legislative program outlined in his message. After a conference with Senate leaders he agreed to delay the appeal for public support in order to see if something definite would be undertaken by the Senate.

February 21, 1930: The marked differences in opinion existing between the President and Senator Grundy were brought to the attention of the Senate by Senator Pat. Harrison, of Mississippi, ranking minority member of the Committee on Finance. In a characteristic speech Senator Harrison referred to Senator Grundy as having appealed to his Old-Guard colleagues to fight the President because of the more moderate protection views of the latter and his efforts for a limited revision. Senator Grundy likewise objected to the flexible tariff. Ultra-conservative and high protectionist, he found himself allied for the time being with low tariff Democrats and Progressives in his fight against a Tariff Commission clothed with adequate flexible revision powers. The Republican "Young Guard" senators protested at the Old Guard's failure to defend the President.

February 22, 1930: The President spent much time with Senate and House leaders in endeavoring to bring about a conclusion to the tariff legislation, because of the uncertainties it was creating in a business world already shocked by the stock market collapse. He urged more moderate views upon the extreme protectionists. The situation appeared to be that about eighty per cent of the members of the Senate had each placed something he had wanted in the bill. Many of these members hoped it would be enacted; but many of them were creating a public impression of opposition. It was apparent that the bill finally would pass.

February 24, 1930: The President invited to breakfast with him Secretaries Mellon and Mills of the Treasury; Senators Watson and McNary; Floor Leaders Smoot and Jones of the Senate; Speaker Longworth and Floor Leader Tilson of the House; and Congressmen Snell, Wood and Hawley, to discuss the legislative situation. The President vigorously stated his views upon the tariff bill and its lack of progress. Economy, banking and other problems also were discussed.

March 10, 1930: The President, as guest at a dinner attended by national leaders in the Boy Scout movement, addressed them as follows: [8]

. . . The priceless treasury of boyhood is his endless enthusiasm, his store of high idealism and his fragrant hopes. His is the plastic period when indelible impressions must be made if we are to continue a successful democracy. We assure ourselves that the cure of illiteracy and the fundamentals of education are the three Rs—reading, rightin' and 'rithmetic. To this we must add one more R and that is responsibility—responsibility to the community—if we are not to have illiteracy in government. The conviction that every person in the Republic owes a service to the Republic; that the Republic rests solely upon the willingness of every one in it to bear his part of the duties and obligations of citizenship is as important as the ability to read and write—that is the only patriotism of peace.

The idea that the Republic was created for the selfish benefit of the individual is a mockery that must be eradicated at the first dawn of understanding. It is true that many of our schools have recognized this obligation. . . . If we look over the Republic today we find many failures in citizenship—we find many betrayals of those who have been selected to leadership. I cannot conceive that these failures would take place if every citizen who went to the polls was a good "scout" and every official who was elected had ever been a real Boy Scout. . . .

March 15, 1930: The Postmaster-General announced contracts for a new service of airmail to South America, to include Cuba, Honduras, Nicaragua, Costa Rica, Panama, Colombia, Ecuador, and Peru three times a week. This service saved from six to nine days in transit to Peru.

On October 11th, the first airmail to Argentina carried the President's congratulations to that government that the pre-inauguration visit had so direct a result. By October 9th of this year Uruguay had been added to the service.

The President for some years had taken an active part in securing

[8] State Papers, Vol. I, p. 219.

airmail connections with South America. His plan now was accomplished.

March 24, 1930: After about ten months' deliberation the Senate finally passed the Tariff Bill by a vote of fifty-three to thirty-one. The bill now went to conference with the House. Most of the Republican Progressives voted for the bill. So did seven Democrats. The bill at this stage, however, contained the "Export Debenture Plan." The President's formula of a flexible tariff had been eliminated to all practical purposes. The Senate provision made the Tariff Commission a fact-finding agency only. The rates in the Senate bill, generally speaking, were higher than when the bill had been reported out by the Senate committee. Responsibility for these increases was not confined to the members of any one political party. For example, during the passage of the bill, individual Democrats and Progressives voted a total of over 1,000 times for increases, or against decreases, of duties. There was much work to be done if the bill was to be improved in conference.

March 31, 1930: The President issued the proclamation legally establishing May 1st as Child Health Day. It had been established informally some years before through the American Child Health Association, of which Mr. Hoover was chairman. The proclamation in part said:[9]

. . . Our children have the right to be born in health, to be well throughout babyhood and the pre-school years; to be surrounded with moral and spiritual inspiration; to work and to play through primary school with well minds based on well bodies; to enjoy and to profit to the utmost by their higher schooling because of wholesome habits of thought and deed; thence to graduate into adult life, strong in body and inculcated with the sense of fair play and of responsibility for the rights of others.

April 8, 1930: The President in speaking to the American Society of Mechanical Engineers upon the subject of recent social and economic changes, said:[10]

With the development of our great national tools—our engines, our railways, our automobiles, our airplanes, our steamships, our electric power, and a score of other great implements, together with the supplies of material upon which they depend, the engineer has added vastly to the problems of government, for government must see that the control of these tools and these materials are not misused to limit liberty and freedom, that they advance and do not retard equality of opportunity amongst all our citizens.

These great discoveries and inventions have brought great blessings to humanity but they have multiplied the problems of government and the

[9] State Papers, Vol. I, p. 222.   [10] State Papers, Vol. I, p. 225.

complexity of these problems progresses with the increase of our population. Every county government, every municipal government, every State government, and the Federal Government itself, is engaged in constant attempt to solve a multitude of public relationships to these tools which the engineers by their genius and industry constantly force to the very doorstep of government. And in solving these problems we have need for a large leavening of the engineering knowledge and engineering attitude of mind and engineering method. These problems of public relation are unsolvable without the technical knowledge of the engineer. They are unsolvable without the fundamental engineers' approach to truth. That is, first to determine the facts, arrange these facts in proper perspective and then distill truth from them in the retort of experience. . . .

April 9, 1930: While Secretary of Commerce, President Hoover had been instrumental in initiating negotiations with Canada for the preservation of Niagara Falls. These negotiations had been successful. He sent to the Senate a report of the subject, from the committee under the chairmanship of J. Horace McFarland and urged that the convention, which had been agreed to and which was before the Senate, be now considered for ratification.[11]

April 10, 1930: The death of Mr. Justice Sanford of the Supreme Court of the United States created a vacancy in that tribunal. President Hoover was a close student of our form of government. No lawyer could have had a finer appreciation of the responsibility and power of a Federal judge and especially of a Supreme Court Justice. The Attorney-General was asked to inquire into the qualifications of a number of lawyers and judges, including those from judicial circuits not then represented upon the Supreme Court. Among those inquired about was United States Circuit Judge John J. Parker of the Fourth Circuit. The Attorney-General advised the President that Judge Parker was a very able, hard-working, fair-minded, impartial jurist with a thorough knowledge of the law, and of unquestionable integrity. This conclusion was based upon an inquiry which included an examination of something like 125 opinions which the Judge had written while sitting on the Circuit Court of Appeals. Justice Sanford had been from Tennessee. His death left Justice McReynolds the only member of the Court from the South. The Fourth Circuit had not been represented upon the Supreme Court for several decades. The personal character, professional standing and judicial qualifications of Judge Parker had been presented or vouched for by the most prominent citizens of his state (North Carolina) without reference to party, and from citizens from every walk of life. With scarcely an exception, every senator from the several States within his circuit had recommended or

[11] See State Papers, Vol. I, p. 227 for the message and text of the treaty.

endorsed his appointment. Included among his endorsers were two United States Circuit judges, ten United States District judges, a large number of State judges, the president and five past-presidents of the American Bar Association, several presidents of State Bar Associations, and many other prominent members of the Bar from both political parties. The President decided to nominate Judge Parker, and did so.

Almost immediately a bitter fight was started against his confirmation. This fight was started by one or more national negro organizations. It was aided by certain groups of organized labor. The negro organizations based their opposition upon a statement claimed to have been made by Judge Parker in 1920 while he was a candidate for governor of North Carolina. The leaders in these organizations wholly ignored the very substantial endorsement of Judge Parker by the leaders of their race in North Carolina. Likewise they ignored at least two of the decisions by the United States Circuit Court, wherein Judge Parker wrote the opinion. These opinions sustain the Constitutional rights of the negro.

Representatives of certain labor organizations found fault with a decision of the Circuit Court of Appeals in the Fourth Circuit, in which Judge Parker wrote the opinion. [United Mine Workers vs. Red Jacket Coal & Coke Co., 18 Fed. (2nd), page 539.] In this case the Circuit Court of Appeals based its decision and opinion upon decisions of the Supreme Court of the United States. Impartial lawyers reading the opinions of the Supreme Court will come to the opinion that Judge Parker and his associates were bound to follow the Supreme Court decisions, regardless of their personal opinions as to whether the Supreme Court had been right or wrong in its conclusions in those cases, and that the Circuit Court of Appeals did so on every point in the case.

As a result of the attacks the Senate refused to confirm the nomination of Judge Parker by the vote of forty-one to thirty-nine. Opposed to his confirmation were a combination of Democrats, Progressives and certain regular Republicans who had a substantial percentage of negroes in their constituencies. Supporting Judge Parker were Republicans and about ten Democrats. The final vote was taken on May 7th. On May 9th the President sent in the nomination of Owen J. Roberts. Several days later the Senate confirmed by unanimous vote.

April 21, 1930: The American Child Health Association completed its report upon the appalling health situation among Puerto Rico children. The President raised some $700,000 from private sources with which to undertake a campaign of betterment, in co-operation with the Puerto Rico Government, under the direction of the American Child Health Association.

April 22, 1930: Speaking from the White House over the radio the President, addressing the citizens of Ponca City, Oklahoma, in honor of pioneer women, said:[12]

There are few men of the West of my generation who did not know the pioneer woman in his own mother, and who does not rejoice to know that her part in building that great civilization is to have such beautiful recognition. It was these women who carried the refinement, the moral character and spiritual force into the West. Not only they bore great burdens of daily toil and the rearing of families, but they were intent that their children should have a chance, that the doors of opportunity should be open to them. It was their insistence which made the schools and the churches.

April 23, 1930: The President sent out invitations to State and local authorities to attend a national conference on street and highway safety to be presided over by the Secretary of Commerce. He conferred today with leaders of various national associations upon their part and the program to be considered. He stated that despite every effort that was being made to the contrary, accidents were steadily mounting until the problem was of real national importance.

April 28, 1930: To expedite action upon his recommendation for legislation, for more effective machinery of law enforcement, the President addressed a special message to Congress:[13]

In my messages of June 6th and December 3, 1929, I placed before Congress the urgency of certain improvements necessary to effective criminal law enforcement. Substantial progress has been made upon some of the measures proposed, yet we are nearing the end of the present session, and I cannot too strongly urge the necessity of action upon all these recommendations before adjournment.

The most important recommendations made by me were five in number.

1. There should be a transfer of the functions of detection and prosecution of prohibition cases from the Treasury Department to the Department of Justice, and thus an ending of divided responsibility and effort. . . .
2. There must be relief afforded from congestion in the courts. . . .
3. There must be extension of Federal prisons with more adequate parole systems and other modern treatment of prisoners. We have already 11,985 prisoners in Federal establishments built for 6,946. The number of Federal prisoners in Federal and State institutions increased 6,277 in the nine months from June 30, 1929, to April 1, 1930. . . .
4. We are in need of vigorous reorganization of the Border Patrol. . . .

[12] State Papers, Vol. I, p. 243.   [13] State Papers, Vol. I, p. 272.

5. The District of Columbia is without an adequate prohibition enforcement law. . . .

Our obedience to law, our law enforcement and judicial organization, our judicial procedure, our care and methods of handling prisoners, in relation to not only Federal Government but also to the State and municipal governments, are far from the standards that must be secured. . . .

April 29, 1930: The President approved the Watres Act authorizing a reorganization of the Air Mail Service, which he had recommended in his annual message. The intricate problems involved had been under examination by Postmaster-General Brown. They arose from the following situation. The commercial airmail contracts had been established as the result of the report of the Morrow Commission in 1925. The commercial air transport industry was then young and experimental. There was but little experience upon which to fix the rates in the contracts, the routes which should be developed, or the conditions which should be required in order to stimulate traffic or serve best in national defense. Of even greater importance was the tremendous progress that had been made in aviation during the intervening years.

Experience had proved the early rates to be too high. Exorbitant profits had been made, some contracts as high as $3.00 per mile. Great speculation in the securities of aviation companies had taken place in expectation of continuance of such rates. Some thirty companies had engaged in the traffic and in consequence many routes were not served by continuous lines. There were no transcontinental routes. The conditions of the contracts had not developed equally the collateral services of passengers and express which it was hoped would bear an ever-increasing part of the costs. The planes were confined largely to purely mail-carrying types of no great speed. As many of the contracts for carrying the mail had in 1930 some years yet to run and could not honestly be cancelled, methods had to be devised to secure their voluntary surrender.

As a result of the amended law and the able administration of Postmaster-General Brown, through negotiation the rates were greatly reduced, the routes were consolidated into a carefully planned national system of commercial airways, the type of plane was entirely changed to passenger and express service, which promised to reduce greatly the volume of subsidy required. The speed, safety and reliability of planes were greatly enhanced. The nation was saved from a hodge-podge of airways similar to the tangle that had grown up in rail transportation, and above all, a great arm of national defense was created.

In the fiscal year ending June 30, 1929, before the act went into effect, commercial aviation companies had flown 10,200,000 miles with the mail and the contractors had been paid $14,600,000 or $1.43 per mile. The airmail receipts were estimated at about $1,700,000, bringing the net cost to the government down to about $1.26 per mile.

In the fiscal year ending June 30, 1933 under the revised legislation, the contractors flew 35,900,000 miles with the mail and were paid $19,400,000, or about fifty-four cents per mile. Due to the greatly improved service, however, airmail receipts increased to about $10,000,000, which resulted in a net cost to the government of about twenty-six cents per mile. The reduction in costs of transportation by the reform had been over sixty per cent on the gross cost per mile and about eighty per cent on the net cost per mile. Of equal importance, the subsidies had been so directed that the whole service was transformed into large passenger and express-carrying planes, from which the revenues outside the government were growing steadily and with the growth of the air mail traffic bade fair soon to reduce the subsidies to the amount of the mail receipts. Passengers had increased from 165,200 in 1929 to 550,000 in 1933. The manufacturing capacity for planes had increased enormously, and furnished the largest capacity in case of war of any country in the world. The planes had so much improved in character and quality, that the mail time between the two seaboards had been reduced from forty-eight hours to twenty-one hours. The number of people directly employed had increased from 15,000 to 35,000, every one of whom in some capacity was a highly trained reserve of personnel in time of war. In military values alone the government would have needed to expend five times the annual sum involved to build up the same organization if it had done so through the military department.

May 1, 1930: The conferees on the tariff were still at odds on the "Export Debenture Plan" amendment. In responding to an inquiry, the President reiterated his views on the subject in a letter to Congressman John Q. Tilson, Republican floor leader:[14]

MY DEAR MR. TILSON:

I have your letter of inquiry as to whether I can see any reason to change the views which I expressed on April 20th [1929] last upon the so-called (Export) Debenture Plan introduced by the Senate into the Tariff Bill. I do not.

Some minor alterations have been made in the plan which do not go in the essential fact that the practical working of it will depress and not elevate prices to the farmer. The plan in the present bill presents an additional objection in that the export subsidies proposed vary with different agricultural products and thus are widely different to different farmers. They vary from about nine per cent upon the cost of production of rye

[14] State Papers, Vol. I, p. 296.

to apparently nearly 100 per cent on tobacco. In the latter case growers could apparently afford to raise their products and export it for the subsidy alone.

Since my previous statement the Tariff Commission has estimated the cost of the plan to the Treasury, if put into operation and on the basis of present exports, of about $280,000,000 per annum.

May 3, 1930: The Tariff Bill again was before the House upon a report from the conferees. The House once more stood by the President by again rejecting the "Export Debenture Plan" by a vote of 231 to 161. Then it refused to concur in the Senate amendments as to a flexible tariff by a vote of 236 to 154. This meant further consideration by the conferees.

May 4, 1930: Some 1,000 college economists memorialized the President to veto the Tariff Bill. The bill was not yet through conference. Many of the rates had not yet been agreed upon. It developed later that the protest was organized behind the scenes by a New York agency interested in promoting free trade.

May 5, 1930: The President, speaking at the opening session of the annual meeting of the American Red Cross, said:[15]

> The past fifteen years have seen a great change in the purpose and an expansion in the benevolent activities of this, our great official association for the administration of national charity. Originally designed for succor in war, it has now become also the national agency for relief of disaster in peacetime, both at home and abroad. The past decade it has distinguished itself a score of times by effective organization of the saving of life and suffering. Its ever-increasing strength represents the growing of the spiritual sense of responsibility of the nation toward those who meet with disaster. . . .

May 13, 1930: Following thorough investigation and after an unsuccessful attempt by moral suasion, the Administration started legal action to dissolve the so-called radio manufacturing trust.

The President signed the first of a series of bills covering the Federal prison reforms which he had recommended to Congress. The Acts provided (a) the creation of a Bureau of Federal Prisons in the Department of Justice, under a director appointed by the Attorney-General with complete authority over all United States prisons and prisoners; (b) a National Board of Parole; (c) medical services in all prisons placed under the Public Health Service; (d) the establishment of a boy's reformatory; (e) establishment of a new prison for vicious offenders; (f) a declaration of policy of classification and segregation of prisoners

[15] State Papers, Vol. I, p. 297.

according to character, offense, etc.; (g) provision for instruction and industrial employment in prisons, the latter to be of non-competitive type, and the creation of temporary camps for prisoners in outside government work with reductions in sentences for faithful work; (h) increase in the number of Federal judges in a number of districts; (i) establishment of a probation system in the United States courts with probation officers under the direction of the Department of Justice; and (j) establishment of the Division of Identification and Information, in the Bureau of Investigation, in the Department of Justice. The acquiring and the exchanging of criminal records with State and municipal authorities was to constitute a major function of the division.

Under this reorganization the Federal Government was able for the first time to concentrate criminal records, also fingerprints, in one unit. It was a very distinct advance in empowering the government to cope with the criminal.

Taking this program, embracing the separate acts and resolutions by Congress, as a whole, no such extensive or enlightened reform in dealing with criminals had been accomplished heretofore in the entire social history of the Federal Government.

May 19, 1930: The Republican Senate conferees, Senators Smoot, Watson, and Shortridge, had voted against the amendments which the Senate had made by inserting the "Export Debenture Plan" and by changing the flexible provisions. They had been compelled to give assurances at the time of their appointment as conferees that they would stand by the Senate amendment. The House was insisting on its position and so were its conferees. One or the other must yield or there would be no tariff bill. Finally the Senate yielded. The votes came upon a resolution which released the Senate majority conferees from their promise to insist on the Senate amendments. The vote releasing them on the "Export Debenture Plan" was forty-three to forty-one. The vote on the flexible provisions was a tie, forty-two to forty-two. Thereupon Vice President Curtis, who was in the chair, cast the deciding vote, making the result forty-three to forty-two. The way had been cleared for an agreement by the Conference Committee.

May 21, 1930: In his campaign for the Republican senatorial nomination Senator Grundy formed an alliance of mutual benefit with former Governor Gifford Pinchot of Pennsylvania. Mr. Pinchot again was a candidate for governor. Opposing Senator Grundy was Secretary of Labor Davis. Mr. Davis was nominated. In a three-cornered contest for governor, Pinchot was nominated.

May 24, 1930: The flexible provisions agreed to in conference proved to be substantially less than the President had wanted. But, when the Conference Report was presented to the Senate, Senator Barkley of Kentucky, for reasons of his own, made several points of order to the report, including the flexible provisions. A day or two later Vice President Curtis, who was presiding, sustained the point of order. This necessitated sending the bill back to conference.

The President demanded the flexible provisions in accordance with his ideas. This was done through the efforts of Senator Smoot, Representative Hawley, and their respective Republican colleagues. In its final form the result was a complete victory for the President in the flexible provisions.

The inclusion of a practical flexible tariff strengthened the bill immeasurably. Where certain rates had been fixed too high, they could be reduced. If other rates had been fixed too low, they could be increased. The proponents must present their evidence in detail. If a case were made out the remedy would follow. The opposition of the Democrats in Congress was largely partisan and also quite inconsistent. Governor Alfred E. Smith of New York, as a candidate for President in 1928, had advocated a Tariff Commission with powers over rates far in excess of the flexible powers asked by and finally granted to the President.

May 27, 1930: The President addressed the open meeting of the Conference on Street and Highway Safety, invited by him on April 23rd. He said:[16]

The great loss of human life in street and highway accidents, and the toll of suffering among surviving victims, is a national concern of grave importance. You thus are gathered here to consider a humanitarian and economic problem which touches every man, woman, and child in the land.

It is encouraging to know that . . . where remedies have been actively applied, the accident increase has been curbed. . . . The way has thus been pioneered. . . .

The Federal Government can properly assist in securing the spread of information and ideas and co-ordination of activities, but it still remains the fact, nevertheless, that the State and local authorities, with the co-operation of the public, must be responsible for the practical application of remedial measures. . . .

May 27, 1930: The President signed the Act consolidating the several prohibition enforcement agencies scattered through various departments, placing them in the Department of Justice. He at once set up the Bureau of Prohibition in that department with personnel chosen by Civil Service examination.

[16] State Papers, Vol. I, p. 300.

May 28, 1930: The Tariff Bill reported by the conferees still was under consideration in the Senate. The discussion was largely on the flexible provisions as finally agreed to by the conferees. The President authorized Senator Watson to state his position upon the flexible tariff. The Senator said:

I never quote the President of the United States, but I want to say that in every talk I have had with the President about the situation he stated that he wanted a tariff commission to have all the authority except that he should sign or veto the report of the commission just as he signs or vetoes bills passed by Congress. The President said "I want a straight non-partisan commission to go into the whole question." I think that so far as it is permissible to make rates and let those rates be submitted to the President of the United States, I want a non-partisan commission. If the tariff can be taken out of politics I want it taken out of politics.

May 30, 1930: After reviewing, from the east terrace of the White House, a parade by the veterans of our wars, in which a few surviving veterans of the Union Army of 1861-65 occupied the post of honor, the President motored to the battlefield of Gettysburg. There he made a Memorial Day address. Upon that historic battlefield where the Union had been saved and speaking from the place where Lincoln had delivered the immortal Gettysburg Address, the President said in part:[17]

Every American's thought of this great battlefield of Gettysburg flashes with the instant vision of the lonely figure of Lincoln, whose immortal words dominate this scene. . . .
. . . Lincoln's counsels sounded strangely when spoken in the midst of war. His was the call of moderation. Our history would be even brighter than it is if his predecessors and his contemporaries had spoken as temperately as he, if they had been moved with charity toward all, by malice toward none.
. . . Since his day reason has not always ruled instead of passion, knowledge has not always been sought instead of reliance upon improvised conjecture, patience has not ever delayed the impetuous feet of reckless ambition, quiet negotiation has not always replaced the clamor of the hustings, prudent counsel has not invariably overcome the allurements of demagogic folly, good will has not always won the day over cynicism and vainglory. . . .
In the weaving of our destiny, the pattern may change, yet the woof and warp of our weaving must be those inspired ideals of unity, of ordered liberty, of equality of opportunity, of popular government, and of peace to which this nation was dedicated. . . .
The weaving of freedom is and always will be a struggle of law against lawlessness, of individual liberty against domination, of unity

[17] State Papers, Vol. I, p. 304.

against sectionalism, of truth and honesty against demagoguery and misleading, of peace against fear and conflict. In the forming of this pattern, the abuse of politics often muddies the stream of constructive thought and dams back the flow of well-considered action.

June 2, 1930: Congress made radical changes in the existing provisions of the laws providing pensions for Spanish War Veterans. Some of these changes the President thought were very unjust and created dangerous precedents. He returned the bill, S. 476, to the Senate, where it originated, without his approval, saying: [18]

I am returning this bill (S. 476) without approval. The bill establishes a new basis for pension of Spanish War Veterans. I am in favor of proper discharge of the national obligation to men who have served in war who have become disabled and are in need. But certain principles are included in this legislation which I deem are opposed to the interest both of war veterans and of the public. My major objections to this bill are these:

1. In the whole of our pension legislation over past years we have excluded from such national award persons whose disabilities arise from "vicious habits." This bill breaks down that exclusion. Certainly such claims for public help cannot be fairly based upon sacrifice to the nation in war and must be opposed to national policy.

2. This legislation lowers the minimum service period from ninety days to seventy days for non-service connected disability pension. Under other provisions of law, men who served only one day and during that suffered injury or impaired health, became eligible for pensions. This law, however, provides that if a man should incur any disability at any time in his life he may claim pension with only seventy days of service. The ninety-day minimum service has been maintained against the Civil War veterans all these years because less service than this was not considered to imply personal danger or risk which warranted pension. If injury or impaired health incident to service is clearly proven, other laws cover such cases.

Congress overrode the President's veto.

June 5, 1930: Senate leaders informed the President that Senator Grundy had concluded not to vote for the Tariff Bill, as he did not consider the industrial rates high enough, and he was opposed to the flexible provisions. Notwithstanding his dissatisfaction with the bill, which, of course, was known, the opponents of protection were referring to the bill in the press as the Grundy Bill. It was becoming more apparent that the bill would pass the Senate, for there were several on the Democratic side who were making an appearance of opposition, but who had obtained sufficient local or regional advantages not to allow it to fail. If they

[18] See State Papers, Vol. I, pp. 302 and 307.

were needed, they would furnish the necessary votes to see that it did pass.

June 7, 1930: Senator Steiwer of Oregon issued a public statement criticizing the Democratic votes for tariff duties on the products of their own States. At the same time they violently condemned the bill in its entirety in the hope of gaining partisan advantage. He cited a long list of such actions.

June 10, 1930: The President signed a bill providing for a Federal charter for the Textile Foundation, a measure he had urged five years before as Secretary of Commerce, for the development of scientific research in connection with the industry. A board, consisting of the Secretary of Commerce and three representatives of the industry, was set up to administer a fund of two million dollars saved from certain war agencies for the purpose.

June 11, 1930: The President signed the Perishable Agricultural Commodities Act, 1930. Its major purpose was to suppress unfair practices in marketing perishable commodities. The need for this he had pointed out in his initial message to Congress in April of 1929. The President in a press statement said:

. . . I have advocated this legislation for some years. It has been supported by the great majority of commission men and dealers in agricultural perishables as well as by agricultural organizations. It is a very important step in protecting both the farmers and the honest dealers as well as the consumer.

June 12, 1930: Senators Reed and Grundy publicly condemned the Tariff Bill on the ground that the industrial rates were too low. Senator Grundy again denounced the flexible provisions. Both, however, stated that they would probably vote for the bill.

June 13, 1930: The Senate finally passed the Conference Report on the Tariff Bill (H.R. 2667) by forty-four to forty-two. Of the Progressive group, Senators Couzens, Cutting, and Johnson voted for it. Of the Democrats, Senators Broussard, Fletcher, Kenrick, Ransdell, and Trammell voted for it. The President was advised that there were other favorable votes in reserve if there had been any danger of failure.

June 14, 1930: The House likewise passed the Conference Report on the Tariff Bill.

June 12-15, 1930: The Tariff Bill was now awaiting Executive approval or disapproval. Hearings upon the measure had commenced in December of 1928. The bill had been under consideration by Congress for a year and a half. During that period no head of a business knew what changes in rates eventually would be agreed upon. The provisions of the bill had been much misrepresented. Some of its proponents had exaggerated its benefits. At the same time most of its opponents, both in and out of Congress, had grossly misrepresented its schedules and rates. Then upon this false premise they told of the dire consequences that would befall the country if the bill became a law. The President received a mass of recommendations as to approval or veto from representatives of a diversity of interests. Among those registering their opposition to the bill were Albert H. Wiggin (chairman of the Chase National Bank); Charles Sabin (chairman of the Guaranty Trust Company); Charles E. Mitchell (chairman of the National City Bank); Thomas W. Lamont (J. P. Morgan and Co.); Oswald Garrison Villard (editor of the *Nation*), Henry Morgenthau, Jr.; Roy Howard (Scripps-Howard newspapers); Jouett Shouse (chairman, Democratic National Executive Committee); John J. Raskob (chairman, Democratic National Committee); and Stephen H. Love (president United States Beet Sugar Association).

Those urging approval of the bill included the directors of the American Farm Bureau Federation; Louis J. Taber (master of the National Grange); Clarence E. Huff (president of the Farmers' Union); Matthew Woll (vice chairman American Federation of Labor), and John E. Edgerton (president of National Association of Manufacturers).

June 15, 1930: The President made a public detailed analysis of the Tariff Bill: [19]

I shall approve the Tariff Bill. . . . It was undertaken as the result of pledges given by the Republican Party at Kansas City. . . .

Platform promises must not be empty gestures. In my message of April 16, 1929, to the Special Session of the Congress I accordingly recommended an increase in agricultural protection; a limited revision of other schedules to take care of the economic changes necessitating increases or decreases since the enactment of the 1922 law, and I further recommended a reorganization both of the Tariff Commission and of the method of executing the flexible provisions.

A statistical estimate of the bill by the Tariff Commission shows that the average duties collected under the 1922 law were about 13.8 per cent of the value of all imports, both free and dutiable, while if the new law had been applied it would have increased this percentage to about 16.0 per cent.

This compares with the average level of the tariff under

The McKinley Law of	23.0%
The Wilson Law of	20.9%
The Dingley Law of	25.8%
The Payne-Aldrich Law of....................	19.3%
The Fordney-McCumber Law of...............	13.83%

[19] State Papers, Vol. I, p. 314.

Under the Underwood Law of 1913 the amounts were disturbed by war conditions varying 6 per cent to 14.8 per cent.

The proportion of imports which will be free of duty under the new law is estimated at from sixty-one to sixty-three per cent. This compares with averages under

The McKinley Law of........................	52.4%
The Wilson Law of..........................	49.4%
The Dingley Law of.........................	45.2%
The Payne-Aldrich Law of...................	52.5%
The Fordney-McCumber Law of..............	63.8%

Under the Underwood Law of 1913 disturbed conditions varied the free list from 60 per cent to 73 per cent averaging 66.3 per cent.

The increases in tariff are largely directed to the interest of the farmer. Of the increases, it is stated by the Tariff Commission that 93.73 per cent are upon products of agricultural origin measured in value, as distinguished from 6.25 per cent upon commodities of strictly non-agricultural origin. The average rate upon agricultural raw materials shows an increase from 38.10 per cent to 48.92 per cent in contrast to dutiable articles of strictly other than agricultural origin which show an average increase of from 31.02 per cent to 34.31 per cent. Compensatory duties have necessarily been given on products manufactured from agricultural raw materials and protective rates added to these in some instances.

The extent of rate revision as indicated by the Tariff Commission is that in value of the total imports the duties upon approximately 22.5 per cent have been increased, and 77.5 per cent were untouched or decreased. By number of the dutiable items mentioned in the bill, out of the total of about 3,300 there were about 890 increased, 235 decreased, and 2,170 untouched. The number of items increased was, therefore, 27 per cent of all dutiable items, and compares with 83 per cent of the number of items which were increased in the 1922 revision.

This tariff law is like all other tariff legislation, whether framed primarily upon a protective or a revenue basis. It contains many compromises between sectional interests and between different industries. No tariff bill has ever been enacted or ever will be enacted under the present system, that will be perfect. A large portion of the items are always adjusted with good judgment, but it is bound to contain some inequalities and inequitable compromises. There are items upon which duties will prove too high and others upon which duties will prove to be too low.

Certainly no President, with his other duties, can pretend to make that exhaustive determination of the complex facts which surround each of those 3,300 items, and which has required the attention of hundreds of men in Congress for nearly a year and a third. That responsibility must rest upon the Congress in a legislative rate revision.

On the administrative side I have insisted, however, that there should be created a new basis for the flexible tariff and it has been incorporated in this law. Thereby the means are established for objective and judicial review of these rates upon principles laid down by the Congress, free from pressures inherent in legislative action. Thus, the outstanding step of this tariff legislation has been the reorganization of the largely inoperative flexible provision of 1922 into a form which should render it possible to secure prompt and scientific adjustment of serious inequities and inequalities which may prove to have been incorporated in the bill.

This new provision has even a larger importance. If a perfect tariff bill were enacted today, the increased rapidity of economic change and the constant shifting of our relations to industries abroad will create a continuous stream of items which would work hardship upon some segment of the American people except for the provision of this relief. Without a workable flexible provision we would require even more frequent Congressional tariff revision than during the past. With it the country should be freed from further general revision for many years to come. Congressional revisions are not only disturbing to business but with all their necessary collateral surroundings in lobbies, logrolling, and the activities of group interests, are disturbing to public confidence.

Under the old flexible provisions, the task of adjustment was imposed directly upon the President, and the limitations in the law which circumscribed it were such that action was long delayed and it was largely inoperative, although important benefits were brought to the dairying, flax, glass, and other industries through it.

The new flexible provision established the responsibility for revisions upon a reorganized tariff commission, composed of members equally of both parties as a definite rate-making body acting through semi-judicial methods of open hearings and investigations by which items can be taken up one by one upon direction or upon application of aggrieved parties. Recommendations are to be made to the President, he being given authority to promulgate or veto the conclusions of the commission. Such revision can be accomplished without disturbance to business, as they concern but one item at a time, and the principles laid down assure a protective basis. . . .

. . . It is urgent that the uncertainties in the business world which have been added to by the long-extended debate of the measure should be ended. They can be ended only by completion of this bill. Meritorious demands for further protection to agriculture and labor which have developed since the tariff of 1922 would not end if this bill fails of enactment. Agitation for legislative tariff revision would necessarily continue before the country. Nothing would contribute to retard business recovery more than this continued agitation.

As I have said, I do not assume the rate structure in this or any other tariff bill is perfect, but I am convinced that the disposal of the whole question is urgent. I believe that the flexible provisions can within reasonable time remedy inequalities; that this provision is a progressive advance and gives great hope of taking the tariff away from politics, lobbying, and logrolling; that the bill gives protection to agriculture for the market of its products and to several industries in need of such protection for the wage of their labor; that with returning normal conditions our foreign trade will continue to expand.

The subsequent history of the flexible tariff in the Hoover Administration was that 250 industrial items were reviewed upon request by the commission, and the rates changed in about seventy-five of these items.

June 21, 1930: Democratic leaders continued the attack on the Tariff Bill and the President, although they had voted for increases and against decreases on hundreds of the items.

June 23, 1930: Recently there had passed the House a bill amending the World War Veterans' Act. The Director of the Veterans' Bureau had advised the President that if the bill became law it would involve an immediate additional annual expenditure of $181,000,000 with a growing maximum annual outlay which would ultimately reach $400,000,000. The Senate amended the bill, but as amended it involved an increase in expenditures of over $100,000,000 the first year, and an increase annually thereafter until it would ultimately reach $225,000,000. Equally objectionable with the added cost were the inequalities, discriminations, and injustices which the bill created among the veterans. In many cases service men of substantial overseas service and with disabilities received in combat would receive less money than others with brief service in this country, and whose disabilities did not appear until several years after discharge. The presumptive period date for non-service connected disabilities was advanced from January 1, 1925, to January 1, 1930. Furthermore, the list of these presumptive disabilities was greatly enlarged. The President made an earnest effort further to modify the bill but without success.

June 26, 1930: The President vetoed the Veterans' Bill. The House upheld the veto. His message was as follows: [20]

To the House of Representatives:

I am returning herewith House Bill 10381 without approval.

One of the most repugnant tasks which can fall to this office is to disapprove of measures intended to benefit our sick or disabled men who have served our country in war. Perhaps as much as any other person, I have full realization of the task, the hardships, and the dangers to which the nation ordered its sons. In sentiment and in sympathy I should desire no greater satisfaction than to support just measures which are proposed for their benefit. But I want a square deal between veterans; not unjust discriminations between special groups, and I do not want wasteful or unnecessary expenditures.

The country already generously provides for the 280,000 men whose health or earning power is shown to have been impaired by their service in the war and for 91,000 dependents of the men who suffered or died. That is and should be a first charge upon the nation.

[20] State Papers, Vol. I, p. 323.

This measure except for a small part adds nothing to aid of veterans wounded or disabled in the war. It is a radical departure from our full commitment to provide compensation to men for war disability into the field of pensions to men who have incurred disabilities as the incident of civil life since the war and having no valid relation to their military service. It provides that in respect to veterans who between the years 1925 and 1930 shall have become afflicted with any one of an extensive category of diseases and thus disabled, there is established a "presumption" that these diseases originated from their service, and that they should be "compensated" or pensioned upon the basis of men who suffered as the result of actual military service. This provision would give war disability benefits to from 75,000 to 100,000 men who were not disabled as the result of war. In other words, the bill purports to establish that men who have enjoyed good health for a minimum of seven years (from 1918 to 1925) since the war, or a maximum of twelve years (to 1930) and who have then become afflicted, have received such affliction from their war service.

I am informed by the Director of the Veterans' Bureau that the medical council of the bureau, consisting of most eminent physicians and surgeons, supported by the whole experience of the bureau, agree conclusively that this legal "presumption" that affliction from diseases mentioned in the bill between 1925 and 1930, is not a physical possibility and that the presumption constitutes a wholly false and fictitious basis for legislation in veterans' aid. This is confirmed by a recent resolution of so eminent a body as the American Medical Association.

The spectacle of the government practicing subterfuge in order to say that what did not happen in the war did happen in the war, impairs the integrity of government, reduces the respect for government, and undermines the morale of all the people.

The practical effects of this enactment of a fictitious "presumption" into law are widespread. It creates a long train of injustices and inequalities. The first is to place men of this class who have in fact been disabled in civil life since the war upon the same basis as the men who were wounded in battle and suffered the exposures of the trenches. But a second injustice immediately arises. The Veterans' Bureau estimates that there are somewhere in the neighborhood of 380,000 possible cases of disability incurred in civil life since the war amongst the 4,300,000 living veterans. By this legislation all except somewhere between 75,000 and 100,000 of these men are excluded from this aid by the government except for benefits which they already receive by hospitalization, the bonus, and insurance. This bill would, therefore, create a preferred group of one third among the men who are suffering from disabilities incurred in civil life since the war.

The further injustice of this bill may become more apparent when it is realized that men who were enrolled in the army who remained but comparatively a few days or weeks in service, without ever leaving their home States, will receive aid upon the same basis as those men who passed through the battle of the Argonne. They may come upon the

THE SEVENTY-FIRST CONGRESS 443

government payroll for life in case of total disability at rates from $80 to $200 per month. Beyond this, again, under the provisions of this bill as it affects the existing law, many thousands of men who have in fact incurred their disabilities in civil life may receive larger allowances from the government than the men actually wounded at the front. . . .

This bill departs from the traditional basis upon which we have given support to the veterans of the Civil and Spanish wars. We have always recognized the principle in that legislation that the veterans of less than ninety days' service, unless they have a disability incurred in line of duty, should be excluded from benefits, because such men have not been called to actual war service. Recently in the Spanish War Veterans' Bill, against my protest, this was reduced to seventy days, but in the bill we are here considering there is no requirement whatever of service, and a man with one day's service after enrollment is entitled to all of the benefits. Here we create at once an injustice between veterans of different wars and between men whose lives were endangered and those who incurred no risks.

There is no provision in this bill against men of independent means claiming benefits from the government for these disabilities arising in civil life. Surely it is of vital importance to the taxpayers, who, directly or indirectly, include all veterans themselves, that they shall not be called upon to contribute to such men of independent means. . . .

. . . This bill contemplates compensation for some misconduct disabilities, the whole conception of which must be repugnant to decent family life.

No government can proceed with intelligence that does not take into account the fiscal effects of its actions. The bill in a wasteful and extravagant manner goes far beyond the financial necessities of the situation. General Hines, after renewed examination, reports that this bill as finally passed will cost $110,000,000 the first year; that this will increase to an annual burden of $235,000,000, and continue during the life of these veterans. . . .

These costs are beyond the capacity of the government at the present time without increased taxation. They are larger than the veterans have themselves proposed. . . .

Even if I were able to overlook these burdens, for monetary considerations are indeed secondary, I cannot overlook the discriminations and injustices which this legislation creates, together with its failure to meet the real need that exists today among our veterans in a fundamental and sound manner.

June 26, 1930: It was apparent before the action by the House that a veto would not be sustained unless the President could persuade a substantial portion of the members of his party in the House to accept a substitute. With this in mind the President had been in conference with leaders of the majority in the House. They had come to an agreement on the terms of a World War Veterans' Bill which provided allowances for substantial disabilities incurred in civil life and without discrimination as to those disabilities and the veterans incurring them. That it met a real need among veterans could not be questioned. In this way the very objectionable features of the original legislation were eliminated. Incidentally this more just legislation cost one third of the amount in the bill which was vetoed.

June 27, 1930: As a result of conferences between the President, members of the Cabinet, and Congressional leaders, Congress passed and the President approved a resolution (Pub. Res. No. 98, 71 Congress) authorizing the creation of a commission to study the advisability of amending the Constitution so as to remove the profits from war and to equalize its burden on all citizens. The commission was to be composed of four members each, from the House and the Senate, and six members from the Cabinet.

This War Policies Commission consisted of the Secretaries of War (chairman), Navy, Agriculture, Commerce, and Labor, and the Attorney-General with Senators David Reed, Arthur H. Vandenberg, J. T. Robinson, Claude Swanson, and Representatives L. H. Hadley, William P. Holaday, Ross Collins and John L. McSwain. The Congressional members had had many years of experience in the handling of legislation and appropriations pertaining to our army and navy. The commission considered many plans, including that of Mr. Bernard M. Baruch, and later brought in a full report with recommendations which the President transmitted to Congress March 7, 1932. Legislation was necessary to put the recommendations into effect. Congress took no action upon them.

The Senate cut out of the appropriation bill the funds for the support of the Wickersham Commission on Law Observance and Enforcement. The amount requested was $100,000. The President commented publicly: [21]

> This deleted part of the appropriation is that devoted to investigation into the cause and remedy for crime in general and for the determination of the reform needed in our judicial and administrative machinery....
> ... With growing crime of all kinds and with insistent recommendations from every bar association and public body concerned that we should have an accurate study of the reforms necessary in our whole judicial and administrative machinery, that we should have some constructive program for decrease and control of crime as a whole, I cannot abandon

[21] State Papers, Vol. I, p. 344.

the question for one moment or allow the work of this Commission to cease. I have asked the Commission to proceed with its full program of work and it has consented to do so.

June 30, 1930: The President signed the bill creating the new Federal Power Commission. The old commission was a more or less nominal body, and had consisted of three Cabinet members who were too busy with the duties of their departments to give the necessary personal time to undertake power regulation. Congress refused to follow the request of the President and grant to the commission the authority over interstate power rates, and the accounting and financing of companies engaged in interstate power distributions.

The new commission merely succeeded to the very limited authority given the old commission in the Federal Waterpower Act which was passed in 1920. Briefly the authority was restricted to investigating and reporting on water resources and power projects and the granting of licenses for constructing and operating power projects in navigable waters and on government lands.

The President was indignant at the action of the radical members of Congress in granting only a part of the powers requested. Their ultimate objective, of course, was government operation. They apparently opposed adequate control of private enterprise in the hope that rising public resentment over unjust rates by some greedy corporations would enable them to win their issue. This raised the whole question of private enterprise under regulation versus government ownership and operation, or State socialism.

July 3, 1930: Congress adjourned, the Senate finally had given way to the President's demands on veterans' legislation. Congress had been in practically continuous session for more than a year—since April, 1929.

Within thirty days of the opening the Progressives had formed a coalition with the Democrats against the President and thus reduced the Administration's supporters in the Senate to a minority. With the splendid co-operation of the House and not quite a majority of Republicans in the Senate, reinforced from time to time by occasional Democrats and Progressives, whenever a specific question appealed to them, a large amount of constructive legislation was passed.

The work of the session, aside from the appropriation and other routine bills, included the passage of the Agricultural Marketing Act with the establishment of the Federal Farm Board and the regulation of market practices in agricultural perishables; provided for Congressional re-apportionment; the revision of the tariff, including the flexible provisions, and a reorganization of the Tariff Commission. Also included were the establishment of the Federal Power Commission; the reform of parole and probation and Federal prisons; the establishment of a Federal Criminal Identification Service; the consolidation of prohibition enforcement activities; the organization of a narcotics bureau; the expansion of veterans' hospitals; the establishment of disability allowances to disabled veterans; the consolidation of all veterans' services; the organization into a definite plan of rivers and harbors improvements; a substantial increase in Federal highways; the enlargement of the public buildings construction in the program of the government for housing itself throughout the country; the ratifications of the London Naval Treaty; the reform of airmail services; the defeat of the "Export Debenture Plan," and of unjust and extravagant legislation for veterans.

Moreover, systematic inquiries had been authorized and were in progress looking to important reforms in judicial procedure and law enforcement; in conservation of the public domain; and in the reclamation service. The Senate Committee on Banking and Finance had heeded the President's recommendation and started an inquiry into the banking system. The only substantial failure was in the regulation of interstate electric power.

July 7, 1930: Work was started on the Colorado River Dam.

July 8, 1930: The President issued an executive order consolidating the old Pensions Bureau, the World War Veterans' Bureau, and the National Homes for Disabled Volunteer Soldiers' Bureau (each previously under a separate department of the government) into one independent agency, to be called the Veterans' Administration. General Frank T. Hines was appointed Administrator of Veterans' Affairs. Increased efficiency and a saving of about $10,000,000 a year in administration resulted. Some months before the President had signed a bill which provided nineteen more hospitals for the use of veterans.

July 9, 1930: The President today announced the names of the temporary Advisory Committee which was to study policies both of the merits of rival bids to the Shipping Board for trans-Atlantic services and of the character of ships proposed to be built through government construction loans. Questions had been raised involving the future of the merchant marine and the actions of the Shipping Board, and the President felt that an independent report by a fact-finding committee of outstanding men would be advantageous. The men appointed were Ira A. Campbell, New York; H. G. Dalton, Cleveland; Edward N. Hurley, Chicago; George B. Jackson, Baltimore; and Clarence M. Woolley,

New York. As a result of the committee's report, the policies of the Shipping Board later were changed.

July 29, 1930: The President having in view the reform of the bankruptcy laws, stated to the press:[22]

I have authorized the Attorney-General to undertake an exhaustive investigation into the whole question of bankruptcy law and practice. It will be a most extensive and vigorous investigation. The work will be under the direction of the Solicitor-General and he will be assisted by the Department of Commerce. . . . The purpose of the investigation is, of course, to propose to Congress some essential reforms in the bankruptcy law and practice.

The desire of the President to procure facts before making a decision led him to utilize almost daily the various government statistical agencies. He desired to improve the service and stated:[23]

I am today appointing a committee to advise the government departments on methods for revision of the statistical services for the determination of unemployment. . . .

The question is not as simple as it appears on the surface. . . . The amount of unemployment in the census taken April 1st gives us for the first time an accurate base on which to formulate plans and a knowledge of the whole problem which we have never hitherto possessed. But if we were to attempt such an absolutely accurate determination of employment once every three months it would require a house to house canvass of the entire nation and would cost us ten or fifteen million dollars per annum. On the other hand it has been long recognized that the present Department of Labor statistics are inadequate. . . .

August 1, 1930: The President today announced a White House Conference on Home Building and Home Ownership. He stated:[24]

After wide consultation with interested leaders I have decided to undertake the organization of an adequate investigation and study on a nation-wide scale of the problems presented in home ownership and home building, with the view to the development of a better understanding of the questions involved and the hope of inspiring better organization and removal of influences which seriously limit the spread of home ownership, both town and country.

The conference will be organized by a Planning Committee comprised of representatives of the leading national groups interested in this field. . . .

The conference will deal with the whole broad question of home

[22] State Papers, Vol. I, p. 361.   [23] State Papers, Vol. I, p. 360.
[24] State Papers, Vol. I, p. 362.

construction and home ownership. It will embrace such questions as finance, design, equipment, city planning, transportation, etc. . . .

The finance question, however, is only one of many. Greater comfort and reduction in cost of construction in many parts of the country through improved design, the better layout of residential areas are all of first importance. The expansion and betterment of homes in their bearing upon comfort, increasing standards of living, and economic and social stability, are of outstanding importance.

The Planning Committee of the conference comprised Secretary of Commerce Lamont, chairman; John M. Gries, Chief of the Division of Building and Housing Department of Commerce, executive secretary; and the heads of the following associations—

>American Civic Association
>American Farm Bureau Federation
>American Federation of Labor
>American Home Economics Association
>American Institute of Architects
>Association of General Contractors
>Association of Life Insurance Presidents
>Better Homes in America
>Chamber of Commerce of the United States
>General Federation of Women's Clubs
>National Association of Builders' Exchanges
>National Association of Real Estate Boards
>National Congress of Parents and Teachers
>National Farmers' Union
>National Grange
>Russell Sage Foundation
>Savings Bank Division—American Bankers' Association
>United States League of Building and Loan Associations
>Women's National Farm and Garden Association

This committee was engaged in exhaustive investigation of housing conditions, financial and other methods for extension of home building and home ownership. Its expenses were paid by private subscription and it cost the government nothing. It completed its work with the passage of the Home Loan Bank Bill.

August 6, 1930: The President asked for and issued to the public a report by Secretary of the Interior Wilbur and Commissioner of Indian Affairs Rhoads on the plans and progress of reorganization of the work pertaining to American Indians, looking "towards making the

THE SEVENTY-FIRST CONGRESS 449

Indians self-supporting and self-respecting American citizens. The Indian was to be no longer viewed as a ward of the nation but as a potential citizen." The protection to the Indians from exploitation was greatly extended; educational and health services improved; and other notable advances made in their development.

August 12, 1930: The President announced the successful completion of the work of the commission he had appointed August 13, 1929 to find a solution for the San Francisco-Oakland Bridge problem. While Secretary of Commerce he had endeavored unsuccessfully to compose the differences between the army and navy on the one hand and the local authorities of San Francisco and Oakland on the other. The municipalities were in great need of a bridge and at a convenient and serviceable location. The army and navy were charged with responsibility for the national defense. For years they had opposed the erection of any bridge, although it was entirely possible to meet the needs of defense. After becoming President, Mr. Hoover issued instructions to the governmental agencies to come to an understanding. They did. The commission comprised: Mark L. Requa, chairman; George T. Cameron, vice chairman; Rear-Admiral L. E. Gregory and W. H. Stanley, General G. B. Pillsbury, Colonel E. C. Daley, State Senator Arthur H. Breed, Professor Charles D. Marx and C. H. Purcell. The commission first met on October 7, 1929, and brought in an unanimous report on August 6, 1930. This report was the result of the first real open-minded, comprehensive engineering survey made upon the subject. The commission recommended the Rincon Hill-Goat Island location. The army and navy officers were in frequent conference with the President whose tact and knowledge of the situation finally overcame their opposition. This bridge constitutes the greatest engineering undertaking of its kind, and to the commission is due a great measure of gratitude from the communities served. The President issued a statement reviewing the matter, as follows:[25]

> After several years of delay in settlement of a site for a much needed bridge across San Francisco Bay, due to disagreements between the naval authorities, the army engineers, the municipal and State authorities, the commission, representing all of these agencies, under the chairmanship of Mr. Mark L. Requa, has now come to unanimous agreement, and appears to have found a solution which has commended itself in all directions, and a much needed improvement may now be carried forward. The bridge will be constructed by local authorities. It involves no participation by the Federal Government other than the granting of certain rights of way.

[25] State Papers, Vol. I, p. 367.

It should be added that in 1932, at the suggestion of the President, the bridge authority applied to the Reconstruction Finance Corporation to furnish the capital with which to construct the bridge—the largest in the world. The request was granted.

August 15, 1930: The President was in conference with the four heads of government aviation, Assistant Secretary of War Trubee Davison, Assistant Secretary of the Navy David Ingalls, Assistant Secretary of Commerce Clarence Young, and Warren Irving Glover, Second Assistant Postmaster-General, together with Colonel Charles A. Lindbergh. They spent two days at the Rapidan Camp, in discussion of methods for the encouragement of commercial aviation and also its adaptation to our national defense.

August 23, 1930: The President named Henry P. Fletcher, Pennsylvania, chairman, and later appointed Edgar Brossard, Utah; John Lee Coulter, North Dakota; Lincoln Dixon, Indiana; Alfred P. Dennis, Maryland; and Thomas Walker Page, Virginia, members of the new Tariff Commission. Brossard, Dixon and Dennis had been members of the old commission. Page had served on the Tariff Commission some years previous by appointment from President Wilson.

September 24, 1930: The President met with the Planning Committee, which he had appointed to prepare for the National Conference on Home Building and Home Ownership. He said:[20]

... I would not have asked you to come if I had not felt deeply that there was a real need. For some years the business community, our municipalities, and great numbers of associations devoted to the promotion of public welfare, have interested themselves in the problems of more adequate housing and home ownership. I will say at once that we have a larger proportion of adequate housing than any country in the world, but we still lag far behind our national ideals of homes for all our people. ...

Adequate housing goes to the very roots of the well-being of the family, and the family is the social unit of the nation. It is more than comfort that is involved, it has important aspects of health and morals and education and the provision of a fair chance for growing childhood. ...

The finance of home building ... is the most backward segment of our whole credit system. It is easier to borrow 85 per cent on an automobile and repay it on the installment plan than to buy a home on that basis. ... Part of the difficulty lies in inadequate financial organization and part of it you will find in obsolete laws.

There are other important phases of the problem beyond the financing. ... The problem of creating real and systematic home areas adjacent

[20] State Papers, Vol. I, p. 372.

to industry and to our cities which can be safeguarded from commercial invasion and destruction needs exhaustive consideration.... Such a question at once raises large problems of city and industrial planning.... The automobile has made such communities far more practical than ever before.

I am in hopes you can find the time and organization to go even farther afield than individual home ownership into this whole question of housing. This will at once carry you into the apartment and rural fields as well....

October 7, 1930: The President at the one hundred and fiftieth anniversary of the Battle of Kings' Mountain spoke upon the growth of human liberty. He said:[27]

... My friends, I have lived among many peoples and have observed many governments. Each has its own institutions and its own ideals, its own spirit. Many of them I have learned to respect and to admire. It is from these contrasts and these experiences that I wish to speak today—to speak upon the institutions, the ideals, upon the spirit of America.

In the time since the Battle of Kings' Mountain was fought our country has marched from those struggling colonies on the Atlantic seaboard to the full sweep of the Pacific. It has grown from fewer than 3,000,000 people to more than 120,000,000. But far more inspiring than its growth of numbers has been the unfolding of a great experiment in human society. Within this land there have been builded new and powerful institutions designed of new ideas and new ideals in a new vision of human relations. Through them we have attained a wider diffusion of liberty and of happiness and of material things than humanity has ever known before. Our people live in a stronger security from enemies abroad and in greater comfort at home than has ever before been the fortune of a nation. We are filled with justifiable pride in the valor, the inventions, the contributions to art and literature, the moral influence of our people. We glow with satisfaction at the multitude of activities in the nation, the State, the local community, which spread benefits and blessings amongst us. We may be proud of our vast economic development over these 150 years, which has secured to the common man greater returns for his effort and greater opportunity for his future than exist in any other place on the earth.

In the large sense we have maintained open the channels of opportunity, constantly refreshing the leadership of the nation by men of lowly beginnings. We have no class or caste or aristocracy whose privilege limits the hopes and opportunities of our people. Science and education have been spread until they are the universal tools of the common man. They have brought to him the touch of a thousand finer things of life. They have enlarged the horizon of our vision into the inspiring works of God.

[27] State Papers, Vol. I, p. 395.

This unparalleled rise of the American man and woman was not alone the result of riches in lands or forests or mines; it sprang from ideas and ideals, which liberated the mind and stimulated the exertion of a people. There were other parts of the world even more easily accessible to new invasion by man, whose natural resources were as great as those of the United States, yet their history over this 150 years presents no achievement parallel to the mighty march of the United States. But the deadening poverty of other lands was in the absence of the stirring ideas and ideals which have lightened the path of the whole American people. A score of nations have borrowed our philosophy from us, and they have tempered the course of history in yet a score of others; all have prospered under them.

These ideas and these ideals were in the hearts and inspired the souls of the men who fought the Battle of Kings' Mountain. They had spurred the migration of their fathers from the persecutions and restricted opportunities of Europe, had been sustained by their religious faith, and had been developed in their conflict with the wilderness, and had become the spirit of the American people, demanding for man a larger mastership of his own destiny. Our forefathers formulated them through the Declaration and the Constitution into a new and practical political and social system unique in the world. Devoted generations have secured them to us.

It is never amiss for us to review these principles, that we uphold our faith in them, that we search our fidelity to them, that by stretch of our vision over the vast pageant of our accomplishment we should gain courage to meet the difficulties of the day.

Our political system was a revolt from dictatorship, whether by individuals or classes. It was founded upon the conception that freedom was inalienable, and that liberty and freedom should rest upon law, and that law should spring from the expressed wisdom of the representatives of the majority of the people themselves. This self-government was not in itself a new human ideal, but the Constitution which provided its framework, with the checks and balances which gave it stability, was of marvelous genius. Yet of vastly more importance than even the machinery of government was the inspired charter of the rights of men which it guaranteed. Under them we hold that all men are created equal, that they are equal before the law, and that they should be safeguarded in liberty and, as we express it, latterly, in equality of opportunity to every individual that he may achieve for himself and for the community the best to which his character, his ability, and his ambition entitle him.

No student of American history can fail to realize that these principles and ideals grew largely out of the religious origins and spiritual aspirations of our people. From them spring at once the demand for free and universal education, that the door of opportunity and the ladder to leadership should be free for every new generation, to every boy and girl. It is these human rights and the success of government which has maintained them that have stimulated the initiative and effort in each individual, the sum of which has been the gigantic achievement of the nation. They are the precious heritage of America, far more important, far more valuable, than all the riches in land and mines and factories that we possess. Never had these principles and ideals been assembled elsewhere and combined into government. This is the American system.

We have lived and breathed it. We have seldom tried even to name it. Perhaps we might well abandon efforts to define it—for things of the spirit can be little defined. Some have called it liberalism, but that term has become corrupted by political use. Some have called it individualism, but it is not an individualism which permits men to over-ride the equal opportunity of others. By its enemies it has been called capitalism, and yet under its ideals capital is but an instrument, not a master. Some have called it democracy yet democracy exists elsewhere under social ideals which do not embrace equality of opportunity.

Ours is a system unique with America—an expression of the spirit and environment of our people—it is just American.

Parallel with us, other philosophies of society and government have continued or developed and new ones have come into the world, born of the spirit of other peoples and other environments. It is a function of freedom that we should search their claims with open mind, but it is a function of common sense that we should reject them the moment they fail in the test. From experiences in many lands I have sometimes compared some of these systems to a race. In the American system, through free and universal education, we train the runners, we strive to give to them an equal start, our government is the umpire of its fairness. The winner is he who shows the most conscientious training, the greatest ability, the strongest character. Socialism or its violent brother, Bolshevism, would compel all the runners to end the race equally; it would hold the swiftest to the speed of the most backward. Anarchy would provide neither training nor umpire. Despotism or class government picks those who run and also those who win.

Whatever the merits or demerits of these other systems may be, they all mean the destruction of the driving force of equal opportunity, and they mean the destruction of our Constitution, for our political framework would serve none of them and many of its fundamental provisions are the negation of them. They mean the abandonment of the nation's spiritual heritage.

It is significant that some of these systems deny religion and seek to expel it. I cannot conceive of a wholesome social order or a sound economic system that does not have its roots in religious faith. No blind materialism can for long engage the loyalties of mankind. Economic aspiration, though it strongly marks the American system, is not an end in itself, but is only one of many instruments to accomplish the profound purposes of the American people, which are largely religious in origin. This country is supremely dedicated, not to the pursuit of material riches, but to pursuit of a richer life for the individual.

It would be foolish for me to stand here and say that our political and social system works perfectly. It does not. The human race is not perfect yet. There are disheartening occurrences every hour of the day.

There are always malevolent or selfish forces at work which, unchecked, would destroy the very basis of our American life. These forces of destruction vary from generation to generation; and if we would hand on our great inheritance to our children, we must successfully contend with them.

While we cannot permit any foreign person or agency to undermine our institutions, yet we must look to our own conduct that we do not by our own failure to uphold and safeguard the true spirit of America weaken our own institutions and destroy the very forces which upbuild our national greatness. It is in our own house that our real dangers lie, and it is there that we have need to summon our highest wisdom and our highest sense of public service.

We must keep corruptive influences from the nation.... Crime and disobedience of law are the very incarnation of destruction to a system whose basis is law. Both pacifism and militarism court danger from abroad, the one by promoting weakness, the other by promoting arrogance. Failure of many of our citizens to express their opinions at the ballot box is at once their abandonment of the whole basis of self-government. Manipulation of the ballot is a denial of government by the people. Corruption or even failure of moral perceptions in public office defiles the whole spirit of America. Mere destructive criticism destroys leadership and substitutes weaklings.

Any practice of business which would dominate the country by its own selfish interests is a destruction of equality of opportunity. Government in business, except in emergency, is also a destruction of equal opportunity and the incarnation of tyranny through bureaucracy. Tendencies of communities and States to shirk their own responsibilities or to unload them upon the Federal Government, or of the Federal Government to encroach upon the responsibilities of the States, are destructive of our whole pattern of self-government. But these evils cannot shatter our ideals or subvert our institutions if we hold the faith. The knowledge of danger is a large part of its conquest.

It is the first duty of those of us who believe in the American system to maintain a knowledge of and a pride in it, not particularly because we need fear those foreign systems, but because we have need to sustain ours in purity and in strength....

... We shall not have full equality of opportunity until we have attained that ultimate goal of every right-thinking citizen—the abolition of poverty of mind and home....

... The world about us is tormented with the spiritual and economic struggles that attend changing ideals and systems. Old faiths are being shaken. But we must follow our own destiny. Our institutions are a growth. They come out of our history as a people. Our ideals are a binding spiritual heritage. We cannot abandon them without chaos. We can follow them with confidence.

Our problems are the problems of growth. They are not the problems of decay. They are less difficult than those which confronted generations before us. The forces of righteousness and wisdom work as powerfully in our generation as in theirs. The flame of freedom burns as brightly in every American heart. There need be no fear for the future of a Republic that seeks inspiration from the spirit of the men who fought at the Battle of Kings' Mountain.

November 5, 1930: The Congressional election resulted in a change in the complexion of the House and Senate highly favorable to the opposition, giving it an increased majority in the Senate and reversing the Republican majority in the House to a minority. The election did not affect the short session to follow, as the new members did not take their seats until a year later.

November 9, 1930: Speaking over the radio from Washington to the dinner given by the Heinz Company in honor of its employees throughout the world, the President, after complimenting Mr. Heinz's long record of public service, said:

. . . The anniversary of an establishment which has a record of over 60 years of continued industrial peace . . . [is] proof that there is common ground of mutual interest and humane relations between employer and employee. . . . Mechanization is so distinctive of our modern civilization that even as a mechanical conception we often tend to forget that the most wonderful and powerful machine in the world is the men and women themselves. It is the human being from which achievement is won far more than the tool. . . . Man's conquest of machines is less spectacular than his conquest of his own will. . . . Wars between nations, wars between groups within nations, industrial conflicts, all end in what appears to be victory for one of the contenders, but the real victory arrives only after the battle has been forgotten and when the human nature on both sides meets in cheerful agreement upon a common solution. . . . Industrial conflict is the greatest waste in industry. It not only delays production and diminishes it, but its most hurtful results are inflicted upon the lives and spirits of men. . . . Man learned the art of staying alive long before he learned the art of mechanics. . . . The machine must build him a better life, not alone in time of leisure but in joy of work, than he knew before.

November 15, 1930: In preparation for the forthcoming Child Conference, the White House issued a statement: [28]

The White House Conference on Child Health and Protection, beginning November 19, will, in the opinion of President Hoover, have laid before it the most complete survey ever undertaken in the United States covering all phases of the child problem. . . .

So far over 2,500 delegates have been appointed. A number of committees were appointed for research and investigation and now total over 1,200 members covering every field and phase of child problems.

[28] State Papers, Vol. I, p. 418.

The committees will be able to lay before this conference the most complete survey ever placed before this country on all questions relating to children's health and protection. . . .

President Hoover added: I do not think—I know—that there never has been so exhaustive an investigation and presentation of the subject as will be made at the conference.

November 18, 1930: The President, by an Executive order, extended the civil service or merit system to the appointment of employees of the District of Columbia. For the first time the appointment of these municipal employees was taken out of politics.

November 19, 1930: The President opened the White House Conference, saying:[29]

Something more than a year ago I called together a small group of representative men and women to take the initial steps in organization of this Conference on Child Health and Protection. . . .

. . . You comprise the delegates appointed by our Federal departments and by the governors of our States, the mayors of our cities, and the representatives of our great national associations, our medical and public health professions. In your hands rest the knowledge and authority outside of the home itself.

We approach all problems of childhood with affection. Theirs is the province of joy and good humor. They are the most wholesome part of the race, the sweetest, for they are fresher from the hands of God. Whimsical, ingenious, mischievous, we live a life of apprehension as to what their opinion may be of us; a life of defense against their terrifying energy; we put them to bed with a sense of relief and a lingering of devotion. We envy them the freshness of adventure and discovery of life; we mourn over the disappointments they will meet.

The fundamental purpose of this conference is to set forth an understanding of those safeguards which will assure to them health in mind and body. There are safeguards and services to childhood which can be provided by the community, the State, or the nation—all of which are beyond the reach of the individual parent. We approach these problems in no spirit of diminishing the responsibilities and values or invading the sanctities of those primary safeguards to child life—their homes and their mothers. After we have determined every scientific fact, after we have erected every public safeguard, after we have constructed every edifice for education or training or hospitalization or play, yet all these things are but a tithe of the physical, moral, and spiritual gifts which motherhood gives and home confers. None of these things carry that affection, that devotion of soul, which is the great endowment from mothers. Our purpose here today is to consider and give our mite of help to strengthen her hand that her boy and girl may have a fair chance. . . .

. . . Let no one believe that these are questions which should not stir a

[29] State Papers, Vol. I, p. 419.

nation; that they are below the dignity of statesmen or governments. If we could have but one generation of properly born, trained, educated, and healthy children, a thousand other problems of government would vanish. We would assure ourselves of healthier minds in more vigorous bodies to direct the energies of our nation to yet greater heights of achievement. Moreover, one good community nurse will save a dozen future policemen.

Our problem falls into three groups: First, the protection and stimulation of the normal child; second, aid to the physically defective and handicapped child; third, the problems of the delinquent child. . . .

But that we be not discouraged let us bear in mind that there are 35,000,000 reasonably normal, cheerful human electrons radiating joy and mischief and hope and faith. Their faces are turned toward the light—theirs is the life of great adventure. These are the vivid, romping, everyday children, our own and our neighbors' with all their strongly marked differences—and the more differences the better. The more they charge us with their separate problems the more we know they are vitally and humanly alive.

. . . And also, on the bright side, your reports show that we have 1,500,000 specially gifted children. There lies the future leadership of the nation if we devote ourselves to their guidance.

In the field of deficient and handicapped children, advancing knowledge and care can transfer them more and more to the happy lot of normal children. . . . We must not leave one of them uncared for.

There are also the complex problems of the delinquent child. We need to turn the methods of inquiry from the punishment of delinquency to the causes of delinquency. It is not the delinquent child that is at the bar of judgment, but society itself.

Again, there are the problems of the orphaned children. . . .

There are vast problems of education in relation to physical and mental health. . . . Our children all differ in character, in capacity, in inclination. If we would give them their full chance they must have that service in education which develops their special qualities. They must have vocational guidance.

Again, there are the problems of child labor. Industry must not rob our children of their rightful heritage. Any labor which stunts growth, either physical or mental, that limits education, that deprives children of the right comradeship, of joy, and play is sapping the next generation.

. . . Delinquency increases with congestion. Overcrowding produces disease and contagion. The child's natural play place is taken from him. . . .

Nor is our problem one solely of the city child. We have grave responsibilities to the rural child. Adequate expert service should be as available to him from maternity to maturity. . . .

These are a part of the problems that I charge you to answer. This task that you have come here to perform has never been done before. . . .

There has not been before the summation of knowledge and experience such as lies before this conference. There has been no period when it could be undertaken with so much experience and background. The nation looks to you to derive from it positive, definite, guiding judgments. . . .

May you who are meeting here find in your deliberations new fuel with which to light this flame of progress so that this occasion may be marked with a fresh luster that will set us anew on the road through the crowding complexities of modern life.

November 21, 1930: The conference concluded its deliberations with the adoption of the "Children's Charter." Its original was drafted by the President and it was put in final form by the conference. It was issued over his signature by request of the conference. This document was to have a powerful effect upon awakening the American people to the problems of childhood. It has been estimated that thirty millions of copies have been circulated by the press. And over a million copies were specially printed and distributed by various associations.

The conference completed its work as an investigating body with a series of special reports from the conference committees, which have been published and which form the foundation of our present knowledge of the problems. The investigations and reports represented an expenditure of $500,000 which the President secured from private sources.

The Charter reads:

THE CHILDREN'S CHARTER

President Hoover's White House Conference on Child Health and Protection, recognizing the rights of the child as the first rights of citizenship, pledges itself to these aims for the children of America.

I

For every child spiritual and moral training to help him to stand firm under the pressure of life.

II

For every child understanding and the guarding of his personality as his most precious right.

III

For every child a home and that love and security which a home provides; and for that child who must receive foster care, the nearest substitute for his own home.

IV

For every child full preparation for his birth, his mother receiving prenatal, natal and postnatal care; and the establishment of such protective measures as will make childbearing safer.

V

For every child health protection from birth through adolescence including: periodical health examinations and where needed, care of specialists and hospital treatment; regular dental examinations and care of the teeth; protective and preventive measures against communicable diseases; the insuring of pure food, pure milk and pure water.

VI

For every child from birth, through adolescence, promotion of health, including health instruction and a health program, wholesome physical and mental recreation, with teachers and leaders adequately trained.

VII

For every child a dwelling-place safe, sanitary, and wholesome, with reasonable provisions for privacy; free from conditions which tend to thwart his development; and a home environment harmonious and enriching.

VIII

For every child a school which is safe from hazards, sanitary, properly equipped, lighted, and ventilated. For younger children nursery schools and kindergartens to supplement home care.

IX

For every child a community which recognizes and plans for his needs, protects him against physical dangers, moral hazards and disease; provides him with safe and wholesome places for play and recreation; and makes provision for his cultural and social needs.

X

For every child an education which, through the discovery and development of his individual abilities, prepares him for life; and through training and vocational guidance prepares him for a living which will yield him the maximum of satisfaction.

XI

For every child such teaching and training as will prepare him for successful parenthood, homemaking, and the rights of citizenship; and, for parents, supplementary training to fit them to deal wisely with the problems of parenthood.

XII

For every child education for safety and protection against accidents to which modern conditions subject him—those to which he is directly exposed and those which, through loss or maiming of his parents, affect him indirectly.

XIII

For every child who is blind, deaf, crippled, or otherwise physically handicapped, and for the child who is mentally handicapped, such measures as will early discover and diagnose his handicap, provide care and treatment, and so train him that he may become an asset to society rather than a liability. Expenses of these services should be borne publicly where they cannot be privately met.

XIV

For every child who is in conflict with society the right to be dealt with intelligently as society's charge, not society's outcast; with the home, the school, the church, the court and the institution when needed, shaped to return him whenever possible to the normal stream of life.

XV

For every child the right to grow up in a family with an adequate standard of living and the security of a stable income as the surest safeguard against social handicaps.

XVI

For every child protection against labor that stunts growth either physical or mental, that limits education, that deprives children of the right of comradeship, of play, and of joy.

XVII

For every rural child a satisfactory schooling and health services as for the city child, and an extension to rural families of social, recreational, and cultural facilities.

XVIII

To supplement the home and the school in the training of youth, and to return to them those interests of which modern life tends to cheat children, every stimulation and encouragement should be given to the extension and development of the voluntary youth organizations.

XIX

To make everywhere available these minimum protections of the health and welfare of children, there should be a district, county, or community organization for health, education and welfare, with full-time officials, co-ordinating with a state-wide program which will be responsive to a nation-wide service of general information, statistics, and scientific research. This should include:

(a) Trained, full-time public health officials, with public health nurses, sanitary inspection and laboratory workers.
(b) Available hospital beds.

(c) Full-time public welfare service for the relief, aid and guidance of children, in special need due to poverty, misfortune or behavior difficulties, and for the protection of children from abuse, neglect, exploitation or moral hazard.

FOR EVERY CHILD THESE RIGHTS, REGARDLESS OF RACE, OR COLOR, OR SITUATION, WHEREVER HE MAY LIVE UNDER THE PROTECTION OF THE AMERICAN FLAG.

November 29, 1930: James J. Davis had been elected United States Senator from Pennsylvania. Mr. Davis had been Secretary of Labor under three Presidents. His resignation was submitted. The Secretary of Labor had been traditionally appointed from the ranks of organized labor. The coal miners and the Federation group had been favored in previous administrations. The President believed that the railway employees were deserving of the honor. He announced the appointment of William N. Doak. William Green, President of the American Federation of Labor, protested Mr. Doak's appointment because, though he was a member of the Brotherhood of Railway Trainmen, he was not a member of those unions under Mr. Green's supervision. The President felt it necessary to issue a public statement:

I do not feel that I can consent to the principle of debarment of the railway employees or other labor unions and associations or any labor man in the United States from the opportunities or aspiration to attain any office in this land. I have the highest respect for Mr. Green and the American Federation of Labor, but Mr. Green's enunciation that appointments must come from one organization in fact imposes upon me the duty to maintain the principle of open and equal opportunity and freedom in appointments to public office.

CHAPTER III

THE SHORT SESSION OF THE SEVENTY-FIRST CONGRESS AND THE FIRST SESSION OF THE SEVENTY-SECOND. THE CHECK UPON CONSTRUCTIVE LEGISLATION

DECEMBER, 1930–SEPTEMBER, 1932

THE Seventy-first Congress assembled on December 1, 1930, for the last and short session of that body. The session was largely concerned with relief matters, and the consideration of the annual appropriations. There was no constructive work of consequence.

December 2, 1930: The President sent his message to Congress. This message generally was confined to more urgent economic matters, as it was imperative that recovery of the country should not be disturbed by constant agitation. The introduction of important banking and other reform legislation at the last moment was likely to create situations which would only delay recovery.

In that part of his message to the Congress concerned with social reforms the President stated:[1]

> There is need for revision of our immigration laws upon a more selective basis, flexible to the needs of the country. . . . I urge the strengthening of our deportation laws so as to more fully rid ourselves of criminal aliens. . . .
>
> I urge further consideration by the Congress of the recommendations I made a year ago, looking to the development through temporary Federal aid of adequate State and local service for the health of children, and the further stamping out of communicable disease particularly in the rural sections. The advance of scientific discovery, methods, and social thought imposes a new vision in these matters. The drain upon the Federal Treasury is comparatively small. The results both economic and moral are of the utmost importance.

The President recommended the following economic reforms:

Electrical Power

I have in a previous message recommended effective regulation of interstate electrical power. Such regulation should preserve the independence and responsibility of the States.

[1] State Papers, Vol. I, p. 428, *et seq.*

Railways

We have determined upon a national policy of consolidation of the railways as a necessity of more stable and more economically operated transportation. Further legislation is necessary to facilitate such consolidation. In the public interest we should strengthen the railways that they may meet our future needs.

Antitrust Laws

I recommend that the Congress institute an inquiry into some aspects of the economic working of these laws. I do not favor repeal of the Sherman Act. The prevention of monopolies is of most vital public importance. Competition is not only the basis of protection to the consumer, but is the incentive to progress. However, the interpretation of these laws by the courts, the changes in business, especially in the economic effects upon those enterprises closely related to the use of the national resources of the country, make such an inquiry advisable. The producers of these materials assert that certain unfortunate results of wasteful and destructive use of these natural resources, together with a destructive competition which impoverishes both operator and worker, cannot be remedied because of the prohibitive interpretation of the antitrust laws. The well-known condition of the bituminous coal industry is an illustration. The people have a vital interest in the conservation of their natural resources; in the prevention of wasteful practices; in conditions of destructive competition which may impoverish the producer and the wage-earner; and they have an equal interest in maintaining adequate competition. I therefore suggest that an inquiry be directed especially to the effect of the workings of the antitrust laws in these particular fields, to determine if these evils can be remedied without sacrifice of the fundamental purpose of these laws.

Capital-Gains Tax

It is urged by many thoughtful citizens that the peculiar economic effect of the income tax on so-called capital gains at the present rate is to enhance speculative inflation, and likewise impede business recovery. I believe this to be the case and I recommend that a study be made of the economic effects of this tax, and of its relation to the general structure of our income tax law.

December 13, 1930: The President said in addressing the Gridiron Club:[2]

After the war all the great governments found themselves involved in a great dislocation in agriculture, industry, and labor, with great business activities on their hands which could not be instantly dissolved. In the dual necessity to tide millions of people over these dislocations and to deal with the businesses on hand, the governments everywhere were plunged into a continuation of this centralization of activities. They found them-

[2] State Papers, Vol. I, p. 469.

selves in the presence of disappearing altruism and rising self-interest. Their abilities at successful administration were correspondingly greatly diminished.

From the apparent success of governments in war dealing with great emergencies, there has grown up among our people the idea that the government is a separate entity, endowed with all power, all money, and all resources; that it can be called upon at any hour to settle any difficulty. As a result, there is constant pressure in the face of every problem for the increase of functions of the central government. Steadily, despite our efforts to free ourselves from these influences, the government is being loaded with responsibilities and becoming centralized beyond the ability of men to administer.

We have a vivid manifestation of these problems during the past year. Not an hour has gone by during this last year of depression when there has not been some demand, backed by some important influence, that we should take over more and more responsibilities and more and more functions from the citizens, the States, and municipalities in the hope of remedy to our immediate difficulties. I have considered that it is vital for the future of the American people that each community itself should be roused to the utmost in remedy of its own difficulties, and that the governments should be brought into action only where remedy was beyond local strength. To sustain the spirit of responsibility of States, of municipalities, of industry, and the community at large, is the one safeguard against overwhelming centralization and degeneration of that independence and initiative which are the very foundations of democracy.

The Federal Government can co-operate in assistance in disaster with community and industrial action, and the organization of local responsibility. The country has reason to be proud of the magnificent response of the past year to this stimulation. The nation is being rapidly organized today and, except for some special difficulties where the government must yet act, the people promise to carry their burden. Our people must not go hungry or cold. But no conceivable amount of appropriations from the Federal Treasury for public works can be any but a small per cent of the employment that is afforded by the courageous organizations of construction in industry itself and by our local governments. No doles of the Federal Government can equal, in even a minor per cent, the benefits to the wage-earner and the people at large by the organized maintenance of wage scales, and spreading part-time employment in place of the usual reductions in times of depression that we have witnessed during the last year. No proposal of charity by the government can equal a small part of the sums attained by the thousand earnest local committees now engaged in relief of distress in our counties and towns. I do not believe they will fail, and I believe that we shall again demonstrate the strength and devotion of our people to the fundamentals of our democracy.

Thus our problem is not only a question of prevention of hunger and cold, it is also a question of method by which we maintain local, individual responsibility in the American people to meet their own obligations at their own door, and to abolish the illusion that the Federal Government is a remedy for everything. It is for these high purposes that we must guide our policies so as to stimulate the forces of self-sufficiency of local independence in which lies the hope of our Republic.

December 27, 1930: The California Joint Federal and State Water Commission, appointed by the President and Governor Young, submitted its report. The report proposed a comprehensive basis for the development and conservation of California water supplies and defined the relations of Federal, State, and private action. It exerted a large influence in the plans for the development of the State.

January 10, 1931: The President, in July, 1930, had appointed Dr. George Otis Smith, for twenty years chief of the United States Geological Survey; Claude L. Draper, chairman of the Wyoming Public Utilities Commission; Colonel Marcel Garsaud, formerly chief engineer of the Port of New Orleans; Frank R. McNinch, of North Carolina, and Ralph B. Williamson, of Washington, to be members of the newly created Federal Power Commission. The Senate confirmed the appointments on December 20, 1930. The commission proceeded to remove from the staff left by the old commission, several subordinate officers, which action Senators Wheeler of Montana and Norris of Nebraska resented. On January 5th, 1931, the Senate, at the instance of these senators, sought to remove three of the newly appointed commissioners by recalling their confirmation. The President replied:

I cannot admit the power of the Senate to encroach upon the Executive functions by removal of a duly appointed executive officer under the guise of reconsideration of his nomination.

Also, after advising with the Attorney-General, and conferring with Senator Hebert of Rhode Island, he issued a public statement: [3]

I have today notified the Senate that I will not accede to their resolution. . . .

I am advised by the Attorney-General that these appointments were constitutionally made, are not subject to recall and that the request cannot be complied with by me. In any event, the objective of the Senate constitutes an attempt to dictate to an administrative agency upon the appointment of subordinates and an attempted invasion of the authority of the Executive. These, as President, I am bound to resist.

I cannot allow a false issue to be placed before the country. There is no issue for or against power companies.

It will be recalled that on my recommendation the Federal Power Commission was reorganized from the old basis of three Cabinet members, giving a small part of their time, to a full commission of five members, in

[3] State Papers, Vol. I, pp. 478, 479, 485.

order that adequate protection could be given to public interest in the water resources of the country, and that I further recommend that the commission should be given authority to regulate all interstate power rates. The law establishing the new commission became effective last June, although legislation giving it authority to regulate rates has not yet been enacted.

The resolutions of the Senate may have the attractive political merit of giving rise to a legend that those who voted for it are "enemies of the power interests," and, inferentially, those who voted against it are "friends of the power interests," and it may contain a hope of symbolizing me as the defender of power interests if I refuse to sacrifice three outstanding public servants, or to allow the Senate to dictate to an administrative board the appointment of its subordinates, and if I refuse to allow fundamental encroachment by the Senate upon the constitutional independence of the Executive. Upon these things the people will pass unerring judgment.

Much of the debate indicates plainly that those who favored this resolution are intent upon removing Messrs. Smith, Draper, and Garsaud, not because they are unqualified, but to insist upon the Senate's own selection of certain subordinates. Irrespective of the unique fitness of these commissioners for their positions, and before they have given a single decision in respect to any power company, they are to be removed unless they are willing to accept employees not of their choosing. It is not only the right but it is also the duty of the commission under the law to appoint its own employees. . . .

. . . The resolution raises the question of the independence of the Executive arm of the government in respect of the appointment and removal of executive officials. Many Presidents have had to meet this particular encroachment upon the Executive power in some form. Every one of them has repelled it, and every President has handed on this authority unimpaired. It reaches to the very fundamentals of independence and vigor of the Executive, whose power comes from the people alone, and the maintenance of which is vital to the protection of public interest and the integrity of the Constitution. . . .

I regret that the government should be absorbed upon such questions, as the action of the Power Commission in employment or non-employment of two subordinate officials at a time when the condition of the country requires every constructive energy.

Quo Warranto proceedings at once were started to obtain a judicial decision as to the legality of the appointments. These proceedings were expedited and reached the Supreme Court of the United States. Former United States Senator George Wharton Pepper appeared for George Otis Smith and supported the position of the President. John W. Davis, former Solicitor-General, appeared for the United States Senate. The court, in an opinion to be found in United States vs. Smith, 286 U. S., page 6, fully sustained the President's position.

January 14, 1931: The governors of many States having called State conferences upon Child Health and Protection to implement the work of the White House conference, the President today sent a message to Governor Leslie of Indiana for presentation to the Indiana meeting:[a]

MY DEAR GOVERNOR LESLIE:

I will be obliged if you will express my cordial greetings to the Indiana Conference on Child Health and Protection. . . . There is an especial reason for wishing to speak to this first of many State and regional groups who will carry forward the word of the White House conference. The conclusions of that conference, so far as they propose immediately practical measures in behalf of childhood, depend for their application chiefly upon the States and the local communities. The Federal Government can help with information and research, and toward the creation of administrative agencies and the funds to assist in support of them, but they rest primarily with States and counties, co-operating often with private agencies and dealing with the problem at close range and in the light of local conditions. The work in behalf of children is so intimately a part of the life of the people that its control and direction need to be kept very close to them. I look forward with high anticipation to the success of your conference.

Yours faithfully,
HERBERT HOOVER.

The follow-up program of the conference already had taken definite form in twenty-five States and the Territory of Hawaii. Other States were organizing their field-workers and many colleges were using the conference plans and findings. Parent-teacher associations and groups in the medical and health fields had adopted the charter. The material had been made available in books and programs for club work.

January 20, 1931: The President received the report on Prohibition of the Commission on Law Observance and Enforcement. In brief, the commission voted as a body against outright repeal; the restoration in any manner of the legalized saloon; the Federal or State governments entering into the liquor business; the modification of the National Prohibition Act for allowing the manufacture of light wines or beer as long as the Eighteenth Amendment was a part of the Constitution. It agreed that co-operation from the States was an essential element in enforcement. It found the current organization for enforcement was inadequate and recommended its strengthening, with increase in appropriations and improvement in the laws. The committee, as a whole, agreed that while the Eighteenth Amendment was the law of the land, it should be enforced.

Despite inherent conflict of views, all the members were agreed that if

[a] State Papers, Vol. I, p. 490.

the Amendment was revised, the regulation and prohibition of the manufacture, traffic, transportation, importation, and exportation of liquor should be a power resting with Congress. There was other conflict of views concerning the Eighteenth Amendment filed in separate reports by the individual members. Two of the commission were for its repeal, six for modification, four for further trial of enforcement.

The commission had a difficult task. It is to be regretted that there was lack of unanimity, and also a conflict between its recommendations and reasons, as well as its conclusions. However, the attitude and mind of the public at that time was not dissimilar.

January 21, 1931: Some newspapers having claimed that the President dictated the Wickersham report, the commission promptly issued an emphatic statement that this was "wholly without foundation . . . absolutely false."

January 23, 1931: As a partial correction of the grave injustice of the charges made by Attorney-General Daugherty of the Harding Administration against Benedict Crowell, Assistant Secretary of War in the Wilson Administration, the President today appointed Mr. Crowell a brigadier general in the Officer's Reserve Corps, and stated that he did so in part as a vindication.

February 5, 1931: A vacancy existed in the United States District Court for Minnesota. Senator Schall had been asked for suggestions. He responded, urging the appointment of a certain lawyer. Appropriate inquiry was made by the Department of Justice. The Attorney-General advised the President that he could not recommend the appointment. The Senator was advised that the nomination could not be made. Further suggestions were requested. There was a deadlock for several months. Finally, under local pressure, the entire Congressional delegation from Minnesota joined the Senator in urging the President to send in the nomination. The latter was convinced that the appointment ought not to be made, and refused to do so.

February 18, 1931: The President vetoed a bill (S. 3165) to pay $3,500,000 to certain Indians in a land transaction that had been completed and paid for seventy-five years before. The promoters of the legislation failed in their efforts to secure a reconsideration of the adverse action.[5]

February 28, 1931: The problem of Muscle Schoals had become more and more involved in politics. In view of this and to clarify the issues, the President issued the following statement:[6]

[5] For text of message see State Papers, Vol. I, p. 505.
[6] State Papers, Vol. I, p. 520.

I have received a multitude of telegrams from governors and citizens in the Southern States urging approval of Senator Norris' Muscle Shoals project, and requesting that I express my views upon it. Some of them express dissatisfaction with its principles but consider it expedient to approve it. I have also many telegrams from citizens of the Southern States and other parts of the country protesting against the principles of the bill.

It is obvious from the debate, the press, and these many communications that Muscle Shoals legislation is no longer a question of disposing of a war activity to the advantage of the people primarily concerned. It has by this legislation been transformed into a political symbol and is expected to be a political issue. To be against Senator Norris' bill appears to be cause for denunciation as being in league with the power companies. It appears also to be emerging as the test of views upon government operation and distribution of power and government manufacture of commodities. In other words, its adaptation to the use of the people of the Tennessee Valley and to farmers generally, is now enmeshed in an endeavor to create a national political issue.

One side issue of this political phase is the use which has been made of Muscle Shoals to sidetrack effective action on the Federal regulation of interstate power in co-operating with the States. Before and since taking office I have proposed this as a measure of essential protection to the 75,000,000 consumers and several million investors in power securities in all walks of life, who use and own the 35,000,000 horsepower of the country. This public necessity has been held aside for eighteen months, and time of Congress given to one per cent of the power and the interests of one per cent of the people of the United States, which is the proportion of the Muscle Shoals problem to the whole.

The bill calls for expenditure of ninety or a hundred million dollars from the Federal Treasury, to expand a power plant which has been a by-product of other major purposes of navigation and national defense, into a large undertaking by the government, the major purposes of which is to be the generation and distribution of power and the manufacture of fertilizers.

In acting on the bill I have to consider whether it is desirable to adopt a change in Federal policies from regulation of utilities to their ownership and operation; whether the lease provision in respect to the fertilizer plant is genuinely workable; whether the method proposed in this bill will produce cheaper fertilizers for the farmers; whether the project is required for national defense; whether the proposals in this bill are in reality in the interest of the people of the Tennessee Valley; and in general to consider the commonplace unromantic facts which test the merits and demerits of this proposition as a business.

This happens to be an engineering project, and so far as its business merits and demerits are concerned is subject to the cold examination of engineering facts. I am having these facts exhaustively determined by the different departments of the government and will then be able to state my views upon the problem.

March 3, 1931: The President vetoed the Muscle Shoals Bill. As to the principles involved, the President said:[7]

I am firmly opposed to the government entering into any business, the major purpose of which is competition with our citizens. There are national emergencies which require that the government should temporarily enter the field of business, but these must be emergency actions and in matters where the cost of the project is secondary to much higher considerations. There are many localities where the Federal Government is justified in the construction of great dams and reservoirs, where navigation, flood control, reclamation, or stream regulation are of dominant importance, and where they are beyond the capacity of purpose of private or local government capital to construct. In these cases power is often a by-product and should be disposed of by contract or lease. But for the Federal Government deliberately to go out to build up and expand such an occasion to the major purpose of a power and manufacturing business is to break down the initiative and enterprise of the American people; it is destruction of equality of opportunity amongst our people; it is the negation of the ideals upon which our civilization is based.

This bill raises one of the important issues confronting our people. That is squarely the issue of Federal Government ownership and operation of power and manufacturing business not as a minor by-product but as a major purpose. Involved in this question is the agitation against the conduct of the power industry. The power problem is not to be solved by the Federal Government going into the power business, nor is it to be solved by the project in this bill. The remedy for abuses in the conduct of that industry lies in regulation and not by the Federal Government entering upon the business itself. I have recommended to the Congress on various occasions that action should be taken to establish Federal regulation of interstate power in co-operation with State authorities. This bill would launch the Federal Government upon a policy of ownership and operation of power utilities upon a basis of competition instead of by the proper government function of regulation for the protection of all the people. I hesitate to contemplate the future of our institutions, of our government, and of our country if the preoccupation of its officials is to be no longer the promotion of justice and equal opportunity, but is to be devoted to barter in the markets. That is not liberalism, that is degeneration.

I sympathize greatly with the desire of the people of Tennessee and Alabama to see this great asset turned to practical use. It can be so turned and to their benefit. I am loath to leave a subject of this character without a suggestion for solution. Congress has been thwarted for ten years in finding solution, by rivalry of private interests and by the determination of certain groups to commit the Federal Government to government ownership and operation of power.

The real development of the resources and the industries of the Tennessee Valley can be only accomplished by the people in that valley themselves. Muscle Shoals can only be administered by the people upon

[7] State Papers, Vol. I, p. 526.

the ground, responsible to their own communities, directing them solely for the benefit of their communities and not for purposes of pursuit of social theories or natural politics. Any other course deprives them of liberty.

I would therefore suggest that the States of Alabama and Tennessee, who are the ones primarily concerned, should set up a commission of their own representatives, together with a representative from the national farm organization and the corps of army engineers; that there be vested in that commission full authority to lease the plants at Muscle Shoals in the interest of the local community and agriculture generally. . . .

The Federal Government should, as in the case of Boulder Canyon, construct Cove Creek Dam as a regulatory measure for the flood protection of the Tennessee Valley and the development of its water resources, but on the same bases as those imposed at Boulder Canyon—that is, that construction should be undertaken at such time as the proposed commission is able to secure contracts for use of the increased water supply to power uses, or the lease of the power produced as a by-product from such a dam on terms that will return to the government interest upon its outlay with amortization. On this basis the Federal Government will have coöperated to place the question into the hands of the people primarily concerned. They can lease as their wisdom dictates, and for the industries that they deem best in their own interest. It would get a war relic out of politics and into the realm of service.

March 3, 1931: The Senate upheld the President's veto of the Muscle Shoals Bill forty-nine to thirty-four.

March 4, 1931: Congress adjourned. A filibuster by Senator Thomas of Oklahoma killed the President's rural health program for children, which otherwise would have passed. The filibuster also defeated the Vestal Copyright Bill to protect authors. Both of these had been passed in the House and had substantial majorities favoring them in the Senate.

The President was disappointed. This was particularly true as to the Rural Health Bill. Some years before he had, as chairman of the American Child Health Association, carried forward experiments in developing more effective county organization with respect to the health and care of children. After the Mississippi flood, with private financial aid, he had established a health supervision in more than one hundred counties. The result had been practically to stamp out malaria, plague, typhoid and other diseases in those areas, so long as the supervision was continued, and greatly to aid in better conditions of birth and nurture of children.

The principles of this Rural Health Bill had been those of Federal subsidy to States or counties creating a public health unit of a doctor, a sanitary engineer, and a nurse, with a further subsidy for provision of maternity and children's services. The Federal administration was to be conducted jointly by the Public Health Service and the Children's Bureau.

The failure of the passage of the bill postponed its benefits for many years. The succeeding Congress was so engrossed in legislation necessitated by meeting the problems of the depression, deepened by the European collapse, that it would not give attention to the subject.

March 6, 1931: Alexander Legge, after remaining much longer than he had originally agreed, resigned as chairman and as member of the Federal Farm Board. The President appointed James C. Stone, of Kentucky, to succeed him. Mr. Stone had been serving as vice chairman.

March 8, 1931: The President pocket-vetoed a bill (S. 3060) fostered by Senator Wagner (Democrat), of New York, to give subsidies to the States with which to operate their own State public employment agencies, thereby supplanting the existing Federal Employment Service which had been whole-heartedly co-operating with existing State agencies. The President vetoed it because:

(a) It would destroy the Federal service which had been built up over many years;

(b) It would destroy the interstate co-operation which could be had only through a Federal service;

(c) There was no provision which would prevent the new service from becoming purely political in its operations in the States.

He was convinced that its true inspiration was the attempt to Tammanyize, not only in New York but elsewhere in the country, the agencies which were trying to assist the citizens in the obtaining of civilian jobs. Of course this was another occasion for an attack, wherein the President was charged with being heartless and disinterested in the unemployed. These critics failed to say that the President had secured from Congress, for the Federal Employment Service, an appropriation which was twice the previous amount, and that following the crash in 1929 he had established the service on a more sound and efficient basis than it ever had been. In 1932, the American Federation of Labor, the Veterans of Foreign Wars, and the Disabled American Veterans all endorsed the work of this service at their conventions.

March 11, 1931: To a correspondent who offered advice as to the further extension of government, the President wrote:

Do not think for one moment that I do not value criticism by my friends; I do value it very much.

I have the feeling that if you could sit in the middle of the government and see the tools with which we have to work and the disasters which confront us at all times in the use of these human tools, you would not want us to extend the area of government, but rather to keep the government as nearly as we can in its greatest function—the safeguarding of human rights. Also, if you could sit in the middle of the government you would be even more disheartened than you are now by the wrongs and cruelties that take place through greed and selfishness. To steer a straight course through these rocks is no ordinary task, and is a task that will not wholly be accomplished in one generation.

. . . People are not my friends who agree with me on all points, and I am in need of honest opinion, so do not hesitate to send it along.

March 13, 1931: The President made the following public statement concerning the oil situation: [8]

I have received several hundred telegrams from the West and Southwest either inquiring or making suggestions as to the situation in the oil industry.

In order to make the matter clear I may state:

In order to prevent enormous waste of gas and oil and to prevent the ruin of the independent oil producers, the Federal Oil Conservation Board brought about over a year ago, under the leadership of Secretary Wilbur, an almost entire restriction of production from the newly discovered, great oil pool at Kettleman Hills, California, a large part of which is the property of the Federal Government. The State authorities of Oklahoma have brought about similar restraint upon an enormous new pool discovered at Oklahoma City. Coincident with these efforts, the State commissions working with other producers of California, Oklahoma, and Texas, brought about proration agreements amongst themselves. A third great pool has been recently developed in Eastern Texas, upon which no proration has yet been brought about, but I am advised that the Governor is making an effort to bring it about. The question of prorating of imports has been under agitation as also having a bearing upon the problem.

. . . But such action (in restraint) would have little effect, however, unless the East Texas pool shall be prorated on the same basis as the other new pools. It is believed that if these two results can be brought about, the industry will soon readjust itself.

April 9, 1931: The National Advisory Committee on Illiteracy, appointed by the President, reported that the national percentage of illiteracy was 4.3 per cent of the population, showing also the percentage as of each State. It announced that in forty-three States and districts there were active co-operating committees, with over a thousand leaders co-operating with governors and civic organizations. It recommended further arousing of thoughtful people, working with private funds, since "people closest to their problems are regarded as best equipped to direct their own machinery and resources." It suggested "illiteracy clinics." The committee organized a system of volunteer and State adult education throughout the country.

[8] State Papers, Vol. I, p. 533.

April 13, 1931: At the twenty-fifth annual meeting of the board of directors of the National Recreation Association, President Hoover said:[9]

I am glad to welcome the directors of the National Recreation Association at the White House on this occasion. . . . I have followed the work of the association for many years. It has taken a most significant and a magnificent part in the whole recreational development of the country. Its work today is of increasing importance because of the growing congestion of cities, on one hand, and the increasing leisure of our people, on the other. The whole recreational movement is one not only vital to the public health, but it is vital to public welfare. . . . Many less problems in government arise which concern people while they are at work than while they are at leisure. They do not often go to jail for activities while they are on their jobs. Most of our problems arise when the people are off their jobs.

April 14, 1931: Among those with whom the President consulted from time to time was Dr. R. R. Moton, the head of Tuskegee Institute. In connection with the work of the Haitian Commission, of which Mr. W. Cameron Forbes was the chairman, the President tendered, and Dr. Moton accepted the chairmanship of a Committee on Education. Dr. Moton invited the President to address the Institute on the occasion of the fiftieth anniversary of its founding. The President accepted and said:[10]

It is now over sixty years since the Negro was released from slavery and given the status of a citizen in our country, whose wealth and general prosperity his labor has helped create. The progress of the race within this period has surpassed the most sanguine hopes of the most ardent advocates. No group of people in history ever started from a more complete economic and cultural destitution. . . .

The greatest single factor in the progress of the Negro race has been the schools, private and public, established and conducted by high-minded, self-sacrificing men and women of both races and all sections of the country, maintained by the States and by private philanthropy, covering the whole field of education from primary school through to college and university. These public and private schools particularly, under the leadership of Tuskegee and other universities and colleges, have been the most effective agents in solving the problems created by the admission to citizenship of 4,000,000 ex-slaves without preparation for their new responsibilities. That such a revolution in the social order did not produce a more serious upheaval in our national existence has been due to the constructive influence exerted by these educational institutions, whose maintenance of further development is both a public and private duty.

[9] State Papers, Vol. I, p. 542. [10] State Papers, Vol. I, p. 545.

The nation owes a debt of gratitude to the wisdom and constructive vision of Booker T. Washington, the founder of Tuskegee. His conception of education, based fundamentally upon vocational and moral training, has been worthily continued by his able successor, Dr. R. R. Moton, who likewise deserves the gratitude of the nation for his many contributions to the solution of one of our most difficult national problems. His ability and sanity and modesty have been powerful forces in progress and good will. . . .

The interest of the President in the special problems of the negro had been evidenced by an exhaustive survey of the facts, undertaken during 1930 at his instigation, for a better public understanding of the whole question.

April 22, 1931: From time to time the President had conferred with Professor Wesley C. Mitchell of the National Bureau of Economic Research, on the expediency of that institution making an exhaustive study of the results of unemployment insurance in foreign countries. The British Government having instituted a thorough inquiry into their own and Continental experience, it was today decided to defer our study until the results of the British inquiry were available.

April 25, 1931: The President today created the Council of Personnel Administration to improve the Civil Service. The undertaking was in consequence of an able report by Chairman Thomas E. Campbell of the Civil Service Commission. The order stated:[11]

For the purpose of developing in the Federal Government a more effective and economical system of employment and personnel management, . . . there is hereby established a Council of Personnel Administration, . . .
. . . The President of the Civil Service Commission shall act as chairman of the council. . . .
The Council of Personnel Administration shall:
(a) Establish a liaison system between the Civil Service Commission and the several departments;
(b) With the assistance of advisory committees . . . make available to the government the best developments in personnel administration outside of government service. . . .
(c) Prepare specific plans for improvement and co-ordination of personnel administration. . . .

April 26, 1931: The President issued an order extending preferences to veterans who desired to enter government employment.

April 27, 1931: An appreciation of the efforts of the President toward improving conditions in the cotton and textile industry is shown in the

[11] State Papers, Vol. I, p. 552.

following letter from George A. Sloan, president of the Cotton-Textile Institute, Inc.:

DEAR MR. PRESIDENT:

You will be glad to know the very favorable results which have come to the industry following the conference of a year ago. . . .

As a result of constructive action in the industry, a large human service has been given in that employment of women and minors at night will practically cease. More definite knowledge as to production, stocks, and distribution has been acquired, and greater uniformity of running time throughout the industry has been secured with a view to more stabilized employment and merchandising. Co-operative action was taken in promoting consumption of the products of the industry, and in dealing with other matters of public interest without in any way impairing the competitive character of the industry.

Indeed, there is a feeling that the foundation has been laid . . . for an industry which for many years has been gravely in need of stabilization.

Respectfully yours,
(Signed) GEO. A. SLOAN.

May 12, 1931: The interest of the President in National Defense matters is shown in a statement issued by the President to the press:

About a month ago I requested the General Staff through Secretary Hurley to make a renewed study of the whole question of army posts from the point of view of gaining the maximum efficiency through the concentration of the army, and the important purpose of economy in the War Department. The staff has insisted for great numbers of years that the army must be more largely concentrated if it is to be the most effective body, and it becomes even more necessary now in view of the very large mechanization of the army and the number of subsidiary mechanical services, such as aviation and so on.

We have actually abandoned thirteen posts during the past two years. The staff will probably report between twenty or thirty more posts that should be abandoned if we are to have the most effective army, and if we are to accomplish some very considerable economies. . . .

May 14, 1931: The President, in view of the ample production of wood products from privately owned forests, directed the Department of Agriculture to cease leasing national forests, in order to conserve them for the future.

June 2, 1931: Governor Woodring of Kansas, on behalf of mid-West agriculture, wired the President urging him to full use of the flexible tariff provision for the benefit of agricultural products. He also requested that the President arrange reciprocal agreements with other nations.

In reply, the President called the attention of the Governor to the working of the flexible provision, and continued: "The President has no other power whatever to raise or lower duties by bargaining with foreign countries. You are greatly misinformed as to . . . retaliatory measures against American tariffs . . . one or two instances, and they do not involve agriculture . . . taking Europe as a whole the free list amounts to fifty-one per cent, whereas the free list of the United States runs up to sixty-seven per cent. . . . I assume you do not want the tariff on agricultural products reduced even if legally possible . . . the complaints from foreign countries . . . have been against the agricultural schedules . . . the only bargains that could be made would involve a reduction of agricultural tariffs . . . on industrial products . . . if you will specify the schedules . . . too high, and so advise any Midwest agricultural association, such association has the right to appear before the Tariff Commission and submit its case."

June 4, 1931: The President, having taken great interest with Secretary of the Interior Wilbur in the development of the national parks, today called for a report upon the National Park Service. The important items in the report of the director of the service, Horace Albright, were:

. . . Extraordinary improvements have been made in these wilderness playgrounds in the last few years. New roads have been constructed. . . . New trails have been laid out. . . . Hotels and lodges have perfected accommodations that meet the demands of every pocketbook. Campsites have been made generally available for those who bring their own equipment.

. . . The system comprises 22 parks and 34 monuments. The areas are larger by 266,456 acres now than they were in 1929. . . .

. . . Visitors . . . in 1924 numbered only 1,670,908, whereas the total for 1930 was 3,246,656. . . .

. . . The last two years represent a period of unusual development along all lines. . . .

All in all, the accomplishment, in the field of national park and monument development during the past two years have been greater than during any other two-year period since 1870, when that small band around the Yellowstone campfire were inspired to conceive the national-park idea.

June 5, 1931: The President attended a meeting of the National Editorial Association at Washington. Wickham Stead, former editor of *The London Times,* and "Pertinax" (André Géraud), a French correspondent, were also guests. These gentlemen, in the course of their remarks, blamed the United States for the failures in Europe and made a personal attack upon President Wilson. When President Hoover arose he dropped his prepared manuscript and, instead, paid a high and eloquent tribute to President Wilson. He then proceeded to a discussion of the responsibilities of other nations for their own actions, together with a flat statement that the United States would not assume either their moral or political liabilities.

June 15, 1931: In speaking at Indianapolis, the President said, as to governmental and business reforms: [12]

We can already observe some directions to which endeavor must be pointed. For instance, it is obvious that the Federal Reserve System was inadequate to prevent a large diversion of capital and bank deposits from commercial and industrial business into wasteful speculation and stock promotion. It is obvious our banking system must be organized to give greater protection to depositors against failure. It is equally obvious that we must determine whether the facilities of our security and commodity exchanges are not being used to create illegitimate speculation and intensify depressions. It is obvious that our taxes upon capital gains viciously promote the booms and just as viciously intensify depressions. In order to avoid taxes, real estate and stocks are withheld from the market in times of rising prices, and for the same reason large quantities are dumped on the market in times of depression. The experience of this depression indeed demands that the nation carefully and deliberately reconsider the whole national and local problem of the incidence of taxation. The undue proportion of taxes which falls upon farmers, home owners, and all real property holders, as compared to other forms of wealth and income, demands real relief. There are far wider questions of our social and economic life which this experience will illuminate. We shall know much more of the method of still further advance toward stability, and wider diffusion of the benefits of our economic system.

Some groups believe this plan (national development) can only be carried out by a fundamental, a revolutionary change of method. Other groups believe that any system must be the outgrowth of the character of our race, a natural outgrowth of our traditions; that we have established certain ideals over 150 years upon which we must build rather than destroy.

. . . [We] shall go on with our American system, which holds that the major purpose of a State is to protect the people and to give them equality of opportunity, that the basis of all happiness is in development of the individual, that the sum of progress can only be gauged by the progress of the individual, that we should steadily build up co-operation among the people themselves to these ends . . . [or] we shall directly or indirectly regiment the population into a bureaucracy to serve the State, that we should use force instead of co-operation in plans, and thereby direct every man as to what he may or may not do.

[12] State Papers, Vol. I, p. 581.

THE CHECK UPON CONSTRUCTIVE LEGISLATION

... Shall we establish a dole from the Federal Treasury? Shall we undertake Federal ownership and operation of public utilities instead of the rigorous regulation of them to prevent imposition? Shall we protect our people from the lower standards of living of foreign countries? Shall the government, except in temporary national emergencies, enter upon business processes in competition with its citizens? Shall we regiment our people by an extension of the arm of bureauracy into a multitude of affairs?

The future welfare of our country, so dear to you and me for ourselves and our children, depends upon the answer given. . . .

June 17, 1931: In an address before the joint session of the Illinois Legislature at Springfield, Illinois, wherein he stressed the experience in and contribution to government by the States, the President said: [13]

... A study of national legislation and national action will show that an overwhelming proportion of the ideas which have been developed nationally have first been born in the State legislatures, as the result of the problems which have developed within the States. They have been given trial; they have been hammered out on the anvil of local experience. It is true that not all of the ideas come through successfully. But even the negative values of the trial, especially in some parts of the Union, are of themselves of inestimable value to the nation as a whole. And the ideas which develop with success become of vital importance to our people at large. . . .

Ours must be a country of constant change and progress, because of one fact along with many others, and that is that the constant discoveries in science, and their product in new invention, shift our basis of human relationships and our mode of life in such a fashion as to require a constant remodelling and the remoulding of the machinery of government. That does not imply that the eternal principles of justice, and right, and ordered liberty, upon which the Republic is founded, are subject to change, for they are not. . . .

August 7, 1931: At the request of the President, Assistant Secretary of the Interior Dixon issued a statement on the responsibility of Texas for the oil situation, the other important States having enacted the laws recommended by the administration for the control of the waste from new pools and other bad practices in production. Mr. Dixon said:

... all the other great producing states have placed a curb on oil output, and only Texas has failed to cooperate with the industry at large. ... The State Authorities and Legislatures of California and Oklahoma have, under the leadership of their governments, cooperated to prorate their production as urged by the Federal Oil Conservation Board. Except

[13] State Papers, Vol. I, p. 590.

for the failure of the Texas authorities and legislature so far to co-operate by controlling their big new oil pool in East Texas, the whole oil situation would have been corrected months ago.

August 26, 1931: The International Chamber of Commerce "declared for a determination of definite principles of tariff duties," and the Wiggin (non-governmental bankers') Commission for examining the capacity of Germany to pay its debts, cited tariff barriers as hampering that capacity. Various requests came to the President to promote a re-examination of American tariff duties. In a letter of reply to one of these, the President said:

. . . the International Chamber of Commerce, having declared for a determination of definite principles of tariff, in which I presume they recommended the American principle, should recommend that principle to European nations. If that were adopted it would reduce tariffs all over Europe . . . changes in American tariffs must be made by application and hearings. It is open to any importer of German goods to raise such cases before the Tariff Commission . . . the Wiggin Commission . . . would have been constructive to suggest that such cases be presented and to have supported the recommendation of the International Chamber and the proper reorganization of European tariffs.

September 15, 1931: The President spent the day in conference with the leaders whom he had appointed to conduct the National Conference upon Home Building and Home Ownership as to the result of the special investigations and the practical programs to lay before the conference. There were present Secretary of Commerce Lamont, Secretary of the Interior Wilbur, John M. Gries, Edgar Rickard, Harland Bartholomew, Alexander M. Bing, Mrs. Hugh Bradford, William M. Calder, Frederick A. Delano, Frederick H. Ecker, Frederick M. Feiker, Mrs. Henry Ford, James Ford, W. H. George, Dr. Lilian Gilbreth, William Green, Anton Horst, Mrs. William Lake, Miss Gertrude Lane, Mrs. William Brown Meloney, Robert Pyers, John W. O'Leary, William Parker, Leonard Reaume, Alexander Robinson, Loring Schuler, Mrs. John Sippel, Miss Louise Stanley, French Strother, Miss Frances Swain, Thomas Symons, James S. Taylor, Samuel H. Thompson, and Lawrence Veiller.

The President said:[14]

I wish to announce that the President's Conference on Home Building and Home Ownership for which preparations have been in progress for something over a year will be held in Washington, Wednesday,

[14] State Papers, Vol. I, p. 614.

THE CHECK UPON CONSTRUCTIVE LEGISLATION 481

December 2nd to Saturday, December 5th, inclusive. About 400 persons have assisted in the preparatory work and 1,000 representative citizens from the forty-eight States, associated with building and housing activities, are expected to participate in the conference. The conference has been under the chairmanship of Secretary Lamont, of the Department of Commerce. Dr. John M. Gries is the executive secretary.

A Planning Committee, comprising representatives of some twenty voluntary associations, was created to make the study and set up a national conference for consideration of the data and recommendations of expert committees. . . .

The conference in December will be the first of its kind on this scale in the United States. It will deal with the whole question of home construction and ownership, and of the home environment. It will embrace finance, design, equipment, city planning, household management, and many other aspects. . . .

. . . It, obviously, is not our purpose to set up the Federal Government in the building of homes. But the conference will, I believe, afford a basis for the development of a sound policy and inspire better voluntary organization to cope with the problem.

September 29, 1931: The Garfield Commission upon Conservation of the Public Domain made its report. The congestion of Congress over recovery questions prevented action in the matters recommended, particularly in saving the grazing lands. The report contributed to action subsequently taken in this matter.

October 1, 1931: The joint committee appointed by the President and by the governors of Alabama and Tennessee to recommend a plan for Muscle Shoals brought in a report recommending a lease of the power and the fertilizer plant for private operation under government restrictions as to rates and uses.

October 7, 1931: The President met with a committee of the prospective "Better Homes" Conference to discuss definite plans to be laid before that body for financing of home mortgages. There were present: James L. Madden, Metropolitan Life Insurance Company; W. E. Best, United States Building and Loan League; Hiram I. Cody, Cody Trust Company; H. A. Kahler, New York Title and Mortgage Companies; H. A. Kissell, National Association of Real Estate Boards; S. N. Reep, Home Building and Loan Association of Minneapolis; Ernest T. Trigg, manufacturer; and Clarence M. Woolley of New York.

The President proposed a national system of mortgage discount banks both to relieve mortgage strains and to find new capital for home building and slum clearance. The insurance representatives opposed the whole plan, stating that no home or mortgage relief was necessary.

October 8, 1931: On the question of foreign loans and the circumstances under which they should be made, the President, in speaking before the Fourth Pan-American Conference said: [15]

> There is one lesson from this depression to which I wish to refer, and I can present it no more forcibly than by repeating a statement which I made to this conference just four years ago, when we were in the heyday of foreign loans. I stated, in respect to such loans, that they are helpful in world development, provided always one essential principle dominates the character of these transactions. That is, that no nation as a government should borrow or no government lend and nations should discourage their citizens from borrowing or lending unless this money is to be devoted to productive enterprise.
>
> Out of the wealth and the higher standards of living created from enterprise itself must come the ability to repay the capital to the borrowing country. Any other course of action creates obligations impossible of repayment except by a direct subtraction from the standards of living of the borrowing country and the impoverishment of its people.
>
> In fact, if this principle could be adopted between nations of the world—that is, if nations would do away with the lending of money for the balancing of budgets for purposes of military equipment or war purposes, or even that type of public works which does not bring some direct or indirect productive return—a great number of blessings would follow to the entire world.
>
> There could be no question as to the ability to repay; with this increasing security capital would become steadily cheaper, the dangers to national and individual independence in attempts of the lender to collect his defaulted debts would be avoided; there would be definite increase in the standard of living and the comfort and prosperity of the borrower....
>
> I repeat this today, because had it been followed during these past five years our problems throughout the world would be far different, our difficulties infinitely less....

October 12, 1931: President Hoover in a radio address to the Convention of the International Association of Chiefs of Police, at St. Petersburg, Florida, said: [16]

> ... In the United States a major responsibility rests upon the shoulders of our Chiefs of Police. Ours is a form of government where the task and responsibility of maintenance of organized society through its never-ending battle against crime rests upon each local community. The Chiefs of Police occupy a position of high command in that service. In not a few of our communities the police have been subject to criticism. That criticism arises from the exception and not the rule in police conduct. Moreover, there is a sentimentalism in some people which makes popular heroes out of criminals which needs replacement by a sentimentalism that makes a popular hero of the policeman for the courage and

---
[15] State Papers, Vol. II, p. 7.   [16] State Papers, Vol. II, p. 16.

devotion he shows in protection of our citizens. Instead of the glorification of cowardly gangsters we need the glorification of policemen who do their duty and who give their lives in public protection.

The police perform an unending task, not alone in the mothering of the children on our streets and in the good-humored dissolution of traffic jams, but in this incessant war against criminals. If the police had the vigilant, universal backing of public opinion in their communities, if they had the implacable support of the prosecuting authorities and the courts, if our criminal laws in their endeavor to protect the innocent did not furnish loopholes through which irresponsible, yet clever criminal lawyers daily find devices of escape for the guilty, I am convinced that our police would stamp out the excessive crime and remove the world-wide disrepute which has disgraced some of our great cities.

The police by instinct are the enemies of gang activities, robberies, hold-ups, and ruthless murder. But so long as criminals can proceed with the smug assurance that they can defeat the law there is a constant discouragement to the police. I wonder at times that they maintain the vigilance and courage they do against the odds with which they have to contend. . . .

October 26, 1931: The attitude of the President toward the radio and the continental European system of government broadcasting, as distinguished from our system, is evidenced in his address to the National Convention of the National Broadcasters Association at Detroit, by radio. He said:

. . . The determination that radio channels were public property and should be controlled by the government; the determination that we should not have governmental broadcasting supported by a tax upon the listeners, but that we should give license to use of these channels under private enterprise where there would be no restraint upon programs, has secured for us far greater variety of programs and excellence of service without cost to the listener. This decision has avoided the pitfalls of political and social conflicts in the use of speech over the radio which would have been involved in government broadcasting. It has preserved free speech to the country.

These principles are now strongly imbedded in our law and in our entire public system. The industry has constantly faced new and complex problems in developing policies and practices abreast of development and need. Your association has contributed greatly to their solution. I am confident that you recognize the responsibility which rests upon you in public interest. It is needless to mention the many-sided importance of radio in modern life. Its dissemination of entertainment, of knowledge, and of public opinion and topics of the public welfare, has become an essential element in the intellectual development of our country. It has brought most of the supposed values which were formerly available exclusively to life in the cities, to every home throughout the land, for the treasures of music, of entertainment, and of information have been brought to the loneliest farm and the most remote hamlet. It is an incalculable extension of happiness and contentment. . . .

These were not new ideas for, while Secretary of Commerce, Mr. Hoover had taken an early hand in the building up of this industry. He had expressed this view of its regulation to the Fourth National Radio Conference:

The ideal situation would be a traffic regulation by the Federal Government to the extent of an allotment of wave-lengths and control of power and policing of interference, leaving to each community a large voice in determining who are to occupy the wave-lengths assigned to that community. . . . It cannot be thought that any single person or group shall ever have the right to determine what communication may be made to the American people. We cannot allow any single person or group to place themselves in a position where they can censor the material which shall be broadcast to the public.

October 27, 1931: Secretary of War Hurley returned from the Philippine Islands. He went at the request of the President to get a more definite understanding of the Philippine problem, including the operations of the system of government and first-hand knowledge of the social, economic, political and educational conditions in the islands. In a statement to the press, the President summarized his views on the question of granting independence. He said:[17]

On Secretary Hurley's return, at the Cabinet meeting this morning, we discussed the Philippine question at considerable length. Independence of the Philippines at some time has been directly or indirectly promised by every President and by Congress. In accord with those undertakings, the problem is one of time. In the interest of the Philippine people, the time element involves the necessity that independence must be assured of durability and the Government of the Philippines must be assured of stability. The economic independence of the Philippines must be attained before political independence can be successful. Independence tomorrow without assured economic stability would result in the collapse of Philippine Government revenues and the collapse of all economic life in the Islands. We propose to give further consideration to the whole question during the immediate future.

November 9, 1931: The President sent letters to the mayors of cities inviting their participation in the approaching Home Building and Home Ownership Conference:

This conference follows months of study by committees . . . the subjects considered are construction, financing, design, equipment, city

[17] State Papers, Vol. II, p. 24.

THE CHECK UPON CONSTRUCTIVE LEGISLATION 485

planning, environment, furnishing, home management . . . based on the best experience of those who have special knowledge. . . . I am hopeful that every community will participate. I shall greatly appreciate it if you will appoint representatives . . . that the exchange of experiences and the establishment of standards and methods will encourage home building and home ownership . . . increase employment . . . and promote social stability.

November 14, 1931: President Hoover in addressing the meeting of the Liberal Arts Colleges Association over the radio expressed his views in reference to the small college:[18]

I am glad to express appreciation of the service of the liberal arts college, that is the small college. I do this the more freely because of the more than six hundred such institutions in our land, most of them have little, if any, endowment or State support. In these times of trends toward larger units the difficulties of the unsupported small college multiply, which make their successful operations less hopeful, and, in many cases, a desperate struggle. . . .

The liberal arts college places an emphasis upon personal contacts of teacher and student which render them a vital part of our educational system. . . .

Throughout our history these colleges have been and are now the seed beds of leadership. They have contributed a large part to the presence in our land of nearly two million trained men and women. Theirs is a great honor roll of men and women in our nation. The finest traditions of our country are rooted in their associations and their inspiration. . . .

In the last analysis the chief service to higher education in our country must rest not with the few highly endowed universities but, in large degree, with the more than six hundred smaller colleges for whose future welfare I am now speaking. . . .

That service for the youth is a guarantee of equality of cultural opportunity and a bulwark for the spiritual life of the generation in which our children will have to live, a service I sincerely commend.

December 2, 1931: The President today opened the Conference on Home Building and Home Ownership. He stated:[19]

You have come from every State in the Union to consider a matter of basic national interest. Your purpose is to consider it in its long view rather than its emergency aspects. Next to food and clothing the housing of a nation is its most vital social and economic problem. This conference has been called especially to consider one great segment of that problem—that is, in what manner can we facilitate the ownership of homes, and how can we protect the owners of homes?

[18] State Papers, Vol. II, p. 35.   [19] State Papers, Vol. II, p. 36.

The conference also has before it some phases of that other great segment of housing; that is, the standards of tenement and apartment dwellings. . . .

While the purpose of this conference is to study and advise upon the very practical questions of home design, of materials, of building regulations, of zoning, of taxes, of transportation, of financing, of parks and playgrounds and other topics, yet behind it all every one of you here is impelled by the high ideal and aspiration that each family may pass their days in the home which they own; that they may nurture it as theirs; that it may be their castle in all that exquisite sentiment which it surrounds with the sweetness of family life. This aspiration penetrates the heart of our national well-being. It makes for happier married life, it makes for better children, it makes for confidence and security, it makes for courage to meet the battle of life, it makes for better citizenship. . . .

. . . Over thirty communities embracing the collective skill and experience of our country have been voluntarily engaged for the past year in collecting the best of national experience from every part of the country, in collating it into definite recommendations for your consideration. Like the solution of all practical problems, the facts first must be discovered; they must be assembled in their true perspective; and the conclusions to be drawn from them must be the inexorable march of logic.

It has long been my opinion that we have fairly creditably solved every other segment of our credit structure more effectively than we have solved this one. . . .

. . . To find a way to meet the need is one of the problems that you have to consider; that is, how we can make a home available for installment purchase on terms that dignify the name credit and not upon terms and risks comparable to the credit extended by a pawnbroker. . . .

I recently made a public proposal for the creation of a system of Home Loan Discount Banks. That proposal is familiar to you, and I will not traverse its details at the present time. . . .

And there are many other problems involved in your investigations which bear equal importance to the problem of home financing. The surroundings in which such homes are to be built; the very method of their building; transportation and other facilities which must be provided for them; and the protection that must be given to them from the encroachment of commerce and industry. All of these and many other subjects you will compass. . . .

The conference presented a definite program of national action, with exhaustive reports giving the fact and reason for every recommendation. It laid the foundation for sound and progressive achievements. One of its tangible results was the Federal Home Loan Bank System, and the financing of slum clearance by the Reconstruction Finance Corporation.

Later on, the President, in thanking William Green of the American Federation of Labor for his co-operation in the Home Building and Home Ownership Conference, thus described its objectives:

THE CHECK UPON CONSTRUCTIVE LEGISLATION 487

The conference . . . not only assembled in an orderly manner a great deal of material not heretofore so readily available, but it brought forth a number of new ideas, gave a new setting and a new relationship to principles previously well known, and it offered to interested groups and individuals an opportunity for considering housing problems from the viewpoint of others striving towards a common goal. It marks the beginning of a new effort to raise the housing standards of a greater number of American people to a satisfactory level. . . .

December 7, 1931: The Seventy-second Congress convened. The Democrats, having a working majority, organized the House of Representatives, and elected Representative John N. Garner of Texas as Speaker.

December 8, 1931: The President's annual message dealt in large part with the great emergency situation created by the financial collapse in Europe. The country was absorbed in the problems of the crisis, during which long-view economic and social action, except the question of banking and bankruptcy reform, must wait. The President felt that the work of the session should be confined to recovery matters.

On subjects other than emergency he said:[20]

. . . The railways present one of our immediate and pressing problems. They are and must remain the backbone of our transportation system. . . . In my message of a year ago I commented on the necessity of Congressional inquiry into the economic action of the anti-trust laws. . . . I have recommended in previous messages the effective regulations of interstate power as the essential function of the re-organized Federal Power Commission. I renew the recommendation. It is urgently needed in public protection. . . . I again call attention to my previous recommendations upon this subject (public health) particularly in its relation to children. The moral results are of the utmost importance. . . .

It is inevitable that in these times much of the legislation proposed to the Congress and many of the recommendations of the Executive must be designed to meet emergencies. In reaching solutions we must not jeopardize those principles which we have found to be the basis of growth of the nation. The Federal Government must not encroach upon or permit local communities to abandon that precious possession of local initiative and responsibility. Again, just as the largest measure of responsibility in the government of the nation rests upon local self-government, so does the largest measure of social responsibility in our country rest upon the individual. If the individual surrenders his own initiative and responsibilities, he is surrendering his own freedom and his own liberty. It is the duty of the national government to insist that both the local governments and the individual shall assume and bear these responsibilities as a fundamental of preserving the very basis of our freedom. . . .

[20] State Papers, Vol. II, p. 51.

Many vital changes and movements of vast proportions are taking place in the economic world. The effect of these changes upon the future cannot be seen clearly as yet. Of this, however, we are sure: Our system, based upon the ideals of individual initiative and of equality of opportunity, is not an artificial thing. Rather it is the outgrowth of the experience of America, and expresses the faith and spirit of our people. It has carried us in a century and a half to leadership of the economic world. If our economic system does not match our highest expectations at all times, it does not require revolutionary action to bring it into accord with any necessity that experience may prove. It has successfully adjusted itself to changing conditions in the past. It will do so again. The mobility of our institutions, the richness of our resources, and the abilities of our people enable us to meet them unafraid. It is a distressful time for many of our people, but they have shown qualities as high in fortitude, courage, and resourcefulness as ever in our history. With that spirit, I have faith that out of it will come a sounder life, a truer standard of values, a greater recognition of the results of honest effort, and a healthier atmosphere in which to rear our children. Ours must be a country of such stability and security as cannot fail to carry forward and enlarge among all the people that abundant life of material and spiritual opportunity which it has represented among all nations since its beginning.

December 10, 1931: The President reported to Congress:[21]

Conversations were begun between the Secretary of State and the Canadian Minister at Washington on November 14th looking to the framing of a treaty for the development of the St. Lawrence seaway. The negotiations are continuing. I am hopeful that an agreement may result within a reasonable time enabling us to begin work on this great project, which will be of much importance economically to Canada and to the United States.

January 21, 1932: Charles F. Abbott of New York, and others representing various industrial associations, urged the President to recommend the suspension of the anti-trust laws for two years. The President expressed himself as wholly opposed to anything that would lead to price fixing or creation of scarcity; that such a move might result in business tyranny wholly uncompensated by possible benefits in lessening unfair competition. The President stated that where competition in interstate commerce was unmoral or unsocial, it should be corrected by specific statutory law.

February 11, 1932: A delegation of over one hundred manufacturers headed by Malcolm D. Whitman urged the President to take the lead in suspension of the anti-trust laws. The President did not agree and pointed out that the evils which might grow up would drive the country

[21] State Papers, Vol. II, p. 77.

THE CHECK UPON CONSTRUCTIVE LEGISLATION 489

toward Socialism. He refused to agree to any plan involving price fixing or other monopolistic practices.

February 25, 1932: In a letter to the National Education Association, the President said he desired:

> ... to remind our people that, however the national economy may vary or whatever fiscal adjustments may need be made, the very first obligation upon the national resources is the undiminished financial support of the public schools. We cannot afford to lose any ground in education. That is neither economy nor good government.

February 29, 1932: In a special message to the Congress on reform of the judicial system, the President said:[22]

> On previous occasions I have called the attention of the Congress to the necessity of strengthening and making certain changes in our judicial and law-enforcement machinery. Since then substantial progress has been made both through improved methods of administration and additional legislation. However, there is room for further improvement. . . .

Congestion in the Courts

Improvement has been shown during the past three years through steps taken under direction of the Attorney-General in more efficient organization of enforcement agencies through Congressional action in concentration of the responsibilities in the Department of Justice and through the prison reform laws passed by the Congress. Yet despite every effort there is still undue congestion in the courts in a number of districts.

The following statistics indicate this congestion as well as the progress made:

Criminal cases commenced have increased from 1928 to 1931, but the number pending shows a decrease from 30,400 at the end of 1928 to 27,900 at the end of 1931. In 1931 alone 4,000 more criminal cases were disposed of than commenced, showing a definite gain in this field. There has also been a steady improvement in the quality of the work of the prosecuting agencies. Despite an increase in the volume of criminal cases begun, there has been a steady reduction in the number left pending each year. The results attained show a greater percentage of convictions and a lower ratio of dismissals and acquittals. In 1928, 78.3 per cent of criminal cases terminated were by verdict and plea of guilty, while in 1931 this ratio has increased to 84.2 per cent. In 1928, 21.7 per cent of criminal cases were terminated by dismissal or acquittal, while in 1931 this figure had fallen to 15.8 per cent.

Final results of the more effective work of the Federal agencies for enforcement of criminal laws are evidenced by increase of prisoners. The

[22] State Papers, Vol. II, p. 129.

number of Federal convicts in prison institutions and on parole increased from 19,110 at the end of 1928 to 27,871 on June 30, 1931. During the same period the number on probation increased from 3,500 to 12,000. The total number of Federal convicts under some form of restraint was 39,900 on June 30, 1931, as compared with 22,600 on June 30, 1928. The recent reorganization of the parole and probation systems not only has produced a humane result, but has relieved an otherwise impossible prison congestion. These gains in effectiveness have been the result mainly of improvement in personnel, of administrative effort and re-organization, and not of reforms in judicial procedure. . . .

Reform in Criminal Procedure

The extent of crime is and must be a subject of increasing concern to the government and to every well-disposed citizen. This increase is by no means confined to the violation of new criminal laws.

Some part of all crime is due to confidence of criminals in the delays of the law and to their ability to avoid conviction and to delay penalties by misuse of the procedure and provisions of the law intended to assure fair trial. This is more manifest in procedure in the courts of some States than in the Federal courts. Yet important reforms in the Federal establishment and in the Federal procedure are needed and must be undertaken. Aside from its direct result, the indirect result of high standards in the Federal courts is of nation-wide influence.

The present procedure in criminal appeals to the United States circuit courts of appeal and the procedure in the United States district courts, in preparation for appeals after verdicts of guilty, lend themselves to delay and unnecessary expense. . . .

. . . I suggest that the Supreme Court of the United States be authorized to prescribe uniform rules of practice and procedure in criminal cases for all proceedings after verdicts in the district courts, and for the circuit courts of appeal, including the courts of the District of Columbia. . . .

Legislation should be enacted to permit an accused person to waive the requirement of indictment by grand jury. Where the accused admits his guilt, preliminary hearings and grand-jury proceedings are not necessary for his protection, they cause unnecessary expense and delay. . . .

There have been many instances, some recently in the Supreme Court of the District of Columbia, where indictments, returned after long and expensive hearings, have been invalidated by the discovery of the presence on the grand jury of a single ineligible juror. . . . Legislation should be enacted limiting the time for making motions to quash indictments because of disqualifications of grand jurors. . . .

Each year many juveniles charged with violation of law fall into the custody of the Federal authorities. In the interest of child welfare there should be legislation enabling the Attorney-General to forego prosecution of children in the Federal courts and to return them to State authorities to be dealt with by juvenile courts and other State agencies equipped to deal with juvenile delinquents.

THE CHECK UPON CONSTRUCTIVE LEGISLATION 491

The Constitution provides that the judicial power of the Federal courts shall extend to cases between citizens of different States and the Judiciary Acts have provided for the exercise of this jurisdiction. . . .

I recommend the consideration by the Congress of a measure to modify this jurisdiction to a limited extent by providing that where a corporation, organized under the laws of one State, carries on business in another State it shall be treated as a citizen of the State wherein it carries on business as respects suits brought within that State between it and the residents thereof and arising out of the business carried on in such State. Such a change in the law would keep out of the Federal courts cases which do not really belong there and reduce the burdens of the Federal courts without impairing in any degree the diversity of citizenship jurisdiction which the framers of the Constitution had in mind.

I have hitherto recommended legislation effectively to supplement the prohibition law for the District of Columbia. . . .

Conclusions

Reform in judicial procedure is, for many reasons, a slow process. It is not to be brought about by any single measure. It can best be accomplished by dealing with the subject step by step, the sum of which, in the course of time, will result in definite improvement. . . .

March 8, 1932: The War Policies Commission today submitted its report to Congress. It had been appointed by the President on June 27, 1931, to study the promotion of peace, the equalization of the burdens of war, and the minimization of the profits of war. It recommended a Constitutional amendment empowering Congress to stabilize prices in war times and to eliminate profiteering, providing for a ninety-five per cent capture by taxation on all war-profits of corporations and individuals in excess of average profits of the three years preceding a war. The next day, Senator Vandenberg, one of the commission, introduced in the Senate a resolution asking the Treasury to study this latter recommendation. The change in administrations prevented any action on the report.

March 23, 1923: The President signed a bill which, in a case growing out of a labor dispute, limited a United States Court from granting an injunction or temporary restraining order, except under clearly defined and restricted circumstances and conditions. Among other provisions the act declared the so-called "Yellow Dog" contracts to be contrary to public policy and unenforceable either in law or as a basis for granting equitable relief. The President expressed his approval of the measures. In so doing he was carrying out ideas which he had expressed some years before. During the labor disturbances which occurred during the depression of 1921, Mr. Hoover, while a member of President Harding's Cabinet, had vigorously stated his opposition to the policy of Attorney-General

Daugherty in using the injunctive powers of the Federal courts for the purpose of breaking strikes.

April 5, 1932: The well-worn criticism of the President by his Democratic opponents for appointing a number of commissions was revived in a partisan attack upon him. The White House issued a statement as follows: [23]

> In a business so vast and complex as that of the Federal Government a large part of the research work necessarily is carried out by special commissions and committees, delegated to investigate a given subject and to report to the President or to the Congress. They also act for the coordination of government activities, recommend policies, represent the government abroad or at national functions and exercise semi-judicial or semi-legislative powers delegated by the Congress.
>
> A great majority of these commissions are created, not by the President, but by the Congress upon its own motion. All of the commissions created by the President are for temporary non-administrative purposes as are also a large number of those created by Congress.
>
> The number of commissions set up under recent administrations are:

	By Congress.	President.	Total
President Theodore Roosevelt	..	..	107
President Taft	..	..	63
President Wilson	75	75	150
President Harding	..	..	44
President Coolidge	74	44	118
President Hoover	24	38	62

> A full list of the commissions and committees created under previous administrations was published as a Senate document at the request of Senator Watson.
>
> Of the committees appointed by President Hoover, seven received some appropriations for their work, the others were voluntary or supported by public institutions.

April 9, 1932: Speaking at the semi-annual dinner of the Gridiron Club, the President said: [24]

> Our people are at times discouraged by the apparent partisanship in time of national crisis. But we must again needs remember that ours is a government builded upon political parties. Its vital stability depends upon organized expression of the will of the people through party organization. Other democracies in the despair of these three years have sought to build coalition governments, but if you search their results you will find that they have weakened the national vitality by vacillation, or the impotence of positive action from internal friction, or have degenerated to dic-

[23] State Papers, Vol. II, p. 158.   [24] State Papers, Vol. II, p. 162.

THE CHECK UPON CONSTRUCTIVE LEGISLATION

tatorships. Worse still, if there be no alternative party in time of great strain there may be no answer except violent revolution. Political parties having been elected to majorities whether in the Executive or in the Houses of Congress have a positive responsibility to leadership and to patriotic action which over-rides partisanship. Constructive opposition too is essential to the spirit of democracy itself. The anvil of debate alone can shape the tools of government. . . .

April 25, 1932: Notwithstanding the condition of the country and the tremendous demand upon the Federal Treasury growing out of the depression, there were continued attempts to raid the Treasury. The President today vetoed another of these raids by Indian claim agents: [25]

I am returning herewith Senate Bill 826, "An Act conferring jurisdiction upon the Court of Claims to hear and determine claims of certain bands or tribes of Indians residing in the State of Oregon," without my approval.

The bill limits the claims which can be presented to those "arising under or growing out of any treaty, agreement, Act of Congress, Executive Order," and then throws the door wide open by adding "or otherwise." I cannot assent to the proposition that the government should be obligated after seventy-five years to defend a suit for unknown claims of such ancient origin and for persons long since dead not based upon any treaty, agreement, Act of Congress, or Executive Order.

I want full justice for our Indian wards, and would have no objection to the presentation of claims arising under the treaties named in the bill, both ratified and unratified treaties. I am advised, however, that all funds promised to these Indians under the ratified treaties have been appropriated and paid. . . .

May 11, 1932: With a Presidential campaign in the offing, the Democratic-controlled Congress passed a so-called tariff bill, which was a mixture of politics, reciprocal tariff treaties and destruction of the powers of the Tariff Commission. The President vetoed it and said in part: [26]

My first objection to the bill is the misrepresentation . . . as to its purpose. If the purpose . . . is to secure lower tariffs on the thirty-five per cent of our imports which are not on the free list it would seem that the direct and simple method of so doing would be to recognize that tariffs are duties applied to particular commodities, and to propose definite reduction of the duties on such particular commodities. . . . Alternatively, the Congress is able to direct the Tariff Commission under the "flexible" provisions of the Act of 1930 to act upon such schedules as are believed to be too high . . . there never has been a time in the history of the United States when tariff protection was more essential to the welfare of the American people than at present. Prices have declined throughout the

[25] State Papers, Vol. II, p. 166.   [26] State Papers, Vol. II, p. 181.

world but to a far greater extent in other countries than in the United States. Manufacturers in foreign countries which have abandoned the gold standard are producing goods and paying for raw materials in depreciated currency. . . . If the intent . . . of the proposed bill is to . . . reduce tariff protection there never was a time more inappropriate on account of widespread domestic unemployment.

The second objection to the bill is that it practically destroys the "flexible" tariff through the removal of executive authority to render conclusions of the Tariff Commission effective . . . and thus defeats a reform so earnestly sought ever since its first advocacy by President Roosevelt and finally fully realized in the Tariff Act of 1930. . . .

My third objection to the bill lies in the conditions stipulated for action in an International Conference which it is proposed should be called to deal with trade questions. I wish to say at once that I am in fullest accord with the proposal for an international action or conference to "eliminate discriminatory and unfair trade practices," "preventing economic wars," and "promoting fair, equal and friendly trade and commercial relations among nations." . . .

. . . The proposals . . . raise questions of futility or alternatively of abandonment of essential American policies. The first legislative act of Washington's Administration was a tariff bill. From that day to this, one of our firm national policies has been that tariffs are solely a domestic question in protection of our own people. It is now proposed that an international conference should be called with view to "lowering excessive tariffs." The very implication of calling other nations into conference with view to changing our tariff duties is to subject our tariffs to international agreement. . . .

. . . If the Congress proposes to make such a radical change in our historic policies by international negotiation affecting the whole of American tariffs, then it is the duty of the Congress to state so frankly and indicate the extent to which it is prepared to go. . . .

My fourth objection to the bill lies in the further request that I should "negotiate with foreign governments reciprocal trade agreements under a policy of mutual tariff concessions." . . .

A firmly established principle of the American tariff policy is the uniform and equal treatment of all nations without preferences, concessions or discriminations. . . . No reform is required in the United States in this matter, but we should have at once abandoned this principle when we entered upon reciprocal concessions with any other nation. . . . That is the very breeding ground for trade wars. This type of preferential tariff agreement which exists abroad today is one of the primary causes of trade wars between other countries at the present moment.

It has been the policy of our government for many years to advance "most favored nation" treaties with view to extinguishing these very processes, preferences, and trade frictions, and to secure equal treatment to us by the other nations in all their tariff and economic agreements. We have such treaties or executive agreements with thirty-one nations. If we adopted this complete reversal of policies and now negotiated reciprocal tariff agreements we should either under our "most favored nation" obligations need extend these rights to all nations having such treaties with us, or to denounce such treaties.

The struggle for special privileges by reciprocal agreements abroad has produced not only trade wars but has become the basis of political concessions and alliances which lead to international entanglements of the first order. These very processes are adding instability to the world today, and I am unwilling to enter upon any course which would result in the United States being involved in such complexities and such entanglements.

Of high importance to us . . . is that the principal interest of a majority of the sixty or seventy other nations . . . would be to reduce the American agricultural tariffs. No concessions otherwise than those related to agricultural products would be of any importance to those particular nations . . . demoralize our agricultural industry and render us more and more dependent upon foreign countries for food supply: to drive our farmers into the towns and factories, and thus demoralize our whole national, economic, and social stability.

Moreover, the futility of the Executive negotiating such treaties as reciprocal tariffs has been often demonstrated in our past. . . . Out of some twenty-two such treaties providing for reciprocal tariff concessions, the Congress either refused to confirm or failed to act in sixteen, and two of the remaining six failed of confirmation by other governments. . . .

May 13, 1932: Word came that the son of Colonel and Mrs. Charles Lindbergh had been kidnapped. The President, shocked by this most inhuman of crimes and knowing the parents intimately, immediately called the Colonel by telephone and tendered the services of the government in the rescue of the child and the apprehension of the criminals. The President then called in the Attorney-General and instructed him to put his force on the job, which was done. Later, and when those responsible were still at large, the President said to the press:

I have directed the law enforcement agencies and the several secret services of the Federal Government to make the kidnapping and murder of the Lindbergh baby a live and never to be forgotten case, never to be relaxed until those criminals are implacably brought to justice. The Federal Government does not have police authority in such crimes but its agencies will be unceasingly alert to assist the New Jersey Police in every possible way until this end has been accomplished.

June 11, 1932: The President stated to the press: [27]

I have today signed the bill authorizing the transfer of the cases of juvenile delinquents from the Federal system of Criminal Justice to Juvenile Courts in their home communities, provided these Juvenile Courts are

[27] State Papers, Vol. II, p. 208.

willing to accept them. This measure is an important step forward in that it sets an example through its recognition by the Federal Government of the principle that even the relatively small number of juveniles in the Federal system should be handled on a modern scientific basis. It is also a recognition by the Federal Government of the Juvenile Court as the proper place for the handling of the cases of all juveniles, and is an acceptance of the principle that juvenile offenders are the product of and the responsibility of their home communities.

This step was recommended in one of the reports of the National Commission on Law Observance and Enforcement, was included in the recommendations in the President's message to Congress, and has had the active interest and approval of social workers all over the country.

June 22, 1932: The President today signed the anti-kidnapping bill, the passage of which he had asked members of the House and Senate Judiciary committees to expedite. This act provided a basis for Federal action in certain kidnapping cases. To transport in interstate commerce a kidnapped person who was being held for ransom was made a Federal penitentiary offense. The court was authorized to fix a maximum punishment of life imprisonment.

June 29, 1932: The President today signed an act providing for additional or alternate jurors in certain important and long drawn out criminal cases. This was one of the judicial reforms which he had recommended.

July 8, 1932: A model law against possession and sale of, or concealed carrying of weapons in the District of Columbia without license was embodied in a bill which the President signed. This was a part of the law reforms asked for by the President.

July 10, 1932: Congress had passed, and today the President signed, a bill which made it a Federal crime to use the mails with intent to extort money from any person by threatening to kidnap or otherwise injure the person or property of any person. This concluded the authority he had requested to meet the kidnapping problem.

These laws, together with the re-organization of the Bureau of Investigation in the Department of Justice by the employment of a higher type of personnel and the installation of a system of national criminal records, formed the foundation for the Federal drive, then and later, against kidnapping and organized crime.

July 13, 1932: The President announced the completion of the St. Lawrence Waterway Treaty. As Secretary of Commerce and chairman of the St. Lawrence Waterway Commission he had initiated and himself conducted much of the negotiating that lead to the treaty. He had also addressed himself for many years while Secretary of Commerce to the settlement of disputed and rival engineering methods which had long held up the consummation of the agreement. Upon announcing the treaty he said:

After a long period of intensive negotiations an outline of a treaty was concluded the middle of June; the terms were finally settled yesterday and the treaty is now in process of construction and will be ready for signature at an early date, when a full statement by the governments concerned will be issued.

In the negotiations the Hon. Hanford MacNider, our Minister to Canada, had performed a most essential part.

July 18, 1932: In a statement to the press, the President said:[28]

The signing of the Great Lakes St. Lawrence Waterway Treaty marks another step forward in this the greatest internal improvement yet undertaken on the North American continent. The treaty must yet be ratified by the legislative bodies of the two governments and is not effective unless this is done.

The treaty represents to me the redemption of a promise which I made to the people of the mid-West. It provides for the construction of a twenty-seven-foot waterway from the sea to all Canadian and American points, on the Great Lakes. Such a depth will admit practically ninety per cent of ocean shipping of the world to our lake cities in the States of New York, Ohio, Michigan, Indiana, Illinois, Wisconsin and Minnesota. Its influence in cheapening transportation of overseas goods will stretch widely into the interior from these points. Its completion will have a profoundly favorable effect upon the development of agriculture and industry throughout the mid-West. The large by-product of power will benefit the Northeast. These benefits are mutual with the great Dominion to the north.

The waterway will probably require ten years for completion, during which time normal growth of traffic in the nation will far more than compensate for any diversions from American railways and other American port facilities. The economic gains from improved transportation have always benefited the whole people. . . .

The project is of first importance to the whole continent. The many and extremely complex engineering, legal, commercial, and international problems have been worked out by the representatives of both countries in a spirit of co-operation of which all North America can be justly proud.

The President urged its ratification in his message of December 6, 1932, and again, as a recovery measure involving employment of labor, on February 20, 1933.

July 20, 1932: As a step in his efforts to consolidate government bureaus, and acting under an authority of Congress of June 30, 1932, the

---

[28] State Papers, Vol. II, p. 237.

President directed the consolidation of the radio division of the Department of Commerce with the Radio Commission.

July 28, 1932: A large number of World War veterans, self-styled the "Bonus Army," came to Washington during the early spring to lobby for the bonus. During their stay in Washington they were frequently addressed and harangued by various members of Congress. Their camps naturally attracted a large element of Communists and hoodlums which the saner elements of the veterans themselves were unable to restrain. Prior to the adjournment of Congress on July 16th, the President had asked for and received an appropriation with which to offer the veterans (who might be without means) their transportation home. Between 5,000 and 6,000 availed themselves of this opportunity, leaving some 5,000 to 6,000 of a remnant including the non-veteran disturbers, Communists, and others. On July 28th over 1,000 of them converged from their camps and attacked the police who had, after days of given warning, removed some fifty of their numbers from the occupancy of certain old buildings, the destruction of which for purposes of erecting new government buildings already had been delayed rather than inflict any hardship. The story unfolds itself from this point in the following official documents:

July 28th, 1932.

THE PRESIDENT:

The Commissioners of the District of Columbia regret to inform you that during the past few hours circumstances of a serious character have arisen in the District of Columbia which have been the cause of unlawful acts of large numbers of so-called "bonus marchers," who have been in Washington for some time past.

This morning, officials of the Treasury Department, seeking to clear certain areas within the Government triangle in which there were numbers of these bonus marchers, met with resistance. They called upon the Metropolitan Police Force for assistance and a serious riot occurred. Several members of the Metropolitan Police were injured, one reported seriously. The total number of bonus marchers greatly outnumbered the police; the situation is made more difficult by the fact that this area contains thousands of brickbats and these were used by the rioters in their attack upon the police.

In view of the above, it is the opinion of the Major and Superintendent of Police, in which the Commissioners concur, that it will be impossible for the Police Department to maintain law and order except by the free use of firearms which will make the situation a dangerous one; it is believed however, that the presence of Federal troops in some number will obviate the seriousness of the situation and result in far less violence and bloodshed.

The Commissioners of the District of Columbia, therefore, request that they be given the assistance of Federal troops in maintaining law and order in the District of Columbia.

Very sincerely yours,
L. H. REICHELDERFER, *President,*
Board of Commissioners of the District of Columbia.

July 28, 1932: The President said to the press:[29]

For some days police authorities and Treasury officials have been endeavoring to persuade the so-called bonus marchers to evacuate certain buildings which they were occupying without permission. These buildings are on sites where government construction is in progress and their demolition was necessary in order to extend employment in the district and to carry forward the government's construction program.

This morning the occupants of these buildings were notified to evacuate and at the request of the police did evacuate the buildings concerned. Thereafter, however, several thousand men from different camps marched in and attacked the police with brickbats and otherwise injuring several policemen, one probably fatally.

I have received the attached letter from the commissioners of the District of Columbia stating that they can no longer preserve law and order in the District.

In order to put an end to this rioting and defiance of civil authority, I have asked the army to assist the district authorities to restore order. . . .

Congress made provision for the return home of the so-called bonus marchers who have for many weeks been given every opportunity of free assembly, free speech and free petition to the Congress. Some 5,000 took advantage of this arrangement and have returned to their homes. An examination of a large number of names discloses the fact that a considerable part of those remaining are not veterans; many are Communists and persons with criminal records.

The veterans amongst these numbers are no doubt unaware of the character of their companions and are being led into violence which no government can tolerate.

I have asked the Attorney-General to investigate the whole incident and to co-operate with the District civil authorities in such measures against leaders and rioters as may be necessary.

In a public press interview General McArthur said:

. . . It is my opinion that had the President not acted today, had he permitted this thing to go on for twenty-four hours more, he would have been faced with a grave situation which would have caused a real battle. Had he let it go on another week I believe that the institutions of our Government would have been very severely threatened. I think it can be

[29] State Papers, Vol. II, p. 242.

safely said that he had not only reached the end of an extraordinary patience but that he had gone to the very limit of his desire to avoid friction and trouble before he used force. Had he not used it all that time, I believe he would have been very derelict indeed in the judgment in which he was handling the safety of the country. This was the focus of the world today; and had he not acted with the force and vigor that he did, it would have been a very sad day for the country tomorrow.

I have never seen greater relief on the part of the distressed populace than I saw today. I have released in my day more than one community. . . .

. . . At least a dozen people told me, especially in the Negro section, that a regular system of tribute was being levied on them by this insurrectionist group. . . .

. . . I have been in many riots but I think this is the first riot I ever was in or ever saw in which there was no real bloodshed. So far as I know there is no man on either side who has been seriously injured.

July 29, 1932.

HONORABLE LUTHER H. REICHELDERFER,
Commissioner, District of Columbia,
Washington, D. C.

MY DEAR MR. COMMISSIONER:

In response to your information that the police of the District were overwhelmed by an organized attack by several thousand men, and were unable to maintain law and order, I complied with your request for aid from the Army to the police. It is a matter of satisfaction that, after the arrival of this assistance the mobs which were defying the municipal government were dissolved without the firing of a shot or the loss of a life. . . .

It is the duty of the authorities of the District to at once find the instigators of this attack on the police and bring them to justice. . . .

There is no group, no matter what its origin, that can be allowed either to violate the laws of this city or to intimidate the government.

Yours faithfully,

HERBERT HOOVER.

July 29, 1932: The President said to the press:[30]

A challenge to the authority of the United States Government has been met, swiftly and firmly.

After months of patient indulgence, the government met overt lawlessness as it always must be met if the cherished processes of self-government are to be preserved. We cannot tolerate the abuse of Constitutional rights by those who would destroy all government, no matter who they may be. Government cannot be coerced by mob rule.

The Department of Justice is pressing its investigation into the violence which forced the call for army detachments. . . .

[30] State Papers, Voll. II, p. 245.

The first obligation of my office is to uphold and defend the Constitution and the authority of the law. This I propose always to do.

The misrepresentation of the "Bonus Marchers" incident, for political purposes during the campaign, possibly surpassed any similar incident in American history. Not only had the "marchers" been treated with patient consideration by the President, but also not a single person had been injured or a shot fired after he took command of the situation. Two veterans had been killed by the police, acting under Superintendent of Police Glassford, prior to the President's intervention to preserve order. Yet the President was portrayed as a murderer, the veterans were inflamed to believe he desired their destruction, and that he aspired to military dictatorship.

September 29, 1932: The President, in an address to the Women's Conference on Current Problems conducted by the *New York Herald Tribune Institute,* said upon social questions: [81]

Your meeting is for the purpose of forming programs of work in local advancement during the next year. I have been asked to speak for a few moments on the question of housing and of children. . . .

Second only in importance to the direct problems of childhood are the collateral problems of home surroundings and home ownership. The conference in Washington on Housing and Home Ownership in which many of those present with you this evening participated has established a basis for national thought and progress in the great social and economic problems involved. The work of that conference has already flowered in the creation of a new system of Home Loan Banks which I recommended to the Congress for both emergency purposes and for the permanent advancement of home ownership. The authority in the Reconstruction Finance Corporation Act to make loans for slum clearance in the cities is another evidence of the advance of public thought. To you who are planning ahead programs of work for earnest groups of organized women I strongly commend study of the new data, new ideas and methods and plans envisaged by this most exhaustive conference on housing and homes.

Our most immediate question is the strain of the depression upon the children. . . . The devotion of voluntary effort, the solicitude being given throughout the nation to the welfare of children through this trying distress is a stimulant to the spirit of every one of us. The continuous reports of the Public Health Service showing less infant mortality, less infant disease than in prosperous times, can mark only one thing and that is the most extraordinary devotion to those who would normally be the most hard-pressed. . . .

There is another opportunity growing out of these times to advance the cause of children. . . . [There is] a large increase in what we popularly call "technological unemployment." One answer to it lies in short-

[81] State Papers, Vol. II, p. 289.

ening the hours of labor. . . . But there is also another contribution which can be made—that is the steady elimination of child labor. . . .

. . . We cannot afford to slacken one moment in the preparation of the new day of a generation of Americans stronger and better, not only physically and intellectually, but above all morally.

Latterly I have been much interested in the systematic formulation of the conclusions of the White House conference on problems of children. Out of this conference came the Children's Charter, containing a definite program, a program near to your heart and mine, a program so comprehensive, so varied as to provide a foothold for every kind of organized interest, a program so definite that you can make it a personal and specific undertaking. That it struck a responsive chord in the nation is evidenced by the millions of copies of it which have been reproduced.

CHAPTER IV

EXTRACTS FROM THE SPEECHES OF MR. HOOVER IN THE PRESIDENTIAL CAMPAIGN OF 1932. A SUMMARY OF THE CONSTRUCTIVE POLICIES OF THE ADMINISTRATION

WE have presented in the words of President Hoover a summary of his emergency measures to meet the depression (Part I, Chapter XIV). That he also formulated many other plans to improve the administration of the government and solve many of the current problems is shown in the preceding pages. These plans are further explained by the following extracts from his campaign speeches in 1932.

The following subjects are treated in order:

1. The problems before us.
2. Reform in prohibition.
3. Reform in banking and finance.
4. Reform in government regulation or operation of electric power.
5. Reform in railway regulation.
6. Bankruptcy reform.
7. Reform in immigration.
8. The development of waterways.
9. Conservation.
10. The tariff.
11. The Constitution.
12. The battle for the American people.
13. America *vs.* the "New Deal."

I

The Problems before Us

August 11, 1932: On the subject of permanent reforms the President said in his speech of acceptance:[1]

My fellow citizens, the discussion of great problems of economic life and of government often seems abstract and cold. But within their right solution lies the happiness and hope of a great people. Without such solution all else is mere verbal sympathy.

Today millions of our fellow countrymen are out of work. Prices of

[1] State Papers, Vol. II, p. 263; also following reference under same date.

the farmer's products are below a living standard. Many millions more who are in business or hold employment are haunted by fears for the future. No man with a spark of humanity can sit in my place without suffering from the picture of their anxieties and hardships before him day and night. They would be more than human if they were not led to blame their condition upon the government in power. I have understood their sufferings, and have worked to the limits of my strength to produce action that would really help them. . . .

. . . From the hard-won experience of this depression we shall build stronger methods of prevention and stronger methods of protection to our people from the abuses which have become evident. We shall march to far greater accomplishment. . . .

Through it all our first duty is to preserve unfettered that dominant American spirit which has produced our enterprise and individual character. That is the bedrock of the past, and that is the guaranty of the future. Not regimented mechanisms but free men is our goal. Herein is the fundamental issue. A representative democracy, progressive and unafraid to meet its problems, but meeting them upon the foundations of experience, and not upon the wave of emotion or the insensate demands of a radicalism which grasps at every opportunity to exploit the sufferings of a people.

With these courses we shall emerge from this great national strain with our American system of life and government strengthened. . . .

The problems of the next few years are not only economic. They are also moral and spiritual. The present check to our material success must deeply stir our national conscience upon the purposes of life itself. It must cause us to re-value and re-shape our drift from materialism to a higher note of individual and national ideals.

Underlying every purpose is the spiritual application of moral ideals which are the fundamental basis of happiness in a people. This is a land of homes, churches, schoolhouses dedicated to the sober and enduring satisfactions of family life and the rearing of children in an atmosphere of ideals and religious faith. Only with these high standards can we hold society together, and only from them can government survive or business prosper. They are the sole insurance to the safety of our children and the continuity of the nation. . . .

2

REFORM IN PROHIBITION

August 11, 1932: The President speaking at Washington, said:

The Republican platform recommends submission of the question to the States that the people themselves may determine whether they desire a change, but insists that this submission shall propose a constructive and not a destructive change. It does not dictate to the conscience of any member of the party.

The first duty of the President of the United States is to enforce the laws as they exist. That I shall continue to do to the utmost of my ability.

Any other course would be the abrogation of the very guarantees of liberty itself.

The Constitution gives the President no power or authority with respect to changes in the Constitution itself; nevertheless my countrymen have a right to know my conclusions upon this matter. They are clear and need not be misunderstood. They are based upon the broad facts I have stated, upon my experience in this high office, and upon the deep conviction that our purpose must be the elimination of the evils of this traffic from this civilization by practical measures.

It is my belief that in order to remedy present evils a change is necessary by which we resummon a proper share of initiative and responsibility which the very essence of our government demands shall rest upon the States and local authorities. That change must avoid the return of the saloon.

It is my conviction that the nature of this change, and one upon which all reasonable people can find common ground, is that each State shall be given the right to deal with the problem as it may determine, but subject to absolute guarantees in the Constitution of the United States to protect each State from interference and invasion by its neighbors, and that in no part of the United States shall there be a return of the saloon system with its inevitable political and social corruption and its organized interference with other States.

American statesmanship is capable of working out such a solution and making it effective.

3

REFORM IN BANKING AND FINANCE

Washington, August 11, 1932: [2]

In soil poisoned by speculation grew those ugly weeds of waste, of exploitation, of abuse, of financial power.

This depression has exposed many weaknesses in our economic system. There have been exploitation and abuse of financial power. We will fearlessly and unremittingly reform such abuses. I have recommended to the Congress the reform of our banking laws. Unfortunately this legislation has not yet been enacted. The American people must have protection from insecure banking through a stronger system. They must be relieved from conditions which permit the credit machinery of the country to be made available without adequate check for wholesale speculation in securities with ruinous consequences to millions of our citizens and to national economy.

Indianapolis, October 28, 1932: [3]

. . . this depression has exposed many weaknesses in our economic system. It has shown much wrongdoing. There has been exploitation and abuse of financial power. These weaknesses must be corrected and that

[2] State Papers, Vol. II, p. 257.
[3] State Papers, Vol. II, p. 389 *et seq.;* also following references under same date.

wrongdoing must be punished. We will continue to reform such abuses and correct such wrongdoing as falls within the powers of the Federal Government.

The American people must have protection from insecure banking through a stronger system. They must be relieved from conditions which permit the credit machinery of the country to be made available without adequate check for wholesale speculation in securities, with its ruinous consequences to millions of our citizens and to national economy. . . .

I recommended to the Congress the sane reform of our banking laws. The Democratic House of Representatives did not see fit to pass that legislation in the last session. I shall persist in securing its accomplishment.

New York, October 31, 1932: [4]

. . . democracy must remain master in its own house . . . abuse and wrongdoing must be punished and controlled . . . in the ebb and flow of economic life our people in times of prosperity and ease naturally tend to neglect the vigilance over their rights. Moreover, wrongdoing is obscured by apparent success in enterprise. Then insidious diseases and wrongdoings grow apace. . . . It is men who do wrong not institutions. It is men who violate the laws and public rights. It is men not institutions who must be punished.

Cleveland, October 15, 1932: [5]

There is an agency of protection which we have created which has been near to my heart over many years. That has been the establishment of better opportunity for our people to purchase their own homes and to have a chance to keep them when they have undertaken this great step in life. In November of last year I propounded a plan for a national system of Home Loan Banks. These banks were for the purpose, with the temporary assistance of the government, of mobilizing the resources of building loan, savings banks, and other institutions devoted to home ownership to enable them to borrow collectively on more favorable terms from the investor, and to assure to the borrower long-term payments at more reasonable rates. The literally thousands of heart-breaking instances of inability of working people to attain renewal of expiring mortgages on favorable terms, and the consequent loss of their homes, have been one of the tragedies of this depression. Had the Democratic House of Representatives acted upon this measure at the time of its recommendation, we would have saved hundreds of thousands of these tragedies.

I finally secured the passage of that bill through the Congress. Those banks will be operating by the end of this month. The system is not as perfect as I would wish, yet it has already had one immensely beneficial effect, and there will be others. The anticipation of its aid has largely stopped foreclosing on homes, and with its operation it should enable every man who wants to make a fight to hold on to his home an opportunity to do so.

[4] State Papers, Vol. II, p. 408 *et seq.;* also following references under same date.
[5] State Papers, Vol. II, p. 337 *et seq.;* also following references under same date.

And there is another purpose in setting up this new institution. Despite the tendency of the people in some communities to huddle in depression and therefore to create many vacant dwellings, yet there are other communities where people today wish to build homes but cannot do so because they cannot borrow a portion of the cost. These institutions by furnishing this capital will give renewed employment to many thousands of people.

Indianapolis, October 28, 1932: [6]

In the matter of the Home Loan Banks, the Governor states that this idea was brought out in the middle of the campaign, and, like the instructions to speakers, he makes slurs upon it. That statement falls to the ground in the same slough of untruth as the others when it is recollected that I had founded the Better Homes movement in the United States more than ten years ago, whose activities in over 9,000 different communities through the devoted service of thousands of American women finally blossomed into the White House Conference on Home Building and Home Ownership in December a year ago. On that occasion I proposed the plan for the Home Loan Discount Banks which I had advanced two years before, and secured the support of that conference for the creation of the institution. The bill was drafted and presented to Congress on December 8th last. The refusal of the Democratic House of Representatives to act prevented its passage until the last hour of the session eight months later, when the pressures from women and men devoted to the upbuilding of the American home had become so great that they did not dare defeat it in the face of this campaign.

Had that bill been passed when it was introduced, nearly a year ago, the suffering and losses of thousands of small-home owners in the United States would have been prevented. I consider that act was the greatest act yet undertaken by any government at any time on behalf of the thousands of owners of small homes. It provides the machinery, through the mobilization of building and loan associations and savings banks, by which we may assure to men and women the opportunity to bring up their children in the surroundings which make for true unity and true purpose in American life.

4

REFORM IN GOVERNMENT REGULATION OR OPERATION OF ELECTRIC POWER

Washington, August 11, 1932:

I have repeatedly recommended the Federal regulation of interstate power. I shall persist in that. I have opposed the Federal Government undertaking the operation of the power business. I shall continue that opposition.

[6] State Papers, Vol. II, p. 406.

Indianapolis, October 28, 1932:

. . . I stated as early as seven years ago that "glass pockets are the safety of the industry as well as the public."

New York, October 31, 1932:

Another proposal is that the government go into the power business. Three years ago, in view of the extension of the use of transmission of power over State borders and the difficulties of State regulatory bodies in the face of this interstate action; I recommended to the Congress that such interstate power should be placed under regulation by the Federal Government in co-operation with the State authorities.

That recommendation was in accord with the principles of the Republican Party over the last fifty years, to provide regulation where public interest had developed in tools of industry which was beyond control and regulation of the States. . . .

From their utterances in this campaign and elsewhere we are justified in the conclusion that our opponents propose to put the Federal Government in the power business with all its additions to Federal bureaucracy, its tyranny over State and local governments, its undermining of State and local responsibilities and initiative.

5

Reform in Railway Regulation

Indianapolis, October 28, 1932:

I have repeatedly recommended to the Congress a revision of our railway transportation laws in order that we might create greater stability and greater assurance of this vital service in our transportation. This regulation should be extended to other forms of carriers, both to prevent the cutthroat destruction of their own business now going on amongst them and to prevent their destruction of the other major arm of our transportation. I have set this matter out in numerous messages to Congress. I have supported the recommendations of the Interstate Commerce Commission, which are specific and not generalities. Our opponents have adopted my program in this matter during this campaign, except certain glittering generalizations, as to which they do not inform us how they are to be accomplished, and upon which I enter a reservation.

6

Bankruptcy Reform

Washington, October 12, 1932: Address at the meeting of the American Bar Association:[7]

There is another field of urgent reform in the fields of justice—that is, the laws, the technicalities, the procedure, the cost of civil actions, of management of estates, or bankruptcies, and of receiverships. These laws

[7] State Papers, Vol. II, p. 334.

and procedures have failed to keep pace with all the growing complexities of economic and business life, and they must be simplified that their costs and their economic wastes be reduced.

7
REFORM IN IMMIGRATION

Washington, August 11, 1932:

I favor rigidly restricted immigration. I have by Executive direction, in order to relieve us of added unemployment, already reduced the inward movement to less than the outward movement. I shall adhere to that policy.

8
THE DEVELOPMENT OF WATERWAYS

Washington, August 11, 1932:

I have always favored the development of rivers and harbors and highways. These improvements have been greatly expedited. We shall continue that work to completion. After twenty years of discussion between the United States and the great nation to the north, I have signed a treaty for the construction of the Great Lakes–St. Lawrence seaway. That treaty does not injure the Chicago to the Gulf waterway, the work upon which, together with the whole Mississippi system, I have expedited, and in which I am equally interested. We shall undertake this great seaway, the greatest public improvement upon our continent, with its consequent employment of many men as quickly as the treaty is ratified.

9
CONSERVATION

Washington, August 11, 1932:

I have for years supported the conservation of national resources. I have made frequent recommendations to the Congress in respect thereto, including legislation to correct the waste and destruction of these resources through the present interpretations of the anti-trust laws. I shall continue to urge such action.

10
THE TARIFF

Washington, August 11, 1932:

I am squarely for a protective tariff. I am against proposal of a competitive tariff for revenue as advocated by our opponents. That would place our farmers and our workers in competition with peasant and sweated labor products.

Indianapolis, October 28, 1932:

During the first seven weeks of this campaign he [Governor Roosevelt] not only adopts their historic position and constantly repeats their platform, but re-enforces it by repeated statements:

"I support the competitive tariff for revenue."

"The Tariff Law of 1932 was a drastic revision of the tariff upward, in spite of the fact that the existing tariff levels were already high enough to protect American industries."

"We sit on the high wall of the Hawley-Smoot tariff."

"I condemn the Hawley-Smoot tariff."

"A wicked and exorbitant tariff."

"Sealed by the highest tariff in the history of the world."

"Our policy declares for lowered tariffs."

"A ghastly jest."

Mr. Roosevelt and his party knew that the major increases in the Smoot-Hawley Act were the farm tariffs when their platform was drawn, and he knew of them when he made the statements that I have quoted.

Beyond this the Democratic Party and their candidate propose to enter upon reciprocal tariffs. That idea is not entirely new in our history, although it is a violation of a now firmly established principle of uniform and equal treatment of all nations without preferences, concessions, or discriminations. It is just such concessions and discriminations that are producing today a large part of the frictions of Europe. I suppose our Democratic friends try to blame these European tariff wars on the Smoot-Hawley Bill.

Though reciprocal tariffs are a violation of American principles, this nation has fallen from grace and at times attempted to do this very thing. At one time twenty-two such treaties were negotiated for this purpose. Congress refused to confirm sixteen of them, two of the remaining failed of confirmation by other governments, and four others were so immaterial as not to excite notice. On another occasion Congress conferred on the Executive a limited authority to make such treaties, twenty-two of which were agreed upon, all of which were repealed by tariff acts. This all demonstrated just one thing. In an intelligent democracy you cannot surrender the welfare of one industry or locality to gain something for another.

There is, however, an over-riding objection to reciprocal tariff upon the governor's new shuffle, which requires that he give further assurances to the farmers. The vast majority of the wishes of foreign countries about our tariffs is to get us to reduce our agricultural tariffs, so that they can enter our agricultural market.

In all this discussion about reducing tariffs, it should be remembered that if any one of the rates or schedules of our tariff is too high, it has been open to our opponents during the whole of the last session of the House of Representatives to pass a simple resolution, and thereby secure its review from the Tariff Commission. Did they do that? They did not.

EXTRACTS FROM SPEECHES OF MR. HOOVER

Des Moines, October 4, 1932: [8]

All tariff acts contain injustices and inequities. That is the case with the last tariff bill. Some people get too much and some too little. But those of you who have followed the accomplishments of this administration will recollect that I secured in the last tariff act, twenty-five years after it had originally been advocated by President Theodore Roosevelt, the adoption of effective flexible tariff provisions to be administered by a bipartisan body. . . .

By maintaining that reform the country need no longer be faced with heartbreaking, logrolling selfishness and greed, which comes to the surface on every occasion when Congress revises the tariff.

This bipartisan Tariff Commission has now been engaged for over eighteen months in an effective revision of the tariff. It has heard every complaint. It has found that many rates were just, some were too high, and some too low. But if there are tariffs which are too high and result in some damages to the United States, those tariffs can be readjusted by mere application to the commission. That tribunal is open to all the people.

Our opponents opposed this reform in tariff legislation. They passed a bill last session to destroy the independence of the commission. They promise in their platform to destroy it. . . .

Cleveland, October 15, 1932:

I have for many years advocated high wages as the economic basis for the country. That is the road to economical production and high consumption of products of the farm and factory.

. . . In order to show you what the rates of wages are in the United States compared with other countries, I have this week secured through the Department of Commerce a calculation on a basis which I have used before for purposes of illustration. The actual wages in terms of the currencies of other countries are difficult to compare. We must find a common denominator.

If we say that five per cent of butter and ninety-five per cent of flour form the basis of that useful mixture called "bread and butter," then the weekly earnings in each country would buy, at retail in those countries, the following totals of this useful compound:

WEEKLY WAGES IF APPLIED TO THE PURCHASE OF "COMPOSITE POUNDS OF BREAD AND BUTTER" AS OF OCTOBER, 1932.

	Railway Engineers	Carpenters	Electricians	Coal Miners	Weavers	Day Labor
U. S.	1,069	1,064	1,300	734	565	393
*U. K.	342	253	276	223	161	184
Germany	271	176	169	162	120	106
France	246	183	164	123	86	86
Belgium	288	228	240	180	199	160
Italy	275	118	149	70	67	85
Japan	131	86	90	57	31	55

(* United Kingdom)

[8] State Papers, Vol. II, p. 293 *et seq.;* also following references under same date.

Do you want to compete with laborers whose wages in their own money are only sufficient to buy from one-eighth to one-third of the amount of bread and butter which you can buy at the present rates of wages? That is a plain question. It does not require a great deal of ingenious argument to support its correct answer. It is true we have the most gigantic market in the world today, surrounded by nations clamoring to get in. But it has been my belief—and it is still my belief—that we should protect this market for our own labor; not surrender it to the labor of foreign countries, as the Democratic Party proposes to do. . . .

11

THE CONSTITUTION

October 12, 1932: President Hoover, in addressing the American Bar Association at Washington, D. C., said:

. . . Today, perhaps as never before, our very form of government is on trial in the eyes of millions of our citizens. Economic stresses of unparalleled magnitude have wracked our people, and in their distress some are tempted to lay the blame for their troubles upon the system of government under which they live. It is a not unnatural instinct, however mistaken it may be. It can be a dangerous thing, if wise and trusted men fail to explain to the people how often in history the people's interests have been betrayed by false prophets of a millennium, promised through seductive but unworkable and disastrous theories of government. The menace is doubled by the fact that these vain allurements are today being offered to our harassed people by men of public reputation in economics and even by men in public life. No man can foretell to what lengths the pressure of public clamor may at any time be brought to bear upon those charged with the processes of government to yield to changes which you know, before they are tried, would destroy personal liberty and sweep away the security of savings and wages built up by centuries of experience. All progress and growth is a matter of change, but change must be growth within our social and governmental concepts if it should not destroy them.

You have your duty in this area to expound the history of the painful past through which rights and liberties have been won, to warn of repetitions of old and fatal experiments under new and glamorous names, to defend our system of government against reckless assaults of designing persons. It is your task to prove again what none knows better than you, that the very citadel of the rights of the poor against the oppression of rulers, and against the extortions of the rapacious, is the judicial system of the country, and that the impregnable apex of that system is the Supreme Court of the United States. . . .

And here lies also one of the most delicate relations of our Republic. We must maintain on the one hand a sense of responsibility in the States. It is the local communities that can best safeguard their liberties. We must, therefore, impose upon the States the maximum responsibility in these regulatory powers over economic functions. It may be even necessary in the long view of the Republic that the people of some States, whose governments are negligent of the interests of their own people, should be inadequately protected rather than destroy the initiative and responsibility of local communities and of all States and undermine the very foundations of local government. On the other hand, we must be courageous in providing for extension of these regulatory powers when they run beyond the capacity of the States to protect their citizens.

In the ebb and flow of economic life our people in times of prosperity and ease naturally tend to neglect the vigilance over their rights. Moreover, wrongdoing is obscured by apparent success in enterprise. Then insidious diseases and wrongdoings grow apace. But we have in the past seen that in times of distress and difficulty wrongdoing and weakness come to the surface and our people, in their endeavors to correct these wrongs, are tempted to extremes which may destroy rather than build.

In the separation of responsibilities between the Federal and State governments on matters outside of the economic field, we have constantly to resist the well-meaning reformer who, witnessing the failure of local communities to discharge responsibilities of government, to extinguish crime, and to set up agencies of government free of corruption, to move apace with the thousand social and other advances which the country sorely needs, constantly advocates and agitates that the powers of the Federal Government be applied, that we may have a rigid uniformity of reform throughout the nation. Yet even here it is better that we should witness some instances of failure of municipal and State governments to discharge responsibilities in protection and government of their people, rather than that we should drive this Republic to a centralization which will mean the deadening of its great mainspring of progress, which is the discovery and experimentation and advancement by the local community.

12

The Battle for the American People

Des Moines, October 4, 1932:

We have fought an unending war against the effect of these calamities upon our people. This is no time to recount the battles on a thousand fronts. We have fought the good fight to protect our people in a thousand cities from hunger and cold.

We have carried on an unceasing campaign to protect the nation from that unhealing class bitterness which arises from strikes, and lock-outs, and industrial conflict. We have accomplished this through the willing agreement of employer and labor, which placed humanity before money through the sacrifice of profits and dividends before wages.

We have defended millions from the tragic result of droughts.

We have mobilized a vast expansion of public construction to make work for the unemployed.

We fought the battle to balance the budget.

We have defended the country from being forced off the gold standard, with its crushing effect upon all who are in debt.

We have struggled to save homes and farms from foreclosure of mortgages, battled to save millions of depositors and borrowers, from the ruin caused by the failure of banks, fought to assure the safety of millions of policyholders from failure of their insurance companies, and fought to save commerce and employment from the failure of railways.

We have fought to secure disarmament and maintain the peace of the world, fought for stability of other countries whose failure would inevitably injure us. And above all, we have fought to preserve the safety, the principles and the ideals of American life. We have builded the foundations of recovery.

All these battles, related and unrelated, have had a single strategy and a single purpose. That was to protect your living, your comfort, and the safety of your fireside. They have been waged and have succeeded in protecting you from infinitely greater harm which could have come to you.

Thousands of our people in their bitter distress and losses today are saying that "things could not have been worse." No person who has any remote understanding of the forces which confronted this country during these last eighteen months ever utters that remark. Had it not been for the immediate and unprecedented actions of our government, things would be infinitely worse today.

Instead of moving forward we would be degenerating for years to come, even if we had not gone clear over the precipice, with the total destruction of everything we hold dear.

Let no man tell you that it could not be worse. It could have been so much worse that these days now, distressing as they are, would look like veritable prosperity.

In all these great efforts there has been the constant difficulty of translating the daily action into terms of public understanding. The forces in motion have been so gigantic, so complex in their character, the instrumentalities and actions we must undertake to deal with them are so involved, the figures we must use are so astronomical as to seem to have but little relation to the family in the apartment, the cottage, or on the farm.

Many of these battles have had to be fought in silence, without the cheers of the limelight or the encouragement of public support, because the very disclosure of the forces opposed to us would have undermined the courage of the weak and induced panic in the timid, which would have destroyed the very basis of success.

Hideous misrepresentation and unjustified complaint had to be accepted in silence. It was as if a great battle in war should be fought without public knowledge of any incident, except the stream of dead and wounded from the front. There has been much of tragedy, but there has been but little public evidence of the dangers and enormous risks from which a great national victory has been achieved.

I have every confidence that the whole American people know in their hearts that here has been but one test in my mind, one supreme object in the measures and policies we have forged to win in this war against depression: That test was the interest of the people in the homes and at the firesides of our country. I have had before me but one vision: That is, the vision of the millions of homes of the sort which I knew as a boy in this State. . . .

I have been talking of currency, of gold, of credit, of bonds, of banks, of insurance policies, of loans. Do not think these things have no human interpretation. The happiness of 120,000,000 people was at stake. . . .

I wish I were able to translate what these perils, had they not been overcome, would have meant to each person in America. The financial system is not alone intrusted with your savings. Its failure means that the manufacturer cannot pay his worker, the worker his grocer, the merchant cannot buy his stock of goods, the farmer cannot sell his products. The great clock of economic life would stop. Had we failed, disaster would have translated itself into despair in every home, every city, village, and farm.

We won this great battle to protect our people at home. We held the Gibraltar of world stability. The world today has a chance. It is growing in strength. Let that man who complains that things could not be worse, thank God for this victory and make reverent acknowledgment of the courage and stamina of a great democracy. . . .

These issues rise above the concern of an ordinary campaign. Our cause is not alone the restoration of prosperity. It is to soundly and sanely correct the weaknesses in our system which this depression has brought to the surface. It is the maintenance of courageous integrity in political action and in government. It is the holding of this nation to the principles and ideals which it has had from the beginning. It is to make free men and women.

Finally, let me deal for a moment with the ultimate realities. I have had to describe the complicated processes of currencies, and taxation, and other such dreary things. They are but the tools we use to manage the processes by which we answer the old, old question, wherewithal shall we live? They are necessary tools, but they are not an end in themselves. Our toils and cares are but for a higher purpose.

We are not a nation of 120,000,000 solitary individuals, we are a nation of 25,000,000 homes, each warmed by the fires of affection and cherishing within it a mutual solicitude for kinfolk and children. Their safety is what we are really striving for. Their happiness is our true concern. Our most solemn hope for them is that they may share richly in a spiritual life as well, that puts them not only at peace with their fellows but also in harmony with the will of a beneficent Providence.

Out of our strivings for material blessings must come safety for homes, and schools, and churches, and holding of national ideals, the forming of national character. These are the promises of America, and those promises must be fulfilled.

Cleveland, October 15, 1932:

We have been fighting . . . to relieve distress, to repel impending catastrophes, to restore the functioning of our economic life. This economic system has but one end to serve. That end is not the making of money. It is to create security in the millions of homes of our country, to produce increasing comfort, to open wider the windows of hope, to increase the moral and spiritual stature of our people, to give opportunity for that understanding upon which national ideals and national character may be more and more strengthened.

13
America vs. the "New Deal"

New York, October 31, 1932:

This campaign is more than a contest between two men. It is more than a contest between parties. It is a contest between two philosophies of government.

We are told by the opposition that we must have a change, that we must have a new deal. It is not the change that comes from normal development of national life to which I object, but the proposal to alter the whole foundations of our national life which have been builded through generations of testing and struggle, and of the principles upon which we have built the nation. The expressions our opponents use must refer to important changes in our economic and social system and our system of government, otherwise they are nothing but vacuous words. And I realize that in this time of distress, many of our people are asking whether our social and economic system is incapable of that great primary function of providing security and comfort of life to all the firesides of our 25,000,000 homes in America, whether our social system provides for the fundamental development and progress of our people, whether our form of government is capable of originating and sustaining that security and progress.

This question is the basis upon which our opponents are appealing to the people in their fears and distress. They are proposing changes and so-called new deals which would destroy the very foundations of our American system.

Our people should consider the primary facts before they come to the judgment—not merely through political agitation, the glitter of promise, and the discouragement of temporary hardships—whether they will support changes which radically affect the whole system, which has been builded up by 150 years of the toil of our fathers. They should not approach the question in the despair with which our opponents would clothe it.

Our economic system has received abnormal shocks during the past three years, which temporarily dislocated its normal functioning. These shocks have in a large sense come from without our borders, but I say to you that our system of government has enabled us to take such strong action as to prevent the disaster which would otherwise have come to our nation. It has enabled us further to develop measures and programs which are now demonstrating their ability to bring about restoration and progress.

We must go deeper than platitudes and emotional appeals of the public platform in the campaign, if we will penetrate to the full significance of the changes which our opponents are attempting to float upon the wave of distress and discontent from the difficulties we are passing through. We can find what our opponents would do after searching the record of their appeals to discontent, group, and sectional interest. We must search for them in the legislative acts which they sponsored and passed in the Democratic-controlled House of Representatives in the last session of Congress. We must look into measures for which they voted and which were defeated. We must inquire whether or not the Presidential and Vice Presidential candidates have disavowed these acts. If they have not, we must conclude that they form a portion and are a substantial indication of the profound changes proposed.

I may say at once that the changes proposed from all these Democratic principals and allies are of the most profound and penetrating character. If they are brought about this will not be the America which we have known in the past.

Let us pause for a moment and examine the American system of government, of social and economic life, which it is now proposed that we should alter. Our system is the product of our race and of our experience in building a nation to heights unparalleled in the whole history of the world. It is a system peculiar to the American people. It differs essentially from all others in the world. It is an American system.

It is founded on the conception that only through ordered liberty, through freedom to the individual, and equal opportunity to the individual will his initiative and enterprise be summoned to spur the march of progress.

It is by the maintenance of equality of opportunity, and therefore of a society absolutely fluid in freedom of the movement of its human particles, that our individualism departs from the individualism of Europe. We resent class distinction because there can be no rise for the individual through the frozen strata of classes, and no stratification of classes can take place in a mass livened by the free rise of its particles. Thus in our ideals the able and ambitious are able to rise constantly from the bottom to leadership in the community.

This freedom of the individual creates of itself the necessity and the cheerful willingness of men to act co-operatively in a thousand ways and for every purpose as occasion arises; and it permits such voluntary co-operations to be dissolved as soon as they have served their purpose, to be replaced by new voluntary associations for new purposes.

There has thus grown within us, to gigantic importance, a new conception. That is, this voluntary co-operation within the community. Co-operation to perfect the social organization; co-operation for the care of those in .distress; co-operation for the advancement of knowledge, of scientific research, of education; for co-operative action in the advancement of many phases of economic life. This is self-government by the people outside of government; it is the most powerful development of individual freedom and equal opportunity that has taken place in the century and a half since our fundamental institutions were founded.

It is in the further development of this co-operation, and as sense of its responsibility, that we should find solution for many of our complex problems, and not by the extension of government into our economic and social life. The greatest function of government is to build up that co-operation, and its most resolute action should be to deny the extension of bureaucracy. We have developed great agencies of co-operation by the assistance of the government, which promote and protect the interests of individuals and the smaller units of business. The Federal Reserve System, in its strengthening and support of the smaller banks; the Farm Board, in its strengthening and support of the farm co-operatives; the Home Loan Banks, in the mobilization of building and loan associations and savings banks; the Federal Land Banks, in giving independence and strength to land mortgage associations; the great mobilization of relief to distress, the mobilization of business and industry in measures of recovery, and a score of other activities are not socialism—they are the essence of protection to the development of free men.

The primary conception of this whole American system is not the regimentation of men, but the co-operation of free men. It is founded upon the conception of responsibility of the individual to the community, of the responsibility of local government to the State, of the State to the National Government.

It is founded on a peculiar conception of self-government designed to maintain this equal opportunity to the individual, and through decentralization it brings about and maintains these responsibilities. The centralization of government will undermine responsibilities and will destroy the system.

Our government differs from all previous conceptions, not only in this decentralization, but also in the separation of functions between the legislative, executive, and judicial arms of government, in which the independence of the judicial arm is the keystone of the whole structure.

It is founded on a conception that in times of emergency, when forces are running beyond control of individuals or other co-operative action, beyond the control of local communities and of States, then the great reserve powers of the Federal Government shall be brought into action to protect the community. But when these forces have ceased there must be a return of State, local, and individual responsibility.

The implacable march of scientific discovery with its train of new inventions presents every year new problems to government and new problems to the social order. Questions often arise whether in the face of the growth of these new and gigantic tools, democracy can remain master in its own house, can preserve the fundamentals of our American system. I contend that it can; and I contend that this American system of ours has demonstrated its validity and superiority over any system yet invented by human mind.

It has demonstrated it in the face of the greatest test of our history—that is, the emergency which we have faced in the past three years.

When the political and economic weakness of many nations of Europe, the result of the World War and its aftermath, finally culminated in collapse of their institutions, the delicate adjustment of our economic and social life received a shock unparalleled in our history. No one knows that better than you of New York. No one knows its causes better than you. . . .

In spite of all these obstructions we did succeed. Our form of government did prove itself equal to the task. We saved this nation from a quarter of a century of chaos and degeneration, and we preserved the savings, the insurance policies, gave a fighting chance to men to hold their homes. We saved the integrity of our government and the honesty of the American dollar. And we installed measures which today are bringing back recovery. Employment, agriculture, business—and all of these show the steady, if slow, healing of our enormous wound. . . .

If these measures, these promises, which I have discussed; or these failures to disavow these projects; this attitude of mind, mean anything, they mean the enormous expansion of the Federal Government; they mean the growth of bureaucracy such as we have never seen in our history. No man who has not occupied my position in Washington can fully realize the constant battle which must be carried on against incompetence, corruption, tyranny of government expanded into business activities. If we first examine the effect on our form of government of such a program, we come at once to the effect of the most gigantic increase in expenditure ever known in history. That alone would break down the savings, the wages, the equality of opportunity among our people. These measures would transfer vast responsibilities to the Federal Government from the States, the local governments, and the individuals. But that is not all; they would break down our form of government. Our legislative bodies can not delegate their authority to any dictator, but without such delegation every member of these bodies is impelled in representation of the interest of his constitutents constantly to seek privilege and demand service in the use of such agencies. Every time the Federal Government extends its arm, 531 senators and congressmen become actual boards of directors of that business.

Capable men cannot be chosen by politics for all the various talents required. Even if they were supermen, if there were no politics in the selection of the Congress, if there were no constant pressure for this and for that, so large a number would be incapable as a board of directors of any institution. At once when these extensions take place by the Federal Government, the authority and responsibility of State governments and institutions are undermined. Every enterprise of private business is at once halted to know what Federal action is going to be. It destroys initiative and courage. We can do no better than quote that great statesman of labor, the late Samuel Gompers, in speaking of a similar situation:

"It is a question of whether it shall be government ownership or private ownership under control. If I were a minority of one in this convention, I would want to cast my vote so that the men of labor shall not willingly enslave themselves to government in their industrial effort."

We have heard a great deal in this campaign about reactionaries, conservatives, progressives, liberals, and radicals. I have not yet heard an attempt by any one of the orators who mouth these phrases to define the principles upon which they base these classifications. There is one thing I can say without any question of doubt—that is, that the spirit of liberalism is to create free men; it is not the regimentation of men. It is not the extension of bureaucracy. I have said in this city before, that you cannot extend the mastery of government over the daily life of a people without somewhere making it master of people's souls and thoughts. Expansion of government in business means that the government, in order to protect itself from the political consequences of its errors, is driven irresistably without peace to greater and greater control of the nation's press and platform. Free speech does not live many hours after free industry and free commerce die. It is a false liberalism that interprets itself into government operation of business. Every step in that direction poisons the very roots of liberalism. It poisons political equality, free speech, free press, and equality of opportunity. It is the road not to liberty but to less liberty. True liberalism is found not in striving to spread bureaucracy, but to set bounds to it. True liberalism seeks all legitimate freedom first in the confident belief that, without such freedom, the pursuit of other blessings is in vain. Liberalism is a force truly of the spirit, proceeding from the deep realization that economic freedom cannot be sacrificed if political freedom is to be preserved.

Even if the government conduct of business could give us the maximum of efficiency instead of least efficiency, it would be purchased at the cost of freedom. It would increase rather than decrease abuse and corruption, stifle initiative and invention, undermine development of leadership, cripple mental and spiritual energies of our people, extinguish equality of opportunity, and dry up the spirit of liberty and progress. Men who are going about this country announcing that they are liberals, because of their promises to extend the government in business, are not liberals, they are reactionaries of the United States.

And I do not wish to be misquoted or misunderstood. I do not mean that our government is to part with one iota of its national resources without complete protection to the public interest. I have already stated that democracy must remain master in its own house. I have stated that abuse and wrongdoing must be punished and controlled. Nor do I wish to be misinterpreted as stating that the United States is a free-for-all and devil-take-the-hindermost society.

The very essence of equality of opportunity of our American system is that there shall be no monopoly or domination by any group or section in this country, whether it be business, sectional, or a group interest. On the contrary, our American system demands economic justice as well as political and social justice; it is not a system of *laissez faire*.

I am not setting up the contention that our American system is perfect. No human ideal has ever been perfectly attained, since humanity itself is not perfect. But the wisdom of our forefathers and the wisdom of the thirty men who have preceded me in this office, hold to the conception that progress can be attained only as the sum of accomplishments of free individuals, and they have held unalterably to these principles.

In the ebb and flow of economic life, our people in times of prosperity and ease naturally tend to neglect the vigilance over their rights. Moreover, wrongdoing is obscured by apparent success in enterprise. The insidious diseases and wrongdoings grow apace. But we have in the past seen in times of distress and difficulty that wrongdoing and weakness come to the surface, and our people, in their endeavors to correct these wrongs, are tempted to extremes which may destroy rather than build.

My conception of America is a land where men and women may walk in ordered liberty, where they may enjoy the advantage of wealth not concentrated in the hands of a few but diffused through the lives of all, where they build and safeguard their homes, give to their children full opportunities of American life, where every man shall be respected in the faith that his conscience and his heart direct him to follow, where people secure in their liberty shall have leisure and impulse to seek a fuller life. That leads to the release of the energies of men and women, to the wider and higher hope; it leads to opportunity for greater and greater service not alone of man to man in our country, but from our country to the world. It leads to health in body and a spirit unfettered, youthful, eager with a vision stretching beyond the farthest horizons with an open mind, sympathetic and generous. But that must be builded upon our experience with the past, upon the foundations which have made our country great. It must be the product of our truly American system.

CHAPTER V

CARRYING ON

NOVEMBER, 1932–MARCH, 1933

FOLLOWING the election, the administration in large part was concerned with emergency problems. There was little hope for constructive action upon long-view economic or social questions. Except for banking and bankruptcy reform the President of necessity confined his activities to purely emergency matters.

November 12, 1932: On his return trip to Washington after the election, and after a night visit to the Colorado River dam the President, speaking at Boulder City, Nevada, said:[1]

This is not the first time I have visited the site of this great dam. And it does give me extraordinary pleasure to see the great dream I have long held taking form in actual reality of stone and cement.

It is now ten years since I became chairman of the Colorado River Commission. That commission solved in a unique way the legal conflicts as to water rights amongst six of the States which had long held up any possibility of the realization of these works. This was accomplished after three years of negotiations, finally closing with the Santa Fe compact. It was the first time that a provision in the Constitution of the United States for treaties amongst the several States was utilized on so great a scale. That compact was ratified by six of the States and is held open to the seventh to join at any time it may desire. It cleared out the legal underbrush in a way that enabled the next step to be taken. And I again had the satisfaction of presenting, both as an engineer and as the head of the commission, to President Coolidge and to the Congress, the great importance of these works. And I had a further part in the drafting of the final legislation which ultimately brought them into being.

This legislation required the making of an extremely intricate arrangement by which the Federal Government should advance the money but the by-product of power arising from this dam should be sold in such fashion as to return to the Federal Government its entire cost with interest. That contract for the sale of power was successfully negotiated by the present Secretary of the Interior with my approval and contracts were let for actual construction which was begun during my administration. The work has been carried forward with such rapidity that it is already more than a year ahead of schedule in its progress toward the specified period for its completion. Within a few days the river will be diverted through

[1] State Papers, Vol. II, p. 481.

massive tunnels in order that the foundations of the dam may be laid.

This dam is the greatest engineering work of its character ever attempted by the hand of man. Its height alone is nearly 700 feet, making it more than 100 feet higher than the Washington Monument, and far higher than any other such construction ever undertaken.

To understand its purpose our people must realize that the Colorado River in its freshets from the snows of the Rocky Mountains flows at a rate as great as that of Niagara. In the dry season it diminishes to less than five per cent of its maximum flow. The purpose of the dam therefore is to store the freshet; and the amount of water is so gigantic in its proportions that the lake created behind it is over 100 miles long and will require the entire flow of the river for more than two years to fill it.

The primary purpose of this great construction was not the production of power, but as a by-product to its major purpose it will produce over a million horsepower which will, as I have said, pay the cost of the dam and interest back to the Federal Treasury.

Its major purposes are four in number.

Its first purpose was to stabilize the flow of the river from these gigantic annual floods, thus preventing destruction of the great Imperial Valley and the agriculture which has grown up in neighboring States and in Mexico. Most Americans will remember how President Theodore Roosevelt many years ago had to intervene to stop the break in the levees on the river through which the whole of this river was pouring in torrent into the arena of the Imperial Valley which, being below sea-level, would have been turned into an irredeemable sea. This danger is forever removed by the construction of this dam.

Second, to provide a supply of domestic water accessible to Southern California and parts of Arizona. Southern California has a population grown almost to the point where its entire water supply is absorbed, as evidenced by the periodic necessity to ration water in that quarter. With these new supplies of water its growth can go on for generations. And in this connection I may mention that through loans from the Reconstruction Corporation, work starts at once on the great aqueduct to carry this water into Los Angeles and the surrounding towns.

The third purpose was to provide an adequate supply of irrigation water to the large areas of Arizona, the Imperial Valley and other valleys of Southern California.

The fourth purpose is to preserve American rights in the flow of the river.

But the whole of this translates itself into something infinitely more important. It translates itself into millions of happy homes for Americans out under the blue sky of the West. It will in fact in its various ramifications assure livelihood to a new population nearly as great as that of the State of Maryland.

I know that I express the appreciation of the people of the Southwest to the members of the Colorado River Commission who played so large a part in removing obstacles and in effectively establishing these great works, and to those many others who devoted themselves to securing legislation not only in the Federal Congress but in the legislatures of the different States, and to all those now engaged in direction and work upon this magnificent construction. It will be a source of pride to every man and woman to have had association with so great a work. I hope to be present at its final completion as a by-stander. Even so I shall feel a special personal satisfaction.

The waters of this great river, instead of being wasted in the sea, will now be brought into use by man. Civilization advances with the practical application of knowledge in such structures as the one being built here in the pathway of one of the great rivers of the continent. The spread of its values in human happiness is beyond computation.

November 26, 1932: Secretary Wilbur as its chairman had played a leading part in the work of the Committee on costs of Medical Care which had made an exhaustive examination of methods of spread of medical attention to the people of average means. The President sent to him this message: [2]

When an unofficial organization of distinguished physicians, public health officers, social scientists, and representatives of the general public engaged on a five-year program of research present their final report with its recommendations, it should command general interest.

I wish to extend to the members of the committee my appreciation of their efforts to aid in solving one of the most vital problems facing our people today. I regret that I cannot be present at the meeting of the National Conference on the Costs of Medical Care in the New York Academy of Medicine on November 29th to hear the plans proposed by the committee for the delivery of adequate scientific, medical care to all of our people rich and poor, at costs which can be reasonably met by them in their various stations of life. I commend a careful study of this report to the professional and community leaders throughout the United States.

December 10, 1932: The President, in speaking at the Gridiron Club for the last time, said: [3]

I notice in the press generous suggestions that my countrymen owe to me some debts. I have said in part elsewhere that on the contrary the debt is mine. My country gave me, as it gives every boy and every girl, a chance. It gave me schooling, the precious freedom of equal opportunity for advancement in life, for service and honor. In no other land could a boy from a country village without inheritance or influential friends look forward with unbounded hope. It gave to me a certain measure of success in my profession. It conferred upon me the honor of administering the world's response to the appeal of hundreds of millions of afflicted people during and after the war. It gave me high place in the war councils of the nation. My country called upon me to represent it in the

[2] State Papers, Vol. II, p. 493.   [3] State Papers, Vol. II, p. 542.

reconstruction of human and economic relations between former enemies on the Continent of Europe after the Armistice. It gave me an opportunity for service in the Cabinets of two Presidents. It gave me the highest honor that comes to man—the Presidency of the United States. For this fullness of life—for the chance to serve in many emergencies, I am indebted to my country beyond any human power to repay.

Only a few rare souls in a century, to whose class I make no pretension, count much in the great flow of this Republic. The life stream of this nation is the generations of millions of human particles acting under impulses of advancing ideas and national ideals gathered from a thousand springs. These springs and rills have gathered into great streams which have nurtured and fertilized this great land over centuries. Its dikes against dangerous floods are cemented with the blood of our fathers. Our children will strengthen these dikes, will create new channels, and the land will grow greater and richer with their lives.

We are but transitory officials in government whose duty is to keep these channels clear and to strengthen and extend their dikes. What counts toward the honor of public officials is that they sustain the national ideals upon which are patterned the design of these channels of progress and the construction of these dikes of safety. What is said in this or in that political campaign counts no more than the sound of the cheerful ripples or the angry whirls of the stream. What matters is—that God help the man or group who breaks down the dikes, who diverts these channels to selfish ends. Their waters will drown him or them in a tragedy that will spread over a thousand years.

If we lift our eyes beyond the scene of our recent battle, if we inspect the fate of other democracies under the pressures of the past three years, there is outstanding demonstration of a remark I made at a former meeting of the complete necessity in modern democracies of maintaining two strong political parties. Bloc government among several parties leads not only to negative policies, but to destruction of all responsibility which carries government always on the brink of chaos. Coalition government leads inevitably to danger and often to revolution, for it offers the people no alternative through which to explode their emotions. To carry on competent government there must be a strong and a constructive opposition. The Republican Party now has that duty to the American people. But opposition cannot function without political organization, constancy to principles, and loyalty of men to their party. Likewise, no party in power can serve the country unless the members show loyalty, courage, and a willingness to accept the responsibilities of government.

Nor does this preclude that co-operation which far transcends partisanship in the face of common danger. That great common danger is still in the economic field both at home and abroad. During the past two years we have been fighting to maintain the very foundation of our own stability. That front can be held if no mistakes are made. Today one of the visible evidences of our economic problem is the impassable bridge between debtor and creditor. Either the prices must rise or debts be reduced. Not one but many economic forces have brought this about. To increase prices we must give consideration to the continuing effect of the foreign situation. The vicious spiral of economic and social instability has been continuing in the great majority of foreign countries. If we would make a full and secure recovery, if we would prevent future relapse, we must consider major action in co-operation with other nations. But that co-operation does not imply that it shall be accomplished at the expense of the American people. Others must bear their just burdens and open hope to the people of the United States.

To fulfill these tasks we must maintain a solidarity in our nation. We must maintain that co-operation at home which while it maintains party responsibility yet rises above partisanship. The new administration has my good wishes; it has the good wishes of every American, for in its success lies the welfare of our country. . . .

January 2, 1933: Today the report of the President's Research Committee on Social Trends, Wesley C. Mitchell, chairman, was issued to the public. The report offered the first effort in our history to lay the foundations in fact for a long-view social plan for the nation. The President's statement upon its release was:[4]

. . . The significance of this report lies primarily in the fact that it is a co-operative effort on a very broad scale to project into the field of social thought the scientific mood and the scientific method as correctives to undiscriminating emotional approach and to insecure factual basis in seeking for constructive remedies of great social problems. The second significance of the undertaking is that, so far as I can learn, it is the first attempt ever made to study simultaneously all of the fundamental social facts which underlie all our social problems. Much ineffective thinking and many impracticable proposals of remedy have in the past been due to unfamiliarity with facts in fields related to that in which a given problem lies. The effort here has been to relate all the facts and present them under a common standard of measurement.

I regard these aspects of the report as of far greater significance and value than any of its details, admirable as these studies are.

The committee secured the aid of several hundred specialists and compiled an effective survey of our situation in social and governmental development. The work represented a cost, in paid and voluntary services of fully a million dollars. The funds needed were supplied by private subscription.

As stated by the committee, the President's instructions were: "to examine and report on recent social trends . . . with view to providing . . . a basis for the formulation of large national policies looking to the next phase in the nation's development."

The reports embraced several volumes of fact, upon which the com-

[4] State Papers, Vol. II, p. 560.

mittee indicated conclusions as to the steps to be taken in providing greater personal security through old age pensions and unemployment insurance or reserves. Studies were made of methods for attaining greater economic stability, more effectively to deal with poverty, to improve housing, to advance and perfect educations, to study rural life and the problems presented in religion, morals and attitudes, those presented by increasing leisure, the development of public welfare and social work, insurance, health, crime, increasing governmental functions, relations of government to business, cost of government, the relations of the different elements of government, the functioning of Democracy, and relations with other nations. All these were exhaustively treated in an objective manner.

This report represented not only the President's interest and devotion to social development but also his resolution that, before a program was undertaken, the facts first must be secured. His view was that a measure of recovery from the present depression must come first, and that when this was attained a much wider vision of public relations must be accepted in national development. Public interest in the report was well indicated by the fact that it was carried as news for several columns upon the first pages of the newspapers of the country. It since has had a profound effect upon national thinking.

Coincident with this work the President carried forward that of the Committee on Recent Economic Changes, which he had established when Secretary of Commerce. Arch W. Shaw had succeeded him in the chairmanship and the studies in the development of fact in the economic field were for the same purpose, the determination of sound bases for private and governmental action in economic affairs.

January 5, 1933: The President, at the opening of the Conference on the Crisis in Education, said:[5]

Our nation faces the acute responsibility of providing a right-of-way for the American child. In spite of our economic, social and governmental difficulties, our future citizens must be built up now. We may delay other problems but we cannot delay the day to day care and instruction of our children. . . .

Our governmental forces have grown unevenly and along with our astounding national development. We are now forced to make decisions on the merits of the various expenditures. But in the rigid governmental economies that are requisite everywhere we must not encroach upon the schools or reduce the opportunity of the child through the school to develop adequate citizenship. There is no safety for our Republic without the education of our youth. That is the first charge upon all citizens and local governments.

[5] State Papers, Vol. II, p. 564.

I have confidence that with adequate reduction of expenditures there can be ample amounts obtained from reasonable taxation to keep our school system intact and functioning satisfactorily. Those in charge of the schools must be willing to face conditions as they are, to co-operate in discarding all unnecessary expenditure, to analyze all procedures, and to carry forward on a solid basis of economy. But the schools must be carried on. . . .

January 17, 1933: Congress passed the Philippine Independence Act over the President's veto of January 13th in which he had said:[6]

The Philippine people have today as great a substance of ordered liberty and human freedom as any people in the world. They lack the form of separate nationality which is indeed their rightful spiritual aspiration. They have been encouraged in this aspiration by every President of the United States during the years of our association with the Philippines and by declaration of the Congress.

But in securing this spiritual boon to the 13,000,000 people in these islands the United States has a triple responsibility. That is responsibility to the Philippine people, responsibility to the American people, and responsibility to the world at large. Our responsibility to the Philippine people is that in finding a method by which we consummate their aspiration we do not project them into economic and social chaos, with the probability of breakdown in government, with its consequence in degeneration of a rising liberty which has been so carefully nurtured by the United States at the cost of thousands of American lives and hundreds of millions of money. Our responsibility to the American people is that we shall see the fact of Philippine separation accomplished without endangering ourselves in military action hereafter to maintain internal order or to protect the Philippines from encroachment by others, and above all that this shall be accomplished so as to avoid the very grave dangers of future controversies and seeds of war with other nations. We have a responsibility to the world that having undertaken to develop and perfect freedom for these people we shall not by our course project more chaos into a world already sorely beset by instability. The present bill fails to fulfill these responsibilities. It invites all these dangers. It does not fulfill the idealism with which this task in human liberation was undertaken. . . .

After reviewing these questions in detail the President concluded:

If the American people consider that they have discharged their responsibilities to the Philippine people, have carried out the altruistic mission which we undertook, if we have no further national stake in the islands, if the Philippine people are now prepared for self-government, if they can maintain order and their institutions, if they can now defend their independence, we should say so frankly on both sides. I hold that this is not the case. Informed persons on neither side have made such declarations without many reservations. Nor can these conditions be

[6] State Papers, Vol. II, p. 569.

solved by the evasions and proposals of this bill without national dishonor.

February 8, 1933: At the President's request, Congress appropriated 350,000 additional bales of cotton from the Farm Board to the Red Cross for relief purposes.

February 25, 1933: The President approved the act giving authority to the Supreme Court to prescribe rules of practice and procedure after verdict in criminal cases. He stated:[7]

I have signed with great satisfaction the bill, S.4020, to transfer to the Supreme Court of the United States the authority to prescribe rules of practice and procedure to be followed by the lower Federal courts in criminal cases after verdict. It represents the recommendations of myself and the Attorney-General over the past four years. It realizes, in part, a quarter of a century of demands for reform in Federal criminal procedure. It should prevent well-endowed criminals, who have been convicted by juries, from delaying punishment by years of resort to sharp technicalities of judicial procedure. It will increase the respect for law.

The closing days of the Administration were fully occupied with the efforts President Hoover made to prevent the closing of the banks, due to the panic rapidly approaching as the result of popular fear of the measures and policies of the Roosevelt Administration. The story has been told in earlier chapters of this book.

[7] State Papers, Vol. II, p. 600.

CHAPTER VI

THE CABINET AND THE EXECUTIVE DEPARTMENTS OF THE GOVERNMENT

A VERY large part of the responsibilities of any administration is carried by the heads of great administrative agencies and policies are initiated and executed in their departments. Probity and efficiency in government, in great degree, depend upon them and the subordinates they choose. No record of an administration would be complete without specific reference to the work of these officials.

To the President the administrative responsibility of public officials was not only to hold and improve efficiency in the vast business of government but also to assure beyond all question its probity. His oft-expressed view was that dishonesty in government was far worse than dishonesty in private business, for dishonesty in private business could be measured mostly by money loss and punished by imprisonment; whereas in government, it lowered the whole moral standard of a people. Not a single scandal developed in the whole four years—a record few administrations have equaled, no matter how high-minded were the President and his principal officers.

It is not proposed to describe the routine of these agencies in detail but only to present those items of major activity and policies not mentioned elsewhere.

The secretaries to the President were George Edward Akerson, 1923-1931, and Theodore G. Joslin, 1931-1933; Lawrence Richey and Walter H. Newton.

The total numbers of Federal employees during the Hoover and other recent administrations as reported by the Civil Service Commission were as follows:

Under President Coolidge
June 30, 1928 568,715

Under President Hoover
June 30, 1929 587,665
* June 30, 1930 608,915
* June 30, 1931 616,837
June 30, 1932 578,213
December 30, 1932 564,103

* Increase due to taking 1930 census.

Under President Roosevelt

June 30, 1933	565,432
June 30, 1934	661,094
June 30, 1935	715,000

The State Department

The discussion of foreign affairs is not part of this present volume except in their indirect relation to the economic situation.

Secretary Frank B. Kellogg remained in the Cabinet until Secretary Henry L. Stimson arrived from the Philippines where he had been Governor-General. The Under Secretary of State was, first, Joseph P. Cotton and later William R. Castle, Jr., and the assistant secretaries were Wilbur J. Carr, Francis White, James Grafton Rogers, and Harvey H. Bundy.

A transformation was made in the strained Latin-American relations. This was brought about by President Hoover's visit to South America prior to the inauguration; the announcement of the abandonment of all policies of intervention; the withdrawal of marines from Nicaragua and Haiti; the selection for appointment of career men who knew the language, the country and diplomacy; and the abandonment of "dollar diplomacy" through the announcement that no private concessions would be enforced and no debts collected by military threats.

Unceasing effort for further world limitation of armament brought definite results in the London Naval Conference which was called at the instance of the United States. It was a great and possibly the last practical accomplishment towards disarmament in the present day.

The Kellogg-Briand Pact was transformed from a static to a dynamic force for peace by the "Hoover-Stimson doctrine"—that title to territory annexed in violation of the pact should not be recognized by the signatories to the pact. This great moral sanction was accepted and applied by all of the fifty signatory nations in the case of the attempted encroachment of Russia on China and the Japanese annexation of Manchuria. It remains to be seen whether Mr. Hoover's successors will continue this practical interpretation of morals in world affairs.

After twenty years of negotiation, a treaty was signed with Canada for the construction of the Great Lakes seaway to the Atlantic. It was refused ratification by a Democratic-controlled Senate.

Under the law passed under Mr. Coolidge which strengthened the "career" character of the foreign service, the majority of posts in the diplomatic service (all Latin America and the Far East, with one exception) were placed in this category, thus giving the United States a

Foreign Service of the first rank. Never in our history was peace more assured to the American people or did the United States stand higher in the esteem of the world than on March 4, 1933.

Department of the Treasury

At the Treasury, Secretary Andrew W. Mellon and later Secretary Ogden L. Mills had to receive the brunt of the financial impacts of the depression on the government. The staff of the Treasury embraced Under-Secretaries Ogden L. Mills and later Arthur A. Ballantine, and Assistant Secretaries Walter E. Hope, James H. Douglas, Jr., Ferry K. Heath, and Seymour Lowman, with Director of the Budget J. Clawson Roop.

Certain outstanding accomplishments of the Treasury Department, which do not appear elsewhere, may be mentioned. The enormous public building program undertaken partly to relieve unemployment, but mainly to provide quarters for the government at a saving of rents, was administered by the Treasury under Ferry K. Heath. The "triangle" development at Washington is but one of the beautiful results for the nation. That several hundred millions were expended throughout the country in the purchase of sites, designing of contracts, and the erection of over seven hundred buildings—many of great size—without even a charge of graft and with efficiency, is its own testimony. But beyond this, a new era of government architecture was introduced through the engaging of private architects in each locality, rather than the multiplying of architectural employees of the government. This latter had been the practice.

The average rate of interest upon the public debt was reduced from 1929 to 1932 by one half of one per cent, or a saving of fifty million dollars per annum on interest charges.

One of the increased burdens of the depression upon the Treasury Department was caused by the steady decrease in revenues and the consequent necessity constantly to devise and advocate new sources of government income. How severe were these reductions in revenues is indicated by the total ordinary receipts during each fiscal year ending June 30th.

1929	$4,033,250,225
1930	4,177,941,702
1931	3,317,233,394
1932	2,121,228,006

Another of these increased burdens arose from the fact that the supervision of national banks through the Comptroller of the Currency lies in the Treasury Department. While the failures of National banks were proportionately very much less than of State banks, yet every failure added a new burden to the department. This was particularly the case since the secretary and his assistants and the able Comptroller of the Currency, J. W. Pole, used their best efforts to prevent such closings by assisting in negotiations for the sale of weak banks to stronger ones in order to protect the depositors and to secure the reorganization of suspended banks. That these efforts were of great public importance is indicated by the following table of National banks restored:

	Deposits in Restored Banks
1929	$1,404,000
1930	1,517,000
1931	24,717,000
1932	56,267,000

As the Treasury is the accounting arm of the government, it is appropriate here to review the total expenditures during the Hoover Administration. In order to give them usefulness for comparison they have been recast as nearly as possible upon the basis of presentation adopted by the Roosevelt Administration in 1935-36, where they are divided into "general" and "emergency" expenditures. In this new form, general expenditures are given exclusive of trust accounts and of postal services payable out of postal receipts, and inclusive of the Federal contribution to the District of Columbia. Also the statutory debt redemption is included. The "emergency" expenditures include the public works and other construction items in the government on the basis now used, together with loans on security by government agencies.

The recasting of accounts is difficult to attain as a variation of $50,000,000 might be arrived at by different methods.

	Year	General	Emergency
March 1st to June 30th	1929	$1,164,118,042	$118,843,260
	1930	3,293,895,185	569,970,061
	1931	3,320,313,936	926,636,403
	1932	3,086,202,364	1,799,912,736
July 1, 1932 to March 1st	1933	2,055,859,584	1,241,005,635
	Total	$12,920,389,111	$4,656,368,095

Of the emergency expenditures, $2,397,267,363 were loans against security to a net amount of $2,259,100,732. The gross national debt at March 1, 1929, was $17,378,514,363. On March 1, 1933, it was $20,858,055,366, of which, as above, $2,397,267,288 were loans against security. Assuming a five per cent loss in recovery of loans (most of which have been repaid), the net debt burden on the taxpayers was about $18,600,000,000, or an increase of about $1,400,000,000.

The increase in national debt during two years and four months of the Roosevelt Administration, after allowing for recoverable loans, is near $7,000,000,000 and will probably be double this sum before the entire four years have expired. And even this does not include an increase of $5,000,000,000 in government guaranteed bonds.

War Department

At the War Department, Secretary James W. Good died during the first year of the administration, and was succeeded by Secretary Patrick J. Hurley. The major staff of the department were Assistant Secretaries Frederick H. Payne and F. Trubee Davison; Chiefs of Staff, Major-General Charles P. Summerall and later Major-General Douglas MacArthur, and Chief of Engineers, Major-General Lytle Brown. Many of the activities of the department have been referred to elsewhere.

The military machine was improved in equipment, the fortifications were expanded, and the military posts greatly improved. The army was held to the same strength throughout the administration. Under Assistant-Secretary Davison the air strength was increased from 1,273 planes in 1929 to 1,814 in 1932. Such a figure represents but a small part of the development of ground equipment and training of personnel required for the building up of this service.

The War Department under the chief of engineers was given far larger duties through the expansion of the public works program. The new Mississippi Flood Control was initiated; the Ohio canalization was completed to nine feet in depth; the nine-foot channel was completed from New Orleans to Cairo and from St. Louis to Kansas City, and two-thirds completed to Chicago; the new canalization through a nine-foot channel of the upper Mississippi was substantially advanced; the harbors everywhere were expanded and improved. Better to administer these expanded works, the country was divided into districts and the work was decentralized from Washington.

The Navy Department

Charles Francis Adams was Secretary of the Navy throughout the Administration. He was ably aided by Ernest Lee Jahncke and David S. Ingalls, Assistant Secretaries. Admiral C. F. Hughes was Chief of Operations during the first part of the Administration. He was succeeded by Admiral William V. Pratt.

Our naval strength was increased during this period. The modernization of the battleships *Oklahoma, Nevada, Pennsylvania,* and *Arizona* was completed and that of the *New Mexico, Mississippi,* and *Idaho* largely advanced. New cruisers, the *Pensacola, Salt Lake City, Northampton, Chester, Houston, Louisville, Chicago,* and *Augusta* were completed. The keels were laid of seven other cruisers, the *New Orleans, Portland, Astoria, Indianapolis, Minneapolis, Tuscaloosa,* and *San Francisco* and together with the aircraft carrier *Ranger* were in large part completed. Numbers of destroyers and submarines were laid down or completed, and in construction. Yards, docks, and land equipment generally were improved. The useful aircraft were increased from about 800 to about 1,000 and the necessary expansion of ground services provided. The effective strength of our navy was greater at the end of the Hoover Administration than at any time since the Washington Arms Treaty.

DEPARTMENT OF JUSTICE

Attorney-General William D. Mitchell directed the Department of Justice throughout the entire period. His staff first comprised Charles Evans Hughes, Jr., and later Thomas D. Thacher, Solicitor-Generals, John Lord O'Brian, assistant to the Attorney-General, and Assistant Attorney-Generals Charles P. Sisson, Seth W. Richardson, Roy St. Lewis, G. Aaron Youngquist, Monte Appel, Charles Rugg, Nugent Dodds, and Charles W. Lawrence.

A drastic reform of the whole Federal law enforcement machinery was carried out. The most careful scrutiny was given to the appointment of Federal judges and district attorneys. A score of weak district attorneys were removed or failed of reappointment. But, of even more importance, the whole machinery of enforcement was tightened up all along the line. As stated elsewhere, the criminal procedure in Federal courts was simplified and greatly improved. The Criminal Investigation Division under J. Edgar Hoover was built up into a real Scotland Yard, with a personnel of legally trained men instead of the old-fashioned detectives. These men created the spirit of the "G" men who now are the terror of the criminals. The various prohibition enforcement bureaus were consolidated into the Department of Justice. The Lindbergh kidnapping law was passed and the use of income tax evasions and prohibition law violations made possible effective drives against well known gangsters over the nation.

The public interest in the prohibition question and the work of the Wickersham Commission on that problem overshadowed other and more effective work which was accomplished. From the recommendations of the commission and from the co-operation of the Attorney-General, criminal procedure in the courts was reformed, as already stated.

Through the persistent endeavors of the Attorney-General and

Sanford Bates, Director, Bureau of Prisons, the whole prison system was reformed, the probation and parole systems were transformed, reformatories built for women and for young prisoners, and new prisons erected at Lewisburg, Pennsylvania; New Orleans; Billings, Montana; and Detroit, and open air prison camps installed at Camp Lee, Virginia, and El Paso, Texas.

The investigation, recommendation for legislation and final enactment by Congress of reform in bankruptcy laws have been referred to.

It is difficult to demonstrate the tangible results of this vigorous administration of the Department of Justice. Some indication of the increasing thoroughness of law enforcement is shown by the comparative increase in cases instituted and terminated by the department:

	Fiscal Year 1929	1932
Civil Cases Commenced	24,307	34,189
Civil Cases Terminated	21,733	29,591
Criminal Cases Commenced	86,348	91,174
Criminal Cases Terminated	85,324	96,949

This, however, by no means tells the whole story, for it is the convictions which count most in criminal law enforcement. This is indicated by the prison "population."

Federal Convicts as at June 30, each year

	1929	1930	1931	1932
In Federal Prisons	9,694	13,269	13,657	13,698
Other Institutions	(Unknown)	13,438	12,283	12,891
On Parole	963	1,939	2,628	3,327
On Probation	(Unknown)	4,222	3,327	23,200
Total		32,868	41,891	53,116

The long-term convicts were sent to Federal prisons and short-term to local jails. That these increases were not due alone to more vigorous enforcement of the Prohibition Act is indicated by the fact that the number of prohibition violators sent to Federal prisons during the fiscal year, 1929, was 3,589, for 1930 was 4,722, for 1931 was 4,815, for 1932 was 4,833. Yet the long-term convicts in this period increased from 9,694 in 1929 to 13,698 in 1932. The prohibition acts were given a full trial of enforcement by the Federal authorities. The consolidation of all prohibition enforcement agencies into the Department of Justice during President Hoover's Administration, the transformation of the personnel from political appointees to trained civil service employees all contributed to give as full force to the acts as was possible. The following tables indicate the vigor of action:

*Jail sentences for violation of prohibition laws—
year ending June 30,*

1929	21,602
1930	27,709
1931	30,108
1932	44,678

Convictions which resulted in fines, civil proceedings, padlocking and confiscations increased in the same ratios.

And upon some of the larger aspects of the Attorney-General's work, one comment alone is necessary. While under the Attorney-General's advice several legislative acts were vetoed by the President because they were unconstitutional, no single law signed by Mr. Hoover out of the host of those enacted in his Administration has been declared unconstitutional by the Supreme Court.

Post Office

Walter Folger Brown was Postmaster-General, Arch Coleman, W. Irving Glover, Frederick A. Tilton, and John W. Philp were Assistant Postmaster-Generals. The depression greatly affected the volume of mail and the postal receipts, and presented a most difficult administrative question. The department's expenditures were largely for salaries and the government could not set the example of the discharge of faithful employees, but did, in fact, preserve a living basis for them throughout the period. The economies made and the reorganization in methods carried through substantially reduced the amount of increasing deficits.

The Post Office is a routine department where close and efficient management offers little opportunity for interesting development. The oustanding work in this direction was the development of commercial aviation, the extraordinary accomplishment in which has been described.

Department of the Interior

Ray Lyman Wilbur was Secretary of the Interior throughout the Administration. Former Senator Joseph H. Dixon and John H. Edwards were Assistant Secretaries and Edward C. Finney was Solicitor. Horace M. Albright was continued in the National Park Service from the leadership of which Stephen Mather had retired, due to ill health after years of devotion to that service. On the death of William Spry, C. C. Moore succeeded to the Land Office, Charles J. Rhoads the Indian commissionership and J. Henry Scattergood was Assistant Commissioner. Lawrence M. Judd succeeded to the governorship of Hawaii and George A. Parks continued as Governor of Alaska. Elwood Mead continued as Commissioner of Reclamation, William J. Cooper as head of the Bureau of Education and George Otis Smith as the Director of the Geological Survey, until he was made chairman of the Federal Power Commission, when he was succeeded by William C. Mendenhall.

The activities of the department, beyond matters mentioned elsewhere and its routine administrative work, were largely a special development of the Indians toward self-support with view to their gradual absorption into the population; the development of definite policies for conservation of the grazing ranges on the public domain; the conservation of minerals in the public domain by withdrawal of prospecting and development licenses for fuel minerals—oil, coal, and shales; the conclusion of agreements among oil producers for conservation of oil and gas through unit operations in the newly discovered fields such as Kettleman Hills; the advancement of State legislation in prevention of waste in oil production (this was attained in each major oil-producing State); the advocacy of interstate compacts for joint action in prevention of oil waste (a proposal at the time resented by oil producers, but now advocated by them); the development of potash supplies in Texas and New Mexico; and the development of the national parks.

Extensions were made to sixteen of the national parks and monuments. New parks and monuments were created at Bandelier and Carlsbad, New Mexico; Arches in Utah; Canyon de Chelly in Arizona; the Great Smokies in North Carolina and Tennessee; Shenandoah Park, George Washington's Birthplace and Colonial National Monument in Virginia; the Great Sand Dunes in Colorado; and Death Valley in California. The area of parks and monuments was extended by over 3,000,000 acres during the Hoover Administration, or over forty per cent.

The policies of the Reclamation Service were directed by President Hoover and Secretary Wilbur to the conservation of water by large reservoir construction. It was part of these policies to delay expansion of irrigation areas until the farm products were needed by the country, but to take in hand projects for which years of preparation and construction were necessary. President Hoover's view long had been that the Federal Government should confine itself to dam construction, leaving irrigation development to the States without imposing any charge for dam construction. This policy had become imperative, as of the total area susceptible of irrigation—3,300,000 acres—only fifteen per cent was public lands, the balance being State or private lands. The largest project upon which construction was initiated was the dam on the Colorado River. Engineering investigation of the Grand Coulee in the State of

Washington and the great central valley water projects in California were carried forward.

Department of Agriculture

This department has been under great pressure ever since the War. Like the period following the Napoleonic Wars the disparity between agricultural prices and industrial wages has been continuous.

The Secretary of Agriculture during the Administration was Arthur M. Hyde, former Governor of Missouri. In addition to his duties in the Agricultural Department, he was an active member of the Federal Farm Board, the work of which, with the many other activities of the department, has been discussed elsewhere. Among the exceptional activities of Secretary Hyde, during this period, were the initiation of certain vital investigations with a view to determination of important agricultural conservation policies. These embraced an exhaustive study of land use to develop a national policy for better land settlement, and of turning marginal lands into forestry and other forms of national land utilization. Following these investigations, a national conference was called by Secretary Hyde, in 1932, at which national policies were definitely formulated. R. W. Dunlap was Assistant-Secretary of Agriculture.

The forests are under this department. Their conservation was pushed vigorously. The total acreage in nationally owned forests was increased from about 156,000,000 acres in March, 1929, to about 188,000,000 acres in March, 1933. A great deal of marginal land was thus absorbed.

An exhaustive study of erosion also was initiated at this time. And Secretary Hyde initiated a thorough inquiry into utilization of farm by-products and the cultivation of plants for industrial use which might supplant excessive crops. Headway was made in this direction.

Secretary Hyde was particularly active in establishing wider credit institutions for farmers. The extension of farm credit associations and the creation of the Agricultural Regional Credit Banks through the Reconstruction Finance Corporation were in large part due to his efforts. The department had the burden of administering the government aid in the drought of 1930. For this purpose, a total of 385,192 loans for seed and feed were made, aggregating $47,055,761. Again in 1931-32, the department administered on behalf of the R.F.C. $64,203,777 which was loaned to 507,643 farmers to enable them to get into crop production.

The work of the Federal Bureau of Public Roads, ably administered by Thomas H. McDonald, was greatly expanded as a measure of unemployment and agricultural relief. During Secretary Hyde's administration nearly 50,000 miles of Federal aid highways were built. The number of persons given employment varied from 200,000 in the off-seasons to 390,000 at the intensive seasons. The drive of President Hoover and Secretary Hyde for State co-operation in increasing construction of non-Federal aid highways created the largest road building activity in our history and gave wide employment.

Department of Commerce

This department had been built up greatly during Mr. Hoover's secretaryship from 1921 to 1928. Its Bureau of Foreign and Domestic Commerce had been developed until it had become a great agency for the promotion of American trade. During the Hoover Administration Robert P. Lamont was secretary for the first three years and Roy D. Chapin for the last year. Dr. Julius Klein and Clarence M. Young were assistant secretaries.

The department had a large routine of duties, in protection to life at sea and in the mines, and large agencies of economic and statistical services and duties in the promotion of industry and trade. Exceptional burdens were imposed upon its economic activities by the depression. Constant investigations into causes and remedies were in progress. Such exceptional activities as the determination of the number of unemployed, the constant investigation of economic situations and trade opportunities abroad, and the development of commercial aviation, already have been referred to.

The entire aeronautic service of inspection of planes, examination of pilots, lighted airways (some 20,000 miles), beacons, 350 emergency landing fields, radio weather service and research divisions, was built up during Mr. Hoover's Administration either as Secretary of Commerce or as President. In the meantime, with these facilities commercial aviation increased from a few miles of annual flying to over 50,000,000 miles.

The radio industry also had developed beyond ship-to-shore use during the period of Mr. Hoover's secretaryship and Presidency. He had organized it first upon a voluntary basis and, subsequently, through legislation recommended by him, the entire regulation and the use of radio channels brought order into the development of broadcasting and other radio uses. It was due to Mr. Hoover that all radio channels, wave lengths, were taken over by the government for public use and assigned to private and other purposes by the government for use but not for ownership, and subject to public regulation.

CABINET AND EXECUTIVE DEPARTMENTS 541

While many services of lighthouse, channel marking, navigation laws, and others affecting the merchant marine were offered by the Department of Commerce, the Shipping Board administered the government-owned lines and the loans for ship construction, and the Post Office Department administered the mail subsidies. In creating the Shipping Board, Congress made it an independent agency apart from the Executive. It then conferred on the Board quasi-judicial and administrative functions. The President ceaselessly recommended the transfer of the administrative functions to the Department of Commerce, where it would be under the direction of the Executive. Such an arrangement would have made for better administration and at much less cost.

Department of Labor

The Labor Department was, for the first twenty-one months of the administration, under Secretary James J. Davis, who was succeeded upon his election to the United States Senate by Secretary William N. Doak in November, 1930. The assistant secretaries were Robe Carl White and W. W. Husband.

The burdens of the department were much increased by the depression. The Employment Service was greatly expanded in April, 1931, and John R. Alpine was asked by the President to undertake its direction. The work of this division is indicated by the increase in placements through its own employment offices and those with whom it co-operated. Together with co-operating State and municipal employment offices 1,104,136 persons were placed in 1931 and 2,174,179 in 1932. The service to agricultural seasonal workers expanded from placing 559,571 persons in 1929 to 886,605 in 1932.

The Bureau of Immigration was given additional burdens through the President's immigration instructions of September, 1930, which limited all immigration to those who would not become public charges. The effect of this order is shown by the following figures:

	Immigrants (inward)	Emigrants (outward)
1929	279,678	69,203
1930	241,700	50,661
1931	97,139	61,882
1932	35,576	103,295

Had not this action been taken by the President, the unemployed in this country would have been increased by at least half a million.

The work of the Children's Bureau was of outstanding interest to the President. Despite the reductions in expenditure in all the other regular bureaus, he steadily increased the resources of this bureau. The expenditures were:

1929	$303,451.86 *
1930	332,776.96
1931	353,011.97
1932	375,823.25

* (Without maternity and infancy appropriations, which expired this year.)

The Conference on Child Health and Protection has been described.

The outstanding accomplishment of the Hoover Administration in labor matters was the unparalleled era of industrial peace which he brought about through the co-operation of employers and employees. The conferences and policies which produced these results already have been described. The tangible proof is in the following table. The record of strikes and lockouts expressed in man-days work lost, as given by the Department of Labor reports, was:

Under President Hoover:

1929	March	1,740,468
	April	1,429,437
	May	1,727,694
	June	1,627,565
	July	1,062,428
	August	358,142
	September	244,864
	October	272,018
	November	204,457
	December	95,541
1930	All	2,730,368
1931	All	6,386,183
1932	All	6,462,973
1933	January	251,829
	February	113,215

This ends a narrative of real accomplishments. Mr. Hoover entered the White House with ideas of great and forward looking, as well as creative, activity, and many of them were carried into effect in spite of the adverse times. They will be of increasing importance through the coming years, and of lasting benefit to the American people.

Mr. Hoover well can afford to await the verdict of history. And his claim to statesmanship is secure.

INDEX

INDEX

INDEX

Adams, Charles Francis, 13, 534.
Addresses, President's: *to Associations, Clubs, etc.*, American Banks Association, 46–47; American Federation of Labor, 49–50; Gridiron Club, 82, 419–420, 463–465, 492–493, 524–526; International Chamber of Commerce, 82–83; Republican Editorial Association of Indiana, 89–90; American Legion, 120; Associated Press, 383–385; American Institute of Architects, 385–386; Community Chest workers, 423–424; Boy Scout leaders, 425; American Society of Mechanical Engineers, 426–427; Red Cross, 432; National Recreation Association, 474; American Bar Association, 508–509, 512–513; *Radio*, 65, 136–137, 174, 181, 429, 455, 483–485; *Miscellaneous*, on his policies, 20, 76–79; on result of election, 276; on international currency relations, 298–302; on gold standard, 317; on Ohio River canal, 409–411; on Negro progress, 474–475; on governmental and business reforms, 478–479; on Colorado River Dam, 522–524; *to Conferences*, Pan-American, 134–135, 482; Governors, 199–200; Business and Industrial Committees of Federal Reserve Districts, 243–244; Wickersham Commission, 390; Federal Farm Board, 397; Child Conference, 398, 455–458; State and Highway Safety, 434; "Better Homes," 450–451, 485–486; Women's, on Current Problems, 501–502; on Crisis in Education, 527–528; *to Congress*, 214–216, 320–321, 327 (*see* Messages); *Acceptance*, 248–250, 503–504; *Campaign*, St. Paul, 250–253, 274, 275; Cleveland, 253–254, 260–263, 268, 506–507, 511–512, 515–516; Fort Wayne, 254; Des Moines, 254–260, 268–270, 511, 513–515; Washington, 255, 266–267, 269, 504–505, 507, 509; St. Louis, 263–264; Indianapolis, 264–265, 269–270, 505–508, 510; Detroit, 265–266, 270–272; New York, 270, 506, 508, 516–521; *Inaugural*, 374–375; *Memorial*, to Thomas A. Edison, 408–409; Memorial Day, 86–87, 435–436; anniversary of Battle of King's Mountain, 451–455; *to Legislatures*, Illinois, 479.
Administrative agencies, 530–542.
Aeronautics: National Advisory Committee on, 418; service, improvement in, 540.
Agricultural: Marketing Bill, 24, 38, 168, 378, 386, 387–388, 391–392, 407, 445; Credit Banks, 152, 234, 244, 258, 370, 539.
Agriculture, Department of, 13, 539–540.
Air: Mail, 425, 430–431, 446, 537; strength, increase in, 534.
Akerson, George Edward, 530.
Alabama, 471, 481.
Alameda (Calif.), 400.
Alaska, 538.
Albright, Horace M., 537.
Alpine, John R., 67, 111, 541.
American: Federation of Labor, 34, 36, 49, 472 (*see* Addresses and Green, William R.); Economic Association, 60; Telephone and Telegraph Company, 71; Legion, 119–120 (*see* Addresses); Institute of Architects, 385; Relief Association's Children's Fund, 399; Child Health Association, 419, 426, 428, 471; Medical Association, 442; Bar Association, 508, 512; Red Cross (*see* Red Cross).
Amtorg, 45.
Anti-trust laws: and oil industry, 378; President on, in message to Congress, 463; President opposed to suspension of, 488–489; and conservation of national resources, 509.
Appel, Monte, 35.
Argentina, 44, 101, 256, 261, 425.
Arizona, 396, 523.
Armaments, 5, 83, 94, 301, 403, 531.
Arms Conference, 293, 403.
Army Engineer Corps, 239.
Asia, 57.
Associated Press, *see* Addresses.
Association of Railway Executives, 185.
Atlanta, 399.
Australia, 16, 261.
Austria, 5, 70, 74, 84–87, 89, 91, 96–97, 106, 111, 122, 170, 236, 291.
Aviation: President in summary on, 414–415; President's conference with four heads of government, 450. *See* Air Mail and Aeronautics service, improvement in, etc.

Baker, Newton D., 241, 244–245.
Ballantine, Arthur A., 532.
Baltimore, 274, 362.
Baltimore Sun, The, 203, 289, 341.
Bank for International Settlement, *see* World Bank.
Bank of United States, 59, 64.
Banking: Reform bills, 166–167, 171, 179–180, 184, 188, 235, 317, 320–321, 352, 363; System, President in summary on, 415.
Bankruptcy laws, 42, 180–181, 303, 321–324, 352, 447, 508–509, 522, 536.
Banks, United States: panic of February–March, 1933, 4, 276, 302, 313, 328, 331–332, 344–346, 347–367 *passim*, 529; organization of, 6–7, 18, 125; failures, 7, 71, 107, 112, 115, 118, 122–123, 126, 128, 142, 144, 159, 166–167, 195, 214, 271, 316, 326–327, 339, 347–367 *passim* (*see* Bank of United States); and short-term world loans, 74, 80, 101; loan guarantee proposed, 118; centralized, 233; reform of, 303, 315–328 *passim*, 505–507, 522 (*see* Federal Home Loan Banks, etc.); separation of commercial and investment, 319; holidays, 347–367 *passim*; figures, 348–349, 358, 533; guarantee of deposits, 356, 359–360, 362–363, 365; percentage opened after holiday, 367; inquiry into banking system, 446.
Baruch, Bernard M., 282, 336, 444.
Basel, 100, 157.
Bates, Sanford, 536.

545

Baton Rouge, 398.
Belgium, 5, 97, 101-102, 291, 511.
Bestor, H. Paul, 129, 135, 140, 164-165, 387.
Better Business Bureau, 16.
"Better Homes in America," 134, 507. *See* Home Building and Home Ownership, White House Conference on.
Billings (Mont.), 536.
Bolivia, 122.
Bonus: Bill, 64-69, 71, 85; resolution of September 21, 1931, 119-120; President to Press on, 267-268; and Democratic proposals, 273; "Army," 498-501.
Borah, 130-131, 392, 397.
Border Patrol, 429.
Boston, 348.
Boulder: City (Nev.), 522; Dam (*see* Colorado River Dam).
Brazil, 51, 135, 261.
Briand, 98.
British Stabilization Fund, 334.
Brown, Lytle, 41, 534.
Brown, Walter F., 13, 391, 403, 430, 537.
Bruening, Chancellor, 87, 100, 103, 105.
Budget: Expenditures and revenue, 34, 39-40, 51, 58, 125, 140-141, 149-150, 152, 156-157, 159-160, 162-163, 182, 187, 190-191, 195-199, 201-237 *passim*, 212-215, 222, 224, 235-236, 251, 253, 266-267, 270, 273, 303-314 *passim*, 330, 339-340, 352-353, 369, 513, 533-534; Economy Program, 157; National finances, figures (*see* Statements, financial).
Buenos Aires, 57.
Buffalo Courier, The, 22.
Bundy, Harvey H., 531.
Bureaus: Labor Statistics, 51; Federal Prisons, 432; Investigation, 433; Prohibition, 434. *See* World War Veterans' Bureau, etc.
Burma, 261.
Burton, Theodore E., 129.

California, 396, 400, 465, 473, 479, 523, 538-539; Joint Federal and State Water Commission, 400, 465.
Camp Lee (Va.), 536.
Campaign speeches, 248-274, 503-521.
Canada, 96, 101, 151, 170, 230, 257, 261, 316, 383, 414, 427, 531.
Capital: Gains Tax, President on, in message to Congress, 463; flight of (*see* Gold, international movement of).
Carr, Wilbur J., 531.
Castle, William R., Jr., 89, 98-100, 107, 531.
Census: employment, 36; Bureau, 123; of 1890, 376; of 1920, 391; of 1930, 391; Bill, 391, 393.
Challenge to Liberty, The, 373.
Chamber of Commerce, United States, 155, 245-246, 362.
Chamberlain, Neville, 229.
Chapin, Roy D., 241, 540.
Chicago, 25-26, 45, 53, 56-57, 88, 136, 164, 166, 219, 223, 365, 376, 509, 534.
Chicago: Evening Post, 183 n.; *Daily News, The*, 376.
Child: Health Day, 377, 426; Health and Protection, White House Conference on, 396, 417, 455-461, 542.

Children's: Bureau, 407, 417, 471, 541-542; Charter, 458-461, 502.
Chili, 110, 122.
China, 116, 261, 531.
Citizens Reconstruction Organization, 183 n.
Civil Service: 375, 386-387, 434, 456, 475, 530; President in summary on, 418.
Civil War veterans, 436, 443.
Clayton Act, 119.
Cleveland, Grover, 333; (Ohio), 60, 253, 260, 355, 362, 506, 511, 515.
Coleman, Arch, 537.
Collier: Bill, 272; Chairman, 306-307.
Colorado: River Dam, 35, 40-41, 242, 391, 395, 446, 471, 522-524, 538; Springs, 391.
Columbia, 122, 425.
Commerce, Department of, 13, 540-541.
Commissions: in recent administration, statistics, 492. *See* by titles, *e.g.*, Civil Service, Conservation of the Public Domain, etc.
Committees, *see* by titles, *e.g.*, Aeronautics, Recent Economic Changes, etc.
Communists, 45.
Conferences, President's: with railroad presidents, 25, 246; with industrial leaders, 26, 34; with labor leaders, 27, 34, 51; with building and construction leaders, 28; with agricultural leaders, 30; with public-utility leaders, 30; with governors and Federal officials for drought relief, 43; with New York Clearing House and insurance leaders, 125-127; with Congressional leaders, 126, 129-130, 176-177, 203, 220, 283, 425; on mortgage discount banks, 133; on proposed currency stabilization, 138; on hoarding, 168; with members of New York Stock Exchange, 175; on financial assistance to railways, 185; House Economy Committee, 193-194; with political leaders on recovery, 200, 204-205; Rapidan Camp, 217-219; with Mr. Roosevelt, 365-366. *See* by titles, *sub* Addresses, etc.
Congo, 261.
Congress, achievements of: Seventy-second, 234-236; Seventy-first, 445-446. *See sub* Conferences, Messages, various bills by title, etc.
Conservation: of the Public Domain, Commission on, 407-408, 416, 481; President in summary on, 416. *See* Oil, conservation of.
Constitution, 231, 352, 354, 419, 428, 444, 505, 512, 522.
Construction, public, *see* Public works.
Coolidge, Calvin, 12, 24, 62, 106, 216, 266, 388, 492, 522, 530-531; Dam, 40.
Cooper, William J., 538.
Copenhagen, 57-58.
Costa Rica, 89, 425.
Costigan-LaFollette Bill, 174.
Cotton: Co-operatives, 24; Joseph, 531.
Couzens, 230, 326, 357.
Cove Creek Dam, 471.
Crime statistics, 384, 399, 489-490. *See* Law enforcement.
Criminal Investigation Division, 433, 535. *See* Law enforcement.
Crissinger, Daniel R., 10.
Crowell, Benedict, 468.
Crowther, Samuel, 406.
Croxton, Fred C., 113, 241, 247.

INDEX

Cuba, 261, 399, 425.
Cumming, Hugh S., 113, 160.
Czechoslovakia, 74, 96, 291.

Daugherty, Attorney-General, 468, 491-492.
Davis, James J., 13, 36, 433, 461, 541.
Davison, F. Trubee, 534.
Dawes, Charles G., 69-70, 93, 99, 106-108, 163, 171, 179, 219, 239.
De Groot, William A., 386.
Debts: War, 4-5; post-war, 8-9; intergovernmental, 83, 88, 93-94, 133, 135, 139, 217, 226, 268, 278-303 *passim*, 336, 343; national, 313-314, 533-534; inflated, 321-324; public, 532-533. *See* Moratorium and World War Debt Commission.
Deficiency Bill, 422.
Deflation, attempts to offset, 24; definition of, 259.
Democratic: National Convention, 223; proposals, 1932, 272-274; platform, 1932, 303; National Committee, 421.
Denmark, 122.
Department of National Defense, 176.
Deportations, 84, 462. *See* Immigration.
Depression of 1929: two major stages of, 3; a slow downward movement, 3-4; acute characteristics of, 4; causes of, 4, 6-9, 57, 260-264; effect of World War on, 4, 6, 73, 260; relief, 4-6, 109-117 *passim*, 123, 160; effect of European post-war situation on, 7; introduced by stock speculation, 14, 73, 260, 262; first symptoms of, 17; forerunners of, 17-18; four definite periods of, 18; crises, 19, 142, 236-237, 350; mental unpreparedness for, *quotations*, 21-22; turns in, 23-24, 71-72, 81, 142, 144, 166, 184, 270-272, 347; and government revenues, 42; grain market collapse, 54; breadlines, 62; lowest points, 73, 76, 236-237; and war debts, 285-286; wage cuts, 121; reviews of, 147-152, 248-250; panic character, 214; emergency actions, 250-253; overcome, 366-367. *See* Inflation and Gold, international movement of, etc.
Depressions, past, 3, 6, 72, 491.
Des Moines, 172, 254-255, 263, 268-270, 511, 513.
Detroit, 119-120, 187, 265, 270-271, 339, 348-349, 355, 358, 362, 408, 483, 536.
Detroit Free Press, 288.
Devaluation, *see* Inflation.
Dictatorship, 339, 352.
Dingley duties, 263, 438-439.
Disabled American Veterans, 472.
Disarmament, 276. *See* Arms Conference.
District of Columbia, 362, 385-386, 423, 430, 456, 533. *See* Washington.
Dixon, Joseph, 479, 537.
Doak, William N., 461, 541.
Dodds, Nugent, 535.
Douglas, James H., 532.
Drought, 42, 57-60, 63, 66, 148, 257, 513, 539.
Dunlap, R. W., 539.

Economic: reviews of Hoover Administration, 368-369; Trends, Committee on, 527.
Economics of Recovery, The, 369.
Economy: Act of 1932 (*see* Economy Committee); Committee, 178, 182, 192-194, 196, 198, 201, 219, 223, 231, 305.
Ecuador, 113, 261, 425.

Edge, Walter E., 95-96, 99, 101.
Edison, Thomas A., 408-409.
Education, Conference on the Crisis in, 527-528.
Edwards, John H., 537.
Egypt, 261.
Eighteenth Amendment, 374, 376, 384, 389, 399, 418, 467-468.
El Paso, 536.
Electrical Power Regulation, President on, 416, 462.
Employment, 5, 8, 17, 26-27, 30, 35, 52-53, 58, 60, 63, 71, 86, 110, 114, 125, 142, 150, 159, 162, 166, 198, 205, 212-213, 218, 221, 247-248, 271, 338-339, 351, 353, 364, 368, 420, 447, 509, 519, 540.
Enemy Trading Act, 364.
England, *see* Great Britain.
Esthonia, 291.
Europe, collapse in, 3, 12, 14, 16-19, 26, 54, 56-57, 70, 72-73, 81-108 *passim*, 110-111, 124, 142, 144, 236, 249, 260-261, 263, 319, 338, 352, 477, 519.
European Economic Conference, 85.
Excise taxes, *see* Taxes, sales.
Expenditures, *see* Budget.
Expenses, *see* Budget.
Export Debenture Plan, 381-383, 387-388, 391-392, 393, 408, 411, 426, 431, 433, 446.
Exports, American, 121, 123-124, 140, 144, 211, 271, 276. *See* Export Debenture Plan.

Far East, 170, 531.
Farm: Board (*see* Federal Farm Board); Credit Administration, 165; Loan Act, proposed amendment to, 140, 164-165; Loan Bank (*see* Federal Farm Loan Banks).
Farmers' National Grain Corporation, 24, 45.
Fascists, 45.
Federal Reserve Bulletin, 69, 71.
Federal: Reserve System, 7, 9-12, 14-16, 23-24, 33, 35-37, 45, 71, 85, 101, 111, 115, 118, 122, 125-126, 128-129, 131-133, 143-145, 149-150, 152, 154, 159, 161, 166, 168-172, 178-179, 184, 202, 207, 219-220, 236-237, 239, 252, 258, 272, 315-316, 321, 332, 334, 336, 342-343, 351, 354, 357, 359, 362-363, 365, 368-369, 478, 518; Farm Board, 24, 34-35, 37, 45, 54, 58, 116-117, 148, 168, 181, 185, 219, 224, 240, 256, 370, 381-382, 385, 388, 392-394, 396-397, 399, 445, 472, 518, 529, 539; Farm Loan Banks, 58, 127, 129-130, 135, 140, 219, 240, 246, 258, 316, 387; Stabilization Board, 66, 123-124; Employment Service, 67, 111, 417, 472, 541; Land Banks, 129-131, 144, 149, 153, 161, 179, 231, 235, 252, 258-259, 370, 518; Home Loan Banks, 142-145, 149, 150, 153, 161, 166, 217-218, 220, 230-235, 240-244, 252, 315, 321, 369-370, 448, 481, 486, 501, 506-507, 518; Power Commission, 151, 416, 445-446, 465-466, 487, 538; Trade Commission, 156; Intermediate Credit Bank, 218; Revenue Board report, January 1, 1933, figures, 332 (*see* Federal Reserve System); Reserve Bank's (New York) memorandum on effect of devaluation, 334; Prisons, President on, 418, 429; Criminal Identification Service, 433, 446; Prisons, new, 536; (*see* Leavenworth, Atlanta, Lewisburg, etc.); Waterpower Act, 445; employees, comparative statistics under recent administrations, 530-531;

Bureau of Public Roads, 539; building program (*see* Public works); Oil Conservation Board (*see* Oil, conservation of); Public Buildings program (*see* Public works); Reserve Act (*see* Federal Reserve System); Reserve Advisory Council (*see* Federal Reserve System).
Fess, Simeon D., 342, 351.
Fine Arts Commission, 414.
Finland, 5, 96, 291.
Finney, Edward C., 537.
Fisher, Governor (Pa.), 423.
Five-day week, *see* Furlough system.
Florida, 404–405.
Ford, Henry, 355, 358.
Fordney-McCumber Law, 438–439.
Foreign Service, 532.
Forests, conservation of, 539.
Fort Wayne, 254.
France, 5, 70, 75, 81, 85–89–91, 95–104, 106–107, 110–111, 115–116, 121, 138, 163, 170, 212, 220, 230, 282, 287, 289–291, 511.
Furlough system, 194, 196, 219, 221, 238.

Garner: bills (*see* Garner, John N.); John N., 55, 91, 130, 219, 221, 272–273, 306–307, 324–325, 329, 352–353, 421, 487.
Geneva, *see* Arms Conference.
Geological Survey, 48, 538.
Georgia, 377–378.
German-Austrian Customs Agreement, 70, 81, 84, 86, 90–91, 96, 116.
Germany, 5, 70–71, 74–75, 83, 85–108 *passim*, 110–111, 115, 117, 122, 139, 144–145, 157, 169–170, 193, 211–212, 217, 236, 270, 284–285, 480, 511.
Gifford, Walter S., 112–115, 124, 136–137, 140, 241, 245.
Glass, Carter, 144–145, 165, 172, 217, 230, 315, 335, 337, 340, 342, 345, 350, 354, 358, 365; Banking Bill (*see* Banking Reform bills); Steagall Bill (*see* Banking Reform bills).
Glover, W. Irving, 537.
Gold: standard, 6, 19, 119, 121–122, 126, 135, 139, 154, 159, 169, 172, 184, 212, 214, 220, 235–236, 252, 278, 297–303, 319, 329–369 *passim*, 369, 514; international movement of, 7–9, 75–76, 93, 100, 110–111, 116, 119, 121, 142, 159, 163, 170, 173, 180, 214, 220, 236, 252, 261, 271, 298, 331, 334, 336–337, 339, 341, 343, 346, 348–368 *passim*; situation, 169–173, 220; "free," 169, 172; foreign, in United States, 169–170; proposed embargo on, 169; monetary, in United States, 170; profits from international movement of, 334; defaults on (*see* Gold standard); hoarding (*see* Hoarding).
Goldsborough credit inflation bill, 200, 236, 353.
Gompers, Samuel, 519.
Good, James W., 13, 129, 395, 412–413, 534.
Governmental structure, reorganization of, 244, 305, 307, 310.
Grand Coulee (Wash.), 538.
Great Britain, 5–6, 16, 19, 70, 75, 81, 86–92, 95–96, 100–104, 106, 109–111, 115, 117, 119, 121–122, 124, 126, 140, 142, 144, 156, 163, 166–167, 169–170, 193, 211–212, 216–217, 220, 236, 280, 282, 287, 291, 297, 316, 475.
Great Lakes: improvement, 410; seaway (*see* St. Lawrence waterway).
Greece, 96, 122, 291.

Green, William R., 39, 42, 51, 247, 326, 461, 486. *See* American Federation of Labor.
Grundy, Joseph W., 423–424, 433, 436–437.

Haiti, 531; Commission, 474.
Harding, Warren G., 175, 468, 492.
Harrison, Pat., 306, 424.
Hatry affair, 16.
Hawaii, 467, 537.
Hawley-Smoot tariff, *see* Smoot-Hawley tariff.
Heath, Ferry K., 532.
Henderson, Arthur, 98.
Herald Tribune, *see New York Herald Tribune, The*.
Highways: President in summary on, 414; improvement, 539–540.
Hindenburg, von, President, 90–91.
Hines, Frank T., 67–68, 443, 446.
Hoarding, 107, 111, 115, 120, 122, 135, 142, 144, 159, 167–169, 173, 175, 178, 180–181, 183, 195, 214, 236, 252, 271, 316, 327, 331, 334, 336, 338–339, 341, 343, 346, 348–367 *passim*, 368.
Holland, 103.
Home: Building and Home Ownership, White House Conference on, 142, 145, 149, 447–448, 450–451, 480–481, 485–487, 507; Loan Discount Banks (*see* Federal Home Loan Banks).
Honduras, 425.
Hoover, Herbert: his leadership within Constitution, 3, 20; as Secretary of Commerce, 9–10, 25, 52, 134, 156, 376, 389, 395, 397, 409, 427, 437, 449, 484, 491, 527, 540; and relief, 10, 26–27, 52–56, 62, 72, 110, 112, 124, 152, 177, 215, 378–379; Cabinet, 12–13; attempt to prevent collapse, 14–16; and situation in 1929, 18–19; policies and achievements, 19–20, 42, 76, 248, 251–253, 369–370, 373–375; opposition to, 21, 32, 46, 125, 146–147, 159, 163, 171, 176, 178–179, 181, 184, 201, 212, 236, 304, 315, 347–367 *passim*, 421, 423, 445, 492; apprehensive of boom, 23, 26; makes ocean-mail contracts contingent upon ship construction, 31; a liberal, 32–33; and expenditures, 35, 42, 51, 178; address to United States Chamber of Commerce, 36; and employment census, 36; advocates independent farmer-marketing, 39; on Rivers and Harbors Bill, 41; and bankruptcy law, 42; and immigration, 44–45; experience in relief, 52, 64, 113; and Democrats, 55, 146–147; and recovery plans, 57–58, 153–154, 239–240; and "made" work, 59, 154, 177; and Bonus Bill, 68, 187; vetoes, 68, 198, 226, 312–313, 468, 470–473, 493–495, 528–529; to France on moratorium, 97; on home situation, July 10, 1931, 99–100; on London conference, 105; on deficits, 109–110; on Swope plan, 119; summary of third great crisis, 124–125; campaign, 142, 201, 238, 248–274; and taxes, 144, 378; economic program, December 8, 1931, 148–152; statement to deputation of unemployed, 162; on Reconstruction Finance Corporation, 163–164; on Federal Land Banks, 164; disapproves issue of fiat money, 165; recommends preferring American goods, 165; directs fleet to land at Shanghai, 166; on Banking Reform Bill, 166; meetings on gold reserve, 171; on Economy Committee, 178; on hoarding, 178, 183; on Glass-Steagall Bill, 179–180; on reduction of appropriations, 182; and merchant marine, 188–189,

INDEX

415; bill signatures, 219, 223, 393–394, 432–434, 434; compromise proposal on Relief Bill, 229; plans for slum clearance, 240, 245; urges livestock loans, 244; on induction of Newton D. Baker to relief organization, 244–245; and tariffs, 246, 390–392, 396–397, 421–422, 438–441; administration over on November 9th, 276; international negotiations, 276; and increase in national debts, 312–313; work to reopen Michigan banks, 349–350; urged to reply publicly to Roosevelt's failure to co-operate, 358; efforts to prevent panic, 359–367; and Federal banking holiday, 364–367 *passim;* and secrecy of tax refunds, 375–376; publishes recommendations of eleven judges, 381; on nomination of postmasters, 386–387, 418; first definite setback, 393; declines to allow United States participation in World Bank, 395; on Colorado River Dam, 395–396; to Western governors on Reclamation, 401–402; pension-insurance proposal, 405–406; and commissions, 419, 492; founder of American Child Health Association, 419; and law enforcement, 423, 432–433; considers appeal for public support, 424; invites conference on street and highway safety, 429; forms Veterans' Administration, 446; on Senate's recalling their confirmation of officers, 465; stops leasing of national forests, 476; and objectives of Better Homes Conference, 486–487; his opportunities, 524–526; number of federal employees under, 530; and Latin-American relations, 531; and reduction in interest of public debts, 532; and extension of parks and monuments, 538; view of irrigation, 538–539; and radio industry, 540; conferences (*see* Conferences); Dam (*see* Colorado River Dam); messages (*see* Messages, President's); Plan (*see* "Standstill proposal").

Hoover, J. Edgar, 535.
Hoover-Stimson doctrine, 531.
Hope, Walter E., 532.
House, Edward M., 282, 296; Economy Committee (*see* Economy Committee).
Howe, Louis McHenry, 282.
Hughes, Charles Evans, 265, 395, 423; W. P., 404; C. F., 534; Charles Evans, Jr., 535.
Hull, 345.
Hungary, 74, 84, 96–97, 100, 111, 122, 170, 291.
Hurley, Patrick J., 413, 476, 484, 534.
Husband, W. W., 541.
Hyde, Arthur M., 13, 43, 45, 135, 408, 539.

Illinois, 177, 497.
Illiteracy, National Advisory Committee on, 412, 417, 473.
Immigration: 44–45, 84, 148, 151, 376, 462, 509, 541; Restriction Act of 1924 (*see* National origins clause).
Imperial Valley, 523.
Independent Offices Appropriation Bill, 312–313.
India, 122, 261.
Indian: claims bills, 272; Bureau, 422; Affairs, 448–449; claim agents, 493; self-support, 538.
Indiana, 467, 497.
Indianapolis, 89–90, 264, 269–270, 274, 478, 505, 507–508, 510.
Indies, 261.
Inflation: its effect on production, 4; currency, 5, 214, 217, 230, 269, 273, 327, 329–346 *passim,* 348–367 *passim;* in farm-land prices, 6; war, 8; credit, 9–12, 73, 200, 414; its effect on depression, 17–18.

Ingalls, David S., 534.
Insull, 245.
Insurance, old age and unemployment, 405–406, 475.
Interior, Department of, 13, 537–539.
Intermediate Credit banks, 258.
International: Chamber of Commerce, 82–83, 480; Wheat Conference, 85; monetary and economic conference, 211–212, 216–217; Association of Chiefs of Police, 483.
Interstate: Commerce Commission, 60, 135–136, 150, 154, 161, 185, 323, 387, 508; compact proposal (oil), 392.
Iowa, 246.
Italy, 5, 96, 101, 103, 121–122, 170, 291, 511.

Jahncke, Ernest Lee, 534.
Japan, 96, 101, 103, 119, 154, 166, 511, 531.
Joint Stock Land Banks, 130, 258, 316.
Jones-White Law, *see* Merchant Marine Act.
Joslin, Theodore G., 530.
Judd, Lawrence M., 537.
Judicial reforms, *see* Law enforcement.
Justice, Department of, 13, 535–537.

Kansas City, 381, 388, 438, 534.
Kansas City Star, The, 15 n.
Kellogg, Frank B., 13, 531.
Kellogg-Briand Pact, 138, 531.
Kemmerer, E. W., 121.
Kent, Frank R., 45–46, 421.
Kettleman Hills, 473, 538.
Kidnapping, 235, 496, 535.
Klein, Julius, 240, 540.
Knox, Frank, 167, 178, 183 n.
Kreuger collapse, 184.

Labor, Department of, 13, 541–542.
Ladies' Home Journal, 406.
Laissez faire, 520.
Lamont, Robert P., 13, 23, 34, 240–241, 403, 481, 540.
Land Banks (*see* Federal Land Banks).
Latin America, 170, 531.
Latvia, 291.
Lausanne Conference, 139, 157, 163, 212, 217, 225–226, 229, 236.
Laval, Premier, 103, 121, 131, 133, 135, 137–138, 211.
Law: enforcement, 374, 383–385, 389, 399, 418, 421–422, 429–430, 434, 446, 496, 504–505, 535–537; Commission members, 389; President in summary on, 418; statistics, 536–537; Observance and Enforcement, National Commission on, 495–496. *See* Eighteenth Amendment.
Lawrence, Charles W., 535.
League of Nations, 70, 81.
Leavenworth, 399, 401.
Legge, Alexander, 24, 37–38, 472.
Legislative Economy Program, 157.
Léon, René, 333.
Leslie, Governor (Ind.), 467.
Letters and telegrams: *President to,* Alexander

INDEX

Legge, 38-39; Eugene Meyer, 116-117, 145; George Harrison, 127-129; Frank Knox, 178; correspondents, 189, 197-198, 207, 356, 472-473, 480; John McDuffie, 192; Herbert S. Crocker, 208-211; Borah, 230; Governor Turner (Iowa), 246; Franklin D. Roosevelt, 280-281, 290-291, 295-296, 338-340, 360; Arch W. Shaw, 317-320; David A. Reed, 341; Mills, 343-344, 361; Simeon D. Fess, 351-354; Federal Reserve Board, 355, 359, 364-365; Senator McNary, 382-383; a Florida Republican, 405; heads of mutual life insurance companies, 405; J. Clawson Roop, 407; W. O. Thompson, 421; John Q. Tilson, 431; Governor Leslie (Ind.), 467; Governor Woodring (Kansas), 477; mayors, 484-485; National Education Association, 489; L. H. Reichelderfer, 500; Wilbur, 524; *Others to President*, Dawes, 69-70; Von Hindenburg, 90-91; Franklin D. Roosevelt, 282, 293-297, 344-345; Federal Reserve Board, 357, 362-363; George A. Sloan, 476; L. H. Reichelderfer, 499; *Miscellaneous*, A. Harry Moore to W. Warren Barbour, 328.

Lewisburg (Pa.), 536.
Lindley, Ernest K., 330.
Lithuania, 291.
Liverpool, 54, 56.
Loans, short-term, 74-75, 80, 85, 101.
London Conference: Relief, 85, 104-105, 108; Naval, 446, 531.
London Times, The, 477.
Long, Huey, 317.
Longworth, Nicholas, 129.
Los Angeles, 523.
Louisiana, 135.
Lowman, Seymour, 532.
Luther, Herr, 99, 107.

MacArthur, Douglas, 499-500, 534.
MacDonald, Ramsay, 94, 211-212.
Maine, 368.
Manchuria, 119, 531.
Manufacturers' sales tax, *see* Tax, sales.
Maryland, 355, 358.
Mather, Stephen, 537.
McKinley duties, 263, 438-439.
McNary Equalization Fee Bill, 388.
Mead, Elwood, 538.
Meat-packing industry, 408.
Medical Care, National Conference on the Cost of, 524.
Mellon, Andrew W., 13-14, 23, 25, 88, 90, 95-96, 101-102, 107, 125-126, 168, 212, 532.
Mendenhall, William C., 538.
Merchant Marine, 188-189, 403, 446; President in summary on, 415.
Messages, President's, to Congress: on economic questions, 33, 57-58, 147-152, 160-161, 414-418; on moratorium, 152-153; on economy, reorganization, and the budget, 175-176, 190-191, 201-202, 304-305, 309-311; on bankruptcy laws, 180-181, 322-323; on Unemployment Relief Organization, 225; on World Economic Conference, 289; on war debts, 291-293; on reorganization of banking system, 315-316; on farm relief and tariff, 379-381; on aeronautics, 418-419; on law enforcement, 422-423, 429-430; on Veterans' Bill veto, 441-443; on social and economic reforms, 462-463; on emergency and permanent measures, 487-488; on reform of the judicial system, 489-491. *See* Budget.

Mexico, 523.
Meyer, Eugene, 44, 107, 116-117, 126-127, 145, 163, 179, 239, 357, 363, 365, 387.
Michelson, Charles, 45 n., 46.
Michigan, 177, 337, 349-350, 355, 357-358, 497.
Miller, Charles A., 239.
Mills, Ogden L., 88, 98-100, 107, 126-127, 138, 168, 207, 282-283, 333, 343-345, 351, 355-356, 361, 365, 532.
Minneapolis, 57.
Minnesota, 468, 497.
Mississippi, 377-378; Flood Relief, 52, 471, 534; system, 410, 414, 509-510.
Missouri, 539.
Mitchell, William D., 13, 321-322, 364, 378, 535.
"Mobilization of Private Charities for Human Need, The," *see* Unemployment Relief Organization.
Moley, Raymond, 282, 365.
Moore, A. Harry, 326, 328; C. C., 537.
Moratorium, 90-108 *passim*, 110, 133, 135, 144-145, 152, 155, 157, 226, 281, 292, 370.
Morrow, Dwight, 98-99, 107, 129; Commission, 430.
Mortgage discount banks, *see* Federal Home Loan Banks.
"Most favored nation" treaties, 495.
Muscle Shoals, 69, 352, 468-471, 481; President in summary on, 415.
Mutiny in British Navy, 117, 119.

Narcotics Act, 399, 446.
National: Industrial Conference Board, 37, 369; Drought Relief Committee, 43; Credit Association, 126-129, 131-132, 135, 139-140, 144, 148-149, 154, 159, 251, 369; Education Association, 178, 489; Bureau of Economic Research, 262, 264, 475; origins clause, 376, 380-381, 393; Law Enforcement Commission (*see* Wickersham Commission); Association of Life Insurance, 405; Board of Parole, 432 (*see* Law enforcement); Homes for Disabled Volunteer Soldiers Bureau, 446; Recreation Association, 474; Defense, 476; Park Service, 477; Editorial Association, 477-478; Broadcasters Association, 483; Radio Conference, Fourth, 484; Conference on Home Ownership and Housing (*see* Home Building and Home Ownership, White House Conference on).
Navy: League, 122; Department, 13, 534-535.
Negroes, 474-475.
Netherlands, 170.
New Deal, 324, 341, 347, 516-521.
New England, 238.
New Hampshire, 238.
New Mexico, 538.
New Orleans, 534, 536.
New York: state, 16, 262, 265, 386, 497; Board of Trade, 35; Stock Exchange, 51-52, 175-176, 178, 192-193; State Chamber of Commerce, 167; City, 270, 280, 298, 357, 365, 506, 508, 516; Bar Association, 378; Academy of Medicine, 524.
New York: American, The, 15 n.; *Times, The*, 21-22, 35, 45, 56, 66, 71, 88, 95, 203, 282, 306-307, 333, 336, 340, 342, 344, 369; *Journal of Commerce, The*, 22; *World, The*, 47; *Herald Tribune, The*,

INDEX

288–289, 328, 335–337; *Herald Tribune Institute*, 501–502.
New Zealand, 96.
Newton, Walter H., 94, 530.
Niagara Falls, 427.
Nicaragua, 425, 531.
Non-governmental bankers commission. *See* Wiggin Commission.
Norman, Montagu, 9–10, 107.
North Carolina, 428.
Norway, 96, 122.
Noyes, Alexander Dana, 333, 336.
NRA, 119, 246.

Oakland, 400.
O'Brian, John Lord, 535.
Ohio: 177, 497; River canal, 409, 534.
Oil: shale lands scandals, 47–49; conservation of, 376, 378, 391, 402, 416, 473, 538; representatives, conference of, 391.
Oklahoma, 473, 479.
Omnibus: pension bill, 236, 272; Economy Bill (*see* Economy Committee).
Ontario, 383.
Oregon, 231.

Packers and Stockyards Act, 408.
Panama, 425.
Pan-American Conference, Fourth, 482.
Parker, John J., 395, 428.
Parks, George A., 537.
Patman Bonus Bill, 119, 220–221, 235, 353.
Payne-Aldrich: duties, 263, 438–439; Frederick H., 534; Judge, 61–62, 185.
Pennsylvania, 124, 347; Railroad, 208–209.
Pensions, 198, 200; Bureau, 198, 446. *See* Civil War veterans, Spanish War veterans, Bonus, etc.
Periods in economic history, 1931–1933, 352–353.
Perishables, agricultural, 437, 445.
Personnel Administration, Council of, 475.
Peru, 70, 425.
Philippines, 189, 484, 528–529.
Philp, John W., 537.
Pinchot, Governor (Pennsylvania), 124, 433.
Poland, 74, 96, 291.
Pole, J. W., 533.
Pomerene, Atlee, 239, 325, 327, 350.
Ponca City (Okla.), 429.
Portland, 267.
Post Office: deficit and expenditures, 66, 182, 309; postal savings, 150; postage increase, 304; postmasters, 386–387, 418; system of accounting, 391; Department, 13, 537; subsidies, 541.
Porter, M. C., 178.
Power Commission, 320.
Pratt, William V., 534.
President's Unemployment Relief Organization, *see* Unemployment Relief Organization.
Press and public statements: *On Conference and Committees*: railway, 25–26; labor, 28; Congressional, 131; with Laval, 137–138; Rapidan Camp, 217–219; New England, 238–239; Federal Reserve, 242; Social Trends, 526–527; *Miscellaneous*: on relief, 43–44, 59, 63–64, 111, 115–116, 221–223, 226–229, 232–233, 381, 450–451; on railways, 61, 185; on Bonus, 69, 267–268, 499, 501–502; on moratorium, 92–94; on currency stabilization, 138–139, 333; on home ownership, etc., 143–144, 233–234, 480–481; appeal for co-operation, 162; on hoarding, 167, 175; on stock exchange, 176; on budget, expense, economy, etc., 182, 187, 191–194, 196, 202–203, 221, 223–224, 312; on Reconstruction Finance Corporation, 204–206, 325; on public use of surplus credit, 207; on pork barrel legislation, 212–213; on the Council of National Defense, 219–220; on war debts, 226, 283–287; on public works, 244, 400, 449; on his correspondence with Franklin D. Roosevelt, 297; on reorganization of government bureaus, 308, 312; Independent Offices Appropriation Bill, 312–313; on Republican organization in South, 377; on Child Health and Protection, 396, 455–456; on Leavenworth riots, 399; on limitation of armaments, 403; on tariffs, 404, 411–412; on Public Lands, 407–408; on death of Good, 412; on Indian Bureau, 422; on vetoing Spanish War pensions, 436; on Perishable Agricultural Commodities Act, 437; on Wickersham Commission, 444–445; on bankruptcy laws, 447; on statistical agencies, 447; on appointment of William N. Doak, 461; on Senate's recalling confirmation of officers, 465–466; on Muscle Shoals, 468–469; on oil situation, 473; on creation of Council of Personnel Administration, 475; on National Defense, 476; on Philippine independence, 484; in defense of commissions, 492; on juvenile delinquents, 495–496; on Lindbergh kidnapping, 495; on St. Lawrence Waterway Treaty, 597; on criminal procedure, 529. *See* Proclamations.
Price-fixing, 269, 272, 489.
Proclamations: on "national origins" plan, 376; on Child Health Day, 377, 426. *See* Press and public statements.
Prohibition, President in summary on, 18. *See* Eighteenth Amendment and Law enforcement.
Public: works, 25, 34–36, 40, 44, 53, 55, 57, 62–63, 114, 123–124, 150, 153, 155–157, 162, 177, 198, 206, 208–211, 213, 222, 226, 232, 235, 244, 251, 273–275, 352–353, 401, 446, 513, 532–533; Works Administration, 151; Works, Committee for expansion of, 156–157; health, 124, 417, 432, 471, 501; health, President in summary on, 417–418; buildings, President in summary on, 414 (*see* Public works); lands (*see* Public works); roads program (*see* Public works). *See* Rivers and Harbors program.
Puerto Rico, 419, 428.

Radio: Commission, 498; Commission, President in summary on, 415; Manufacturing Trust, 432.
Railway Credit Corporation, 185.
Railways: construction, 25–26, 31; consolidation of, 60–61; increase in rates, 135–136; reorganization, 323–324; President in summary on, 415; employees, 461; President on, in message to Congress, 463; reform in regulation, 508.
Rainey Bill, 273.
Rapidan Camp, 217–219, 450.
Raskob, 46.
Reapportionment Bill, 391, 393–394.
Recent Economic Changes, Committee on, 388–389.
Reclamation Service, 401–402, 416, 446, 538.
Reconstruction Finance Corporation, 152, 154, **158**,

161, 163, 165–166, 169, 171–172, 179–180, 184–185, 187, 195, 204–208, 213–214, 216–219, 221–223, 225, 227–228, 233–236, 239–241, 244–246, 252–253, 258, 265–266, 269, 313–314, 316, 321, 323, 324–328, 339–340, 347, 349–350, 352–353, 355, 369, 450, 486, 501, 523, 539; Board of Engineers, 241.
Red Cross, 58, 60, 62–63, 65–66, 148, 168, 181, 185, 224, 235, 432, 529.
Reed, David A., 98–99, 340.
Reflation, see Inflation.
Relief bill, 221, 225, 232.
Republican: National Convention, 381, 388, 438; platform, 387–388.
Revenue: Act of 1924, 152; Bill of March–April, 1932, 186, 188, 200–201; total ordinary receipts, 1929–1932, 532. See Budget.
Rhoads, Charles J., 537.
Richardson, Seth W., 535.
Richey, Lawrence, 530.
Richmond (Va.), 199.
Rist, Charles, 10.
Ritchie, Albert C., 355.
Rivers and Harbors program, 34–35, 40–41, 446.
Roberts, Owen J., 428.
Robinson, Henry M., 243–244, 246.
Rogers, James Grafton, 531.
Roop, J. Clawson, 532.
Roosevelt, Franklin D., 19, 35, 155, 275–314 *passim*, 326, 329–346 *passim*, 350–367 *passim*, 434, 510, 529, 531, 533; Dam, 40; Theodore, 396, 408, 492, 511, 523.
Roosevelt Revolution, The, 330–331.
Rugg, Charles, 535.
Rumania, 96.
Rural Health Bill, 471–472.
Russia, 4–5, 57, 85, 261, 318, 531.

Sackett, Ambassador, 83, 87, 89, 100.
St. Lawrence waterway, 151, 230, 257, 410, 414, 488, 496, 509, 531.
St. Lewis, Roy, 535.
St. Louis, 263, 534.
St. Paul, 250, 271–272.
St. Petersburg (Fla.), 482.
Salaries, federal, Constitution on, 231.
Salt Lake City, 39.
San Francisco, 348, 400: Bay Bridge, 242, 399–400; Bay Bridge commission, 449.
Sanford, Justice, 427.
Santa Fé compact, 522.
Sarajevo, 70.
Scattergood, J. Henry, 537.
Schacht, Hjalmar, 10.
Schurman, Jacob Gould, 97.
Scribner's Magazine, 45–46.
Shanghai, 166.
Shearer, William, 403.
Sheppard-Towner Act, 417.
Sherman Act, 119, 463.
Ship construction, 31, 44.
Shipping Board, 151, 188, 403, 447, 541; policies; Advisory Committee on, 446–447.
Shouse, Jouett, 45 n., 46, 186.
Sisson, Charles P., 535.
Smith, Alfred E., 434.
Smoot-Hawley tariff, 260–263, 510.

Social Trends, Research Committee on, 420–421, 526–527.
Socialism, 489.
Soldiers' adjusted compensation certificates, see Bonus Bill.
South, 469.
South America, 16, 57, 74, 425.
South Carolina, 135, 377–378.
Soviet Government, see Russia.
Spanish: War veterans, 69, 436, 443; Revolution, 81.
Speculation, history of, as forerunner of depression, 14–19, see Depression.
Springfield (Ill.), 479.
Spry, William, 537.
"Standstill proposal," 102–104, 110, 370.
State: aid, 215–216, 222, 229, 232, 247, 252–253; Department, 13, 531–532.
Statements, financial: July 1, 1930, 39–40; July 24, 1931, 109; current business, September 30, 1931, 122; July 3, 1932, 224; proposed for 1933–1934, 310. See Treasury Department and Budget.
"Sterling bloc," 159.
Stimson, Henry L., 13, 88, 96, 100, 102, 107, 138, 211–212, 531.
Stock market crash of 1929, 3, 17, 19, 236.
Stockton, Gilchrist B., 87.
Stone, James C., 472.
Street and Highway Safety, Conference on, 429, 434.
Strikes and lockouts, comparative statistics, 1929–March, 1933, and March 1933–1935, 542.
Strong: Benjamin, 9–10, 12; Walter, 376.
Sumatra, 261.
Summerall, Charles P., 534.
Supreme Court, 274, 427–428, 466, 512, 529, 537.
Sweden, 96, 122.
Switzerland, 103.
Swope, Gerard, 119, 155.

Taft, William Howard, 423, 492.
Tariff: 200, 379–381, 399, 401, 421, 440–441; Commission, 246, 251, 272, 388, 424, 426, 432, 434, 438–439, 446, 450, 477, 480, 493, 510–511; protective, 255–256, 263, 509; reciprocal, 272; competitive, 274; bills and laws, 387–388, 390, 392, 406–407, 411–412, 426, 431–432, 435–436, 440–441, 493–495, 510; persons for and against, 438; President's analysis of, 438–440; flexible, 397, 401, 404, 406–407, 411, 424, 426, 432–440, 446, 476, 493–494; injustice of, 511. See Export Debenture Plan, Smoot-Hawley tariff, etc.
Taxes: 162, 203, 213, 222; capital gains, 7, 463; income, 109, 120, 152, 182, 196, 199, 216, 245, 308, 310, 376, 378, 463; increase in, 149, 215, 533; estate, 152, 216; luxury, 152; sales, 174, 182, 186, 188, 306–309, 311, 440; state and local, 199; bill, 218–219; land and real property, 257; excise, 310; customs, 310–311; refunds, 375–376.
Tennessee, 352, 427, 469–471, 481.
Texas, 473, 479, 538.
Textile Foundation, 437.
Thacher, Thomas D., 535.
Thomas, Senator, 335.
Tilton, Frederic A., 391, 537.
Toledo (Ohio), 112.
Trade and tariff review, 263.
Traylor, Melvin A., 223, 340.

INDEX 553

Treasury: fund for stabilization of foreign exchange, 327; Department, 13, 532-534.
Tugwell, 356.
Turner, Dan W., 246.
Tuskegee Institute, 474-475.

Underwood Law of 1913, 439.
Unemployment: conferences, 25, 238; Relief Organization, 53, 60, 112, 114, 153, 219, 225, 241, 253; Relief Act, 325. See Employment.
United: Mine Workers vs. Red Jacket Coal & Coke Co., 428; Kingdom, 511. See Great Britain.
United States: Chamber of Commerce (see Chamber of Commerce, United States); Public Health Service (see Public health).
Uruguay, 135, 425.

Valley Forge, 86-87.
Vancouver, 51.
Venezuela, 261.
Vestal Copyright Bill, 471.
Veterans: Bureau, 67-68, 182, 201, 441-442, 446; of Foreign Wars, 472; preference, 475.
Von Hoesch, Ambassador, 90.

Wages, world comparison of weekly, 511.
Wagner bill, 221.
Wallace, Henry A., 329, 335-336.
War: Finance Corporation, 129-130, 132, 149; Policies Commission, 444, 491; Department, 13, 534; debts (see Debts, intergovernmental); profits (see War Policies Commission).
Washington (D. C.): 248, 255, 266, 269, 504-505, 507-508, 522, 532. See District of Columbia.

Washington: Post, The, 94-95; *Herald,* 335.
Waterways, President in summary on, 414.
Watres Act, 430.
Watson, Senator, 172-173.
Webster, Daniel, quoted on tampering with currency, 269.
White: Francis, 531; Robe Carl, 541; House Conference (see Child Health and Protection, White House Conference on).
Wickersham Commission, 390, 444-445, 467-468, 535.
Wiggin Commission, 480.
Wilbur, Ray Lyman, 13, 40-41, 47-48, 378, 391-392, 407, 412, 422, 448, 477, 524, 537-538.
Wilson: Dam, 40; Law, 438-439; Woodrow, 450, 468, 478, 492.
Winant, Governor (N. H.), 238.
Winnipeg, 56-57.
Wisconsin, 497.
Women's: Bureau, 407, 417; Conference on Current Problems, 501-502.
Woodin, William H., 343-345, 351, 355-356, 361, 365.
Woods, Arthur, 52-53, 60-61, 112-113, 245.
World: Bank, 15-16, 73-74, 84, 100, 103-104, 395; Court, 116; Economic Conference, 226, 277-302 *passim,* 343; War Debt Commission, 152-153, 154-155, 236; War Veterans' Bill, 441-444; War Veterans' Bureau, 446.

"Yellow Dog" contracts, 491.
Young: Roy A., 12, 14-16, 23, 44; Owen D., 63-64, 93, 115, 217, 296; Plan, 87, 96, 395; Governor (Calif.), 400, 465; Clarence M., 540.
Youngquist, G. Aaron, 535.

/973.916M992>C1/

DATE DUE